WOODWORK Made S

The Made Simple series
has been created
especially for self-education
but can equally well
be used as
an aid to group study.
However complex the subject,
the reader is taken
step by step,
clearly and methodically,
through the course. Each volume
has been prepared by experts,
taking account of
modern educational requirements,
to ensure the most
effective way of
acquiring knowledge.

In the same series

Accounting
Acting and Stagecraft
Additional Mathematics
Administration in Business
Advertising
Anthropology
Applied Economics
Applied Mathematics
Applied Mechanics
Art Appreciation
Art of Speaking
Art of Writing
Biology
Book-keeping
Britain and the European Community
British Constitution
Business and Administrative Organisation
Business Calculations
Business Economics
Business Law
Business Statistics and Accounting
Calculus
Chemistry
Childcare
Child Development
Commerce
Company Law
Company Practice
Computing Programming
Computers and Microprocessors
Cookery
Cost and Management Accounting
Data Processing
Economic History
Economic and Social Geography
Economics
Effective Communication
Electricity
Electronic Computers
Electronics
English
English Literature
Financial Management
French
Geology
German
Housing, Tenancy and Planning Law
Human Anatomy
Human Biology
Italian
Journalism
Latin
Law
Management
Marketing
Mathematics
Metalwork
Modern Biology
Modern Electronics
Modern European History
Modern Mathematics
Modern World Affairs
Money and Banking
Music
New Mathematics
Office Administration
Office Practice
Organic Chemistry
Personnel Management
Philosophy
Photography
Physical Geography
Physics
Practical Typewriting
Psychiatry
Psychology
Public Relations
Public Sector Economics
Rapid Reading
Russian
Salesmanship
Secretarial Practice
Social Services
Sociology
Spanish
Statistics
Technology
Teeline Shorthand
Twentieth-Century British History
Typing
Woodwork

WOODWORK Made Simple

Tom Pettit, FRSA, MRST

Made Simple Books
HEINEMANN : London

Filmset in 'Monophoto' Times 9 on 10 pt. and
printed in Great Britain by
Richard Clay (The Chaucer Press), Ltd.,
Bungay, Suffolk
for the publishers William Heinemann Ltd.,
10 Upper Grosvenor Street, London W1X 9PA

First edition, June 1977
Reprinted, January 1980
Reprinted (with revisions), September 1984

British Library Cataloguing in Publication Data

Pettit, T.
Woodwork made simple.—(Made simple books, ISSN 0265–0541)
1. Woodwork—Amateurs' manuals
I. Title II. Series
684'.08 TT185

ISBN 0–434–98605–4

Preface

Every piece of wood, even from the same species of tree, has its own individual characteristic features. The most noticeable of these are grain and colour, but not until the wood is being worked do we become really aware of its degree of hardness, its strength, weight and smell, which in some timbers is very aromatic. Its beauty, both as a living tree and as a material with which to work, is to be admired. There is no doubt as to why so many enthusiastic amateur and professional craftsmen find such satisfaction in creative woodwork. They see an idea develop perhaps from only a simple sketch or a more detailed drawing. In seeing the various pieces take their shape, in assembling them, and in giving the work its final finish they experience that sense of personal achievement only to be derived from bringing work to a successful conclusion. There is at the same time a personal appreciation of the skills involved. Ultimately this leads to a much wider appreciation of design, of woodworking tools and materials, and also of the skill of other craftsmen.

Within this book there is available to the reader a ready source of woodworking information, the tools with which to fashion wood, the techniques by which it may be joined, and the finishes appropriate to particular types of work. There is a comprehensive account of the modern portable electric machine tools that will form part of the home or school workshop, metal and plastic fittings used in woodworking, and metal fasteners. Other chapters deal with manufactured boards; tool maintenance; wood carving, wood turning; veneering; laminating; bending; upholstery and safety—so presenting to the reader a really comprehensive woodwork book. It is sufficiently detailed to satisfy the needs of examination students, and at the same time presented in such a way that it will appeal to the absolute beginner, the 'do-it-yourself' enthusiast and those to whom woodworking is a rewarding leisure-time activity. All will find this book both informative and instructive.

TOM PETTIT

Acknowledgements

The author wishes to thank the following for their most valuable and willing assistance in making the preparation of this manuscript possible:

Tools and machines: Messrs. Bahco Record Tools; Kango Wolf Power Tools; Stanley Tools; Spear & Jackson; Copydex; William Whitehouse & Co.; Neill Tools; Harefield Rubber Co.; Denford Machine Tools; Anders Lervad & Son, Denmark; Alec Tiranti.

Timber: The Timber Research and Development Association; The Forest Research Products Laboratory; The Forestry and Timber Bureau of Australia; United Africa Company International; Finnish Plywood Development Association; Chipboard Promotion Association; Fibre Building Board Development Organisation; A and C Black (Publishers).

Hardware: Messrs. Isaac Lord; Spegelstein & Son; Unico Components; GKN; Rawplug Co.; James Collins (Birmingham); Alexander (Silverthorne); Contour Manufacturing Co.; Hillaldam Coburn.

Adhesives: Messrs. Ciba-Geigy (UK); Humbrol; Dunlop Chemical Products Division.

Finishes, etc.: Messrs. Rustin's; W. W. Hill, Son & Wallace; ICI; Wilcot Co.

Miscellaneous: Messrs. Arborite; Norton Abrasives; English Abrasives; Cintride; Pirelli (Progress Mercantile Co.); British Standards Institution; Dalescraft Furniture; Cumberland Pencil Co.; P. W. Blandford (PBK Small Craft Plans, Newbould-on-Stour, Warwicks.); the Asbestos Information Committee; Associated Examining Board; Royal Society for the Prevention of Accidents; Department of Education and Science.

Addresses of some of the manufacturers and suppliers of knock-down fittings mentioned in the text are as follows:

Isaac Kord, Desborough Rd, High Wycombe, Bucks.
Spegelstein & Son, 80–84 Wallis Rd, London E9.
Unico Components, 101 Walnut Tree Close, Guildford, Surrey, GU1 4UQ.

Contents

PREFACE v

ACKNOWLEDGEMENTS vi

1 WOOD 1
- Structure 1
- Distribution 5
- Conversion 8
- Seasoning 8
- Shrinkage 11
- Seasoning Faults 11
- Natural Defects 12

2 MANUFACTURED BOARDS 13
- Plywood 13
- Blockboard 16
- Laminboard 16
- Chipboard 16
- Fibre Building Boards 16
- Plastic Laminates 17

3 DESIGN 18
- Sketching 20
- The Ergonomics of Design 25

4 HANDTOOLS FOR WOODWORKING 32
- Measuring and Simple Testing Tools 33
- Handsaws 44
- Backsaws 49
- Saws for Cutting Curves 51
- The General-Purpose Saw 55
- Log Saw 55
- The Hacksaw and Junior Hacksaw 56
- Files, Rasps and 'Surform' Tools 56
- Chisels 59
- Bench Planes 65
- Rebate Plane 71
- The Multi-Plane 77
- The Block Plane 79
- The Circular Plane 79
- The Router 82
- The Fibreboard Plane 82
- The Scratch Stock 83

The Hand Drill 83
The Joiner's Brace 83
Wood-Boring Tools 87
Hammers 91
Screwdrivers 95
Bradawls 99
Stanley Knives 99
Spokeshaves 100
The Pushpin 100
Pincers 100
Pliers 102
Punches 102
Spirit Level 102
Adjustable Spanner 102
Holding Tools 102

5 ELECTRICALLY POWERED TOOLS 121
Pedestal Drill 122
Portable Jig-Saw 124
Portable Circular Saw 126
Portable Machine Planes 129
The Machine Router 130
Power Sanders 132
The Portable Electric Drill 136
'Do-It-Yourself' Attachments for Portable Power Drills 139
General Workshop and Electrical Precautions 143

6 TOOL MAINTENANCE 147
Oilstones 147
Grindstones 149

7 SAFETY IN THE WORKSHOP 167

8 CONSTRUCTIONS 171
Flat Frame Joints for Stool and Table Constructions 173
Box and Carcase Construction 183
Wide Board Construction 199
Slab Constructions 203
Fixing Tops 207
Lids 207
Carcase Backs 207
Simple Doors 208
Sliding Doors 208

9 FIXING 211
Nails 211
Woodscrews 219
Coach Screws, Cup Square Carriage Bolts and Nuts 223
Fixing to Solid Walls and Floors 226
Fixing to Hollow Walls 229
Adhesives 229

10 Metal and Plastic Fittings 234
Cabinet Handles and Pulls 234
Hinges 235
Catches 244
Bolts 247
Locks 247
Shelf Fittings 248
Stays 249
Thin Plates and Stampings 252
Mirror Fittings 252
Fittings for Sliding Doors 255
Height Adjusters 257
Glides, Castors and Wheels 260

11 Knock-Down (K/D) Fittings 261

12 Woodcarving 277
Carving Tools 277
Holding Tools 279
Carving Techniques 279

13 Veneering, Laminating and Bending 288
Cutting and Peeling Veneers 288
Applying Veneers 288
Laminating 292
Bending Timber 293

14 Woodturning 295
The Woodturning Lathe 295
Tools for Woodturning 296
Turning Between Centres 299
Faceplate Work 301
Measuring Tools 304
Tool Rests 304
Finishing 304

15 Finishing and Finishes 306
Cleaning Up 306
Abrasives 306
Surface Preparation 307
Choice of Finish 307
Finishing Tools 308
French Polish 308
Paints 310
Oil Polishing 310
Wax Polishing 311
Semi-Wax Polishing 311
Clear Varnishes and Lacquers 312
Stains 313
Preservatives 313
Stripping 314

16 Upholstery 315
Upholstery Tools 315
Foams 315
Covering Materials 317
Supports 317
Cushions and Seats 321

Appendix 1: Suggestions for Making Leisure-Time Equipment 324
Fishing Punt 324
Dinghy 327

Appendix 2: Reference Tables 328
General Sizes and Thicknesses of Manufactured Boards 328
Woodscrews 329
Finishes for Screws 332
Spacing of Woodscrews 333
Abrasives: Comparison of Grit Numbers 333
Summary of Gap-Filling Adhesives (Aerodux and Aerolite) 334

Index 336

1

WOOD

Each tree is an individual plant within its own species, and although it will have certain features in common with others of its kind, the timber it produces, due to variations in growth and the way in which it is sawn from the log, will have characteristics of grain peculiar to itself. Like other plants, trees maintain their growth by absorbing carbon dioxide through the leaves, and water plus mineral salts through their roots. Water transpiration from the leaves and capillary action within the cells of the wood produce a flow of sap from the roots to the leaves. The leaves contain chlorophyll, and by photosynthesis—the action of sunlight on this chlorophyll—the carbon dioxide and the sap are converted by the leaves into sugar, starch, fats, gums and resins. This new solution is then carried away from the leaves and forms the food from which the tree continues to grow.

All trees have roots, stem and a crown. The roots, some of which are very powerful and penetrate deep into the ground, firmly anchoring the tree, extract food and moisture from the soil by means of the smaller, younger hair roots. Branches, twigs and leaves together form the crown of the tree, which is supported by the trunk or stem, from which the bulk of usable timber is obtained.

As trees grow taller the girth of the stem is increased each year until maturity is reached, when the rate of growth decreases and the tree gradually decays. When fully mature, a healthy tree produces the most and the best timber, the rate of annual growth depending upon the climate, the location of the tree in relation to the physical features of the ground, the kind of soil and the species of tree. From the cross-section of a tree trunk the structure can be seen and the various parts easily identified.

Structure

Pith. The first year's growth from seed. Located at the base of the trunk and at its very centre, the pith is soft and spongy.

Annual rings. Wood cell growth is faster in spring than in late summer and autumn. Differences of size and density show as annual rings, the lighter coloured spring wood contrasting with the darker later growth. They indicate the age of the tree. It should be noted that the growth of many subtropical and tropical trees is almost regular throughout the year and no distinct rings are produced.

Medullary rays. These are almost invisible in some timbers but in others, such as oak, are very pronounced. They are cells which radiate from the centre of the tree storing and conveying food horizontally. It is of interest that in Australia, for example, the heart of many trees is decayed and useless. The

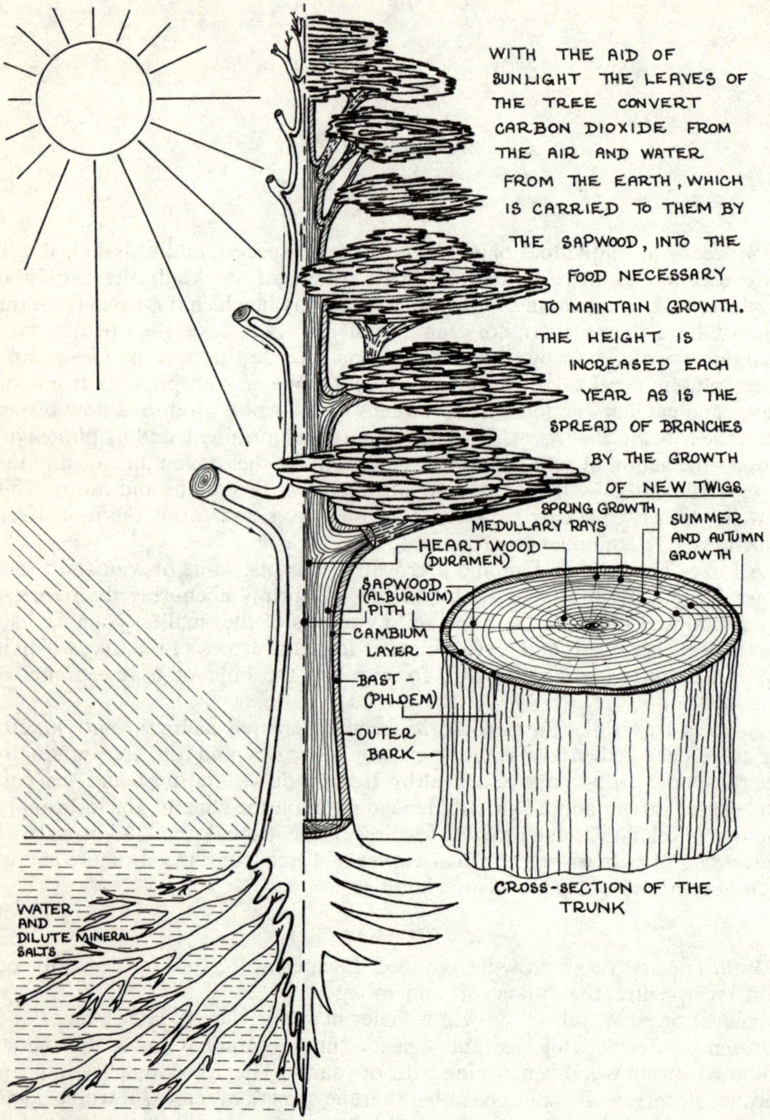

Fig. 1. How a tree grows.

term 'truewood' has been adopted to describe the sound part of the tree between the 'heart' and sapwood from which the bulk of the usable timber is obtained.

Heartwood (duramen). Usually darker in colour as it becomes inactive, the heartwood becomes a firm core supporting the remainder of the trunk, and produces the best timber.

Sapwood (alburnum). This comprises the outer growth rings between the heartwood and the bark by which sap is carried from the roots to the leaves. The sapwood is usually much lighter in colour and softer in texture than the heartwood. As such, it is more vulnerable to decay and attacks by insects or fungi than is heartwood and should not be used for high-class joinery and cabinet making.

Cambium. This is where the new cells of wood are formed, increasing the girth of the tree. The layer, which is a sticky solution, adds cells to the sapwood and to the bast.

Bast (phloem). Food sap produced by the leaves is conveyed by the bast to all growing parts of the tree.

Bark. The cambium layer adds new cells to the bast, the outer layers of which form the bark protecting the tree against weathering and attack by insects, birds and animals.

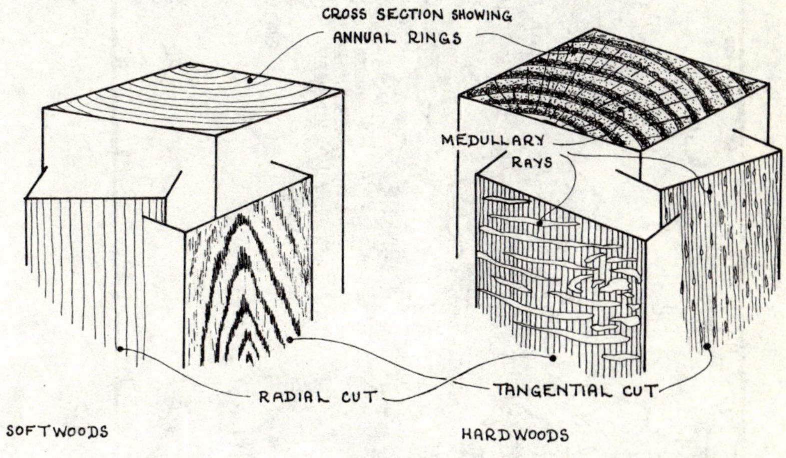

Fig. 2. *Left*: Softwoods (conifers)—the medullary rays are tiny and not normally visible. *Right*: Hardwoods (broad-leaved)—on many the medullary rays appear quite clearly however the timber is cut. They are very pronounced as on oak.

Botanically trees belong to two major class groups: **Gymnosperms** and **Angiosperms.** Their technical equivalents are softwoods (conifers) and hardwoods (broad-leaved trees). Most hardwoods are harder than the softwoods but there are exceptions, balsa and obeche being notable ones, and conversely pitch pine and yew are very tough softwoods.

As might be expected, the hardwoods are more difficult to work and are generally more expensive. They are therefore mainly used for furniture

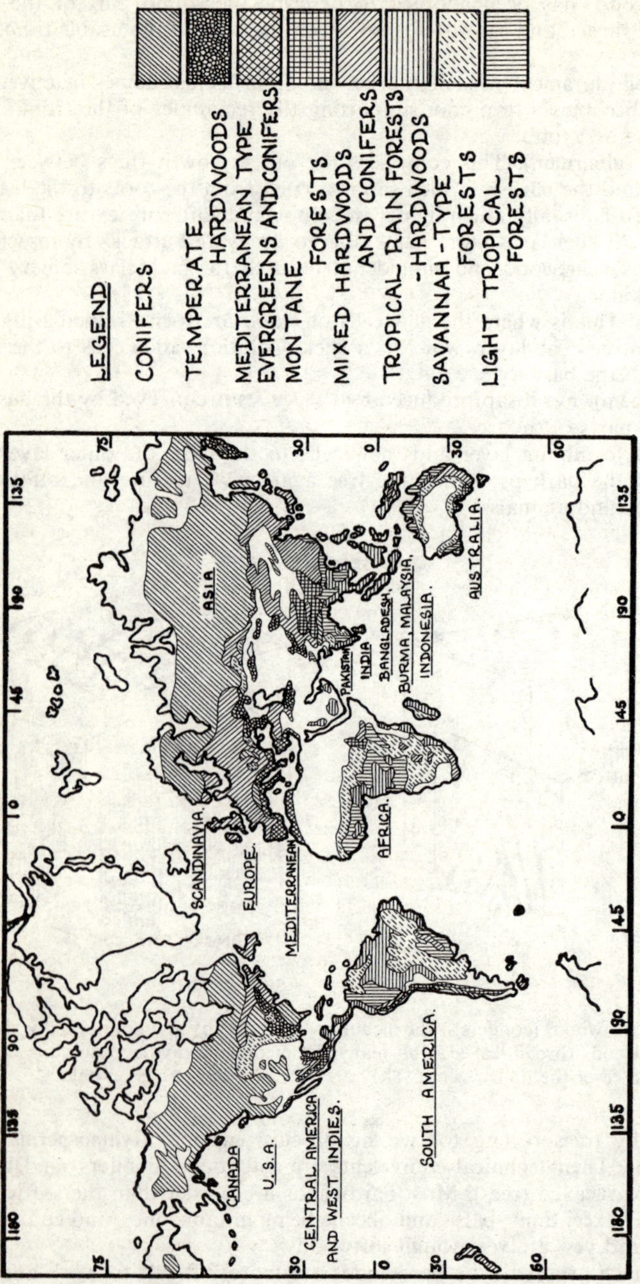

Fig. 3. Forest regions of the world.

making and high-class work, the softwoods being employed for carpentry and joinery. The coniferous softwoods grow in colder, drier and in general poorer conditions than the hardwoods. They have needle-like leaves which are dropped at all times of the year with the exception of larch, which is deciduous. Hardwoods are in three groups: deciduous, which grow in temperate climates, their broad leaves being dropped in autumn; a small group of temperate evergreen, such as holly and laurel, with shiny broad leaves dropped throughout the year; and tropical evergreens which grow in hot, wet climates and whose broad leaves are dropped at all times of the year.

It is estimated that there are up to 6,000 common names for various timbers throughout the world, of which more than 2,000 are in everyday use. Well over 60 pines can be named, between 40 and 50 different mahoganies and over 20 oaks. The widest variety of timber is produced by India, Sri Lanka, Burma and the Andaman islands, their total being over 300. South America produces about 200 varieties and Australasia alone can boast over 130. Included in these are pines such as kauri, hoop, radiata and huon, with hardwoods having such exciting names as blackbutt, bloodwood, ironbark, jarrah, karri, stringybark, wandoo, candlenut and quandong.

There are, in addition, the more usual timbers such as ash, oak, mahogany, alder, beech and birch. It is in Australia where there are the great forests of the Eucalyptus family numbering over 50 species, many being 'gums' such as southern blue gum, mountain gum, sugar gum and yellow gum. Australian softwoods are described as non-pored timbers, and the hardwoods as pored timbers (Eucalypts) and pored timbers (Non-Eucalypts).

Distribution

Around the world are two great belts of forest land which are of tremendous economic importance. In the northern hemisphere this consists of mixed hardwoods and conifers, while in the southern hemisphere there are huge areas of equatorial rain forests producing tropical hardwoods.

The tremendous area of conifers and, to a lesser extent, mixed hardwoods in the northern hemisphere is obvious from Fig. 3. The classification of the various regions is largely self explanatory with the exception of Montane forests, which are on the mountain slopes of the tropics in Central and South America, Africa, Asia and Indonesia. They are cooler and drier than tropical rain forests, the temperatures not varying greatly throughout the year (25–30° C) and the rainfall of 1·00 to 2·00 m per year being evenly distributed. Tropical Montane forests are composed mainly of large and medium-sized broad-leaved evergreen trees with fewer species than tropical rain forests. Riverain forests are those pertaining to a river or its vicinity. Tropical or subtropical grasslands containing scattered trees and shrubs, with fairly heavy rainfall areas of 1·00–1·5 m per year interrupted by distinct seasons, are classed as Savannah-type forests. The main areas are in Africa, South America, India and Australia.

The following gives some indication of the varieties of wood produced by the main timber regions of the world.

Canada and U.S.A. Douglas fir, hemlock, western red cedar, larch, spruce, yellow pine, pitch pine, red and white oak, hickory, hornbeam, walnut, canary, maple, beech, birch, ash and elm.

Central America and West Indies. Mahogany, greenheart, ebony, rosewood, lignum vitae and balsa.

South America. Box, balsa, greenheart, mahogany, laurel, rauli, parana pine.

Europe. Alder, ash, beech, birch, chestnut, elm, hornbeam, lime, oak, poplar, walnut, willow, sycamore, yew, larch, spruce, scots pine.

The Mediterranean. Acacia, cork oak, evergreen oak, olive, cypress, Corsican pine, cedar.

Africa. Mahogany, iroko, obeche, sapele, tola, mansonia, agba, adigbo, utile, afrormosia, walnut.

Asia. Elm, oak, alder, beech, birch, cherry, cinnamon, holly, hornbeam, aspen, pines, spruce, caucasian and common firs.

Pakistan, India, Burma, Sri Lanka, Malaysia, Indonesia. Ebony, teak, meranti, rose-wood, tulip-wood, pedanki, deodar, cypress, juniper.

(Australian timbers have been mentioned above.)

Fig. 4 illustrates some of the varied forms trees take if allowed to grow freely and assume their natural shape. It is interesting to consider in some detail a typical study of a tropical hardwood tree and the author is indebted to the Forestry and Timber Bureau of Australia for the following account of brush box, *Tristania conferta*.

Brush box is commonly a large tree, usually 120–140 feet in height and 3–6 feet in diameter. The trunk is straight and of good form. The main occurrence of this tree is in eastern coastal Australia near Newcastle, New South Wales, to Fraser Island, Queensland. It extends, as a smaller and less common tree, as far north as the southern slopes of the Atherton Plateau. The altitudinal range is mainly from near sea level to under 2,000 feet, but on the coastal escarpment of the Northern Tablelands of New South Wales its distribution attains 3,000 feet. The climate of the region where it is most common is subtropical. Coastal areas are frost free, but 10–25 frosts a year occur at the highest altitudes. The annual rainfall is 35–65 inches, with the maximum precipitation in summer. It prefers valleys and flats in locations varying from coastal lowlands to mountains and the coastal escarpment of tablelands. It is not common on ridges and other exposed situations. Best development is on rather heavy, fertile soils, especially alluvials. It will grow, however, on a wide range of soils, including poor, sandy types derived from sandstones, provided that they are not too shallow.

Brush box is most common in mixture forming a transition between rain-forest and eucalypt forest. Under these conditions it may be associated with flooded gum (*E. grandis*), tallowwood (*E. microcorys*), and turpentine (*Syncarpia glomulifera*) or various rainforest species.

The timber works and dresses well, but dulls tools quickly. It has satisfactory wearing qualities for use as bridge and wharf decking. It is used for flooring and general construction, while special uses include mallets, woodworking planes and pulley blocks. Brush box is a hardy, ornamental, densely foliaged tree well suited for street and park planting. It will tolerate heavy and repeated pruning.

It has been planted on an experimental scale in a number of countries and has shown promise for ornamental and avenue planting. Growth has been satisfactory for such purposes, but there are probably more suitable faster-growing species for timber production in the climatic areas which it prefers. It should not be planted where winter frosts are severe.

Bark. Persistent on the lower part of the trunk, light grey or brown, shortly fibrous and tending to be scaly. Shed from the rest of the trunk and branches, leaving an orange-brown or red-brown surface.

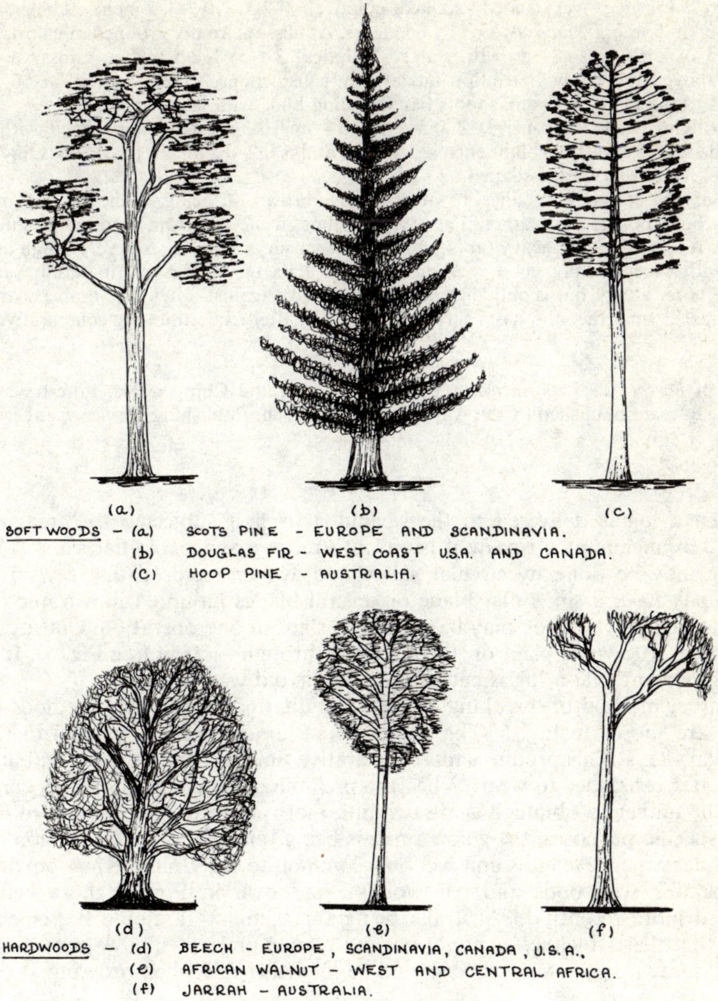

Fig. 4. A selection of tree types.

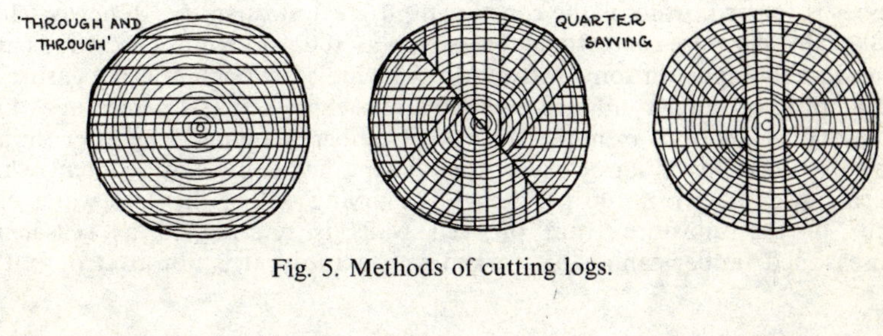

Fig. 5. Methods of cutting logs.

Leaves. Juvenile—very shortly stalked, elliptical, 1–2·5 × 0·7–1·5 inches. Underside of leaves and young stems covered by fine hairs. Adult—alternate, grouped in whorls at the end of each season's growth, stalked, elliptical 2–6 × 1–2·5 inches. Glossy dark green above, dull below. Venation moderately conspicuous, widely spaced, at 60–80 degrees to the midrib. Young shoots hairy, resting buds with large scales.

Fruit. Three-celled capsules, 0·3–0·5 × 0·3–0·4 inches, ovate or bell-shaped with a smooth surface and three blunt enclosed valves. Stalks 0·2–0·5 inches long. Seeds few in each cell, narrowly wedge-shaped.

Wood. The colour is usually brown or pinkish-brown on being sawn, but becomes greyish on exposure to weather. The texture is fine, while the grain tends to be interlocked. It is moderately heavy (about 56 lb/cu. ft. air dry), strong, stiff, very tough and hard with exceptionally good wearing qualities. It is fairly resistant to termite and marine borer attack but is only of moderate durability against fungi. The timber works well, finishes smoothly and has a shrinkage which is, after reconditioning comparatively low.

(From *Forest Trees of Australia*, by Hall, Johnson and Chippendale, Forestry and Timber Bureau, published by the Australian Government Publishing Service, Canberra, 1970.)

Conversion

When a log is delivered to the sawmill it is first subjected to 'breaking down'. By means of a ripsaw it is cut into more manageable flat slabs. The cutting may be done by circular saw, bandsaw, or reciprocating saw. The latter may have a single flat blade or several blades mounted in a frame, in which case the whole log may be sawn into slabs in one operation. Cutting in this way is known as plain or 'through and through' sawing (see Fig. 5). It is very important that a log is cut with care to avoid waste.

Another method of 'breaking down' is by quarter sawing, two methods of which are shown in Fig. 5. The timber is cut almost radially parallel to the medullary rays. This produces more decorative timber with improved stability and better resistance to wear. When the preliminary 'breaking down' is complete the timber so obtained is re-sawn into more accurate sizes to be used for more specific purposes, the whole process being referred to as 'conversion'.

Standard metric lengths and sections, common to the United Kingdom and Europe, for softwoods and hardwoods are shown in Fig. 6, those being adopted more recently in Australia being very similar. It should be remembered that these thicknesses are basic, and planed timber will always measure less than sawn sizes. Allowance should be made for this when ordering.

Seasoning

In addition to the chemical compounds from which the woody tissue of timber is formed, water is the constituent in greatest quantity. In newly felled timber this **moisture content** may be as high as 100 per cent in hardwoods and considerably higher in some softwoods. (The moisture content is a measure of the amount of water contained in wood and is expressed as a percentage of its oven-dry weight. For example, a piece of timber weighing 5 kg after drying may well have lost 7 kg of water, thus having had a moisture content when green (unseasoned) of 140 per cent.) The drying out of this free water and some of the moisture from the cell walls is referred to as **seasoning**. Unseasoned timber cannot be worked satisfactorily; it is not as strong; it is

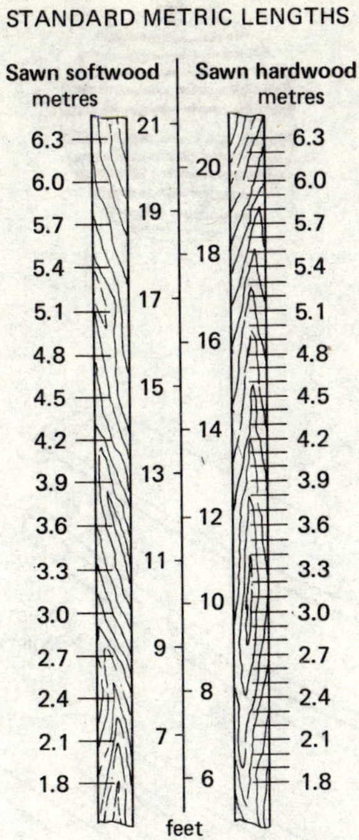

LENGTHS

Sawn softwood

The standard range of lengths supplied from the mills begins at 1.8 metres and increases in steps of 300 millimetres (300 mm) to 6.3 metres. Shorter and longer lengths can be obtained.

Sawn hardwood

The standard range begins at 1.8 metres and increases in steps of 100 millimetres (100 mm). Some hardwoods are imported in lengths shorter than 1.8 metres.

STANDARD SECTIONS

Sawn softwood

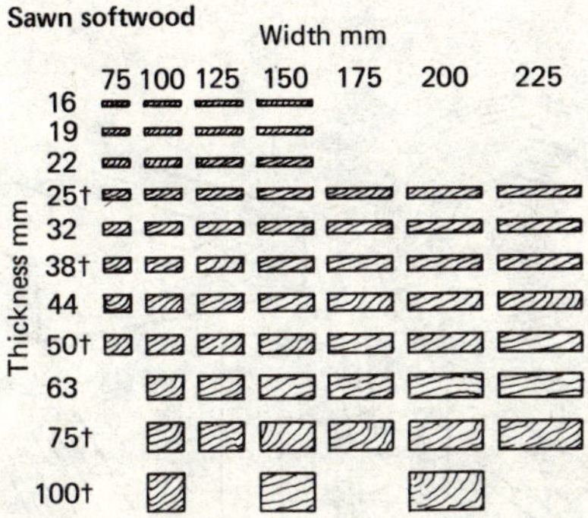

Sawn hardwood

Thickness mm: 19, 25†, 32, 38†, 50†, 63, 75†, 100†, 125

Widths are normally 150 mm and up in steps of 10 mm

Widths of strips and narrows are 50 mm and up in steps of 10 mm.

†Australian preferred metric sizes. Recommended widths are very similar to the above.

Fig. 6. Standard wood lengths and sections.

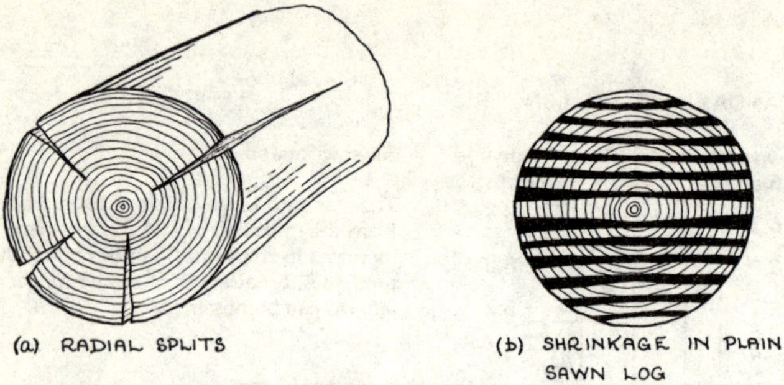

Fig. 7. Shrinkage in logs.

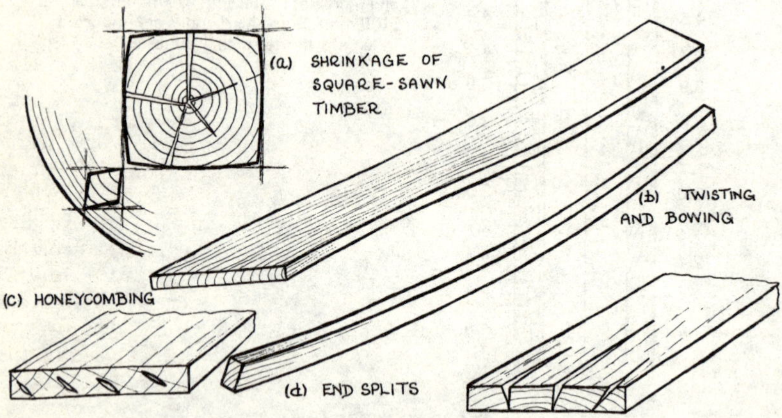

Fig. 8. Seasoning faults.

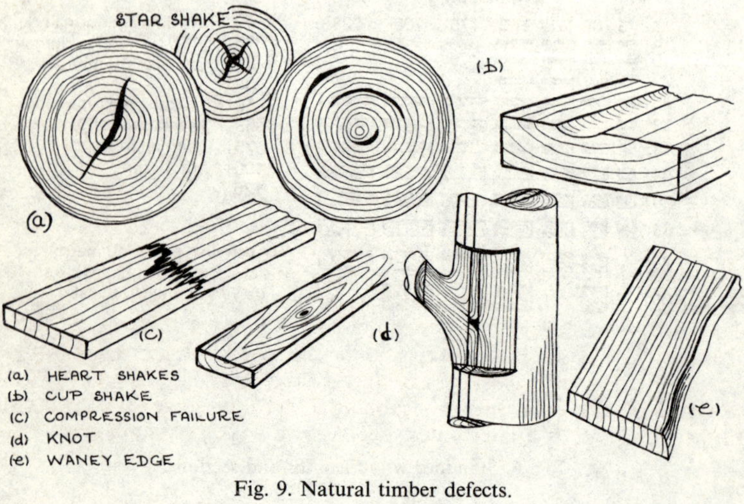

Fig. 9. Natural timber defects.

more susceptible to decay; and would shrink and split badly *in situ*. To avoid this the moisture content must be reduced to an acceptable level depending upon the use to which the timber is to be put. This can be done by **air-seasoning**, with the wood stacked on a dry base of concrete or cinders, bricks being used to support the bottom boards. The remaining boards are then stacked; 'stickers' of seasoned wood, 25 × 25 mm, placed directly above each other to prevent the boards from twisting, separate each layer and allow free circulation of air. A waterproof roof is then placed over the whole stack to shed water. Seasoning in this way may take many years and the moisture content is not predictable. On the other hand, the final required moisture content can be determined if the timber is **kiln-dried**. Here the timber is loaded on to low trolleys which are wheeled into brick kilns. Heating pipes, jets of steam and fans which keep the air circulating gradually reduce the humidity and increase the heat until the timber is seasoned: for example, 16–19 per cent moisture content for external use, 10–12 per cent where there is central heating, and as low as 8–9 per cent for wood block flooring over heating elements.

Shrinkage

Water contained in the log begins to evaporate and the cells of the wood contract immediately a tree has been felled. To reduce the moisture content of some tropical trees, and at the same time reduce their weight to make handling easier, they are '**girdled**'. A notch is cut through the sapwood with an axe round the whole circumference near the base of the trunk, several years before felling. This cuts off the supply of new sap to the tree and the leaves continue to transpire, further reducing its moisture content and gradually drying out the trunk until the tree dies, when it is felled. Conversion should take place as soon as possible after felling or the log will lose moisture most quickly at its porous ends, which could result in radial splits developing, causing considerable waste (see Fig. 7*a*).

Timber always contracts along the line of the annual rings; in other words the annual rings tend to shorten. This is called **shrinkage**, and its effect on slabs produced by plain sawing is indicated in Fig. 7*b*. Timbers shrink very little in length during seasoning, with a very few exceptions (the chief one being the kauri pine of New Zealand). Winter felling of timber is advisable when both moisture content and temperature are low.

Seasoning Faults

Once converted, not only will individual boards shrink, but they will '**cup**' or '**warp**' as the annual rings shorten. Correct stacking for seasoning can help to control this, and at the same time prevent twisting and bowing (see Fig. 8*b*).

The effect of shrinkage on square sawn sections as the annual rings shorten is indicated in Fig. 8*a*. If cut from the heart, the sides tend to become convex, while that from nearer the outer circumference assumes a lozenge section. Star shakes may also develop, or in boards the outer layers may dry out quickly causing end splits to occur. Less frequently the outer surface 'sets' without contracting a great deal, thereby trapping a wet inner core. When this subsequently dries out at a later date, splits known as 'honeycomb checks' may occur.

Natural Defects

Heart shakes (Fig. 9*a*) are single splits occurring in the standing tree and not obvious until it is felled. The shake crosses the pith and the wood fibres are torn apart due to the heartwood drying out and shrinking. A number of such shakes radiating from the pith is known as a star shake, which, as indicated earlier, may also occur during seasoning. If annual rings separate, **'cup' or 'ring' shakes** develop, which on conversion of the log may result in quite large curved sections becoming completely detached (Fig. 9*b*). **Compression failures** (Fig. 9*c*) are usually confined to tropical timbers such as African mahoganies, and are zig-zag cracks across the grain near the heart. Sometimes known as 'thunder shakes', it is thought that they may be due to high winds or some other force bending the tree in the early stages of growth, or due to the excessive jarring of the trunk as the tree is felled. They are a serious defect, making the timber quite useless if a number are present, and affected planks often break in two when lifted.

The growth of a branch forms a **knot**, distorting the grain of the timber and thereby weakening the board, but at the same time may make it more decorative. Some are 'sound' (solid and free from decay), others are 'loose' and liable to drop out as the timber seasons, while in the case of conifers which have lost decayed branches during the years many 'dead' knots are found. These are hard, brittle and often loose (Fig. 9*d*).

Boards which still retain their outer profile even after conversion are said to have a **waney edge** (Fig. 9*e*). Such timber is often used for weather boarding, but for cabinetwork it is detrimental as it means that the edge of the board consists of sapwood.

Many timbers are naturally durable—particularly yew, oak and sweet chestnut. Examples of drain pipes many hundreds of years old made of elm have been found, and although basically the hard timbers are the most durable, the very soft western red cedar is a notable exception. Fallen red cedar logs with mature trees growing over them have been found to be quite sound, obviously due to some feature of their chemical components. This ability to resist the possible attack by timber-destroying fungi is very important since most timbers are prone to attack if their moisture content is above 20 per cent. This may occur due to lack of proper protection by paint or other preservatives, or insufficient ventilation. The most insidious of these fungi is *Merulius lacrymans*, which causes dry rot in buildings. Timber is also prone to attack by wood boring beetles, the three most common being furniture beetles, deathwatch and powder post. Termites are a serious pest in tropical and subtropical countries. Affected timber should be burned when possible or treated expertly with proprietary insecticidal fluids capable of deep penetration.

2

MANUFACTURED BOARDS

The boards dealt with in this chapter include plywood, blockboard, laminated board, chipboard, fibre building boards (which include hardboard and insulating board) and plastic laminates. Metric sizes.for these products are gradually being adopted by most countries and the reader is referred to the tables in Appendix 2. Each of these boards have their own special qualities, but all have several features in common, giving them advantages over natural solid timber. They are economical in that they are cheaper. They may be faced with veneers cut from very expensive timbers and still be purchased at a modest price. In this way the full beauty of natural wood is possible while at the same time world supplies of the more exotic woods are conserved. Large areas such as partition walls may be covered by boards with the minimum of joints because of the large sizes available. Manufactured boards are stable and resist the tendency to twist or warp with atmospheric changes in temperature and humidity. The plastic laminates are available in a very wide range of colours, wood-grain finishes and textured surfaces, all of which are heat- and moisture-resisting, making them extremely suitable for interior cladding of walls or the surfacing of commercial and domestic furniture.

Plywood

Now accepted as commonplace, plywood as we know it is a comparatively modern material although there is evidence of it being used by the Egyptians about 3,000 B.C. Plywoods are made up of an odd number of wood veneers so arranged that the grain of each alternate layer crosses the others at right angles. Glued together in this way, the board is extremely stable, rigid and tremendously strong, overcoming the inherent weakness of timber to split along the grain as there is now no line of cleavage. This gives it a high resistance to impact: its insulation properties are the same as those of the wood from which it is made. It is basically fire retardant and can be made even more so by chemical processes. Special plywoods, used for constructions subjected to high stress, are made with alternative plies at 45 degrees to each other, achieving an even closer distribution of strength.

The number of veneers used in its manufacture is never less than three and may be as many as 19. When the middle veneer is thicker than the two outer ones the board is known as **stout heart.** Boards with more than three laminations are **multi-ply**. Standard board thicknesses range from 3 mm to 25 mm but thinner or thicker plywoods can be obtained for special purposes.

The manufacture of plywood is basically the same throughout the world but specifications do vary. The plies are peeled from cylindrical logs of good girth and clear straight grain. These requirements often make it necessary for a manufacturer to import logs to supplement indigenous supplies. Therefore plywood made from the same timber may be obtained from different parts of the world, manufactured to quite different specifications.

To be peeled logs are softened by soaking in 'log ponds' or by being boiled or steamed in vats. They are then placed in a machine resembling a lathe and are rotated against a knife along the length of the log. The knife advances at a uniform rate, peeling off veneers of constant thickness which are then dried, cut into the required lengths and glued together under pressure. The best veneers are used for the faces, glue is applied by roller, and the press electrically heated to reduce the setting time to a minimum. The boards are then 'trimmed' accurately to size, the faces sanded and, following inspection, given a final grading depending upon the quality of the face veneer. British manufacturers produce plywood to BS 1455:1963 with standard grades of 1, 2, 3 and 4. European beech plywood, for example, is graded as follows:

A	Special selection of faces virtually without blemish.
B	Some pin knots and discoloration allowed and face veneers may be jointed.
BB	Small sound knots, plugs and joints allowed, some streaks and discoloured wood is permitted provided it is sound.
BBBC	Permits broken knots, gaps, splits, rough finish but well glued.

The adhesives used to bond the plies are of the utmost importance since their properties determine the final characteristics of the plywood and the use to which it can best be put. For grades intended for interior use, animal or casein glues are employed since such plywood needs to be well glued but does not necessarily require resistance to moisture or water. When plywood is used externally, however, exposure to the atmosphere requires an adhesive capable of withstanding all the various changes of climatic conditions. Phenolic resins have high strength properties under all conditions of exposure and have been proved to make joints highly resistant to weather, micro-organisms, cold and boiling water, steam and dry heat. They are also very resistant to common solvents, wood preservatives, fire retardant chemicals and most acids. Plywood bonded with such phenol-formaldehyde resins (PF) are classed as 'weather and boil proof' and are graded WBP. For example, Cresta plywood is made of selected West African hardwoods with mahogany or sapele facings bonded in this way, and in addition to ordinary external use is recommended for boat building (see pages 230 and 324). Not only must the glue be suitable for exterior use, but so too must the wood itself, which may also be treated with preservatives or paints.

Plywood may be obtained in any combination of grade and type of adhesive to meet requirements. When ordering a sheet of plywood it is understood that the first dimension indicates the run of the grain on the face; thus a board 2440 × 1220 is 'long grain' whereas a board 1220 × 2440 is 'cross grain', which is often specified for veneering or bending purposes. Alder, beech, birch, gaboon and Douglas fir are timbers frequently used to make plywood in the Western world while in Australasia, hoop pine, kauri, bunya pine, maple, sycamore, coachwood and radiata pine are used.

Plywood can be worked in much the same way as solid timber; care is necessary, however, in planing the edges to avoid splitting the ends. Some

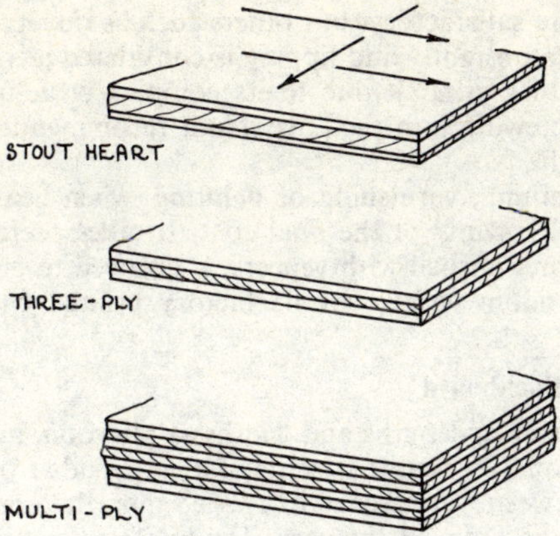

Fig. 10. Types of plywood.

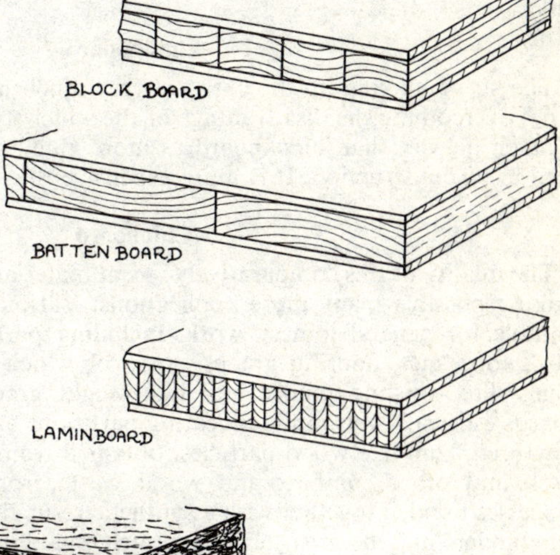

Fig. 11. Laminated boards.

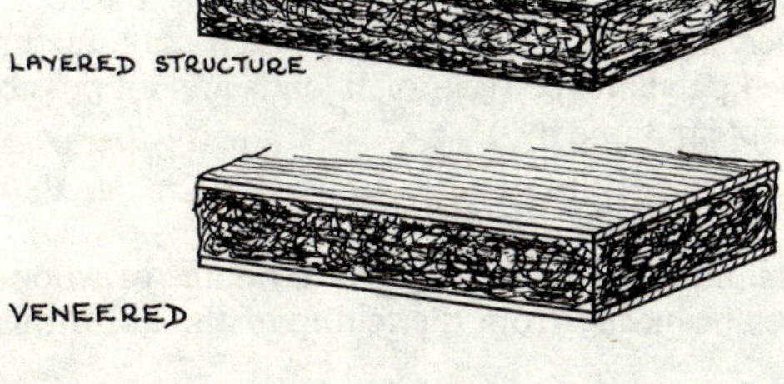

Fig. 12. Chipboard.

joints such as housings and laps are satisfactory, but others such as dovetails are impracticable. The edge is often unsightly and lipping is considered advisable in most cases. Pinning is rather difficult due to its compact structure unless the holes are pre-drilled. Screwing into the edge is not recommended, but twin-fast screws hold well in the face.

Plywood may be finished by staining, varnishing or painting, when heavy undercoats are advisable to avoid 'crazing' of the final coat. It takes preservative stains very well. It may be pre-finished with veneers, V-grooved to give the impression of planking in random widths, or be factory printed with wood-grain effects.

Blockboard

Blockboard is manufactured in similar lengths and widths as plywood, and in thicknesses of 12, 16, 18, 22, 24 and 25 mm. It consists of a core made from strips 25 mm wide sandwiched between outer veneers of 2–3·5 mm, the grain always running at right angles to the grain of the core. The line of the strips making up the core is sometimes 'telegraphed' through the outer veneers and is difficult to conceal. Because of this tendency blockboard should not be used for high-class work. Battenboard is built up from strips not more than 75 mm wide.

Laminboard

The strips making up the core are very much narrower, only 1·5 to 7 mm wide, overcoming the disadvantage of the wider strips used for blockboard. It is much heavier than blockboard as more glue and denser timbers are often used in its construction. It is more expensive thus limited to high-class work.

Chipboard

The quality of this comparatively recent material has been rapidly improved making possible many more applications. Various grades are now available suitable for general joinery work, including partitions, panelling, cabinets, work tops, etc., flooring grades, some of which have tongue and grooved edges, fire resisting grades and lightweight grades which are low-density boards especially for non-loadbearing partitions and roof cladding. It is manufactured from fine wood particles, obtained from forest thinnings of spruce, larch and other conifers, and wood waste from other timber-consuming processes bonded together with a synthetic resin glue under heat and pressure. The binders may be urea, phenol or melamine formaldehyde resins.

Some boards have a single layer consisting of chips of similar size bonded at random. Others have outer layers of finer chips to give a smoother face over a core of coarser particles. Chipboards are available faced with natural wood veneers or plastic coatings in various colours, wood-grain effects and in some cases metal. Veneers are applied to both sides of the board to balance each other, preventing bowing (see Chapter 13). As with other manufactured boards, the edges require to be lipped and conventional joints are not possible. (The reader is referred to Chapters 8 and 11.)

Fibre Building Boards

These are sheet materials manufactured from the actual fibres of wood or woody plants bonded together primarily from the felting of the fibres themselves and their own inherent adhesive properties. Raw timber is reduced to its fibres and any necessary additives such as adhesives are mixed with it in water. This watery pulp is fed on to a forming machine and gradually dries out by gravity and suction as it moves along on a web or mat.

Insulating board is made from this so-called 'wet lap' simply being passed between rollers to produce the required thickness and cut to sheet sizes which are then dried and trimmed. **Hardboard** is produced by subjecting the cut sheets to great pressure in a hydraulic press, and it is this hot pressing which gives the sheet its special characteristics of density, smoothness and strength. There are three grades of hardboard depending upon their density: medium, standard and tempered. The last has greater strength and improved moisture resistance by the addition of oils or resins. Both insulating board and hardboard are available with a number of factory applied surface textures and finishes. In addition to enamelled, plastic and wood grain type facings, moulded hardboard, which is embossed with a pattern in the press, and perforated hardboard (pegboard) are available.

Being a timber-based material, fibre boards can be cut and used in a similar manner to timber. A fine-toothed saw should be used to cut into the face, and the edges cleaned with plane, file or glasspaper. Insulating board is best cut with a sharp trimming knife and can be grooved and bevelled with the Record fibreboard plane (see Chapter 4). For fixing, nails or screws should be at 100 mm centres round the edges of the board and at 150–200 mm centres along intermediate fixings.

Plastic Laminates

Arborite is a high pressure thermoset plastic surfacing material consisting of multi-layers of specially processed papers impregnated with synthetic plastic resins. Intense heat and pressure fuse these layers into a homogeneous solid panel. Phenolic or melamine resins are used to impregnate the layers of kraft paper, to which are added a pattern paper and a sheet of alfa cellulose paper, both of which are also impregnated. The pattern paper is the one which gives the sheet its colour or wood grain effect, and the cellulose overlay paper is the vehicle for carrying an extra working surface of melamine and becomes transparent during lamination. It is in this form that the lay-up or 'books' of sheets are fed into the press. The number of kraft papers in a lay-up determines the thickness of sheet to be produced. Arborite manufacture decorative laminates from 0·8 to 31·75 mm thick. Initially the sheet will have a glossy surface, which is rubbed down mechanically with pumice powder and water if a semi-matt finish is required. The back of each sheet is sanded to provide a key for the adhesive when the sheet is eventually bonded.

Cutting should be done with a hacksaw blade in a pad handle or with a Stanley saw knife: the hard laminate would quickly blunt a tenon saw. Final trimming of the edges can be with a file and glasspaper, or in some cases with a plane. Sawing must always be into the face to avoid chipping. Contact adhesives are satisfactory for most applications but a resin glue may be used providing adequate overall pressure can be applied during the setting time. The laminate may be cleaned with a damp cloth and the original lustre maintained by occasional applications of glass or furniture polish. Coarse abrasive cleaners or steel wool should not be used, and although laminates are heat resistant, very hot dishes should preferably be placed on a table mat.

3

DESIGN

The design of a piece of woodwork involves many considerations before the work can begin. Some motivation must exist which makes the need for a particular item apparent. This might arise from a natural creative instinct, or simply from plain necessity. Method is important if waste of time and possibly materials are to be avoided. No work, however simple, should begin until specific requirements such as choice of wood, overall dimensions, proportions, appearance, construction, necessary metal or plastic fittings, finish and cost have been considered. The material may be natural timber, manufactured board or a combination of both, with occasionally additional materials such as glass, metal or plastic laminates. Overall dimensions will have limitations imposed on them depending upon what the work is expected to do—for example, it may be a cupboard which has to fit into a limited space, or a box which has to hold a number of specific items, or something to be sat on which immediately restricts the height. Joints, nails, screws and glue may all be included in the construction and the use of each requires careful thought, as does the possible use of heavier metal fixings such as bolts, brackets and other commercially made fittings as hinges, locks and handles.

The proportions of materials used in relation to each other and the shape and size of other fitments used all affect the appearance of the work. Not only is appearance important, of course, but so is the efficiency of the finished piece, which is usually related to strength, not only of individual members but of the construction as a whole. Efficiency also means that the piece will do what is expected of it. Finish is important because this may affect the choice of materials, particularly if the completed work has to fit in with an established furnishing scheme. If this has a 'natural' finish the timber used may simply have to be of the same kind as existing pieces, but if it is to be painted there may be more freedom of choice. In some cases overall cost may be a limiting factor in the choice of materials, but even if necessity makes the price of no consequence it is always good practice to cost the items beforehand.

All these problems of design should be settled in advance in the form of notes, freehand sketches or more detailed diagrams when necessary. For very many years, when faced with a design problem the author has successfully adopted the following procedure bearing in mind the preceding considerations. Ideas are recorded in the form of freehand sketches and accompanying notes, several alternative designs being drawn. Even for the most simple objects, such as a stick on which to wind string, or a shelf, this is quite possible. Then by a process of selection and rejection the one considered to be the most suitable is chosen. If necessary at this stage more detailed workshop drawings are then made.

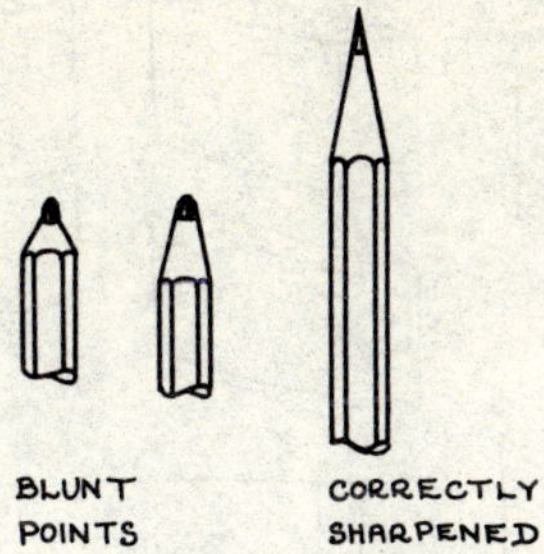

Fig. 13. Pencil points.

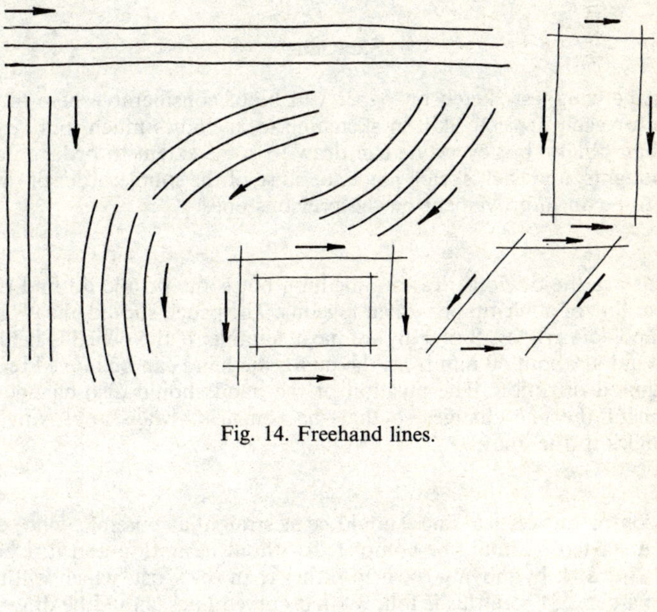

Fig. 14. Freehand lines.

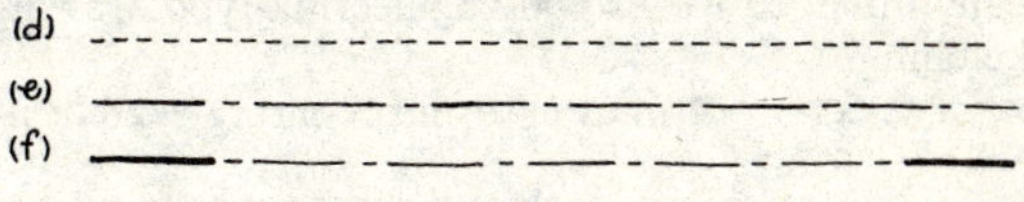

Fig. 15. Types of lines.

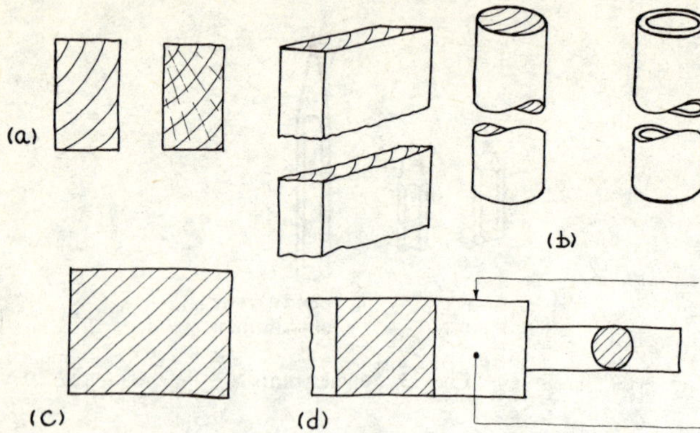

Fig. 16. Conventional representation.

Sketching

Even the roughest sketch on paper will be of considerable help to clarify designs for each project. Skill in sketching ideas comes much more easily to some than others, but everyone can draw to some extent in order to express their thoughts, and each sketch made, because of the simple order of things, is bound to be an improvement on the previous one.

Pencils

Pencils are the obvious drawing medium but some people do find the bolder, freer line of a felt-tip pen advantageous. The pencil should always be kept sharp, and soft grades, B or HB, are most suitable. If the pencil is held as for writing and at about 40 mm from the point, the hand can be moved readily in any required direction. The position of the hand should also change as the direction of the line changes so that the pencil is always approximately at right-angles to the line.

Lines

Horizontal and vertical lines should be as straight as possible. Once the line has been started it should be completed without hesitation and it is better if the line is drawn by moving the arm rather than the wrist, which will tend to produce a curve. From this it follows that curved lines should be drawn from the wrist, the pencil preferably moving towards the body. BS 308, Part 1: 1972 (General Principles) and Part 2 (Dimensions and Tolerancing of Size) make various recommendations regarding the use of different types of line, which although basically intended for use on engineering-type drawings can well be adopted for sketching.

Fig. 15 shows a selection of lines used in preparing sketches.

a. Visible outlines and edges—a continuous line of 0·7 mm thickness.

b. Outlines of adjacent parts, or revolving sections; dimension and leader lines; hatching—a continuous line 0·3 mm in thickness.

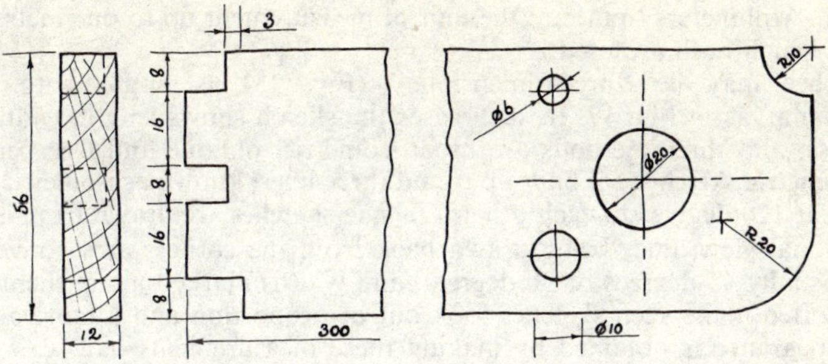

Fig. 17. Dimensions, diameters and radii in two-dimensional sketches.

c. Limits of partial views of sections when the line is not an axis—continuous irregular lines of 0·3 mm.

d. Hidden outlines and edges—short thin dashes (0·3 mm).

e. Centre lines and extreme position of movable parts—chain, thin (0·3 mm). Use of a centre line where items are symmetrical means that only half the work need be drawn.

f. Cutting planes—chain lines, thick (0·7 mm) at the ends and at changes of direction, thin (0·3 mm) elsewhere.

Further Recommendations

Other common features for which conventional representations are adopted and which are valuable in making sketches, often being space-saving too, are illustrated in Fig. 16 as follows:

a. End grain, softwood, and hardwood where the medullary rays are indicated.

b. Interrupted views where space on the paper does not permit the full length to be drawn. Timber, round rod—such as long handles, and metal tube; for example, the hanging rail in a wardrobe.

c. 'Hatching': a method of indicating sectional shapes.

d. A square rail with a round peg at its end. Note how the sections are indicated within the shape and how attention can be drawn to certain features: the arrowhead indicates an edge and the dot a surface.

Sketches of small work may be approximately full size, but obviously those of larger work will not be. Full-size measurements must be shown in both cases; often these have to be worked out as the design proceeds with the aid of a rule or steel tape, and in many cases measurements *in situ*. BS 308 recommends that dimensions, diameters and radii should be indicated as shown in Fig. 17, and be so placed that they are readable from the bottom of the drawing or right-hand side. 'Projection lines' are extensions of the drawing from which they should be separated by a small space. 'Dimension lines' are drawn between them and terminate in a small arrowhead touching the projection line. Millimeters (mm) are the unit of measurement up to one metre (m), beyond which both are used.

Sketches may be 'three-dimensional' (Fig. 18) as opposed to 'two-dimensional' as in Fig. 17. In such cases the sketch shows length, width and thickness, and three methods are used: isometric, oblique and free perspective. **Isometric sketches** are built up round three lines, known as isometric axes, pitched at 120 degrees to each other. **Oblique sketches** are drawn from a two-dimensional view, lines being drawn back from the corners at a convenient angle, usually 45 degrees or 30 degrees, and widths marked along them. Full widths often make such sketches look out of proportion and a more acceptable appearance is obtained by making these measurements half-scale. **Free perspective sketches** are similar to isometric, except that lines are drawn towards two imaginary 'vanishing points' some considerable distance away. This type of sketch is often more acceptable to the eye as it gives quite a true representation, but is usually used for the sketching of larger items such as stools, tables, cupboards etc.

In making sketches by any of the above methods it is often useful first to draw a 'box' or 'crate' of thin lines at the requisite angles in which the design for the proposed work can be constructed. This is particularly applicable to circles (see Fig. 19). The addition of light colour tints by pencil or brush often helps to improve visual appreciation of the design sketch.

Unfortunately, it is very difficult to show hidden details on any three-dimensional sketch with accuracy. Any attempt to do so results in a complicated and confused drawing, and this is why it is common practice to show only those parts which can be seen. This difficulty is overcome by drawing a number of two-dimensional views showing the various parts of the work in relation to each other. These two-dimensional views are so arranged that it is possible to project details from one to the other in what is known as **orthographic projection**, the usual form of which is 'first angle'. This generally consists of three views—front elevation, end elevation and plan—but when necessary a second end elevation may be used or a complete section to show the inner construction, details of which may be drawn on the same sheet to a larger scale. The scales used in the metric system are full-size (1:1) and, for reduction, 1:2, 1:5, 1:10 and 1:20 (used in reverse for enlargements). Many examining boards now include problem-solving design questions in their craft education examinations. These may be answered satisfactorily if the preceding techniques are adopted. The following is a typical example, reproduced by courtesy of the Associated Examining Board.

CRAFTWORK – WOOD

Design

(Two hours allowed for the design and half an hour for making a tracing and two lists.)

Make complete working drawings and a list of materials required. Indicate the 'finish' of your choice.

All rough sketches leading up to your final design, together with any explanatory notes, must be attached to your drawing.

When the electricity supply fails as a result of a 'blown' fuse in the domestic fuse box, the immediate requirements are: fuse wire, a small screwdriver, and almost invariably a

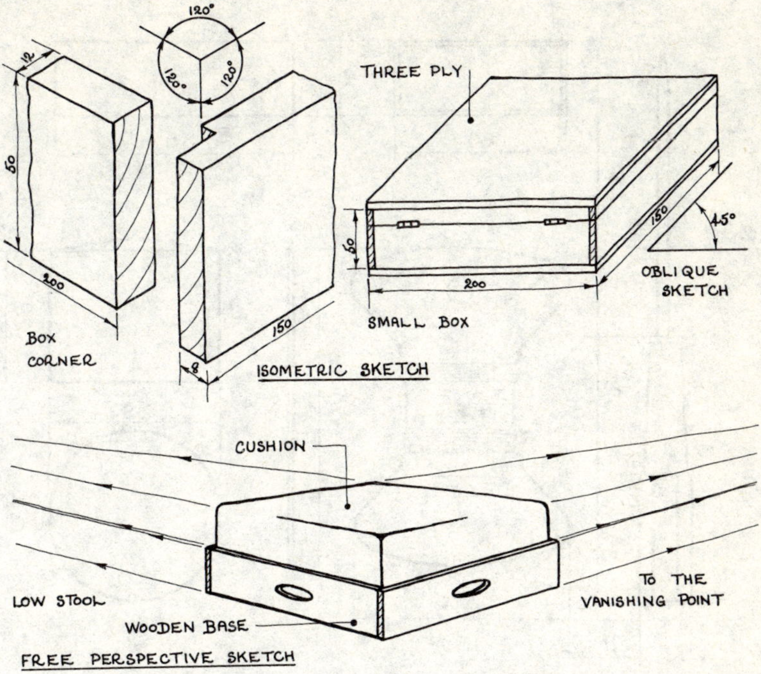

Fig. 18. Types of three-dimensional sketches.

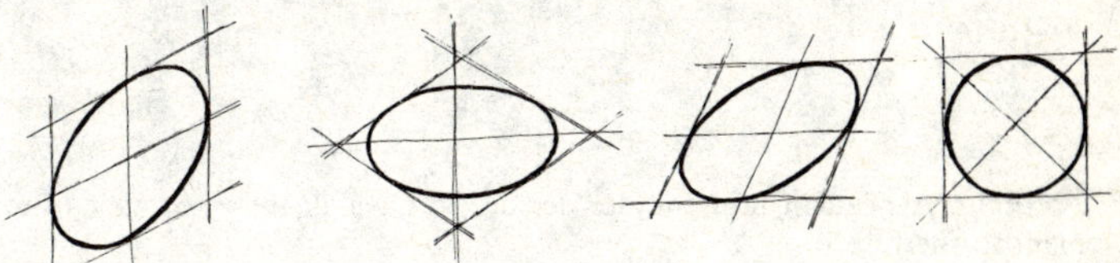

Fig. 19. Sketching circles.

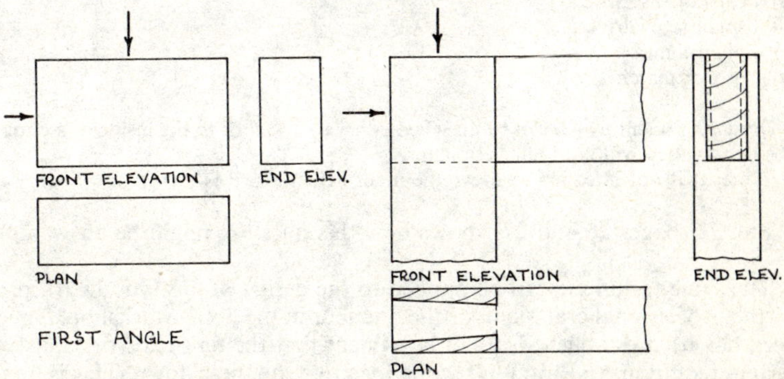

Fig. 20. Orthographic projection: usual arrangement of views.

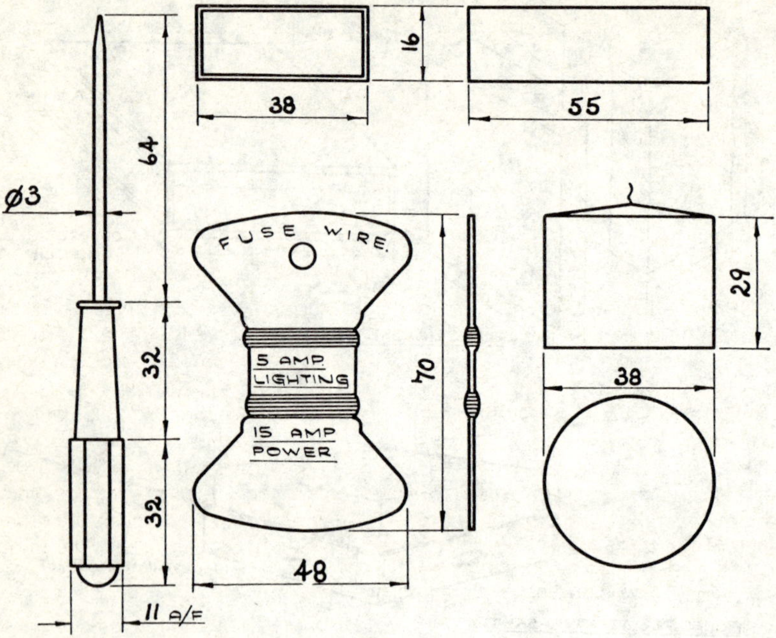

Fig. 21

source of light. A prudent householder decides to have all these together in one place convenient to the fuse box.

Fig. 21 shows:

(*a*) a card of fuse wire;
(*b*) a small screwdriver;
(*c*) a night light;
(*d*) a box of matches.

Design a fitment which can be attached either to a wall or to the inside of a cupboard door and which will hold all these items.

(Note: It is not intended to move the night light when it is used.)

Fig. 22 (pages 26 and 27) shows how this question might be answered.

The same technique can be applied to the design of any woodwork project by the professional craftsman or the amateur in the home workshop. Once the need has been established it will be evident that the finished work must meet certain requirements, and it is a good idea to write these down. This is how the design for an occasional table might be worked out.

Requirements

1. The table should have modern styling.
2. It should be low in keeping with the design of the existing furniture.
3. Big enough in area to hold crockery, etc., for light hot meals, afternoon tea, supper, etc.
4. It should be easy to move and not be too heavy.
5. Stable.
6. Easy to clean.
7. Surface proof against heat and liquids.
8. Good overall appearance.
9. The wood should be light in colour.
10. 'Natural finish'.

Several alternatives within the limits of the brief have been sketched in Fig. 23, each in good proportion and being three-dimensional to give a fair indication of how they would look when completed. They are all of modern design employing modern materials and modern methods of assembly as well as some traditional methods. Proposed dimensions are shown and each design is reinforced by written notes or more detailed sketches of the construction.

Precise details of the construction of the table are shown in Fig. 24, an orthographic projection in first angle. Accurate measurements are shown, as are the overall proportions and the relationship of each member to the others. Part of the top has been cut away from the plan in order to show the underframing more clearly. Materials required are listed clearly, as is the possible finish. The deep purple of the anemone Arborite will contrast well with the natural finish of the beech. Constructional details of the various proposed designs such as the helicoil screws, the capped screws and the barrel nuts provide decorative features. So too does the careful choice of colour between timber and the Arborite laminate.

More traditional designs might rely on surface features such as simple carving, mouldings or edge treatments as chamfers and bevels. On many occasions a scale model is a useful extension to a drawing before being committed to the actual work. In this way proportions can be checked and if colour is added to the model an even better impression of the design is obtained. Offcuts of wood, hardboard, card, etc., which can all be glued easily may be used for such models and poster paint is a suitable colouring medium.

The Ergonomics of Design

As a science, ergonomics is comparatively recent, the word being derived from the Greek *ergon* (work) and *nomos* (law) and interpreted as fitting the work to be designed to the person who has to use it. This, in an effort to ensure efficiency in use, and to avoid fatigue from the strain put on muscles which have to maintain some unnatural posture over a vice, hunched over a worktop or for ever having to stretch up to shelves which are far too high. The common church pew, for example, is an ergonomic nightmare!

Many major industrial concerns and university faculties have carried out ergonomic research and this information is applied extensively to design by architects and manufacturers of tools and household utensils, domestic and industrial fitments and furniture. Handles are designed which fit the hand and give maximum efficiency—for example, the squared plastic handle of the

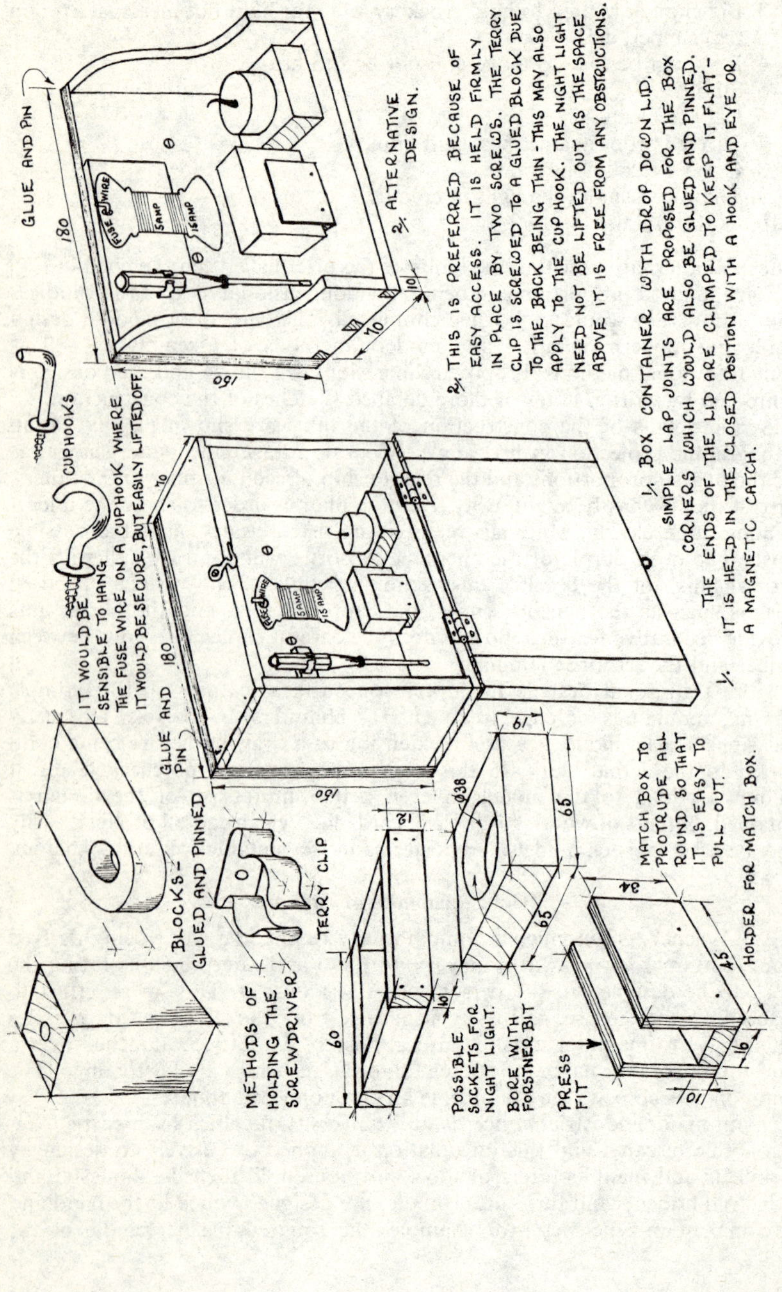
GLUE AND PIN
180
160
70
10
FUSE WIRE
5AMP
15AMP
2/. ALTERNATIVE DESIGN.
2/. THIS IS PREFERRED BECAUSE OF EASY ACCESS. IT IS HELD FIRMLY IN PLACE BY TWO SCREWS. THE TERRY CLIP IS SCREWED TO A GLUED BLOCK DUE TO THE BACK BEING THIN - THIS MAY ALSO APPLY TO THE CUP HOOK. THE NIGHT LIGHT NEED NOT BE LIFTED OUT AS THE SPACE ABOVE IT IS FREE FROM ANY OBSTRUCTIONS.
CUPHOOKS
IT WOULD BE SENSIBLE TO HANG THE FUSE WIRE ON A CUPHOOK WHERE IT WOULD BE SECURE, BUT EASILY LIFTED OFF.
GLUE AND PIN
180
70
160
1/. BOX CONTAINER WITH DROP DOWN LID.
SIMPLE LAP JOINTS ARE PROPOSED FOR THE BOX CORNERS WHICH WOULD ALSO BE GLUED AND PINNED.
THE ENDS OF THE LID ARE CLAMPED TO KEEP IT FLAT-
1/. IT IS HELD IN THE CLOSED POSITION WITH A HOOK AND EYE OR A MAGNETIC CATCH.
BLOCKS - GLUED AND PINNED
TERRY CLIP
METHODS OF HOLDING THE SCREWDRIVER.
POSSIBLE SOCKETS FOR NIGHT LIGHT.
BORE WITH FORSTNER BIT
Ø38
60
18
10
65
65
19
PRESS FIT
MATCH BOX TO PROTRUDE ALL ROUND SO THAT IT IS EASY TO PULL OUT.
34
45
16
10
HOLDER FOR MATCH BOX.

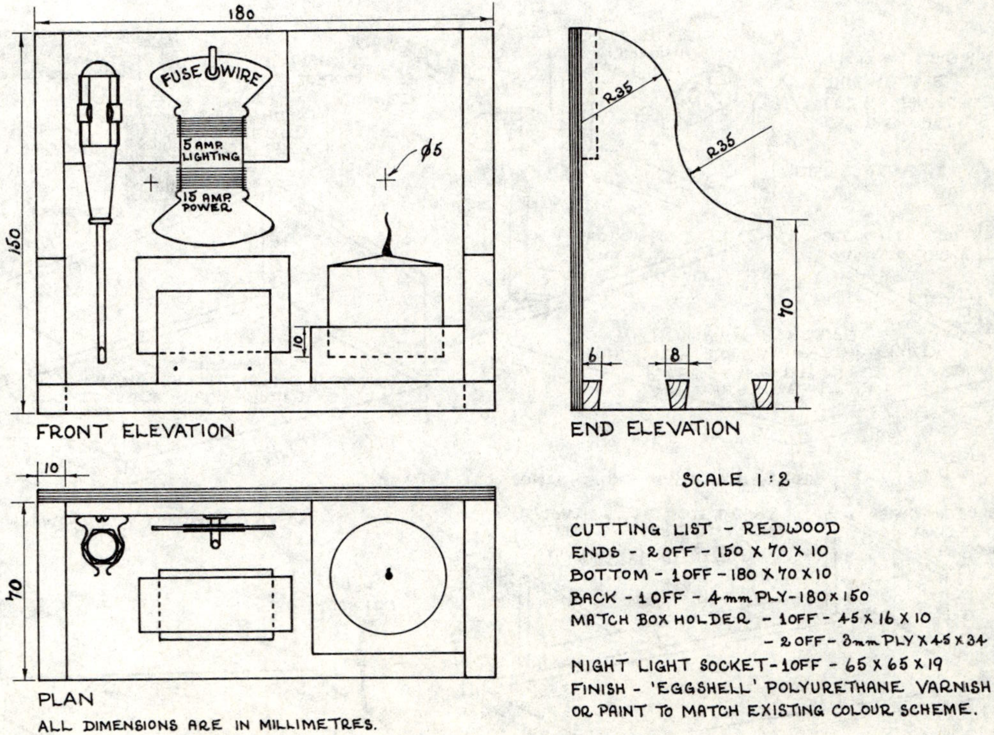

Fig. 22. Suggested ideas leading to solution of the question on page 22.

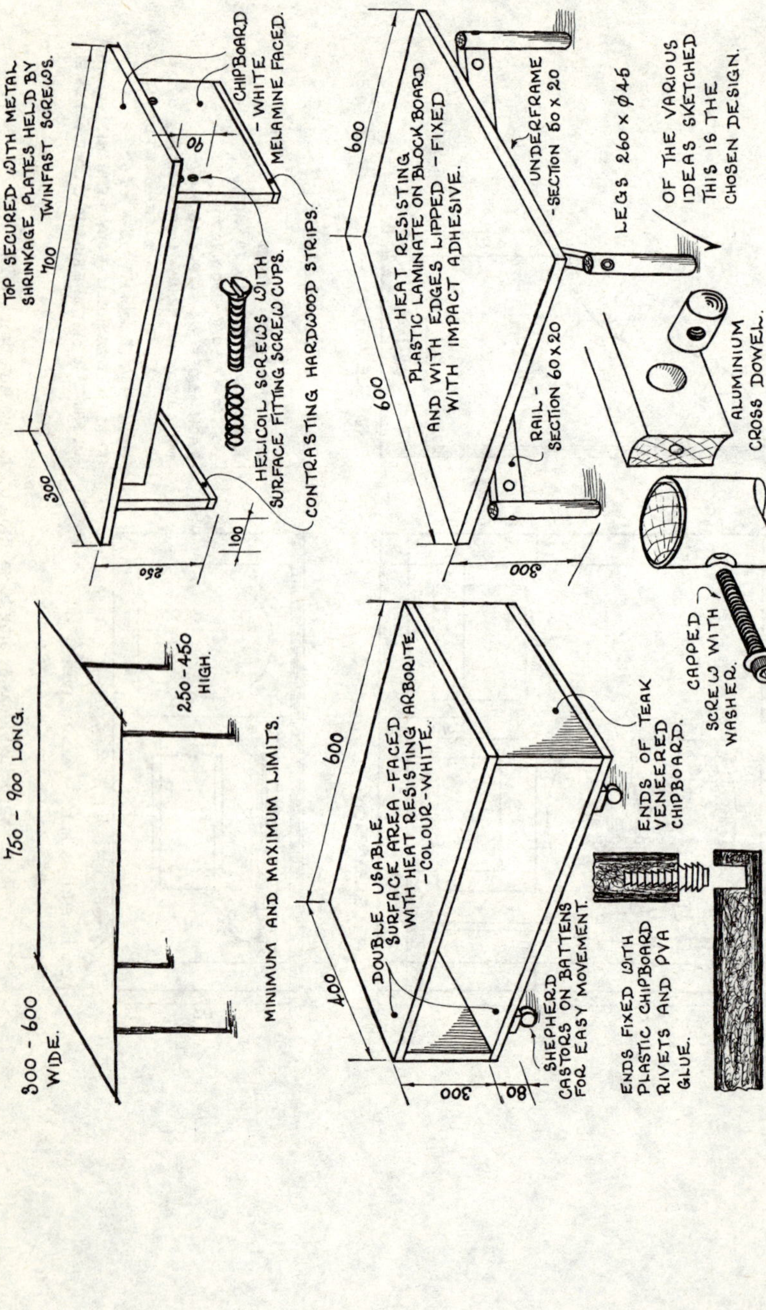
300 - 600 WIDE.
750 - 900 LONG.
250-450 HIGH.
MINIMUM AND MAXIMUM LIMITS.
TOP SECURED WITH METAL SHRINKAGE PLATES HELD BY TWINFAST SCREWS.
700
300
250
100
40
CHIPBOARD - WHITE MELAMINE FACED.
HELICOIL SCREWS WITH SURFACE FITTING SCREW CUPS.
CONTRASTING HARDWOOD STRIPS.
400
600
300
80
DOUBLE USABLE SURFACE AREA - FACED WITH HEAT RESISTING ARBORITE - COLOUR - WHITE.
SHEPHERD CASTORS ON BATTENS FOR EASY MOVEMENT.
ENDS OF TEAK VENEERED CHIPBOARD.
ENDS FIXED WITH PLASTIC CHIPBOARD RIVETS AND PVA GLUE.
600
600
300
HEAT RESISTING PLASTIC LAMINATE ON BLOCK BOARD AND WITH EDGES LIPPED - FIXED WITH IMPACT ADHESIVE.
RAIL - SECTION 60 x 20
UNDERFRAME - SECTION 60 x 20
LEGS 260 x ∅45
OF THE VARIOUS IDEAS SKETCHED THIS IS THE CHOSEN DESIGN.
CAPPED SCREW WITH WASHER.
ALUMINIUM CROSS DOWEL.

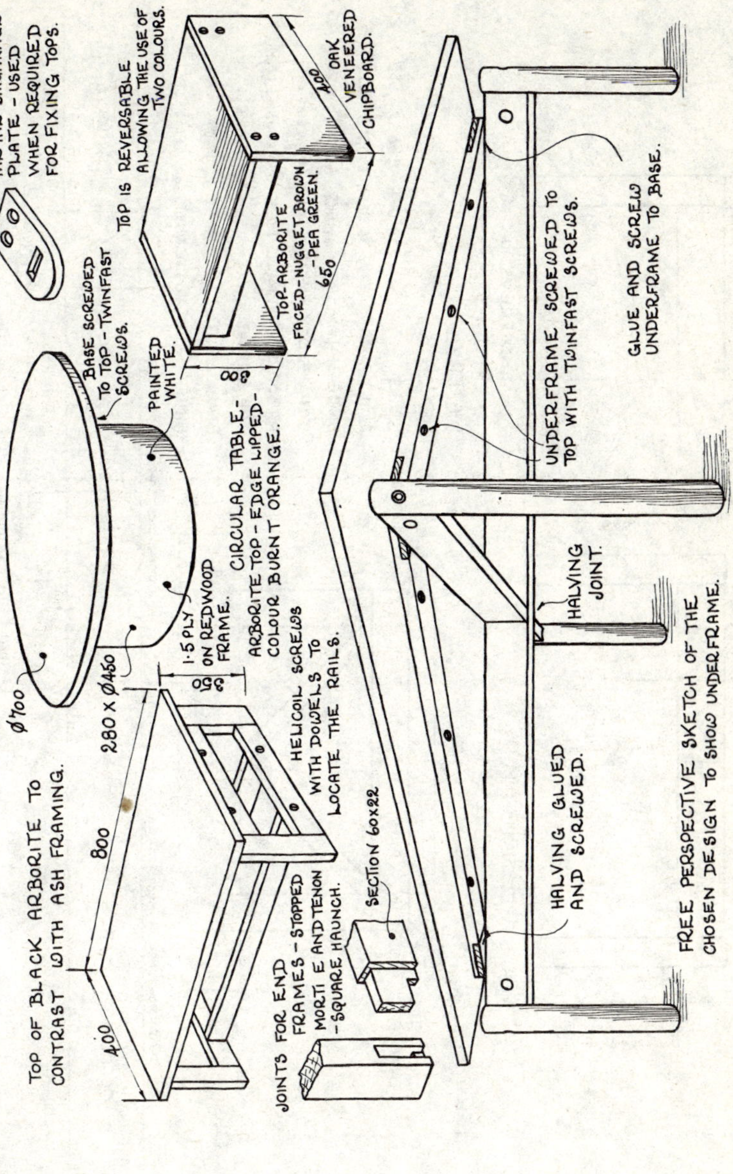

Fig. 23. Alternative approaches to making an occasional table.

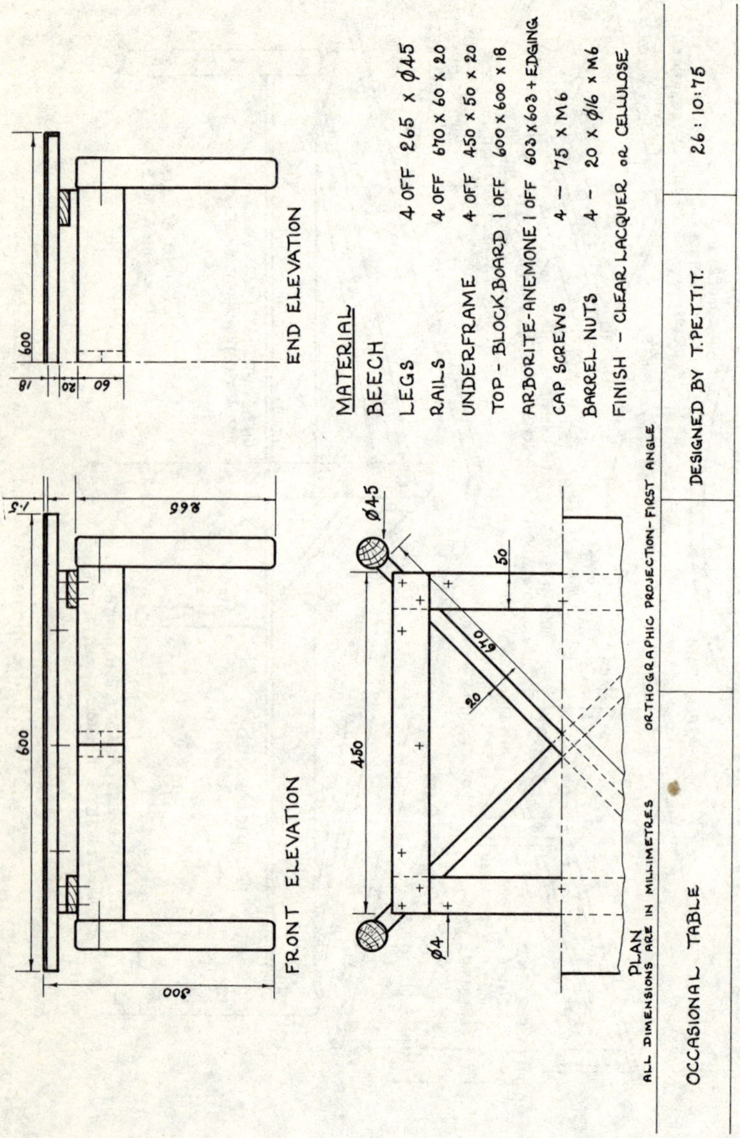

Fig. 24. Design of an occasional table.

Marples 'Blue Chip' range of chisels (see Chapter 4); worktops should be a suitable height on which to work bearing in mind that not all people are alike; and modern chairs are becoming more and more comfortable to sit on.

The professional or the amateur designer must take into account the ergonomics of whatever is designed, albeit a simple object like a salad spoon, the position of a handle on a door or a complex item such as a chair. In many ways in the past, the role of ergonomics as an essential factor of design has been ignored either through lack of knowledge, added cost or at the expense of appearance. It is now an aspect of design which no one should ignore.

4

HANDTOOLS FOR WOODWORKING

When reaching for a handhold on a ledge, a friend rock climbing in the English Lake District about 20 years ago picked up what was quite obviously a stone age axe. On a subsequent visit the author found further specimens in the same area, and also flat topped rocks which had equally obviously been used as work benches, the ground around them being strewn with small flakes of stone which had been chipped off while the axes were being fashioned. The hill slopes around have since yielded many more such examples which are approximately 240 mm long, 80 mm wide and 40 mm thick. The axes were made from a volcanic tuff, a hard igneous intrusion which emerged on the face of the mountains at a high level around the valley. It is believed that pieces of granite were imported into the area with which to chip the axes to shape, and at what has now become known as the 'Langdale Axe Factory', rejects, thrown aside because of faulty workmanship or flaws in the rock, are still to be found. Examples of these axes have been identified in different parts of the country indicating that they were transported from the Lakeland site and that they could well have been a part of some form of trading system. It is quite remarkable that neolithic man, a primitive inhabitant of the Lake District, should have recognised the use to which this rock could be put and devised a means and developed the skill by which it could be worked. Equally remarkable is the fact that this important archaeological site should have remained undiscovered throughout thousands of years until such a short time ago.

Quite probably the granite used to shape these axes would initially be held in the hand, as would the axes themselves, being used as a general-purpose tool to cut, to use as a weapon and for primitive cultivation. Later, the addition of a handle, made by binding the axe head with leather thongs into a split at the end of a stick, increased its efficiency. Obviously, hammers too would develop in a similar way and as tools were developed from his primitive weapons so too Man became for ever separated from his fellow animals.

Archaeological excavations and occasional 'finds' have in fact confirmed this development of primitive tools and examples have been discovered throughout the world. Originally man made use of and adapted as tools whatever objects he found around him. For example, flakes of flint were used as scraping and cutting tools, and later, with crude, uneven serrations in the edge, as saws. In using materials which were simply 'to hand', he had little choice of design and tools of this nature found in burial mounds of northern England, French caves, and excavations in Sweden, Denmark, Switzerland and Italy vary in length from 40 to 230 mm and were not capable of making deep cuts due to their thickness. Even when mounted on wood or horn, as some were, this problem was not solved. The snout of the sawfish, the notched edges of shells and shark's teeth have all been used as saws in various parts of the world.

Eventually the discovery of metals by Man made him independent of natural materials and objects. He was able to determine the kind of tools he needed, and so design them to meet particular requirements. Archaeological discoveries and studies have enabled us to trace the development of tools throughout the various periods of history, and this development has been such that in many cases even our most modern tools bear a distinct resemblance to the hammers, axes, chisels, saws and planes of several hundred years ago. One obvious difference is the introduction of modern plastics for tools such as folding rules, marking gauge screws, chisel, screwdriver and saw handles, etc. Most households have a small, basic number of tools, possibly inherited, or acquired more recently to perform a particular task, or to be available should minor emergencies arise. These may consist of no more than a screwdriver, a hammer and a pair of pliers. However, for anyone intending to do even the most simple woodwork little can be done with these alone, and cutting tools such as chisels, saws, planes and drills will also be required. Careful thought and consideration should be given to the purchase of each tool, as such a wide variety is now available from which to select. It is sound practice to buy good-quality tools, which will be found to give good service, durability and efficiency, and will, in the long term, be worthwhile investments. Just as the best work is produced by using the best materials available, so too the finest workmanship is made possible by the use of good tools. It is the purpose of this chapter, not only to give a detailed account of the handtools in regular use, but also indicate to the reader those which the author has found to meet the above requirements.

Measuring and Simple Testing Tools

The Bench Rule

Some **hardwood** bench rules are still found in woodworking use. These were of a sturdy section, quite rigid, and with the ends protected by brass clamps to prevent undue wear since it must be possible for this type of work to make accurate measurements right from the end of the rule; for example, taking a measurement from inside a corner. On these rules the graduations were well defined, but nevertheless, being of wood, the surface was susceptible to wear and to disfiguration by glue, stains and paints. These could not be removed without the danger of destroying the graduations. Further, any wear along the edge of the rule made it useless for testing the truth of straight edges or small flat surfaces, a use to which the bench rule is often put.

Steel rules have almost entirely superseded the wooden ones and are superior in that they withstand wear much better and smaller measurements can be marked on them more accurately. With the introduction of the metric system, which is becoming more and more universal, this is a very important consideration. The 300 mm rule illustrated in Fig. 25 is typical of the modern styles being manufactured. Tough and springy so as to retain straightness, the deeply cut black graduations are easily readable against the satin-chrome finish. That they should be easily readable is a most important feature of a rule and the sawtooth arrangement of the measurements on this example ensures that this is so. One-metre rules are also available.

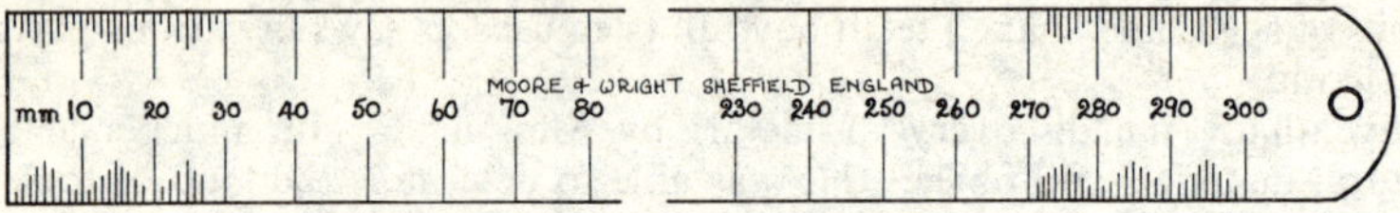

Fig. 25. The steel rule.

Fig. 26. The folding rule.

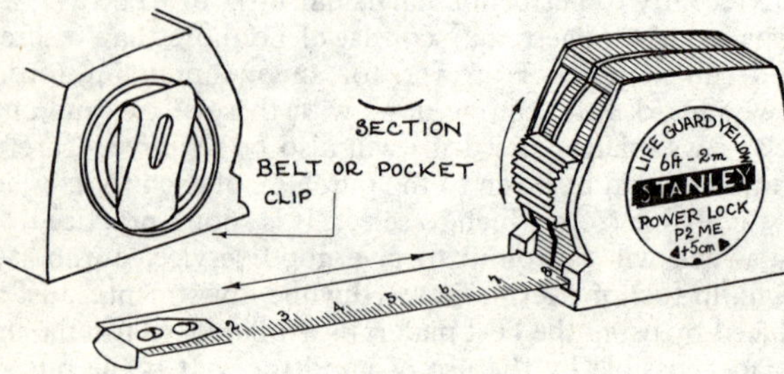

Fig. 27. The flexible rule.

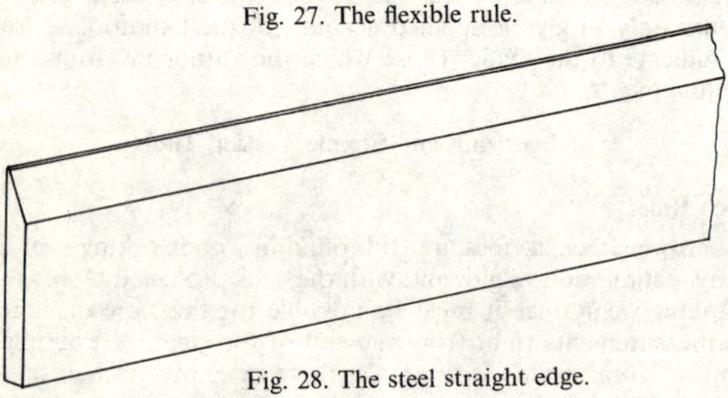

Fig. 28. The steel straight edge.

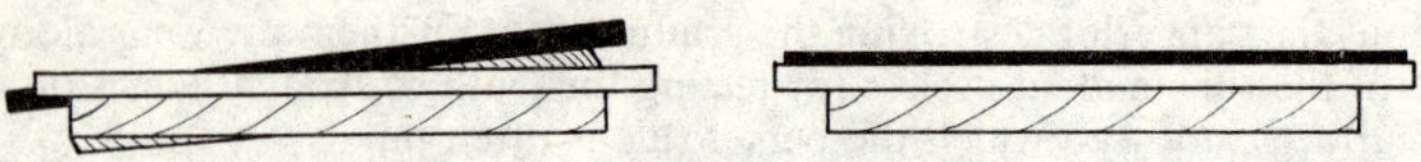

Fig. 29. Winding strips.

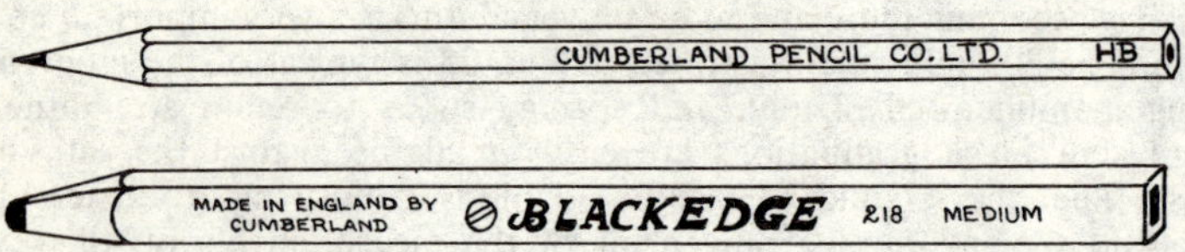

Fig. 30. Pencils for use on wood.

The Folding Rule

Folding rules are very convenient in that they can be easily carried in the pocket, and are equally useful for making measurements at the bench or 'on site'. Originally of boxwood with brass endplates and hinges, **plastic** is now being used. The Marples Shockproof Rule illustrated in Fig. 26 is moulded from white Makrolon which, being both tough and flexible, resists breaking and splintering. The accuracy of the rule is unaffected by atmospheric conditions, and the numerals and graduations are clearly marked, deep cut and long lasting. Accurate measurements can be made from the end of the rule, the tips of which are of stainless steel, as are the hinges. Unfolded, the rule will measure up to one metre in units of one millimetre, five millimetres and tens of millimetres.

The Steel Tape

There is a whole range of steel tapes from which to choose, all being accurate, but each having different features largely governed by cost. For example, some have plastic cases, others more expensive metal ones. Available in various lengths of up to three metres, tape is more suitable for some work than the folding rule as the greater range of measurement reduces the possibility of errors. Two other big advantages are its compactness, being retractable, and also making possible the taking of accurate measurements between two fixed surfaces, e.g. across an alcove in a room. (The 50-mm length of the bottom of the case must then be added to the length of the rule protruding from the mouth.) Although the rule is coiled within its case, because of its concave section it becomes rigid when extended, although still sufficiently flexible to measure round both internal and external curves of quite small radius.

Stanley rules have what the makers describe as a 'true-zero' hook at the tip of the blade which slides on studs to compensate for its own thickness, thereby ensuring accurate measurements whether the hook is pushed in, as it would be if measuring from inside a corner, or pulled out, as when it is hooked on to the edge of a board to measure the width. They also have a 'true-view' mouth which enables the exact measurement to be read at a glance, and most have yellow or white blades on which the graduations are clearly printed. The Stanley tape is completed by bonding to the blade an overall film of clear, tough polyester which is highly resistant to abrasion, most acids, alkalis, oils and solvents. Each tape is spring-loaded so that after use it retracts automatically into its case, but some models are provided with a locking catch which will hold the blade positively in any position to prevent inaccuracies occurring when in use. A clip by which the rule may be hung on to a belt or the edge of a pocket is also provided on the rear of the case of some rules. If not required, the clip can be easily taken off by the removal of the Pozidriv screw.

Straight Edges

These are rigid, rectangular-sectioned, flat steel bars with one bevelled edge. Usually one metre in length, with a hole near one end by which they may be hung up, they can be used for drawing straight lines; as a guide for the knife when trimming veneers; testing the edges of long boards for truth; or testing across the surface of wide boards which have been glued together to check that they are lying flat.

Winding Strips

These are a simple home-made tool consisting of two identical strips of hardwood planed accurately to the same width and thickness. When placed across the width of a board near to each end, a quick glance along will soon tell whether the board is flat, depending upon whether the strips are 'in winding' or their top edges are parallel. They are very useful when planing a wide board to thickness.

Pencils

For general work an HB pencil will be found satisfactory but the point must be kept sharp so that all setting out and marking is done accurately. Being a soft grade, the pencil will mark the wood without damage to the surface—a distinct advantage when the work is being cleaned up later. To ensure accurate marking, the pencil should be inclined so that the point is in close contact with the edge of the guiding tool. Also, measurements may be marked off from the rule more accurately if it is tipped up so that its edge is resting on the surface of the wood.

For very fine, delicate setting out it may be desirable to use a pencil of a harder grade so that the lines are not so easily rubbed off accidentally as the work progresses. For very heavy work on timber which might possibly be unplaned, the Cumberland 'Blackedge' carpenters' pencil, which has rectangular leads, is recommended. These are available in three grades; soft, medium and hard. Pencils with flat sides are preferable to round ones since they do not roll off the bench quite so easily, so preventing broken points. Brightly coloured pencils can be seen more readily among the shavings and tools which tend to accumulate on the bench as the work progresses.

The Marking Knife

The angled steel blade of a marking knife is either fixed by two rivets into a slot in the rosewood handle or it may run the full length of the handle, in which case a piece of wood is riveted to each side. It is ground and sharpened at the same angle but on the off side only, the other side being kept perfectly flat. Used to sever the surface fibres of the wood, thereby enabling the saw to present a clean cut, the marking knife cuts across the grain and is guided by the edge of a try-square blade, or by a sliding bevel if the cut is at an angle (see Fig. 31). The cut does to some extent also enable the saw to begin cutting rather more easily. Double cut lines, the width of the saw kerf apart, should be made at any point where the wood is being cut into two or more parts, as distinct from sawing off waste at the ends.

Some woodworkers recommend that the knife should be used for setting out whenever possible rather than the pencil, but it should be pointed out that a wrong cut line cannot be removed easily and might in fact make a piece of wood quite useless for its intended job if it was so disfigured. The marking knife is ideal for cutting across the shoulders of tenons, for example, but if in doubt it is advisable first to set out in pencil and then cut over the pencil lines.

Compasses

With one leg sharpened rather like the marking knife so that its inner face is flat, presenting a cutting edge to the wood, **wing compasses** produce a cut circle or arc (see Fig. 32*a*). This is an advantage if the line has to be sawn to or

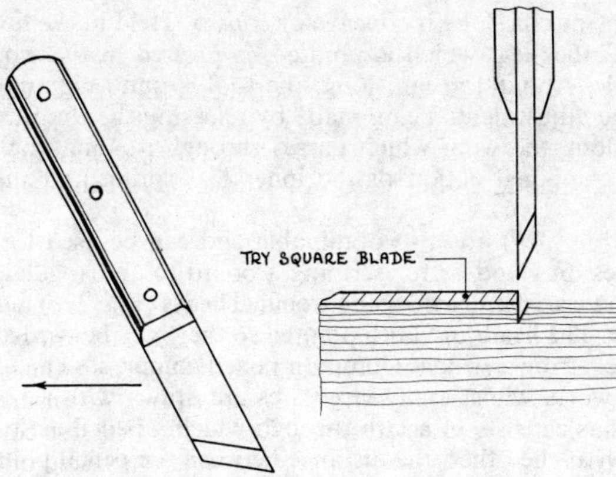

Fig. 31. The marking knife.

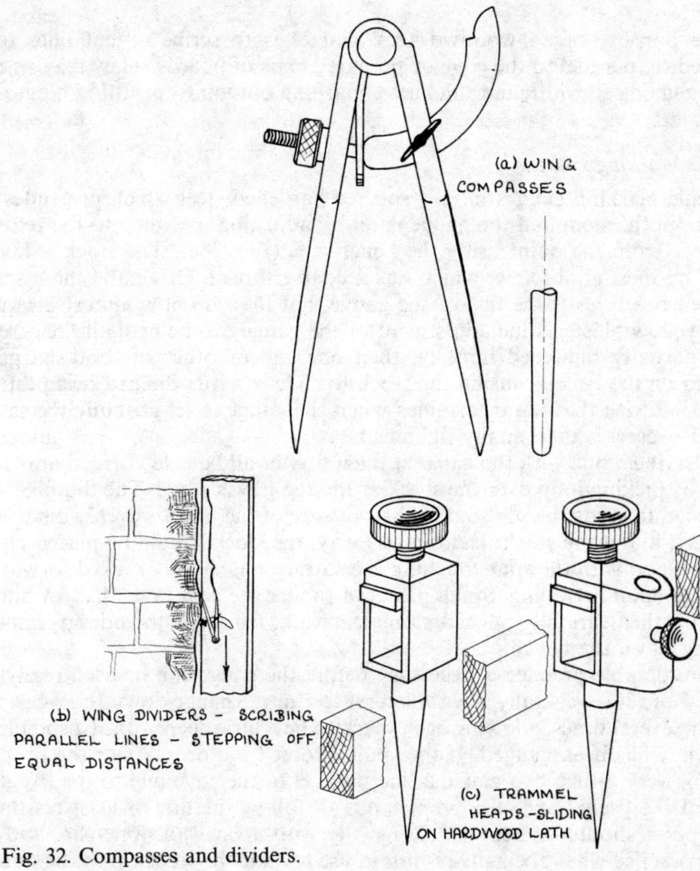

Fig. 32. Compasses and dividers.

cut to with a gouge or chisel, be it concave or convex. Held in the normal way when in use, the other leg, which is pointed, is pressed in the wood at the centre of the circle. About 150 mm long, the tool is quite big and heavy in construction, large adjustments being made by releasing the thumbscrew and moving the leg along the wing which passes through it. Fine adjustment is obtained by the combined action of the inner leaf spring and the circular knurled nut.

Wing dividers (Fig. 32*b*) are also obtainable and can be used for stepping out equal distances on wood or for scribing a board to an irregular surface.

Large circles and arcs are drawn using **trammel heads** (Fig. 32*c*) mounted on a hardwood beam. The heads are both pointed so they may be used as dividers and one has a socket for a pencil. Common pencil compasses can, of course, be used for light work, whilst really large arcs are drawn with a home-made beam compass. This consists of a lath through which a pencil is fitted at one end and a bradawl at the other, the distance between the pencil point and the bradawl being the radius of the arc.

Gauges

The purpose of all woodworkers' gauges is to scribe or cut lines to be worked to, parallel to the edge or prepared ends of boards. They may be used when planing to width and thickness, marking out joints, or fitting hinges and locks, etc.

Single Marking Gauges

Single marking gauges have a spur of hardened steel which protrudes 2–3 mm from the stem and the gauge is set by adjusting the stock to the required distance from the point using the bench rule (Fig. 33*a*). The stock is held in place by the thumbscrew, which has a coarse thread. Originally these screws were of beech, as is the rest of the gauge, but they are now almost always of clear yellow plastic. Fine adjustment of the gauge can be made if the screw is only partially tightened initially, then one end or other of the stem gently tapped on the bench causing the stock to slide towards the end being tapped. Checking with the rule determines when the gauge is set absolutely correctly and the screw is then finally tightened.

To scribe a line with the gauge it must first of all be held correctly, which is done by picking it up over the stock as though it was a ball. The thumb is then extended towards the pin so that the pressure of the hand is evenly distributed between it and the stock. Held in this way, the stock should be placed closely to the wood with the spur touching the surface but slightly rocked forward so that the point is trailing. Small pieces of timber are held in the hand while the gauge is then carefully pushed along the wood from end to end; larger pieces are rested on the bench.

Considerable practice is necessary before the gauge can be used really efficiently and it is generally advisable first to run the gauge down the wood very lightly several times, allowing each mark to be a little deeper until a sufficiently clear line has been gauged. If the spur is forced too deeply into the timber it may be very difficult to gauge a line parallel to the edge due to the irregularities of the grain, since the point tends to follow the line of least resistance. This point should be kept sharp, usually with a small oilstone slip, and it is good practice when the gauge is not in use to slide the stock up to the point in order to protect it, leaving the thumbscrew just sufficiently tight to hold the stock in place. Some gauges are made with brass strips recessed into the face to combat wear.

It may be added that in the absence of a gauge a pencil line may be drawn parallel to an edge if the pencil is held as though for writing, the point placed the requisite distance from the edge of the wood and moved along, the other fingers acting as the stock of a gauge. Pencil lines can be gauged further from the edge by holding the folding rule in the left hand, with the thumb nail rubbing on the edge of the wood. The rule must extend the required distance across the board, a pencil placed against the end of it, and, maintaining this position, the two are drawn along the wood. Lines drawn by either of these two methods are suitable for sawing on when wide boards are being reduced to workable widths.

The Mortise Gauge

As the name implies, this gauge is used to set out the parallel lines of mortise and tenon joints. Usually made of rosewood with brass fittings, it has two spurs, one of which is fixed and the second mounted in a slide which can be adjusted by means of the thumb screw at the rear (Fig. 33*b*). The two spurs should be close to the ends of the T-sectioned strip so that they can be set to quite small distances.

Chisels supposedly of the same size are inclined to vary a little in width. It is therefore advisable to set the two spurs by actually putting the tip of the chisel between the extreme points and adjusting them to the exact width of the cutting edge. Once this has been done the stock must be set so that the two points fall into the correct position on the wood. This must be done carefully with the bench rule as it is not advisable in this case to obtain fine adjustment by tapping the ends of the stem on the bench which might result in damage being caused to the mechanism of the gauge.

The stock is held in place by the knurled screw, or a slotted screw working in a brass shield. Gauging must always be done from the face side of the wood for both mortise and tenon to ensure that the joint goes together with the face sides fitting flush. The gauge illustrated in Fig. 33*b* has a third spur fitted which allows it to be used as a single marking gauge.

The Cutting Gauge

A simple cutter, sharpened on one side only and held in place by a small brass wedge, is the only difference between the cutting gauge and the single marking gauge (see Fig. 33*c*). The cutter is sharpened on one side only; it may be set to any required depth and may be used with the flat side facing, or away from, the stock, depending upon the work in hand. Primarily intended for slitting thin wood up into strips, the gauge can be used to particular advantage when marking out across the grain—for example, when setting out lap joints. When used for slitting, successively deeper cuts are made from each side of the wood until they meet.

A few hints regarding gauges. A thin convex cheek of wood slipped onto the stem of the single marking gauge between the stock and the spur enables it to be used on concave edges. Alternatively, a plate similarly placed and having two vertical brass rods silver-soldered to its outer edges allows the gauge to be

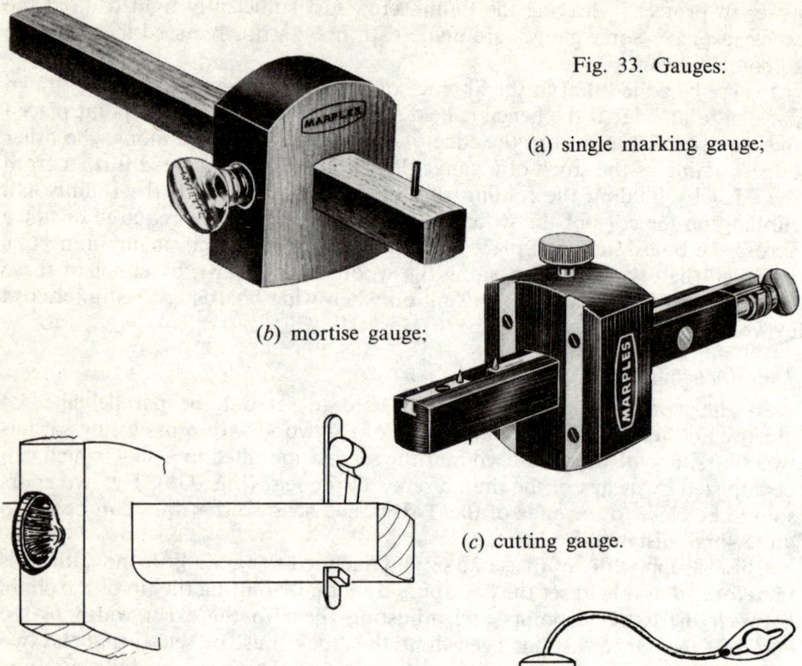

Fig. 33. Gauges:

(a) single marking gauge;

(*b*) mortise gauge;

(*c*) cutting gauge.

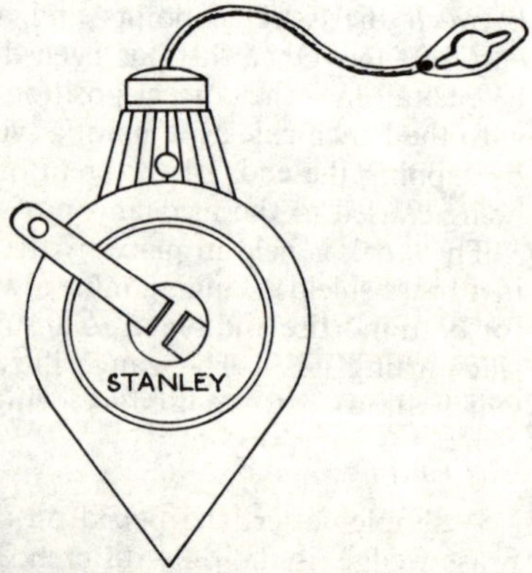

Fig. 34. The chalk-line reel.

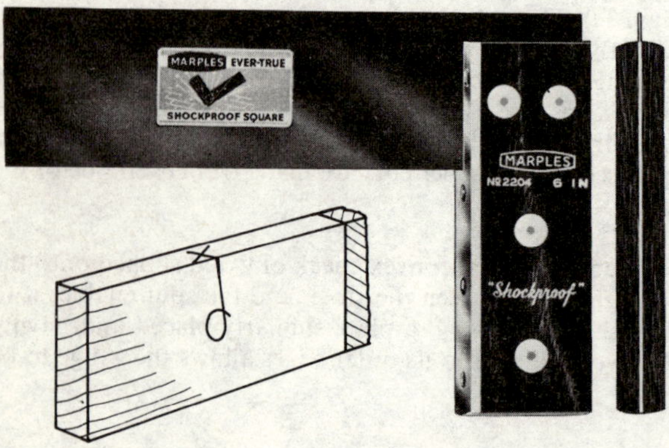

Fig. 35. The try square.

used successfully on both internal and external curves. The so-called butt gauge has three spurs and is used primarily by joiners to set out for butt hinges on doors and frames.

Chalk Line Reel

It is quite common for wide boards to have irregular or waney edges so that straight lines along them cannot be gauged in the normal way with a rule and pencil. The chalked line is placed in a saw-cut at one end of the board—the hook underneath so that the cord does not come out—and it is then stretched tightly along the board to a corresponding mark at the other end. A quick flick of the cord with finger and thumb then deposits a chalked line along the timber. The same method is also very useful for marking off a straight edge across the ends of tongue-and-groove boards where they have been used to cover a large area—for example, at the eaves of a shed roof when the ends can then be sawn straight before the bitumen felt is laid. As the line is pulled from the reel it is chalked automatically; three colours—red, white and blue—are available. With a strong die-cast aluminium body, the reel can also be used as a plumb bob when suspended.

The Try Square

Without any doubt, the try square is one of the most important basic tools, and is really necessary for even the most simple construction work. The tool consists of a hardened and tempered steel blade set at right angles to a stock, which is generally of hardwood with a brass plate on the inner face to cut down wear that would make the tool inaccurate. Other materials such as cast iron or plastic may be used by different manufacturers.

The try square has two important duties to perform, in testing for squareness and in marking out lines at right angles. When individual pieces of wood are being prepared for use, the better wide side must first be planed flat. This side will be the one which is already the flatter, with even grain, and is as free from knots, shakes or other faults as is possible. If it is a short length it can be tested for truth using the back of the try square blade, standing it on edge from alternate corner to corner. When held up to the light, discrepancies will be observed below the blade. On wider pieces it is also a good idea to test across the wood. Longer pieces can be tested in the same way with the bench rule, and even longer ones with steel straight edge and winding strips. Whichever method is used, when it is quite certain that the surface is flat, it should be marked as indicated in Fig. 35. This is then known as the **face side**.

The face side mark should be run off on to the better of the two edges, which will be selected using the same criteria as for the choice of the face side. Using the jack plane or the try plane (jointer), depending upon the length of the edge, it should then be planed flat, testing in the same way as for the face side. In addition, the stock of the try square must be held tightly against the face side and the blade held across the edge, because not only must the edge be flat; it must also be at right angles to the face side. When this has been achieved by careful planing the edge is marked with a cross running off on to the face side with one line of the cross meeting the end of the face side mark. This is then known as the **face edge**.

The wood is subsequently gauged to width from the face edge with the single marking gauge and the try square used for testing once more as the waste is planed away down to the line. Similarly, this is followed by gauging to thickness from the face side and planing down to the line. It is important that all timber intended for framing, and in some cases carcase work, is reduced to the correct width and thickness using this sequence of operations, and that strict accuracy is observed. Failure to do this will become more obvious as the work proceeds: inaccuracies will become accentuated and 'out of square' will be evident during assembly.

The try square is also used to test internal and external right angles when frames, boxes, and carcase work are being assembled. The squareness of large frames and carcases may be checked with the 'diagonal rod'. This is placed alternately from corner to corner and the assembly adjusted until each diagonal is the same length.

Accurate marking out is quite impossible without the try square, and pencil or cut lines can be made using the try square blade as a guide. To ensure complete accuracy the stock must always be held tightly against either the face side or face edge. Waste wood to be sawn or chiselled away should be marked as such with diagonal lines. Ends being sawn or planed square can also be tested. The Ever-True square in Fig. 35 (by Marples) has an L-shaped steel blade which extends down the full length of the hardwood stock and is secured by four steel rivets with brass washers. Complete rigidity of the blade within the stock is thereby ensured. For different sizes of work, blades of 150, 230 and 300 mm are obtainable, each with correspondingly larger stocks.

The Mitre Square

The mitre square (Fig. 36) has to a large extent been superseded by the metal mitre templet (or template). Constructed of the same materials as the try square, its use is limited in the workshop to marking and testing the angles to which the blade is set—namely, 45 degrees and 135 degrees—in other words the mitres at the corners of a right-angled frame. The bottom of the stock is protected by brass plates riveted to each side.

The Sliding Bevel

Being free to move on its pivot, the steel blade, which is slotted, can be set to any required angle and adjusted so that it can be used to its full length across a board or shortened to mark off the angles of dovetails. A locking lever, which is operated by the thumb and first finger, fixes the blade in place. Like the mitre square, the end of the hardwood stock is protected by brass plates.

Angle Divider

The angle divider is a special-purpose tool made by Stanley Tools. It is most useful for taking off the angle for mouldings which have to be mitred and fitted inside a corner which is at an angle other than 90 degrees—for example, skirting boards or mouldings round a panel in an irregular frame. The straight blade enables the tool to be used as a try square. The all-metal combination square, the stock of which carries a 300 mm rule which can be extended fully to one side or the other, is becoming increasingly popular with woodworkers. The stock is such that mitres at 45 degrees can be marked off or tested, and there is also a built-in spirit level which enables the truth of horizontal or vertical surfaces to be tested.

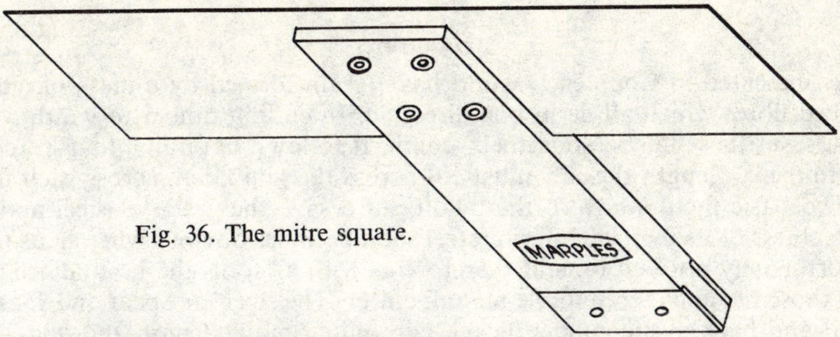

Fig. 36. The mitre square.

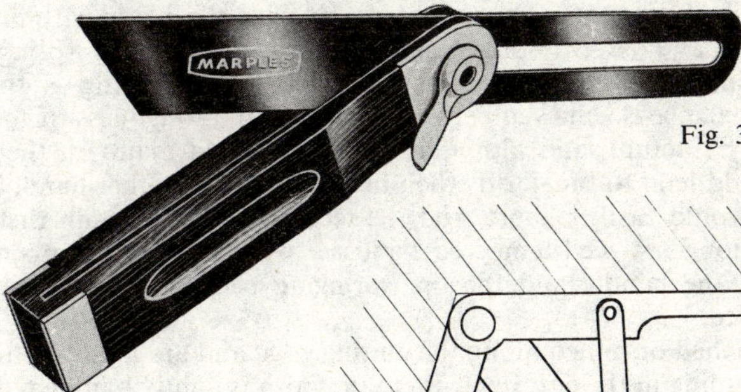

Fig. 37. The sliding bevel.

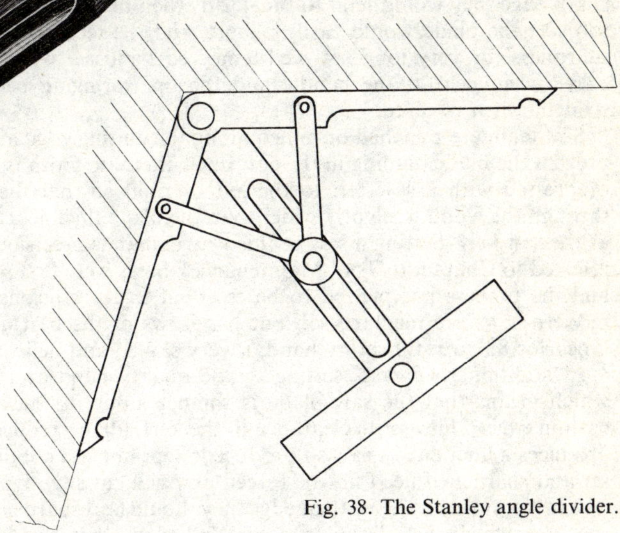

Fig. 38. The Stanley angle divider.

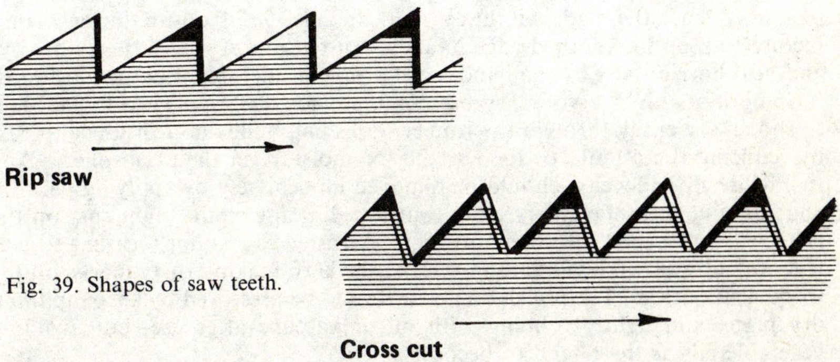

Fig. 39. Shapes of saw teeth.

Handsaws

As indicated in Chapter 1, wood has a grain formed by a mass of closely packed fibres which all lie in one direction. In cutting timber to width a saw must sever these fibres along their length. It follows, naturally, that in reducing timber to length the saw must cut across the grain; i.e., across each fibre.

Two basic factors govern the quality of a saw: the grade of steel and the correctness of its temper. Inferior steel soon becomes obvious when in use, but unfortunately not before, and therefore as with all tools the best advice is to buy those made by a reputable manufacturer. The steel for Spear and Jackson hand and backsaws contains nickel, chromium, molybdenum and vanadium in accurately prescribed amounts. These elements provide the blade with excellent wear-resisting and edge-holding characteristics, and can be spring-tempered and tensioned to give fast, accurate cutting. (Tempering is the process by which a balance is achieved between hardness and toughness. If too hard, the blade may fracture, and although the teeth would maintain their sharp edge they would tend to break off when being set. On the other hand, if too soft the blade would easily distort, and the teeth would not retain their sharpness for very long.) A well-tempered handsaw will bend in a uniform curve when held at the handle and the tip, springing back to be perfectly straight when released.

Saw teeth are punched or milled along the cutting edge and are then 'set' to prevent the blade binding in the cut. Each alternate tooth is lightly hammered, or pressed with a saw set, to the left or right so that the width of the cut through the wood is slightly wider than the blade thickness. This cut is known as the **saw kerf**. Setting a saw in this way demands precision and the reader is referred to Chapter 6 (Tool Maintenance). Saws were first set in Roman times and the process has proved to be essential to the efficiency of a saw. Most modern saws are machine set, but handsaws of the best quality such as the 'Spearior 88' are still set by hand, a very skilled and delicate operation.

In addition to expert 'setting', good-quality handsaws are taper-ground, which means that the saw blade is thinner along its back edge than at the cutting edge. This assists clearance in the kerf, allows reduced set and thereby produces a finer cut. A saw so produced, kept in good condition and correctly set and sharpened need not be forced and will cut sweetly and efficiently.

As soon as the teeth lose their edge they should be resharpened to avoid forcing the saw, which may result in a buckled blade that can be very difficult to straighten since the blade will have been expanded in its centre during manufacture to keep the toothed edge in a state of tension. A saw turned sideways and held horizontally by the handle will drop considerably if badly tensioned.

Smooth sawing is assisted by making the blade finely polished to enable it to slide more easily through the timber. Polishing builds up resistance to rust by reducing the affinity of the surface for moisture in the atmosphere. Any rust which does develop should be removed immediately by applying paraffin and rubbing with fine emery cloth, but avoiding the teeth. Light rust on the teeth will be cleaned off as the saw cuts. A rusted saw is not pleasant to use, will not cut well, and will tend to bind in the kerf, making rusty marks on the wood as it does so. The polish on a saw should be preserved by keeping it in a dry place, and lightly rubbing with oil or vaseline after use, but avoiding vegetable oils as these tend to become sticky.

Of equal importance to the efficiency of the saw is the design and fit of the handle. Hardwood handles should be of sound, knot-free, close-grained timber and fixed tightly to the blade. Modern saws often have plastic handles moulded directly on to the blade. The handle should be so set that the line of thrust is to the centre of the cutting edge. To help preserve the truth of the blade the handle is a convenient means by which it may be hung up when not in use, with the teeth protected by a 'tooth guard' (plastic ones are often provided with new saws). Failing this, a strip of wood as long as the blade and slotted along its length can easily be made in the workshop; this can be held in place by a piece of string fitting through a hole near its centre and tied over the back of the saw.

Handsaws of the above specifications are used for the preliminary cutting of wood to size from planks, and in heavy woodwork for sawing large joints. There are two kinds: the **rip saw** for cutting 'with the grain' and the **cross-cut** and **panel saws** for use 'across the grain'.

The Rip Saw

The rip saw is for cutting along the grain, and the teeth are cut so that each is 60 degrees at the point with the leading edge perpendicular, or slightly backed, but never more than 3 degrees from the vertical (Fig. 39).

If vertical, cutting will be rapid and the finish coarse; backing off makes the cutting slower but smooth, the angle being sometimes known as the **pitch**. The rip saw is so sharpened that each tooth works with a plane or chisel action, making cuts at right angles to the blade. The teeth are not bevelled but filed square, and ranged like a series of chisels alternately one behind the other to cut the wood at the most efficient angle. The rip saw is one of the longest handsaws with blades of 650 mm and five points to the inch. This means that if an inch rule is held against the teeth there will be five points to the inch, which includes the two touching the inch marks at each end. Therefore there is always one more point per inch than there are teeth per inch, e.g. 5 points = 4 teeth. This is a rule that applies to all saws (see Fig. 40).

The Cross-Cut Saw

When a marking knife is used to make a double cut where a piece of timber is to be sawn accurately into two, you will notice that the grain between the two cuts is very short and the wood will crumble away as the cuts are made deeper. A finger rubbed across the surface is often sufficient to break the wood away. In a similar way, the teeth of the cross-cut saw are 'bevel-sharpened' into knife-edge points and being 'set' cut two knife lines close together. As the saw is drawn backwards and forwards the wood crumbles in the gullets between the saw teeth and is carried away as sawdust. The teeth of cross-cut saws are angled back from the leading edge at about 14 degrees, the actual angle of the point again being 60 degrees (see Fig. 39). Cross-cut saws with blades 450, 500, 550 and 600 mm long and 6 to 8 points to the inch are manufactured (see Fig. 40).

The **panel saw** is a cross-cut usually 500 or 550 mm long with 8 to 10 points to the inch (Fig. 40). Being shorter and therefore lighter, they are pleasant saws to handle and to use. The smaller teeth are more suitable for hardwoods, giving a smoother cut, and for smaller sections such as thin boards and plywoods since they also cause less splintering, particularly of the underside.

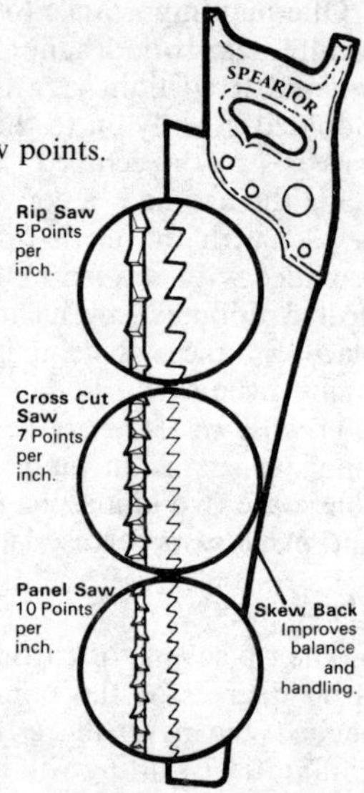

Fig. 40. Measurement of saw points.

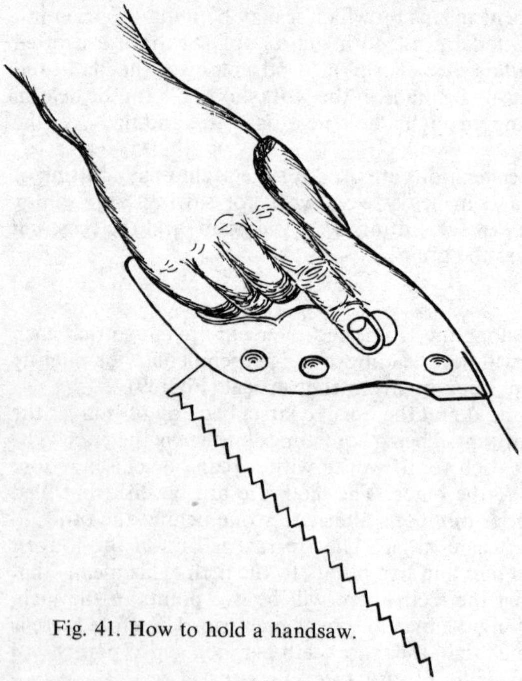

Fig. 41. How to hold a handsaw.

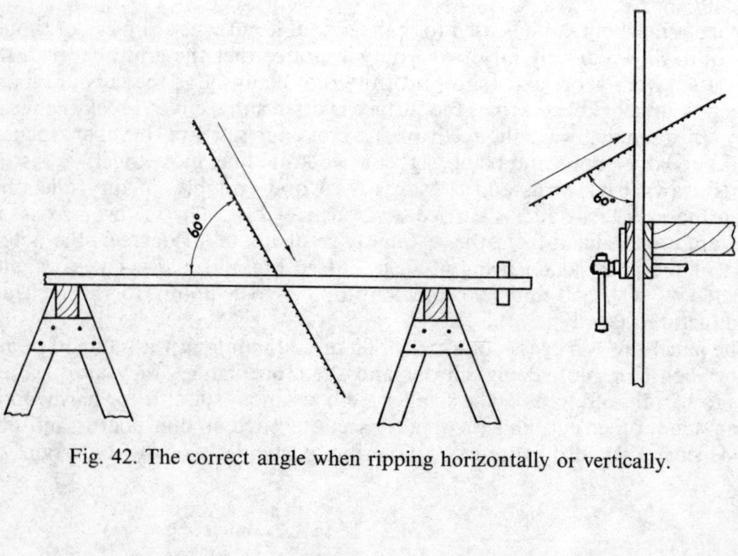

Fig. 42. The correct angle when ripping horizontally or vertically.

Due to the way in which rip saws are sharpened they cannot be used for cutting across the grain as this would cause excessive splintering; but cross-cuts will saw with the grain although not so well as rip saws.

Use of the Handsaw

All handsaws have closed handles which are grasped tightly in the hand when in use with the index finger pointing forward and the wrist held firm so that movement of the arm is from the elbow and shoulder (Fig. 41). The thumb is extended down the other side of the handle in line with the index finger. Because of the 'set' of the saw teeth which produces a kerf to allow the saw blade to follow easily through the wood, sawing should always be done on the waste side of the line to which you are cutting. If this practice is not observed the piece of wood sawn off may be smaller than intended by as much as the full width of the saw kerf.

To start either the rip saw or the cross-cut saw, the left hand should grip the timber and the thumb be used to guide the saw at the point where the cut is to begin. The saw must now be drawn backwards carefully at least once and perhaps several times until a small guiding cut is established in the edge or end of the board. This must never be done quickly or the saw may jump, nor should you attempt to start the cut by pushing down immediately instead of pulling up. Once the guiding cut is established, the normal cutting strokes may be made using as far as possible the full length of the blade to ensure smooth cutting and even wear of the teeth.

When a board has to be ripped along its length (see Fig. 42) it may be done horizontally if very long or vertically if reasonably short. In the first instance the board should be supported across two trestles, held firmly with the knee and the cut commenced. As soon as the cut is long enough the first trestle should be moved forward and a small wooden wedge dropped into the cut. This wedge is then used to keep the saw cut open and prevent the saw from binding as the cut increases in length. Finally, the second trestle must be moved forward to allow the saw to complete the cut. If ripping is being done vertically in the vice, the board should be placed so that the vice is supporting the part being sawn as much as possible. Initially it should be placed low in the vice to limit vibrations, then lifted up a little at a time as the cut becomes deeper. The most suitable angle between the saw and the work for either method is 60 degrees.

Cross-cutting a board can again be done on trestles or by holding it horizontally in the vice. The saw must be started off in the normal way, care being taken to saw on the waste side of the line, and a cross-cut or panel saw chosen depending upon the thickness of the wood. If held in the vice, it is better to have the board flat rather than on edge, since in this way it is easier to follow the line and cutting is smoother as more saw teeth are in the wood at any one time due to the angle at which the saw is held (Fig. 43). There is also less vibration since the board is given more support, being held across its full width rather than only along its bottom edge. Extra wide boards will obviously have to be supported on trestles or, if these are not available, strong wooden boxes may be used.

Once the beginning of the cut has been made by drawing the saw backwards, it must then be held firmly and downward pressure applied to the blade

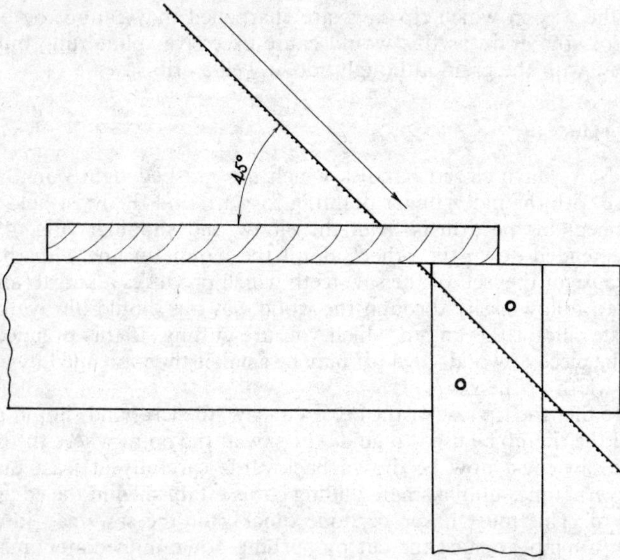

Fig. 43. The correct angle between the saw and the work when crosscutting with the handsaw.

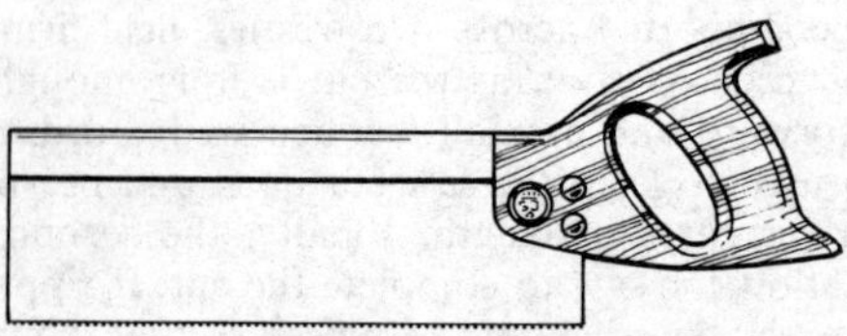

Fig. 44. The tenon saw.

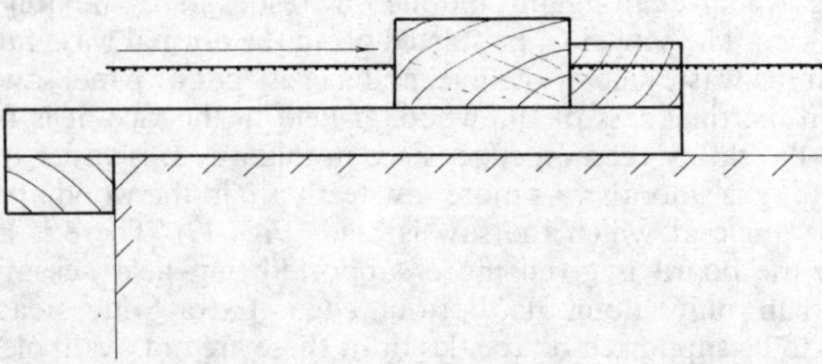

Fig. 45. The bench hook.

taking care that the saw is held vertically (test with try square if necessary) and that it is at right angles to the edge of the wood. The saw should now start easily and cutting be continued with long, steady strokes, using as much of the full length of the blade as is possible from toe to heel, and pressure being relieved on the backward pull. If the saw is held loosely it is difficult to cut to a straight line so should the blade wander the grip must be tightened and by carefully twisting the handle the direction can be gradually corrected. If this is not sufficient the saw should be taken back and by using short strokes at the point of deviation sawing should be recommenced along the original line of cut.

It is quite common for the saw cut to close up as the board is being sawn across due to the natural tension within it. This causes the blade to be nipped and to bind in the wood. If this occurs and attempts are made to force the saw forward, complete jamming of the blade can happen quite suddenly, resulting in it being buckled. Should this happen, unskilled hammering may make matters worse by spoiling the tensioning and the only safe course is to return the saw to the manufacturers for expert attention. If it becomes obvious that jamming may happen, the saw should be withdrawn completely and the cut made again, right from the beginning thereby widening the saw kerf; held open with a wedge if this is possible; or with the assistance of a second person holding the board apart.

When sawing, a comfortable stance must always be adopted so that full freedom of the sawing arm is possible and so that by looking over the saw, the cutting edge and the line to which the cut is being made can both be observed clearly throughout the operation.

If cross-cutting is done between trestles, when the cut is almost complete the board is weakened and will sag under its own weight. This too will cause the kerf to close, nipping the saw, and must be prevented by supporting the board with the left hand. Assistance may also be required as the cut is completed to prevent excessive splintering as the two pieces fall apart. When the board is held in the vice it is possible for the person sawing to give this support more easily. If the cut has to be made very close to the end of the board it may become difficult to keep the saw in line due to the waste continually splitting away. A piece of scrap wood clamped to the underside of the board and sawn through as the required cut is made will keep the saw in line.

A saw should always cut freely under virtually its own weight. Failure to do so generally indicates that it requires to be sharpened. Accidental damage to the teeth from contact with the vice, other tools, nails and screws, etc., should be avoided. An angle of 45 degrees between the saw and the work is considered to be suitable for cross-cutting. The short grain of wooden handles used on the best quality saws is often strengthened with a piece of beech dowelling.

Backsaws

Backsaws are required for finer and more accurate work at the bench, which is largely confined to cutting joints. Because of this requirement a thinner gauge of steel is used for the blade and the teeth are much finer than those of the handsaw. Since the blade is thin and comparatively narrow a very heavy steel or brass 'back' grips it along its whole length to keep it rigid (Fig. 44). It is from this feature that such saws derive their name. By tradition the better quality saws have always been given brass backs, which most craftsmen still believe to be superior. The weight of the back considerably reduces the pressure necessary for cutting, and in fact for some light cuts the weight of the saw itself is quite sufficient.

To do its work efficiently the blade must be perfectly flat, free from twist and the cutting edge perfectly straight. The back and the blade must both be fitted securely into the handle so that the whole tool is rigid; the handle of most modern backsaws is of the closed variety. The teeth have 60 degree points, are pitched at 16 degrees and must be evenly set and sharp.

For general work at the bench, the **tenon saw** needs to cut both with and across the grain. The teeth are therefore sharpened as cross-cut teeth with a bevel since these will rip when necessary, whereas teeth sharpened for ripping will not make clean cuts across the grain. Some modern saws are coated with Teflon*S, which gives excellent cutting performance by reducing friction and is also rust resisting. The handle is usually of polypropylene moulded directly on to the blade.

Because the teeth of the backsaw are small great care must be taken when sharpening to keep them even in size and their condition should always be such that there is never any need to force the saw to cut, for this may result in distortion of the blade. Any slight distortion which may occur can often be corrected if the blade is supported vertically on a piece of wood and the back struck gently with a hammer at the ends. This forces the blade further into the back and springs it into truth once more. Should this not be successful more serious damage must have occurred, possibly both the blade and the back being twisted, and advice should be sought from the maker.

Backsaws are held in exactly the same way as handsaws but are almost invariably used horizontally—that is, with the blade vertical and the cutting edge parallel to the bench top. The wood being sawn is held in the vice or on the bench hook, which may be placed against the front of the bench or in the vice, where it is even more secure (Fig. 45). In all cases the wood must be held firmly: if movement occurs, buckling of the saw blade may follow. When work is held on the bench hook the ball of the left hand presses down on the near corner to hold it in place against the back of the hook and the fingers rest across the top. The thumb of this hand then guides the saw. First, as it is drawn backwards to establish the cut, and then, as the cut becomes deeper, the saw is lowered into a horizontal position. A similar procedure is adopted if the work is held in the vice, the thumb being pressed on to the wood and being used to guide the saw while the fingers are curled up inside the palm of the hand to keep them behind the saw and therefore out of danger.

Bench hooks should be of all-timber construction, the ends pegged to the board with wooden dowels to prevent any possible damage to the saw teeth. The saw must always cut through on to the bench hook, and to make this possible for anyone who is left-handed it may be necessary to cut off a little of the back at the opposite end. At all times care must be taken, and particularly when sawing joints, to cut up against the line but always in the waste portion. Failure to do this will result in badly fitting joints due to the width of the saw kerf. Backsaws are useful for cutting all thin wood including plywood and hardboard because of their fine teeth which minimise splintering of the underside. Because of their rigid blades they are also useful for cutting mitres, particularly in conjunction with the mitre box.

The **dovetail saw** is a smaller version of the tenon saw. The blade is even thinner, the teeth smaller, and, as its name implies, it is used for cutting small dovetail joints and other equally fine and necessarily accurate work. Being so fine, the cut made by a marking knife provides a suitable groove in which the saw will cut with clean shoulders to joints.

The **bead saw** and the even smaller **jeweller's saw** are members of the back-saw family. Used for very fine work indeed, bead saws range from 100 mm to 300 mm; and jeweller's saws are 200 mm in length and have straight wooden handles rather like those for files and chisels. The jeweller's saw, for example, has very fine teeth: 24–32 points per inch which are not set. In the thin wood for which the saw is intended, this gives a very smooth cut which needs little or no finishing.

Similarly, the **veneer saw** has very fine teeth, sharpened as for cross-cutting but not set, only having to cut through the thickness of veneers. The edge of the blade is slightly curved to avoid the danger of its corners damaging the veneer. The back, to which the blade is attached, is of wood, straight along its length, but moulded in section to form a handle by which the saw is held.

Saws for Cutting Curves

Whereas the saws described previously have been designed for the express purpose of sawing to a straight line, there will obviously be many occasions when it is desirable to be able to saw to a curve. To enable the saw to do this the blade must be very narrow in comparison to the width of the handsaw and backsaw, both of which have deep blades to help them maintain the straightness of the cut. The width of blade behind the teeth therefore governs the size of curve it can negotiate; the narrower the blade the smaller the curve. Naturally it follows from this that the smaller blades are more fragile and must therefore be used for only the lightest work.

The Coping Saw

Blades for coping saws are 150 mm long and have short steel pins set into small holes near each end (Fig. 46). The blades are up to 3 mm wide and are hard and brittle, which makes them liable to snap easily. They are expendable and when blunt are thrown away. In view of their limited length, and the above characteristics, they are only suitable for light work on wood up to perhaps 16 mm thick, plywood and hardboard.

As with all very narrow blades they must be tensioned in order to keep them straight when in use and this is achieved by stretching the blade within the saw frame. The pins on the blade are fitted into the two slotted pins carried by the frame. This is made possible by unscrewing the handle so that one pin can be advanced into the frame. The frame itself, which is of flat sectioned steel, is tensioned so that it too tends to pull the blade tight as the handle is screwed up once more. By easing off the tension, the saw blade can be rotated within the frame to any required angle but care must be taken at all times to ensure that the two pins carrying it are in line or the blade will be twisted.

The handle, which carries the threaded steel ferrule, and may be of wood or plastic, should be held in both hands when in use. For horizontal sawing the work is generally held in the vice, the thumb and index finger of the right hand point in the direction of the blade, while the remaining fingers grip the handle. The left hand is then wrapped round the right with the thumb again pointing

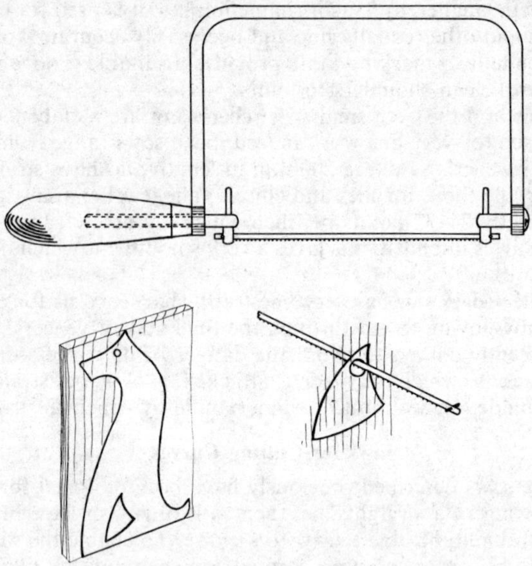

Fig. 46. The coping saw.

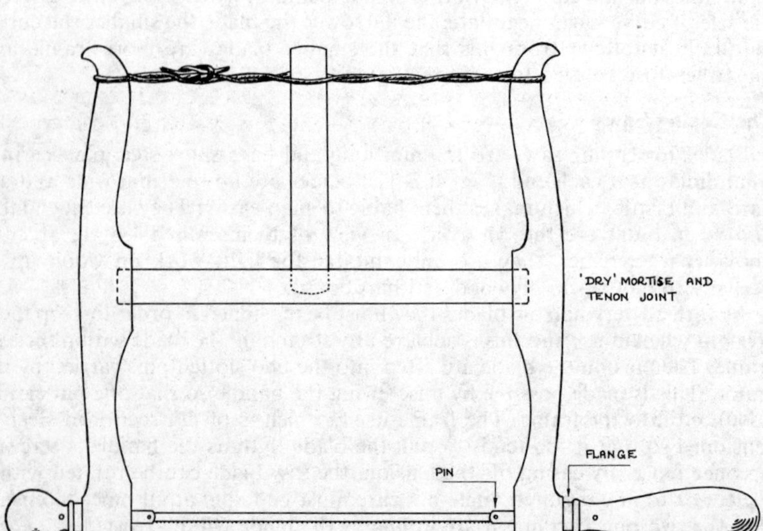

Fig. 47. The bow saw.

forward. The blade can then be drawn backwards and forwards through the wood using its full length. For this kind of work some craftsmen prefer to have the teeth pointing towards the handle so that the cut is made on the pull stroke, maintaining the tension of the blade. The disadvantage to this is that since the shape to be sawn is usually set out on the best side of the wood, any rag formed by the saw is on the face of the work. The alternative is to have the teeth pointing forwards so that they cut when pushed, which then has a slight tendency to buckle the blade. It is evident that each method has advantages and disadvantages and the one selected is very largely a matter of personal choice.

The coping saw can also be used vertically if the work is clamped in a horizontal position overhanging the bench edge. The saw handle is grasped in the right fist and the left hand wrapped around it. Cutting is then achieved by pulling the saw downwards, in which case the teeth of the blade must point towards the handle. It is advisable to sit down when working in this way to maintain steady, even cuts, keeping the blade quite vertical and so avoiding breakages. The position of the work will need to be changed from time to time as the sawing proceeds.

Coping saws are also most useful for removing some of the waste wood when joints are being cut—for example, between dovetails and dovetail pins. When an internal cut has to be made as opposed to sawing round a profile, a hole is drilled in the waste, the blade threaded through and re-attached to the frame (Fig. 46). It is good practice to slacken off the tension on the frame and blade when the saw is not in use.

The Bow Saw

The Romans used an arch of wood to hold a narrow blade in tension, then later held the blade between two arms of wood drawn apart by a tightly twisted cord across their opposite ends. This was known as the frame saw and present-day bow saws are very little different in style and construction (Fig. 47). Made of beech, the middle rail or beam is fitted into the shaped ends by a dry mortise and tenon joint. These joints act as a fulcrum at each end of the beam so that as the cord is twisted tightly by the wooden lever the blade is pulled into tension, the lever then being checked by the beam.

Different sizes of frames are available to hold blades of different lengths, one of 250 mm being suitable for most general purposes. Steel pins, which in practice often means bent nails, are used to hold the blade into slots in the brass rods which are used to connect the handle and knob of the frame. These rods, which are really part of small brass castings, have large flanges immediately outside the arms which thereby take the strain set up in the frame as the cord is tightened. Both handle and knob should be fastened to these castings with brass pins. The brass rods, being circular in section, are free to turn in the frame. This means that like the coping saw, the blade can be turned through 360 degrees by turning both the handle and the knob at the same time. Care must again be taken to avoid twisting the blade when in use or inaccurate sawing will result.

Bow saw blades are bigger and tougher than those of the coping saw, with teeth like those of the cross-cut saw, and are capable of quite heavy work. The depth of cut possible with the bow saw depends upon the size of throat—that is, the distance between blade and beam. In use the work being cut is held in

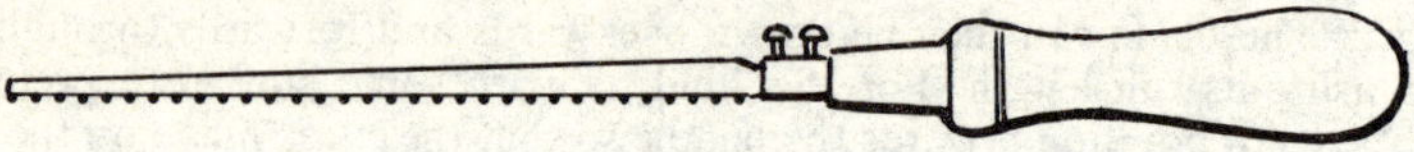

Fig. 48. The keyhole saw or pad saw.

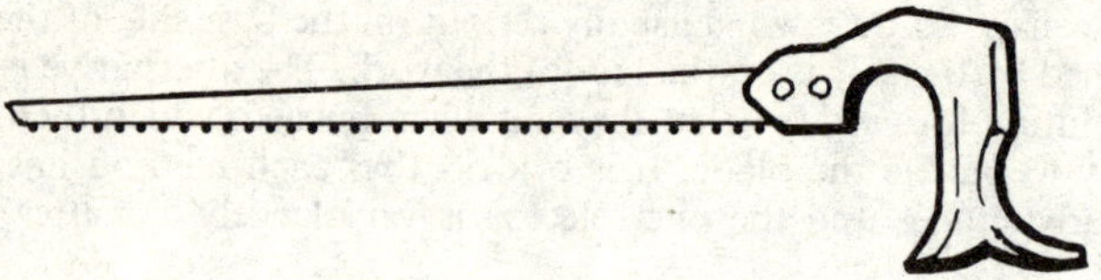

Fig. 49. The compass saw.

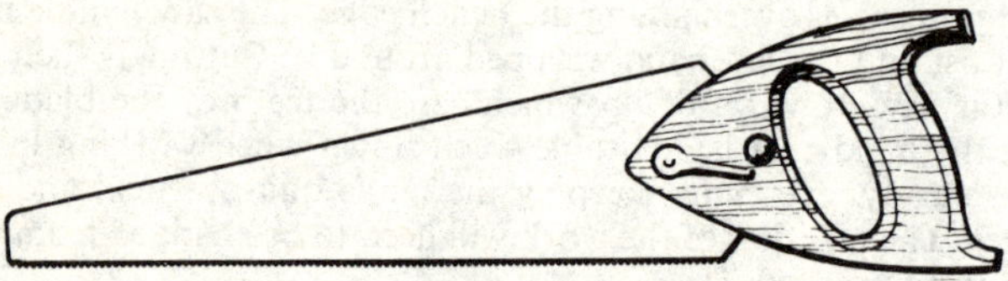

Fig. 50. The general-purpose saw.

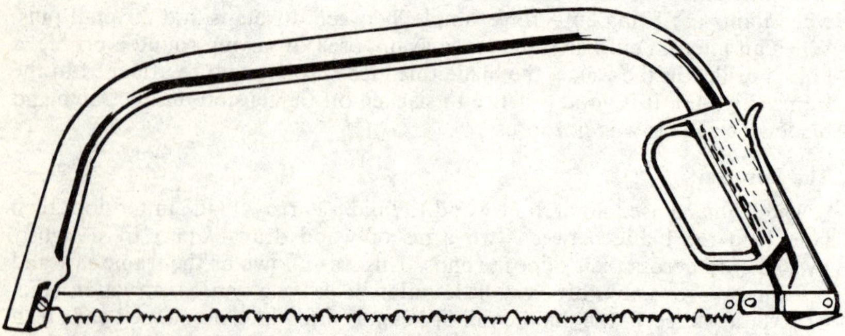

Fig. 51. The tubular-frame or log saw.

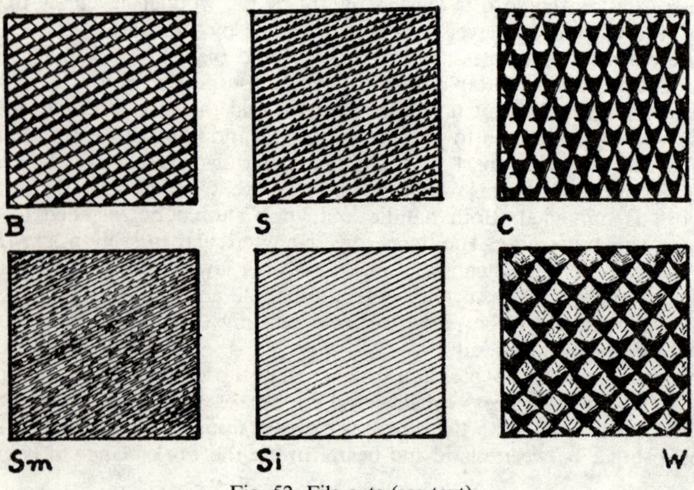

Fig. 52. File cuts (see text).

the vice, sawing being done as low as possible to prevent vibration, with the saw held in a similar manner to the coping saw but bearing in mind its extra weight.

The Pad Saw or Keyhole Saw

This saw (Fig. 48) can be used for internal cuts in wood which are too far from the edge for the bow saw to reach, a starting hole always being necessary. Its name indicates that it may be used to saw out the straight part of a keyhole after the round hole has been drilled at the top. The saw blade relies upon its own strength to keep it straight and therefore for any particular job no greater length of blade should be used than is necessary or it may become buckled or even snap off. The unused portion of the blade can be slid back into the handle, the two fixing screws in the ferrule then being tightened to hold the blade in place. To help maintain rigidity of the blade it is made quite thick so that it is not really capable of making fine cuts, although the back edge of the blade is generally thinned off to allow it to follow curves more easily. The lengths of blades available are 200, 230, 250 and 300 mm and the teeth are of the cross-cut variety but with little or no set. The saw is held in much the same way as the coping saw.

The Compass Saw

This is a saw similar in some respects to a handsaw, and is used for making curved cuts in quite large work which could not be attempted with the bow saw (see Fig. 49). Various sizes of saw are made, and the blades taper to a point and are kept as narrow as possible bearing in mind the type of work they are intended to accomplish. Because they are narrow, the blades are made thicker than is normal to add to their strength, but this in turn makes more effort necessary when sawing. The teeth are similar to those of the panel saw, the length of blade being 300–450 mm.

The General-Purpose Saw

General-purpose saws are of quite recent manufacture. They have a tough blade 350 mm long, with teeth which are induction-hardened and will successfully cut mild steel and non-ferrous metals as well as wood, laminates, plastics, chipboard, blockboard and other abrasive materials. A quick-release screw enables the blade to be fixed at five different angles to the handle, which often makes it possible to work more easily in awkward situations (Fig. 50).

Log Saw

The oval-section tubular steel frame of the log saw is fitted with a plastic hand grip and guard. Plain or Teflon*S coated blades are available and are held in place by screws at the ends and tensioned by a lever device (Fig. 51). The blades are thin, narrow and flexible, the teeth being designed to cut both on the forward and backward strokes. They have extra deep gullets at regular intervals to carry out the damp sawdust and debris produced when sawing green timber. The teeth are usually induction-hardened, giving them a long, effective cutting life—up to five times the life of an untreated blade. If coated with PTFE (polytetrafluoroethylene), which is rust and abrasion resistant, the build-up of sap and possibly resin on the blade is reduced. The Spearfast blade is a typical example and is supplied with or without the PTFE coating to fit

534, 610, 760 and 915 mm saws. The teeth are double-bevel sharpened, but being induction-hardened they cannot be sharpened with a file. The smallest tubular frame saw, 534 mm, has a round-section frame tapered quite sharply towards the toe which makes it possible to be manipulated in restricted spaces.

The Hacksaw and Junior Hacksaw

Although basically metalworker's tools, the woodworker will often find hacksaws useful to shorten bolts and screws, cutting off or through nails and fitting other pieces of hardware either of metal or plastic. Hacksaw blades are usually 200 or 250 mm long with 18, 24 or 32 teeth per inch. The larger teeth are better for soft metals such as aluminium, brass and mild steel, but harder alloys require the smaller teeth to bite into them. They cut on the forward stroke and are tensioned by means of a wing nut at the front of the frame. The junior hacksaw is a most useful little tool with a 150 mm blade, 32 teeth per inch. The frame has to be compressed as the blade is inserted, which is then tensioned when the frame is released.

Quite recent introductions to the Spear and Jackson range are the 500 mm Tufcut Black Prince with induction-hardened teeth of cross-cut shape, ten points to the inch. The teeth are brought quickly to bright red by induction-heating and then cooled. This leaves them very hard and therefore particularly suitable for cutting composite materials such as plywood, chipboard, etc.

The Hardpoint Black Prince has a blade 560 mm long with eight points to the inch, but the teeth have quite a different form. Both edges of each tooth are at the same angle and the teeth have deep gullets. Each tooth is longer than normal, bevel sharpened on both edges and is intended for cross-cutting softwoods. The tooth form is known as the Fleam tooth, or as in France, the 'dent du loup' (the wolf's tooth). Originally of Scandinavian design, it will cut effectively on both push and pull strokes and is therefore fast cutting but does not give quite as fine a finish as the normal cross-cut.

Files, Rasps and 'Surform' Tools

Standard metal workers' files have a place in the woodworker's kit of tools. In addition to the sawfile, which is designed for a specific purpose, they are useful for the general maintenance of tools such as wood-boring bits and cabinet scrapers, and for removing sharp edges from metal and plastic fittings and possibly in making adjustments to them. They can also be used for final shaping and smoothing in difficult corners not easily accessible to other tools. It should be remembered, however, that they basically have comparatively small teeth intended for cutting metal so that when used on wood the teeth soon become choked. They can be cleared quite quickly by brushing vigorously across the file in the direction of the cut of the teeth with a wire brush or file card. These brushes are made up of short lengths of tempered steel wire set into a woven backing which in turn is tacked on to a wooden back to keep it rigid. It should be borne in mind that once a file has been used on metal it becomes even less effective on wood.

Depending upon their section and cut, files range in length from 100 to 405 mm. 'Spearfiles' are made from the finest grade Sheffield tool steel and are specially finished by a sand-blast method designed to improve their cutting

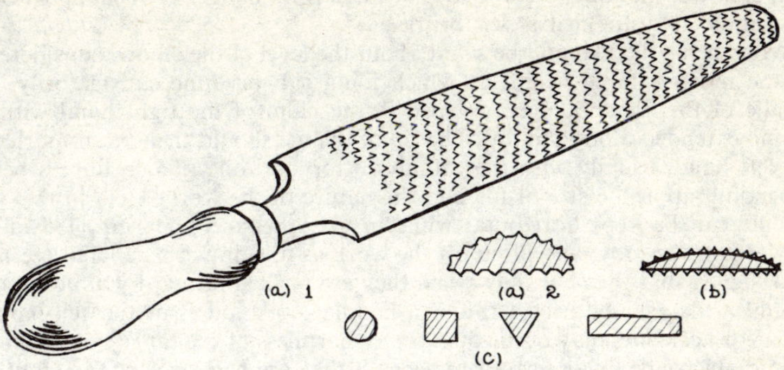

Fig. 53. Wood rasps.

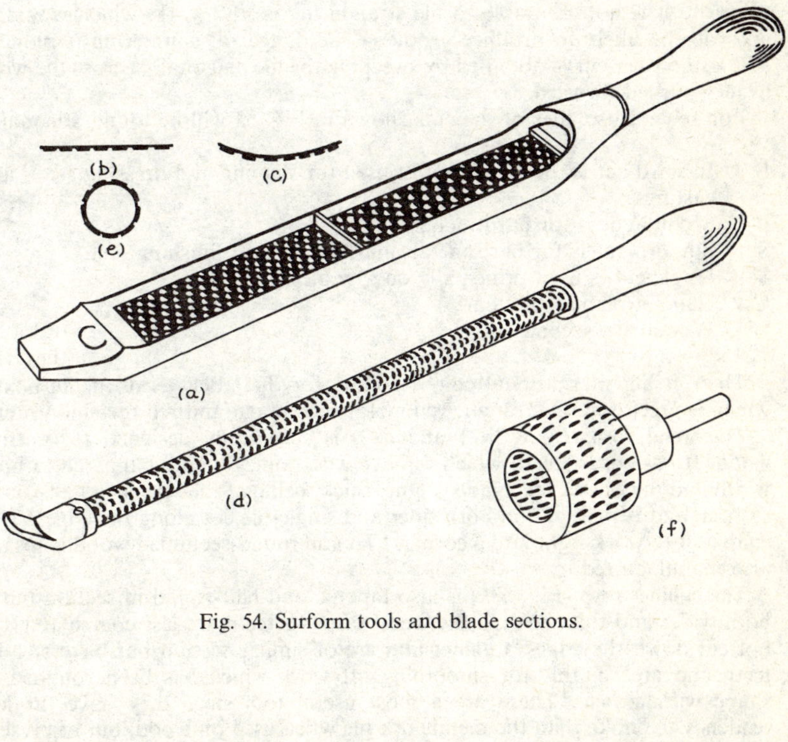

Fig. 54. Surform tools and blade sections.

efficiency and lengthen their effective life. The file blades are hardened and tempered but the tang left soft so that there is no danger of it snapping off in the handle as it might if it was brittle.

Work being filed should be set at about the level of the elbow, considered to be the most suitable height at which filing can be done satisfactorily. The handle of the file should be grasped in the palm of the right hand with the thumb extended along the top. The tip of the file should then be supported by the left hand, usually with the thumb on top and one or two fingers below, depending upon the size of file and the nature of the work. Held in this way, the file can be kept horizontal while in use, pressure being applied on the forward stroke only, and lifted off the work as it is drawn back. The teeth are so designed that they cut only when they are pushed forward. On no account should a file ever be used without a handle—unless it is of the self-handled type—or accidents may occur due to the sharpness of the tang. Loose handles should always be made firm or replaced if they are badly worn. Fine finishing cuts can be made by holding the file at right angles to the work and drawing it backwards and forwards along the full length of the surface being prepared.

Convex curves are produced with a flat-sided file and concave shapes with a file having a convex side. When working on wood, filing should always be from the short grain to the long—that is, 'with the grain' so that a smooth surface is produced. Care must be taken to avoid splintering the edges and therefore it is not advisable to file straight across the work, which would in any case be likely to produce grooves. The danger of splintering is reduced and a smoother curve obtained by sweeping the file diagonally across the work as it is pushed forward.

For general use, files of the cuts shown in Fig. 52 will be found adequate.

B Bastard cut is the standard cut used for shaping and dressing steels and castings.
S Second cut is for hard metals.
Sm Smooth cut is for hard metals and for use as a finishing file.
Si Single cut is used principally on saw files.
C Cabinet rasp second cut.
W Wood rasp second cut.

There is an international colour coding for the labels used on file boxes, which is green for bastard cut, yellow for second cut and red for smooth cut.

The wood rasp (Fig. 53*a*–1 and *a*–2) is specifically designed for cutting wood. It has coarse teeth which remove wood quickly and is tapered in both width and thickness. The blade is quite thick, being of the standard half-round section, and is rasp-cut on both sides and single-file cut along the edges. This enables it to work right into a corner. Flat and round-sectioned wood rasps are also manufactured.

The cabinet rasp (Fig. 53*b*) is also tapered and half-round in section but is both wider and thinner than the wood rasp. Its teeth are less coarse and it is not cut down the edges. **Cabinet files** are of similar section but have smaller teeth and are suitable for smoothing off work which has been roughed to shape with a rasp. These are a most useful tool since they have far less tendency to choke than the metalwork file when used on wood, but at present are most difficult to obtain.

Fig. 53*c* indicates the sections of **metalworking files** which are likely to prove most useful to a woodworker.

The range of Surform tools introduced by Stanley Tools (Fig. 54) can still be regarded as comparatively new. Each blade has many small cutting teeth, each of which acts rather like a chisel or small plane. Being cut right through the blade, which is quite thin, the teeth are not inclined to choke easily since the swarf cannot build up in front of them. The steel blade provides fast and easy cutting on wood, plastics and plastic laminates, nylon and fibre glass, light building blocks and soft metals. The blades are disposable and when blunt must be replaced. Flat, convex and round blades are available. The Surform tools include planes, files and a drum cutter for use with a power drill. These tools are very popular for sculptured work.

Chisels

For the purpose of this chapter, we shall include the plain and bevelled-edge firmer chisels, mortise chisels and gouges. The complete chisel consists of three main parts: the blade, the handle and ferrule. The blade is of tool steel; the ferrule of brass, with the exception of the registered pattern mortise chisel, where it is steel; and the handle of ash, boxwood or plastic.

Steel for the blade is in flat bar of various sections depending upon the size of chisel to be made. Suitable lengths are cut and heated to bright red in gas-fired furnaces. They are then forged between dies by one of three methods: on a spring hammer; on a series of spring hammers with each having a separate die; or on a die-forging hammer, a method which is now gradually replacing the other two. After forging, any strains or stresses set up in the metal are relieved by further heating in a furnace, following which the blade is hardened. This is carried out by heating the blade to redness and quenching in cold water or oil. This makes the steel very hard and at the same time very brittle, which could lead to fracturing during use. The brittleness is reduced by tempering, which is done in an automatic oven that heats the blades to a predetermined temperature, after which they are allowed to cool naturally. The resulting blade must be hard enough to keep a sharp edge and yet not break under pressure when in use. It should be noted that the tang is left soft so that there is no danger of it snapping off in the handle. The blades are then checked for hardness using the Brinell test. A diamond point is pressed into the metal up to a certain pressure and the degree of hardness read off from a dial. A modern crack-detecting machine is also used to check each blade for flaws created during forging. The neck and bolster of the chisel are ground by hand, but the flat faces are ground on a surface grinder producing a finished surface which is perfectly flat. The final processes are demagnetisation and inspection. Wooden or plastic handles are fitted to the blade with a pneumatic press.

Chisel size is determined by the width of the cutting edge, which must be absolutely straight and is formed by grinding (see Chapter 6, Tool Maintenance). At all times this cutting edge must be perfectly sharp so that the work can proceed easily and good surfaces be produced. A 'dulled' chisel is both difficult to guide and very dangerous in use due to the excessive force required to make it cut.

For light cuts in both hard and soft woods, hand pressure should be sufficient, but for heavier cuts it may be necessary to use a joiner's mallet with which to strike the chisel handle. Whether the chisel is used with the bevel down or the bevel up depends upon the work being done. The bevel does guide the chisel out of the wood, so that if a considerable amount has to be roughed off quickly it would be used bevel down so that the waste wood is scooped away. To finish the surface the chisel should then be turned over, presenting its flat face to the wood and light cuts taken down to the required line. Such work is usually done horizontally, the wood being held in the vice when possible. When the mallet is used, the chisel should be grasped firmly in the left hand and the mallet in the right. However, if the mallet is not being used the chisel should be held in the right hand, which then supplies the necessary force to make it cut, and the left hand used in whatever way is convenient to support the chisel near its cutting edge. This will depend upon the nature of the work being done, but at no time should the hands be so positioned that there is danger of them being cut. Horizontal paring, as this is called, must always be with the grain to avoid splitting. An easier cut is possible and a smoother surface produced if the cutting edge of the chisel is presented at a slight angle to the direction of cut, so giving it a slicing action. Long tapers, housings, chamfers and bevels, even convex surfaces, can all be produced in this way. Sometimes the removal of the waste is made easier by putting a series of saw cuts across it first.

Vertical paring, as opposed to horizontal, is usually done on ends and corners. The work must be placed flat on a piece of smooth scrapwood and held down firmly with the left fist. The index finger of this hand is then wrapped round the chisel and the thumb placed behind it so that the chisel is held vertically with the bevel outwards. The handle must now be grasped in the right hand and the right shoulder used to press the chisel down so that it cuts off the wood. Each cut must be light, gradually working back to the finished line. The direction of the grain must always be observed and cutting should be such that if a split does occur it runs into the waste wood. For very light cuts pressure may be applied by the right thumb instead of the right shoulder.

A shearing cut can be made if as the chisel is forced down it is brought from a slightly slanting to a vertical position. Similarly, a slicing action can be produced if the chisel is kept perfectly vertical but is slid very slightly in the direction of the grain as it is pushed down.

The purpose of the scrapwood on which the work rests is to provide a surface to which the chisel can cut and at the same time prevent the back of the wood being splintered.

The **drawer lock chisel** is a special tool made entirely of steel and cranked at right angles at each end to form two short blades. It is used with the hammer to cut out lock recesses in narrow drawers and the mortice in the rail to receive the tongue of the lock.

The Plain Firmer Chisel

These are bench chisels intended for general purposes, of quite sturdy dimensions and strong enough to be used for joint cutting in conjunction with the mallet. Rectangular in section, the blade is strong but its thickness often limits the use to which it can be put.

Ash-handled with brass ferrule (Fig. 55*a*). The handle is round in section, highly polished and comfortable to hold; the blade is fitted to it by means of a tang. Care must be exercised when the handle is struck with the mallet to avoid splintering. This is prevented at the lower end of the handle by the ferrule, brass being used for this to avoid rust. The blade has a strong bolster or shoulder on which the handle is seated and is forged from high-quality tool steel. The chisels are usually provided sharpened ready for use with a protective plastic edge guard.

The 'Blue Chip' Firmer Chisel (Fig. 55*b*) has a square section handle, the corners being nicely radiused to give a comfortable grip, made from high-impact resistant plastic in a distinctive shade of blue. The blade has a tang which fits into the handle, which in turn fits into the conical socket. This chisel really does handle very well indeed, the squaring of the handle itself giving greater manual control whereby any tendency for the chisel to twist while cutting can be prevented. The blade is of equally high quality and is forged from tool steel.

The Boxwood Carving Handled Firmer Chisel (Fig. 55*c*). The blade is similar in shape to the ash-handled variety, of quality tool steel carefully hardened and tempered, as are the blades of the whole range of chisels by Marples. Handles are turned from well-seasoned boxwood and are beautifully smooth to handle.

Oval splitproof-handled chisels are available in the same range from 3 mm to 51 mm wide. These have standard blades but the handle is moulded from a special plastic which is virtually indestructible, the oval contour of which affords a comfortable grip. The cuo-tone finish of the handle is quite distinctive.

The Bevel-Edge Firmer Chisel

Fig. 56 (*a–c*) shows the oval splinterproof handle, the Marples Blue Chip, and the boxwood carving handled chisels. Each of these has blades whose edges are bevelled off along their length. An examination will show that the bevels are slightly different in each case and this is to do with the overall design of the chisel by the manufacturer, who is concerned with weight, strength, balance, appearance and efficiency in use. Naturally, the bevel does weaken the chisel blade and this is most noticeable in the narrower sizes, which must only be used by hand and never levered. All three are similar in construction to the firmer chisel, but with the bevelled edge they can accomplish more delicate tasks, such as cleaning out the corners of dovetail pin sockets for which the blade of the firmer chisel would be too thick.

Paring chisels are a special kind of bevel-edged chisel with very long blades, 250 mm, giving a long reach. In comparison, the Marples Harlequin range has blades of only 65 mm. Being short, these are particularly useful for young people and with craftsmen who need a short blade for maximum control, the widths being 6, 13, 19 and 22 mm. The handle is of top-quality impact-resistant plastic. Standard chisel blades are 125 mm in length, but it must be remembered that all get shorter in use due to grinding and sharpening!

Blade widths for both firmer and bevel edge chisels are within the following range: 3, 6, 10, 13, 16, 19, 25, 32, 38 and 51 mm.

Mortise Chisels

Mortise chisels are used for chopping out joints—in particular mortise

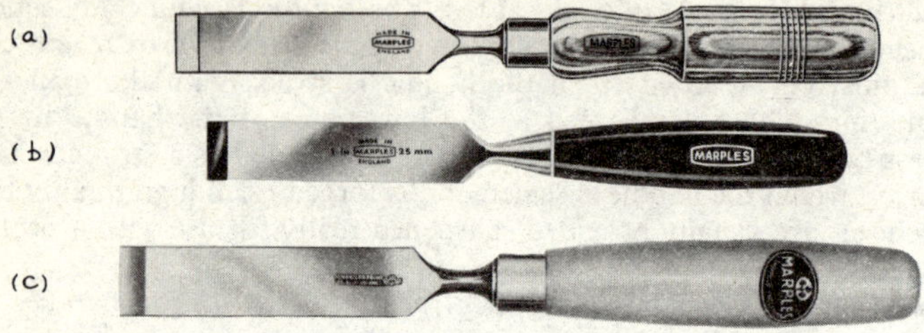

Fig. 55. The plain firmer chisel.

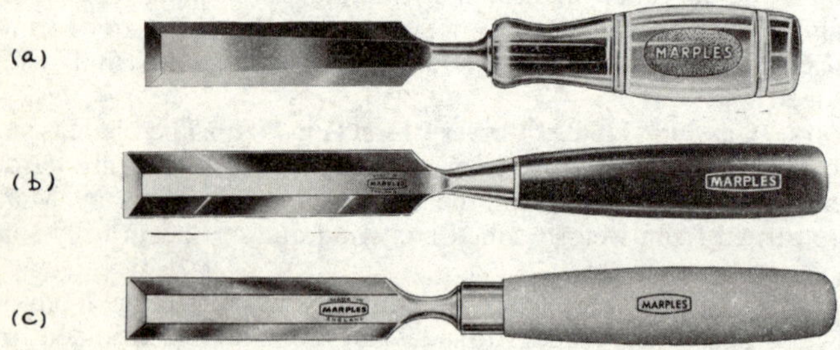

Fig. 56. The bevelled edge firmer chisel: (*a*) the oval splinterproof handle; (*b*) Marple Blue Chip; (*c*) boxwood carving handled.

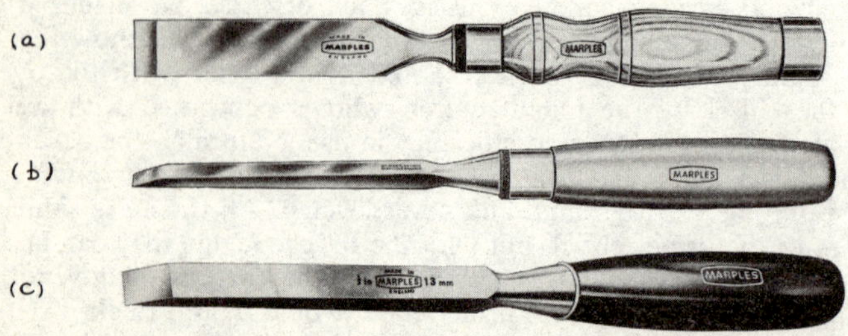

Fig. 57. The mortise chisel.

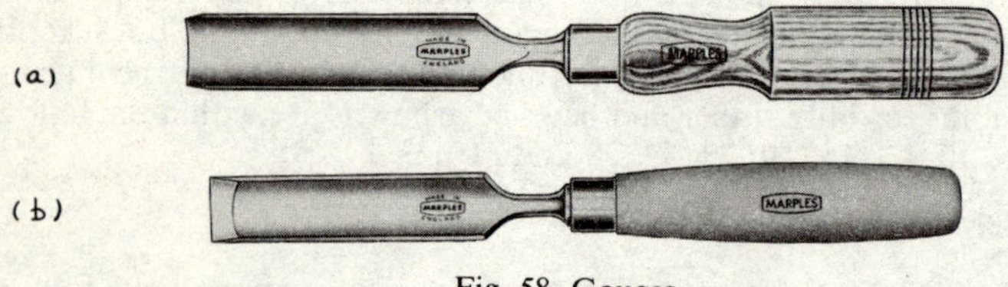

Fig. 58. Gouges.

joints as their name suggests. They are used in conjunction with the mallet and are strongly built to withstand this kind of heavy use and the leverage to which they are subjected. They should always be used vertically with the flat face towards the body, working outwards from the centre of the mortise, and after being driven into the wood leverage is then forward.

Registered Chisel (Fig. 57*a*). The round handle of selected hardwood, which is traditionally ash, has a strong steel hoop at the striking end in addition to the normal ferrule above the bolster. This top ferrule is to prevent mushrooming and splintering of the wood due to the successive mallet blows to which the handle is subjected when the chisel is in use. The blade is specially tempered and is of greater thickness than the normal firmer chisel to stand up to this heavier work of mortising and to resist the shock of the mallet blows. A leather washer fitted between the bolster and the handle absorbs the shock to the hand. The size range is 3, 5, 6, 8, 10, 12, 13, 16, 19, 22, 25, 32 and 38 mm blade width.

Sash Mortise Chisel (Fig. 57*b*). This is often referred to as the 'London pattern' and is used exclusively for mortising work. The blade is long for deep mortising and is stoutly made for this kind of heavy work. The boxwood handle is of the carving pattern and has a leather shock washer between bolster and ferrule. Blade widths are 6, 8, 10 and 13 mm.

'Blue Chip' Mortise Chisel (Fig. 57*c*). This blade is identical to that of the sash mortise chisel and available in the same widths. There is a nylon shock-resisting washer between the blade bolster and the 'blue chip' square-section handle. Being of high impact-resistant plastic this can be struck with the mallet.

Gouges

Gouges are really a special form of chisel, the principal difference being that the blades are rounded in section and have a curved cutting edge. They are used in the same way as chisels but produce curved surfaces as opposed to flat ones.

The Out-Cannel (Fig. 58*a*). This is also known as the **firmer gouge** and has the cutting bevel ground on the outside. Because of this, the tool has a scooping action, the corners not being so liable to dig in. This makes the gouge suitable for hollowing out and cutting recesses for finger grips in cabinet work. It is also most useful for roughing out treen work such as hand-cut bowls and other types of wood sculpture (see Chapter 12).

The In-Cannel (Fig. 58*b*). These gouges are ground and honed on the inside of the curve. Grinding, at 25 degrees, is by means of a thin stone with a convex edge, taking care not to draw the temper by overheating the blade. An oilstone slip is then used with which to produce the fine cutting edge. The curve of the slip should as far as possible be the same as that of the gouge, burrs being removed from the back. In-cannel gouges are used for cutting mouldings and other concave curves, generally by vertical paring as with a chisel. They are also known as **paring** or **scribing gouges.**

Both types of gouge are available with either selected hardwood or boxwood handles in widths from 6 to 25 mm (Fig. 59). Both are also available in a long version as paring gouges with boxwood handles and in this case are specified as being ground to cut circles of the diameters stated: for example, 6 mm gouge to 6 mm circle; 10 mm gouge to 13 mm circle; 25 mm gouge to 32

Line drawings shown are actual size and shape of cutting edge.

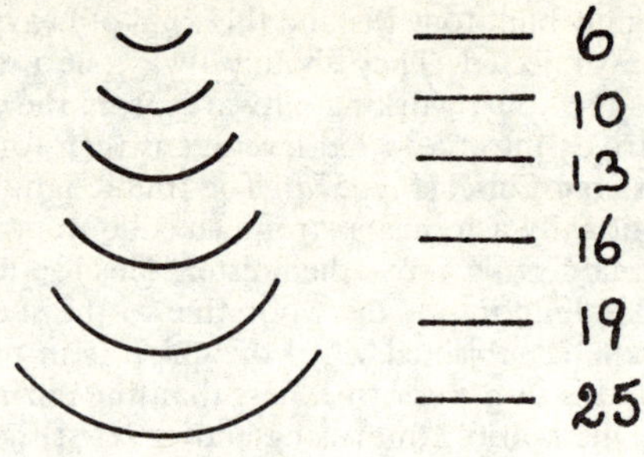

Fig. 59. Gouge sizes.

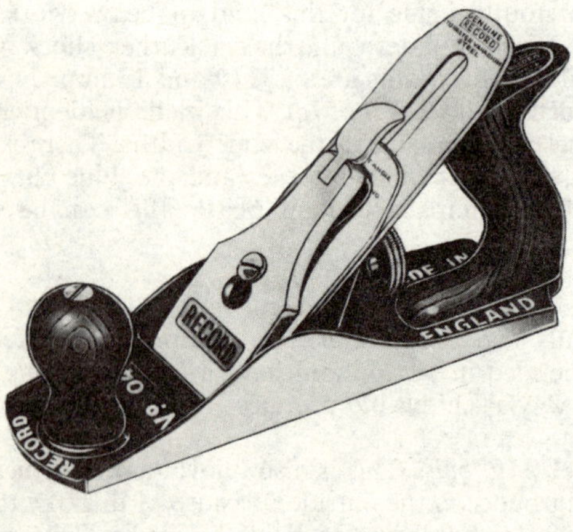

Part Ref.	Description
A	Body
B	Frog with Parts M, N, O, R
C	Cutter
D	Cap Iron
E	Lever Cap
F	Cap Iron Screw
G	Lever Cap Screw
H	Nut and Screw for Knob
J	Knob
K	Nut and Screw for Handle
L	Handle (and Toe Screw $04\frac{1}{2}$–08, 010 & T5)
M	Lateral Adjusting Lever
N	"Y" Adjusting Lever
O	Cutter Adjusting Nut
P	Frog Screw with Washer
Q	Frog Adjusting Screw
R	Cutter Adjusting Screw (not illustrated)
S	Handle Toe Screw (not illustrated)
T	Side Handle, T5 only (not illustrated)

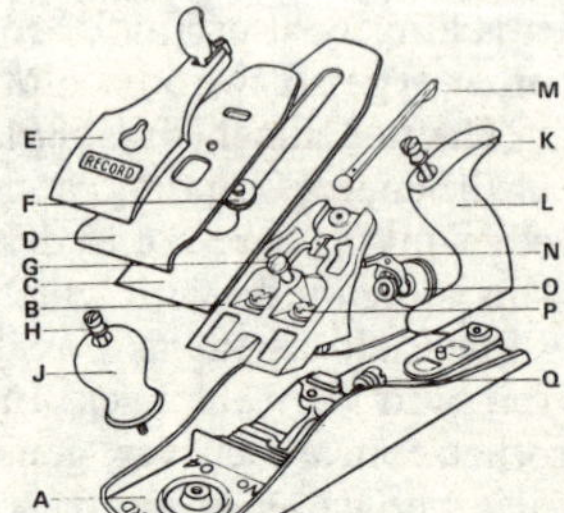

Fig. 60. The plane.

mm circle, etc. There is a range of 13 sizes up to 32 mm gouge to 150 mm circle.

Bench Planes

Early craftsmen reduced rough sawn timber to required sections with the adze, which produced what might be described as a scalloped surface. Having a convex blade, the adze produced a face which, although it was flat overall, was irregular, consisting of smooth hollows scooped out by each swing of the blade. This 'adze finish' is much prized by some collectors of antiques and is applied by some present-day manufacturers of furniture. Further smoothing was necessary to produce a completely flat surface, which was probably done by some method of abrasion. It would appear that the plane was developed from this need to make surfaces which were both smooth and flat. The earliest known examples are of Roman origin, both wood and metal being used in their construction. They are quite easily recognised as planes, the dimensions comparing remarkably with those of modern tools.

Basically the plane has two purposes: to smooth off rough surfaces and in so doing reduce the timber to a required size. Very many different kinds of planes are now made, each designed to do a special kind of work, and most are largely of 'all-metal' construction, which has now almost entirely superseded the range of wooden tools made from beech. They include moulding planes, try plane or jointer, jack plane and smoothing plane. The latter could quite well be the first plane which the would-be craftsman adds to his tool kit as it is probably the most useful for the amateur.

Metal planes such as the range of bench planes produced by Record have bodies of high-grade cast iron and tungsten–vanadium steel cutters. This steel is capable of retaining its fine edge during prolonged use on the hardest of woods. Tungsten and vanadium are metallic elements used in the manufacture of the hardest steels. Tungsten unites with the carbon of the steel to form tungsten carbide, which is the main constituent of all high-speed cutting materials used in modern machine tools for metal working, such as lathes, milling machines, etc. It has the capacity to cut at very high spindle speeds, even when working on hard steels. Obviously then, a plane iron containing the correct amount of tungsten will be harder and more resistant to wear. Its use in Record planes has proved that it will take a keener cutting edge and hold it for a longer period than ordinary steel. The correct and skilful introduction of tungsten in steel prevents what is known as 'grain growth'. In the fully hardened cutter this means that the steel is of very small grain size, and because of this it is more resistant to shock. This ensures that the keen edge of the plane iron will suffer less damage in use—in other words, it will stay sharper longer than other steels.

Precision engineering is employed at every stage in the production of the blade and the various components of the plane, resulting in an efficient complete assembly. This reduces particularly looseness and chatter when the plane is in use, which would result in scarred and irregular surfaces. The cutter is hardened and tempered under scientific control, using very sensitive instruments that record the slightest variation of temperature to ensure accurate and uniform hardness. Each one is subjected to a hardness test, enabling the makers to guarantee the quality of every individual blade which leaves the works. These tungsten steel blades are superior to the cast steel blade that was fitted to wooden planes in that they are less bulky and they keep their cutting edge much longer. Metal planes, which are now most widely used by professional and amateur craftsmen, and by schools in general, have other advantages. They are easier to hold, less bulky, well balanced and with well designed, strong and comfortable handles which are so positioned that the tool can be used efficiently with the minimum of effort and fatigue.

Adjustment of the blade is also much easier and much more positive. Setting the wooden plane depends upon the careful use of the mallet or hammer on toe or heel to alter the depth of cut. The blade is then kept in place with a wooden wedge which has to be tapped home by hammer. Lateral adjustment of the blade must then again be made by hammer, light blows being given on its edge near the top end whereby it is moved from side to side until a cut of equal depth is obtained across the full width.

The blade assembly of metal bench planes enables precision adjustment to be made mechanically. Depth of cut is adjusted by means of a large-diameter knurled brass nut which operates a lever which in turn is engaged in a slot in the cap iron (see Fig. 60). Turning this screw forward towards the front of the plane withdraws the whole of the blade assembly—that is, the cutter and cap iron which slide between the frog and lever cap. The blade is pushed out, increasing the depth of cut, by turning the screw backwards towards the handle. This fine adjustment can be made quite readily with the index finger while the plane is in use if it is found necessary to vary the 'cut' being used on a particular piece of wood in order to produce the surface finish required. To ensure that the blade protrudes an equal amount across its width a lateral adjustment lever is pivoted near the top of the frog. A circular metal pad at the lower end of this lever fits into the slot of the blade which can then be moved laterally as the lever is pushed from side to side. Failure to adjust this correctly may result in one corner of the blade being very much lower than the sole of the plane, resulting in the surface of the wood being gouged. Shavings of unequal thickness might also choke the throat of the plane. The position of the cutting edge in relation to the sole—in other words, depth of cut—may be seen if the plane is held upside down with the sole level with the eye. The cutting edge of the blade can then be observed protruding from the mouth. It appears as a dark line contrasting with the polished bottom of the plane. It is good practice to inspect a plane in this way if it is being used for the first time on a particular piece of work, and is absolutely essential if it is being reassembled after sharpening. Several factors determine the set, or hook, as it is sometimes known. Generally, the best results are obtained by taking off very fine shavings, but to remove the initial roughness of a sawn board the set might be increased, or if it is desirable to remove a considerable bulk of timber quickly when planing to size. Whether the wood is hard or soft and the nature of the grain are also factors to be taken into consideration.

The cap iron is an integral part of the blade to which it is attached by means of a large, flat-headed screw. The edge of the cap iron, which is common to the so-called bench planes, must fit closely across the full width of the flat side of the blade and be set a little back from its cutting edge. The purpose of the cap iron is to break the shaving as it leaves the cutting edge and in so doing deflect it away from the plane. It also lifts the shaving to leave the cutting edge clear and free to do its work. By pressing down on to the blade when fully tightened, the curved shape of the cap iron strengthens the cutting edge and thereby helps to eliminate chatter. It is usual to set the cap iron closer to the cutting edge if the wood is hard, or with a difficult grain pattern or for fine finishing. For softwoods it can be set a little further back, but the most suitable distance for any particular set of circumstances is soon learnt from experience. Both cap iron and cutting iron must always fit closely together so that no shavings lodge between the two or the plane may be choked.

The sole of the metal plane is much harder and therefore less subject to wear than that of the wooden plane. In turn, this means that the width of the mouth is less likely to be affected by wear of the sole. The forward edge of the mouth must hold the wood down in front of the blade to ensure that shavings are cut off as the plane is pushed along the wood rather than split off, which would result in a rough surface.

On a wooden plane the leading edge of the mouth often becomes worn and rough from use, making it less efficient. In the days when such planes were in frequent use it was often necessary to remouth them. This entailed recessing the sole and in so doing cutting away the forward edge of the mouth and gluing in a block of beech which extended back into the throat and mouth, reducing their widths. Once the glue had set the sole was trued along its full length with the try-plane, making sure that it was also at right angles to the near side by testing with the try square. By adjusting the frog of the modern metal plane, the position of the whole blade assembly can be changed, opening or closing the mouth and throat. The finer the planing being done—and this depends upon the nature of the work—the narrower the gap should be between the cutting edge and the forward edge of the mouth. This adjustment can only be made by first removing the lever cap, cap iron and cutter. The screws fixing the frog are then accessible and should be slackened to enable the movement of the frog with its own adjusting screw. Once the required position has been obtained these screws must be fully tightened again or the blade will chatter in use and move out of place.

Wood to be planed must be held firmly. Long pieces are normally placed on the bench top with the front end against the bench stop and the board turned so that planing is with the grain. Shorter work may be held in the vice. A well-balanced stance is necessary when planing, usually with one foot forward so that the left hand, which holds the knob of the plane, can press the front of the sole onto the wood. At this stage the blade should not be touching the timber. The right hand, which is going to provide the motive power, grasps the handle with the index finger extended down the edge of the blade assembly. This is the same grip as for the handsaw and is adopted so as to give greater directional control of the plane. The plane is then pushed forward and equal pressure is used on both knob and handle to hold it down on to the wood. This is to keep the plane flat so that it produces an equally flat surface.

As the planing stroke is nearing completion pressure should be eased off, particularly on the knob so that the front of the plane does not tip downwards. This would result in the end of the board being planed away below the level required. Similarly, when beginning the stroke slightly more pressure should be applied to the knob than the handle to avoid rounding off the back end.

For the method to follow in planing a piece of timber to size, the reader should refer to the section on the use of the try square (page 41). Squaring the edge of a very narrow board may present quite a problem due to the tendency for the plane to tilt. Clamping a strip of flat wood along one or both sides to thicken the edge, giving the plane a wider surface on which to work, often provides a solution. Planing across the end grain of wood also requires special techniques to avoid the splitting off of edges by over-planing. The ends of small sections are usually planed on the shooting board, while the ends of wider sections and boards are smoothed with the block plane or smoothing plane respectively. Planing is usually done from the outer edges towards the centre, but where necessary a piece of scrap wood clamped to the far end will prevent splintering and allow the full width to be planed. If the far corner is bevelled off this too relieves pressure on the last fibres.

Although wooden planes are generally much more bulky and in the main less efficient they do have one advantage. There is less friction between wood and wood than between metal and wood. They are, therefore, easier to push along the timber. Metal bench planes are available with corrugated soles to reduce the surface area in contact with the wood, which in turn reduces the friction and makes movement easier, particularly when working with resinous timber.

The Record group of bench planes includes the smoothing plane, jack plane, fore plane and jointer. Each type, with the exception of the fore plane, is available with different widths of cutter and in different lengths, and therefore weights. High-quality materials are used for each part. The body, which is ribbed for strength and rigidity, the frog and lever cap are accurately machined castings. The cutter is of tungsten–vanadium steel, precision ground on all faces and is tested and guaranteed to be the right temper. High-quality steel to withstand the tension imposed on it is used for the cap iron. The finely polished handle and knob are of selected hardwood. Body and frog are stove-enamelled Record blue and the body sole and the sides are accurately machined and smoothly finished. The machined faces of the frog are screwed firmly on to similar machined faces on the body to eliminate chatter.

Although only the smoothing plane is illustrated in Fig. 60, each plane in the range is constructed similarly and consists of similar parts. The best early experience of planing is probably obtained from the use of the smoothing plane. Of short length—240, 245 and 260 mm, and cutter widths of 45, 50 and 60 mm—it is of reasonably light weight (1·5, 1·7 and 2·2 kg respectively). This makes it suitable for a young person to use at school to clean up pre-planed timber, or for the amateur craftsman involved with light constructions in the home, where again he is only concerned with the final finishing of timber which he purchased already machine-planed.

Before a new plane can be used the cutter must be honed, which means that the blade assembly must be taken apart. The cam lever on the plated lever cap must be lifted, releasing pressure on the cutter assembly, which allows the lever cap, cap iron and blade to be lifted away from the frog and plane body. The cap iron must now be unscrewed from the cutter and this is best done by placing the blade flat on the bench, holding it firmly with the left hand, while the right is used to keep the screwdriver vertical as the screw is slackened off. Done in this way there is no danger of an accident should the screwdriver slip from the screw. A large screwdriver with a wide blade should always be used for this purpose.

Though honing is dealt with in detail in Chapter 6 (Tool Maintenance), brief reference may be made here. A good-quality oilstone which is perfectly flat must be used and lubricated with a thin machine oil. The ground bevel is placed flat on the oilstone and the cutter raised to form a honing angle of 30 degrees. By pushing the cutter forward and then pulling it back several times along the full length of the stone a burr is formed on the flat side. By turning the cutter over so that it is flat on the oilstone, a few light strokes along the stone should remove the burr. Should it still remain the whole process must be repeated until the burr has been worn off by the cutting action of the oilstone.

When reassembling the plane, the cap iron must be screwed on to the back of the blade and set parallel with the cutting edge. For softwoods the cap iron should be set back approximately 1·5 mm from the cutting edge, but for finishing hard or curly grained wood it should be set as close as possible. As the cutter assembly is placed back into the plane, care must be taken not to damage the newly sharpened edge on the frog or body of the plane. Care must also be taken to make sure that the lateral adjusting lever is fitted into the slot in the blade, and that the lever controlling the depth of cut is also fitted into its slot in the cap iron. The lever cap can then be placed in position over its retaining screw and the cam lever snapped into place. Final adjustment of the blade can then be made by using the knurled brass nut to give the required depth of cut, and the lateral adjustment lever to position the blade parallel to the base of the body to produce shavings of equal thickness. If it is also considered that adjustment to the width of the mouth is necessary to help give the required finish to the work in hand, the position of the frog must be changed. Fine setting of the mouth in conjunction with fine setting of the cap iron is advised to obtain satisfactory finishing of difficult woods. From Fig. 60 it will be seen that this can only be done when the cutter assembly is removed.

Once the plane is reassembled and the set of the blade inspected, it should be tested on a piece of scrap wood of the same type and with similar grain to that on which the plane is to be used. Any necessary final adjustments can be made at this stage. The cutting edge of the smoothing plane should be quite straight with the corners dubbed off so that wide, thin shavings of even thickness are removed. To obtain the finished surface on a piece of work with the smoothing plane, planing should begin at the near side and successive shavings taken off moving across the width of the work until the whole surface has been covered. Planing must always be light and with the grain. Should the plane fail to produce a smooth surface in a particular place, this may be due to a change in grain direction, and the direction of planing must be changed accordingly. With the blade set correctly, and the cap iron set fine to give the correct chip effect, shavings will rise from the throat and curl away sweetly from the plane, producing a smooth silky surface on the work. This is one of the most simple and yet most satisfying aspects of woodworking.

The Jack Plane

One disadvantage of the short smoothing plane is that it will tend to follow rather than remove any irregularities there may be in a long length of timber. For this reason it should be used for final finishing and the initial preparation of any rough timber carried out with the jack plane. These are considerably longer, 355 and 380 mm, with blade widths of 50 and 60 mm and weights of 2·2 and 2·7 kg respectively. The longer length of the jack plane makes is easier to produce a straight flat surface. Because of its length the plane at first only removes the high spots; then gradually as these are planed away the wood is planed along its full length.

Adjustment, care and maintenance of the jack plane is exactly the same as for the smoothing plane with the exception that the blade is sharpened to a gentle curve across its full width. This makes the removal of waste material quicker and easier as the curve of the blade scoops the wood away. The curve of the blade does, however, produce grooves along the length of the timber with ridges between them which are quite visible. If they are not removed the ridges become even more obvious when the work is completed, whether with paint or a clear natural finish. Part of the work of the smoothing plane is to clear away the marks left by the jack plane.

The Fore Plane

The fore plane is longer still than the jack plane (455 mm) with a 60 mm cutter width and a weight of 3·2 kg. Being longer, it produces an even more accurate surface than the jack plane, particularly as the cutter is sharpened square in the same way as the smoothing plane.

The Jointer

Jointers are exceptionally long planes used to produce very accurate edges on long timber. Because of their extra length, the castings for both the fore plane and jointer are made with an inner rib running from end to end to give increased strength and greater rigidity. Large framed assemblies such as doors, sawn edges of manufactured boards to be used for carcase construction and the edges of boards which have to be glued together, are examples of the type of work for which the jointer may be used.

The planes are 560 and 610 mm in length, with cutters 60 and 70 mm wide and weights of 3·6 and 4·1 kg. Like the fore plane and the smooth plane, the jointer is sharpened square across the blade, the corners only being dubbed off to avoid deep scoring of the surface.

The Technical Jack Plane

This Record plane has been specially designed for schools and technical colleges. The design of the body casting provides extra strength around the blade assembly, the sides being made deeper at this point. They in turn are reinforced by an enlarged forward web above the mouth. The deep sides minimise any tendency there may be to tilt the plane and at the same time provide a wide, steady bearing surface which makes the plane ideal for use on the shooting board. A straight handle, which can be screwed in at right angles to either side just behind the blade, is provided for when the plane is being used for shooting. These planes are quite long and very sturdy, 330 mm with a 50 mm blade and weight of 2·3 kg.

The Bench Rebate Plane

The sides and forward web of this plane are also very much deeper than is normal and the mouth extends across the sole from side to side. This enables the specially shaped blade to cut the full width of the plane body, i.e. 54 mm. In this case the body is of malleable iron to compensate to some extent the loss of strength due to the mouth being extended through the sides. The body is 330 mm long and the assembled plane has an overall weight of 1·8 kg. Large rebates from which the bulk of the waste has been sawn, can be quickly cleaned out by this plane. Smaller rebates can be cut out completely, providing suitable fences are clamped to the wood with which to guide the plane and to limit its cut. If used across the grain, a saw cut must first be made to sever all the fibres of the wood.

Of all the wooden planes, possibly the **jack** is the only one which some craftsmen still prefer to use. It does have advantages in that it is light to use and rough-sawn timber can be planed to size relatively quickly. Of its disadvantages, retruing the sole, remouthing, repairing or replacing damaged handles spring readily to mind, coupled with the somewhat difficult method of adjustment.

Metal planes are precision tools and their fine adjustment provides very accurate cutting. The so-called suction between the accurately ground sole and the wood, particularly as it becomes flatter, does tend to cause the plane to drag, making planing a little more difficult, but, as stated earlier, if this presents a serious problem planes with corrugated soles are available. Alternatively, rubbing the sole lightly with a wax candle does lubricate it and reduce friction. It must always be borne in mind that should the metal plane be dropped, being made of cast iron which is brittle, there is a distinct possibility that the body will break across the mouth.

Rebate Plane

The rebate plane (Fig. 61) will cut rebates up to 38 mm in width, lesser widths being controlled by the parallel fence which is adjustable, and may be used on either side of the plane. Two fence arms facilitate accurate setting of this fence. A depth stop, which is adjustable, allows rebates to be cut to 18 mm deep when working with the fence on the face edge. If the depth stop is removed completely very much deeper rebates can be cut but in this case the required depth must be gauged clearly and planing be stopped when the line is reached. In some cases it is necessary to cut the rebate on the far side of the wood still working from the face edge. The rebate is then known as a **fillister** and is cut in this way to ensure that the wood remaining between it and the face edge is of the correct width and is parallel. When used to cut a fillister the fence arms limit the depth to which it can be cut and if a greater depth is required the fence and arms must be removed. Planing is then continued down to a gauge line as the depth stop is not operative in this position.

The plane is fitted with a spur which is used when rebating across the grain. The spur is located in front of the blade and severs the fibres ahead of the cutting edge. There is a neutral position to which the spur may be turned when it is not required—that is, when working with the grain—and both fence and depth stop may be removed completely when the plane is required for 'square plane' work only. It is essential to remember that for all rebate work the side of the cutter against the rebate must be level with, or possibly protrude very slightly from, that side of the plane body. On no account must it be set in or the resulting rebate will not have a square side.

Two cutter positions are provided and for normal rebating and fillistering the cutter should be at the rear, which is provided with a fine-adjustment screw operating in a slot near the top of the blade. By means of this screw the cutter may be raised or lowered to regulate the thickness of shaving being

Part Ref.	Description
A	Body
B	Lever Cap
C	Lever Cap Knurled Screw
D	Cutter
E	Lever Cap Screw
F	Fence with Knurled Screw(s) H
G	Fence Arm(s)
J	Depth Gauge with Screw and Washer K
L	Spur and Screw
M	Cutter Adjusting Lever on 078
M	Cutter Adjusting Nut on 778
N	Cutter Adjusting Screw (778 only)
O	Body Arm Set Screw(s)

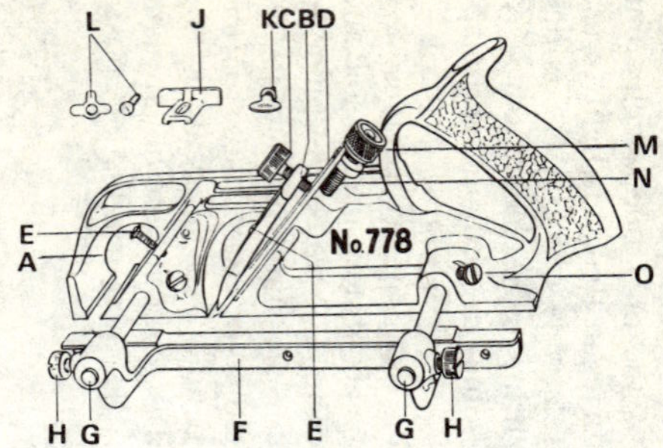

Fig. 61. The rebate plane.

Part Ref.	Description
A	Body (with Adjustable Mouth J—073 only)
B	Lever Cap with Screw D
C	Cutter
E	Cutter Adjusting Screw
F	Cutter Adjusting Nut
G	Mouth Locking Screw and Washer
H	Mouth Adjusting Screw

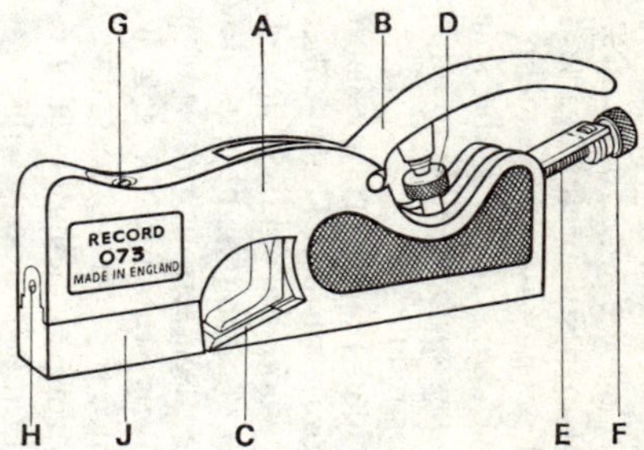

Fig. 62. The shoulder rebate plane.

removed. It is essential that the edge of the cutter is always sharpened dead square since virtually no lateral adjustment is possible. The blade is plain with no back iron and is held in position by means of a screw-operated lever cap.

To prepare the plane for use, once the cutter has been honed and positioned the two fence rods should be inserted into the holes and secured with the two set screws, taking care not to allow the rods to protrude beyond the off-side of the plane body. The fence must now be set on the rods to give the required width of rebate, and the depth stop adjusted with the thumbscrew so that the rebate is cut to the necessary depth. These measurements are checked with the steel rule, taking care not to damage the fine cutting edge of the blade. The thickness of shaving is adjusted by raising or lowering the blade by turning the cutter adjusting nut after slightly easing the knurled lever cap screw. When the blade is set satisfactorily this screw should then be re-tightened, but only finger tight to avoid any possible damage to the components. For bull-nose work—that is, cutting tight up to a corner—the blade should be placed in the forward position, the amount of set noted by sighting along the sole as for a bench plane and the blade made firm with the lever cap and screw. In this position the cutter adjusting nut is not operative. If necessary the sole, fence and the face of the depth stop can be lubricated by rubbing lightly with a wax candle as for the bench planes.

The handle of the rebate plane closely resembles that of the handsaw and the plane should be held in just the same way, the index finger again being extended down the side of the plane to steady and to guide. The left hand should be used to steady the front of the plane and to apply side pressure to keep the fence tight to the wood. The plane must be kept upright at all times to ensure that the rebates being cut are square. It must always be remembered that, as with all planes of this type, the cut must begin on the far end of the wood, and the plane brought a little further back after each successive shaving until the rebate has been completed. By this method the rebate will be cut accurately.

The Shoulder Rebate Plane

The body and lever cap of the shoulder rebate plane are of bright finished castings, the base and sides of the body being accurately machined and ground so that it will lie flat on either side and can be used by either the right or left hand. The Record 073 illustrated in Fig. 62 incorporates an improved screw adjustment to the mouth which gives a wide range of adjustment for fine or coarse work. The depth is regulated by screw adjustment of the blade, which is then held in place by the lever cap screw. As this screw is tightened down on to the top of the blade, the front end of the lever is in turn pressed down on to the front of the cutter to hold it firmly in position.

Two widths of blade are available, 19 and 32 mm, and the planes are 200 and 204 mm long, 1·1 and 1·8 kg in weight. The blade must be sharpened perfectly square so that it will line up with the sole of the plane. In common with most small planes, the blade is set with the bevel uppermost, the frog being at a low angle varying from 12 to 20 degrees depending upon the type of plane. Shoulder planes are used, as their name suggests, for trimming the shoulders of wide tenons, truing rebates and fine work in general, particularly across the grain.

Part Ref.	Description	
A	Body (with Nose G—077 only)	
B	Lever Cap with Screw D	
C	Cutter	
E	Cutter Adjusting Screw	Not applicable to 076
F	Cutter Adjusting Nut	
G	Detachable Nose	
H	Nose Locking Screw	
J	Mouth Distance Pieces	

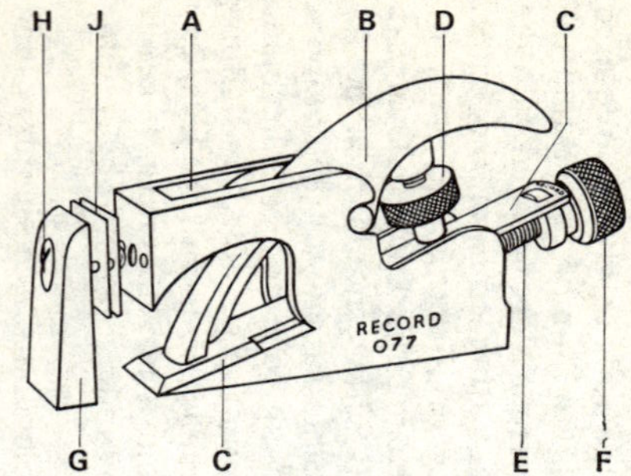

Fig. 63. The bull-nose rebate plane.

Part Ref.	Description
A	Body with Nose B and Screw C
C	Nose Screw
D	Cutter Clamp with Screw and Washer E
F	Cutter (Right Hand)
G	Cutter (Left Hand)
H	Knob
J	Depth Gauge with Screw and Washer K

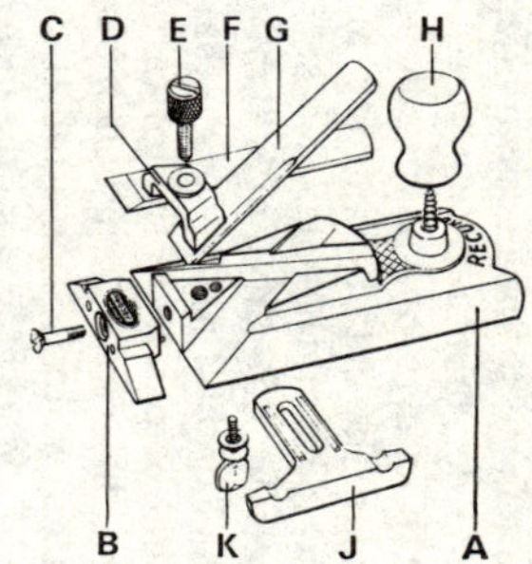

Fig. 64. The side rebate plane.

Part Ref.	Description
A	Body and Cutter Adjusting Screw
B	Cutter Clamping Bracket and Screw
C	Fence
D	Fence Knurled Screw
E	Fence Arm
G	Depth Gauge and Stem
GKL	Depth Gauge Complete
H	Cutter
J	Cutter Adjusting Nut
K	Depth Gauge Locking Screw
L	Depth Gauge Expander
T	Fence Arm Set Screw
W	Cutter Clamping Nut
Y	Handle
Z	Handle Fixing Screw

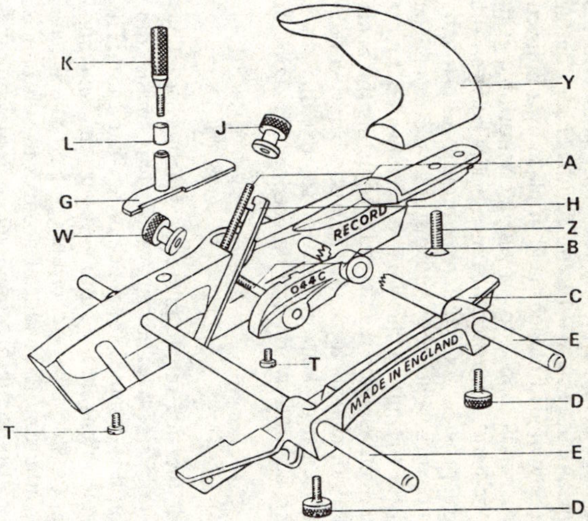

No. 045C CUTTERS

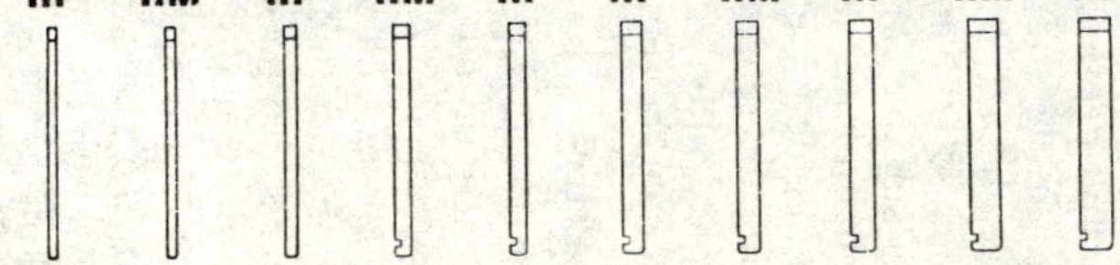

Part Ref.	HP	HM	HP	HM	HP	HP	HM	HP	HM	HP
Size inches	1/8		3/16		1/4	5/16		3/8		1/2
mm	3·2	4·0	4·8	6·0	6·4	7·9	9·0	9·5	12·0	12·7

Fig. 65. The plough plane.

The Bull-Nose Rebate Plane

This plane is designed particularly for fine work where extreme accuracy is required, and will plane into corners and other difficult positions such as finishing off a stopped chamfer or a stopped rebate. It is very similar to the shoulder plane, but only about half its length—102 mm with 29 mm cutter width and 0·8 kg (Fig. 63). The low-angled blade is held in place by a knurled wheel and screw, while the lever cap is shaped to provide a comfortable grip, fitting nicely into the palm of the hand. Two steel distance pieces between the detachable nose and the body provide four different mouth adjustments for very fine or slightly coarser work. The nose and distance pieces can be removed completely to convert the tool into a chisel plane which will cut right up to a vertical face. The depth of cut is again regulated by adjusting the blade with a screw which operates in a slot near its top end. The wood being worked must be clamped firmly to the bench or held in the vice so that this small plane, which is capable of such accurate work, can be used with maximum efficiency.

The Side Rebate Plane

The body and depth stop of the side rebate plane are machined castings with a plated finish, and the knob is of selected hardwood. This small, compact plane weighs only 0·3 kg and is designed for right- or left-hand use. The thin blades are set at a low angle to enable the cutting of very fine shavings. The plane is suitable for accurate side rebating, cleaning up grooves made with the plough plane, and for adjusting the width of grooves to suit panels, glass and sliding doors, etc. It is also useful for trimming damaged mouldings and for easing the rebate of a door frame while the door is still *in situ*. The plane is supplied with two cutters, an adjustable depth stop which is reversible, and the nose may be removed for working close into corners.

The Plough Plane

The Record 045C plough plane (Fig. 65) is an entirely new design and is capable of carrying out a wide variety of work, including the making of grooves in which to fit hardboard to plywood panels, grooves for sliding doors, etc., rebates, and for removing the waste wood from housings. (In this case a strip of wood must be fixed across the work to act as a fence.) The open, modern styled plastic handle of cellulose acetate has been designed for greater ease of use and more comfortable handling.

The plane is fitted with a double arm bridged fence which may be used on either side of the plane and an improved fully adjustable depth gauge. This incorporates a unique nylon expander which makes possible immediate, positive locking as a one-hand operation. The depth gauge enables the plane to cut accurate grooves to a depth of 16 mm, which, using the long double arms of the fence, may be made up to a maximum of 127 mm from the working edge. Ten tungsten steel cutters are supplied with the plane, so that it will plough grooves ranging from 3·2 to 12·7 mm in width. The wider blades have a notch near the top so that their depth of cut may be varied with the knurled cutter adjusting nut. The cutter clamping nut must be eased slightly before any adjustment is made. As with the rebate plane, cutting must be started at the far end of the wood gradually working back to the near end. A conversion kit now enables this plane to do the work of the multi-plane.

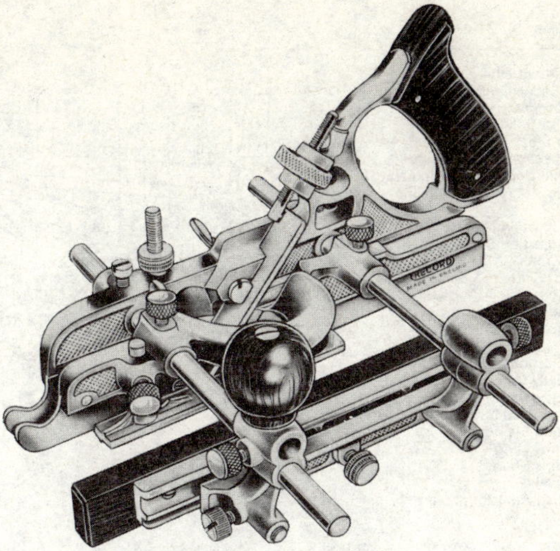

Fig. 66. The multi-plane.

The Multi-Plane

The multi-plane (Fig. 66) is often referred to as the 'universal' plane due to the multiplicity of the work for which it may be used. Ploughing, rebating, housing, tonguing, fillistering, edge and centre beading, sash moulding and slitting can all be carried out.

Housing is often referred to by some craftsmen as trenching or dadoing. The plane is fitted with an adjustable fence and depth gauge, two sets of fence arms (long and short), beading stop, slitting cutter, sliding section depth gauge, cam steady and spurs for cross-grain working. Using these spurs, which are fitted in the body and the sliding section, housings may be cut across the grain. Since the tool is not working from an edge in this case it is not possible to use its own fence. A strip of wood which will act as a fence must therefore be fixed across the work to the right of the plane, making it difficult to use the main depth gauge. In such a case the second depth gauge on the sliding section is used. To begin the cut the plane should be drawn backwards a few times so that the spurs will cut through the grain on the surface of the wood. The groove can then be ploughed out, cutting from the far side and working gradually deeper and backwards to the near edge. Any tendency there may be to splinter at the ends of the housing may be reduced by making small saw cuts down the edges of the groove, on the waste side of the line. When grooving with the grain, the blade of required width is placed in the main body, and except for the narrowest cutters the sliding section is added as well to give extra support to the back of the blade. The cutter must not be set in at all from the outer sides of these two sections otherwise the plane will jam in the groove being cut. It is better, in fact, if it stands very slightly proud of each. Once the blade has been set to cut what is considered to be the correct thickness of shaving, it must be locked in place with the cutter bolt and wing nut. Both the main depth gauge and the fence should then be set accurately

Part Ref.	Description
A	Body without Fittings
B	Sliding Section without Fittings
C	Fence Complete with Fittings
D	Knob with Bolt and Nut
E	Beading Stop
F	Sliding Section Depth Gauge
G	Adjustable Depth Gauge and Nut H
H	Adjusting Nut for Depth Gauge
I	Cutter
J	Cutter Adjusting Nut and Screw K
K	Cutter Adjusting Screw
L	Slitting Cutter
M	Screw for Slitting Cutter Stop
N	Cutter Bolt
O	Cutter Bolt Wing Nut
P	Cutter Bolt Clip and Screw
Q	Spurs
R	Sliding Section Screws
S	Cam Steady Complete
T	Arm Setscrews
U	Hardwood Slide for Fence
V	Fence Slide Set Screw
W	Fence Arms Long
X	Fence Arms Short
Y	Fence Screws
Z	Fence Slide Adjusting Screw

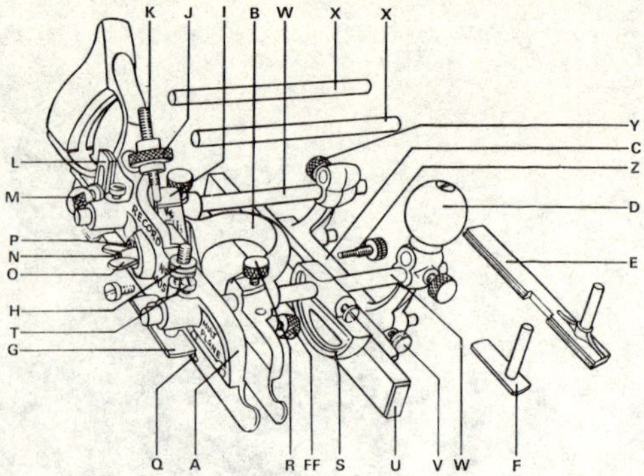

No. 405 STANDARD CUTTERS

	Plough and Dado													Fillister
Part ref.	IP	IM	IP	IM	IP	IP	IM	IP	IM	IP	IP	IP	IP	IP
Size inches	1/8		3/16		1/4	5/16		3/8		1/2	5/8	3/4	7/8	1 1/4
mm	3·2	4·0	4·8	6·0	6·4	7·9	9·0	9·5	12·0	12·7	15·9	19·0	22·2	32·0

	Beading					Tonguing		Ovolo		Slitting
Part ref.	IB					IT		IO		IS
Size inches	1/8	3/16	1/4	3/8	1/2	3/16	1/4	1/4	3/8	
mm	3·2	4·8	6·4	9·5	12·7	4·8	6·4	6·4	9·5	

No. 405 ADDITIONAL CUTTERS

	Sash		Reeding							
Part ref.	IS	IS	IR2	IR3	IR4	IR5	IR2	IR3	IR4	IR5
No. of Beads										
Size inches	1 1/2	1 3/4	1/8	1/8	1/8	1/8	1/4	1/4	1/4	1/4
mm	38·0	45·0	3·2	3·2	3·2	3·2	6·4	6·4	6·4	6·4

	Fluting					
Part ref.	IF					
Size inches	3/16	1/4	3/8	1/2	5/8	3/4
mm	4·8	6·4	9·5	12·7	15·9	19·0

Special Bases and Nosing Tools Number and Type	Part ref.
No. 6 Hollow and Round	6HR
No. 8 Hollow and Round	8HR
No. 10 Hollow and Round	10HR
No. 12 Hollow and Round	12HR
No. 5 Nosing Tool	5NT
Extra Cutters for Hollows or Rounds / Extra Cutters for Nosing Tool	5NTC

Fig. 67. Parts and cutters for the multi-plane.

with the aid of a steel rule, measuring carefully from the edge of the blade. Once again, cutting must begin at the far end of the wood, and if the groove is very wide the amount of effort necessary to cut it can be considerably reduced by using a narrower blade twice, it only being necessary to readjust the fence.

Moulding cutters, such as the ovolo, are set up in a similar way as for rebating but it must be remembered that the end of the cutter is not square as for normal working.

For **rebating**, a cutter wider than the width of the rebate should be used so that it stands proud from the edge of the wood. The sliding section should then be set so that it bears on the surface of the wood, so increasing the stability of the plane. The depth gauge must be set accurately on the main body of the plane, measuring carefully from the cutting edge of the blade. Finally, the fence has to be placed in its lower position so that it will slide below the blade and can be set so that the rebate is cut to the correct width.

In addition to the 24 cutters supplied with the plane as standard equipment, others are available as extras (see Fig. 67); for example, special bases and nosing tools, a hollow and its cutter to form a round, a round and its cutter to form a hollow. A nosing tool and its cutter will form a round such as is required on the edges of stair treads. Each plane is supplied individually packed in a wooden box complete with a very comprehensive instruction booklet.

The Block Plane

Record block planes (Fig. 68) vary in length from 140 to 203 mm and apart from the one short plane which has a cutter width of 35 mm the remainder are 42 mm. Weights vary from 0·3 to 0·8 kg. The bodies are stove-enamelled castings, machined and polished on base and sides.

These small planes, which fit easily into the palm of the hand, are very convenient and easy to use. The blade is ground at 25 degrees and sharpened at 30 degrees; it is set with the sharpening bevel upwards and is held by the lever cap at the low angle of 20 degrees. The simplest versions can only be adjusted by releasing the lever cap and making manual adjustments, but the more expensive can be adjusted mechanically in much the same way as the bench planes can be adjusted both laterally and for depth of cut. In addition, the width of the mouth may be set for coarse or fine working. Since the blade is set so low and with this range of adjustments—in particular being able to set the mouth so close—the plane is invaluable for trimming fine work, chamfering and especially for planing end-grain. It is also most effective when used on small shooting boards. Some of the larger sizes are equipped with a wooden front knob, and there is one plane which is double-ended, with two mouths. Both the cutter and the lever cap can be reversed to form a bull-nose plane.

The Circular Plane

Often referred to as the **compass plane**, the circular plane is designed for use on concave and convex surfaces, such as formers for laminated work or circular table tops (Fig. 69). The cutter assembly is similar to that of the bench planes, providing both lateral and depth of cut adjustment. However, as the direction of the grain can vary considerably in the curved shapes which the plane has to cut, the blade is pitched at a higher angle than is normal to reduce the tendency to tear the wood. When setting the blade, the spring steel sole

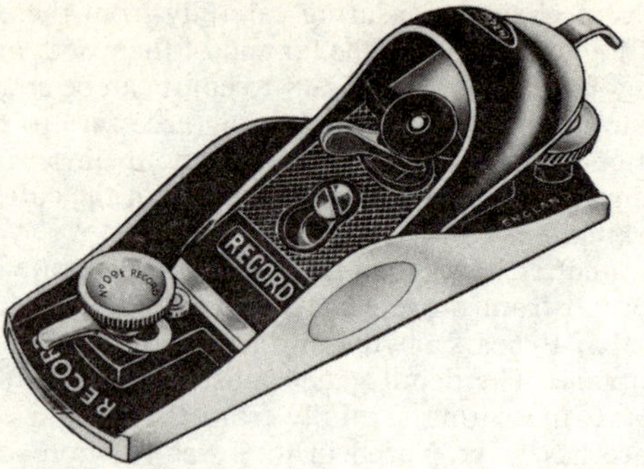

Part Ref.	Description
A	Body (with Adjustable Mouth Plate)
B	Lever Cap
C	Lever Cap Screw
D	Cutter
F	Cutter Adjusting Screw
J	Cutter Adjusting Nut
L	Lateral Adjusting Lever
M	Mouth Knob Screw
N	Adjustable Mouth Quadrant
O	Cutter Adjusting Lever

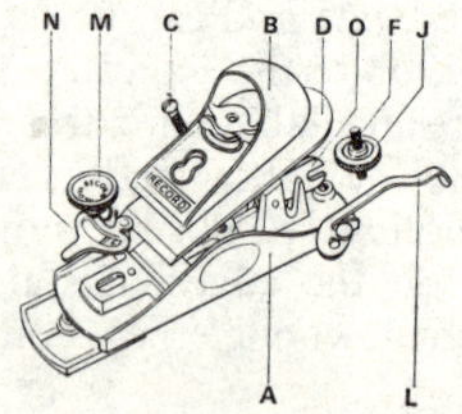

Fig. 68. The block plane.

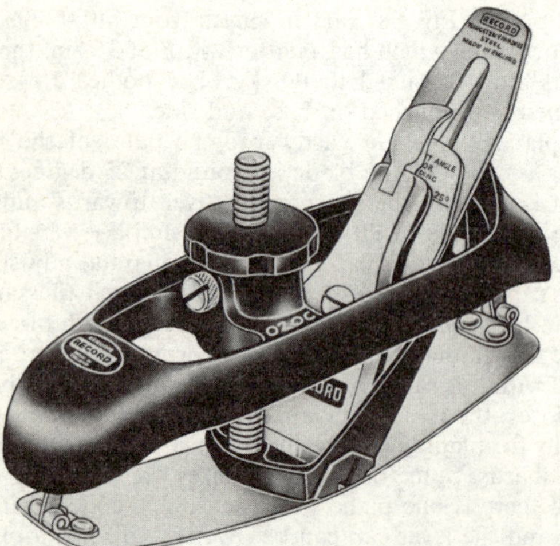

Part Ref.	Description
A	Body
C	Cutter $1\frac{3}{4}$" (45·0 mm)
D	Cap Iron
E	Lever Cap
F	Lever Cap Screw
G	Sole Adjusting Screw
H	Sole Adjusting Nut
K	Sole with Hinges and Frog

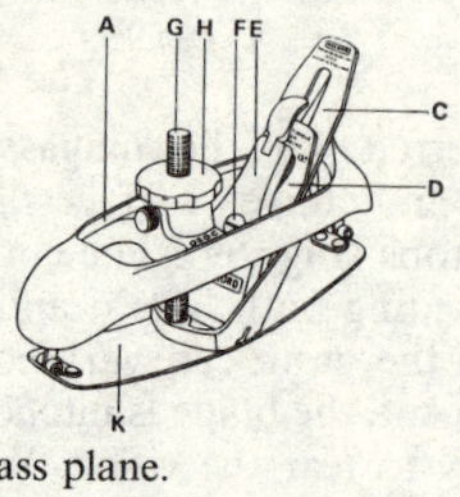

Fig. 69. The compass plane.

Part Ref.	Description
A	Body with Screws H and R
B	Cutters: $\frac{1}{4}''$ (6·4 mm)
	$\frac{1}{2}''$ (12·7 mm)
C	Smooth Cuter
E	Knobs
F	Bolt and Nut for Knob
J	Cutter Adjusting Nut
K	Clamping Collar and Screw L
M	Depth Gauge with Shoe and Screw N
O	Fence with Screw and Washer P

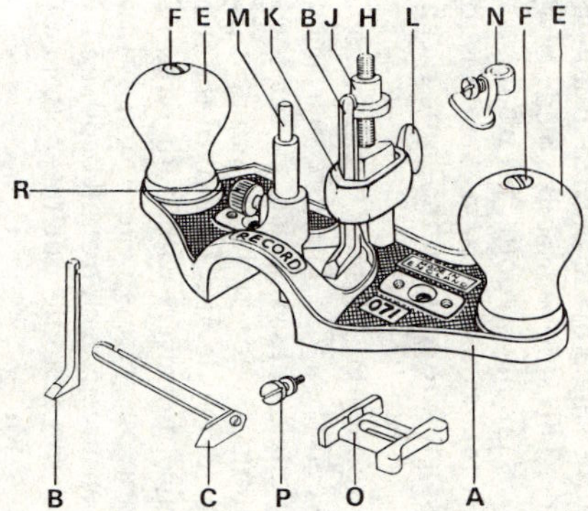

Fig. 70. The router plane.

Part Ref.	Description
A	Body
B	Fence
C	Cutters (Razor Blade Type)
D	Fence Screw with Washer
E	Cutter Clamp and Screws F
G	Handle
H	Handle Bolt and Nut
J	Depth Adjustment Screws
K	Grooving Attachment Body
L	Hardboard Cutter
M	Front Knob with Screw

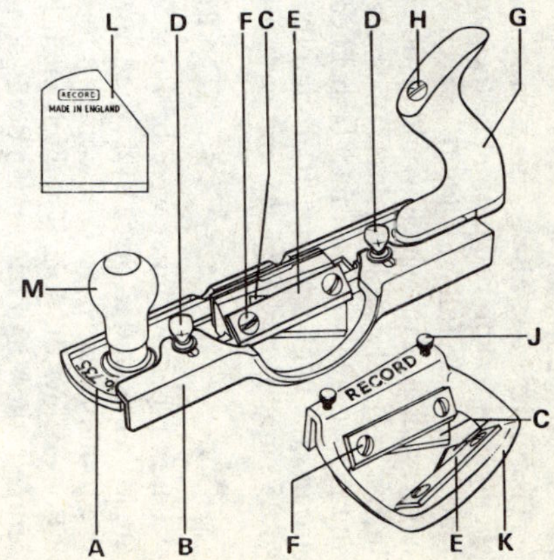

Fig. 71. The fibreboard plane.

should be flat, the amount of curvature then being quickly set by means of the centre screw adjustment.

The plane must always be used parallel to the edge of the wood, avoiding slicing cuts which would damage the surface. Lateral adjustments must also be made very carefully to avoid uneven cuts and to prevent the possibility of corners digging in, which would again cause damage to the surface. When not in use it is advisable to leave the sole flat. The body is a smooth casting, suitably curved so that it may be held comfortably by wrapping the right hand around the back and the left around the front. The plane has an overall length of 250 mm; the blade is 45 mm wide and total weight 2 kg.

The Router

Older types of router were of wood with the single blade pitched at a high angle, being held in place by a wooden wedge. This stout chisel-like blade gave rise to names such as 'Old woman's tooth' or 'Granny's tooth', protruding as it does below the sole. The high pitch is advantageous in that its action is to scrape rather than cut, and in doing so is less liable to tear out the grain. It can also work in quite restricted spaces.

More modern routers are of metal with wooden handles and their cranked blades work almost horizontally with the wood (Fig. 70). They are sharpened on their top side so in fact they are low-angle cutters which, if not used carefully, may lift out the wood with a splitting action rather than cut it. If necessary the blade can, of course, be lowered a little at a time until the full depth has been reached. It is sound practice, however, with both types of router to remove the bulk of the waste from any recess being worked with either a chisel or gouge, using the router to ensure an even overall depth and a smooth finish. Routers are frequently used for cleaning out the bottom of housings, the sides of which have first been sawn.

It is usual for modern routers to have an adjustable fence for right- or left-hand use which enable grooves to be cut parallel to either side of the tool post for general or bull-nose work, the square section cutter fitting into a V-shaped groove. An adjustable shoe allows the throat to be closed for working on narrow surfaces, the rod of which may be used either end up as a guide for the blade. If detached completely from the plane body, the rod and shoe combination form an efficient depth gauge. A considerable amount of effort is necessary in using the router, which is held in both hands and is almost invariably pushed forward. The wood being worked must therefore be clamped down securely.

The Fibreboard Plane

The fibreboard plane (Fig. 71) is a comparatively new tool developed for use on soft insulating boards and hardboard. On insulating board it will bevel up to 10 mm depth at 45 degrees, or slit up to 13 mm thickness. Vee grooves up to 10 mm deep can be cut if the grooving attachment is fitted. On hard or tempered board it will bevel up to 5 mm depth at 45 degrees.

The plane, which is 260 mm long and weighs 1·5 kg, is supplied complete with detachable fence, grooving attachment, six razor-blade type cutters for use on soft insulating board, and one cutter for hardboard.

The planes described above are representative of the wide variety manufactured, and even with only some, rather than all of these, craftsmanship of a very professional standard can be achieved.

The Scratch Stock

The scratch stock is a home-made tool which is always similar in form to that illustrated in Fig. 72 and consists of a blade, filed or ground to shape from an old saw blade, which can be clamped at right angles to the work. The shape of the blade is exactly the reverse of the shape of moulding required. When set, the tool is drawn backwards and forwards along the edge of the work, an even downward and, at the same time, inward pressure holding it to the wood. The vertical face of the stock must not be allowed to wander away from the edge or the shape being worked may be damaged. The blade is sharpened straight across, maintaining the profile, but so that there is no bevel, and therefore the waste is removed by a scratching action only. It is always advisable to test the scratch stock on a piece of scrap wood of the same kind as that to be worked before beginning on the real thing. A single marking gauge can be adapted as a scratch stock by slitting the stem and fitting the scratch blade in a similar way to that illustrated.

Small arrises of different radii can be taken off corners by the **Stanley cornering tool**. This is held in the palm of the hand and worked backwards and forwards along the work. This is very useful on softwood which has to be painted, where sharp corners would be easily damaged. It is also difficult to paint a sharp corner satisfactorily as the paint draws back from the edge.

The Hand Drill

Sometimes referred to as the wheelbrace and originally designed for metalworking, the hand drill (Fig. 73) is now accepted as an essential tool for woodworking also. Still using conventional metalworking twist drills, small-diameter holes to accommodate nails and screws can be drilled quickly and accurately in wood. A set of drills ranging from 1·0 mm by 0·5 mm to 8·0 mm will be found most useful. The chuck has three hardened steel jaws which are spring-loaded. These are opened by holding the shell of the chuck in one hand and turning the crank forward sufficiently to allow the shank of the drill to be inserted between the jaws. Tightening is then done by retaining the grip on the shell and turning the crank in the opposite direction.

Held either horizontally or vertically, the drill is convenient to use, and if necessary for work in a restricted space, the side handle can be unscrewed. So that the drills cut on centre it is advisable to give them a start by first making a small hole with a bradawl. Where it is necessary to drill to only a certain depth, a wooden sleeve from which the required length of drill protrudes can be quickly made from a little scrap wood or dowel. This is left on the twist drill and acts as a depth stop. Double pinions and a ball thrust bearing mounted in the malleable iron frame give a really smooth, positive action. The woodworker will also find the hand drill very useful for light drilling in metal and plastics.

The Joiner's Brace

When small diameter holes are required this is a tool which has been almost entirely replaced by either the hand drill or by the electric drill. Both are more

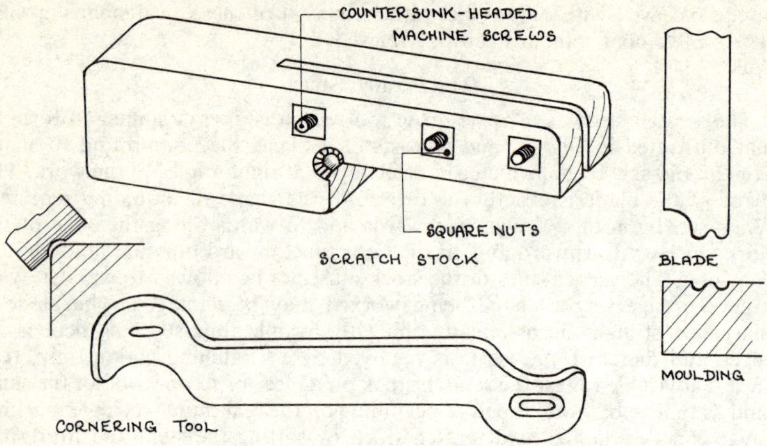

Fig. 72. The scratch stock and cornering tool.

Part Ref.	Description
A	Frame
B	Handle
D	Bevel Pinions
E	Side Knob
F	Gear Wheel
G	Crank Handle complete with Screw and Washer H
J	Chuck Spindle
K	Chuck complete
L	Gear Wheel Spindle

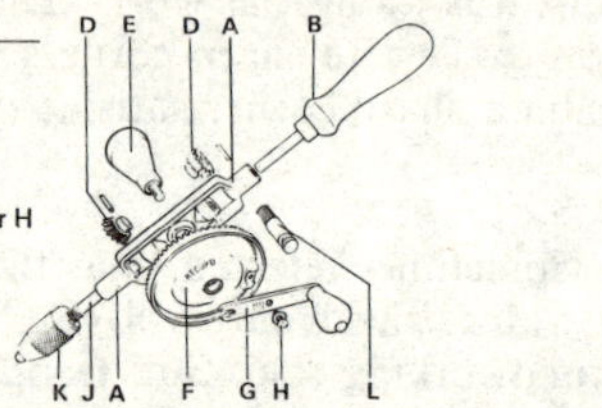

Fig. 73. The hand drill.

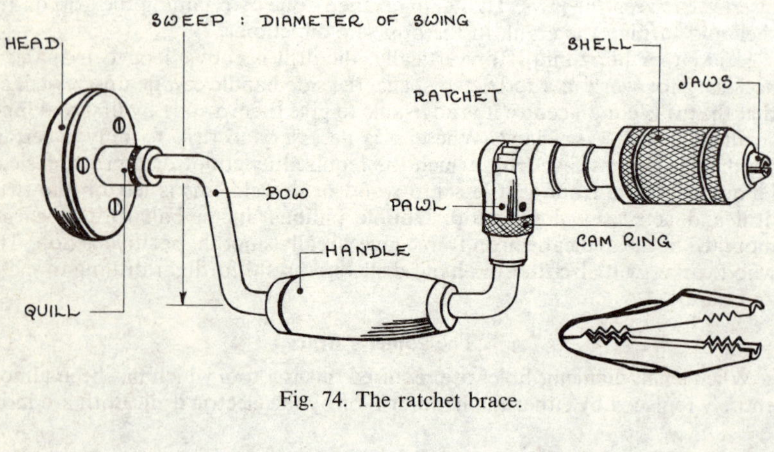

Fig. 74. The ratchet brace.

compact and will drill the required holes more accurately and certainly more quickly. However, for larger holes say of 10 mm diameter and above, the brace and bit is still an essential tool (Fig. 74). For drilling large-diameter holes where space is not restricted, a plain brace with a large sweep is quite adequate. If the working space is limited so that it is impossible to make complete turns of the bow the ratchet brace is necessary. A cam ring controls the direction of the cut so that if the ring is turned to the right the bit is turned into the wood. Once the bit really begins to bite the bow can be swung back and the ratchet operates leaving the bit stationary, to be turned forward once more on the forward sweep. If the ratchet action is necessary when the bit is being withdrawn, the cam should be turned to the left when the second pawl will be disengaged and the first one will re-engage, reversing the motion. With the cam ring central, both pawls are engaged and the brace then works just as a plain one.

Brace bits are held in the chuck, the shell of which controls the operation of the spring-loaded jaws. If the shell is grasped firmly and the bow turned anticlockwise the jaws are allowed to open, and when sufficiently wide apart the tang of the drill may be inserted. Turning the bow hard in a clockwise direction then secures the bit firmly in the chuck. Naturally, the operation is reversed to remove the bit. Wood boring bits usually have square sectioned taper tangs which fit standard 'alligator' jaws. Brace chucks fitted with so-called 'universal' jaws will take all bits with No. 1 Morse-taper shank and straight shank bits in addition to the standard square taper tang.

When in use, the brace is generally held at right angles to the work, either horizontally or vertically. The ability to do this accurately gradually develops with experience. It is quite easy to tell whether the brace is leaning to left or right, but much more difficult to judge whether or not it is bearing away from or towards you. Because of this it is always best to stand at the end of the work to ensure that the drill is not leaning to one side or the other. In this way any possibility of the bit breaking out of the side of the work can be avoided. Verticality can, of course, always be checked by a companion, or with the try square, or at times by clamping guides to the sides of the wood by which it is possible to judge whether the bit is vertical.

Boring holes at angles other than right angles in wood can be quite difficult due to the tendency for the drill to 'run with the grain'. This can be avoided by making a simple jig from a block of wood which can be clamped to the work. The block should first be drilled in the normal way and then bevelled with saw or plane to pitch the hole at the required angle. A little time spent in doing this can prevent a great deal of frustration.

Just as with the hand drill, depth stops are often necessary. These may be home made, a wooden sleeve fitting over the bit to restrict the depth to which it can cut, or two pieces of hardwood clamped to the bit by means of wood-screws near their ends which, when tightened, draw them together. Alternatively, they may be commercially made of metal, which again clamp to the bit. Whenever a depth stop is used care must be taken to avoid scoring the surface of the wood.

Brace heads are invariably of hardwood but most handles are now made of plastic, as in the Stanley range which are available with sweeps of 150 (the electrician's brace), 200, 254, 305 and 355 mm.

(a)

(b)

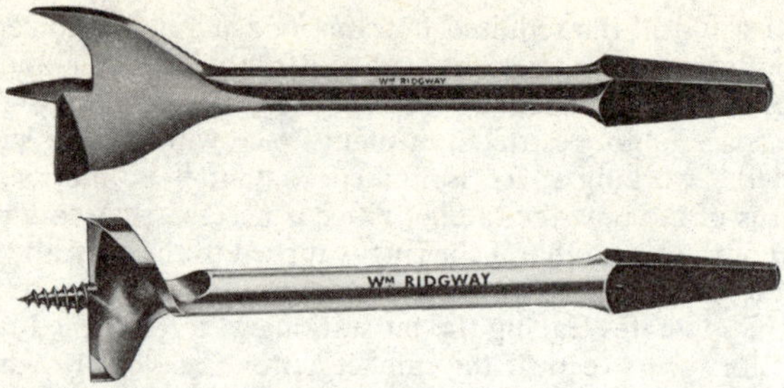

Fig. 75. (*a*) Plain centre bit. (*b*) Quick-cutting centre bit.

(a)

(b)

(c)

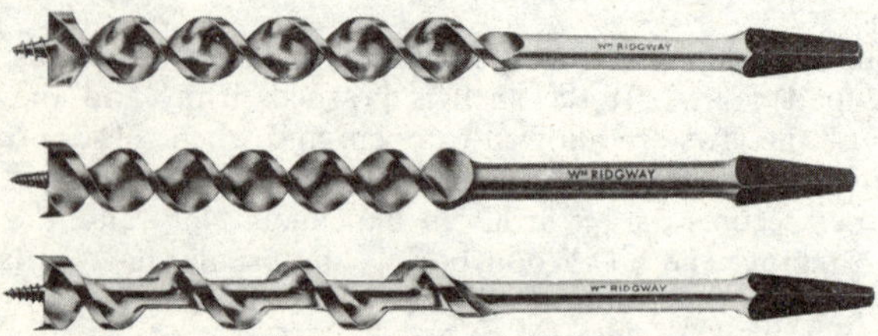

Fig. 76. Twist bits: (*a*) Scotch auger; (*b*) Jennings pattern; (*c*) solid centre.

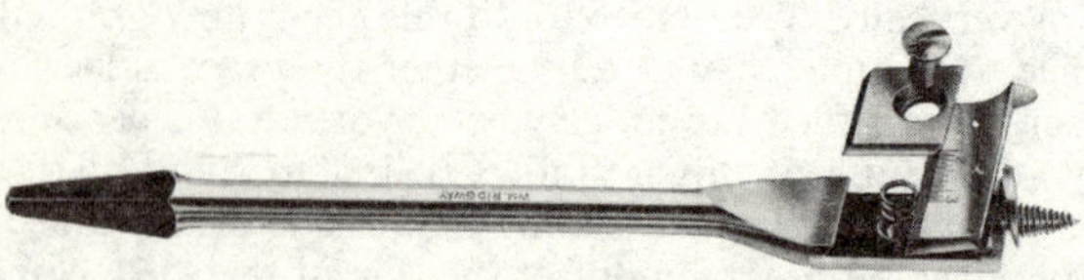

Fig. 77. The expansive bit.

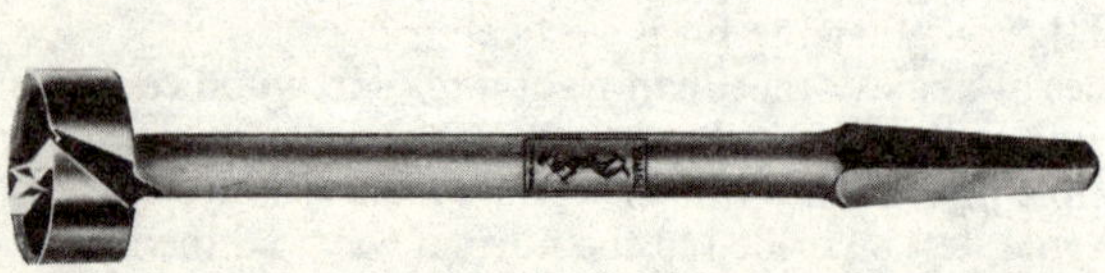

Fig. 78. The Forstner bit.

(a)

(b)

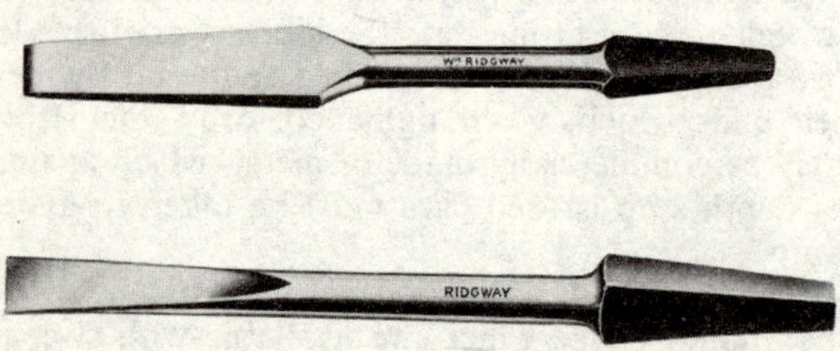

Fig. 79. (*a*) Turnscrew bit. (*b*) Cabinet turnscrew.

Wood-Boring Tools

Wood-boring tools are invariably referred to as **bits**, and a wide selection is available, all designed to bore holes under different circumstances to a variety of sizes and depths.

Centre Bits

Two patterns of centre bit are obtainable (see Fig. 75): the old type, with which the rate of cut is entirely under the control of the craftsman, depending solely on the pressure which he applies to the brace and the rate at which it is turned; and the new type with a screw point which draws the bit into the wood. At times the action of the latter may be found to be a disadvantage, the rate of cut being somewhat coarse. Each type centre bit has one spur which scribes the diameter of the hole and this is followed by the single cutter which lifts out the waste wood.

Centre bits are best suited to making large blind holes. As with all wood boring, if the hole is cut right through the timber there is a distinct possibility of the edges around the far side of the hole being badly splintered. This must be avoided either by working from both sides, turning the wood round once the point of the drill protrudes from the back side, this indicating the centre of the hole, or by clamping a piece of scrap wood to the back side into which the bit cuts, leaving the required hole clean and crisp. Centre bits are not suitable for cutting down end-grain as the point is liable to follow the grain when the bit will drift out of truth. This is because there is no wide portion to the drill behind the cutting edge to maintain the direction of the hole once it assumes any appreciable depth. The old pattern centre bit is excellent for cutting holes in thin material such as hardboard and plywood.

Twist Bits or Auger Bits

The long spiral of twist bits (Fig. 76) bears against the side of the hole being cut, maintaining the direction of the bit and thereby the accuracy of the hole. Such bits are therefore suitable for boring in any direction of the grain.

The following are points to observe when purchasing an auger bit for a specific purpose. It should be straight and all parts symmetrical about the axis; tang, shank, twist and screw point all being in line. The screw must be cleanly formed and should lead smoothly into the cutting edge. When seen in profile against the light, the tips of the spurs must be level and slightly ahead of the cutting edges, which must also be level. Each side will then do an equal amount of work. The throat of the bit must be well formed and cleanly polished so that the flow of chips away from the cutting edges is not obstructed. The diameter of the twist should be slightly less than that of the cutting diameter to prevent the bit from binding in the hole being made.

A good, well balanced bit will draw itself easily into the wood, cutting a clean hole and turning easily without having to be forced unduly. In action the screw point pulls the bit into the timber, the spurs scribe the diameter and cut the wood fibres in advance of the cutters, which then lift the chips and feed them up the twist from which they escape at the top of the hole. When boring a hole, you must be sure that the timber is free of any obstructions such as screws and nails which would damage the bit. It may be quite impossible to make good any harm which these might do and the bit would never again be really efficient.

Bahco Record suggest that bits are often sharpened more than is necessary and the effective life of many considerably shortened by incorrect filing. The original shape should be retained so that each side of the bit does an equal amount of work; therefore each must be filed equally to keep the balance of the nose. Only as little metal as is necessary should be removed by filing lightly with a smooth file. Rules to observe are: always sharpen from inside or underneath—never outside; maintain the original shape and angles by using a suitable smooth file.

The scotch auger bit (Fig. 76*a*) is specially designed and sharpened for boring hardwoods. Bits such as this, without spurs, are also considered best for accurate boring into end grain. Jennings pattern bits (Fig. 76*b*) provide perfect smooth boring and are much preferred by cabinet makers and craftsmen in general for fine work. The solid centre bit (Fig. 76*c*) is excellent for general purpose work.

Twist bits vary in length from 200 mm to 255 mm, depending upon their diameter, but special scotch types are 320, 355, 380 and 480 mm long. On the other hand, short so-called dowel bits of the Jennings pattern are available, as it is seldom necessary to drill much more than 50 mm deep for this type of joint. They are only 125 mm long. The various patterns of auger bit are manufactured within the diameter range 5 to 40 mm. Eyed augers are much longer, some being more than 600 mm in length, and are turned by means of wooden cross handles fitted in the eye which replaces the tang on this type of bit.

The Expansive Bit

Each expansive bit is supplied with two interchangeable cutters which are fully adjustable. Each cutter is serrated along its top edge and the serrations engage with those along the bottom edge of the spring-loaded packing. This ensures that once the packing screw is tightened the cutter cannot slip. The scale on the cutter assists in setting the tool up but before the finished hole is bored a trial should be made on scrap wood. On no account should the maximum on the cutter scale be set beyond the limit mark on the packing. If this is exceeded both bit and cutter will be damaged. Expansive bits are really designed for use on softwoods so that their use on hardwoods should be limited to comparatively small holes. A big advantage is in that one expansive bit is equivalent to having a range of centre bits, particularly of the larger sizes.

The threaded point of the bit carries its own spur and cutter, which work as an independent tool. Cutting ahead of the larger outer cutter they relieve it of considerable strain and reduce the effort necessary when drilling these large-diameter holes. Several sizes are available and with the appropriate cutters enable holes up to 150 mm diameter to be drilled.

Forstner Pattern Bits

Although the Forstner bit has a small point, this is more to start the bit at the required centre rather than guide it (Fig. 78). The bit is in fact guided by its circular rim, and holes bored are clean, true and flat-bottomed. Being unaffected by knots or the run of the grain, holes can be overlapped without difficulty. Forstner bits are made in the range 10–32 mm and are quite unequalled for all kinds of fine and delicate work and pattern making.

Turnscrew Bits

The name and shape of turnscrew bits (Fig. 79) make their purpose obvious—namely, to enable screws to be entered rapidly, the brace making it possible to exert considerable leverage. Like screwdrivers, they are also equally valuable when screws have to be extracted. The larger the screw, the larger the sweep of the brace should be. To withstand the strain which is imposed upon them they are made of high-grade carbon tool steel specially heat-treated for toughness. Blade widths are from 5 to 16 mm, one variety being double-ended with a square section blade at each end resembling a tang which is bevelled across the diagonal. Care must be taken to see that the blade end fits the screw slot well or it may ride out and cause considerable damage to the wood.

Countersink Bits

These bits are used to recess the top of a hole to accept a screw head. The rosehead (Fig. 80*a*) is suitable for use on softwoods and non-ferrous metals, such as brass, copper and aluminium, since it is quite often necessary to enlarge the countersinkings in metal and plastic fittings. The snail horn (Fig. 80*b*) is best used on hardwood, which it is less likely to tear. It is often good practice lightly to countersink the top of a dowel hole so that no splinters foul the joint and the dowel can be led in easily. For a similar reason, lightly countersink the underside of the clearance hole for a screw shank so that any burr turned up by the screw thread as it enters the second piece of wood does not prevent the two from being drawn tightly together. Screw heads may be flush with or slightly below the surface of the wood.

High-Speed Steel (HSS) Countersinks

These countersinks (Fig. 81) are designed for use with the hand drill, electric drill or pedestal drill. Although available in carbon tool steel, HSS is better having a much longer life particularly if used on metal. The Stanley two-flute pattern is intended for use on the pedestal drill and is reputed to be chatter-free. Average sizes are 13 mm diameter head only, 40 mm overall length, shank diameter 6 × 20 mm and included angle of 90 degrees.

The Screw Mate Range

The combination sets provided by Stanley Tools enable several operations to be carried out simultaneously when work is being screwed together. In each case the correct diameter drill must be selected for any particular gauge of screw. All are intended for use with the electric drill.

The pieces of wood being joined must be clamped together and the bit in Fig. 82*a* enables pilot hole, clearance hole and countersinking to be performed in one operation. With the bit in Fig. 82*b* pilot, clearance, countersink and counter bore are all cut at the same time. In this case a depth stop (Fig. 82*c*) of suitable size should be used to give the precise bore depth each time. Counter-bored holes so produced usually require stopping, and the range of plug cutters which go with the counterbore combinations allow cross-grained plugs

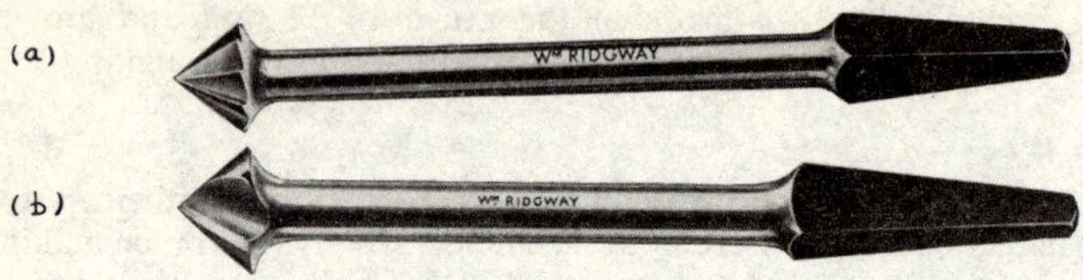

Fig. 80. Countersink bits: (*a*) rosehead; (*b*) snailhorn.

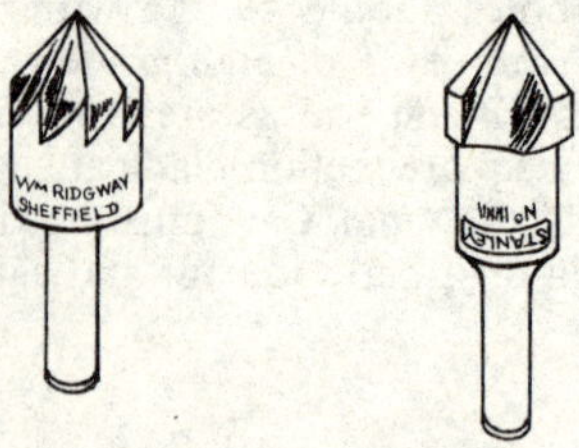

Fig. 81. High-speed steel countersink bits.

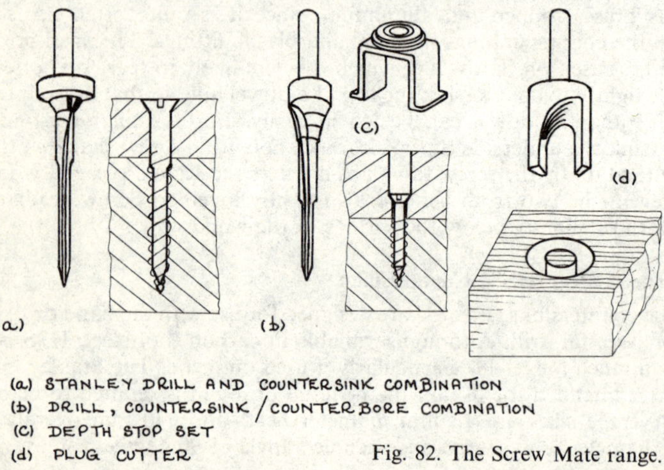

Fig. 82. The Screw Mate range.

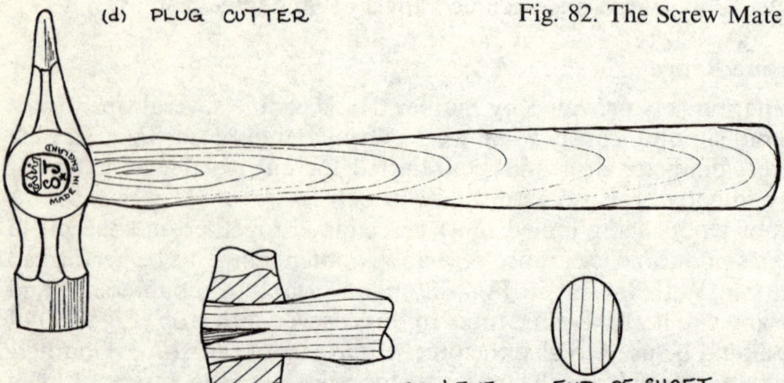

Fig. 83. The Warrington pattern hammer.

to be cut from scraps of the timber being used. Plugs such as these match the grain of the wood and are almost invisible when finished off (Fig. 82*d*).

Many other bits are also available to the woodworker: shell; nose; spoon; shell auger for end-grain boring; single twist auger with screw point and brace tang; and dowel trimmer. This last is used to chamfer the ends of dowels to make fitting easier. For any particular problem regarding boring holes the reader is advised to consult the catalogues issued by the various manufacturers.

Hammers

A good hammer will be forged from selected and guaranteed carbon steel. The dies in which the head is formed are perfectly accurate and well polished. Lengths of hammer steel are heated to a forging temperature and are placed between the dies, which are set in a drop-stamping machine. As the work progresses the head gradually takes shape and the eye is punched through. (This is the hole into which the shaft will be fitted and is made with a pair of dies which work from the upper and lower surfaces of the head to give a double taper or waisted effect.) Any surplus steel which has been squeezed out between the two dies is ground off. The temperature at which the steel is forged is sufficient to ensure that the steel is soft enough to be formed by the dies without causing internal faults in the structure of the metal or defects in the hammer head. To relieve any stresses and strains which may be set up in the steel, however, and to refine its grain structure, the heads are placed in electric furnaces for an hour at a temperature in excess of 800°C. This normalising process is followed by further grinding during which the face is made slightly convex. British Standard specifications permit a maximum convexity resulting from a radius of approximately 255 mm. The edges of the face are also chamfered at this stage. The correct balance between hardness and toughness is obtained by further heat treatment when the striking surfaces are hardened to a depth of three millimetres by partially immersing them in molten lead and then quenching in water. The metal is then very hard, but unfortunately very brittle, and is corrected by tempering in a bath of molten salt or in hot air ovens. This hardening and tempering process produces a hammer head with hard but tough striking surfaces backed up by a slightly softer steel. This absorbs the shock imposed on the faces when the hammer is used, and also resists cracking and chipping of the faces and fractures around the eye.

Final polishing and painting makes the heads ready to have their handles fitted. The best handles are of hickory, which is more resilient and better suited to heavy use than ash, but is more expensive and often difficult to obtain. Both woods are, however, tough and long-grained, and are well able to withstand the strains exerted on them in the course of normal use. Timber for hammer shafts is seasoned, and to prevent shrinkage of the shaft by any subsequent drying out, which would cause the head to become loose, that end of the shaft is impregnated with oil. The handle is tapered to fit the taper of the eye, and is left thicker behind the head so that the two bind snugly together. A hardwood wedge, usually of hornbeam, is then driven into a slot in the forward end of the shaft, spreading it into the eye. Any surplus timber remaining is removed and the end smoothly finished. Steel wedges are then fitted at right angles to the wooden wedge, completely filling out the eye. This

Fig. 84. The engineer's hammer.

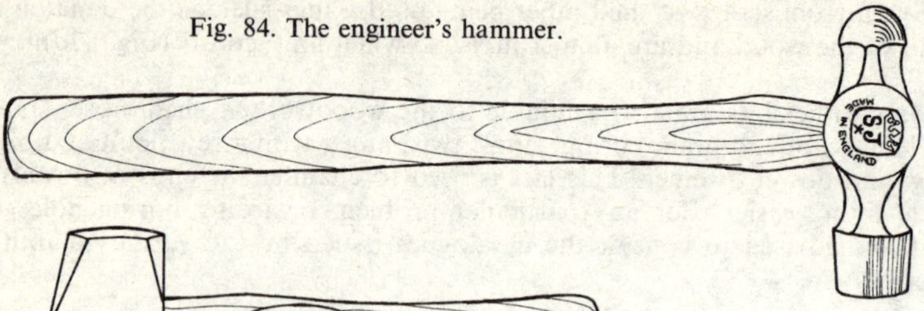

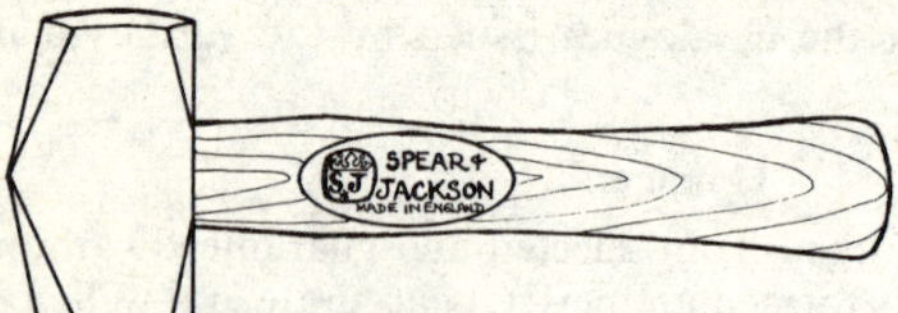

Fig. 85. The club hammer.

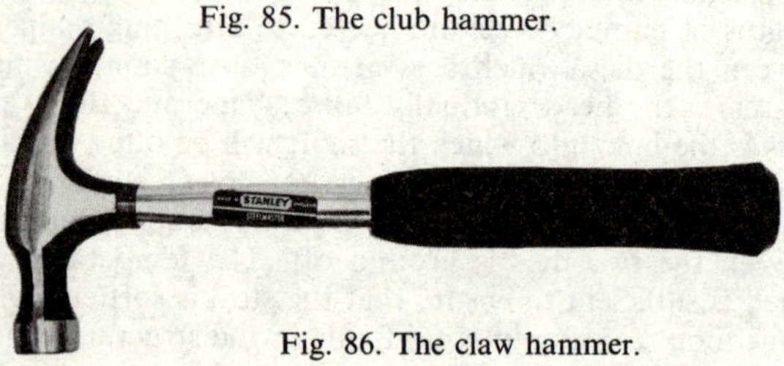

Fig. 86. The claw hammer.

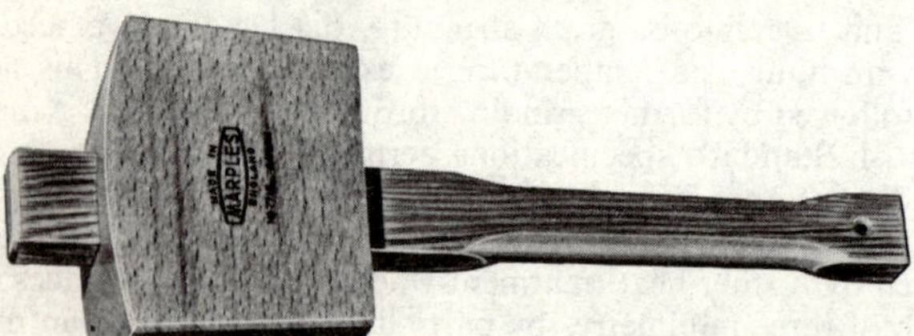

Fig. 87. The joiner's mallet.

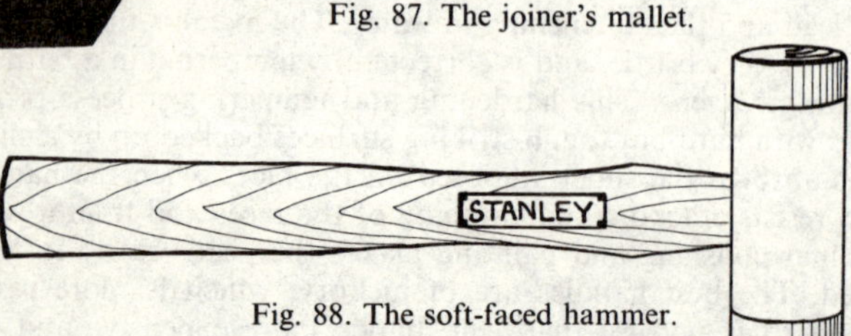

Fig. 88. The soft-faced hammer.

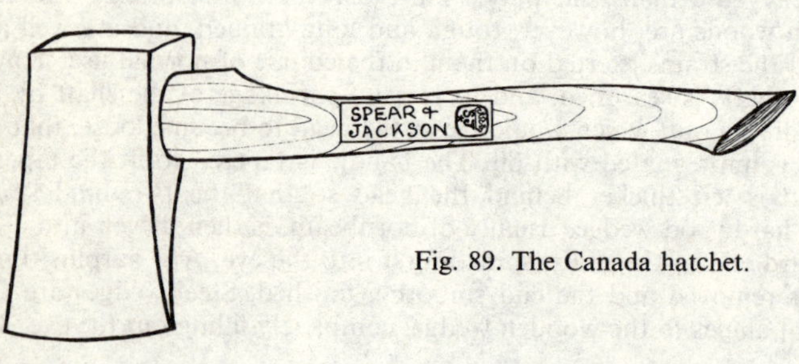

Fig. 89. The Canada hatchet.

combination of tapered eye and the spreading of the wood by the wedges eliminates all risk of the hammer head being flung off in use.

It will be realised from the obvious care and skill which goes into the making of a hammer that far from being the simplest and crudest of hand tools, as imagined by some, the hammer is a well-balanced tool, solid forged for maximum strength and durability. The design of the head has gradually developed over the years, as has the handle, which on the modern hammer is always smooth, comfortable to hold and features a well-shaped grip. In use, the shaft should be grasped firmly near its end with the thumb extended along the top to exercise maximum control. The slightly convex shape of the face on the majority of hammers allows nails to be driven into the wood flush with the surface without leaving hammer marks. On fine work it is better, however, if the nail is left a little proud, being sunk in finally with hammer and nail punch.

The Warrington Hammer

This pattern of hammer (Fig. 83) is much favoured by craftsmen and also is probably the most useful hammer for the householder. It has a cross pein, which is a relatively narrow striking edge set at right angles to the handle. This cross pein can be used to start small nails when they are held between finger and thumb. It is also useful for nailing in grooves or corners where the face of the hammer cannot reach and other places with restricted access. Usually with ash handles, they are available from No. 00 (170 g) to No. 4 (455 g).

Fig. 83 also indicates the section through the eye, showing how it is waisted and how the wedges spread the end of the shaft. Handles are stronger and less likely to split if the annual rings of the timber run as near vertical as possible. This is a point to look for when purchasing a hammer.

The Engineer's Hammer

The ball pein of the engineer's hammer is often useful for light metal beating and riveting. When riveting, the hammer is held close behind its head so that short, sharp blows may be given which will spread the rivet evenly. The handle may be of ash or hickory. Weights range from 155 g to 905 g, the larger being most useful for heavy carpentry and joinery (see Fig. 84).

Club Hammer

Also known as the lump hammer, the club hammer (Fig. 85) is most useful for striking short heavy blows—for example, drilling holes in walls or solid floors to accept heavy-duty rawlbolts. Three sizes are available in weights of 1,135 g, 1,360 g and 1,815 g.

The Claw Hammer

Claw hammers (Fig. 86) are intended for quite heavy work. The ripping claw hammer illustrated has longer claws than is normal and at a straighter angle, which makes them suitable for work such as taking up floorboards, opening packing cases and snapping wire binding. The conventional shape claw hammer is more suited to withdrawing nails as well as driving them in, the larger curve of the claw giving more favourable leverage. Both are available in 445 g and 570 g weights in the Stanley Steelmaster range, which features modern style tubular steel handles with shock-absorbing rubber grips.

Claw hammers with wooden shafts are also manufactured: the ones with socket-type heads which extend back along the handle are strongest (known as 'adze eye' claw hammers).

Joiner's Mallet

These are necessary tools for the woodworker. They are of a suitable size and weight to tap chisels lightly for fine work, and yet strong enough and sufficiently heavy to drive larger chisels into the wood when joints are being cut. Both head and handle may be of beech or, as in Fig. 87, of a selected hardwood. The socket for the shaft is tapered and the shaft is deeper at the front than the back. This means not only that the mallet handle is very strong, but that the head cannot possibly fly off in use; the further the head moves forward the tighter it is wedged on the shaft.

The Stanley Soft-Faced Hammer

Rated between a steel hammer and a mallet, these soft-faced hammers (Fig. 88) have ash shafts and heads of mazak (a zinc/aluminium alloy). The nylon faces are replaceable when worn and are obtainable in diameters of 32, 38 and 45 mm. They permit the hammer to deliver blows of considerable force without damage to the surface, providing it is as hard as, or harder than, the nylon face. For example, damaged metal fittings can be trued without the danger of hammer marks.

Canada Hatchet

The head of the Canada hatchet is polished for half its depth; the shaft is of weatherproofed ash (Fig. 89). It is an ideal tool for householders who have gardens with trees and shrubs to lop. It is useful for rough surfacing of timber, lopping off small branches and trimming bark from green timber being stored for seasoning, roughing off of waste timber before large wood carvings are commenced, pointing stakes, cutting large wedges, shaping plugs for brickwork, etc.

In addition to the hammers listed here, there are very many more so-called 'percussion tools', each designed for special types of work by various skilled craftsmen requiring tools developed according to the needs of their particular discipline. In spite of the generally heavy nature of their work, hammers should be treated with care. A hammer which is too light for the work expected of it will display a bouncing effect which could lead to metal fatigue and fracture of the shaft and possibly the head. Two hammer faces should never be struck together because of the danger of the edges chipping and small pieces flying off at high speed which are a positive hazard. To avoid the possibility of edge fractures some hammer heads are rim-tempered—that is, they are somewhat softened around the rim, losing their brittleness but retaining their toughness. The cheeks of the hammer are soft and it is bad practice to use them for striking instead of the peins. Handles should never be treated roughly—above all they should retain their smoothness and be comfortable to handle. They should never be used as levers, which could result in subsequent shattering, when a wrecking bar would be appropriate. Similarly, the claw hammer should not be expected to do excessive work more suited to the wrecking bar. It is obviously advisable to obtain a tool which is of adequate weight and the correct one for the work to be done, and then to use it for the purpose for which it was designed.

Screwdrivers

Screwdrivers tend to be one of the most abused tools; they are used as levers to lift bent nails or the lids from tins; they are used most unsatisfactorily as chisels for wood or brick; the handles are hammered or, worse still, used as hammers. The temptation to misuse a screwdriver in any of these ways must be avoided. The tip of the blade must be cared for so that it fits the screw head, and the handle must be smooth and comfortable to hold.

The average tool kit should contain a number of screwdrivers of different sizes to deal with different sizes of screw. The largest must be long enough and strong enough to allow both hands to be used to exert sufficient pressure and power to drive home large-gauge screws, while the smallest should be suited to light work with short, small-gauge screws. The tip of the blade should be cross-ground, square to the axis of the blade, and should fit snugly into the screw slot—some workers prefer to have the corners taken off to prevent possible scoring of the work. Should a blade be used which is too narrow, excessive force will be required to turn the screw, and the blade may be damaged, as will the screw. Should the blade be too wide, the wood will be damaged as countersunk-headed screws are driven home. Badly shaped tips which fit loosely into the screw will ride out under pressure with very unfortunate consequences. Correct shapes should be maintained on the emery wheel or grindstone, but avoid drawing the temper.

The Cabinet Screwdriver

The cabinet screwdriver (Fig. 90*a*) is fitted with a turned oval-sectioned hardwood handle fitted with a steel ferrule to prevent splitting. The round blade is cross-ground to a parallel tip and is flattened to form a tang where it enters the ferrule and handle, which enables it to withstand the strain exerted on it in use. The blade is of chrome–vanadium steel from 75 to 250 mm long and with tip widths of 5·55, 7·14, 8·00, 8·70, 10·30 and 11·90 mm.

The Blue Grip

The well-designed handles of high-impact plastic of blue grips (Fig. 90*b*) withstand maximum leverage without the added reinforcement of a ferrule. The blades are of chrome-vanadium steel, plated for rustproofing. The general-purpose range with flared tips are from 75 to 250 mm blade length, and 6·50 to 9·50 tip width. They are also available in Electricians' and Instrument ranges with parallel tips and blade lengths of 75, 100, 150 and 200 mm with widths of 4·80 and 3·15 mm respectively.

Further Screwdrivers

The **London pattern** (Fig. 91*a*) is very robust; its strong flat-sectioned blade and wide tip are very efficient when turning large screws. It is also suitable for removing or replacing plane cap irons when sharpening.

The ratchet screwdriver (Fig. 91*b*) is at its best on small screws as it can be operated with one hand while the other is used to steady the work. Changing the position of the ratchet control enables the tool to be used for inserting or

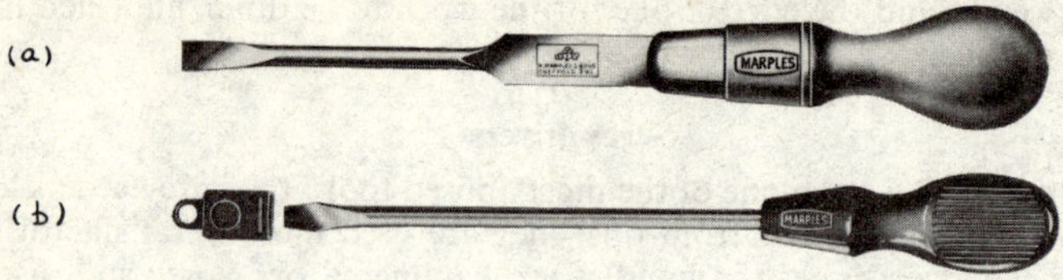

Fig. 90. Screwdrivers: (*a*) cabinet; (*b*) blue grip.

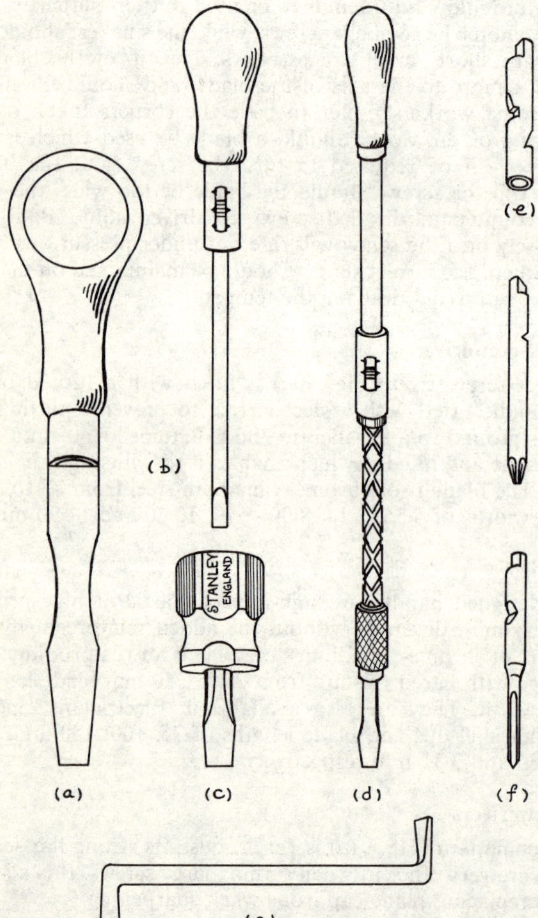

Fig. 91. Screwdrivers: (*a*) London pattern; (*b*) ratchet type; (*c*) stubby; (*d*) 'Yankee' ratchet; (*e*) chuck adaptor; (*f*) Pozidriv bit and drill point; (*g*) double-ended offset.

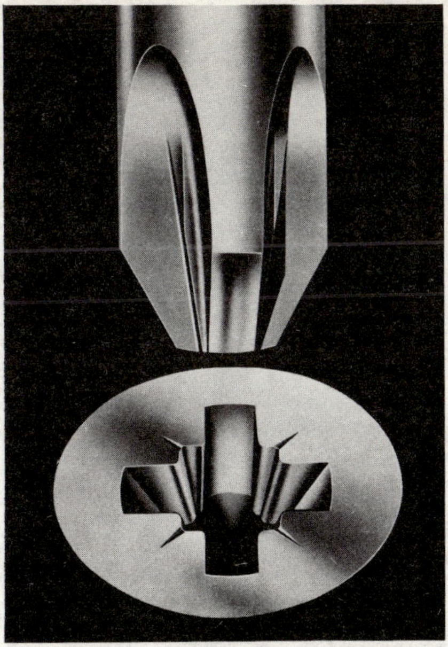

Fig. 92. The Pozidriv point and screw recess. This is now superseded by the Supadriv recess—which has a smaller included angle and sharp inner corners so fitting more closely to the screwdriver point.

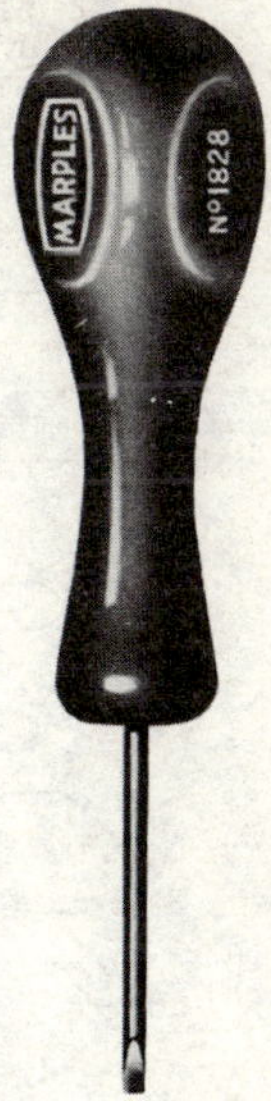

Fig. 93. The tri-grip bradawl.

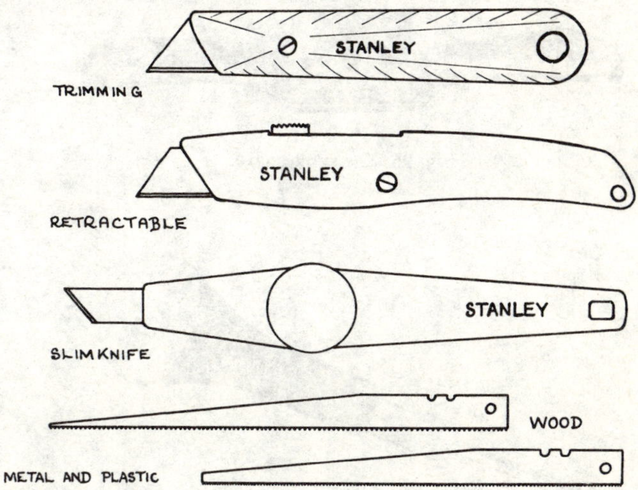

Fig. 94. Stanley knives.

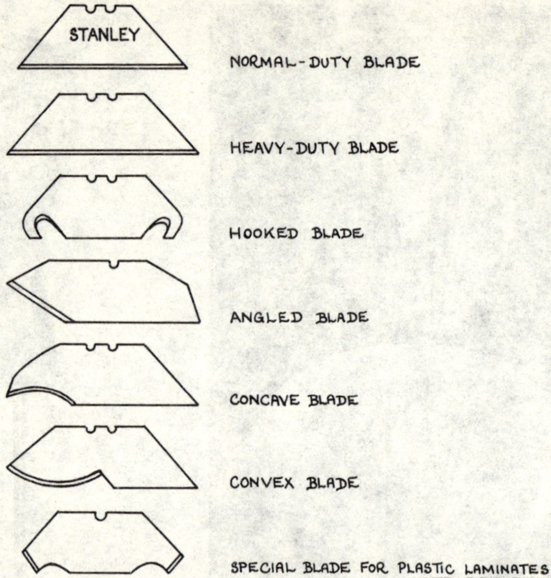

Fig. 95. Stanley knife blades.

Fig. 96. The spokeshave.

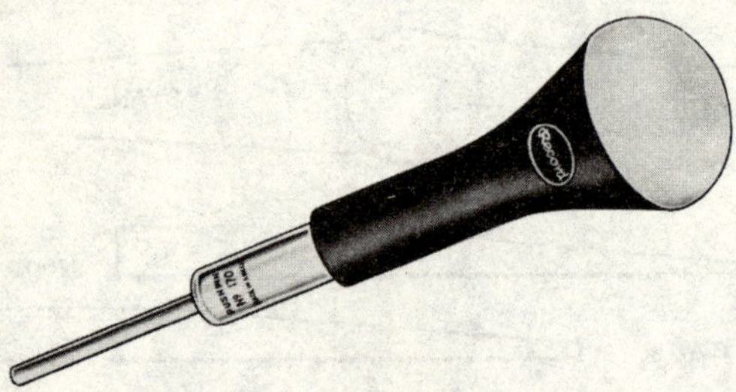

Fig. 97. The pushpin.

withdrawing screws, or as a normal fixed blade. It is available with flared and parallel tips and lengths of 75–200 mm.

Being very short, the **stubby pattern** (Fig. 91*c*) is an excellent tool for use in restricted spaces, the large diameter handle giving plenty of torque to make up for the lack of length.

As the **'Stanley' Yankee ratchet screwdriver** (Fig. 91*d*) is pushed the screw is driven home or withdrawn, depending upon the setting. The tool may be used locked in either the long or short position, and can be used as a normal ratchet screwdriver.

Some models require **chuck adaptors** (Fig. 91*e*) to enable accessories such as Pozidriv bits, countersinks and drill points to be used. Fig. 91*f* illustrates a **Pozidriv** bit, available in Nos. 1 to 4 and drill points in eight sizes of 1·5 to 4 mm.

The **double-ended offset screwdriver** (Fig. 91*g*) is used where there is insufficient space for a normal screwdriver. It can also be obtained for use with screws with recessed heads.

The Pozidriv Point and Screw Recess

'Pozidriv' and the new 'Supadriv' are registered trade marks of GKN Screws and Fasteners Ltd. Screws with this type of head are now in widespread use in British industry and because of their superior driving characteristics have entirely replaced the Phillips recess head, which is now obsolete. The vertical driving faces of these recesses further reduce the risk of the screwdriver 'riding out' and damaging the surface of the work, and also make it possible to drive the screw home firmly and efficiently.

Point sizes 1, 2, 3 or 4 fit the whole range of screws gauge 5–10. Pozidriv screwdrivers by Stanley Tools Ltd. have blue handles of solid high-impact plastic which fit comfortably in the hand and are designed to give a strong positive turning action. The blades are high-quality alloy steel and lengths vary from 25 to 250 mm. Pozidriv screwdrivers fit the Supadriv recess which has improved definition (Fig. 92).

Bradawls

The Tri-grip bradawl illustrated in Fig. 93 has a triangular section handle which prevents it from rolling off the bench top. The handle is of plastic, and is moulded on to the blade so that it can never become loose or pull out. Different colours of handle indicate different blade sizes; blue, small width—35 mm; red, medium—40 mm; yellow, large—45 mm. Bradawls with wooden handles of various shapes. some with the tang of the blade pinned through the handle and some with square section blades known as birdcage bradawls, are obtainable.

The purpose of the bradawl is to make small holes in which to drive nails or pilot holes for screws, particularly when fittings are being attached to the work. It is also used for marking the centres of holes to be bored. So that the bradawl does not split the wood, it is sharpened to a chisel point which is then pressed into the wood across the grain. In this way the fibres are cut across, and the hole is produced by twisting the bradawl as it is pressed further into the wood. The flat tang resists any tendency for this twisting to loosen the blade.

Stanley Knives

Four Stanley knives of use to the craftsman and do-it-yourself enthusiast are manufactured (Fig. 94). The original **trimming knife** comes in two versions: grey-painted finish with serrated grip and red stove-enamelled with smooth grip. Five double-ended blades are supplied. So that it can be safely carried in the pocket, the **retractable blade** type was developed. By pressing the button on the top of the handle the blade can be slid in or out. Also supplied with five assorted blades, the **Slimknife** is light, versatile and sharp. It is tough enough for all general-purpose cutting and yet accurate enough for close, careful work such as modelling.

Fig. 95 indicates the range of blades suited to the trimming and retractable blade knives with which it is possible to cut, slice, pare, score, scoop, chisel or carve. The saw blades shown in Fig. 94 fit the trim knife and are suitable for light work on wood, metal and plastics.

Spokeshaves

The cutting action of the spokeshave (Fig. 96) is similar to that of the plane, except that there is no back iron to the blade, the lever cap both holding the blade in position and breaking the shavings. The sole of the spokeshave is, however, very short to enable it to follow curves, and the general practice is to use flat-soled spokeshaves for convex curves and round-soled on concave surfaces. The blade on the best of modern spokeshaves can be adjusted laterally by means of two knurled screws engaged in slots near the top of the blade by which means the corners of the blade may be raised or lowered as is necessary. Depth of cut is also controlled by the same two screws. The handles at each side of the sole are part of the main body casting of malleable iron, and are so shaped to fit comfortably into the hand with a convenient position for the thumbs so that the hands have complete control over the tool, and the wrists can apply the strong pushing action which is required.

Cutting must always be done with the grain and in practice it will be found that very fine setting is best to avoid 'chatter marks' on the wood. In working convex curves it will be necessary to change the direction of cut to produce the required shape. This is because of the need always to cut with the grain, and although ideally the spokeshave should be held at right angles across the wood it will very often be found that a smoother surface can be produced if it is slightly angled so that it makes a slicing cut. Wooden spokeshaves, the blades of which were held in place by a tang at each end, are rapidly being superseded by the metal versions, which have blade widths of 45 and 54 mm depending upon the pattern.

The Pushpin

The pushpin is a comparatively recent tool providing an easy way to drive panel pins into hardboard or plywood simply and quickly without bending them (Fig. 97). The body and barrel are of brass, and the pin which has to be driven is dropped head first into the barrel where it is held in place by a magnetised steel plunger. The end of the barrel is held in place and a firm push on the handle drives the pin home. On releasing the pressure the plunger is withdrawn by a compressed spring and the tool can be reloaded. The handle is of polypropylene, and maximum pin capacity 32 mm.

Pincers

Obtainable in a range of sizes, pincer jaws wrap around nails to be extracted (Fig. 98*a*). If the nail head is close to the wood, the bevel on the inside of the

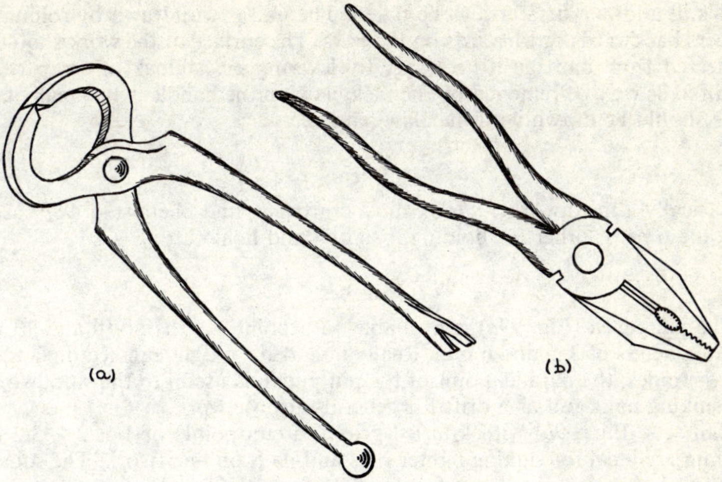

Fig. 98. (*a*) Pincers. (*b*) Pliers.

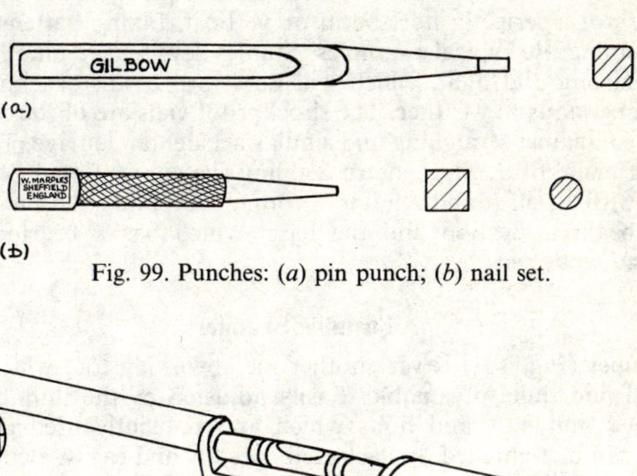

Fig. 99. Punches: (*a*) pin punch; (*b*) nail set.

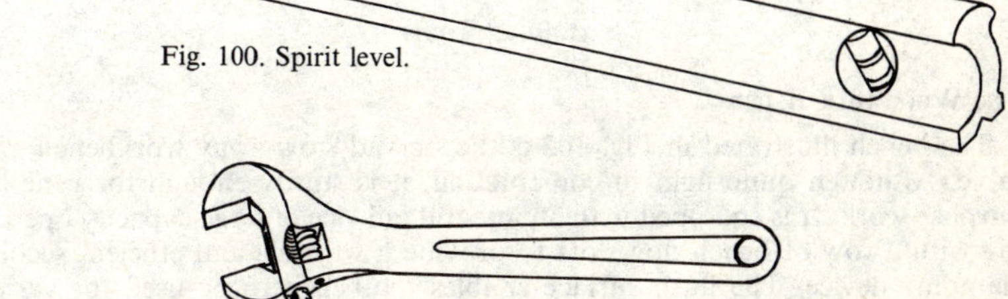

Fig. 100. Spirit level.

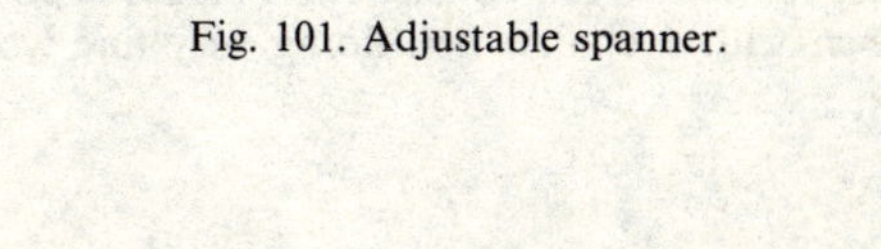

Fig. 101. Adjustable spanner.

jaws still allows a firm grip to be taken. The nail is withdrawn by rolling the pincers backwards or forwards on the jaws. The surface of the work should be protected from damage if necessary by levering on a block of scrap wood. Small nails may be removed by the tack claw on the handle, while really large nails should be drawn with the claw hammer.

Pliers

Basically a metalworker's tool, most craftsmen find pliers (Fig. 98*b*) useful at some time or other for holding, bending and light cutting.

Punches

The **pin punch** (Fig. 99*a*) is available with point lengths of 10 and 13 mm and diameters of 3, 5 and 6 mm. Really intended for light engineering and the motor trades, the parallel point of the pin punch is useful to the woodworker for sinking nails and as a drift for general-purpose work.

Nail sets (Fig. 99*b*) with knurled grip and cup points of 1·6, 2·4, 3·2 and 4·7 mm are ideal for sinking lighter pins and nails on finer work. The squared section of each prevents them from rolling from the bench.

Spirit Level

The craftsman or the practical householder frequently finds the need to be able to set work perfectly horizontal or vertical. Fixing battens to walls or erecting framing are typical examples. Stanley levels have aluminium bodies which are strong and light, which will not warp or distort, and which are virtually impervious to weather. The shockproof vials are of tough plastic and are protected against scratching and similar accidental damage. There are two types, both made of acrylic, one resembling the conventional bent glass vial but larger with an all-round reading through 360°, and solid block vials. The body is I-beam in section and the base, which has a bearing surface of 230 mm, is V sectioned.

Adjustable Spanner

The spanner (Fig. 101) is yet another metalworking tool which the woodworker will find quite invaluable. Easily adjusted by the thumb and finger, coach screws and nuts and bolts which are frequently used in woodwork assemblies can be tightened or slackened speedily and easily. Being adjustable avoids the need to have several spanners.

Holding Tools

The Woodwork Bench

The bench illustrated in Fig. 102 is the Lervad stow-away workbench and table. Although quite light in construction, it is sturdy enough for general-purpose work. It is equipped with an integral tail vice of large capacity operating with a row of bench dog slots to provide a versatile and efficient second clamping device. The flush surface enables the bench to be used for varied craft activities, while the centre rail construction makes it possible to sit comfortably at the bench with a chair when doing very fine work such as light

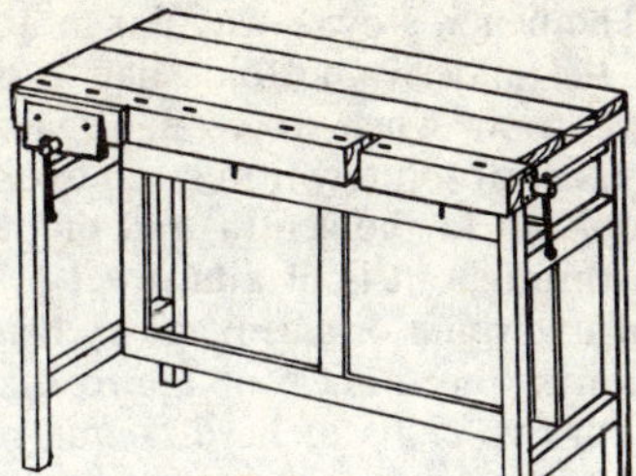

Fig. 102. Woodwork bench.

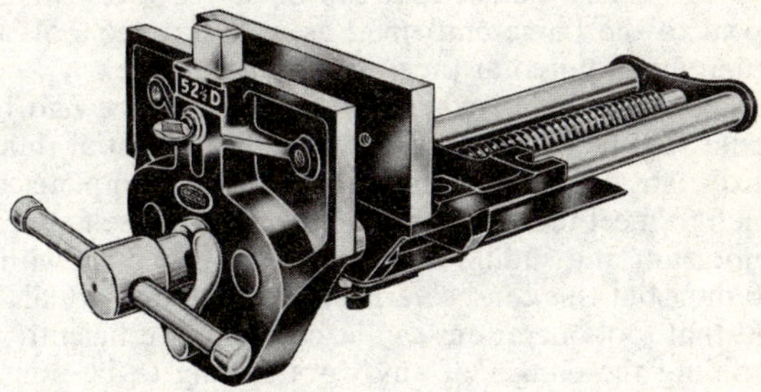

Fig. 103. Woodwork vice.

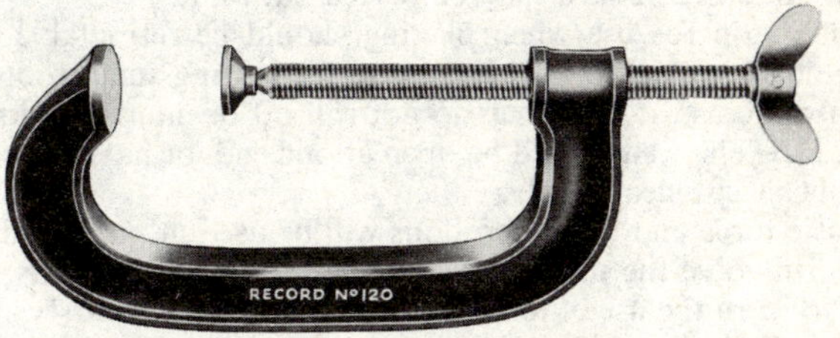

Fig. 104. The G cramp.

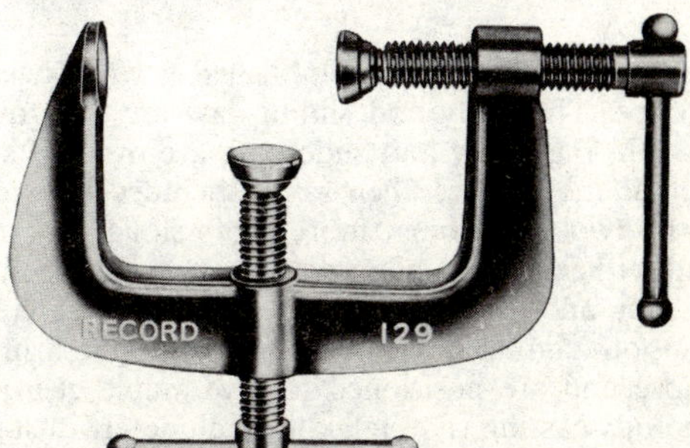

Fig. 105. The edging cramp.

carving and jewellery. The bench stows away flat in a few seconds. Once the top has been lifted off the underframe folds flat in one piece and the two components take up little room when stored flat against a wall. Assembly is just as quick and the bench is absolutely firm when in use. Movable cupboards and/or tool racks to hook on to the central rail of the underframe are also available. Construction throughout is of kiln dried prime Danish beech and the top is proofed against warping or shrinkage by being totally immersed in linseed oil, which soaks into the timber for approximately 6 mm all round. They are then sealed with two coats of hard lacquer to prevent any further change in moisture content and maintain perfect flatness of the working surface under all normal conditions.

A flat, solid surface on which to work is essential and a bench such as that described above or similar models that can be stored away when not in use could well appeal to the home craftsman as well as to schools where a few extra benches may be required at times in a limited space.

Alternatively, considerable personal satisfaction may be had by making a bench. This could well be a first major project. The essential thing to bear in mind is a sturdy, strong construction, resulting in complete rigidity. The design of a bench to meet individual requirements is in itself very worthwhile.

Length is important and should be in the order of 1·5 m, with a height of 760 mm to 840 mm, but this can be varied to suit the individual. It should be of such a height that tool operations can be carried out efficiently and without discomfort, avoiding the danger of any work having to be done in such an awkward way that an accident might result. The bench top needs to be quite wide—say 760 mm—and without surface obstructions so that wide slabs of modern manufactured board may be placed flat on it.

Any bench stop for use when planing should be retractable and a 'well' towards the back of the top is very useful for storing small tools, etc., when not in immediate use so that they do not roll off or interfere with the overall level of the top. The well should be open at one end, or have bevelled fillets so that it can be swept clean easily.

Many basic tools and tool operations will be used in making the bench; no doubt it will involve the use of nails, screws and possibly bolts. There is no better way to learn the use of tools than by using them to satisfy an immediate need. There will also have been the satisfaction of designing the bench, and the experience of specifying and purchasing the materials.

Woodworker's Vice

Record woodworker's vices have established a world-wide reputation for reliability of service. The body and sliding jaw are high-quality castings of guaranteed strength, the screw and slide bars are of solid steel, as are other components such as the handle. Their range includes five vices, three suitable for light work and two for heavier, more professional woodwork. These two are available with either dual or plain screw action. The body and sliding jaw are of robust design, and the slide bars operate in accurately machined housings, giving a smooth sliding movement and a straight firm grip. These bars cannot work loose and are positioned to give ample clearance for gripping large work. The body casting is designed to exclude sawdust and dirt from the working parts and the dual action models include a fitted screw cover. This action has been proved satisfactory over many years. When the trigger is pressed the jaws may be opened or closed instantly, and a half turn on the handle grips or releases the work immediately. Plain screw action may be used as required.

The vice illustrated in Fig. 103 incorporates an adjustable dog in the front jaw plate, a feature which is rapidly growing in popularity, and which, when used in conjunction with a stop fixed on the bench, operates as a most useful and simple cramping device. Two sizes are made with jaw widths of 175 mm opening to 205 mm and weighing 9·1 kg, and 230 mm opening to 330 mm weighing 16·3 kg.

The vice will hold wood firmly while it is being worked and should preferably be bolted to the bench top over or as near to a leg as possible so that it is really solid. It should be mounted so that the metal jaws are at least 10 mm below the level of the bench top to avoid accidental damage to any tools. Hardwood cheeks screwed to the inside of the jaws then raise the level to that of the bench top. The moving parts of the vice should be lubricated regularly to ensure smooth working and to minimise wear.

G Cramps

The popularity of G cramps is reflected in the number of types and sizes available. Apart from its obvious normal use when work is being glued, it is most useful for holding wood down on the bench when it is being worked. Depending upon the type of work for which they are intended, frames are of malleable iron or drop-forged steel with screws turned from solid steel. The standard G cramp (Fig. 104) has a frame which is ribbed for strength, and a 'deep throat' or long reach version is made which is twice as deep. The 'Spingrip' can be operated by one hand while the other steadies the work. A knurled nut in that part of the frame through which the screw passes can be operated by one finger sufficiently to hold the cramp in place when it can then be tightened in the normal way. All cramp screws are fitted with swivel shoes which adapt to angular surfaces. Cramp 'take-in' sizes vary from 50 to 80 mm, and screws may be fitted with wing heads, fixed tommy bars or drop handles.

Edging Cramp

This is an obvious development from the G cramp which has been introduced comparatively recently (Fig. 105). It will cramp edging strips and lippings to straight or curved work, avoiding the use of nails, screws or larger sash cramps. It is fitted with drop handles and swivel shoes which adjust easily to bevelled faces. It has a 'take-in' capacity of 61 mm and throat depth from centre of screw of 32 mm.

Sash Bar Cramps

Long cramps of this kind (Fig. 106) are mostly used in pairs when frames, doors and carcases are being glued together. More than two may be used, however, if long boards are being joined, and possibly only a single cramp if the boards are short. It should be realised that if heavy cramps are used on light frames their weight may pull the framework out of truth. Similarly, a heavy cramp may cause a light frame to appear true when being glued, only to have it spring out of truth when released from the cramps.

Bars are of cold-drawn mild steel, head and slides of malleable iron, with screw and handle of high-quality steel. Capacity lengths are from 460 to

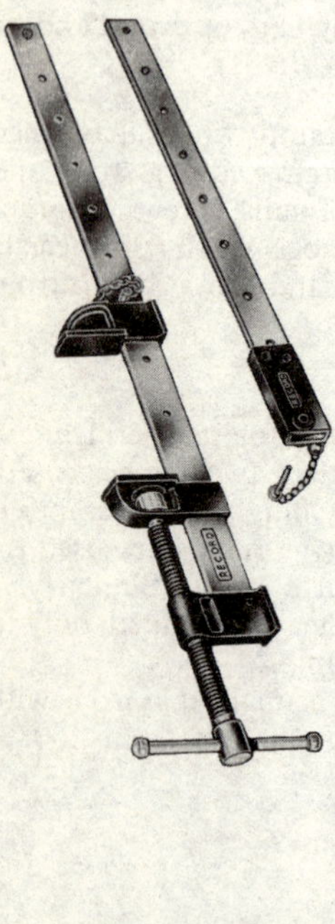

Fig. 106. Sash bar cramps.

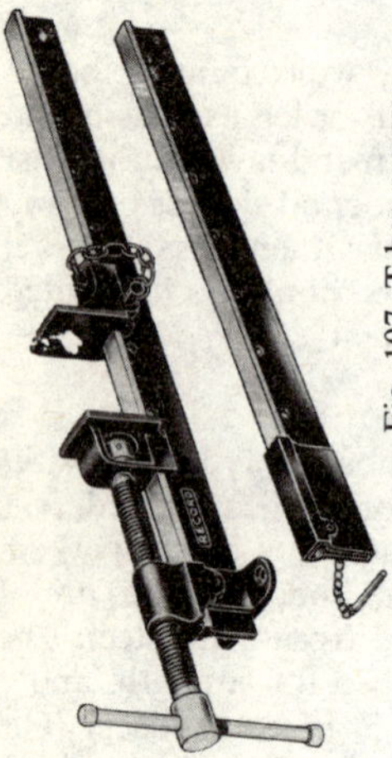

Fig. 107. T-bar cramps.

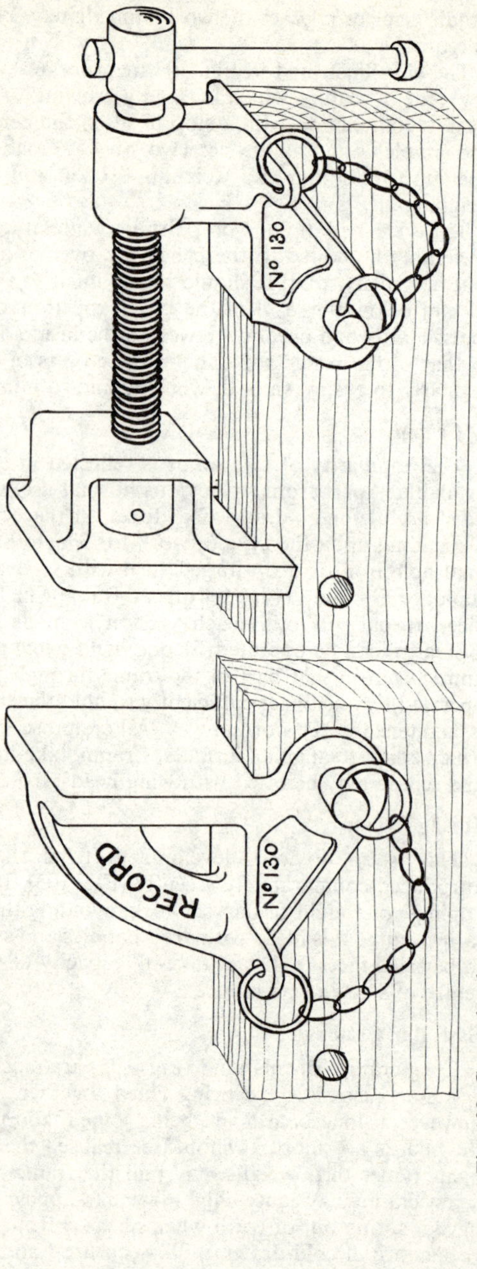

Fig. 108. Cramp heads.

1370 mm. Rail slides are usually positioned by a peg and chain, which often in practice becomes detached and lost. The Deacon Tail Slide, which operates by means of a spring-loaded catch, the pin automatically selecting the next stop when released, is superior.

Work being glued should always be protected from possible marks resulting from the pressure of the cramp heads by inserting pads of scrap wood. Once frames have been cramped up their truth must be carefully checked. Squareness may be tested with the try square for small work, or the diagonal rod on larger assemblies. Care must also be taken to ensure that they are not in winding. Careful adjustment of the cramps will usually correct any faults. When boards are being glued edge to edge, it is good practice to put alternate cramps under and over to prevent any tendency there may be to bow. Battens cramped across the ends also help. A single cramp held in the vice can be used to hold narrow work for shaping, moulding, etc. The cramps should be lubricated, but kept free of excessive oil or grease and also glue, with which they may be fouled during use.

T-Bar Cramps

T-bar cramps (Fig. 107) are made of the same materials but the T-section of the bar makes them much heavier and much stronger. They are ideal for really heavy work. Various lengths of extension bars are available for both sash and T-bar types with which to increase their overall capacity.

Cramp Heads

Cramp heads (Fig. 108) are used in conjunction with a length of hardwood, which must be 25 mm thick and of a suitable width to withstand the strain without distortion, to make bar cramps of any length. The working slide is efficient, the pegs are of a stout diameter and are securely attached by welded steel chains. They are a good economic buy if exceptionally long cramps are required which would not be used frequently. It should be noted that all Record vice and cramp main screws, previously of single-start Acme threads, have now been changed to two-start for improved performance.

The Jet Clamp

Recently introduced by Record–Ridgway Tools Ltd, the jet clamp consists of two clamping arms which slide into any position on a standard bar (Fig. 109). A positive grip is provided by the action of a spring-loaded jamming wedge which locks the clamp firmly on the exact point at which it is set. The action of the wedge provides firm locking during clamping but allows instant release by forward pressure of the arm against the spring. One of the pair of clamping arms incorporates a plastic tightening bar, and when this is turned a swivel arm slides in a small slot to move the wedge and apply the clamping force. Any number of arms can be used on one bar in conventional form or as one pair gripping while others are used to jack or hold components. A swivel bracket is attached to each arm to which various types of snap-on clamping pads can be fitted. These locate through a hole in the bracket and are retained by a spring clip. They also allow the clamp to be swivelled on its clamping axis without releasing the load. The swivel bracket also allows for angled clamping. Pads are provided to suit almost every application, giving the correct gripping surface, improving efficiency and making it virtually impossible for

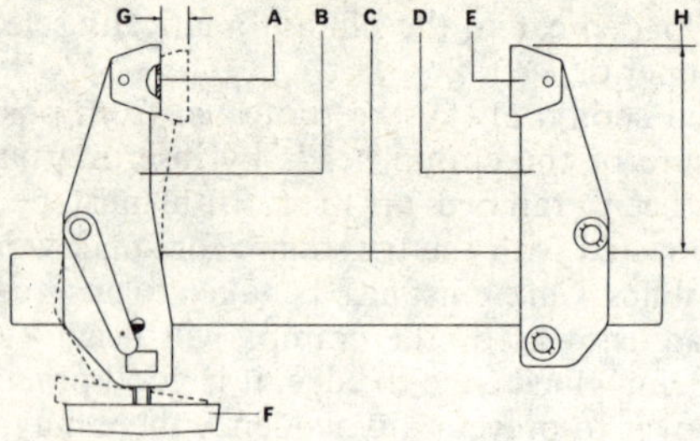

A Clamping Pad Hole.
B Swivel Arm.
C Bar
D Clamping Arm.
E Swivel Bracket.
F Tightening Bar.
G Swivel Arm Movement ½ in. (12.7 mm) maximum.
H Take-in 3⅝ in. (92 mm) maximum.

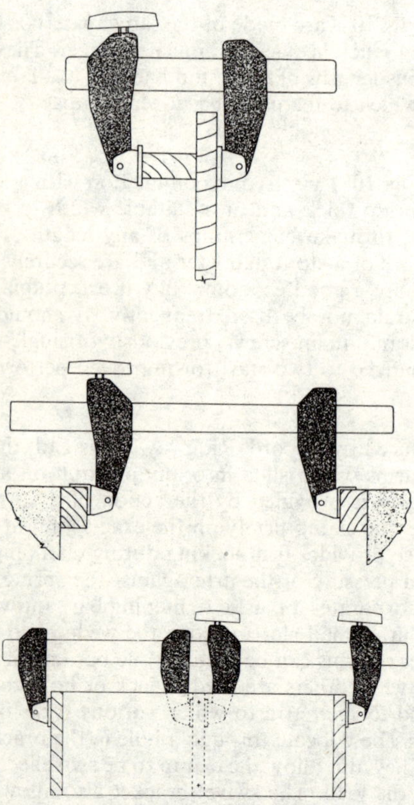

Fig. 109. The 'jet' clamp.

Fig. 110. The corner cramp.

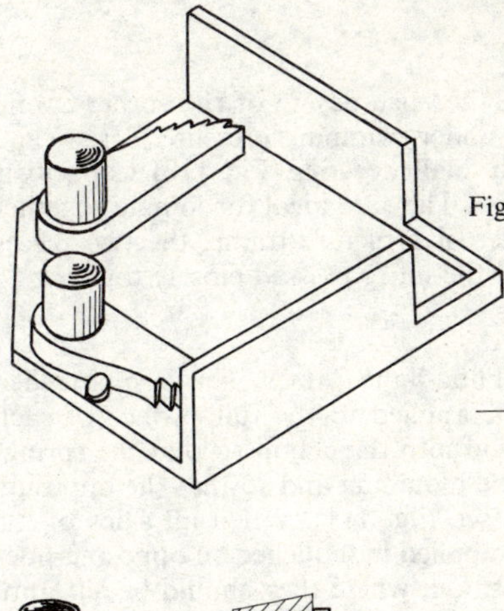

Fig. 111. The Copydex mitre clamp.

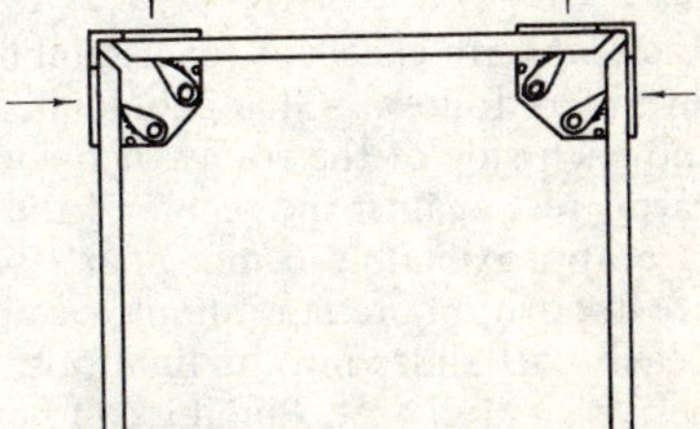

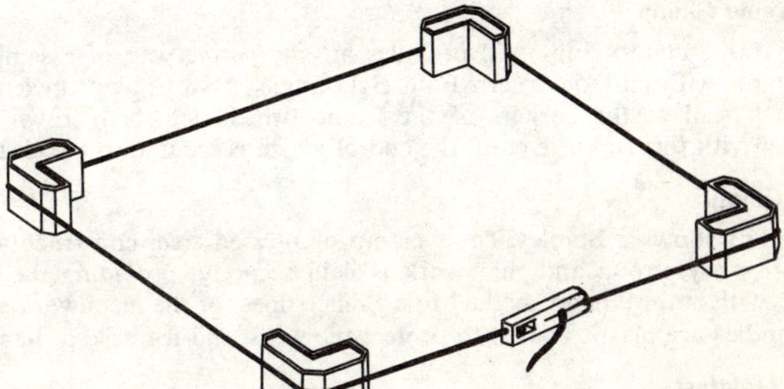

Fig. 112. The frame cramp.

the clamp to vibrate or slip off the work. Plain and serrated pads are for general use on rough surfaces or any work needing the maximum grip. To protect finished work when clamping and to avoid the use of clamping blocks, Neoprene faced pads are provided; 90 degree angle pads, which provide good edge location, are excellent when gluing up frames.

Suggested uses are as a work holdfast, gluing up frames (either parallel or angled), gluing up carcases, locating shelves for screwing or nailing, clamping boards when gluing, and, for metalworkers, as a welding clamp. The general specifications include bars of 305, 610, 915 and 1,220 mm of standard section 32 × 6 mm. The arms have take-in depth of 75 mm and the length capacity is only limited by the length of the bar.

The Corner Cramp

Often referred to as the mitre cramp, the open design of the corner cramp makes it possible to glue and pin joints under cramping pressure. Screws and handles are of steel, and the body is a high-quality casting (Fig. 110). Capacity is 50 or 108 mm, depending upon the model. They are ideal for joining together mitred joints such as those at the corner of a picture frame, the two pieces being placed together on the cramp and the mitre pressed closely together.

The Copydex Mitre Clamp

These clamps are excellent for assembling light frames. The recommended procedure is as follows. Glue should be applied to the full surface of each mitre and each side of the frame then slid into the clamp so that the spring-loaded arms rest against the rebate of the moulding and so that the opposing mitres are approximately 6 mm apart (see Fig. 111). When all sides of the frame are in position pressure should be applied in sequence on opposing sides so that each part slides into its final position, where they should be left until the adhesive has fully set. Pinning can be done immediately after assembly if necessary by turning the frame on to its edge and driving in the pins at the exposed corners. If staples are used they should be inserted from the back once the glue has set and the frame removed from the clamps. A packing strip should be placed against the rebate to ensure a tight grip of the clamp arms if a frame made from thin moulding is being assembled.

The Frame Clamp

The frame clamp (Fig. 112) provides an alternative way of assembling a light frame with mitred corners. Four right-angle jaws of polypropylene plastic are placed at the corners of the frame, which are then drawn tightly together with the Terylene cord, the end of which is secured in the cleat.

Hand Clamp

Fig. 113 shows a Stanley Tools clamp of pressed steel construction. The spring is very strong and thin work is held securely, providing the woodworker with 'a third hand' as the Mole wrench does for the metalworker. Jaws and handles are plastic coated to protect the work and for ease of handling.

Bench Holdfast

This tool too is as good as an extra hand (Fig. 114). It holds the wood firmly to the bench top enabling work to be carried out which could not be

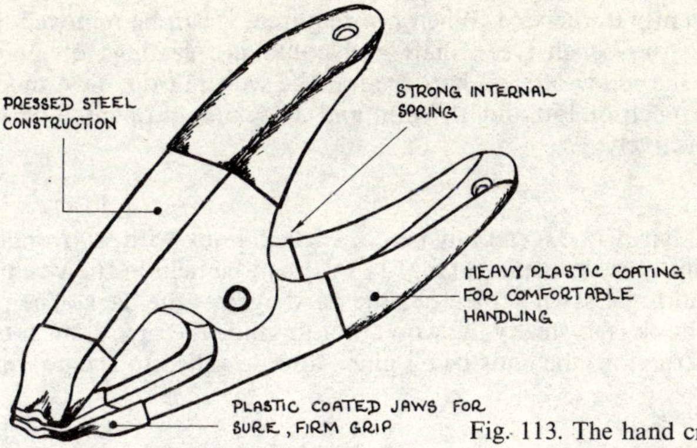

Fig. 113. The hand cramp.

Fig. 114. A bench holdfast.

Fig. 115. Bench hook.

done conveniently in the vice. When not required, it can be removed from its collar leaving the bench free. Shaft and collar are castings of guaranteed strength and the screw of steel hardened at the working tip. Two models are made with a reach of 150 and 180 mm and a maximum opening of 175 and 195 mm respectively.

Bench Hook

Made from hardwood, generally beech, a bench hook with an overall size of 150 × 250 mm is recommended (Fig. 115). It can be held in the vice if necessary; the wood to be sawn is then pressed hard against the back. The purpose of the bench hook is to steady the wood, not to guide the saw. It must be of all wooden construction, the ends being glued and dowelled to the board.

The Mitre Block

Three cuts are provided in the mitre block which are intended to guide the saw so that small mouldings can be cut at 45 degrees and other small sections at 90 degrees (Fig. 116*a*). There are various ways in which the two pieces forming the block may be glued and jointed together but whatever method is used the saw kerfs should not be cut too deep, thereby weakening the back. A piece of scrapwood should be placed on the base to raise its level to that of the bottom of the saw cuts. This avoids the saw cutting into the base.

The Mitre Box

Larger mouldings to be sawn are placed in the mitre box (Fig. 116*b*), care being taken that sawing is always done on the waste side of the line—otherwise the moulding will be too short. Also, it is advisable to saw into the face of the moulding to avoid splintering of the front. To position the adjustable saw guides the screws should be slackened and the saw placed in the kerf. They must be slid up against the saw so that when fastened they hold the saw blade firmly but not too tightly. The saw must then always be withdrawn from the kerf or placed in it from the side. It must not be pulled out through the guides or pushed down through them, otherwise damage will be caused both to the saw and the guides due to the set of the teeth.

As with the mitre block, sawing should be done on to a piece of scrap wood in the bottom of the box, both appliances being held in the vice when in use. A length of 250 mm is suitable for both box and block, with a depth of 50 mm and widths of 75 and 100 mm, depending upon requirement.

Sawing Trestle

This is yet another holding device, for use when ripping or cross-cutting boards (Fig. 117). It is best to have a pair identical in height so that the board is well supported and can be held down by the knee. They should be sturdy and robust so that they remain rigid in spite of the stresses and strains to which they are subjected. It is a worthwhile experience to design and make trestles in the workshop in the same way as the bench might be made. Beech is excellent for the purpose but a good-quality redwood could be used.

Shooting Boards

At a suitable length for general-purpose work of 600 mm, the shooting board can be home-made from beech, and its purpose is to guide the plane

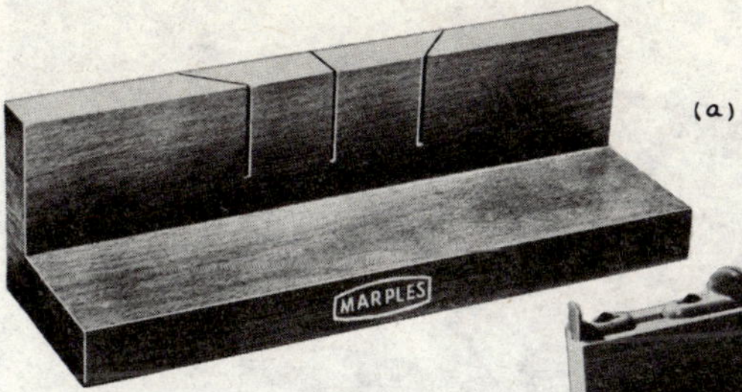

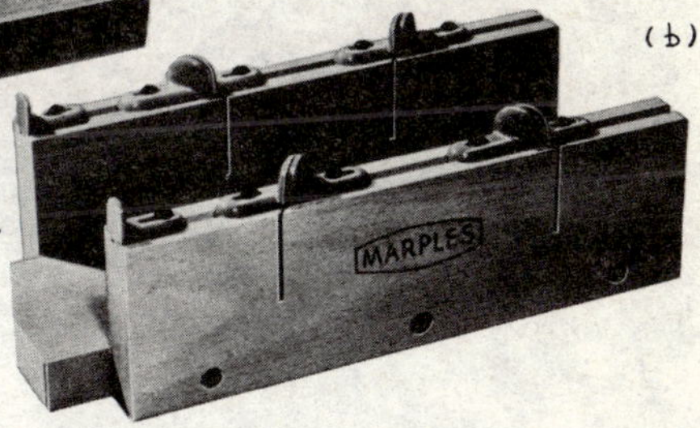

Fig. 116. (*a*) Mitre block. (*b*) Mitre box.

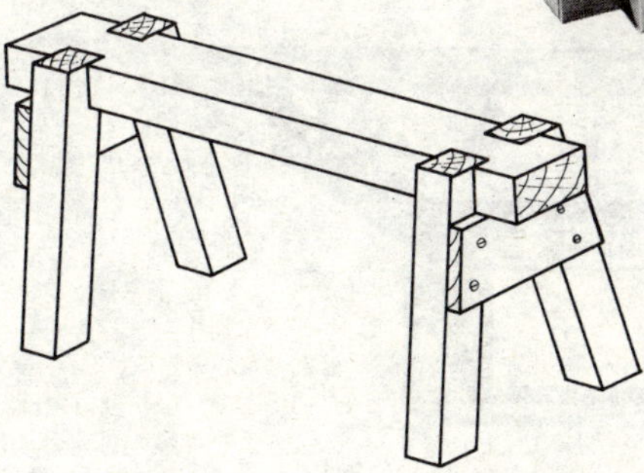

Fig. 117. A sawing trestle.

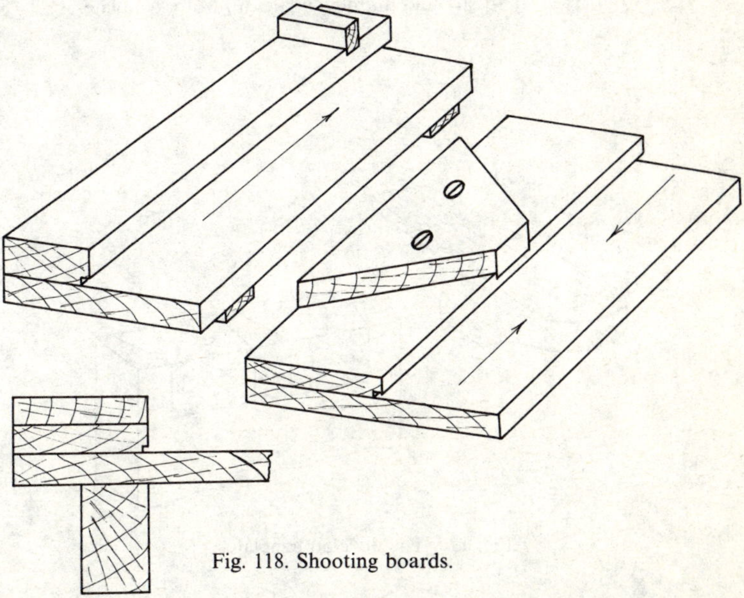

Fig. 118. Shooting boards.

(a)

(b)

Fig. 119. (*a*) Square and mitre template. (*b*) Mitre template.

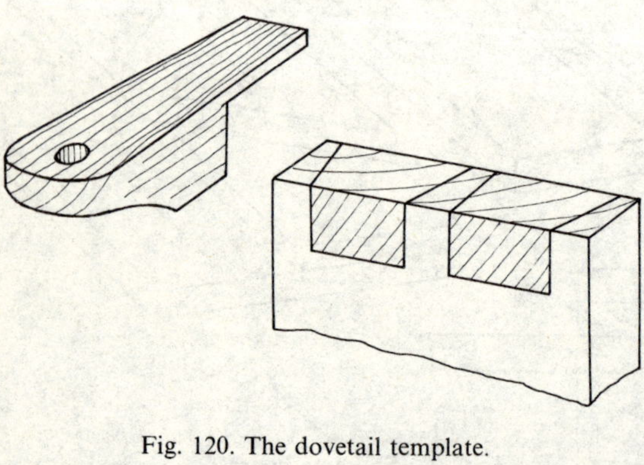

Fig. 120. The dovetail template.

(Fig. 118). The Record technical jack plane with side handle is ideal for the purpose. The plane runs in the rebate formed by the two boards, the corner of which is 'cleared' so that there is no accumulation of waste material which can prevent the plane from working accurately. The upper board is fitted with a stop, the working face of which must be at right angles to the direction of the plane. If the stop is tapered it will make a tight fit. The edges of thin boards can be planed straight and square or the ends of wood trimmed. The accuracy of these depends upon the squareness of the stop. To avoid the back corner being split off it is advisable to pare it away first with the chisel.

Mitre shooting boards can be made in a similar way but the centre stop must be at 45 degrees. In each case it must be possible to hold the board firmly either on the bench or in the vice.

Square and Mitre Templates

These small tools of nickel-plated iron castings are excellent for squaring lines round small square and rectangular sections, and for marking mitres (Fig. 119). Being quite thick they are very safe to use with the marking knife for making cut lines, there being little possibility of the knife overriding the edge. Each is 150 mm long.

The Dovetail Template

Depending upon the woodworker's preference for cutting dovetails or dovetail pins first, simple hardwood templates (Fig. 120) can be made by which the dovetail angle can be marked off (see dovetail joints, page 187). Being small and compact, they can be moved quickly and easily along the wood once the positions of the joints have been marked. With care, they can also be used to guide the chisel if necessary when paring to these angles.

The Copydex Mimic

This is an ideal tool for both the amateur and professional craftsman. With it, profiles can be copied quickly and accurately, and it has many uses other than for woodworking, such as fitting floor coverings around mouldings and pipes, model making and checking the profile of car-body repairs, etc.

The Record 148 Dowelling Jig

This is a versatile tool which enables dowel holes to be drilled very accurately with the minimum of marking out, ensuring that frame and carcase constructions can be assembled easily and without error (Fig. 122). It is designed for 6·3, 8 and 9·5 mm dowels and is supplied with two standard slide rods accepting boards up to 152 mm wide. Additional rods of 305 and 460 mm capacity are also available.

The jig consists of hardened steel drill bushes N, O or P held in carriers M by retaining screws B (see Fig. 123). The carriers are fitted with double fences J and are mounted on two slide rods S which enable the carriers to be placed at convenient distances across boards and small sections. The rods S are grooved at one end to position a reference head A held in place by the two screws R. From A all measurements are set. An adjustable head C, which can be fixed in any position along the rods with its nut E, carries two screws G which are fitted with nylon swivel shoes H. These may be tightened with a coin or screwdriver, clamping the jig securely to the work. On the bush carriers are

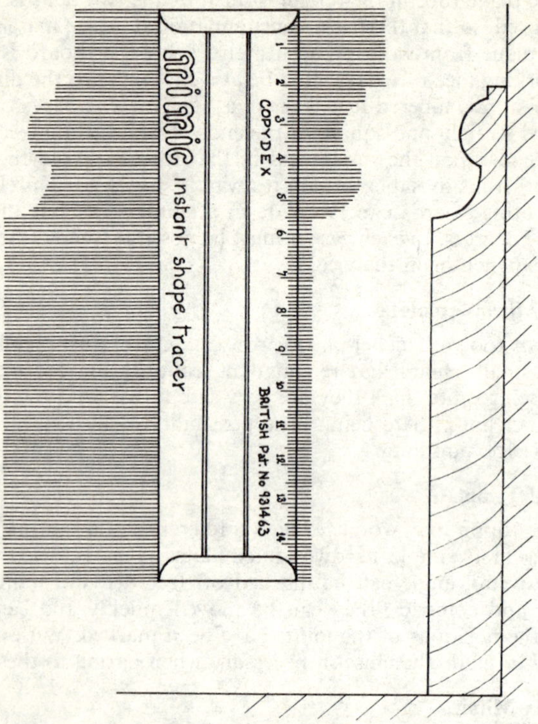

Fig. 121. The Copydex mimic.

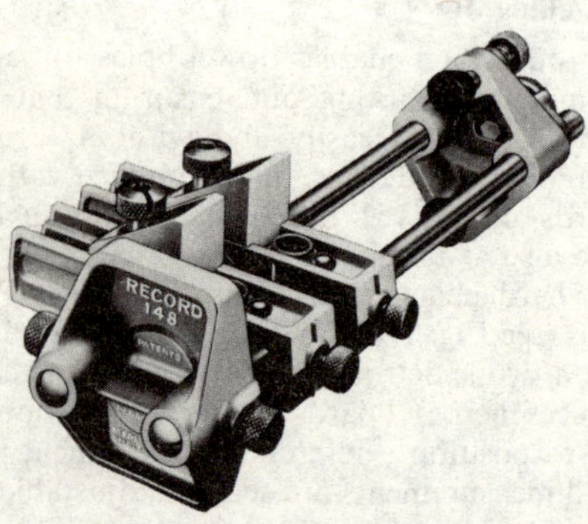

Fig. 122. The Record dowelling jig.

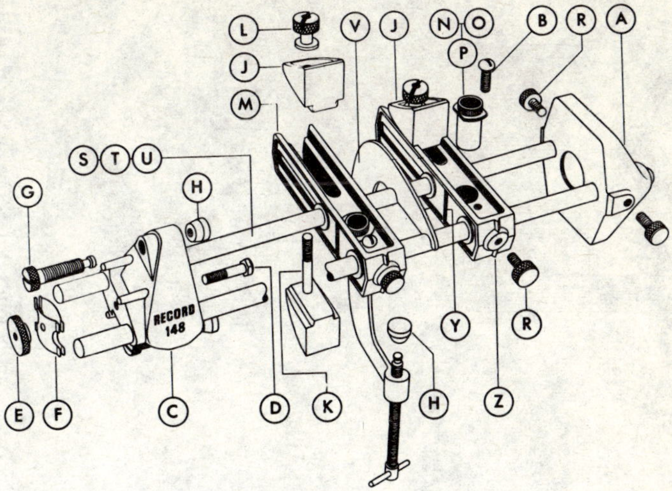

A. Reference Head
B. Drill Bush Retaining Screws (2)
C. Adjustable Head
D. " " Bolt
E. " " Nut
F. " " Springs (2)
G. " " Screws (2)
H. Swivel Shoes (3)
J. Fences (2)
K. Fence Screws (2)
L. Fence Locking Nuts (2)
M. Drill Bush Carriers (2)
N. Drill Bush $\frac{1}{4}$in. (6·3mm) (2)
O. " " $\frac{5}{16}$in. (8mm) (2) (Optional Extra)
P. " " $\frac{3}{8}$in. (9·5mm) (2)
***R.** Reference Head Retaining Screws (2)
***R.** Drill Bush Carrier Fixing Screws (2)
S. Standard Slide Rods (2)
T. Medium Slide Rods (2) (Optional Extra)
U. Long Slide Rods (2) (Optional Extra)
V. Jig Clamp
Y. Bush Carrier Datum Lines
Z. " " " "

* Common Components

Fig. 123. Parts list for the Record dowelling jig.

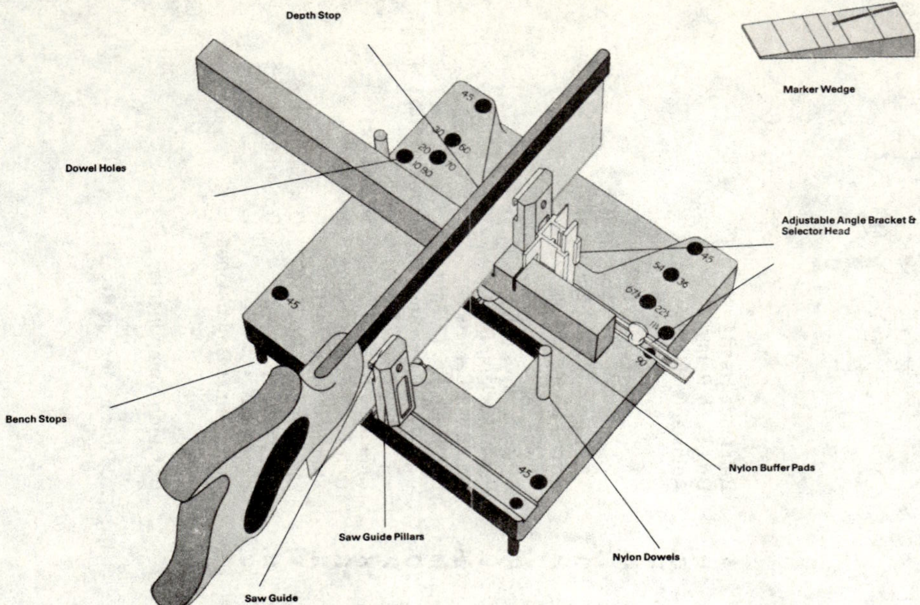

Fig. 124. The Jointmaster.

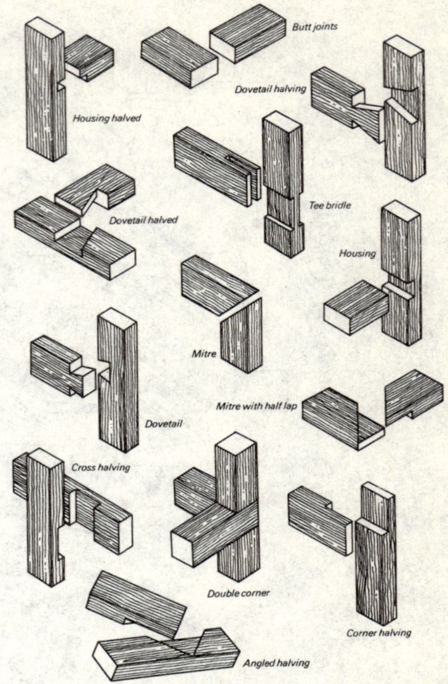

Fig. 125. A selection of joints that can be made with the Jointmaster.

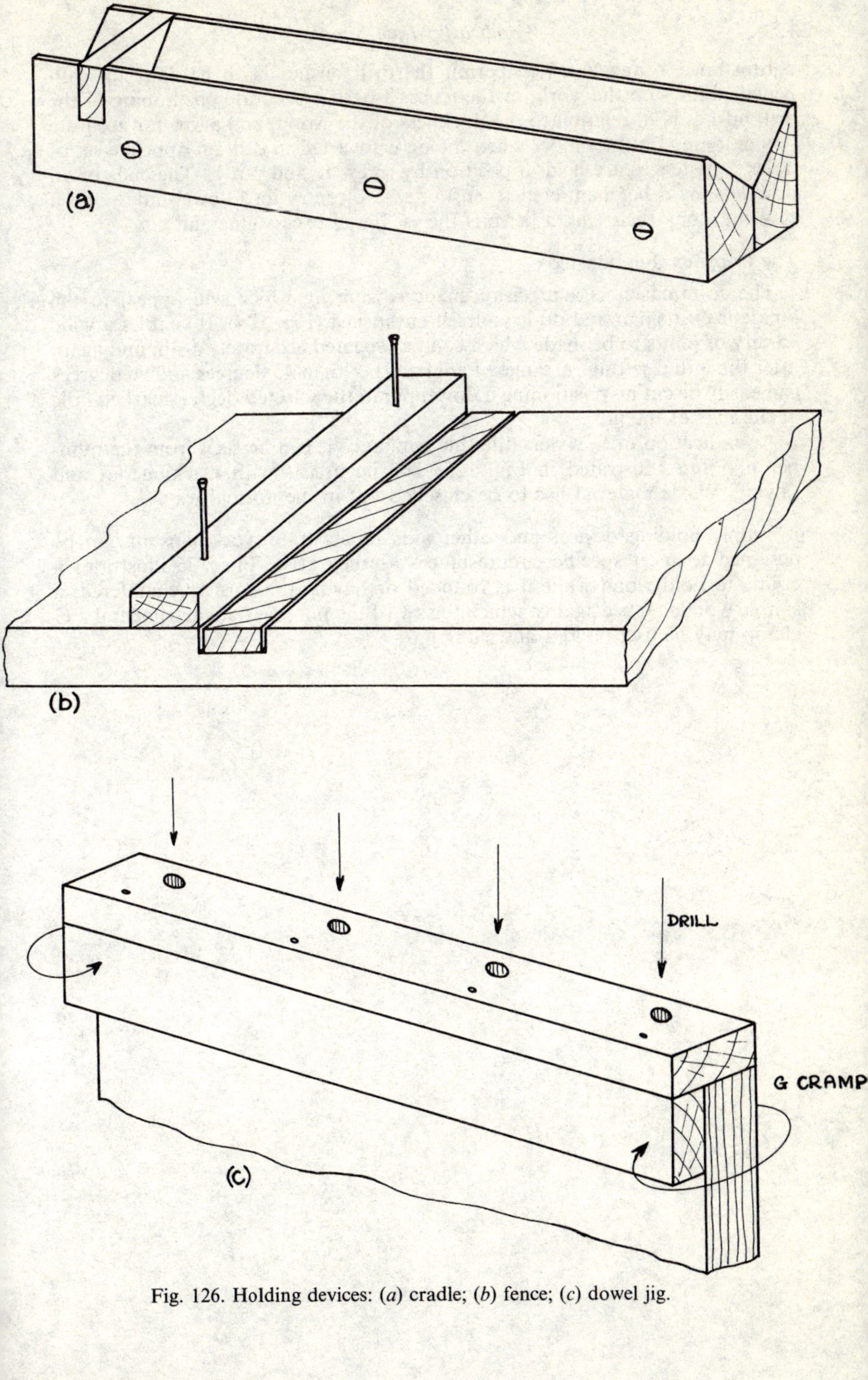

Fig. 126. Holding devices: (*a*) cradle; (*b*) fence; (*c*) dowel jig.

datum lines Y and Z which permit the drill bushes N to be lined up with pencilled lines on the work, or the fences J permit accurate positioning of the drill bushes N in relation to the thickness of the wood, and allow for accurate repositioning on the timber when the jig is inverted to drill an opposite set of holes. The fences are held in position by screw K and nut L. The ends of all dowels should be chamfered to ensure ease of entry into dowel holes, and a saw cut along their length permits the escape of excess glue and air.

The Copydex Jointmaster

The Jointmaster is a precision-made sawing jig which will appeal to the amateur craftsman and do-it-yourself enthusiast (Fig. 124). It enables a wide variety of joints to be made which can be repeated accurately again and again after the initial setting. A range of angles other than 45 degrees and 90 degrees can easily be cut by positioning a dowel pin in the selected degree-marked hole at the rear of the jig.

An indication of how versatile this appliance is can be seen from the number of joints illustrated in Fig. 125. The jig assists with marking out and sawing. Waste material has to be chiselled out in the normal way.

Simple holding devices and other aids to accurate workmanship can be designed to meet specific circumstances as they arise. Fig. 126 illustrates a cradle to hold wood while it is rounded or having the corners chamfered, a simple wooden fence against which to saw (if the pin holes are detrimental a G clamp may be used) and a dowelling jig.

5

ELECTRICALLY POWERED TOOLS

Very little modern woodworking is now done entirely by hand. For many years, use has been made of woodworking machinery in industry, and these machines have now become so sophisticated that they have practically taken over from the traditional craftsman. Work ranging from greenhouses and garden sheds to doors and windows for buildings, from garden furniture to high-quality furniture for the home, is made more quickly and more cheaply by machine tools. In some respects it can also be said that they are made with more accuracy. The preparation of the timber, rebating, moulding, jointing and assembling can be done almost entirely by machines, the successful operation of which requires much of the care and skill previously displayed by the hand-craftsman. Modern technology is such that smaller versions of the heavy industrial machines are now available for use in the school or home workshop. As bigger projects are undertaken—or perhaps where considerable precision is required in what might be termed 'wood-engineering', where 'knock-down' fittings (see Chapter 11) have to be positioned with extreme accuracy—the value of these electrically powered machines will be readily appreciated.

It is naturally of the utmost importance that comprehensive practical instruction must be obtained before any power tool is used. Serious injury can be caused both to the operator and to those nearby if power tools are operated carelessly or incorrectly. It is also essential that the tools are professionally serviced so as to be in perfect working condition. Protective clothing such as aprons should be worn to protect clothes from dust caused by the machines, and it is always advisable to wear goggles to protect the eyes from flying slinters.

Ideally, power tools which are designed to do only one specific task should be purchased, and in schools it is essential to adhere strictly to this principle. No power tools are cheap, but some are cheaper than others. In making a choice from the many available it should be remembered that a power tool must be regarded as a long-term investment from which it is hoped to get many years of service. It is important to make sure of just what it will or will not do, remembering that the machine will give longer and better use if it is well built and strongly made.

For the home workshop, a power drill with attachments is usually quite sufficient where its use is restricted to only one or two people. However, most attachments are not as sturdy or as convenient to use as the single-purpose machine. In schools the constant changing of accessories and the use made of them by many students of varying degrees of skill would quickly produce undue wear and tear, soon resulting in machines becoming unserviceable and dangerous.

The types of work power tools can do efficiently within the school and home workshop when correctly maintained are drilling, sawing, planing, sanding and grinding. Of the basic fixed machines, one would without doubt use the pillar drill, either floor or bench mounted. The use to which portable tools are put depends upon the discretion of the teacher and the views of the education authority, whereas one's own experience of the 'do-it-yourself' attachments to power drills will be a family concern.

The purpose of this chapter is to give an indication of the popular range of power tools which might conceivably be available to the woodworker at school or at home, how these are controlled and what safety precautions should be observed for each tool.

Pedestal Drill

Of the fixed electrically powered tools which may be installed in the school workshop, such as the band-saw and circular saw, the pillar drill (Fig. 127) is the one which a student would be expected to use. Being an expensive tool, it is unlikely that this or the others are likely to feature in the home workshop, where portable tools or do-it-yourself attachments to the power drill are more popular.

Holes can be drilled very accurately with the pedestal drill, which was originally considered a metalworking machine, but with the development of 'wood-engineering' and the need to fit 'knock-down' fittings very exactly it is now a very necessary piece of equipment in the woodwork shop. The development of a whole range of machine woodworking bits designed to perform various tasks has also widened the scope of the work possible on the machine, thus making it still more popular. Its general sturdy construction, basically for drilling metals, furthers its accuracy as a woodworking machine.

When selecting the machine bit best suited to the work in hand, careful consideration should be given to the kind of timber to be bored; the type of work, i.e. cabinet or rough constructional work; diameter and depth of hole required; and the speed of the machine. Boring hard or resinous woods, for example, is quite a different proposition to working on soft woods, and a bit suitable for one will not necessarily be satisfactory for the other. The penetration speed of a bit with a screw lead depends on the machine spindle speed and the pitch of the screw lead. This is measured by the number of turns necessary to bore through 25 mm and varies according to the size of the bit and the timber. Some bits are made with single and some with double start screw leads according to the size of bit and the work for which it is intended.

The screw lead is of little use if the bit is to be used at a very high spindle speed and a tool with a brad point should then be used. The brad-pointed tool is much easier to control since the penetration speed is governed entirely by the pressure applied to the feed handle of the machine by the operator. Any tendency for the tool to 'get hold of the wood' and run out of hand is avoided completely.

Six popular types of machine bit are illustrated in Fig. 127. These are:

No. 1. **The Scotch or square-nose pattern twist bit**, which is suitable for boring hardwoods, rough timbers and heavy constructional work.

No. 2. **Jennings pattern, double spur with extension lip**, which bores easily and cuts a very smooth hole. It is suitable for cabinet-making and all fine

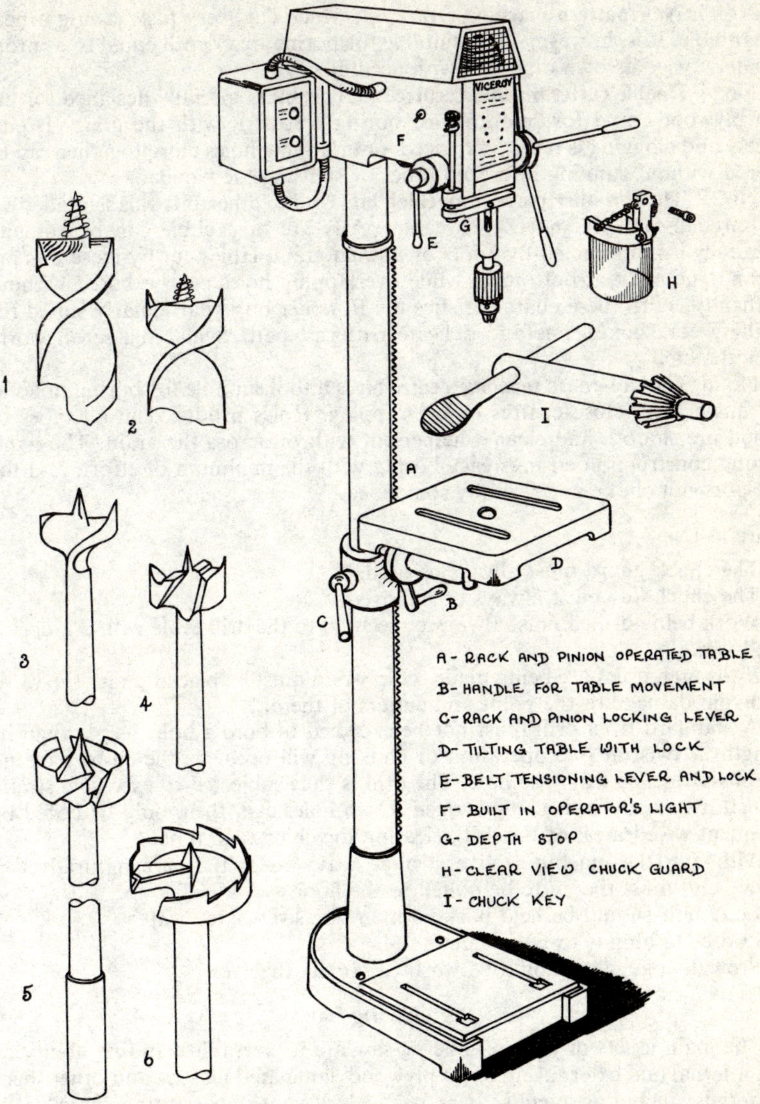

Fig. 127. Pedestal drill and machine bits for wood boring.

work. Both these types can be obtained with brad point (plain, square section—not threaded) if required.

No. 3. **New pattern machine centre bit**, which cuts very fast leaving a neat clean hole. It is, however, only suitable for boring to a depth equal to approximately twice its own diameter with accuracy.

No. 4. **Double cutter machine centre bit**. This bit is specially designed for use on plywoods, and for smooth, fast boring across or with the grain. It cuts freely and clogging is not experienced. Overlapping holes close together can be bored without running into each other or splitting the wood.

No. 5. **The Forstner pattern machine bit**. Unlike other bits this is guided by its circular rim and not by its centre. Any arc of a circle can be cut and accuracy is not affected by knots or uneven grain. Holes cut by these bits are clean, true and flat-bottomed, while overlapping holes can be bored without difficulty. With these characteristics the Forstner bit is particularly suited for drilling core boxes, fine and delicate patterns, pattern making, scroll work, veneers, etc.

No. 6. **The saw-tooth machine centre bit** is a tool suitable for boring holes at an angle, with close centres or overlapping. Holes produced in all types of wood are smooth and clean whether cut with or across the grain. The light, strong construction ensures easy boring with the minimum of effort, and the bit does not choke and is easily sharpened.

Care in Use

The chuck guard must always be used.

The chuck key must always be removed.

Work being drilled must always be secured to the drill table with cramps or drill vice.

If through holes are being made scrap wood must be placed under the work to avoid damage to the point and cutters of the bit.

A standard twist drill must not be expected to bore a hole deeper than its length of twist at one operation or choking will occur as the chips have no means of escape from the hole. The drill is thus subjected to excessive strain, which may result in it being broken. Deep holes can, then, only be bored by frequent withdrawal of the drill, clearing the chips each time.

Although the machines have strong, heavy bases they are naturally top heavy and must therefore be bolted to the floor.

Long hair should be held back with an industrial safety cap.

Loose clothing is to be avoided.

Protective goggles should be worn to protect the eyes.

Portable Jig-Saw

The main assets of the portable jig-saw are its versatility and its ability to cut internal and external curves in plywood, laminated plastics and other sheet materials, including metals. It is particularly suited to cutting large work which could not be easily supported and sawn by the band-saw or permanent jig-sawing machine. Vibration and chatter from the reciprocating action of the saw should, in a good tool, be at a minimum in order that the saw kerf is as smooth as possible. The blade cuts on the upward stroke, tending to pull the saw down on to the work, but to minimise the possible risk of damage to the outer surface of the wood, which may be pre-veneered or surfaced with a

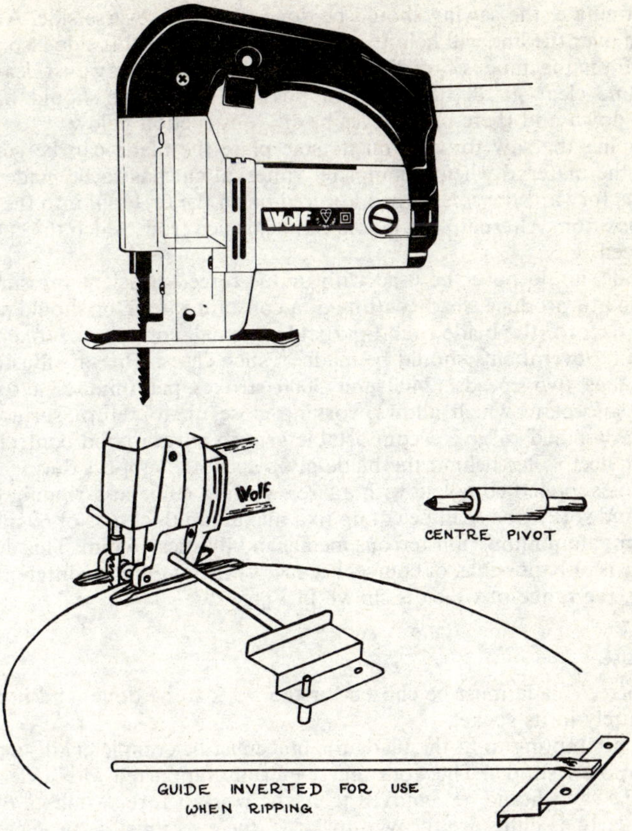

Fig. 128. The portable jig-saw and the circle cutting guide and ripping fence.

	Tooth Pitch	Material and Capacities
	2.5 mm (10 t.p.i.)	Hard and softwood up to 30 mm
	4.0 mm (6 t.p.i.)	Hard and softwood up to 60 mm
	3.0 mm (8 t.p.i.)	Mild steel from 3 to 6 mm thick. Aluminium up to 16 mm thick. PVC and acrylics up to 13 mm thick. Maronite up to 25 mm thick. Arborite up to 22 mm thick (curves in wood).
	1.2 mm (20 t.p.i.)	Mild steel from 1.5 to 4 mm thick. Aluminium from 1.5 to 4 mm thick. Plywood and hardboard up to 16 mm thick.
	0.7 mm (32 t.p.i.)	Stainless steel sheet up to 1 mm thick. (Material should be supported on wooden base during cutting operation.)
	2.0 mm (12 t.p.i.)	Aluminium up to 6 mm thick. Mild steel from 3 to 6 mm thick. Plywood and hardboard up to 32 mm thick. Synthetic resin bonded fabric up to 16 mm thick.

Fig. 129. Jig-saw blades.

plastic laminate, the sawing should be done from the reverse side. A strip of Sellotape over the line will help to reduce splintering on this side also. The air flow from the machine is carefully directed to blow away sawdust, leaving the cutting line clear at all times. When possible, the work should be firmly clamped down and there must never be any obstruction below.

By tipping the saw forward on its sole plate the blade can be gently fed through the material when a completely internal cut has to be made. As the blade cuts forward the sole is then lowered on to the material into the normal cutting position. Alternatively, a hole can be drilled from which the cut can be commenced.

The tool should never be used with undue force, sufficient pressure being maintained to produce steady cutting at a constant rate. Nor should attempts be made to force the blade round particularly small corners or broken blades may result. Several cuts should be made in such cases. The saw illustrated in Fig. 128 has two speeds (2400 and 3000 strokes per minute) and a two-position sole plate which allows working close up to return surfaces. The handle is designed to give a comfortable grip to ensure good control, and a hardened steel roller behind the blade gives accurate support during cutting. The unit is supplied complete with a circle-cutting guide and ripping fence.

Hard and soft woods can be cut up to a maximum thickness of 60 mm; mild steel 6 mm; aluminium, non-ferrous metals and plastics 16 mm. This degree of versatility is only possible, of course, because of the number of different blades available, the range of which is shown in Fig. 129.

Care in Use

The correct blade must be chosen for the work to be done, and it must be fixed securely in its socket.

Before attempting to fit the blade the unit must be completely disconnected from the power supply. The work must be firmly supported with a clear space below. The saw should be removed from the work before switching off.

Particularly as chips are thrown upwards, the eyes must be protected.

Portable Circular Saw

In saving up to 90 per cent in time for most sawing operations which would otherwise be done by hand, and a similar amount of physical energy, the provision of a portable saw in the workshop justifies serious consideration (Fig. 130).

Even where a standard fixed circular saw is installed, the portable saw scores heavily in that it can be taken to the work. A very simple example of this would be in cutting a working length from a board which can then be handled more easily. Skill in using the power saw develops with practice, as with all tools, and once the operator is familiar with the various built-in guides and adjustments considerable accuracy can be achieved. The saws are known by their diameter of blade, which is 150 mm for the do-it-yourself attachment and 184 mm or 235 mm for the purpose-built unit. The larger one is recommended for heavy industrial use only. A blade of 184 mm diameter will make a vertical cut of approximately 58 mm and a bevel cut at 45 degrees of approximately 45 mm.

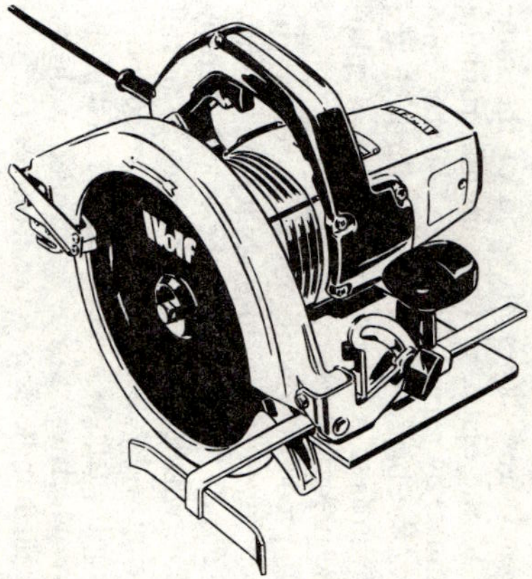

Fig. 130. The portable circular saw.

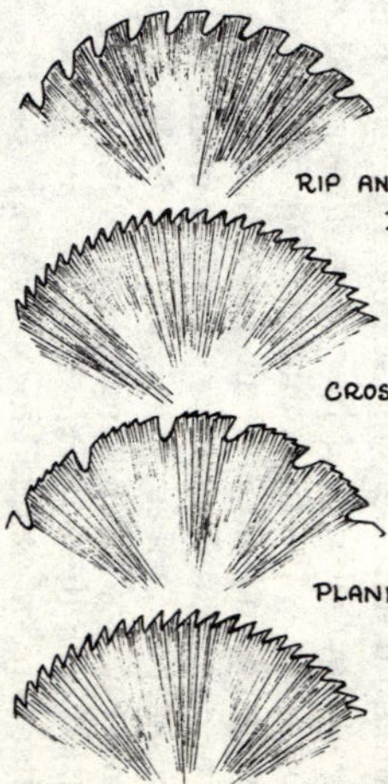

Fig. 131. Blades for the portable circular saw.

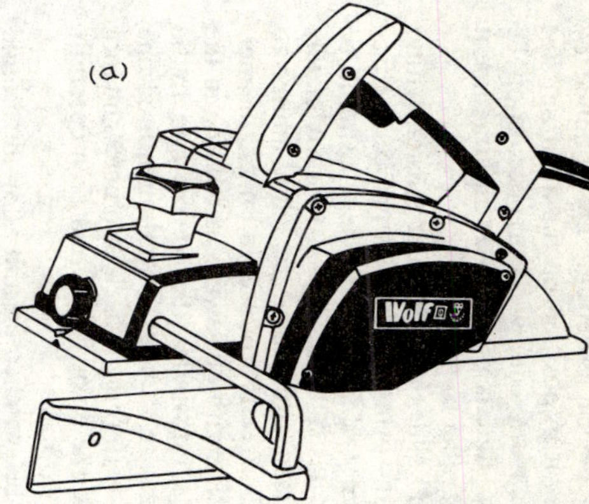

Fig. 132. Planerette (*a*) and heavy-duty machine plane (*b*).

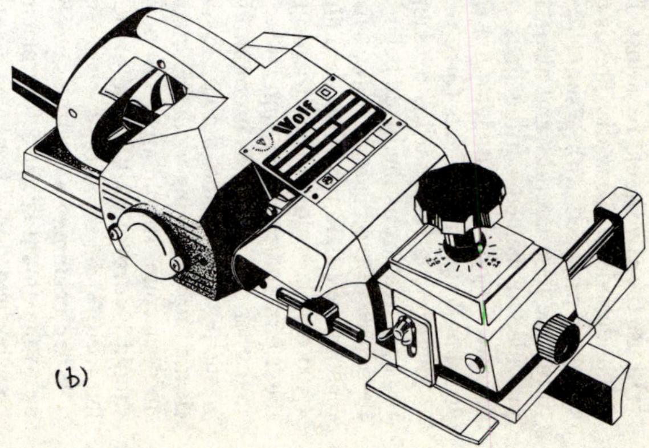

In use the saw should be adjusted so that the blade only just breaks through the underside of the work. This is done by raising or lowering the sole plate, which is provided with a simple locking device. Bevel cuts are obtained by tilting the base laterally and again locking it in position on the quadrant slot provided. Pencilled cutting lines on the work can, with practice, soon be followed easily, but in addition a ripping guide is provided as an attachment enabling long straight cuts to be made parallel to an edge.

The lower blade guard is telescopic and slides round under tension within the upper casing as the blade begins to cut, springing back into place to cover the whole of the blade once the saw is removed from the timber. It should be remembered that the purpose-built saw has a higher speed (approximately 4,400 r.p.m. no load) than the do-it-yourself attachment, which is limited to the r.p.m. of the drill unit. The higher speed produces a much cleaner, smoother cut, which, as is common practice with all sawing, should be in the waste portion of the timber, leaving the remainder the correct size to be cleaned up. If during a cut the blade is seen to wander from the required line on no account should any attempt be made to force it back into line. The tool should be drawn back to the point where the error began and then carefully fed forward once more.

When beginning a cut, the saw should be switched on and allowed to build up to maximum speed before placing it on the timber. The sole plate should then be held down firmly on to the wood and the blade advanced steadily along the line of cut; avoid stalling the saw as a result of attempting to cut too quickly. Different species of timber, and even pieces of wood of the same species, will offer different resistance to the blade, and the normal running speed should be maintained at all times by varying the rate of feed and pressure applied. As with the jig-saw, the blade cuts upwards through the wood, so the face side should be downwards to reduce the possibility of splintering. For the same reason it is a wise precaution to wear goggles.

The portable saw can be readily adapted for sawing out large rebates by attaching a sole plate extension which gives increased stability on narrow edges. Alternatively, a block can be clamped to the side of the wood, thereby increasing its thickness. The second cut, which then allows the waste to fall away, is made from the face which, being wider, gives the saw more support.

The saw is started by gently squeezing the trigger switch incorporated in the handle. This is an efficient method by which the saw is controlled with the minimum of effort, assisted by a second handle above the front of the sole plate. When the choice of saw is being considered, the comfortable feel and position of the handle and switch are important, as are the weight and balance of the whole unit, since it is imperative that such a potentially dangerous tool as the circular saw should be handled with the maximum control and the minimum of fatigue. The weight of the saw illustrated in Fig. 130 is 6·4 kg.

A number of special blades are available for cutting materials other than wood, such as plastic laminates, aluminium sheet, aluminium extrusions, and corrugated and flat steel sheets. Abrasive discs of silicon carbide for cutting flat or corrugated asbestos sheets, or of aluminous oxide for cutting cast iron, steel sheet and tubes, are also available. In order to meet the Abrasive Wheels Regulations of 1970, flanges larger than the standard saw-blade flanges must be used with these discs.

Blades recommended for woodwork (see Fig. 131) are the combined rip and crosscut, the crosscut (both of which are Teflon*S coated) and the planer and mitre blade, which gives an extremely smooth finish to rip and crosscut work. A so-called flooring blade of special temper which will cut occasional nails that may be encountered when taking up floor boards, or in reclaimed timber, etc., can also be obtained.

Care in Use

The timber being sawn must be held firmly so that it cannot possibly move while the cut is being made.

There must be no obstruction below the timber.

The saw blade must not be in contact with the work when the machine is switched on.

Hold the saw in both hands by the handles provided. In this way hands cannot come into contact with the blade.

The saw must be supported at all times by the work, both during and after the cut. It must not be supported by the timber being cut off or this will fall away, possibly leaving the saw out of control.

The saw must be removed from the wood before being switched off, and the blade should stop before the machine is put down.

The power cable should be slung over the operator's shoulder and clear of the saw at all times, and disconnected completely from the supply once the sawing has been completed.

Portable Machine Planes

Planerette and Heavy Duty Plane

The planing width of the Planerette (Fig. 132*a*) is 81 mm and depth of cut up to 1 mm. In comparison there are two heavy-duty models (Fig. 132*b*) with planing widths of 81 mm and 136 mm and depths of cut up to 3 mm. Lengths are 286 mm, 388 mm and 430 mm respectively, and weights 2·5 kg, 4·9 kg and 7·4 kg. These are important factors to consider in choosing a particular model to meet certain requirements. All three models work on the same principle as the floor-mounted planing machine and have twin cutters mounted in a cylindrical block which rotates at 15,000 r.p.m. on the small model and 16,000 r.p.m. on the larger ones.

Although often used for installation work when fitting joinery such as doors and screens 'on site', they have many uses in the workshop where a hand plane might be used. They are precision tools on which the depth of cut can be controlled accurately. Providing the blades are kept sharp, the high-speed rotation of the cutter block coupled with the flat sole plate will produce a fine surface on really difficult grain. The depth of cut is adjusted by raising or lowering that part of the sole plate in front of the cutters.

To commence the cut, the front portion of the sole plate should be rested on the wood, with the cutter blade clear of the end of the board. The trigger switch, which is similar to that of the power saw, is mounted in the handle and should be squeezed in and the full r.p.m. allowed to build up before the plane is pushed smoothly but firmly over the wood. Obviously, the work must be held firmly to avoid movement during the cut. A series of parallel cuts must be made if wide boards are being planed. The rate of feed will depend upon the hardness of the timber and the depth of cut. The machine should always be fed forward with sufficient pressure to keep it cutting but not so much that the cutters are slowed down too much or rough work will ensue. Where possible, planing should be done with the grain as is normal practice. When planing edges, use should be made of the fence, keeping it tight up against the side of the wood to ensure squareness of the edge.

Care in Use

As with all portable tools, keep the supply cable clear of the machine cutters at all times.

Do not switch off until clear of the wood.

Do not put the machine down until all rotation has stopped.

Put the machine across the well of the bench or some suitable place so that the cutters are not in contact with anything which will damage them.

Disconnect the power supply immediately the machine is not required.

Keep the work free of waste chips so that they are not squashed into the surface of the wood making unnecessary indentations.

The Machine Router

Long grooves, stopped or cut throughout the length of the wood, housings across the grain, mortise and tenon joints, rebates and mouldings on straight edges or curved, can all be worked accurately with the router (Fig. 133) and give an indication of how versatile this tool really is. Consisting of a powerful electric motor mounted above a wide circular base, the machine is designed to cut into the surface of the wood, routing out areas, the shapes of which may be governed by working to templates; or making other surface or edge cuts, the shapes of which are determined by the shape of the cutter used.

The depth of the cut is adjusted by raising or lowering the motor, and since the cutter is attached directly to the motor spindle by a collet chuck, the cutter is also raised and lowered. This adjustment can be carried out quickly and accurately using the micrometer scale built into the machine. Two comfortable handles diametrically opposed and built on to the base ensure good control of the machine, and the wide cut-away in the base allows accurate observation of the work being done. This is further assisted on some models by a light mounted behind the machine to illuminate the throat and cutter. A guide fence (Fig. 134) is used when cutting parallel to an edge (as for grooving) and this too has a fine adjustment mechanism so that the cut can be positioned with great accuracy.

Using the correct methods, and providing the cutters are properly sharpened, the surface produced by the router will require little or no sanding; this is because of the high speed of rotation—in the region of 18,000–27,000 r.p.m.—and also because of this cuts can be made in any direction of the grain, although when working on a convex edge it is advisable to cut in an anticlockwise direction which helps the cutter to remain close to the wood.

Router bits must be held tightly in the chuck, again because of the high cutting speed, and the spanner provided for this should always be used. There are two basic types of bits: those for making grooves below the surface of the wood, their shape being that of the groove which they are intended to

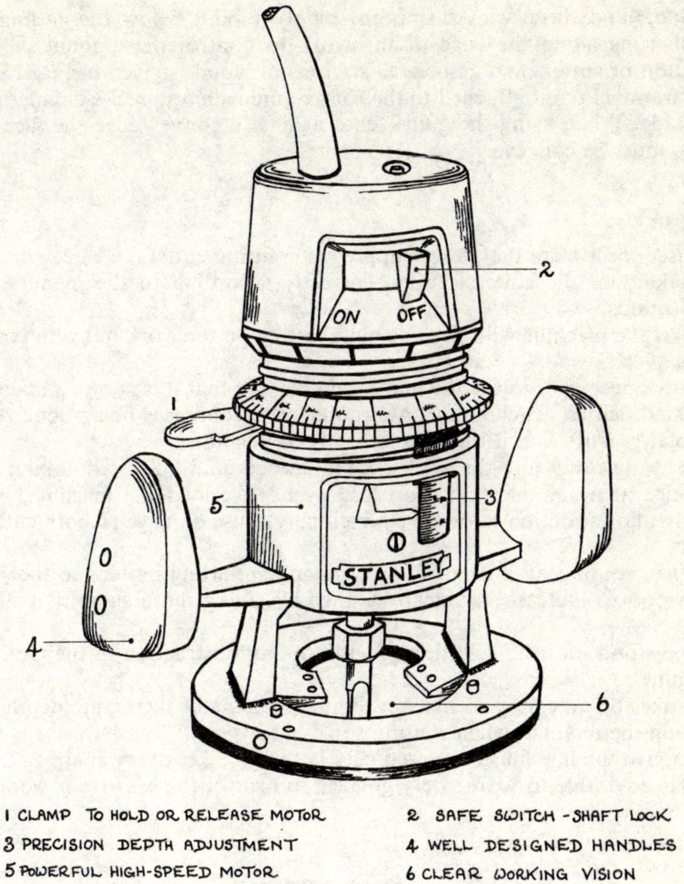

Fig. 133. The machine router.

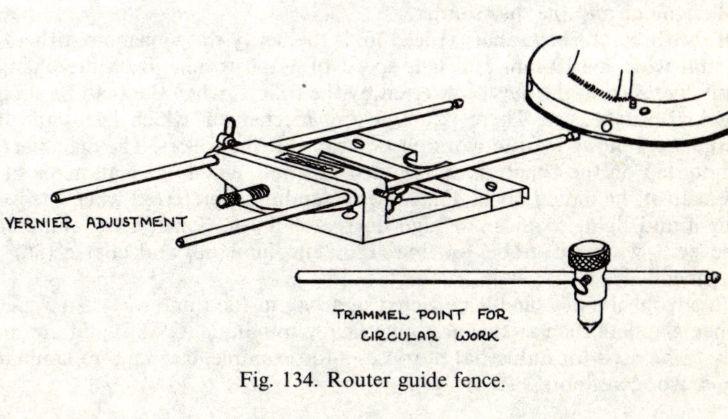

Fig. 134. Router guide fence.

produce; and those with a smooth spigot or pilot below the cutting edges which runs along the edge of the work to control the amount of cut. A selection of cutters and associated sections of wood is given in Fig. 135.

A trammel point attached to the router guide allows precise circular cuts to be made. When using the guide fence against a convex edge the face of the guide must be concave.

Care in Use

Disconnect from the power supply when fitting cutters.

Make sure the cutter is fitted correctly according to the manufacturer's instructions.

Start the machine with the sole plate resting on the work but with the cutter clear of the wood.

If it is necessary to use the guide fence ensure that it is secure and correctly adjusted before switching on. Alternatively, if routing is being done round a template ensure that it too is held firmly in position.

Feed the cutter into the work once it has acquired full speed, taking care to advance at a suitable rate. Too fast would overload the machine, but too slowly allows friction to develop which may cause damage to both cutter and work.

When routing on a narrow edge, clamp supporting battens to the sides of the wood to increase its thickness, thereby giving more support to the sole plate.

The wood must be held firmly, without any obstruction in the path of the machine.

It may be necessary to make a number of cuts of increasing depth before making the final cut when routing some hardwoods.

To give the fine finish required cutters must be kept very sharp.

It is advisable to wear safety goggles to protect the eyes from wood chips and dust.

Power Sanders

Three types of purpose-built power sanders are made: the belt sander, the orbital sander and the disc sander.

Of the three, the **belt sander** (Fig. 136) is the heavy-duty machine with a belt 100 mm wide × 610 mm and belt speed of 1,150 ft/min. Belts are changed simply by relaxing the tension exerted by the rollers, when they can be slipped on or off very easily. There is a tracking mechanism which keeps the belt centred, preventing it from working sideways off the rollers. The machine can be mounted on the bench in an inverted position, enabling small items to be held against the moving belt. This type of sanding is preferred when the work is small and light, requiring a high degree of finish. 'Open coat' aluminium oxide belts with grit grades of fine (120), medium (60) and coarse (36) are recommended.

Dust from the machine is collected in a bag in the same way as a vacuum cleaner. Sanders such as this are quite heavy to handle (6·9 kg) and are most likely to be used for industrial purposes—for example, cleaning up laminated beams, wooden floors, etc.

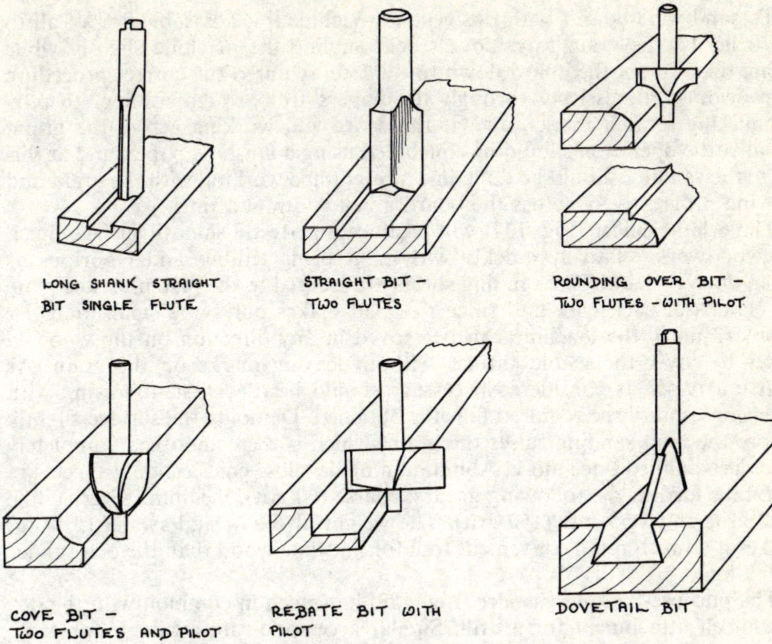

Fig. 135. A selection of the many router cutters.

Fig. 136. The belt sander.

To sand wide boards with this type of machine it is advisable first of all to work across the grain to remove stock, angling the machine slightly while doing this. To get the board down to the level required the correct procedure is to work progressively through the papers from rough to fine, thereby eliminating scratch marks, and at this stage still working across the grain. Finally, the operation should be concluded using a finishing paper, and at this stage the sanding should be done in a straight line working with the grain and moving progressively across the board a belt width at a time.

The **orbital sander** (Fig. 137) will produce a perfectly smooth surface finish on woodwork relatively quickly without it being tedious and laborious as when done by hand. The sanding sheets are secured to the platen or sole plate by clamps at each end, and since this pad makes only very small diameter orbits (3 mm), the machine can be moved in any direction on the wood in order to cover the whole surface without leaving marks on the grain. As coarse a paper as considered necessary should be used first, following with finer grades until the required finish is obtained. Damping the surface slightly before the final sanding raises the grain, which is then smoothed completely when it is sanded once more. Aluminium oxide 'close coat' sanding sheets are recommended in the following grades: coarse (60 grit), medium (80 grit), fine (100 grit) and very fine (150 grit). The weight of the orbital sander (2–4 kg) makes it a much more convenient tool for finishing wood than the belt sander at 6·9 kg.

The purpose-built **disc sander** (Fig. 138) has much in common with the do-it-yourself attachment for a drill. Similar accessories are available for each, but being designed solely for one purpose the handles are well positioned to make the machine even more efficient in use. It also has the advantage of higher operating speeds, ranging from 4,200 to 5,200 r.p.m. running light, and 2,570 to 3,000 r.p.m. on full load, depending upon the model. A machine such as this must comply with the Abrasive Wheels Regulations 1970. By the addition of a grinding pack, comprising a depressed centre-grinding disc (178 × 5 × 22 mm bore), a 178 mm guard assembly, flanges and spanner, it can be converted to a disc grinder. For woodworking, 'open coat' aluminium oxide reinforced sanding discs should be used. Grades 0, ½, 1, 2 and 3 are recommended (80, 60, 50, 36 and 24 grit respectively). Further accessories include grinding wheels and guards, wire brushes, felt pads and lambswool mops for polishing. Abrasive belts, sheets and discs may also be of garnet crystals, silicon carbide, or, hardest of all, tungsten carbide.

Care in Use

Belt sander. Always choose good-quality belts of a suitable grade for the work to be done.

Do not use torn belts.

Ensure that the belt is running true by adjusting the tracking device when necessary.

Do not apply excessive pressure—usually the weight of the machine alone is sufficient.

Orbital sander. The abrasive paper must be held tightly to the sole by the end clamps. Failure to do this prevents the sole plate from transmitting its motion to the sanding sheet, which cannot therefore do its work.

Only apply sufficient pressure to keep the abrasive cutting.

Fig. 137. The orbital sander.

Fig. 138. The disc sander.

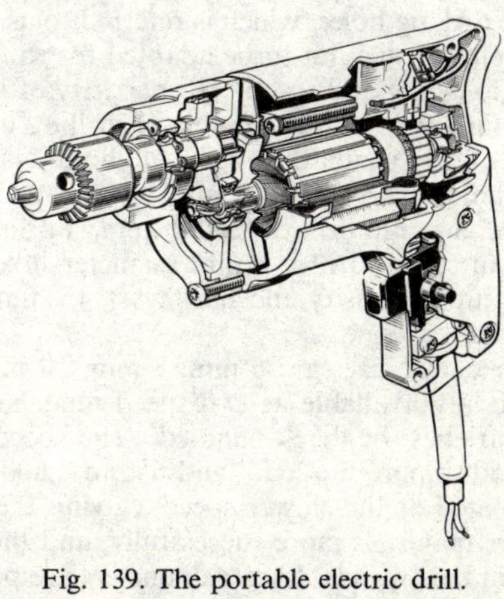

Fig. 139. The portable electric drill.

Disc sander. The circular motion of the disc tends to cut grooves in the surface of the work unless great care is taken.

Tilt the wheel slightly so that only part of the disc is working at any one time. The machine is difficult to control if attempts are made to use the whole face of the disc at once.

Only use very light pressure.

The sanding disc must be firmly fixed to the backing pad.

All sanders. Always switch off the power at the machine and at the supply before making adjustments, i.e. changing abrasive belts, sheets or discs.

Never leave the machine standing on the work.

If switched on accidentally, damage may be done to the work, or the machine may be flung off with resultant damage to itself.

Always lift the machines by the handle(s).

Care must be taken to avoid rounding off corners intended to be square.

Use fine grits on plywoods and veneered panels, taking care not to cut through the top laminate.

Work systematically, avoiding unnecessary re-sanding.

In general work with the grain. This applies particularly to finishing cuts.

Do not allow the sanding sheet to become choked due to waste material clogging the grit. If this happens it should be cleared and the reason for it investigated.

Keep the machines free from dust by regular cleaning.

Eyes and nose should be protected against dust with goggles and respirator, particularly when working indoors or stripping old paint work.

Protective clothing must be worn to ward off the dust.

The Portable Electric Drill

In all probability the power drill (Fig. 139) will be the first portable machine tool provided for any workshop. This is a very simple statement, but the decision as to which drill it should be is by no means as simple. Manufacturers' catalogues present a bewildering array of choice and much careful thought is necessary to select the most suitable one. The selection must be made with careful consideration to what work the drill will be expected to do. Basically this will be drilling holes, which is referred to as 'capacity', but a few simple attachments enable the unit to be adapted for sanding, buffing, grinding, wire-brushing, polishing and so on. The capacity of the drill is defined as the diameter of the largest hole it is capable of drilling in steel, which is also the largest diameter of drill shank the chuck will hold. Naturally, as wood is a milder working material than steel, its maximum capacity in wood will be greater. For example, a 6 mm drill of 2,500 r.p.m. 'no load' and 1,650 r.p.m. 'full load', at 420 watts, will drill a 6 mm diameter hole in steel, 10 mm in masonry (depending upon density and hardness), 13 mm in light alloys, and 16 mm in hardwoods.

The most popular chuck sizes are 6 mm, 8 mm, 10 mm, and 13 mm. The larger ones are generally available as two-speed models of the usual 'pistol' grip or palm grip varieties, or 'back handled'. The speeds of these machines vary from 950 to 2,500 r.p.m. 'no load' and 650 to 1,600 r.p.m. 'full load'. A greater torque is created at the slower speeds, giving the machines sufficient power to drill harder materials more successfully, and they will drill holes up to 22 mm diameter in hardwoods. Larger diameters are possible in softwoods.

Jacobs type chucks, operated by a chuck key, are most serviceable. The extra tightening power provided by the chuck key ensures that the drill bits do not come loose during use.

How comfortably and well the drill can be held when in use is a further consideration, as are its overall dimensions and weight. A detachable side handle is usually available for most models, and some incorporate a depth gauge.

Providing they are really sharp, twist drills of the variety used for metal working will give perfectly satisfactory results when used for drilling wood with the power drill. The centre for the hole should be punched similarly to the way used when drilling holes in metal, and the drill point put into this punch mark before the machine is switched on. Alternatively, the centre can be marked with a bradawl. Another method is to make a drilling jig from an offcut of timber. A hole of the required size is drilled through the jig, which is then clamped over the work in the exact location of the hole to be drilled. A second offcut of timber clamped behind the work will prevent splintering of the wood around the hole as the drill bursts through. The use of a jig of this nature is almost always necessary if drilling has to be done at an angle.

There is a variety of wood-boring bits specially manufactured for use in electric drills (Fig. 140). The range includes the straight shank **cobra bit** of 3 mm diameter, which is ideal for fast boring holes for screws or nails in both hard and soft woods. **Solid centre, single spur brad points** are twist bits from 100 mm to 125 mm in overall length. Their diameters are from 6 mm to 19 mm and the shank 6 mm diameter by 25 mm long. **Flat bits** or **spade bits** are very versatile tools also designed especially for use with electric drills of 6 mm capacity or more, and will bore quickly and cleanly in both hardwoods and softwoods. The shank has three flats ground on it, making it triangular in section so that it fits firmly into the chuck. This is necessary as the drill operates best at very high speeds. Because of this the point of the bit should be located on the wood before switching on the drill and it will be found that only moderate pressure is then required to make the drill cut efficiently. Through holes must be drilled from each side of the wood, the drill being switched off and allowed to stop rotating once the point is showing on the reverse side. It should then be withdrawn from the timber, the point located on the centre thus produced, and drilling recommenced. In this way the hole is drilled accurately on centre without the drill 'wandering'. Again the drill must be switched off and all rotation cease before the bit is withdrawn through the hole. Failure to do this may result in damage to the bit and certainly to the wood around the edges of the hole. As with every other wood-boring bit, sharpness is essential for good cutting and this should be maintained with a smooth file or a slipstone.

For drilling holes in awkward locations, an angle-drill attachment (Fig. 141) pitches the drill bit at 90 degrees to the axis of the machine for drilling which could not otherwise be attempted.

Care in Use

Apply steady pressure in line with the axis of the drill sufficient to maintain the cutting action. Too little pressure may result in excessive friction at the tip of the drill, resulting in the temper of the metal being drawn.

Avoid sideways pressure as this may snap the drill in the hole.

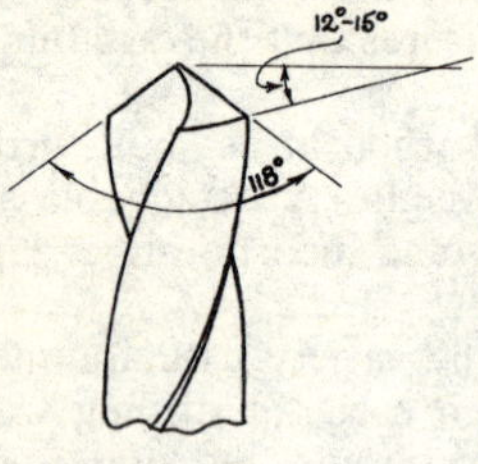

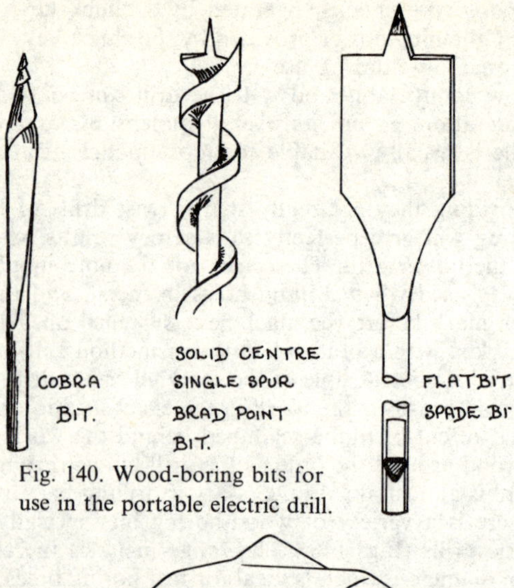

Fig. 140. Wood-boring bits for use in the portable electric drill.

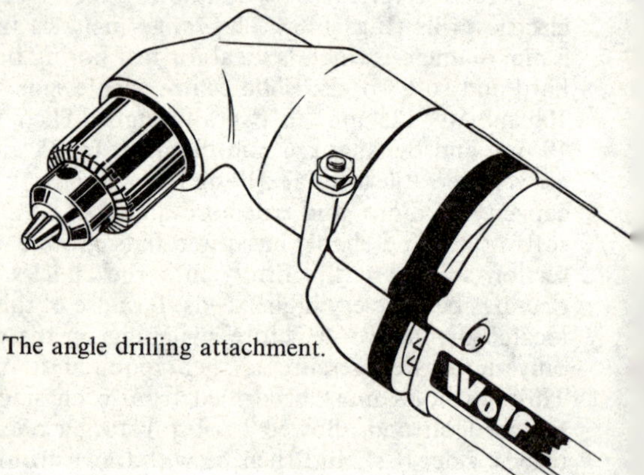

Fig. 141. The angle drilling attachment.

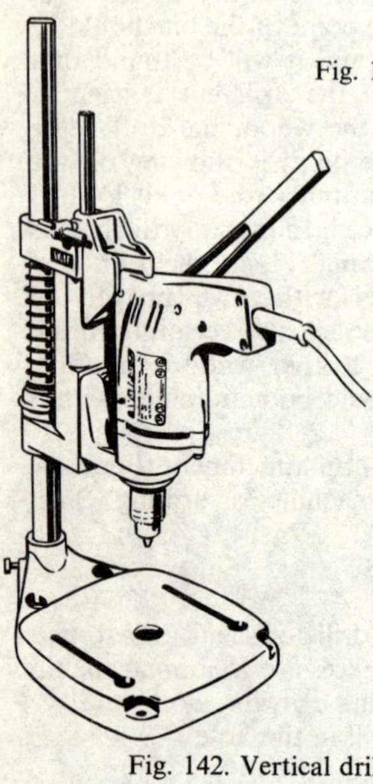

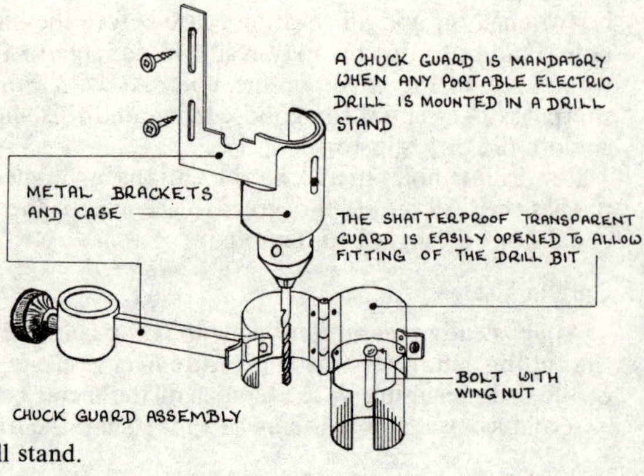

Fig. 142. Vertical drill stand.

All work, large or small, must be held firmly to avoid damage to both it or the drill due to sudden movement.

Always remove the key from the chuck.

Make sure that all three chuck jaws are gripping the drill shank and so hold it centrally.

Power cables to the machine should be kept short. If this is not possible they should never trail on the floor but be slung from the ceiling.

Before bits are changed the machine must be disconnected from the supply.

If the machine is two-speed, allow it to stop before attempting to change the speed.

Use both hands to hold and guide the machine, using the side handles if necessary for heavy work.

Goggles must be worn if there is any danger at all from flying splinters.

'Do-It-Yourself' Attachments for Portable Power Drills

Purpose-built power tools are obviously preferable for the school workshop. They are subjected to fewer changes in use, they are often better balanced and easier to handle, and this in turn leads to better control. A further important consideration is that the on-off switch is a built-in feature of the design and is incorporated in the handle where it is immediately accessible. However, the do-it-yourself attachment, being powered by the drill unit, relies upon the drill switch for starting and stopping. On some models this can be rather inconveniently positioned and somewhat remote. Nevertheless, for the home craftsman who gets to know his own tools well, the acquisition of a set of attachments for this drill increases his woodworking facilities and therefore his work capacity for a very modest outlay.

When choosing a drill it is obviously sensible to study the specifications of the manufacturer's range of attachments to see if these meet possible future needs. Then, when required, buy only those attachments which are specifically designed for that particular drill. Finally, it should be remembered that small-capacity drills of, say, 6 mm for which most attachments are designed are considerably less powerful than the motor of the single-purpose machine and therefore their performance is more limited.

Vertical Drill Stand

This stand holds the drill unit accurately at right angles to the table on which the work rests (Fig. 142). The drilling head is adjustable along the full height of the column, with a depth of feed of 75 mm. With this attachment the drilling of holes for dowels in frameworks, for example, can be done accurately and easily.

A further slight modification to the head of some models of drill permits mortises to be cut using hollow square chisels and mortise drill bits (see Fig. 143). The hollow square chisel is bolted into the extension to the drill clamp and is forced down into the wood while the drill bit rotates inside and slightly ahead of the chisel. In this way a square hole is produced and the complete mortise is made by moving the wood along progressively in the base clamps as a series of connecting cuts is made. The depth of cut is regulated by adjusting the depth stops on the pillar of the drill, and waste material is ejected through the slots in the chisel. You should also note the special shape

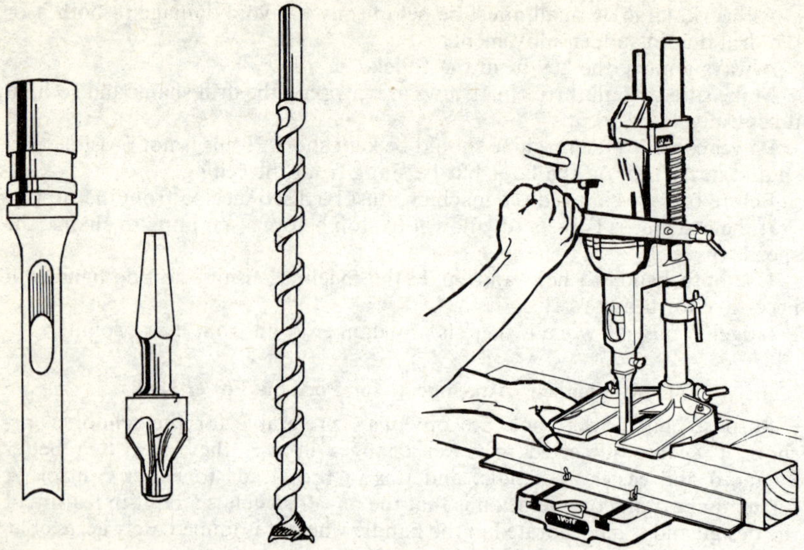

Fig. 143. Mortising attachments and drill stand.

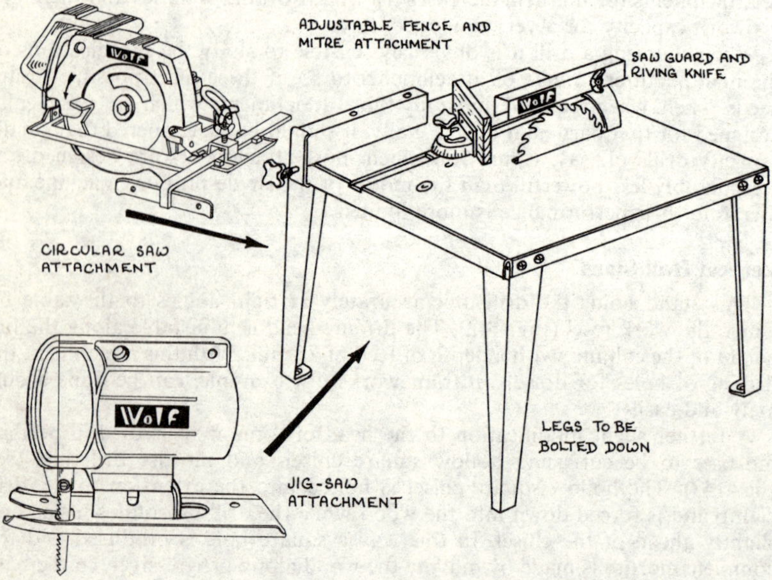

Fig. 144. Circular saw attachment and saw bench.

of the end of the drill bit, which produces the flat-bottomed hole essential when making stopped mortises.

Setting the chisel and bit up correctly is all-important to achieve efficient and accurate cutting. The procedure is to secure the chisel in its socket with a temporary spacer between the socket face and the shoulder of the chisel. The spacer should be 1·5 mm thick—often a coin or a washer is suitable. The bit should now be pushed as far as possible into the chisel and the shank fixed into the drill chuck. The spacer should now be removed and the chisel pushed fully home in its socket, again tightening the locking screw. In this way the bit is slightly in advance of the cutting edge of the chisel and sufficient clearance is provided for it to run smoothly in the chisel. If the mortise is to be cut right through the wood a piece of scrap timber should be placed underneath to protect the cutters.

The chisel is sharpened by using the special tool provided, which fits into a joiners' brace. The chisel should be held vertically in a vice and a few turns of the tool will produce a fine cutting edge. The tool does, however, still leave the inside corners of the chisel thick and these must be cleared with a fine file. *On no account* should the chisel ever be sharpened on the outside: this will cause it to bind in the hole. Should the bit require sharpening, small, smooth, square or flat files should be used to sharpen the spurs again, working on the inside only. The cutters must be sharpened from below using a smooth half-round file in the throat of the bit.

The base of the drill stand must always be bolted firmly to the bench top.

Circular Saw Attachment and Saw Bench

The 150 mm diameter blade of the usual circular saw attachment (Fig. 144) provides quite a workmanlike tool with which both soft and hardwoods, as well as laminated plastics, can be cut with ease and precision. The blade is usually adjustable between 90 degrees and 45 degrees with maximum depths of cut of 43 mm and 35 mm respectively. Saw guard, adjustable sole plate and quadrant, telescopic safety guard and adjustable ripping fence are all inclusive features of the attachment. Adjustments to the depth of cut are achieved by raising or lowering the sole plate, and then locking it in position, usually with a simple wing nut. To fit the attachment the drill chuck has to be removed, the saw casing fitted and locked to the drill body with set screw and shoe and the blade is then fitted with saw flanges directly to the spindle of the drill unit. The flanges and blade are secured with a nut which must be tightened with the spanners provided. As this is potentially the most dangerous of all the attachments, exceptional care must be exercised in its assembly and use. Combined rip-crosscut blades and fine-toothed crosscut blades are available, the latter being more suitable for cutting thin materials. Within the limits of its power, the saw is used in the same manner as the larger, purpose-built saw.

The provision of a saw table, under which the drill and saw attachment can be fitted, converts it into a saw bench (see Fig. 144). The saw retains all its previous refinements but the depths of cut are slightly reduced to 37 mm at 90 degrees and 29 mm at 45 degrees. A saw fence for long parallel cuts and a mitre sawing guide are included as standard. As with the drill stand, the saw bench must be bolted down to the bench top.

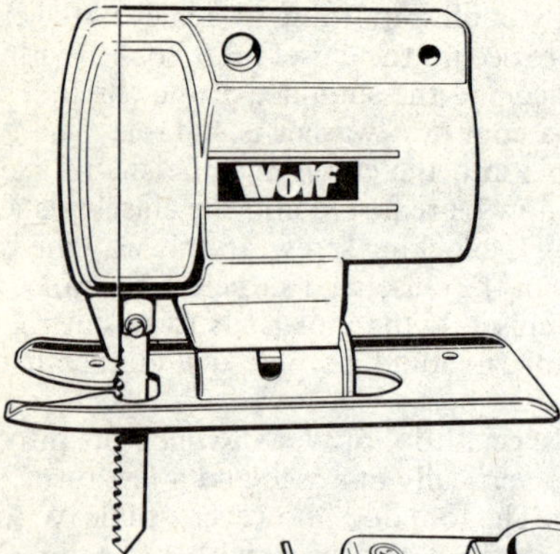

Fig. 145. The jig-saw attachment.

Fig. 146. The orbital sanding attachment.

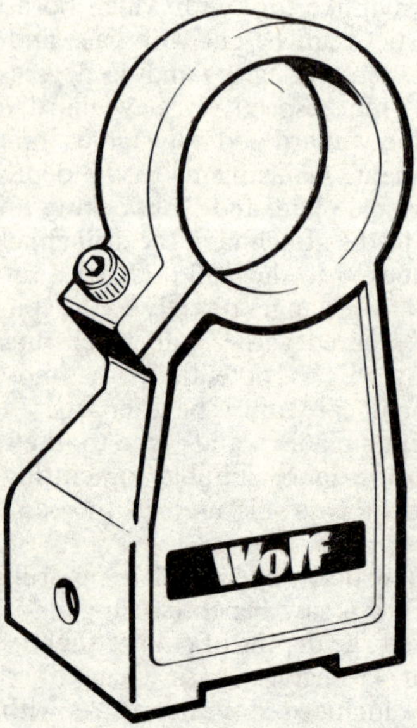

Fig. 147. The bench clamp.

The Jig-saw Attachment

This attachment (Fig. 145) must be fitted to the drill as carefully as the circular saw and can be used in the same manner as the standard portable jig-saw. By adjusting the angle of the sole plate, cuts are possible at all angles between 45 degrees and 90 degrees, where the maximum depth of cut is 38 mm. It is an advantage if the drill unit has two speeds because blades for cutting metal are also available. With them non-ferrous metals can be cut up to 8 mm thick on the higher speeds and steel up to 1·5 mm on the lower ones.

The Orbital Sanding Attachment

The sanding attachment (Fig. 146), which is fitted directly to the body of the drill, quickly converts the unit to an efficient finishing sander. Using the appropriate sanding sheets, it will produce a superfine finish with none of the risk of damage to the work that can arise with disc sanders. Quite recently silicon carbide grits in three grades—coarse, medium and fine—bonded to an open material which allows the dust to fall away from it quite freely, have become available. In this way, the problem of clogging, which is associated with ordinary abrasive sheets, is overcome.

The Bench Clamp

The bench clamp (Fig. 147) enables the drill to be held horizontally to the bench, providing a powerful work head. It should be mounted so that the chuck is over the edge of the bench, leaving a clear space in which sanding discs are free to rotate. By fixing the drill in this way, both hands are left free to control the work. This is a distinct advantage if the work pieces are very small. It is also useful to design and make a sanding table which can be set up in front of the discs.

Other items which can be used with the drill mounted in this way, or using the drill 'freehand', are the drum sander, for which three grades of belt are available, the flexidisc, the paint and varnish remover, and the cup wire brush, which is part of the grinding and buffing set (Fig. 148). The drum sander and the flexible rubber disc will mould themselves to curved surfaces, which makes them particularly useful. On flat surfaces, care must be taken to raise the front edge of the flexidisc before advancing it across the work to avoid gouging. All grades of grits can be used with the flexidisc as well as the lambswool polishing bonnet. Most manufacturers also produce a paint-stirring device to be fitted in the drill chuck to speed up the preparation of paint ready for use.

General Workshop and Electrical Precautions

Advice has been given above on personal safety in using both fixed and portable electrically powered tools. The manufacturer will also be deeply concerned that the design of his products ensures mechanical and electrical safety. This does not, however, relieve the user of the need for care and common sense in using them. It must be remembered that a power tool, because it is electrically driven, is much more dangerous than the equivalent hand tool. The rules regarding workshop dress must be strictly adhered to; machines should be expertly maintained; they must be fitted with the proper guards; cutting tools must always be kept sharp; and machines kept clean. The attention of anyone using a machine must never be distracted.

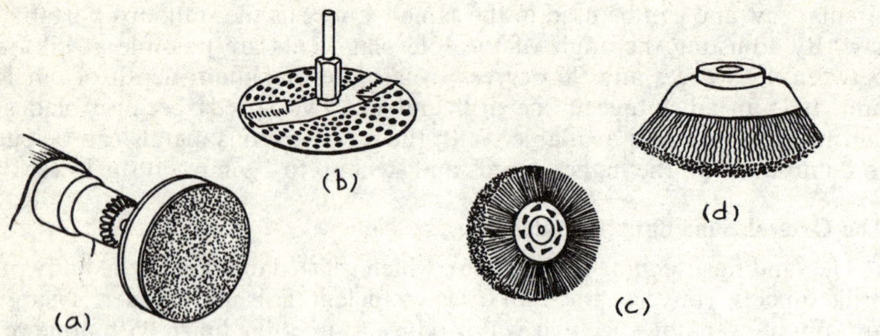

Fig. 148. (*a*) Flexidisc, (*b*) paint and varnish remover, (*c*) flat wire brush, and (*d*) cup wire brush.

Fig. 149. Portable power point.

The electrical safety of machines in the workshop at school or at home is paramount. Machine tools fixed permanently into place are wired into the mains supply; the electrical circuit of the machine is built in by the manufacturer and the supply fed to the machine through rigid conduit, and where it enters the machine possibly through flexible conduit. Under normal circumstances this wiring will not be subjected to any movement and in practice it gives little or no trouble. Such machines are fitted with shrouded starting buttons which it is difficult to operate accidentally, whereas the stop button is mushroom-headed and protrudes so that it can be located quickly and easily, simply by touch. On many modern machines the stop button is locked in the 'off' position and the starting button will not operate until the stop button has been released. A foot-operated safety pedal is also a feature of modern machines which, when depressed in the event of an emergency, cuts off the electrical supply to the machine. In addition, around the walls of school workshops there are emergency stop buttons which cut off mains supply to the fixed machinery. All students should be conversant with the *proper* use of these switches and be taught to use them should the occasion arise.

Portable powered machines present quite different problems of electrical safety. In the United Kingdom they are usually plugged into 13-amp sockets supplying 240 volts from the mains, but many authorities are now providing low-voltage circuits with suitable sockets within the workshop, or alternatively a transformer to step down the voltage to 110. The minimum specification for such a transformer should be as follows: double-wound with an earthed screen, double-impregnated, with the secondary suitable for 110 volts and fitted with a centre tap available for earthing, supplied enclosed in a ventilated sheet steel case. The transformer should be permanently secured to the same mounting surface as the socket outlet, and the input lead must not be extended. The supply to the transformer should be switched off after use. This procedure offers the minimum risk to the operator and limits the possible electric shock to a potential of 55 volts above earth. It is advisable that the plugs used for portable tools should be of hard rubber as these will not fracture if dropped. They must also be three-pin (live, neutral and earth) and be fused in the live lead. This fuse will usually be of 3, 5, 10 or 13 amps but it is advisable to check with the manufacturer's instructions.

Regulations making it a requirement by law that all portable electric tools used in industry in the United Kingdom were to be 'earthed' were introduced by the Factories Act of 1908. At that time the earth wire was the only available means of providing efficient electrical safety in the event of a breakdown in the insulation of the tool. (The earth wire then conducts the current directly to earth and not through the body of the operator.) In theory this is absolutely safe, providing the system is correct in the first instance and is correctly maintained and serviced from then on. Unfortunately, this does not always happen in practice, and hazards do occur due to changing of plugs, incorrect connections being made within them; the earth cable or perhaps only a single strand working loose within the plug and contacting the live terminal, which in turn could make the appliance 'live'. Where an earth wire broke or became disconnected anywhere in the circuit it would mean there were no safety precautions at all if the insulation happened to break down. If the 'live' lead became disconnected and contacted the metal outer case of a power tool this would present a lethal hazard if earthing was not 100 per cent efficient.

It was because of these and other potential dangers that 'double-insulated' electric tools were developed. Wolf double-insulated tools, for example, do not rely on an earth wire for safety. They cannot be incorrectly wired up because only two-core cable is used. This eliminates the danger of incorrectly connecting the earth wire to a live terminal. The bodies, switch, handles and side handles are constructed from tough, non-conductive material. The polyester body completely envelopes the unit, which avoids any possibility of electrical contact with the operator. Chucks, spindles, and exposed metal parts are also insulated by a patented nylon chuck spindle. The operator is therefore afforded the extra protection of holding only a non-conductive shell in his hands should an internal fault occur in the tool, or a fault develop in the plug or socket.

Accidental damage to cables, cable connections within machines, and plugs and sockets, which could lead to electrical faults, can be caused if cables are dragged across floors where they might be walked upon, or trapped in doors if they pass from one room to another. Preferably the cable should be suspended, finally dropping down over the operator's shoulder to the appliance. In this way it is unlikely that damage will be caused to the cable by the machine. Plugs should never be pulled from their sockets by tugging on the cable, nor should the cable ever be in tension. When not in use, the lead to the tool and any extension cable used should be coiled, preferably on a purpose-built reel (Fig. 149).

Wolf Electric Power Tools were the first to be awarded the British Standards Institution 'Kite Mark', indicating that they comply with the amended Factories Act (Electrical Regulations) 1968. In addition, they bear the appropriate international approval seals of official testing authorities throughout the world:

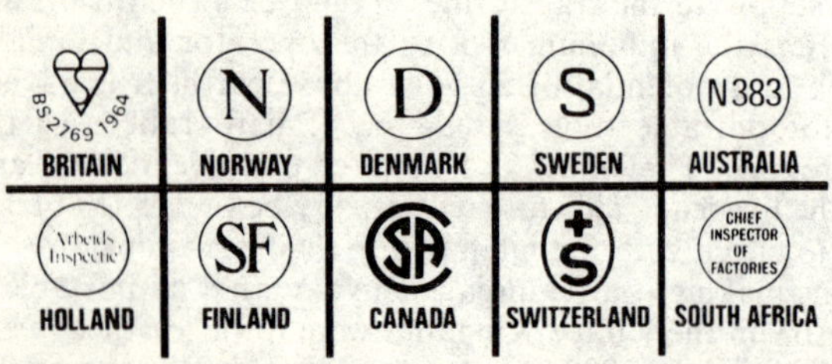

6

TOOL MAINTENANCE

The hard, smooth feel of oak when pared with a really sharp chisel, the silkiness of pine from the smoothing plane and the geometrical simplicity of a hole drilled clean and true may be commonplace in the life of the craftsman. Nevertheless, not only do these and other similar experiences give him satisfaction of the hand and eye, but they also add to the quality of his work. They are the result of using tools which are cared for and properly maintained. It is obvious, however, that in the course of everyday use, simply in doing the job for which they are designed—that is cutting timber—woodworking tools are going to become blunted. The moment this happens, tools become less safe because there is a tendency to try to force them; at the same time the quality of the work begins to decline. Unfortunately, unforeseen accidental damage to cutting edges also occurs at times: contact with another tool, a hidden nail, or simply a hard knot may chip the fine cutting edge of chisels, planes and gouges. It is, therefore, necessary to maintain tools in a first-class working condition in order to achieve satisfactory results.

Oilstones

Normal 'dulling' of the cutting edge of a tool is usually corrected with a suitable oilstone. However, if after being re-sharpened in this way for several times the cutting edge becomes too thick or if a chipped edge cannot be corrected on the oilstone, then it will be necessary to grind the blade before sharpening.

Oilstones may be of natural stone or artificial. Natural varieties such as Washita or Arkansas—which, in particular, gives a very fine edge—are products of America and are quite expensive. Artificial stones—made in three grades: fine, medium and coarse—are of various standard sizes, 200 × 50 × 25 mm being most common. The materials from which they are made, such as corundum, alundum and silicon carbide, are produced in an electric furnace and then crushed, the grits graded, moulded to the required size and refired. Double-sided stones of the same overall size are available with one coarse side for quick rubbing down, and one fine to give a keen edge. These save some initial expense and are perhaps an advantage for use 'on site' since only one stone rather than two has to be carried. Since oilstones are brittle and thus liable to easy fracture it is common practice to protect them in a box made from two pieces of hardwood. Recesses are routed in these to form a base and a lid, so that the stone fits tightly into the base and the lid loosely over it (Fig. 151). Oilstone boxes made in this way can be held on a board hooked over the bench top, so that they do not move when pressure is applied to them as tools are sharpened.

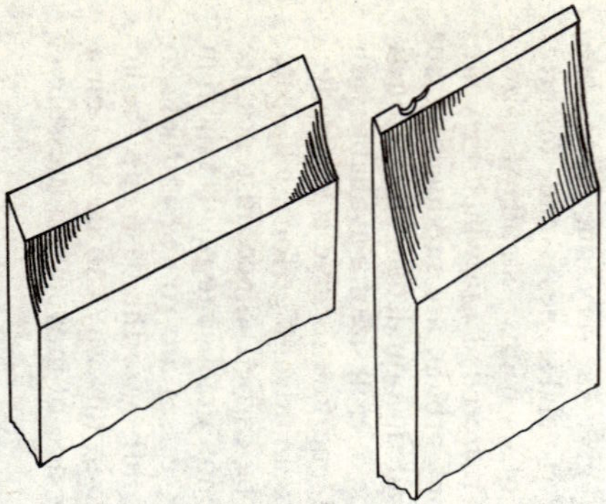

Fig. 150. Thick and damaged cutting edges.

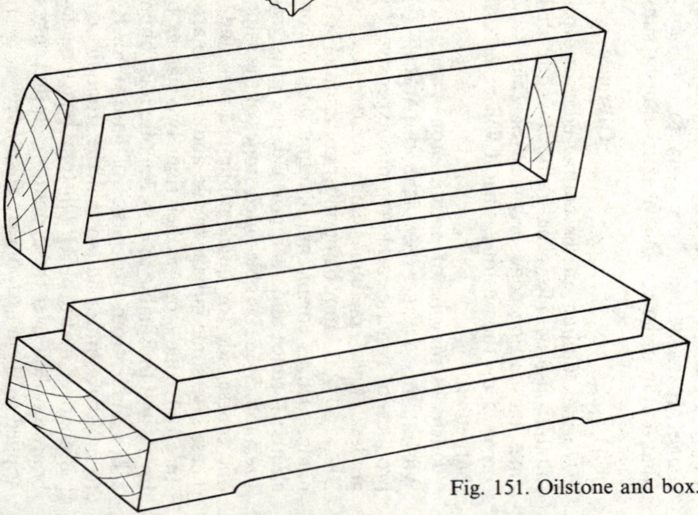

Fig. 151. Oilstone and box.

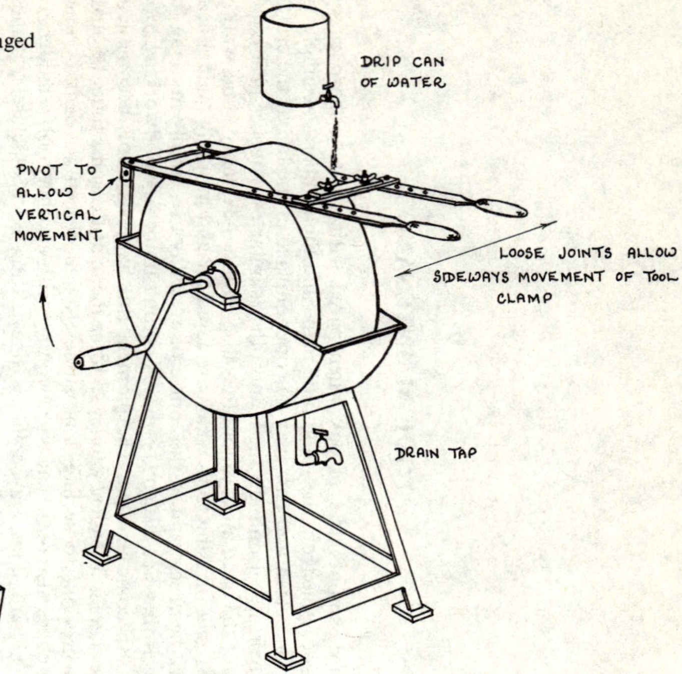

Fig. 152. A simple traditional grindstone.

Every effort should be made to ensure even wear of the stone so that edges produced on it are straight (more will be said about this later). The blade of any tool being sharpened, particularly narrow ones, should be moved evenly over the whole surface to avoid forming grooves. A very light oil should always be applied, which then floats away the tiny particles of metal and grit; this keeps the stone keen and prevents it from becoming choked. Occasionally it may be necessary to give the stone a thorough cleaning and the method is to wash it in paraffin or petrol and then allow to drain before putting it back into use. If at any time it is necessary to 'dress' the surface of a natural stone as a result of uneven wear, it should be inverted and rubbed level on a flat piece of sandstone lubricated with water. Alternatively, a paste of silver sand and water on a piece of heavy plate glass can be used.

Grindstones

Sharpening a cutting blade on the oilstone is referred to as **honing** or **whetting**, and the more frequently this is necessary the wider the sharpening bevel will become, until eventually the tool has to be reground. As might be expected, grindstones were originally of a natural quarried sandstone—York stone is a common example—and first of all were turned by hand or treadle (Fig. 152) then later motor-driven (Fig. 153). The tool being ground is kept cool and the particles of metal and grit washed away by water which drips on to it from a container supported above the stone. An adjustable clamp is used in which the blade of the tool is held near to the top of the stone, which is then rotated. The grindstone is supported by its axle above a trough, the sludge and water from which should be drained off immediately after use. Failure to do this results in the submerged part of the stone absorbing water, thereby becoming soft and consequently resulting in uneven wear. A big advantage of these grindstones is that they run slowly with little or no danger of overheating the tool and 'drawing the temper'. Movement of the tool across the stone prevents further uneven wear.

It is now quite common practice to use an electrically powered bench grinder (Fig. 153) in place of the traditional grindstone. These are usually double-ended, with fine and coarse wheels of materials similar to artificial oilstones. Grinding is done dry and quickly, and can easily result in the tool becoming overheated with resultant loss of hardness to the cutting edge. The thinner the edge of the tool becomes as grinding proceeds, the greater is the danger of this happening due to heat building up at the edge, where it will be observed as a blue discoloration. Unfortunately, this will result in the new edge being too soft to retain its sharpness when in use. Further careful grinding for quite some way further back may be necessary until the softened metal has been removed, which of course shortens the life of the tool. Precautions such as very light pressure and frequent dipping of the tool in a dashpot of water should be taken, and as long as the danger of 'burning' is kept in mind grinding wheels can be used very successfully, although they are basically a metalworker's machine.

Tool blades should be moved from side to side across the edge of the wheel so that all parts are ground evenly and the wheel kept true. At no time should the side of the wheel be used for grinding as this may cause bursting strains within it and subsequent danger to the user. Grinding machines must comply with the Abrasive Wheels Regulations 1970, some of the requirements of which are that: wheel guards should be constructed to contain the wheel in

Fig. 153. Double-ended bench grinding machine.

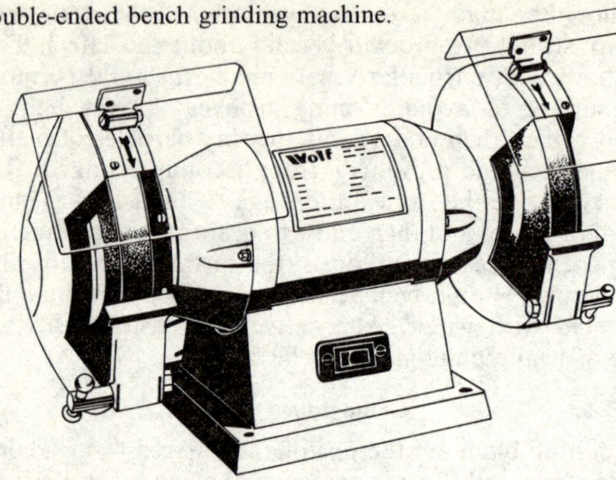

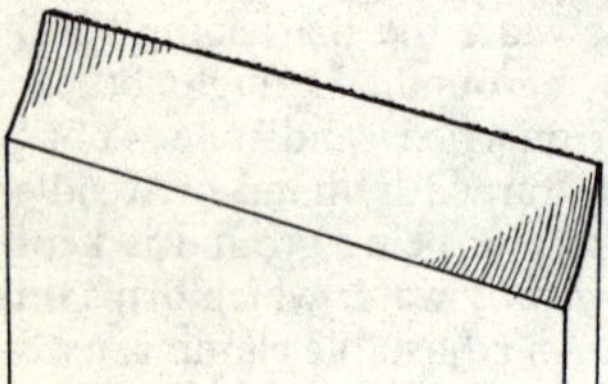

Fig. 154. A hollow-ground edge with small burr left from grinding.

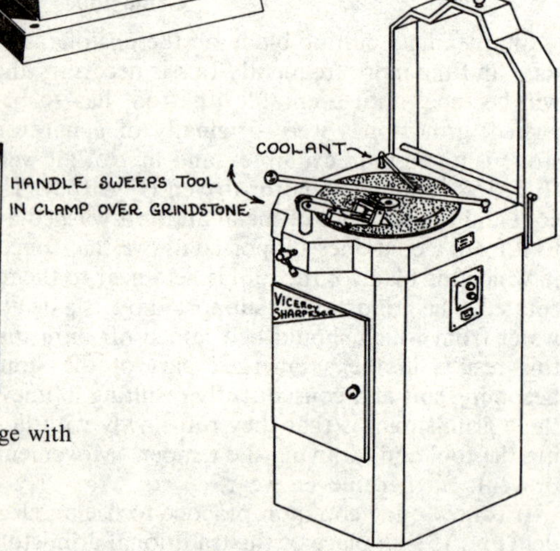

Fig. 155. The horizontal grinding machine.

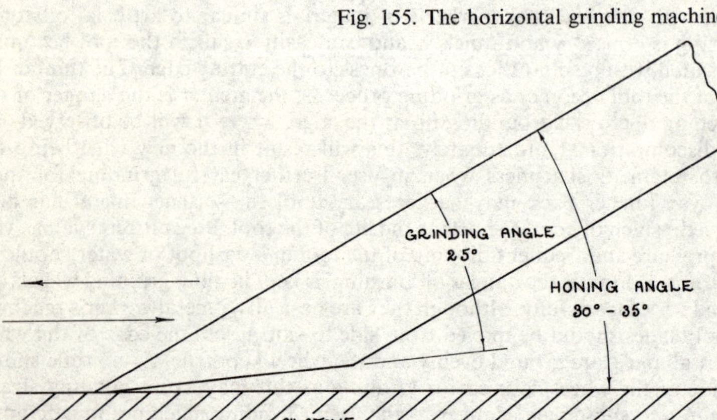

Fig. 156. General-purpose grinding and honing angles.

(a)

(b)

(a) Brush Box (*Tristania conferta*), Australia.

(c)

(b) Taking detailed diameter measurements of *Pinus radiata* (Australia). **(c)** Obtaining bark depth on *Pinus radiata* with the aid of a Swedish bark gauge. (All by permission of the Forestry and Timber Bureau, Australia)

Houses being constructed of *Pinus radiata*. (By permission of the Forestry and Timber Bureau, Australia)

Manufacture of laminated beams at Waipa Mill in Rotorua, New Zealand. The jig is seen on the right. In the centre is a beam just removed from the jig and on the left is a planed beam. (By permission of Ciba-Geigy (UK))

The arched beams of *Pinus radiata* in course of erection. (By permission of Ciba-Geigy (UK))

The rotunda represents symbolically the form and shape of a living tree. The arches and other laminated members are glued with Aerodux. (By permission of Ciba-Geigy (UK))

The completed rotunda. Construction of new laboratory buildings for the New Zealand Forest Research Institute at Rotorua. (By permission of Ciba-Geigy (UK))

Felling a giant African hardwood tree with a power saw. (By permission of United Africa Co.)

Veneer being peeled from a sapele log in a Nigerian mill. (By permission of United Africa Co.)

The six-skinned hull of Sir Francis Chichester's *Gipsy Moth IV* was bonded throughout with Aerodux 500. The boat, built by Camper & Nicholsons Ltd, withstood especially heavy seas during her famous round-the-world voyage—a proof of the excellent qualities of the adhesive. (By permission of Sun/Ciba-Geigy (UK))

Australian Blackbean wall panelling, the Clydesdale Bank, Lombard Street, London, by Messrs. William Mallinson & Sons.

Occasional tables in Burma teak. Note the different surface 'finishes'.

Coffee table in Burma teak.

The Ercol Windsor sideboard, length 1300 mm, depth 460 mm, height 760 mm. Made of solid English elm throughout, each sideboard is unique because of the beauty of the grain which is a record of the life of the original tree. (By permission of Ercol Furniture Ltd)

(a)

(b)

(c)

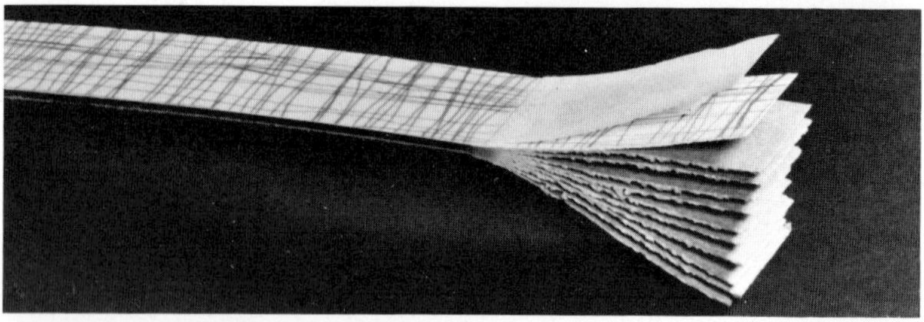

(d)

Fig. 157. Honing, flatting and stropping a plane blade.

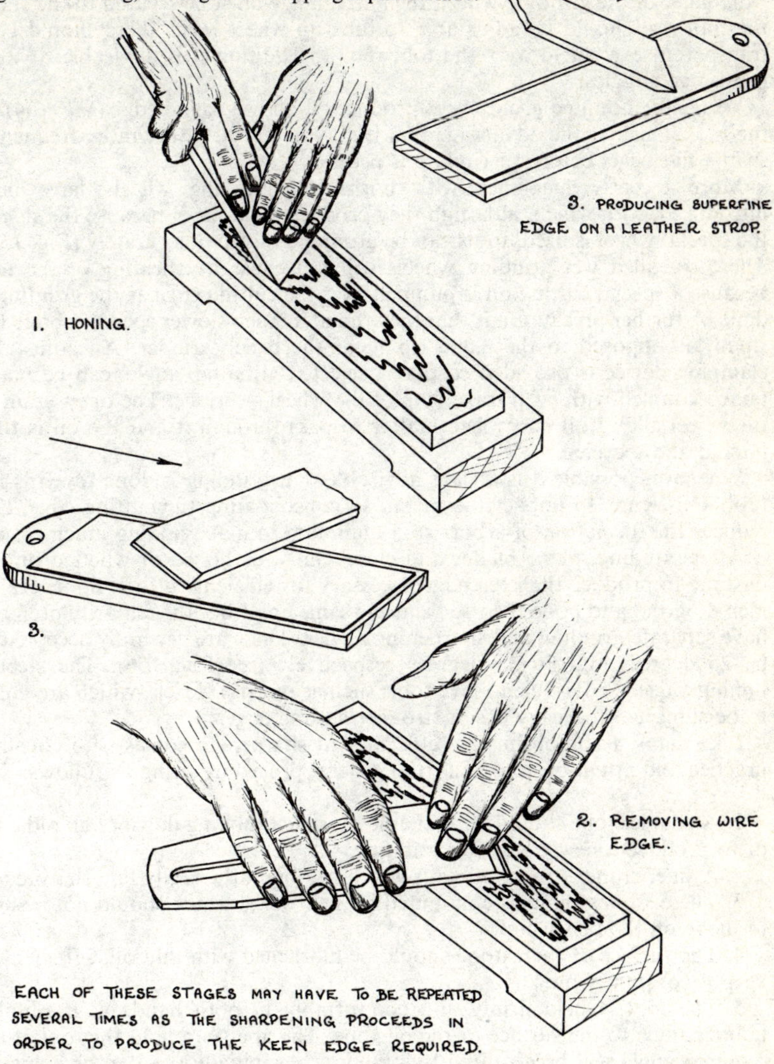

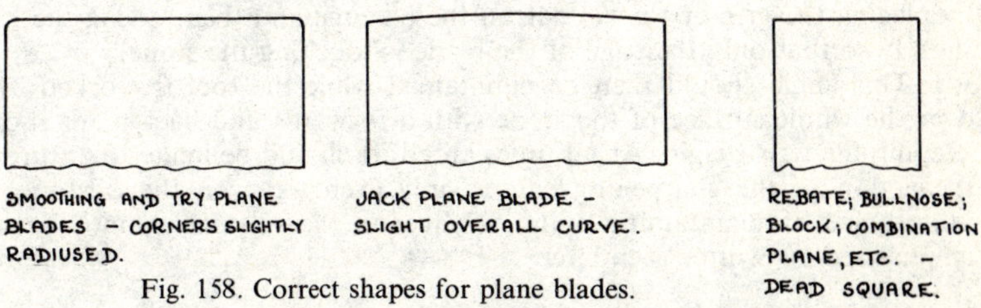

Fig. 158. Correct shapes for plane blades.

the event of it bursting; clamping flanges to be of equal diameter and at least $\frac{1}{3}$ diameter of the grinding wheel; the inner flange must be secured to the shaft; the tool rest should be adjustable to take up wheel wear; there should be a transparent eye shield over the tool rest. In addition it is advisable to wear protective goggles.

Vertically mounted grindstones produce a hollow ground edge (Fig. 154) on the tool. This has the advantage that it may be honed rather more frequently than a flat bevel before regrinding is necessary.

More recently machines with horizontal grinding wheels have been introduced, with which, although they produce a flat bevel because the side of the special wheel is used, tools can be ground easily and accurately (Fig. 155). These so-called wet grinding wheels will not cause overheating of the tool because a special cutting oil is pumped over the cutting edge as the grinding is done. A further precaution is that they run at a much slower speed—about 150 r.p.m. as opposed to the 3,000 r.p.m. of the bench grinder. An adjustable clamping device is provided so that a selected grinding 'angle' can be maintained coupled with even traversing of the wheel's surface. The open grain of the wheel allows oil and waste matter to pass through it and the oil is then filtered and recycled.

Whenever possible it is always advisable that grinding is done towards the tool. This tends to impact the metal, so consolidating the cutting edge, and reduces the formation of a burr to a minimum to make honing much easier.

After grinding, plane blades and chisels must be honed or whetted on the oilstone to produce the keen edge necessary for efficient cutting. Some craftsmen do grind and hone their tools at the same angle but the majority prefer to have separate grinding and sharpening angles. These are generally accepted to be 25 degrees and 30–35 degrees respectively (see Fig. 156). The steeper honing angle is advisable to give tools such as mortise chisels, which are going to be subjected to heavy use, a stronger cutting edge.

Like many accomplishments efficiency at sharpening comes with constant practice and attention to details, the general procedure being as follows:

1. A coarse stone should be available for quick rubbing down of an old edge or to produce a new edge after grinding.
2. A finer stone is required with which to obtain the really fine sharp edge.
3. These stones should be mounted in their boxes which should not be able to move on the bench top.
4. The surface of each stone should be lubricated with thin oil, sufficient to keep it constantly moist.
5. The tool is held firmly and comfortably in both hands at a suitable honing angle to the surface of the oilstone. The ability to hold the tool at the required angle will be acquired by practice, but initially this can be achieved by placing the grinding bevel flat on the oilstone and then raising the hands slightly so that only the edge of the blade is touching the stone.
6. This angle should then be maintained while the tool is worked evenly over the whole surface of the stone with a forwards and backwards motion, keeping the wrists rigid. At all times an effort should be made to ensure that the action of the sharpening causes only even wear on the oilstone. The importance of maintaining a flat surface on the oilstone cannot be overemphasised, as will be seen later.

7. As the honing proceeds any burr produced by grinding will be seen to double back towards the flat side of the tool. If an edge is simply being re-sharpened the oilstone will produce a smaller burr, the presence of which can be felt with the thumb; this also indicates that the tool has been whetted sufficiently.
8. The blade should now be turned flat side down and rubbed along the full length of the oilstone, turning the burr back again.
9. Honing and flatting in this way should now be repeated until the burr, which at this stage is sometimes referred to as a 'wire edge', is worn away or detaches itself from the tool.
10. The final edge can be obtained at this stage by light whetting on the fine stone, taking care not to produce another burr.
11. A superfine edge can be had by stropping the tool on leather charged with oil and a fine abrasive such as grinding paste or jeweller's rouge.
12. Wipe all oil and dirt from the oilstone.

It is possible to tell if an edge is sharp merely by looking at it. An edge which is still 'dull' or in which there are still small defects will reflect light. A really sharp edge cannot be seen by the naked eye—try it with a razor blade. As was stated previously, every effort should be made to keep the oilstone flat. This will be a tremendous help in the correct sharpening of chisels and the cutting irons of the rebate, block and combination planes, which must have a dead square cutting edge. Blades for the smoothing plane and try plane should also have a dead square cutting edge but the corners should be slightly radiused to prevent them leaving sharp edges on the wood when planing wide boards. The blade of the jackplane, which is used for quick preparation of timber, is slightly curved for rapid cutting.

The sharpening bevel of a **plane blade** may become rounded if the hands and wrists are not kept firm during the honing process. A parallel motion must be maintained in order to keep the bevel flat. Any rocking of the tool during honing will round the bevel, possibly to such an extent that the tool will not cut (see Fig. 159). If the oilstone becomes hollow along its length, it becomes difficult to preserve the flat backs of plane blades and chisels and this will impair their efficiency (see Fig. 160). It may result in the presence of a small gap between the cap iron and the plane blade in which small shavings collect, causing larger ones to choke the mouth. A **firmer chisel** will not cut accurately if the back is not flat as there is a tendency for it to be lifted away from the timber. In both cases the cutting angle is increased slightly, making the tools less efficient.

The **spokeshave**, **marking knife**, **block plane**, **shoulder plane**, **bullnose plane**, **rebate and combination planes** are all examples of tools which have simple blades that are generally ground and sharpened at the same angle. This is to give the cutting edge maximum strength in relation to the thinness or narrowness of the blade. The short blade for the metal spokeshave is particularly difficult to sharpen, and the normal practice is to make a wooden holder into which it can be fitted during honing (Fig. 161). Again care must be taken to ensure that the back of the blade for each of these tools is absolutely flat, and this again reflects the importance of keeping the oilstone flat.

Gouges are ground and sharpened to the same angles as chisels and plane blades but their curved section presents special problems. The scribing gouge

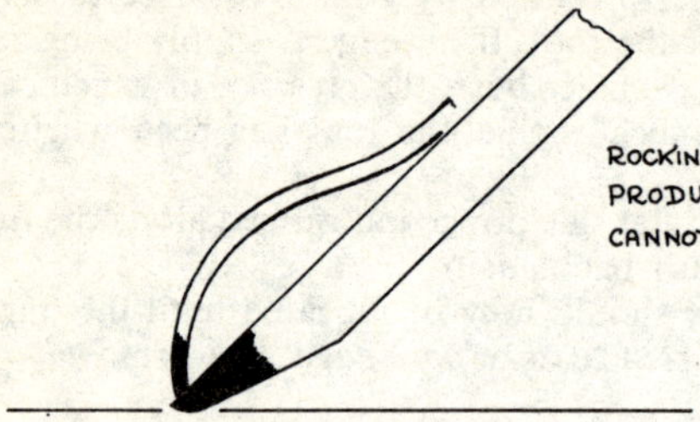

Fig. 159. Incorrect honing produces an inefficient cutting edge.

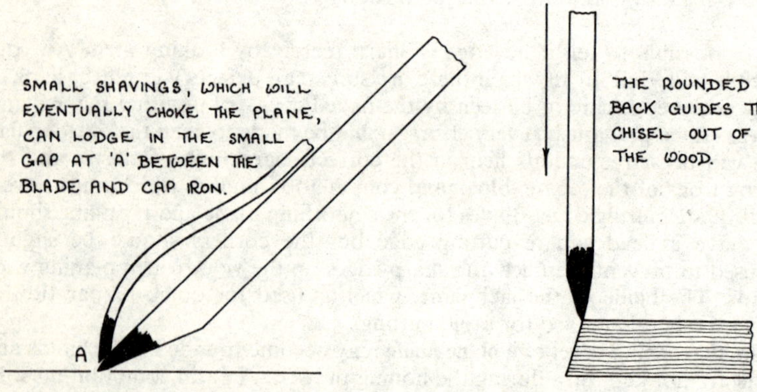

Fig. 160. Rounding effect on the backs of the blades if the oilstone is hollow.

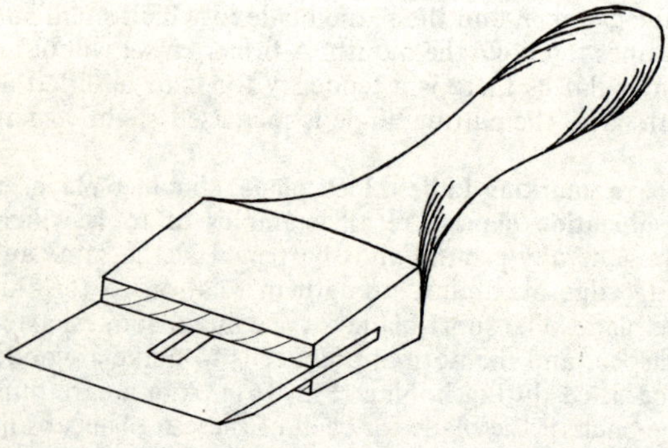

Fig. 161. Wooden holder for use when sharpening spokeshave blades.

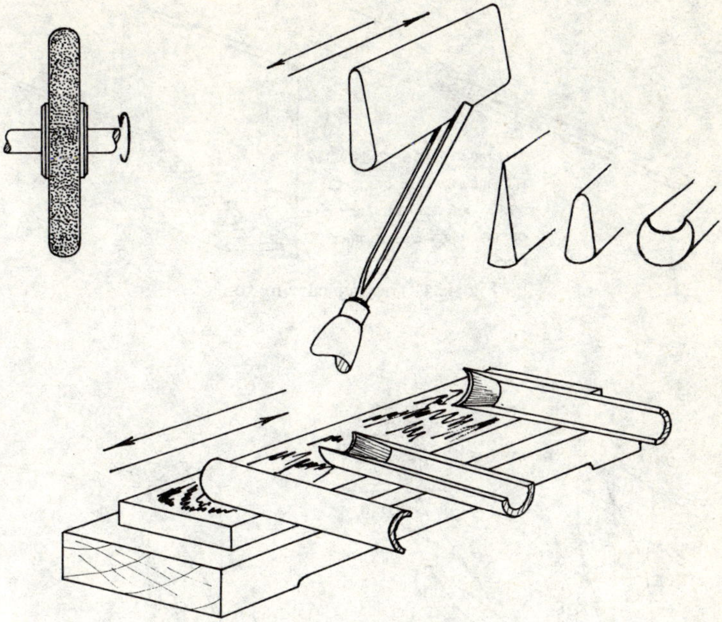

Fig. 162. Sharpening the scribing gouge.

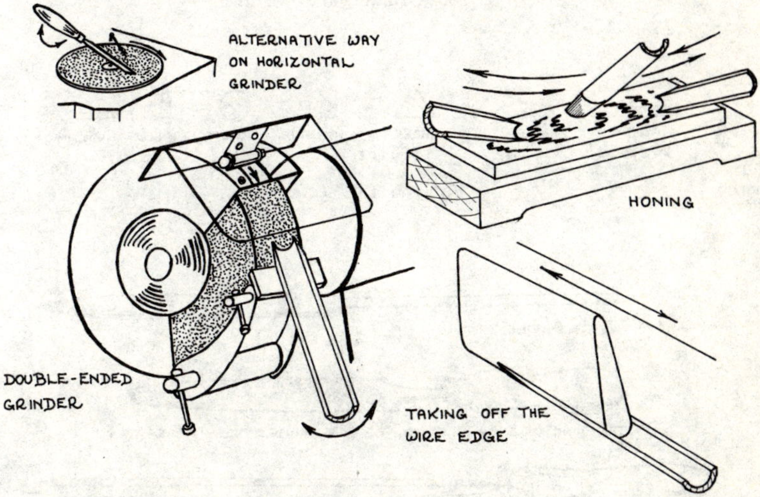

Fig. 163. Grinding and honing the firmer gouge.

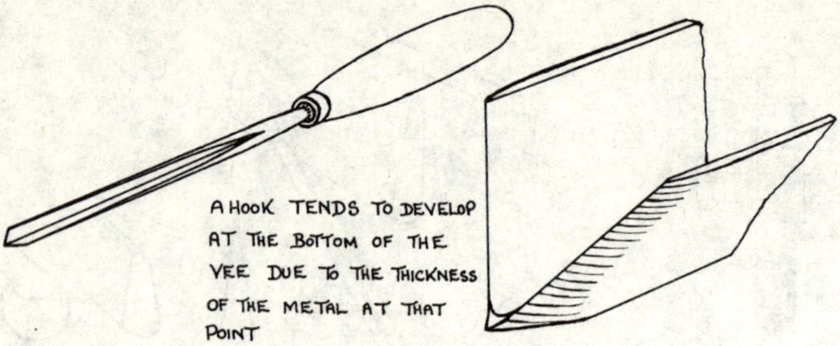

Fig. 164. The Vee carving tool.

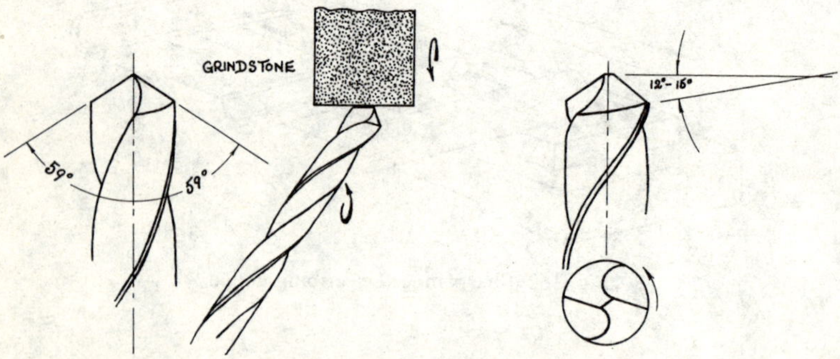

Fig. 165. Grinding the twist drill.

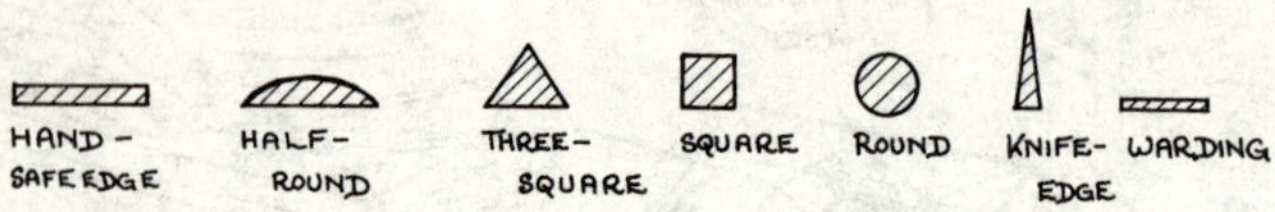

Fig. 166. File sections.

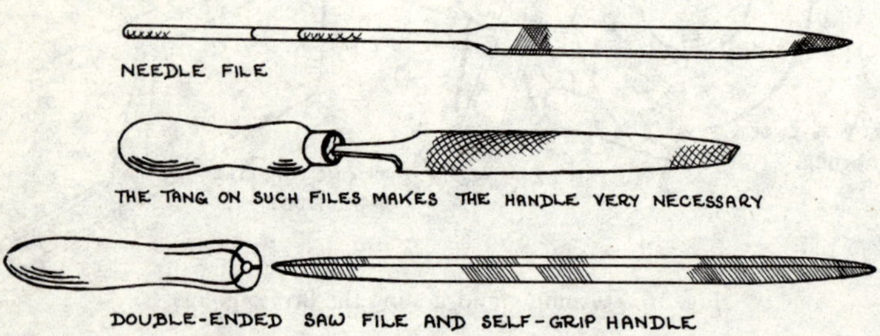

Fig. 167. Examples of the types of files used in sharpening.

can only be ground satisfactorily on its inner side on a grinding wheel with a convex edge. Honing is then completed on the inside with a round-edged oilstone slip, and care should be taken to maintain a constant angle along the whole of the curve as the slip is rubbed to and fro. The wire edge is then removed from the back of the gouge by holding it flat on the oilstone and gently rocking the gouge round as it is rubbed backwards and forwards along the stone (Fig. 162).

Grinding and sharpening the **firmer gouge** is rather the reverse (see Fig. 163). The outer bevel can be ground quite easily on the grindstone by turning it from side to side and then honing in a similar way on the oilstone. The wire edge is taken off on the inner face with the oilstone slip. Care should be taken in this case to hold the slip flat to the curve at all times.

Oilstone slips are manufactured in the same grades as artificial sharpening stones, in a wide range of sizes, and should be lubricated in the same way as an oilstone when in use.

Woodcarving tools are ground and sharpened in a similar way to gouges, but the **Vee tool** (Fig. 164) requires a knife-edge oilstone slip with which to backoff the inside of the Vee. This is a particularly difficult tool to sharpen as a small hook develops on the underside of the Vee which for efficient cutting must be removed by working on the outside with the oilstone and inside with the slip. As a whole, carving tools are quite unique in that some craftsmen prefer to sharpen them with a bevel on both sides, the inner being about one quarter of the outer. A fine-grade stone should always be used, finishing off by stropping from both sides. Grinding and sharpening angles are lower than normal to give an easier cut.

Twist drills, **wood boring bits** and **augers**, in common with all woodworking tools, require to be sharpened from time to time. The twist drill, which is basically a metalworking tool, now enjoys equal favour with the woodworker. Because of its extreme hardness, sharpening is done on the grinding wheel, care being taken not to overheat the metal. The cutting edges are held in turn across the edge of the wheel and the drill lifted with a rocking action against the direction of rotation. This sharpens the edge and in turn 'backs it off' to give clearance to the cutting edges. Skill is required to ensure that the web between the cutting edges is kept as short as possible and that the lips are of equal length (Fig. 165).

Other wood-boring tools are generally of a softer nature, designed for cutting wood only at a low speed. These are sharpened with fine-toothed files of suitable sections appropriate to the shape of the bit (Fig. 166). Jeweller's needle files are small, keen and self-handled, making them most suitable for filing in restricted places and difficult corners on the smaller sized bits. Larger metalworking files are more appropriate for heavier filing on larger sizes. On no account should a file ever be used without a handle due to the danger of the tang injuring the palm of the hand. Special three square files which are double or single ended are used for saw sharpening.

In sharpening any drilling tool the original outer diameter must always be strictly maintained to prevent any possibility of the tool binding in the hole being drilled. For example, the spur of a plain or fast cutting centre bit should never be sharpened on the outer side. If this was done clearance would be lost and the bit would tend to drill an undersized hole. If this happens with an auger bit there would be a positive danger of it binding in the hole as it

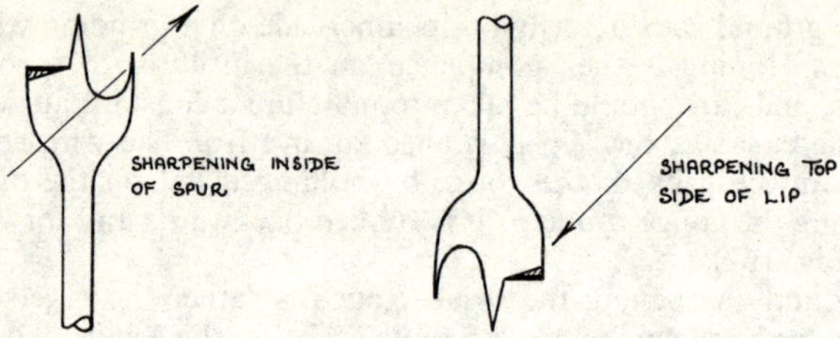

Fig. 168. Sharpening the centre bit to avoid reducing the overall diameter.

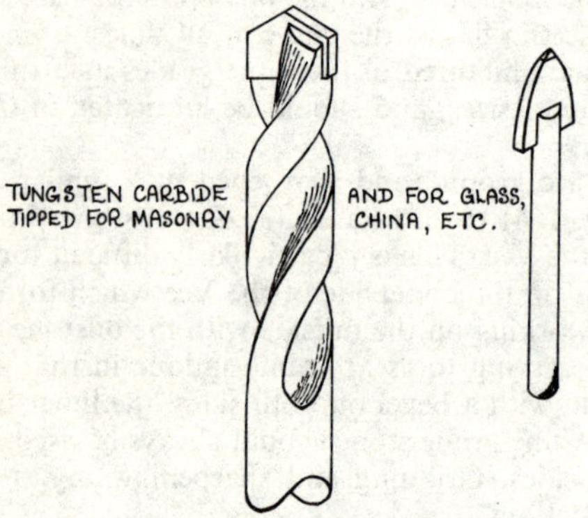

Fig. 169. Special drills.

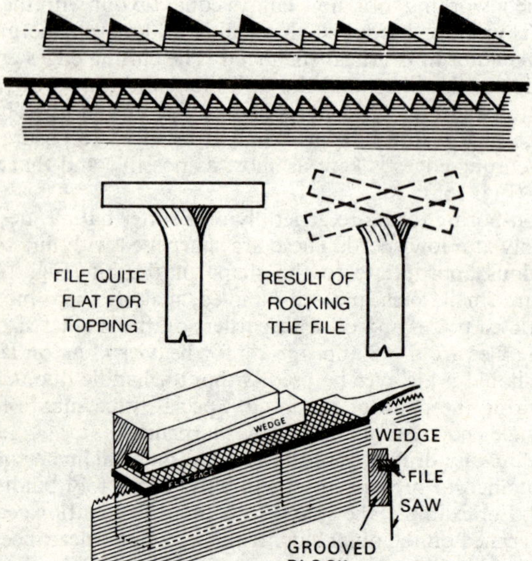

Fig. 170. 'Topping' saw teeth.

penetrated deeper. Spurs then must be sharpened on the inside only (see Fig. 168).

Masonry drills with tungsten carbide tips are ground in a similar way to the twist drill on special grinding wheels of silicon carbide green grit, grade 80.

Woodworking saws in everyday use in the workshop are for sawing across the grain of the wood (i.e. crosscuts) or with the grain (rip-saws). Saw maintenance comes under four headings: topping, shaping, setting and sharpening. When saw teeth are worn, or badly sharpened so that they are at different heights, they require 'topping' (Fig. 170); in other words, they are levelled by running a 10 inch second-cut flat file along the saw as it is held in a saw vice. The teeth are then filed to shape giving them a uniform pitch with a suitable saw file (Fig. 171). To prevent the file from becoming badly worn the width of each face of the file should be a little more than twice the depth of the teeth. The pitch is the angle at which the leading edge of the tooth leans forward—as much as 14 degrees for a crosscut but only 3 degrees for a rip-saw. When the shaping is complete any flats formed on the teeth by topping will have been removed and each tooth brought to a point. No bevels are cut on the teeth at this stage. The range of saw points (inclusive) per inch is: 5 (rip), 6, 7–8, 10–12. Taper saw files are used in lengths of 250, 178 and 150 mm.

Setting (Fig. 172) will produce a saw kerf just wide enough to clear the blade—approximately 1½ times its thickness. Saw manufacturers employ skilled men who set down alternate teeth along the whole length of the blade using a fine cross-peined hammer with the saw held on a bevelled anvil. The saw is then turned over and the remaining teeth are set. At school and at home the usual practice is to use a plier-type saw set. Care must be taken to have a uniform set along each side so that the saw cuts accurately. Slight irregularities of set can be rubbed down by running an oilstone slip along each side as the saw is laid flat on the bench.

The final sharpening depends upon whether the saw is crosscut or rip. For **crosscuts** (Fig. 173) each tooth must be bevelled with the file to produce knife edges on the outer side which will sever the fibres of the wood. The saw is held in the saw vice, handle to the right and teeth protruding 6 mm. The saw is then 'topped' again very lightly to put a very small 'flat' on each tooth. Place the file to cut on the leading edge of the first tooth set towards you (A in Fig. 173). The file will then cut on the back edge of the tooth to its left, this being set away. The file handle is then moved to the left making an angle of 65–75 degrees with the line of the saw blade. This angle must now be maintained and each alternate tooth given two or three steady strokes of the file until half of the small 'flat' is removed from each. When the full length of the saw has been done it must be turned in the saw vice, the file swung this time to the right at 65–75 degrees so that filing is again done towards the handle. Sharpening now begins once more on the front edge of the first tooth (B in Fig. 173) set towards you—i.e. of those teeth not previously sharpened—and is completed throughout the length of the saw removing the other part of the small 'flat' on each tooth.

The **tenon saw** has much smaller teeth but these too are sharpened in just the same way as for the crosscut handsaw, using a file of appropriate size. The blade of the tenon saw is 'backed' to keep the cutting edge perfectly straight for accurate cutting of joints, etc., at the bench. If by chance the blade does

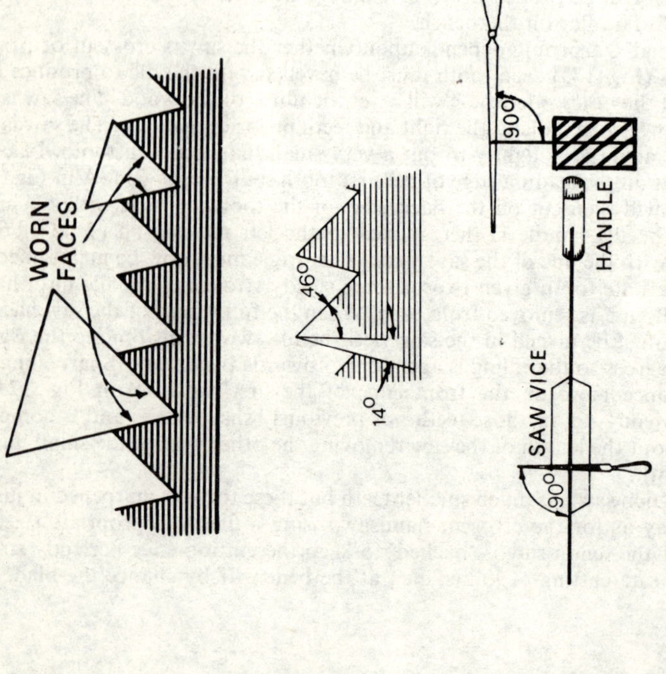

Fig. 171. Filing saw teeth to shape and with correct pitch.

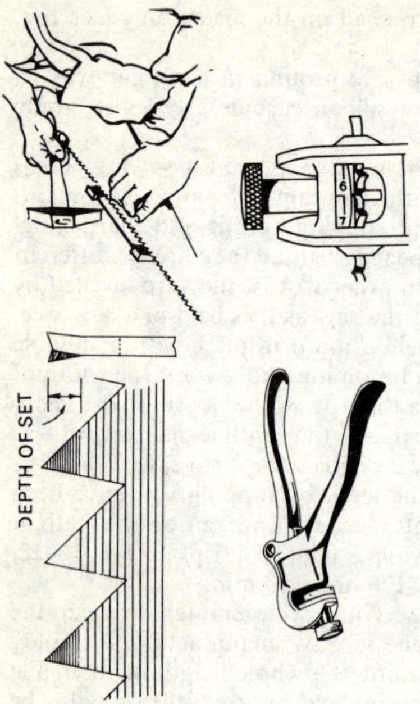

Fig. 172. Setting saw teeth.

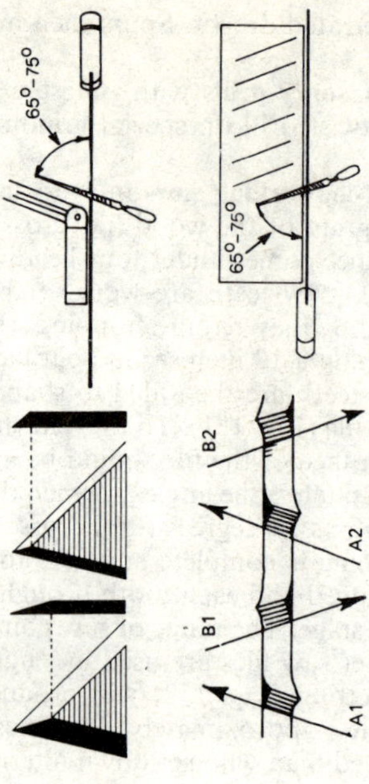

Fig. 173. Sharpening cross-cut teeth.

become distorted it can be trued by striking the back gently at A or B (Fig. 174) while the saw is supported on a flat piece of timber.

Rip-saw teeth must be filed to produce chisel edges which cut along the fibres of the wood. The saw is held in the saw vice, the teeth lightly topped but on this occasion the file is held horizontally for the whole process (see Fig. 175). Each alternate gullet is filed, the saw reversed and the intermediate teeth which were missed previously are now sharpened. Side dressing the saw with an oilstone slip will remove any burrs from the teeth.

For really fine finishing on hardwoods, **cabinet scrapers** will improve on the surface produced by the smoothing plane. Even the most difficult timbers with interlocking or curly grain, or where the flow of the grain is destroyed by knots, can be scraped smooth with these most simple tools. They are made in two shapes of varying sizes from cold-rolled high carbon steel about 0·80 mm thick (Fig. 176). It is important to know how the scraper is used in order to appreciate how it should be sharpened. The edge of the scraper has to be burred over, producing a tiny sharp edge. This edge is then applied to the wood, the scraper slightly inclined forward at its top edge and forward pressure applied to the middle of the scraper. As it is pushed along the timber in this way the burr removes fine shavings, leaving a very smooth surface (Fig. 177).

To sharpen the scraper, the edges must first of all be made straight and square. This is done by draw-filing with a smooth file, holding the scraper in the vice; at the same time the corners should be slightly radiused (Fig. 178). The edges should now be honed on a fine stone (Fig. 179). Lubricant should be applied to the side of the oilstone and the scraper slipped in between the lid and base of the oilstone box. Holding them closely together in one hand, the scraper is rubbed backwards and forwards with the other. Any burr so formed is then removed by rubbing the scraper sides on the flat of the oilstone.

A burnishing tool or 'ticketer' (see Fig. 180) is used to draw out the edge of the scraper, which should be laid flat on the bench top, held down with the thumb and fingers outstretched and the burnisher drawn firmly along three or four times. This must be repeated for both corners of each edge. To form the burr the scraper can now be held in the vice or either vertically or horizontally on the bench. Practice will soon determine the easiest method. The edges are turned back with the ticketer at an angle of 80–85 degrees (Fig. 181). This angle is gradually obtained by slightly changing the position of the burnisher with each stroke, although some craftsmen advocate that this should be done by one stroke only. A little lubricant should be applied to the ticketer on each occasion it is used. As the burrs become 'dulled' it is possible to restore them several times by repeating the burnishing, first of all flatting and then turning back the burr. Eventually this will cease to be effective and the scraper must be filed and honed once more. Curved scrapers are sharpened in a similar way but the honing of the edge is done with an oilstone slip.

The blade of the **scraper plane** is ground and honed at 45 degrees rather like a spokeshave blade (Fig. 182). It is then placed in the vice and burnished so that a burr is gradually turned over towards its flat side.

The **Skarsten scraper** (Fig. 183) has patented replaceable blades which fit into a combined holder and handle and are sharpened with a dead smooth file. A toothing cutter is also supplied which is useful for preparing ground work to be veneered.

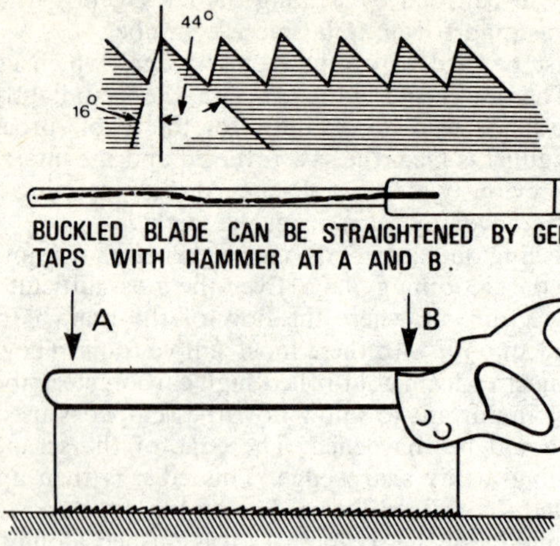

Fig. 174. Tenon saw: correcting distortion.

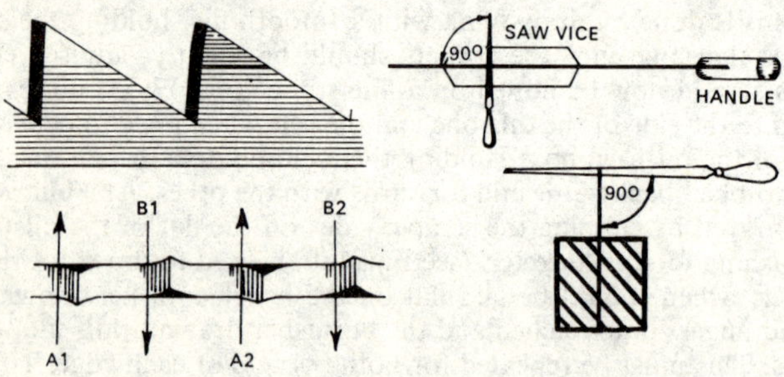

Fig. 175. Sharpening ripping teeth.

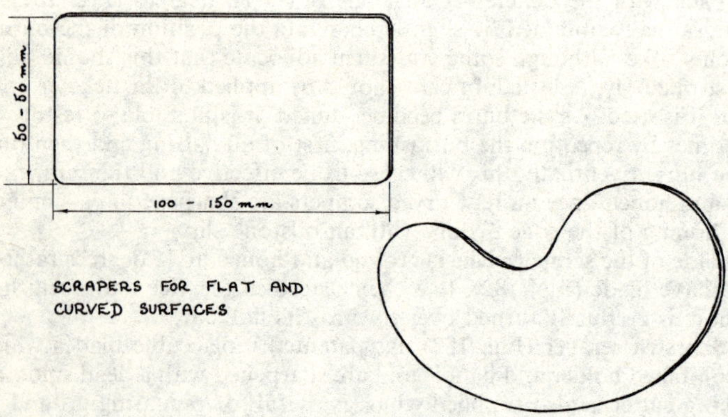

Fig. 176. Cabinet scrapers.

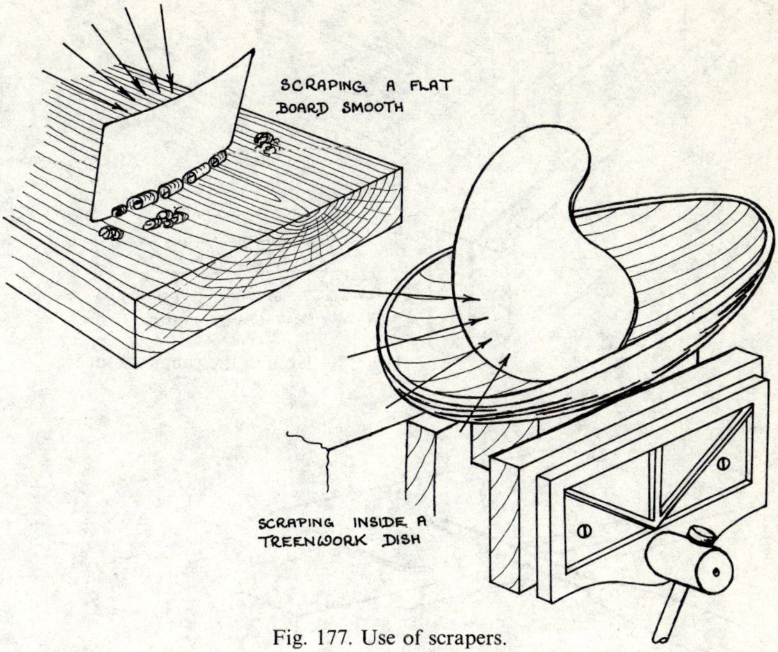

Fig. 177. Use of scrapers.

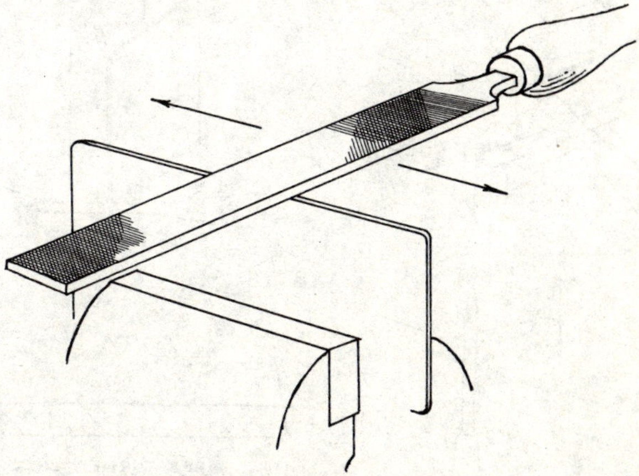

Fig. 178. Draw-filing.

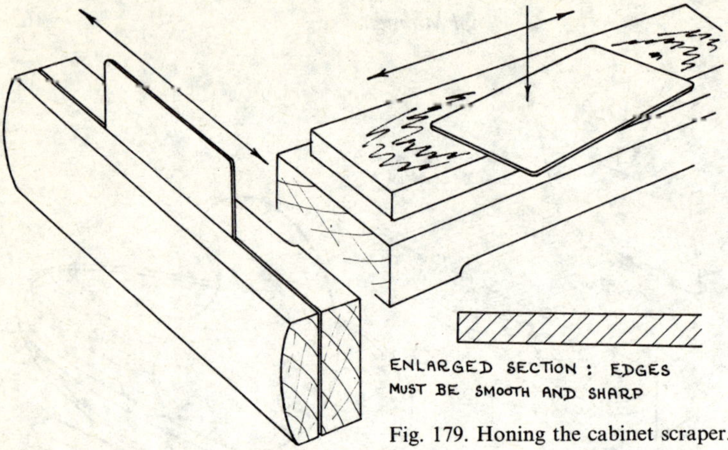

Fig. 179. Honing the cabinet scraper.

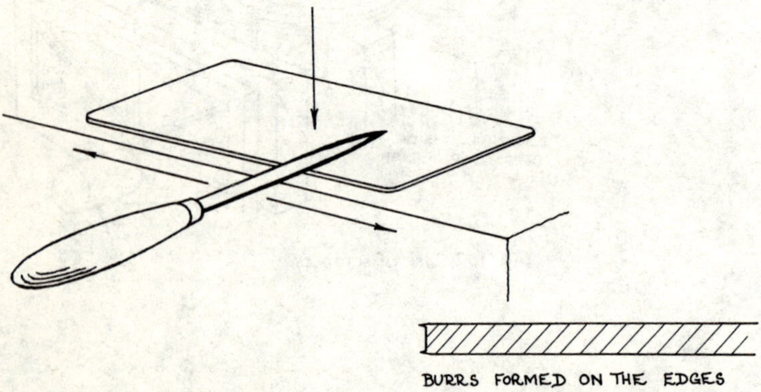

Fig. 180. Forming the burrs with the ticketer.

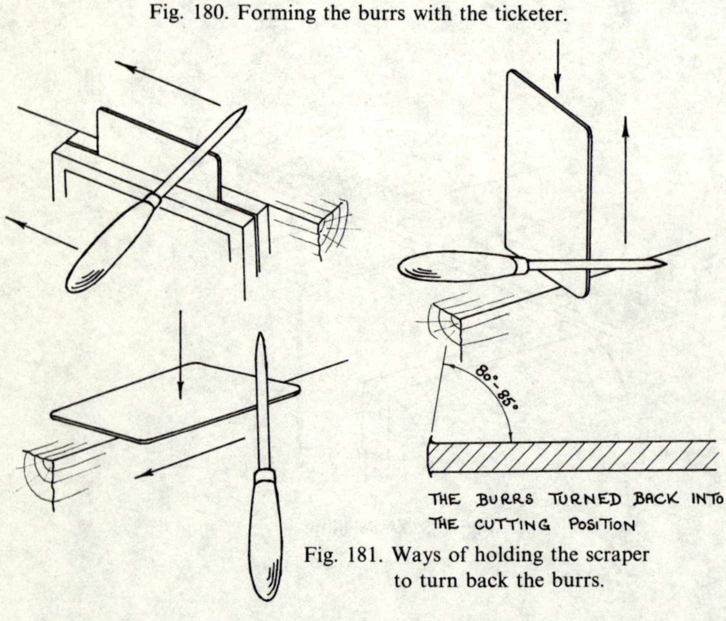

Fig. 181. Ways of holding the scraper to turn back the burrs.

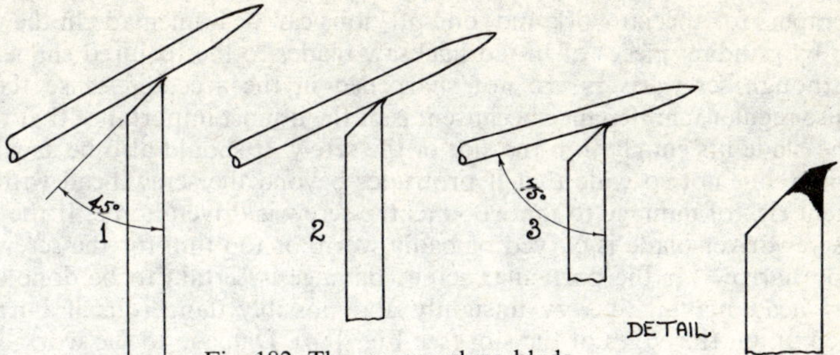

Fig. 182. The scraper plane blade.

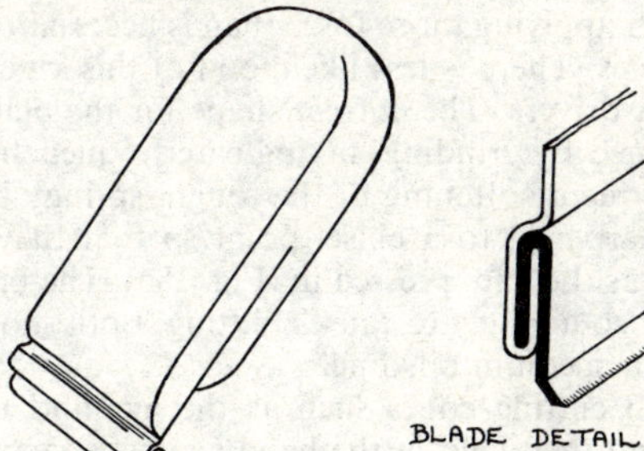

Fig. 183. The skarsten scraper.

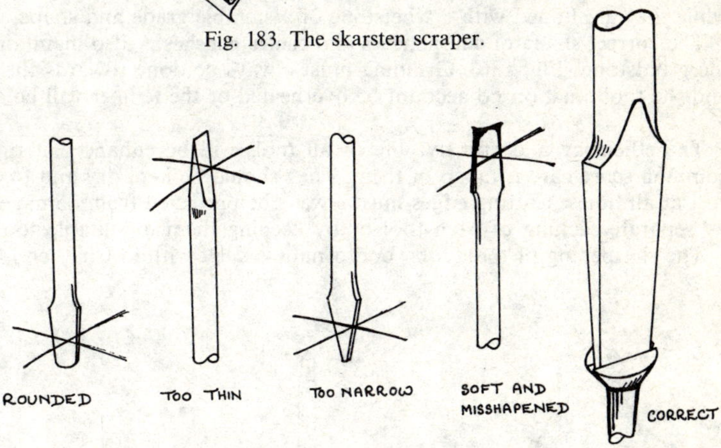

Fig. 184. Bad screwdriver blades will not turn the screw effectively; they will damage the screw head and possibly the wood as well.

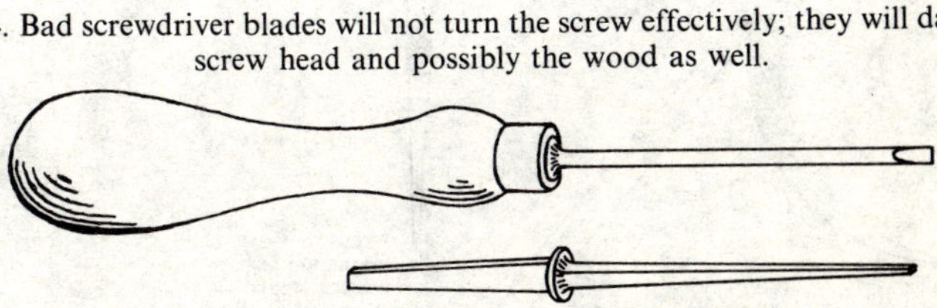

Fig. 185. Bradawl blades.

Scrapers for special work and 'one-off' jobs can be homemade in the workshop by grinding pieces of broad hacksaw blades to the required shape.

Although **screwdrivers** are not sharpened in the accepted sense they do require regular maintenance because it is of the utmost importance that the tip of the blade fits snugly into the slot of the screw. It should also be as wide as possible, but not so wide that it protrudes beyond the screw head with consequent risk of damage to the wood as the screw is driven home. If the tip of the screwdriver blade is curved or badly worn, or too thin for the screw slot, or too narrow for the particular screw, damage is certain to be done to the screw head making it very unsightly and possibly dangerous if burrs are turned up on the edges of the slot (see Fig. 184). Damage to the work, which might be in an almost finished state, is equally certain to happen if the screwdriver slips through applying more force than is necessary in an effort to make up for its deficiencies. There is less likelihood of this kind of thing happening with Pozidriv screwdrivers. The correct shape for the plain screwdriver blade should be maintained by grinding, taking care to quench frequently to avoid burning and subsequent softening of the tough, springy blade.

Bradawls are sharpened to a chisel point so that they will cut across the fibres of the wood as they are pressed in (Fig. 185). The birdcage awl, being of square section, is also unlikely to cause splitting. Both should be sharpened on a fine grindstone or medium oilstone.

Large tools with cutting edges such as the **axe** and the **adze** are ground when necessary, and then held in the hand against some appropriate support while they are honed with a whetstone of a suitable grade and shape.

The correct shape of **nail punches** and **centre punches** is also maintained on the grindstone (Fig. 186). Grinding must always be done towards the point, and the tool must on no account be overheated or the temper will be drawn.

The efficiency and effective life of all tools will be enhanced if ordinary common-sense care is taken of them. They should be kept dry and free from rust at all times. Cutting edges must always be protected from damage either by separate racking of each tool or by keeping them in suitable tool rolls.

The sharpening of tools for woodturning is dealt with in Chapter 14.

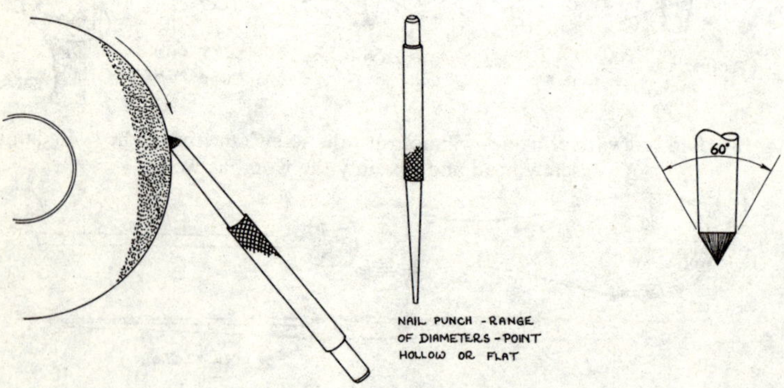

Fig. 186. Grinding punches.

7

SAFETY IN THE WORKSHOP

Quite rightly more attention than ever before is being given to the physical safety of the individual engaged in practical work. This need for increased care is acknowledged at government level and by professional and industrial organisations. Possible hazards and safety precautions to be taken are now more than ever clearly displayed on many products and it would be quite irresponsible for the user to ignore these.

Furthermore, by the development of modern materials and modern techniques, many of which have created their own technologies, a much wider range of creative materials is now available to schools, colleges and craftsmen in general, whether they are in industry or working at home during leisure time. Each new material and new technique demands a thorough knowledge of the special requirements necessary to work them satisfactorily, albeit perhaps only a comparatively simple matter of how to cut them correctly, or perhaps the need to use a particular grade of adhesive. Many of these modern products are commonly used and accepted as being part of woodworking and the user should make himself aware of any attendant hazards in using them. For example, **aerosol paint sprays** should not be used near exposed flames or in confined areas, nor should they be stored in hot rooms or in direct sunlight, nor the tins punctured or burnt because of the risk of explosion.

Glass fibre can irritate the skin tremendously and should be washed off under running water. There should be no attempt to rub it off or the fibres may penetrate the skin. The solvent, or thinner, normally used for glass fibre work is **styrene**, the evaporation of which constitutes a toxic hazard which affects the eyes. As styrene fumes are liberated into the air during the production of GRP articles, good ventilation is necessary, bearing in mind that the evaporation rate is greater in hot weather.

Modern **synthetic resin glues** which are in frequent use can cause dermatitis and a wet cloth should be applied frequently to prevent glue from setting on the hands. Use of rubber gloves or a suitable barrier cream may be advisable.

In order to bond together some of the exotic hardwoods now in use, or to make the best use of modern epoxy resin glues to bond metal to wood, it is essential to degrease thoroughly both the metal and the timber. It is advised that 1.1.1-**trichloroethane** should be used for this purpose, as it is the least toxic of the chlorinated hydrocarbons. To avoid the corrosion of metals, and in particular aluminium and its alloys, the grade known as 'inhibited' should be used. This is marketed by ICI as **Genklene**.

Dust from timbers such as mansonia, opepe and teak may produce skin irritation or irritation of the nasal and upper respiratory passages in some people. If such conditions occur in industry it may be necessary to use extractor fans; where their use would be more limited at school or in the home, wear a simple dust respirator. Similarly, face shields and goggles of various descriptions should be worn to protect the face and eyes where there is any danger from **flying particles** of wood, metal, building materials, **irritant vapours** or **chemical splashes**.

It is known that **asbestos dust** can cause lung diseases and there are strict regulations governing the manufacture and commercial use of asbestos products. As a precaution you are advised to avoid creating and breathing asbestos dust. The safest way to do this when using asbestos products is to follow a few simple rules.

1. Damp the work; wet dust does not become airborne and is not inhaled. For instance, do not sand wall-plugging compounds unless damped.
2. Damp any dust which falls to the floor and pick up as soon as possible, preferably with a vacuum cleaner equipped with a disposable inner bag.
3. Work in a well ventilated space, if possible outdoors, when sawing, drilling, filing or sanding.
4. Use hand saws and drills, which produce less dust than power tools.

The above gives some indication of a topic which has never been neglected, but which is now being given the thorough consideration which it deserves, both at school and in industry. The person who is now most vulnerable is the home craftsman, since there is no one but himself to impose safety regulations upon him. A particularly disturbing aspect of industrial accidents is the number which occur to young people under eighteen, often in the early weeks of their first employment; it will thus be realised that safety education is an essential part of the work of the school. There must be safety rules applied within each workshop and the reasons for them should be explained so that students work sensibly and safely in pursuing their craftwork.

There must be a **First Aid Box** which should be easily accessible in every workshop, and should include at least scissors, various bandages, triangular bandage to use as a sling,. adhesive plasters, sterilised cotton wool, sterilised gauze, antiseptic cream, safety pins and an eye bath.

Suitable **workshop dress** is essential and the use of an apron very necessary. This must be in good condition as loose tapes or torn material can be a source of danger. Jackets should be removed, shirt-sleeves rolled up and ties removed or made secure. Strong footwear to protect the feet from tools or timber dropped accidentally, or chemical splashes, is also very important. In particular the protection of eyes should be regarded as part of the normal procedure. Long hair must be held back out of the eyes for all workshop activities so as not to obscure vision, and to be clear of the moving parts of machines.

There are many obviously potential sources of danger to be guarded against when using **machines**, among which the following can be included:

Sharp edges on machines, equipment, material in stock, cutting tools, saws, etc.

Closing movements on hand tools and machines where skin or clothing may be nipped.

Rotating parts of machines and hand tools which can draw in clothing, hair, fingers, etc.

Uncontrolled sources of heat, sparks, fumes and dust should be avoided. **Fire extinguishers** should be easily accessible. The student should be aware of, and guard against the potential dangers of chemicals, solvents, petroleum, mixtures, bleaches, synthetic resins, degreasing agents, etc.

Hand tools are less dangerous if they are well maintained. For example, a chisel which has to be forced through the wood to produce a cut is more likely to cause an injury than one which is functioning normally, and the same can be said of saws and planes. All tools must be used correctly and serviced regularly so that hazards such as loose hammer heads, loose file handles, dangerous burrs, worn bench stops and bench hooks are avoided.

The ends of **wall drills** and **cold chisels** are inclined to mushroom over as a result of hammering. The ragged edge so formed can result in unpleasant cuts to the hand holding the tool or even more serious injuries if the mushrooming is allowed to become so bad that pieces of metal chip off under the force of hammer blows. In these circumstances they are a particular danger to the eyes. This danger should be averted by grinding off any such burrs each time the tool is sharpened. Similarly, the hardened faces of **hammers** should never be struck together due to the danger of flying chips of metal which may be spelched off their edges.

The **pedestal drill** and the **wood-turning lathe** are the machines in most frequent use and students should be competent to operate them safely before being allowed to work unsupervised. They must be familiar with the controls, and fully conversant with the correct use of tool-holding methods and work-holding devices. Chuck keys must always be removed when not in use. The use of guards and any other safety features must be observed. There must be adequate working space around the machine and the floor must be level, free from obstructions and in a non-slip condition.

Only one person at a time should be at any one machine and should not be engaged in unnecessary conversation with others. The work is demanding and concentration upon it is essential. Moving work or moving parts of machines should never be handled before they have stopped, and adjustment to machines should never be made until they have been electrically isolated.

Further observations on the safe use of the **lathe** are to be found in Chapter 14, dealing with woodturning, and of the **drill** in Chapter 5.

Any **electrical faults** which occur are a great danger as they may result in electric shocks or interrupt the safe operation of a machine. Everyone should be aware of the position of the emergency stop buttons within the workshop. It must be properly understood that these are to be used only in case of an emergency. Wrong use may result in an emergency.

Lighting must be adequate for work at the bench or close work on machines. Dazzling glare from reflections should be avoided; this can be distracting and create errors of judgement in the use of both hand tools and machines, leading to faulty workmanship or resulting in accidents.

Safety precautions related to **electrically powered hand tools** are detailed in Chapter 5. It is sufficient to say here that for basic school use such tools should be of the single-purpose type operating on 110 volts. The use of woodworking attachments to drills is undesirable in schools, although the situation might be quite the reverse in the home workshop, where work may well be restricted to only the owner of the machines.

In all cases the length of flexible extension cables should be kept to a minimum, and temporary or makeshift connections avoided at all times.

For advice on safety in greater detail the reader is referred to the Royal Society for the Prevention of Accidents, *Safety in Practical Departments*, Department of Education and Science, D.E.S. Safety Series No. 3, and BS 4163: *Recommendations for Safety in Workshops of Schools and Colleges of Education*.

At the time of writing, following the Robens Report, the Government has published the Health and Safety at Work Act, which has two main sections: One, dealing with specific regulations regarding processes and machines at work, and Two, with the employer's responsibility for the health, safety and welfare of employees. It may eventually have very far-reaching effects.

8

CONSTRUCTIONS

Early forms of chest were produced by hollowing out logs with part of the log forming the lid (Fig. 187*a*). At that time chests were the main pieces of furniture a family possessed in which to keep their belongings. It is probable that the masons of the period made such chests as these, which were by their very nature both heavy and cumbersome and very difficult to hew out with the primitive tools available. Gradually they were replaced by chests made of slabs of hand-sawn timber nailed together and often reinforced by iron bands—the product of the carpenter and blacksmith (Fig. 187*b*). At this period the lids were hinged on large staples one through the other. Made in this way, the chests were very much lighter in comparison, easier to construct and more economical in the use of timber. The improved design, however, still proved unsatisfactory as the large slabs of timber were very unstable due to expansion and contraction as their moisture content varied with changes in the atmosphere. The most skilled carpenters became aware of this characteristic of timber and its other physical properties, realising that smaller pieces of wood were much more stable. Eventually these joiners, as they had come to be known, designed light frameworks joined together by pegged mortise and tenon joints. The frames were grooved to carry a number of small panels which were free to expand and contract within the grooves. These constructions replaced the slabs as the sides and ends of chests, producing a more serviceable piece of furniture which became much more elegant as the frames were often beaded and the panels carved.

From these early designs other pieces of furniture evolved, made by cabinet-makers whose improved skill was further assisted by an increased number of better designed tools. The gradually improved design of the chest, which resulted in the construction of **flat frames**, led also to two other clearly defined types of 'construction': namely, the **stool or table** and the **box or carcase**.

At present, due to the problems of world supply and demand and of economics, ever-increasing use is being made of manufactured boards. These are completely stable and not subject to the disadvantages of 'solid' timber, but because of their characteristics have necessitated the development of a whole new range of jointing techniques. Many of these techniques fall into the category of knock-down fittings (see Chapter 11) and it is interesting to reflect that the wheel has now virtually turned a full circle so that modern slab constructions closely resemble the slab constructions of the early chests.

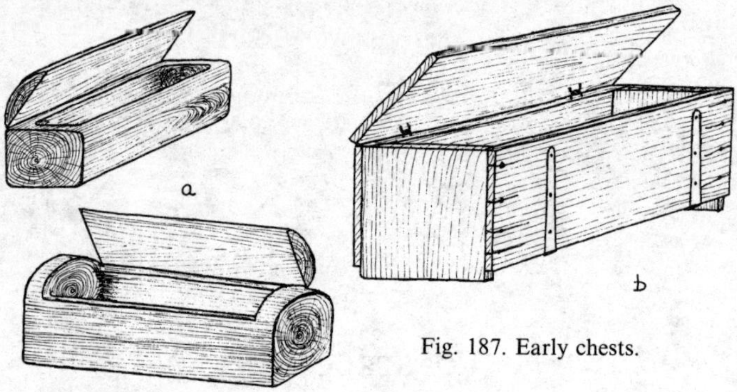

Fig. 187. Early chests.

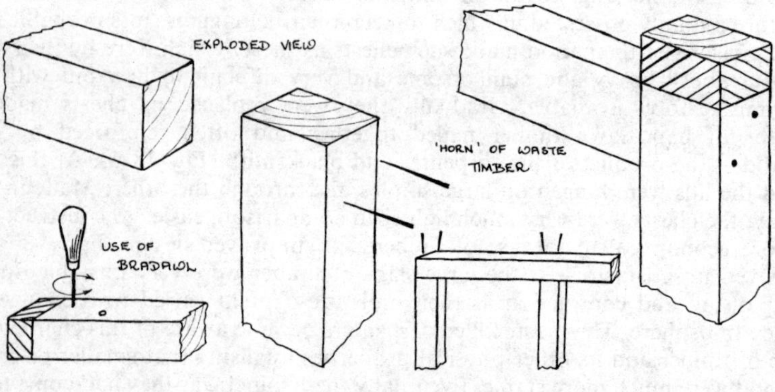

Fig. 188. Nailed butt joint.

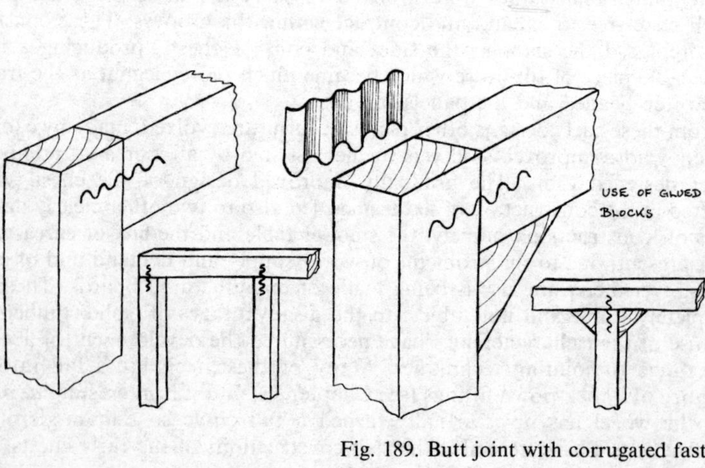

Fig. 189. Butt joint with corrugated fastener.

Flat Frame Joints for Stool and Table Constructions

Butt Joint

The ends of the cross members of the frame must be carefully cut square, and in practice a horn is left on the longer members which is cleaned off after assembling (see Fig. 188). The joint is simply nailed together or may be glued and nailed to give a little extra strength. As a precaution against splitting, holes for the nails can be drilled with the bradawl, placing the blade across the grain and turning it backwards and forwards as it is pressed through the wood. The use of oval nails, which should be staggered and punched below the surface, further reduces the possibility of splitting.

Corrugated fasteners (Fig. 189) may be used as an alternative to nails for frames where it would be a disadvantage to have nail holes showing on the outer edge. Blocks glued to the inside of butt joints make them stronger, but side grain must be glued to side grain as gluing to end grain is not so effective.

Plates of plywood can also be used to strengthen the butt joint (Fig. 190). These are glued and nailed with round wire nails of a suitable length.

Dowelled Joint

Hardwood dowels, grooved to let out trapped air and surplus glue, are fitted into carefully drilled holes (Fig. 191). A dowel jig can be used to ensure accuracy, and chamfering the end of the dowel gives better penetration when the joint is cramped together.

Butt joints and dowelled joints are suitable for simple door constructions, where the frame is strengthened with plywood or hardwood panels, glued and perhaps pinned in place, or for rough frames such as stage flats (see Fig. 192).

Corner and Tee Halvings

Half the timber is removed from each member, leaving large gluing surfaces which are further strengthened by the shoulders (Fig. 193). It is usual to nail, screw or peg as well and the joint is used for strong, simple constructions such as timber framed garages, cold frames, etc. Careless cleaning up of the vertical member of the tee halving will produce a bad fit.

Dovetail Halving

This is a useful joint for binding together a simple frame or where the bottom member of the frame is under strain (see Fig. 194). The dovetail is cut first and the socket scribed from it. The joint may be fixed with glue only, or glue and pins or screws.

Cross Halving

The joint is cut across the thickness or the width of the wood, depending upon the design of the work, and equal amounts are cut from each member which reduces their strength by half (Fig. 195). Any necessary cleaning up of the wood should be done before the joint is cut to avoid making a slack fit. This joint is often used for stretcher rails or the bases of stands, and if it is fixed with screws as well as glue they should be put in from below.

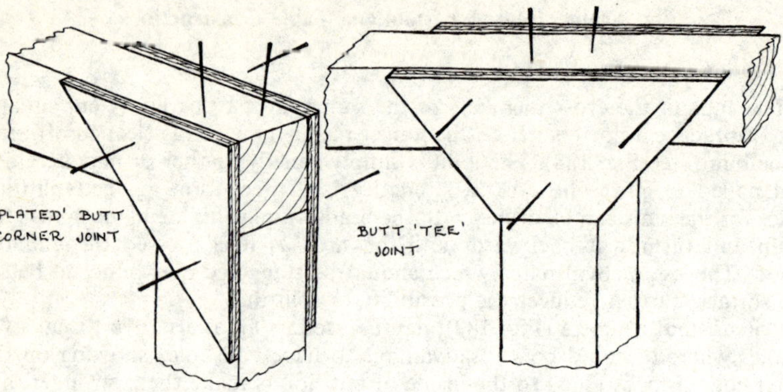

Fig. 190. Using plywood to strengthen the butt joint.

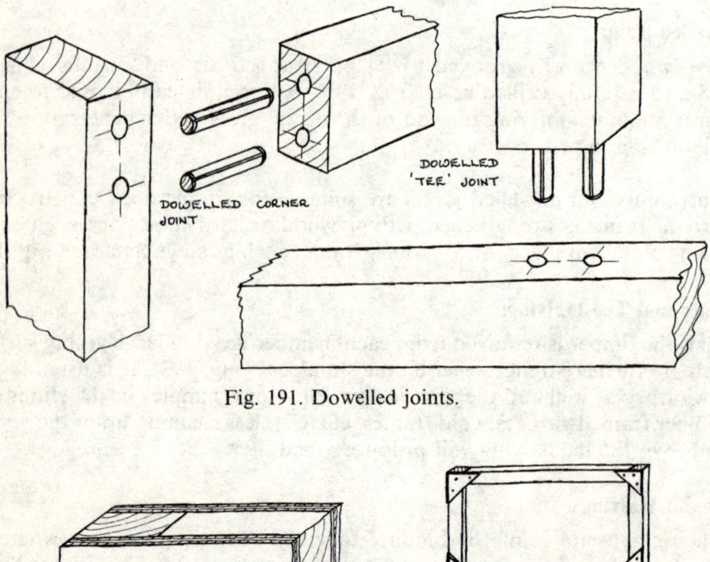

Fig. 191. Dowelled joints.

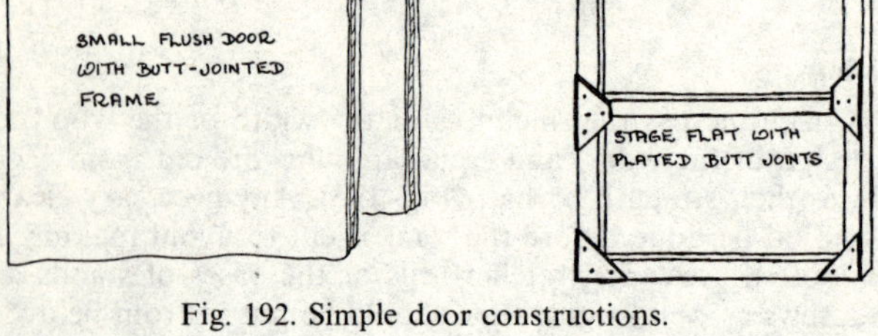

Fig. 192. Simple door constructions.

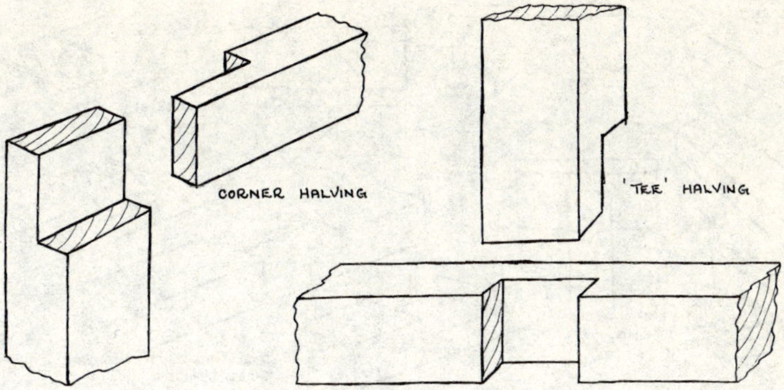

Fig. 193

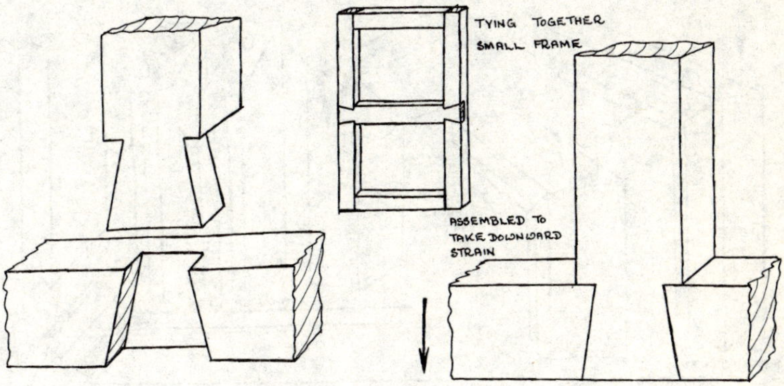

Fig. 194. Dovetail halving.

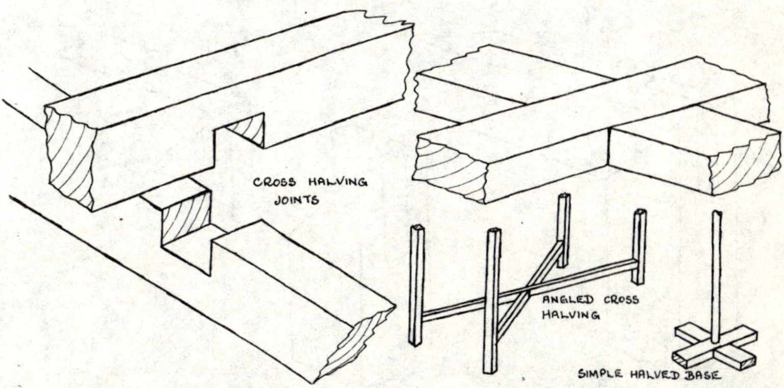

Fig. 195

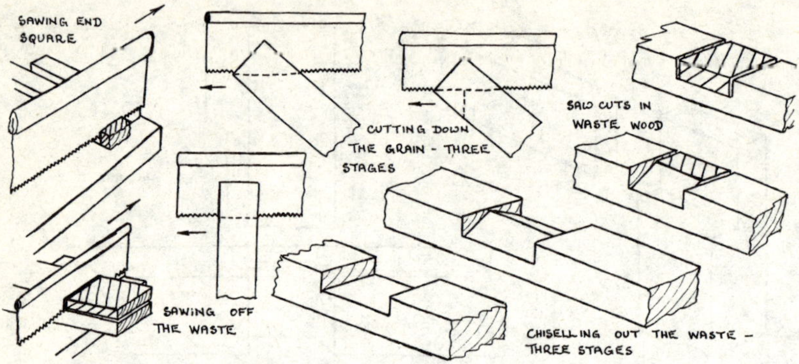

Fig. 196. Tool operations in cutting joints.

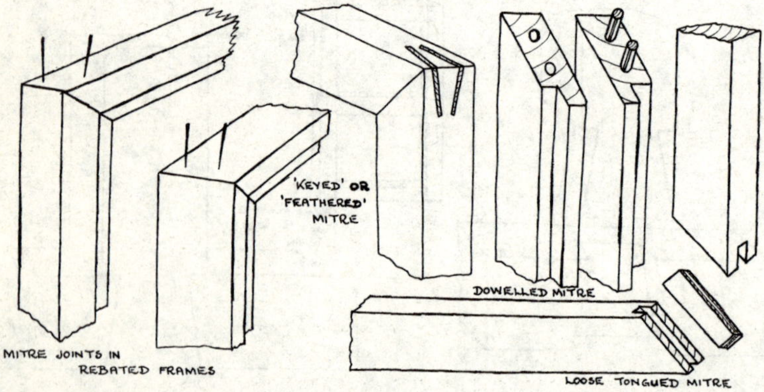

Fig. 197. Mitre joints.

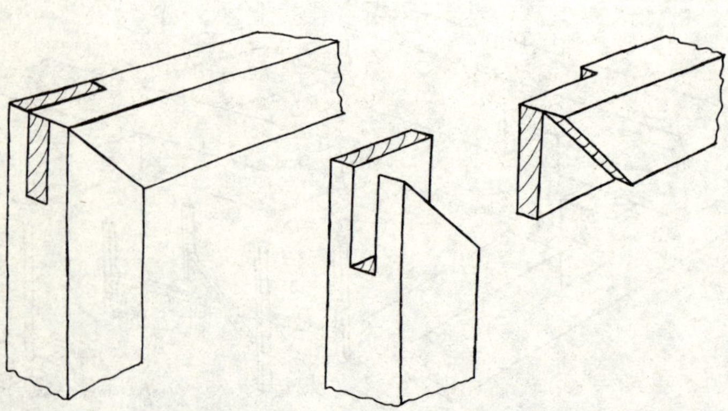

Fig. 198. The mitred corner bridle joints.

The tool operations commonly used in cutting joints such as the above are illustrated in Fig. 196. The wood is held on the bench hook and the end sawn square with the tenon saw. With the work in the vice, long or deep cuts are made just in the waste wood. These are made in three stages to ensure accuracy. The waste is then sawn off completely, taking care not to saw too deeply and weakening the part required. The stages in cutting out the groove for a halving are to saw across the grain, again in the waste wood. If the groove is very wide three or more cuts should be made, then chisel out some of the waste from one side holding the bevel of the chisel downwards. This is then repeated from the other side and the bottom of the notch levelled, this time with the flat side of the chisel downwards. In all cases saw cuts should be made touching the line to be sawn to but in the waste portion to ensure a good fit.

Mitre Joint

The corners of flat frames can be jointed by mitres (see Fig. 197). The wood may be rebated and moulded as for mirrors, picture frames and trays. This is not a strong joint when fixed by glue alone due to the end grain and therefore it is often pinned. Other methods of strengthening are to glue veneers into inclined saw cuts, when it is then said to be 'keyed' or 'feathered'; by using dowels; or by gluing in a loose cross-grained or plywood tongue (this is very strong due to the large gluing area). The mitres are marked out with the mitre square, cut with the tenon saw and trued on the mitre shooting board or end trimmer. The mitre joint has the advantage of not showing any end grain. Mitre cramps are often used during the assembling of a mitred frame.

Mitred Corner Bridle

This is a strong joint—due to the good gluing surfaces—which presents a mitre on the face (Fig. 198). Some end grain shows and it is generally used for heavier frames where a mitre improves the appearance of the face side.

Corner Bridle

The corner bridle is often known as the 'open mortise and tenon'. Joints such as this should fit 'from the saw' by carefully cutting to the setting-out lines and keeping the saw kerf just in the waste portion. Well-fitting sawn surfaces provide good gluing areas. The waste may be removed from the mortise by drilling across the bottom before sawing or by chiselling out after sawing (see Fig. 199). For this a mortise chisel and mallet are used, chopping through from each side and finally paring vertically on to a piece of flat scrap wood. The width of the mortise should be one third of the thickness of the timber.

Tee Bridle

The tee bridle is marked out in the same proportions as the corner bridle (see Fig. 200). Edges 1 and 2 of the inner member should be cleaned up if necessary before the joint is cut to avoid making a slack fit. The grooves are cut out as for the cross-halving, and the sides of the mortise should be left from the saw. When glued the joint is very strong. The end of a simple book rack (see Fig. 200) would be a suitable use for the joint.

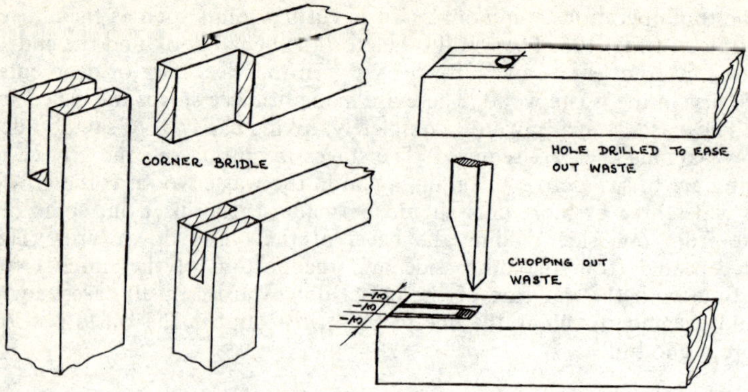

Fig. 199. Removal of waste from corner bridles.

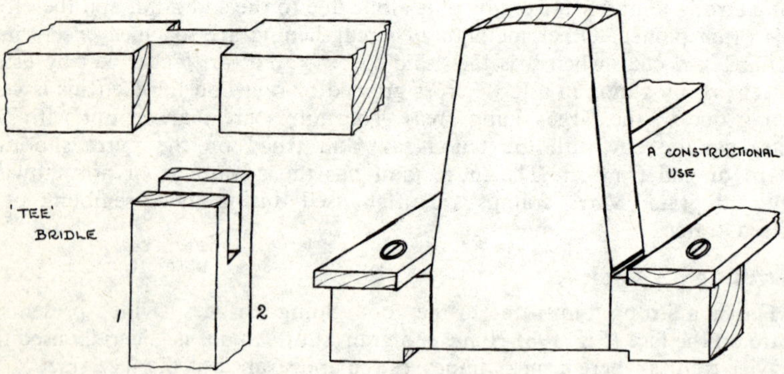

Fig. 200

Fig. 201

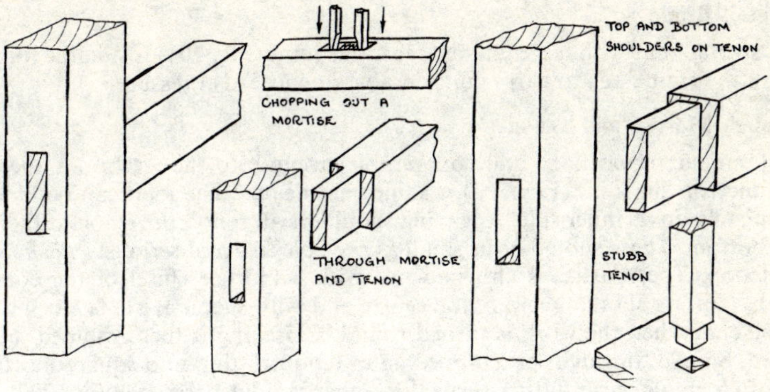

Fig. 202

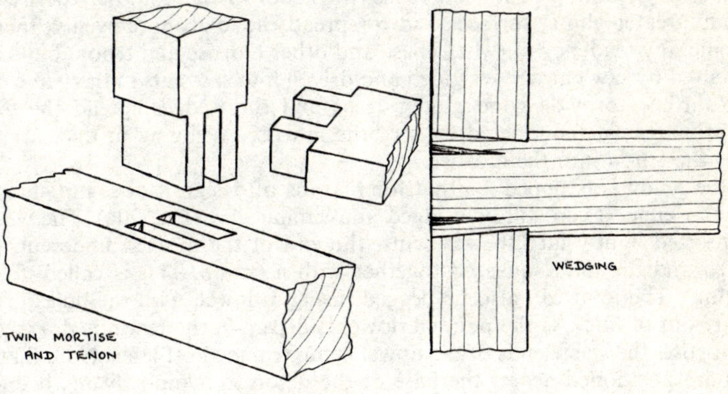

Fig. 203

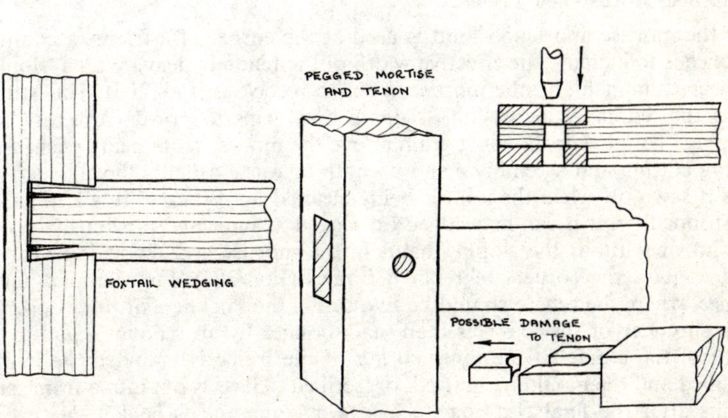

Fig. 204

Dovetail Bridle

A strong joint with large gluing areas, this joint (Fig. 201) is suitable for use where the frame has to carry considerable downwards pressure.

Through Mortise and Tenon

Of similar proportions and comparable strength to the tee bridle, the appearance of this joint (Fig. 202) is somewhat neater. The joint can be hidden completely on its inner side by leaving shoulders all round the tenon at the top and bottom. These should be as small as possible to avoid seriously weakening the tenon. The mortise is chopped out with a mortise chisel of the correct width. Cutting should begin in the centre and with successive cuts work back to the end, when the work is turned round. Chiselling is then resumed in the centre. Simple 'through' or 'stopped' stub tenons fitting into square mortises are often employed in fitting vertical members to flat bases (see Fig. 202).

Twin Mortise and Tenon

For heavy framing or for flat rails, twin tenons (Fig. 203) may be used to provide greater gluing surfaces and to spread the load more evenly, thereby reducing any tendency to twist. These and other mortise and tenon joints may be secured by saw cut wedges glued and driven into saw cuts in the tenon. The sawn surfaces provide good gluing areas and the wedges spread the tenon outwards against the tapered ends of the mortise. Wedging in this way also draws the tenon into the mortise.

If the tenon is 'stopped' so that for reasons of design it does not show on the outer edge, it can still be wedged in a similar way (Fig. 204). The wedges are inserted lightly into the saw cuts, the end of the mortise undercut, glue applied and the joint squeezed together with a cramp. This is called 'foxtail wedging'. The joint can also be pegged, using a dowel, with the holes drilled slightly out of line. As the pointed dowel is driven in the tenon is drawn into the mortise, the waste ends of the dowel being trimmed off later. Note that the holes are positioned nearer the base of the tenon to avoid splitting it due to the pressure of the dowel which could push out the centre of the tenon.

Haunched Mortise and Tenon

If the mortise and tenon joint is used at the corner of a frame, a common practice is to increase the effective width of the tenon by leaving on a 'sloping' or 'secret' haunch and the mortise is cut to receive it (Fig. 205). This strengthens the tenon by increasing its depth and helps to prevent the rail from warping. To prevent the short grain above the mortise from being pushed out during cutting and assembly a short length of waste called a 'horn' is left on. This is sawn off when the joint is being cleaned up. Whether it is a 'through' or 'stopped' joint it can be wedged or pegged as indicated previously.

With or without the sloping haunch, the mortise and tenon joint can be used to joint the corners of rebated frames (Fig. 206); for example, mirror frames, where the rebate should be two thirds the thickness of the wood. The back shoulder of the tenon is then made longer by an amount equal to the depth of the rebate. If the inner corner of the frame is moulded the joint is modified and the moulding 'mitred' or 'scribed'. Glass is put into a frame such as this after the final cleaning up has been done and is held in place by a wooden fillet or bead fixed with panel pins.

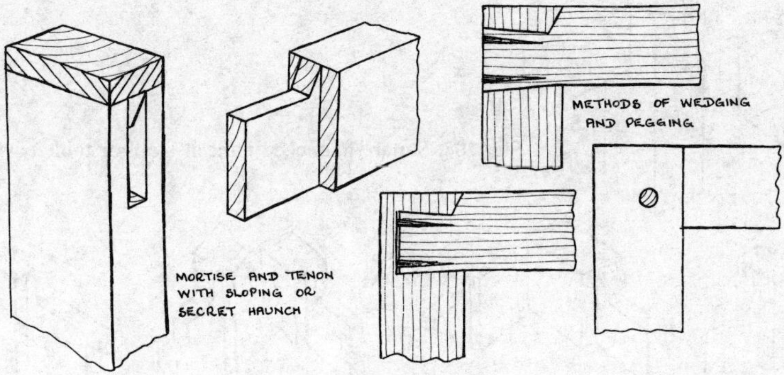

Fig. 205

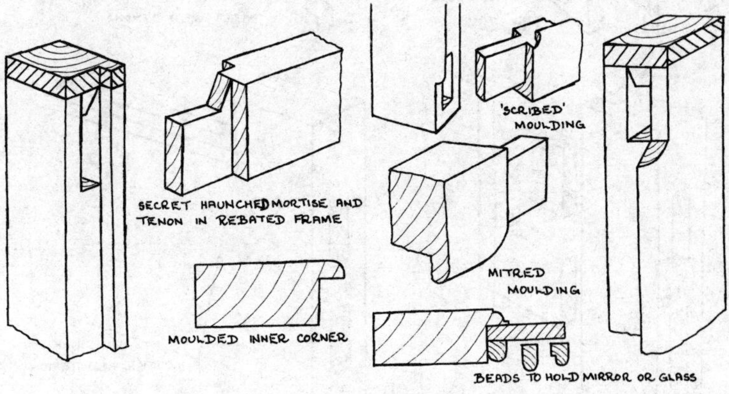

Fig. 206. Use of the haunched mortise and tenon in rebated frames.

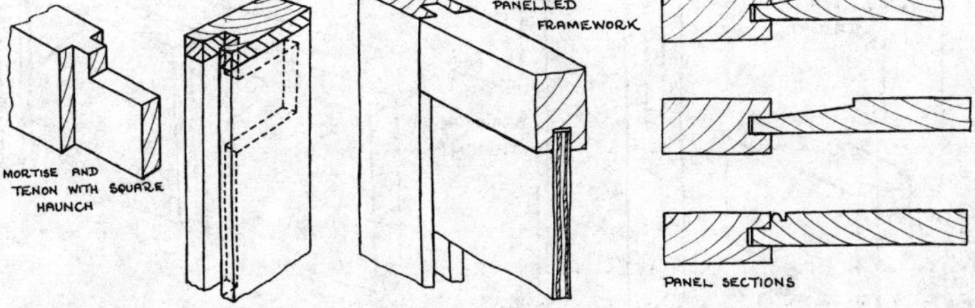

Fig. 207. The square haunch and its use.

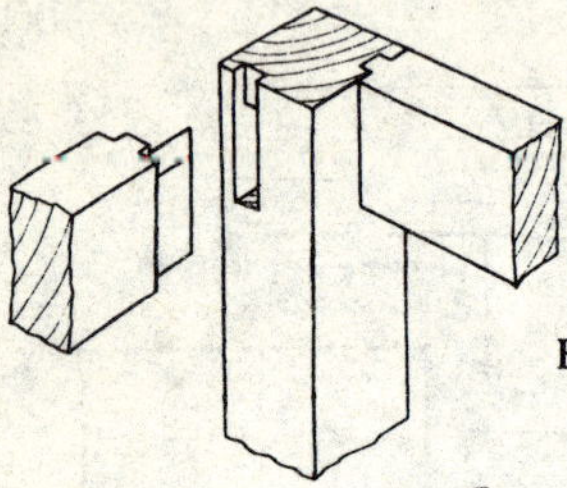

Fig. 208. Square haunched joint at stool or table corner.

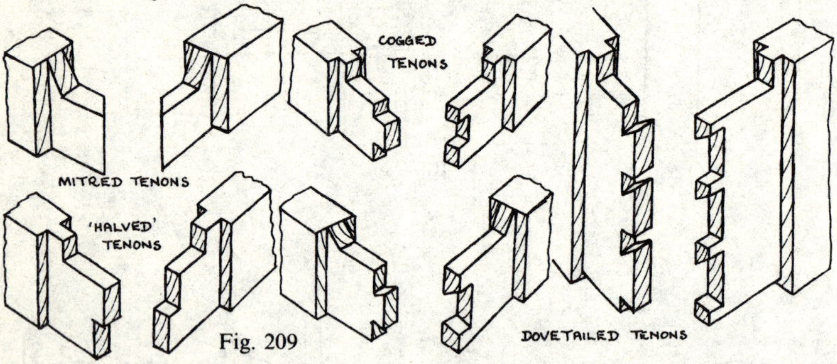

Fig. 209

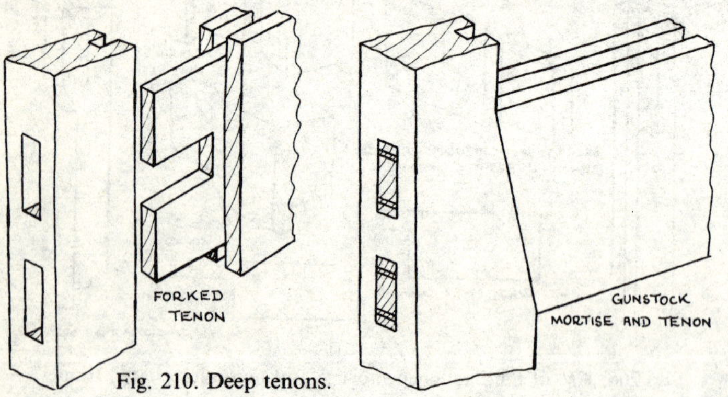

Fig. 210. Deep tenons.

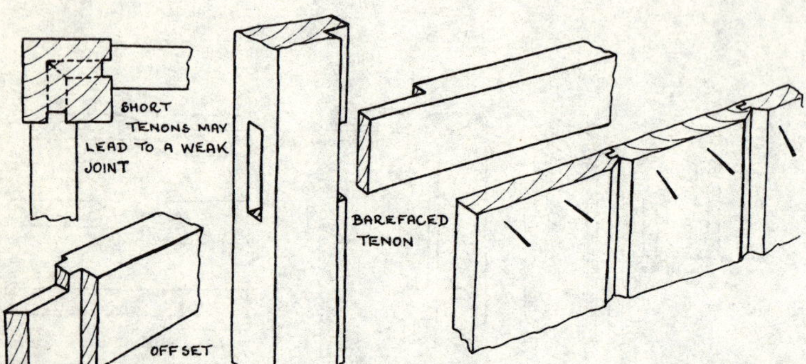

Fig. 211

(e)

(a) Bureau in white melamine-faced chipboard and teak—an attractive contrast. (By permission of Dalescraft Furniture). **(b)** Double bow Windsor chair, width 600 mm, depth 690 mm, and height 1060 mm. The cushion cover can be zipped off for cleaning. Spindles and bows are generally of beech. (By permission of Ercol Furniture). **(c)** Build-up of plastic laminate with Kraft papers impregnated with a melamine resin, pattern paper and overlay. This carries an extra working surface of melamine and becomes transparent during lamination. **(d)** This press at Arborite, North Shields, can produce 240 sheets of 1.5 mm standard laminate per hour. **(e)** Arborite decorative laminates provide hygienic surfaces on kitchen units. **(f)** Edge trims in bending grades of Arborite. (By permission of Arborite)

(f)

The Lervad 700A Tool Cabinet. The adequate storage of tools is an essential factor to good craftsmanship. (Photograph by Colin Elliott)

The Stanley range of Surform tools.

Woodcarving by Michael Smith using Surform tools. (Photographs by Stanley Tools)

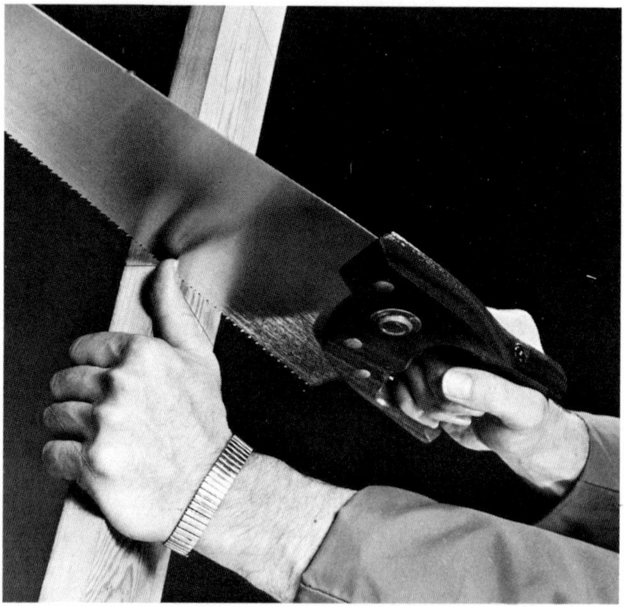

Crosscutting with the handsaw. Note how the thumb is being used to guide the saw at the beginning of the cut.

Using the ripsaw. The index finger is extended down the handle to steady and to guide the saw.

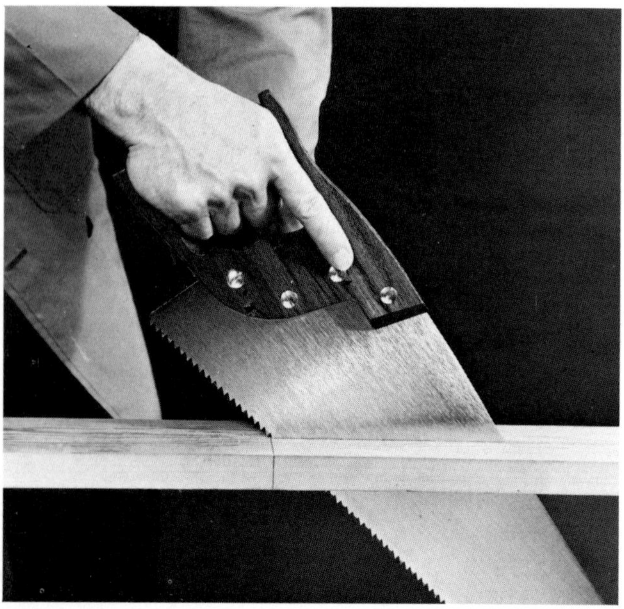

Making long cuts—that is, down the grain—with the tenon saw.

Sawing across the grain with the tenon saw. (Photographs by Spear and Jackson)

(a)

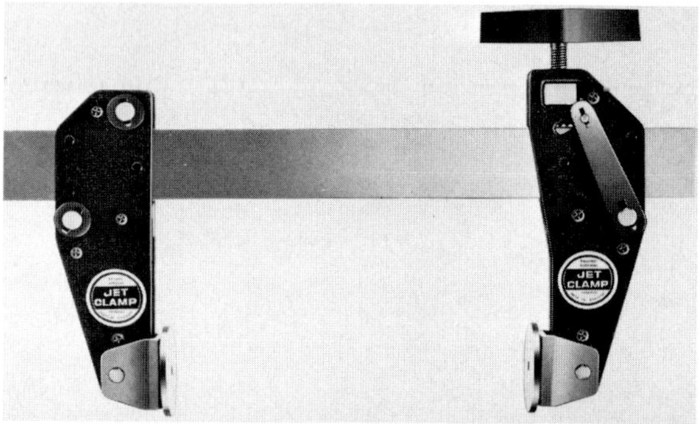

(b)

(c)

(a) The newly introduced Record 'Jet Clamp'. **(b)** Cramping up a flat frame. **(c)** Several clamps employed in cramping up a small carcase.

(a)

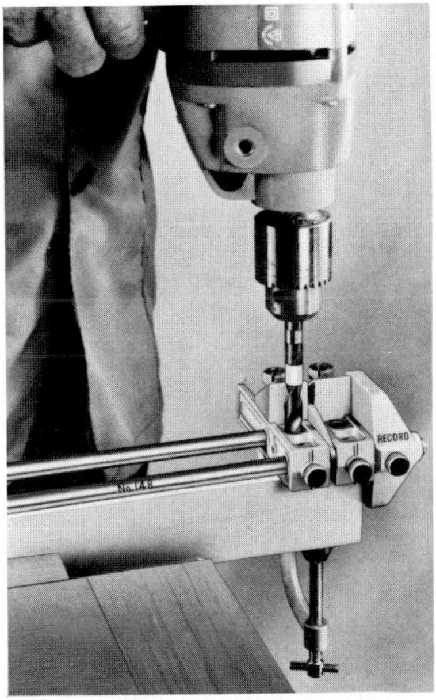

(b)

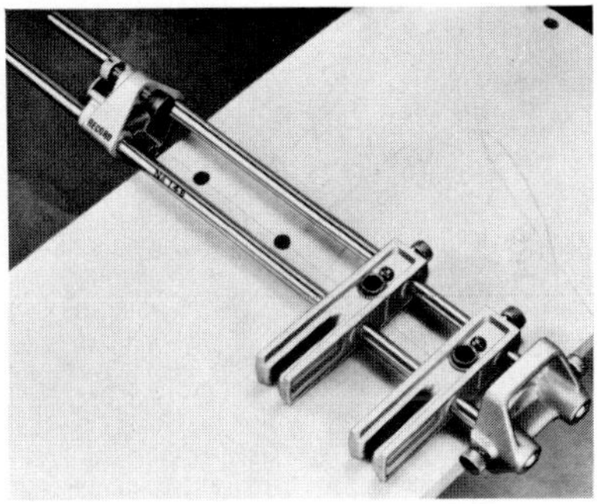

(a) The Record dowel jig.

(b) The jig in use across a wide board as for the carcase.

(c)

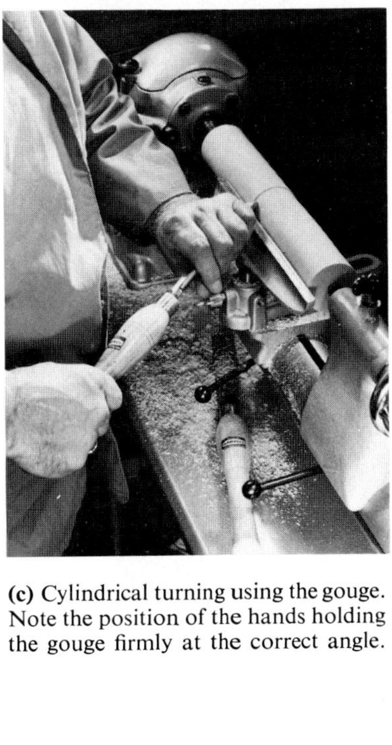

(d)

(c) Cylindrical turning using the gouge. Note the position of the hands holding the gouge firmly at the correct angle.

(d) Turning the outside of a bowl. The bevel of the gouge rubs, so making a cut. (All photographs by Record Tools)

(a)

(a) Smoothing with the skew chisel. The centre of the blade is used and the tool rest set high.

(b)

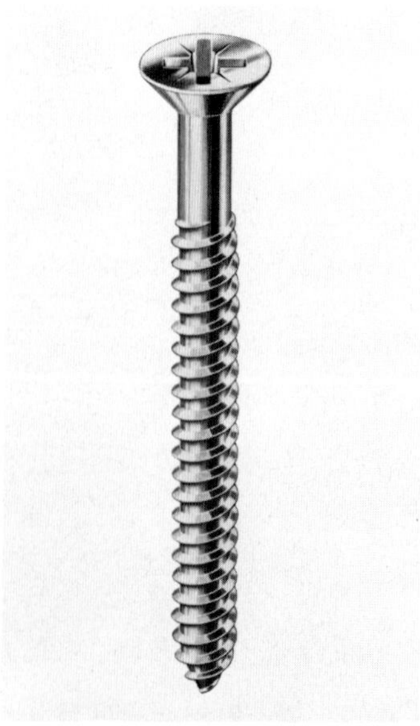

(c)

(b) The Twinfast woodscrew. Note the long parallel thread and parallel shank below the head. **(c)** The Pozidiv recess and screwdriver tip in detail. These provide non-slip driving to ensure against damage to the work. (NB **(b)** and **(c)** are now superseded by the Supadriv recess.) (Photographs by GKN)

As an alternative, the haunch may be 'square' instead of sloping (see Fig. 207). This is stronger still and suitable for use on stools, tables, large doors such as are used in houses, window frames, etc. The square haunch is essential if the frame holds a panel in a groove, when the mortise and tenon are usually cut to the width of the groove, and the panel made to the same thickness. The panels may be simple flat sheets of plywood, pre-veneered or to be painted, or be of solid timber (of which three of the most common sections are shown in Fig. 207). In these cases the edge of the panel can be made to any thickness to suit the required strength of the mortise and tenon. The panel should not be a tight fit in the frame to allow for expansion and contraction, and you should note the space between the panel and the bottom of the groove. The bead on the lower panel would be made with a 'scratch stock'.

The same joint can be used for a stool or table corner (see Fig. 208), in which case the tenons meet at right angles, and the most common practice is to cut the ends at 45 degrees forming a mitre. Where tenons do meet in this way it is important to keep them as long as possible. *On no account should one be cut shorter than the other* as this will seriously affect the efficiency and strength of the joint.

As an alternative to mitring, the joint may be halved or cogged (Fig. 209). For the very best work the author has experimented by dovetailing the ends of tenons, the number of tails depending upon the width of the tenon. In this way the joint becomes virtually indestructible but care has to be taken when gluing up. The whole of the joint must be glued up at the same time, or, if separately, then the piece with the dovetails on it must be glued in first. These jointing methods are stronger than mitring because they increase the effective gluing area on the side grain. Gluing end grain is never very satisfactory.

Deep tenons are often forked and have a centre haunch (Fig. 210). This helps to retain strength and avoids cutting a very wide mortise which would weaken that member of the frame. Joints such as this are often used with sloping shoulders and the width of the stile reduced to make what is known as a 'gunstock' joint.

Barefaced Mortise and Tenon

A disadvantage which might occur where tenons meet is that each may have to be shortened considerably, weakening the joint. This can be partly overcome by off-setting the tenon to allow deeper mortises to be cut. If the tenon is off-set completely to one side it then becomes 'barefaced' (Fig. 211) and is used on work such as gates and 'ledged and battened' doors which are to be boarded on one side. A rebate is cut into the stile to receive the edge of the first and last boards. Barefaced tenons may also be used if the rail is thin and making two shoulders would produce a weak tenon.

Box and Carcase Construction

Butt Joint

Once more the butt joint is the simplest way to form box corners or to position particular partitions within a box (see Fig. 212). The joint may be glued, which gives only limited additional strength (gluing to end grain is never good practice) and therefore requires the additional support of nails or panel pins, depending upon the requirements of the finished work. Whichever

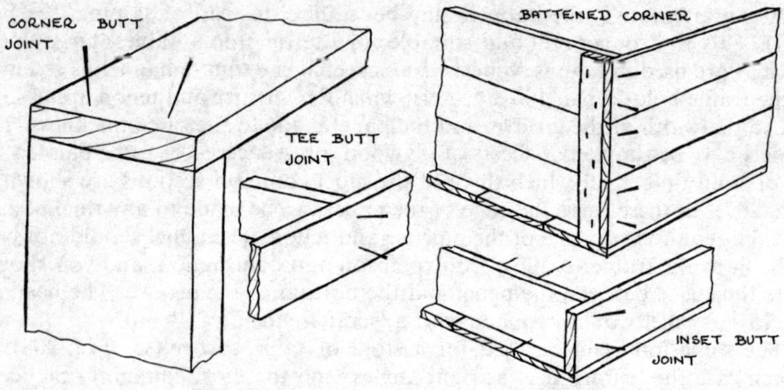

Fig. 212. The butt joint in box corners.

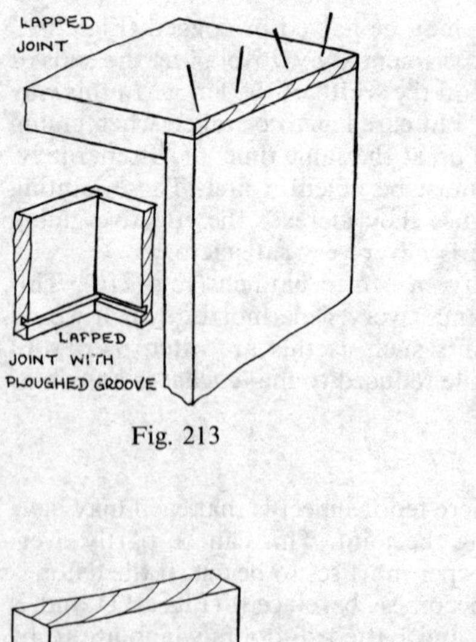

Fig. 213

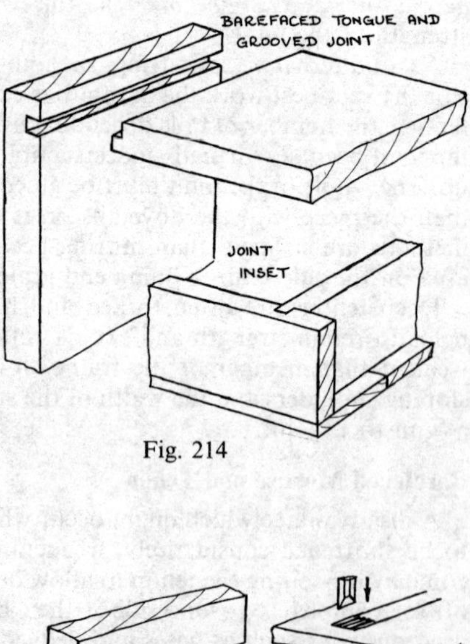

Fig. 214

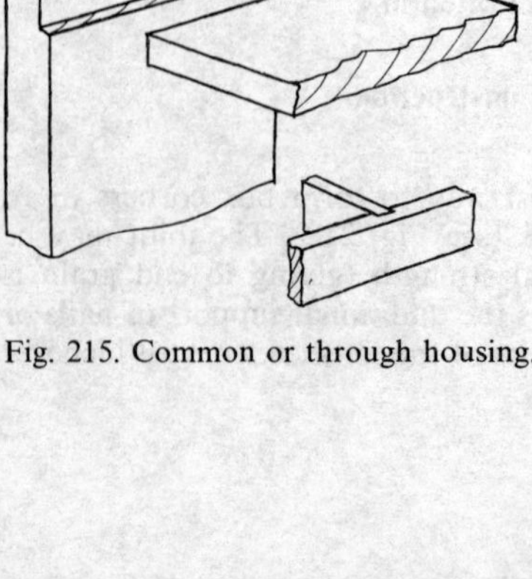

Fig. 215. Common or through housing.

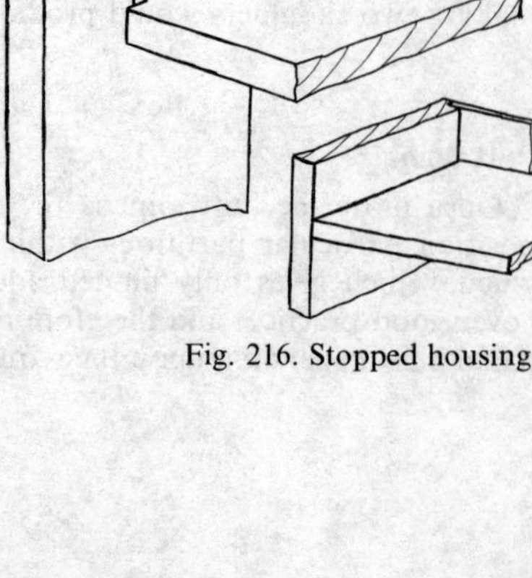

Fig. 216. Stopped housing.

is used, they should be punched below the surface except in the case of round wire nails with flat heads. The nails should be driven in at an angle to give a dovetailing effect, and to prevent splitting the wood can be pre-drilled with a bradawl or small diameter drill. In practice, as a further precaution against splitting, a horn is often left on which is sawn and planed off after assembly. This also ensures a neat joint. The concealed ends of the sides should be squared carefully by sawing and/or planing, possibly on a shooting board, before assembling begins. Glued corner blocks will give additional strength. A stronger box can be made if the ends are set in a little way. For deeper boxes such as packing crates, for example, where the sides are made up of several boards, the ends should be built up first on battens and the nails clenched over. The sides and bottom are then nailed to them. The top may also be nailed on, or held with screws for easy removal.

Lapped or Rebated Box Corner Joint

This withstands stress better than the simple butt joint (see Fig. 213). Again it is usual to glue and nail, punching the heads below the surface, and if necessary stopping the hole with a suitable filler depending upon the nature of the work and the finish to be applied. The ends of the timber should be squared and the rebates cut to a depth of one third the thickness of the timber. The joint can be nailed from either side, or cross-nailed as required, care being taken to avoid splitting. A horn left on to be cleaned off after assembling again produces a neat finish. The joint can be ploughed to hold the bottom of the box and this makes it suitable for simple drawer construction.

Barefaced Tongue and Grooved Joint

This is of greater strength than the butt or lap joints because of its better gluing surfaces, and mechanically it is better able to withstand pressures (see Fig. 214). The short grain on the outside of the grooves is a weakness and is liable to split out. A horn, to be trimmed off later, helps to prevent this or the joint may be used inset, when it is considerably stronger. The tongue should be shaped entirely with the saw.

Common or Through Housing

The groove is sawn and chiselled out right across the wood and may be levelled to a uniform depth with a router (Fig. 215). Its width should be such as to allow for a slight reduction in the thickness of the piece to be fitted into it due to cleaning up before assembling. It can be used near a corner as a box joint or to hold partitions and shelves.

Stopped Housing

This has the advantage of not showing the groove, which may also be concealed at the other end if a back is fitted to the work (Fig. 216). To cut the stopped housing, part of the waste should be chiselled out as for a mortise to give the saw a space into which it can cut. The procedure is then as for the through housing.

Dovetailed Housing

There are many variations of this joint (Fig. 217), which is used on shelves and partitions to tie together the sides of large cabinets, etc., to prevent the

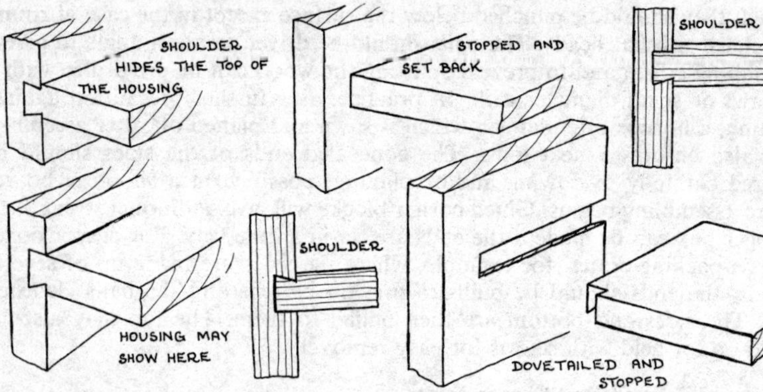

Fig. 217. The dovetailed housing.

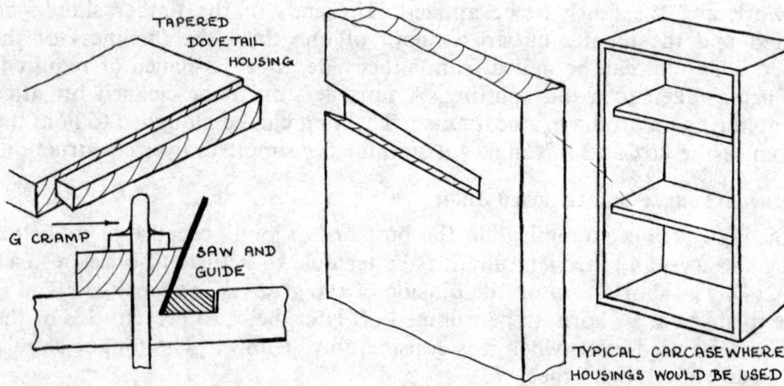

Fig. 218

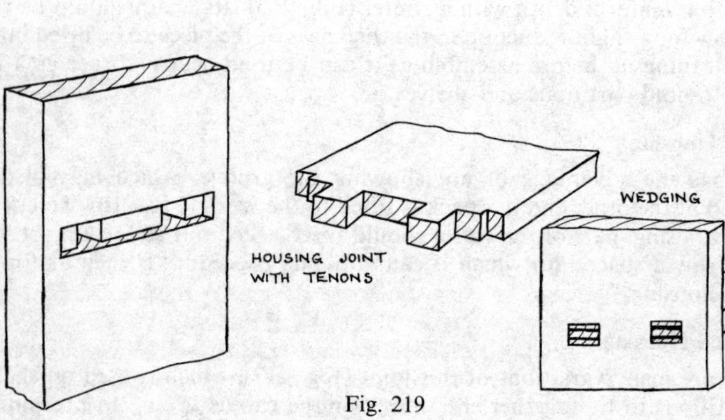

Fig. 219

tendency to bow outwards due to internal pressures. Some have the advantage of a small shoulder along the top which conceals the top edge of the housing that might otherwise show. Others are stopped and set back to allow for a door to be fitted. Joints such as these are usually glued into place after the outer case has been assembled. For each of the preceding joints it is usual to make the depth of the housing approximately one third the thickness of the wood.

Tapered Dovetail Housing

By making the housing and dovetail tapered, the joint becomes easier to slide together from the rear of the carcase. The angle at which to cut the housing can be kept accurately if a saw guide is clamped to the wood. A simple assembly in which these joints might be employed is shown in Fig. 218.

A further variation of the housing joint is to stop both ends and cut near to each end stopped or through mortise and tenon joints (see Fig. 219). These are made as far apart as possible to prevent warping of the shelf. The joints are set out in the usual way with a gauge and the mortises then chopped out with a chisel of suitable width. The chisel must always cut across the grain to prevent splitting, working from each side of the wood until all the waste is removed. The tenons may be wedged with a contrasting wood if desired to form a decorative feature, in which case the top and bottom outer edges of the mortise should be relieved. Wedging must always be done so that the wedge presses against the end grain of the wood, not in line with it or splitting will result.

Pinned Joint

The pinned joint (Fig. 220) can be made by a series of mortise and tenon joints cut across wide boards, and is used as an alternative to housings for fixing partitions. When wedged, they are very strong and are particularly suitable if a heavy downward pull is to be exerted on them. Two wedges are driven into saw cuts in each tenon or if the section of the wood is relatively small the glued wedge may be inserted diagonally.

Comb or Finger Joint

Originally designed as a hinged joint with centre pin and corners rounded to facilitate movement, this joint (Fig. 221) is now used with glue to form an extremely strong corner joint because of its many gluing surfaces. It is also simple to cut and fit as each part is quite straight. The joint lends itself readily to machine-cutting processes, and boxes of thin wood with fine joints, such as cigar boxes, are produced in quantity.

Common or Through Dovetail

This dovetail is very similar to the finger joint but a slope is introduced (Fig. 222). This means that it can only be assembled in one direction and can only possibly pull out in the same direction. It also gains strength from the large gluing area.

The parts of the joint are the 'pins' and the 'dovetails', the sockets for which are between the pins. Machine-cut dovetails have the pins and tails the same size, but the craftsman who cuts them by hand improves the appearance by increasing the tail. Although the slope is missing from only one side of the end pins they are known as 'half pins'. The angle at which the dovetail slope is

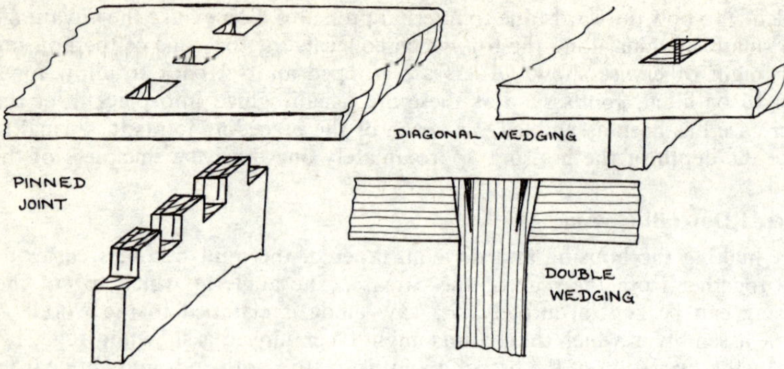

Fig. 220

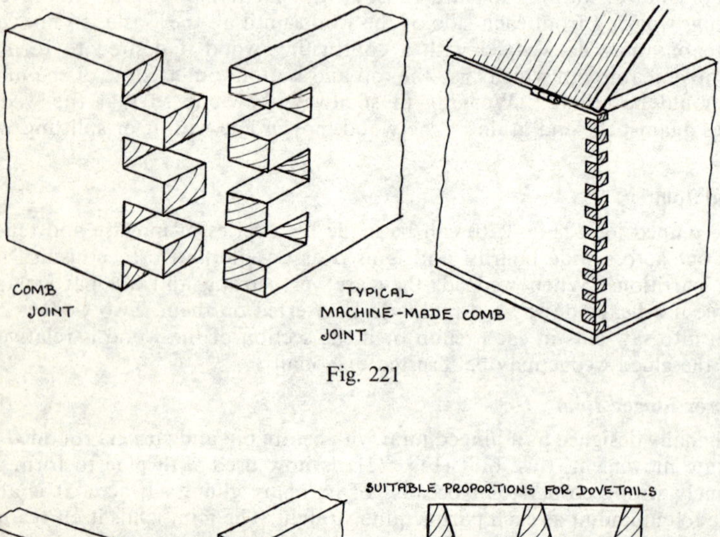

Fig. 221

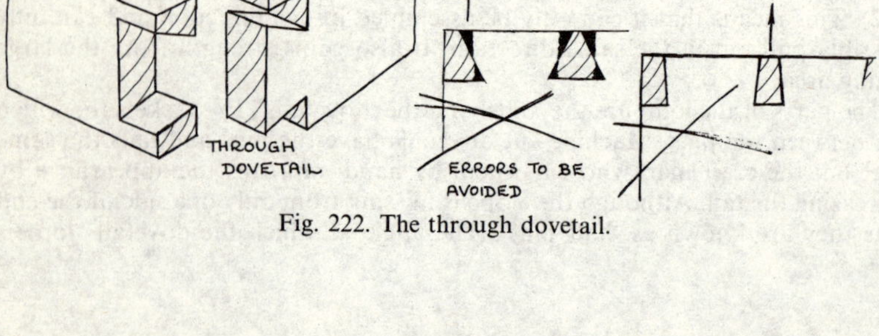

Fig. 222. The through dovetail.

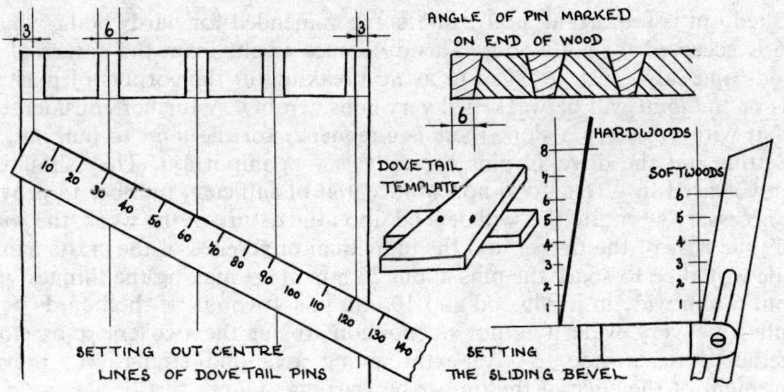

Fig. 223. The through dovetail.

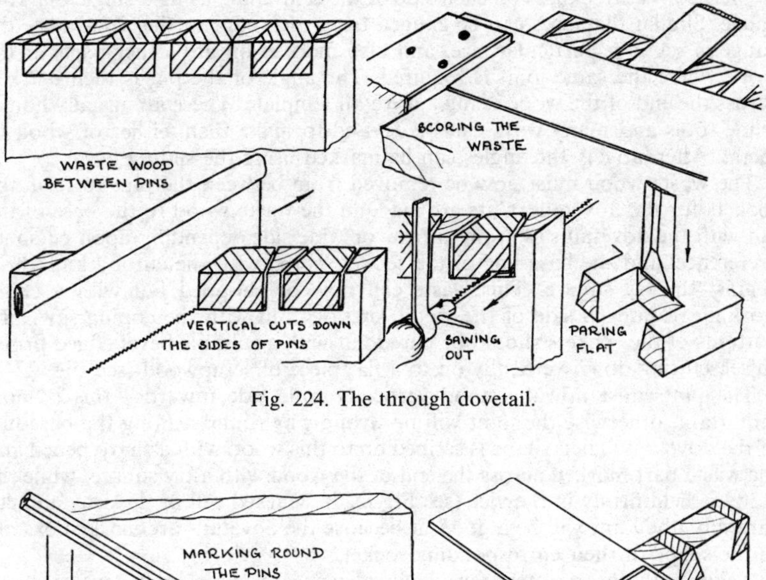

Fig. 224. The through dovetail.

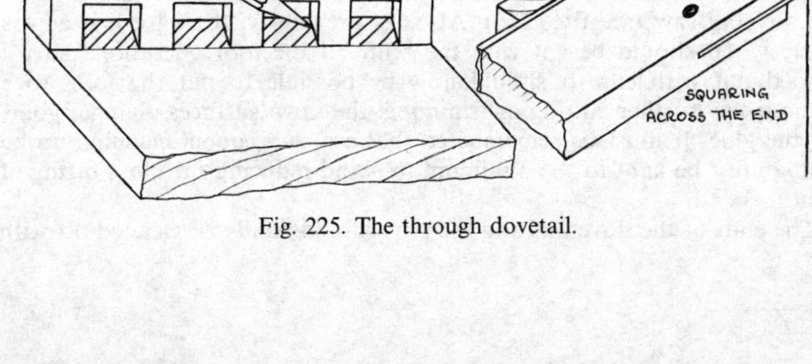

Fig. 225. The through dovetail.

marked out is important, and 1 in 8 is recommended for hardwoods, while 1 in 6 is accepted for softwoods. This difference results from the nature of the woods and care must be taken to avoid breaking off the corners of pins and tails or the joint will be weakened very considerably. A further consideration is that with too steep a slope there is a tendency for the joint to pull out.

Setting out the dovetail pins correctly is very important. They should be evenly spaced to give a good appearance and of sufficient number to provide the necessary strength; this will depend upon the nature of the work, the width and thickness of the timber and the individual preference of the craftsman. A guide would be to space the pins about 25 mm apart making the thinnest part about 6 mm wide in hardwood and 10 mm in softwoods. If the boards being jointed are very wide it is not uncommon to put the two end pins closer together at each side to give extra gluing area and strength to prevent movement of the edge of the timber by warping.

Fig. 223 indicates how the centre lines of the pins can be established for any width of board: because of the two 'half-pins', 3 mm must be allowed at each side to give correct spacing for the size illustrated. The pins are then marked to their correct thickness on each side of the centre line using a single marking gauge. Similar distances can be gauged from each edge of the wood once the gauge is set to a particular size, and also marked on any other parts of the work where the same joint is required. The angle of the pin is then marked across the end of the wood using a dovetail template. These are usually home-made tools and many ways can be devised to make them either of wood or metal. Alternatively the angles can be marked using the sliding bevel.

The waste wood must now be removed from between the pins to form the sockets for the dovetails. Cuts are made in the waste wood to the base of the pin with the dovetail saw from narrow or wide side depending upon personal preference, and the base line of the socket scored with the cutting knife held against the try square. This waste can now be chopped out with a chisel working from each side of the wood, or sawn out with the coping saw. The bottoms of the sockets should be pared flat with a suitable bevel-edged firmer chisel, cutting down vertically on to a flat piece of scrapwood (see Fig. 224).

The pins must now be stood vertically wide side inwards—this is most important, otherwise the joint will be wrong way round—along the base line of the dovetails. Their shape is scribed on to this wood with a sharp pencil and the waste part marked across the end of the wood with a try square, while the wood is held firmly in the vice (see Fig. 225). Marked out in this way and cut carefully, the joint will be a good fit because the dovetails are marked exactly to the shape of their corresponding socket.

Again with the dovetail saw, inclined cuts are made in the waste wood between the dovetails and this waste is then removed as previously with the coping saw and chisel, except at the ends where the half pins are cut off with the dovetail saw (see Fig. 226). Also, as previously, the base line across the waste wood should be cut with the knife. If the tool operations have been carried out with care it should now be possible to put the joint together without any further cutting or trimming, the sawn surfaces giving a good key for the glue. It must be remembered that any subsequent cleaning up before gluing must be kept to the minimum to avoid reducing the close fitting of the joint.

The ends of the dovetails and the pins should finally be cleaned off with the

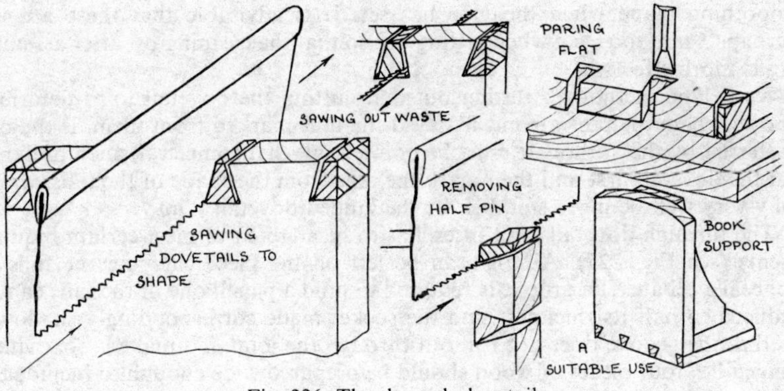

Fig. 226. The through dovetail.

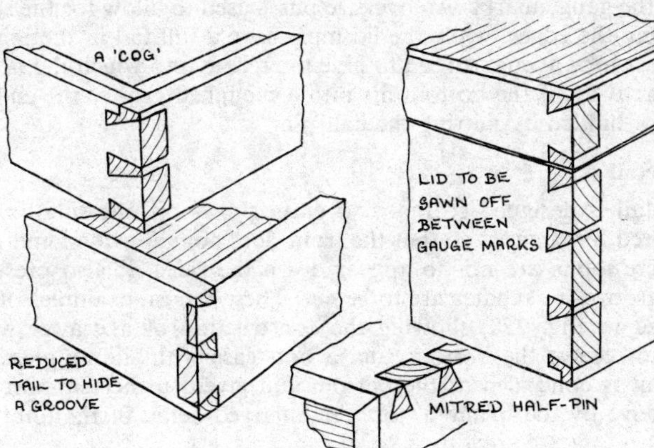

Fig. 227. Adaptations of the through dovetail joint.

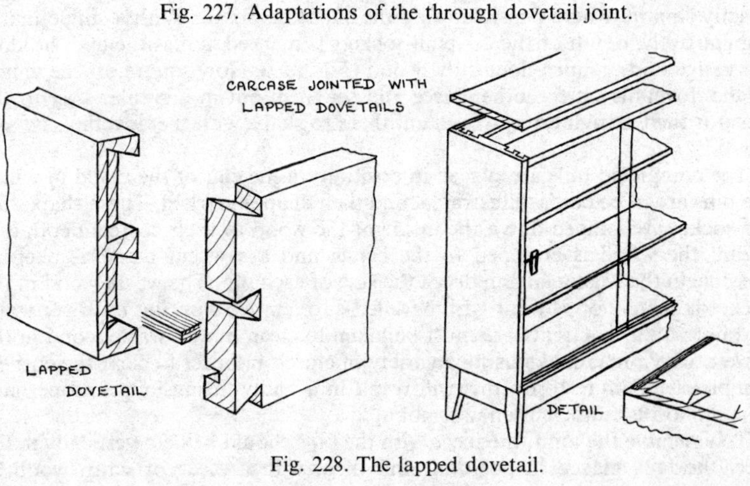

Fig. 228. The lapped dovetail.

smoothing plane when the glue has set. It is advisable that these are left perhaps 1 mm too long when setting out so that the cleaning off after assembling is more effective.

Note: The method of setting out and cutting the dovetail joint described above, where the pins are cut first and the tails marked from them, is the one preferred by the author. It must be pointed out that some craftsmen prefer to cut the dovetail first and then mark the pins from the shape of the tails, which may very well be more suitable for the lapped dovetail joint.

The through dovetail joint often has to be adapted to meet certain requirements (see Fig. 227). A 'cog' can be left on the piece carrying the tails to conceal a rebate. If a groove is required to hold a panel, one of the tails can be reduced to half its thickness and the socket made correspondingly shallower so that the groove does not run out through the joint. To make a box with a hinged lid, four pieces of wood should be prepared wide enough to include the depth of the lid. These are dovetailed together, glued, and the lid then sawn off between the gauge marks. An oversize pin is used to allow for the saw kerf and smoothing the edges, while the lid must have a full tail in the joint. Fig. 227 also shows how a 'cog' is used to hide the rebate into which the bottom is fitted. Alternatively, if the bottom fits into a ploughed groove the end of the groove can be hidden by mitring the half pin.

Lapped Dovetail

This dovetail is designed so that end grain shows on one side only. It is commonly used for drawers so that the front does not show the joint, and for cabinets where joints are not to appear down the sides. It also presents no difficulty if grooves or rebates are to be cut. These typical examples of its use are illustrated in Fig. 228, showing the construction of a drawer with the groove cut to receive the bottom, and a bookcase with sliding glass doors. Here the joint is concealed at the bottom and given further support by the base, and above by the 'planted' top. An enlarged detail of the joint is also shown.

The ends of the wood to be joined by the lapped dovetail must be planed exactly square, where possible using the shooting board. With a single marking gauge the depth of the dovetail sockets is marked across the end, holding the gauge on the inner side of the wood (Fig. 229). Now square off the length of the dovetails on the other piece and set them out in a similar way to the pins for the through dovetail and cut them to shape with the dovetail saw and chisel.

The completed tails are placed in position on the end of the wood in which the pins are to be cut, as illustrated, and their shapes marked. These shapes for the socket are gauged down the inside of the wood to their correct depth and width; the wood is cramped to the bench and a saw cut made as deep as possible in the waste portion down the side of each pin. The waste wood in the socket is then chopped out with bevelled-edge chisels working both vertically and horizontally. Great care must be taken to clean out all waste wood in the socket, which may mean using a variety of chisels in order to clear the corners completely. Failure to do this will result in a badly fitting joint and perhaps damage to the timber when assembling.

To assemble the joint, the piece with the pins should be held vertically in the vice, the tails placed in position, and then, with a piece of scrap wood to

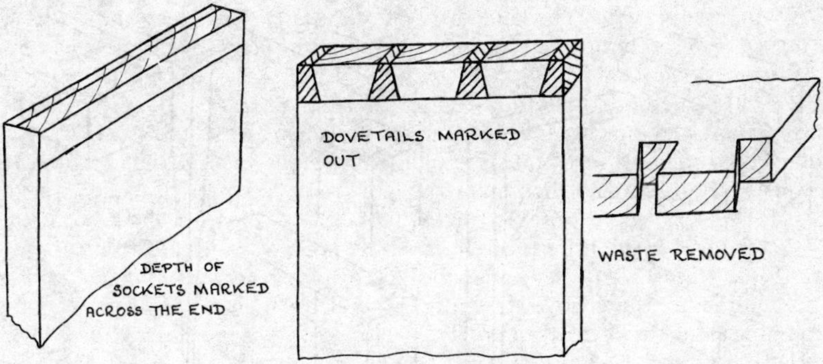

Fig. 229. The lapped dovetail.

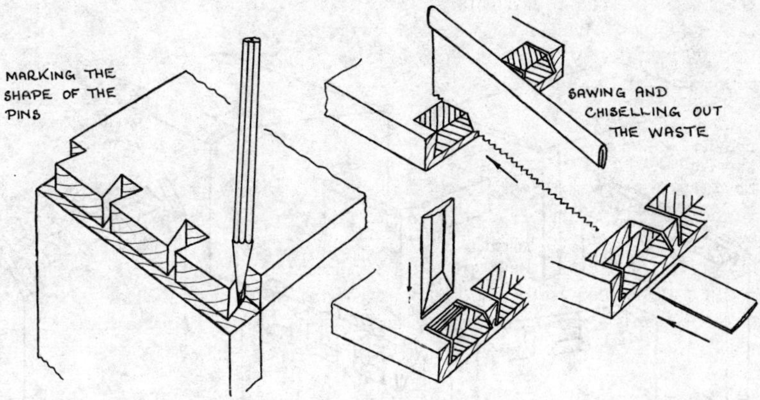

Fig. 230. The lapped dovetail.

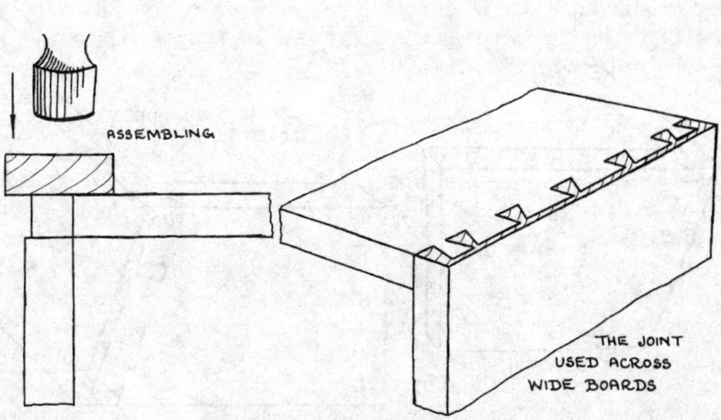

Fig. 231. The lapped dovetail.

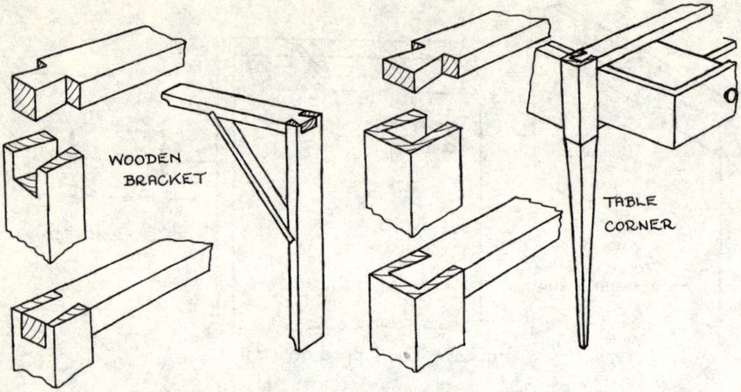

Fig. 232. Uses of dovetail joints.

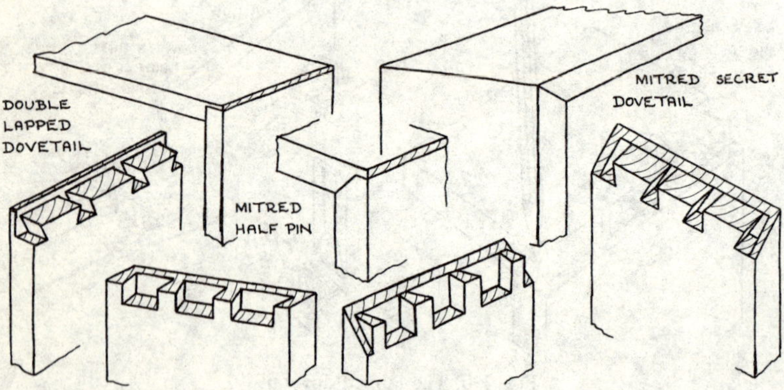

Fig. 233

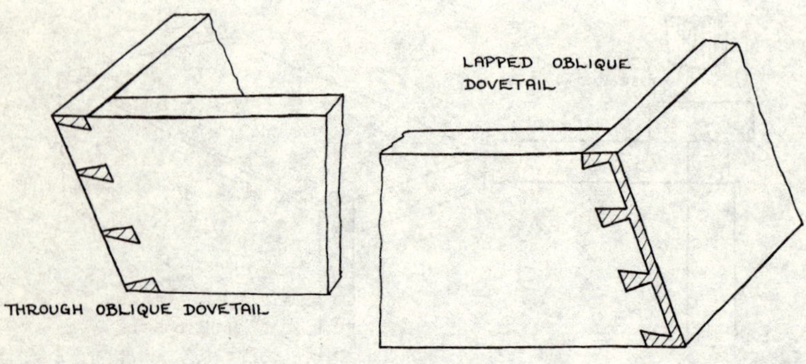

Fig. 234

protect them, lightly tapped into position with the hammer, so completing the joint (Fig. 231). As with all dovetail joints across wide boards, they can be further strengthened and the edges prevented from curling by increasing the gluing area with the inclusion of the narrow dovetails near the sides.

Both the through dovetail and the lapped dovetail can be used singly where high resistance to tension is required. The wooden bracket (Fig. 232) indicates a typical use for the single through dovetail and a construction where the single lapped dovetail is ideal.

Double Lapped Dovetail and Mitred Secret Dovetail

Where design requirements make it undesirable for the joints to show, two further variations of the dovetail joint may be used. The double lapped dovetail shows the end grain of the double lap, while the mitred secret dovetail hides the joint completely (Fig. 233). Yet another variation is to present a mitre on the front face of the double lapped joint. The setting out and cutting of the joint is similar to that for other dovetails, allowances being made for the laps and mitres.

Oblique Dovetails

The design of some work occasionally requires members to be joined at an angle and the through and lapped dovetails can be readily adapted to this purpose. They are then known as Oblique Dovetails (Fig. 234) and can be used for carcase work or for special drawer fronts, etc. You should note how the inner sharp edge is removed from the lapped joint to make it less dangerous to the hand if used for drawer fronts and less liable to splinter off.

Drawer Construction

The construction of drawers is one of the most common uses of dovetail joints, where the lapped dovetail is used at the front so as to present an unbroken surface, providing a strong joint which will withstand the force used in pulling open what might be a very heavy drawer when full (see Fig. 235). The back of the drawer is jointed to the sides with the through dovetail which, due to its large gluing area, is very strong and can therefore withstand the pressures exerted on it by the contents of the drawer. The use of the two joints as described is standard practice but the method of fitting the drawer bottom can vary depending upon the design of the work and the preference of the craftsman, and various alternative methods are possible using grooves or 'slips'.

The inner side of the drawer front is always grooved to receive the bottom and when slips are used a small tongue is cut on them to fit into the groove, while at the rear they are fitted under the back of the drawer (Fig. 236). The advantage of using slips, which are glued to the sides of the drawer, is that they strengthen the drawer side, whereas if it is grooved to take the bottom it is weakened. This weakness may be partially overcome by gluing a slip in the corner between the drawer side and the bottom. In order that this beds on tightly as it is being glued it may be first sawn obliquely into short lengths and each then 'rubbed' into position. All the slips have the advantage of increasing the thickness of the drawer side to a wider bearing surface on which to run.

The traditional drawer bottom was of 'solid' timber, fitted as in Fig. 236 with the grain running from side to side across the drawer. In this case

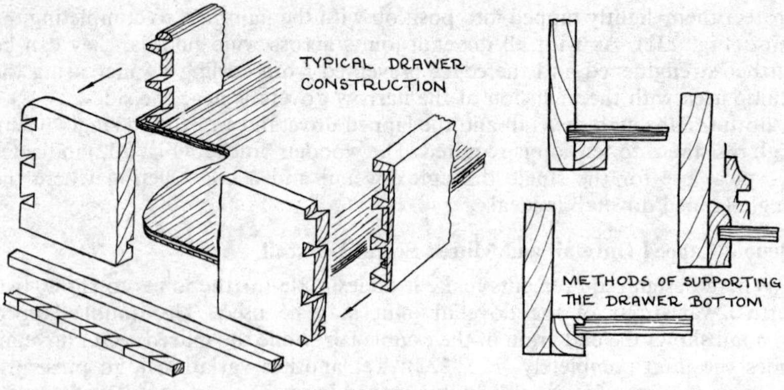

Fig. 235. Drawers.

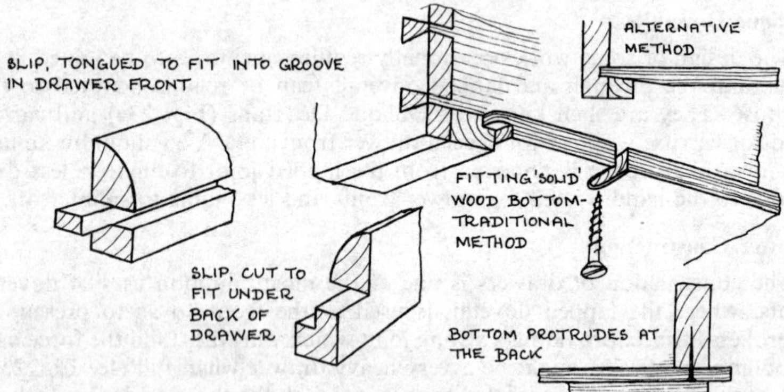

Fig. 236. Drawers.

Fig. 237. Drawers.

provision had to be made for expansion and contraction of the wood, which was achieved by slotting the holes for the screws supporting the back edge. It would be most unusual to adopt this method today as plywood is so much more stable and more readily available in standard thicknesses. The drawer bottom is usually allowed to protrude a little way—about 3 mm—beyond the back of the drawer to enable the screws to give it more support by not breaking out at the edge. An alternative method was commonly used to fit 'solid wood' drawer bottoms. The edge was reduced by a broad bevel so as to fit into the grooved sides and front. The slip then also had to be bevelled before gluing.

Fig. 237 shows an acceptable construction for a simple drawer made in softwood employing the simple lap and through housing joints. The drawer bottom is often given additional support at the front by the addition of one or more glued blocks which are 'rubbed' into position. The number of blocks used depends upon the width of the drawer.

As a general practice drawers with divisions for cutlery are lined with green baize.

Drawer Spaces

Spaces into which the drawers fit within the carcase of a cabinet can be constructed in a number of ways (see Fig. 238). For small cabinets it is sufficient to fit a simple shelf to form a box into which the drawer fits. If the shelf is of manufactured board, however, it may be advisable to glue in hardwood slats on which the drawer will run, in which case the drawer front must be deeper to cover them. Such slats also act as stops for the drawer.

Drawers may also be supported on a front drawer rail and runners. The runners may be slot screwed to the side of the carcase, or a complete frame may be made up carrying a dust panel to prevent dust and dirt falling into the cupboard or drawer below. These frames are housed or stub tenoned into the sides. The inner edge is grooved for the panel and the side members of the frame are tongued into this groove. Small blocks are then glued to the drawer rail as drawer stops.

Modern slab constructions often have hardwood runners glued and screwed to the inside of the carcase. If this is of chipboard, Twinfast wood screws are required to ensure a good hold. The drawers have grooves cut in their sides so that they slide over the strips which then also act as drawer stops. Note that the runners do not touch the back of the cabinet, so preventing a build-up of dust which would eventually affect the fit of the drawer. Single drawers may be underslung on simple rebated runners screwed below the cabinet or table top.

All drawers are prevented from tipping downwards by some form of 'kicker' above them. This may be the cabinet top, or the underside of the shelf, or the underside of the drawer rail or runners.

Deep, Applied and Sloping Drawer Fronts

The styling of drawer fronts can be varied according to the wishes of the designer (Fig. 239). Traditionally the drawer front was fitted exactly into the space constructed to accept it and flush with the carcase around it. To give added interest, however, it was often 'fielded' in the various ways used for panels. More recently deep drawer fronts have been introduced which cover

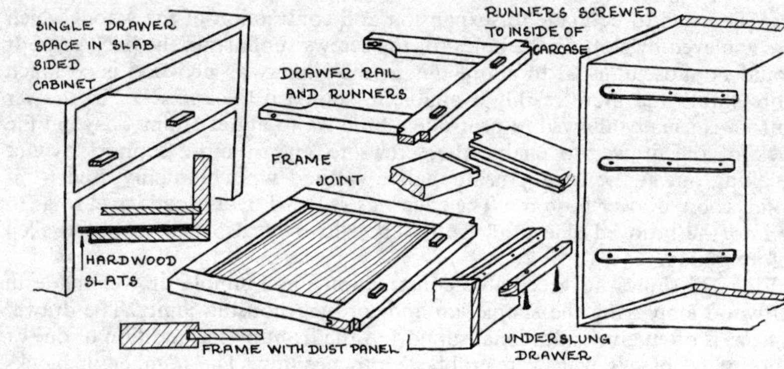

Fig. 238. Drawers.

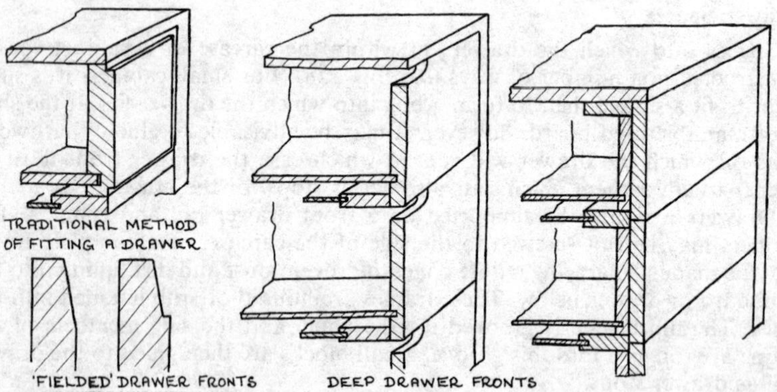

Fig. 239. Drawers.

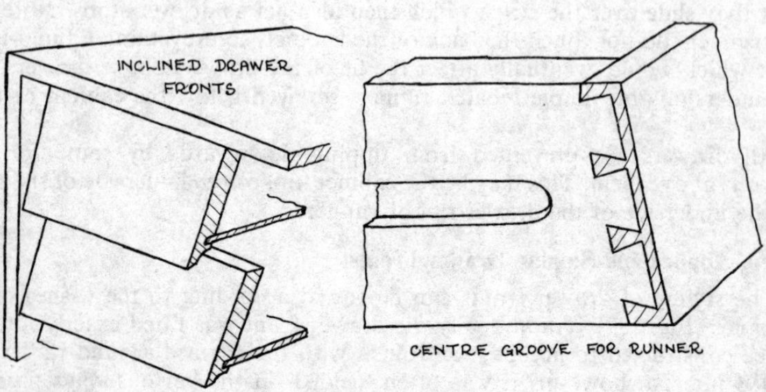

Fig. 240. Drawers.

the drawer rail below them. This allows drawer pulls to be cut in the top edge if desired, doing away with the need for a handle and presenting a flat, almost unbroken surface. This arrangement can be taken a step further by applying false fronts to drawers which have been constructed in the normal way. These fronts are glued in position and, depending upon the finish required, can be of redwood or plywood for painting, solid timber, or pre-veneered board for polishing. In the latter case the edges need to be 'lipped', usually with an iron-on strip of veneer, and handles can be of the recessed variety or screwed on from the inside of the drawer. Neither of these styles requires drawer stops as this function is performed by the drawer front.

A typical example of the use of the oblique lapped dovetail is the construction of an inclined drawer front into the bottom of which a finger grip can be cut if required (Fig. 240). This type of drawer construction, with a centre groove in each side, is ideal for use with drawer runners as in Fig. 238, where the carcase effectively hides the sides of the drawer. To fit drawers to openings, the sides of the assembled drawer should first be planed and cleaned up, then the bottom edges, followed by the top edges until a snug fit is obtained. With all the preceding joints it is good practice wherever possible to leave on 'horns' which are then cleaned off after assembling to produce a neat, smooth and level finish.

Wide Board Construction

A few natural timbers are still obtainable in wide boards, but where the whole of the work is to be of solid wood rather than manufactured board it is usually necessary to joint comparatively narrow widths together. The most simple method of doing this is the 'rubbed' or 'butt' joint (Fig. 241). The edges of the board must be planed absolutely straight and square with the try plane, the adhesive applied and the edges rubbed together to extrude air and surplus glue. The boards are then carefully placed against inclined battens to allow the glue to set prior to cleaning up. Alternatively, after gluing the boards may be sash-cramped together. The success of the joint depends entirely upon the close fitting of the edges and the strength of the glue.

A few simple rules apply to this and other methods of making edge joints. The separate pieces of timber should be arranged so that the heart side of each is alternately up and down. This helps to ensure that the assembled pieces retain their flatness. As the edges are planed and fitted together they should be marked ready for assembling, care being taken to have the grain of each running in the same direction. This too should be marked to facilitate easy cleaning up later. As far as possible, boards should be selected of similar colour and readily matching grain to avoid unacceptable contrasts. The number of sash cramps used on any of these assemblies will vary depending upon the length of the work, and it is advisable to arrange them under and over to prevent the boards from lifting in the middle. The edges of the outer board should be protected from the pressure of the cramp heads with lengths of scrap wood.

Dowelled Edge Joint

By using dowels of hardwood an edge joint (Fig. 242) can be given more strength. The dowels are spaced at regular intervals along the the edge, or may be in pairs, also at regular intervals, again depending upon the size of the

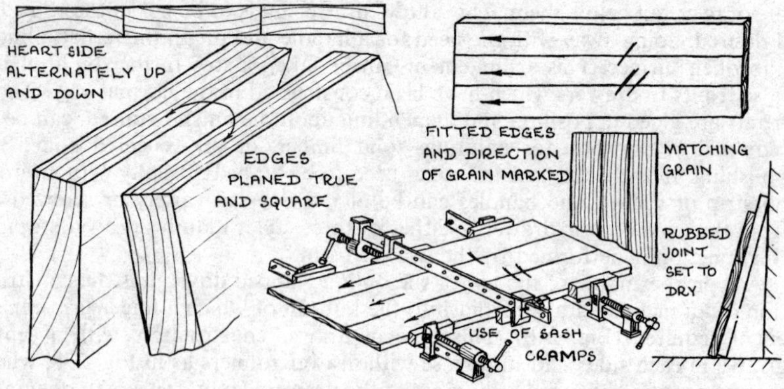

Fig. 241. Wide board construction.

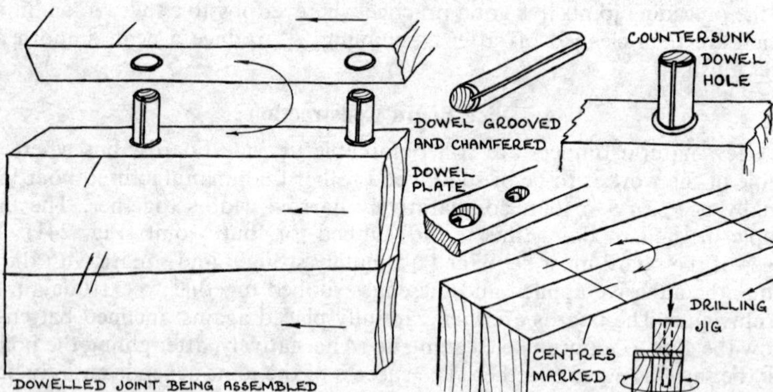

Fig. 242. Wide board construction.

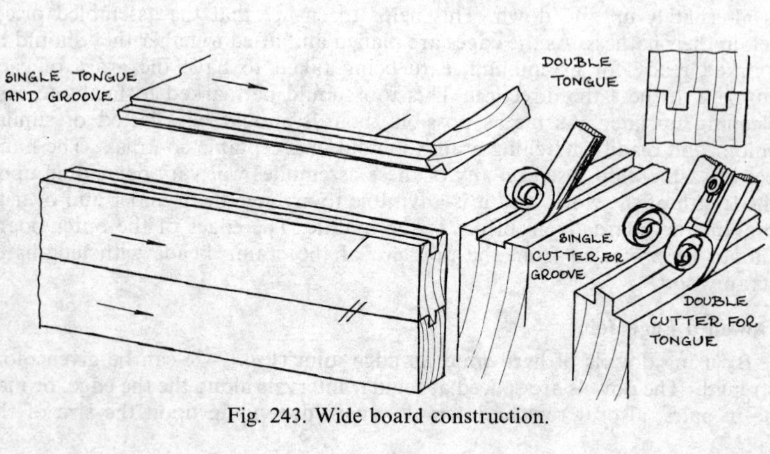

Fig. 243. Wide board construction.

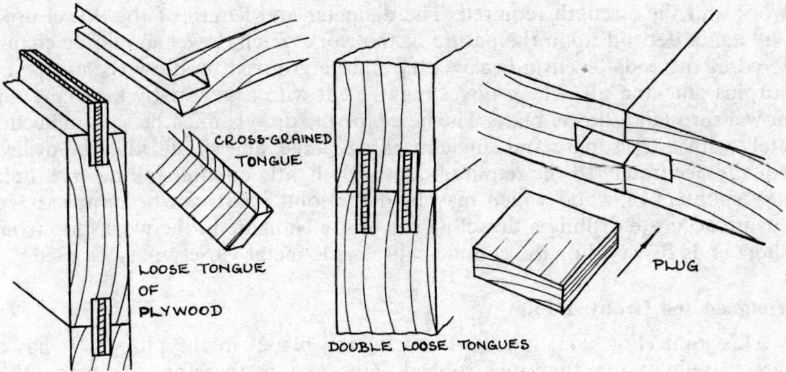

Fig. 244. Wide board construction.

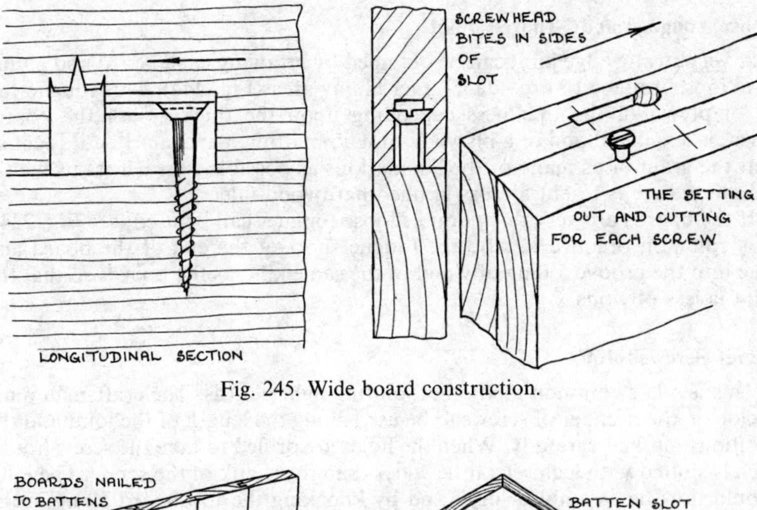

Fig. 245. Wide board construction.

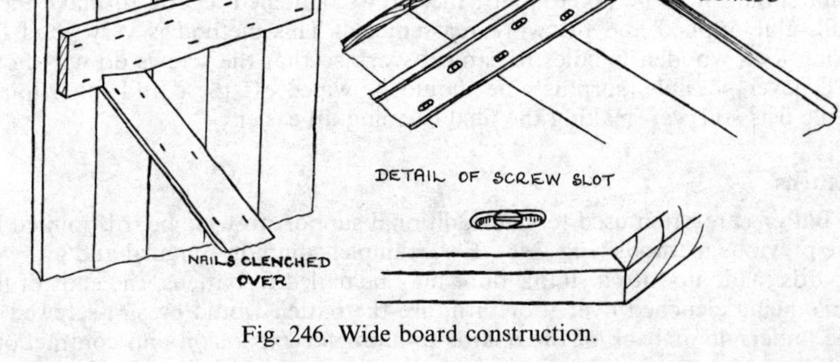

Fig. 246. Wide board construction.

work and the strength required. The diameter and length of the dowel used will again depend upon the nature of the work. Each dowel should be chamfered at the ends to ensure easy entry and be grooved to allow the escape of surplus glue and air. The grooves may be cut with a saw or by knocking the dowel through a dowel plate. The holes for the dowels must be set out accurately with a try square and single marking gauge, and should then be drilled equally accurately to the required depth. By lightly countersinking each hole any splinters of wood which may hold the joint apart can be removed. To ensure accurate drilling a dowel jig can easily be made in the workshop from short ends of wood or the commercially made metal variety may be used.

Tongued and Grooved Joint

This joint (Fig. 243) is cut with matching blades in the plough. It has a larger gluing area than the rubbed joint and is therefore stronger. The thickness of the tongue should be one third of the thickness of the board. For added strength very thick boards may be jointed with a double tongue.

Loose Tongued and Grooved Joint

A very strong edge joint can be obtained by grooving each board and gluing in a 'loose' tongue to provide a larger gluing area (Fig. 244). This tongue can be of plywood, the thickness depending upon the thickness of the board. There is less likelihood of a plywood tongue splitting, particularly if it is cut so that the grain of as many of the laminations as possible runs across its width. An alternative is to cut a cross-grained hardwood fillet.

If the boards are very thick double loose tongues can be used (see Fig. 244). It is common practice to stop the tongue short of the end of the board and glue into the groove a plug of wood of the same kind as the boards so that the joint is less obvious.

Secret Screwed Joint

This is a less common method of jointing light boards. The craftsman must decide on the number of screws to be used along the length of the joint and the positions marked carefully. When the holes are drilled to take the screw heads, each is slotted with a chisel a little wider than the shank of the screw. The joint should now be assembled 'dry', and by knocking the top board along in the direction of the arrow, the slot slides over the screw head (see Fig. 245). The joint should now be taken apart, the screws tightened a little to make them pull, glue applied and the work reassembled. This method is very good for fixing long wooden handles to cabinet work so that the screws do not show. Whenever possible, surplus glue should be wiped off these and other joints while it is still wet, making the final cleaning up easier.

Battens

Battens are often used to give additional support to wide boards jointed by the previous methods (Fig. 246). For example, common tongued and grooved boards made up into a simple door may be nailed to battens, the ends of the nails being clenched over. For furniture the batten would be slot-screwed to the underside or back of the boards to allow for expansion and contraction.

Clamps

An alternative to battens is to use clamps across the ends of the boards, which in turn conceal the joints in the boards (see Fig. 247). This is an ideal method for table tops, for example, as the clamps are flush with the surface and form quite a decorative feature. They can be fitted in a similar way to that used for making edge joints, i.e. tongued grooved or loose tongue, or be made stronger still by being mortise and tenoned.

Slab Constructions

The instability of natural timber, particularly in wide boards, and the limitations of world supply have led to the development and use of more and more manufactured boards. Most of these can be obtained in various qualities and for furniture the surface is prepared for painting or pre-veneered with a balancing veneer on the back, or is plastic coated in white or wood grain effects. Traditional methods of working these boards and jointing them are in many cases simply not suitable and many new and more appropriate ways have been devised. In this respect the reader is directed to Chapter 11. In jointing manufactured boards raw edges are a problem and must be concealed, painted, veneered or lipped, depending upon the work and the type of board.

Butt Joint

Of the many joints used, the butt joint (Fig. 248) is the simplest, initially relying on glue alone for its strength. It may be made stronger by inserting a row of dowels along its length for which a drilling jig should be made for accuracy; by rubbing on glued corner blocks; or by screwing in a corner piece. Adding a back or a bottom to this box construction gives it further strength.

Lap Joints

In plywood, blockboard and pre-veneered chipboard the raw end of the slab left showing in a lap joint (Fig. 249) has to be given a suitable finished surface. Since end grain does not stain well, plywood and blockboard are best painted. The end of pre-veneered chipboard must be veneered.

Mitred Joints

The plain mitred joint (Fig. 249) is best strengthened with corner blocks, but if a clear inner corner is required then the crossgrained loose tongue is ideal. The groove for this is best cut on the circular saw, and as the joint presents a large gluing area it is very strong.

Jointing Slabs to Legs at a Corner

Manufactured boards are excellent for making modern slab-sided furniture such as chests, but present particular structural problems at the corners if legs are required. Several ways are used, as illustrated in Fig. 250. If relatively thin plywood is being used, in which case stout-heart is recommended, then the first three are suitable methods, the plywood being glued and pinned. The tongue and groove is ideal for heavier plywoods, while the loose or cross-grained tongue is more suited to plain or pre-veneered chipboard. All the joints effectively hide the end of the board. An indication is also given as to how the outer and inner corners of the leg can be moulded and shaped as

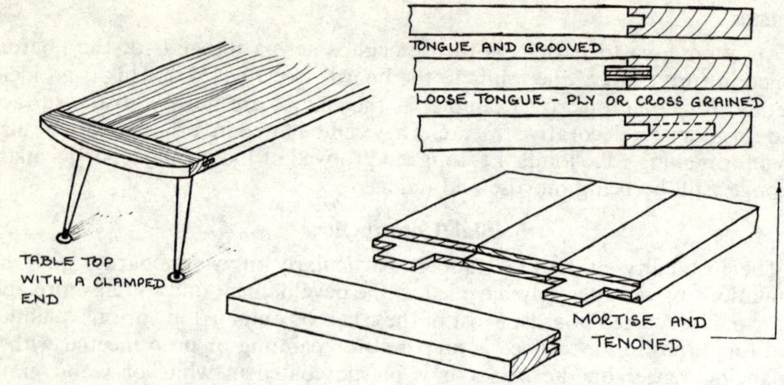

Fig. 247. Wide board construction.

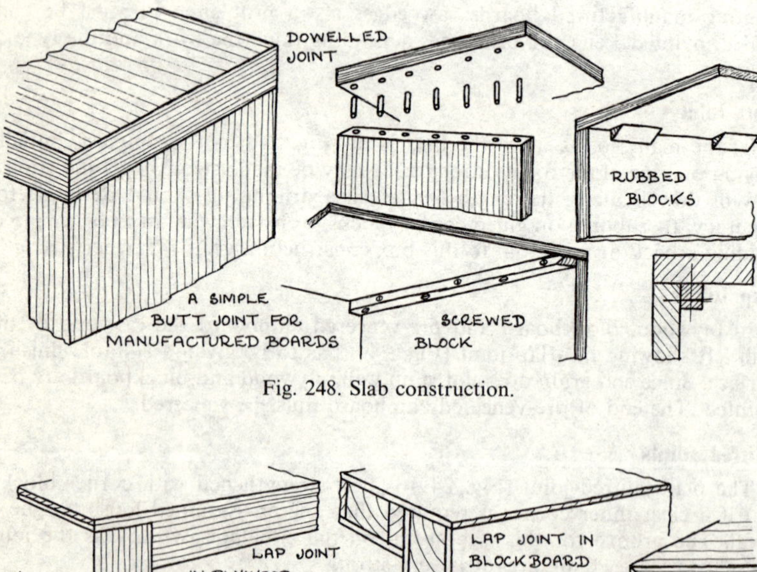

Fig. 248. Slab construction.

Fig. 249. Slab construction.

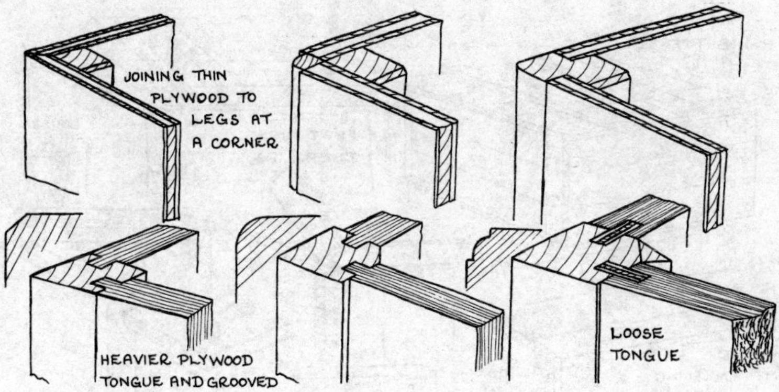

Fig. 250. Slab construction.

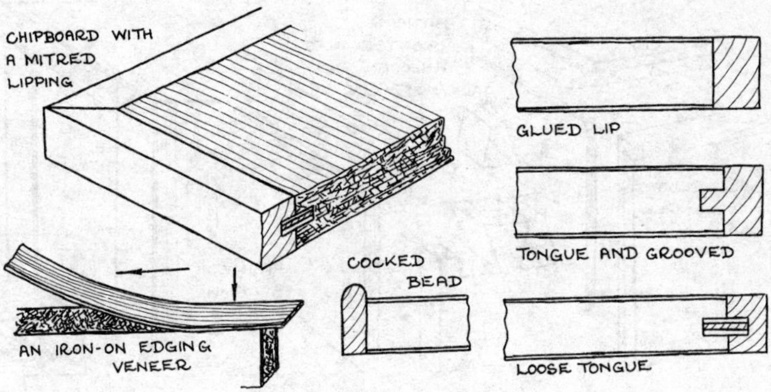

Fig. 251. Slab construction.

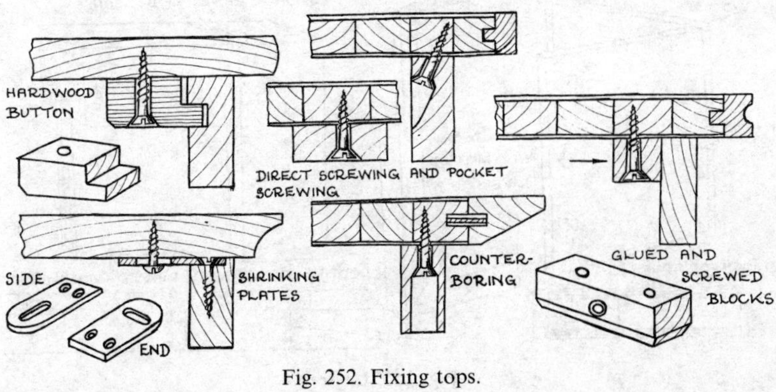

Fig. 252. Fixing tops.

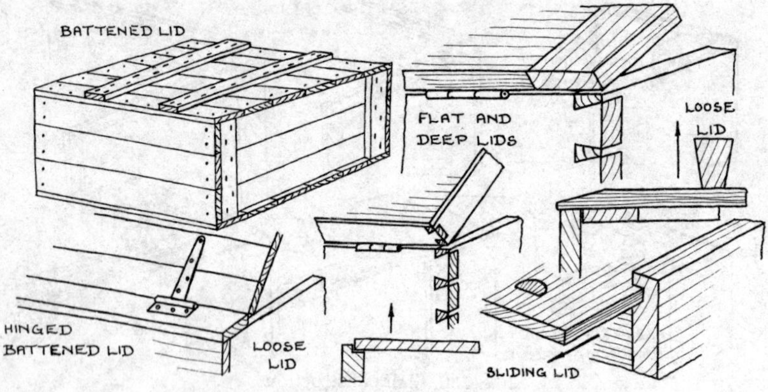

Fig. 253. Lids.

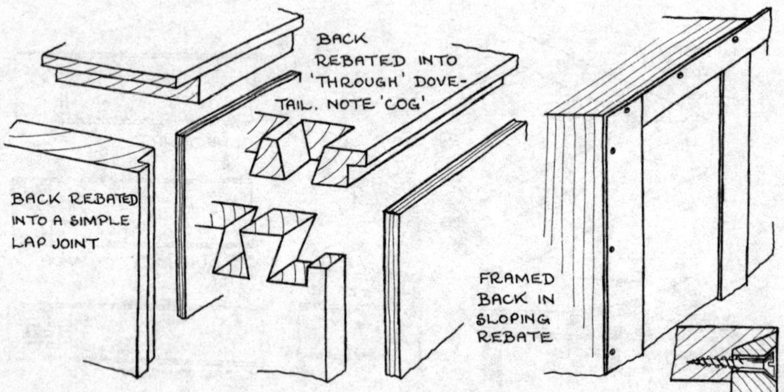

Fig. 254. Carcase backs.

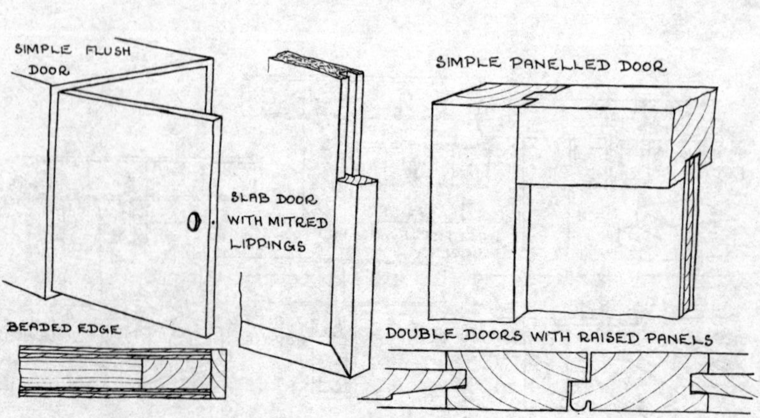

Fig. 255. Doors.

desired. Other variations of the jointing arrangement at such corners are possible and the reader is invited to give some thought to their design.

Lipping Manufactured Boards

It is almost always necessary at some stage of construction when using manufactured boards to 'lip' the edge (see Fig. 251). This is to protect them from damage and to improve the appearance of table tops, shelves, drawer fronts and doors, etc. For pre-veneered chipboard, matching strips of pre-glued veneer are available. This uses hot-press glue and the strips are ironed on with a domestic iron. Waste is cleaned off when the glue has chilled again. These strips are not as substantial as the 'cocked bead' of matching hardwood, or hardwood lippings. These may be jointed and glued on according to the preference of the craftsman.

Fixing Tops

In fixing 'solid' tops provision must be made for expansion and contraction of the timber, which will only occur to any noticeable extent across the grain (see Fig. 252). This can be allowed for by using hardwood 'buttons' screwed to the underside of the top and fitting into grooves in the side of the rail. Metal 'shrinking' plates may be bought or made as an alternative to buttons. The reader should note the difference between that for the side rail and the one for the end.

As manufactured board is so stable it can be screwed directly into place using the most suitable of the following methods: direct screwing, pocket screwing, counterboring, or glued and screwed blocks.

Lids

A number of so-called box constructions require lids. These may be semi-permanent—for example, the packing case where the lid would be screwed or nailed down during transit—or be hinged, sliding or completely loose (Fig. 253). Tee hinges are suitable for use on work such as rough chests, rabbit hutches, chicken runs, etc., where the lid would be battened together. Flat lids with clamped ends and deep lids both require butt hinges. Loose lids which simply lift off can be located by strips of wood, or a second piece fastened underneath, or in a rebate. The arrangement for a simple sliding lid such as might be used for a pencil box is also illustrated in Fig. 253.

Carcase Backs

Plywood is generally used for the backs of carcases. It is screwed or glued and pinned into rebates cut into the back edges of the carcase members. Fig. 254 shows examples jointed with a simple lap and a through dovetail. You should note the wide pin and 'cog' used to conceal the rebate in this case.

If an exceptionally strong back is required it can be built up as a 'framed and panelled' back, in which case it is screwed into rebates with sloping sides. These have a wedging effect as the screws draw the frame in tightly and also allow more wood to be left round the frame to support the screw head and avoid splitting. It should be noted that no rebate is required at the bottom of the carcase.

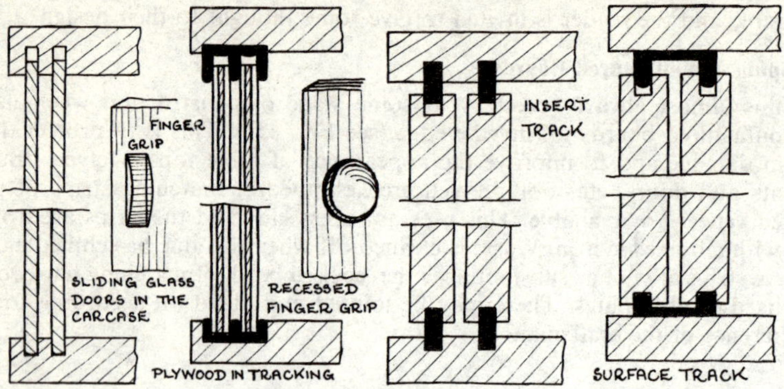

Fig. 256. Doors.

Simple Doors

For cabinets small doors can be constructed in a number of ways (see Fig. 255). **Flush doors** may be built up on a flat frame with hardboard or plywood glued and perhaps pinned to the sides. The joints used for the frame will depend upon the importance of the work and the choice of the craftsman, as will the number of cross members required within the frame to give it adequate strength. Lippings are applied to conceal and protect the edges of the hardwood or plywood. **Slab doors** are made with mitred lippings glued round the edge; the tongue may be cut on the lipping or may be 'loose'. **Framed and panelled doors** have 'raised' or 'fielded' panels and the section in Fig. 255 also shows the arrangement if the doors are double.

Sliding Doors

Sliding doors (Fig. 256) may be comparatively thin, of glass or plywood, and can be run in grooves in the top and bottom of the carcase. Finger recesses can be ground into glass, or simple inserts of wood or plastic pressed into holes cut into the plywood. Nylon or plastic tracking is available for thin doors and can be fastened with screws and a suitable impact adhesive to the surface of the upper and lower carcase members, or into grooves.

For thicker material and larger doors insert or surface tracks of plastic can be used. A plastic runner screwed to the bottom of the door will further reduce both wear and friction. In every case you should note how the space at the top allows the doors to be lifted up and dropped into place.

To conclude this chapter, various pieces of work are shown in Figs. 257 and 258, but no indication is given as to how they would be constructed. You are invited to look at them carefully and consider what joints you would use, again with reference to Chapter 8 where appropriate. In each case you should also consider what type of material they should be made of and the finish which you would employ to make them suitable for their purpose.

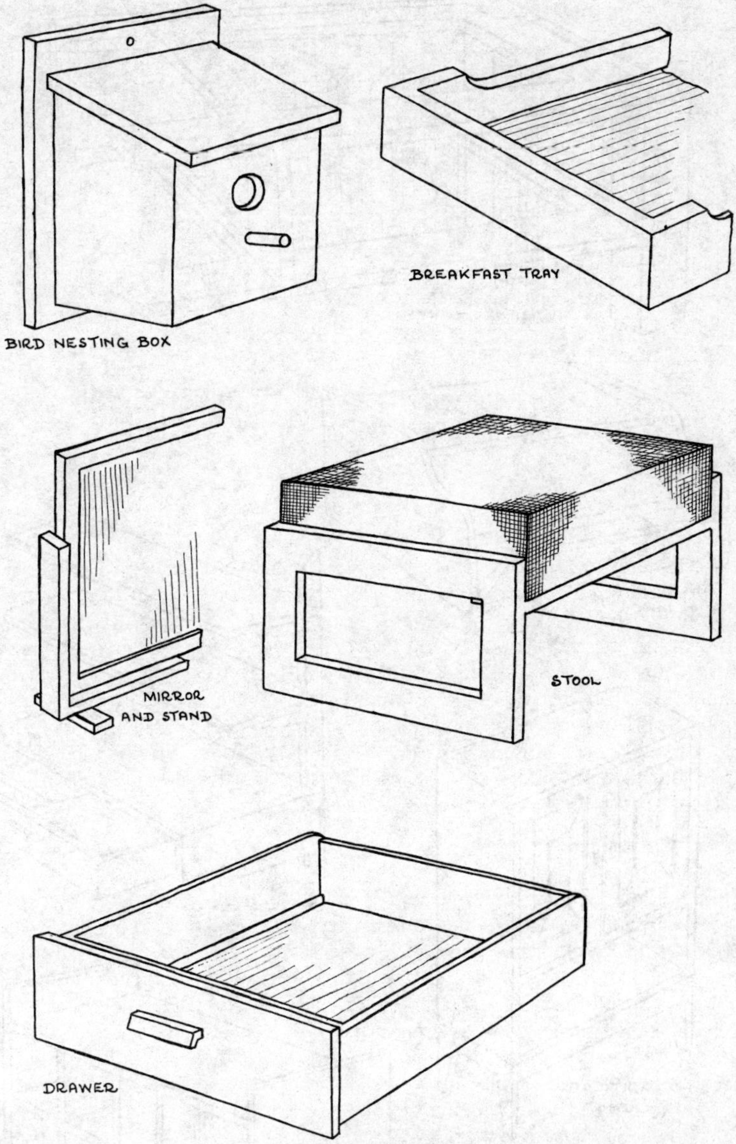

Fig. 257. Suggested work pieces.

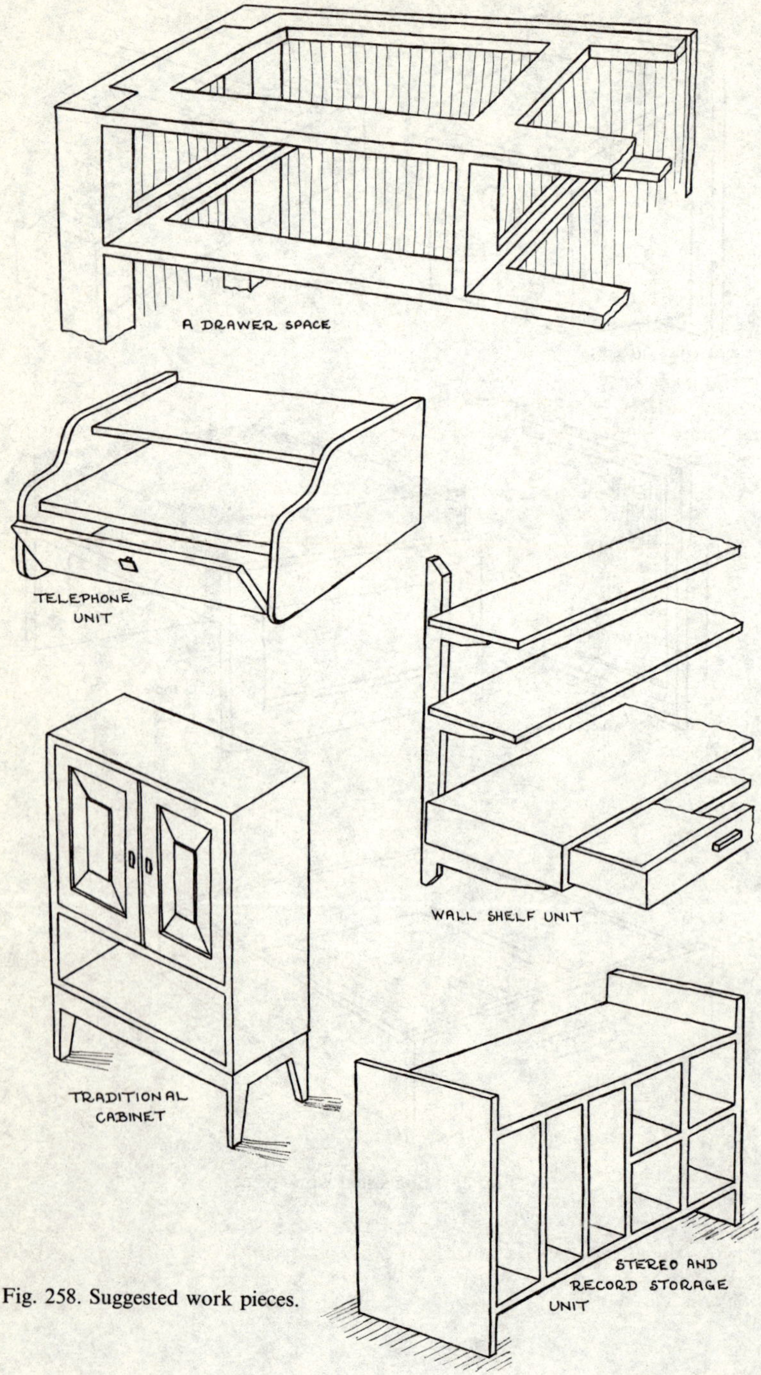

Fig. 258. Suggested work pieces.

9

FIXING

Nails

The common purpose of all nails is to fasten materials together. This they do quickly and efficiently by the friction created between the nail and the material into which it is driven. Generally nails are used to secure wood to wood, but there are special types for fastening metal to masonry, wood to masonry, etc. These various uses have led to many different kinds of nails being made, each associated with different trades' requirements. Nails made from copper and bronze were hammered into shape from the cold metal by the ancient Egyptians, but in this country they were originally forged by hand from iron. A rod of iron was heated, cut into short lengths and one end of each piece forged to a point. Each piece in turn was then placed point downwards into a hole in an anvil (Fig. 259). The hole had a countersunk lip into which the protruding part of the rod was hammered to form the head. After cooling and contraction, the completed nail was then easily removed from the anvil. People so employed were called 'nailers'.

At this time some nails were cast by running molten metal into moulds. These were cheaper than the hand-wrought variety but had the disadvantage of being very brittle. Where it was necessary to clench over nails to give a permanent fixing, as for metal fittings into doors, the hand-wrought type was still superior as the point could be doubled back without fracturing (see Fig. 260). Nails clenched over in this way were said to be **dead** in that it was almost impossible to remove them (hence the saying 'as dead as a door nail').

Cut nails were produced much more quickly and cheaply after the introduction of a machine in 1640 by an Englishman, Richard Foley, which rolled iron into sheets that were then slit into strips. Nails were cut from these strips and soon became widely used for many purposes. They were used extensively for fastening down floorboards. Being flat-sided they could be hammered down into the wood leaving no part protruding (Fig. 261).

The main methods of nail-making up to the mid-eighteenth century therefore were:

Hand-wrought—forged by hand from hot iron (Fig. 262).
Cut nails—cut from iron strip by machine.
Cast nails—molten iron run into moulds.

There is a record of the first automatic nail-cutting machine being in use in the late eighteenth century whereby nails were mass produced cheaply. This in turn led to a method of mass producing nails from coils of wire on fully automatic machines, and although the basic principle of the nail-forming machine has not changed since then, nail manufacture is now one of the most efficient and highly automated of industrial processes.

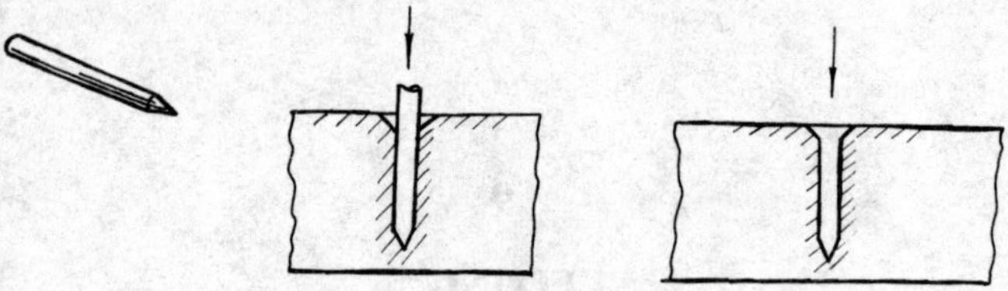

Fig. 259. Method of hand-forging nails.

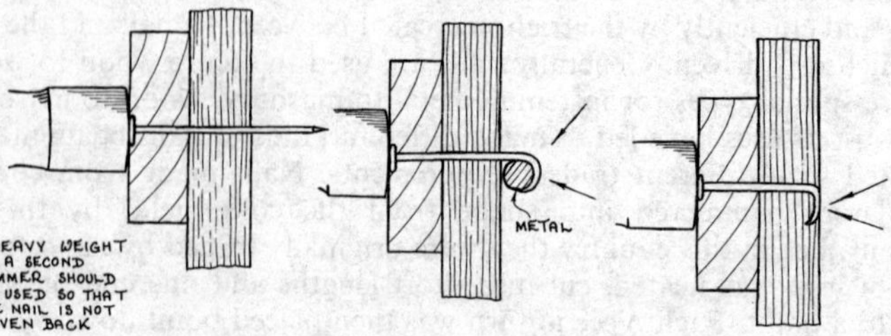

Fig. 260. Clenching over a nail to make it 'dead'.

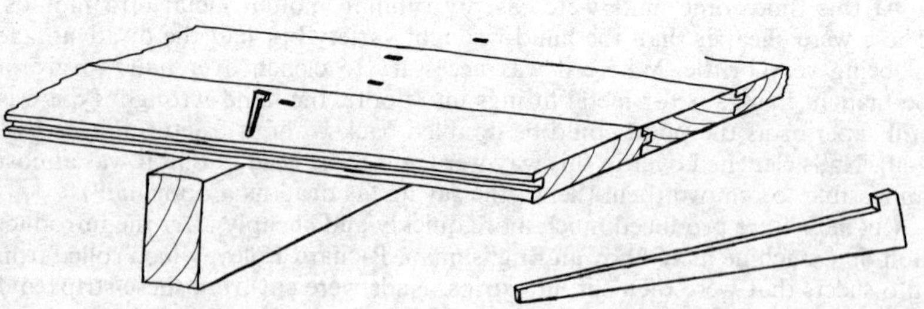

Fig. 261. Cut flooring brad.

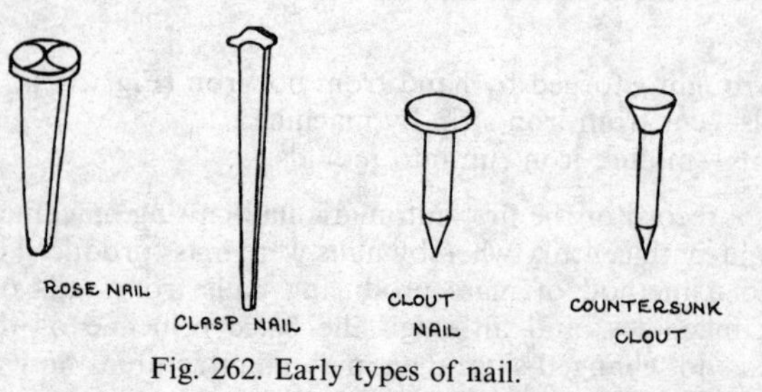

Fig. 262. Early types of nail.

Fig. 263. Automated nail manufacture.

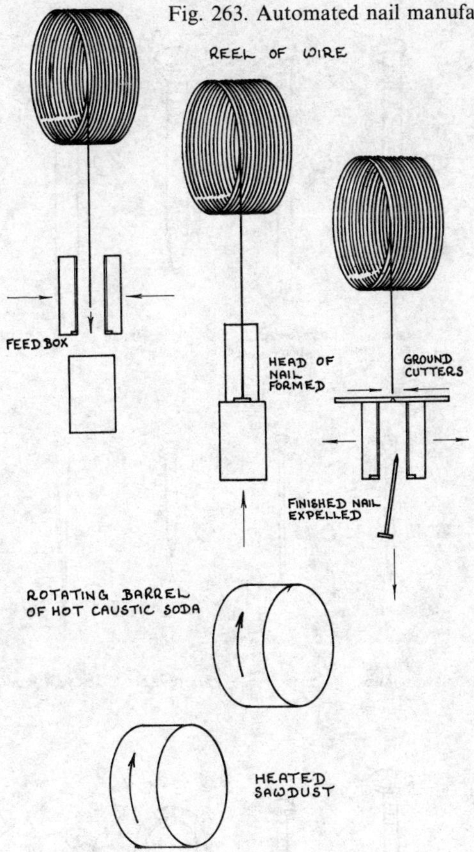

There are five distinct operations (see Fig. 263).

1. Forming the head. Wire is drawn from the coil into the machine and the head is formed by flattening the end of the wire against a die.
2. Feeding the wire. The die opens, and the feed mechanism pushes the wire forward the correct distance (this being the length of the nail).
3. Pinching the wire. The die now closes again, gripping the wire.
4. Cutting off the wire and forming the point. Two cutters which are ground to form a point on the nail move together and chop off the nail.
5. Expelling the nail. When the cutters have opened an expeller knocks the nail into a pan below the machine.

These basic operations can be augmented by additional forming or twisting devices for special nails, such as roofing nails, with twisted shanks and those with helical spirals to give an extra firm grip. By adjusting or changing the

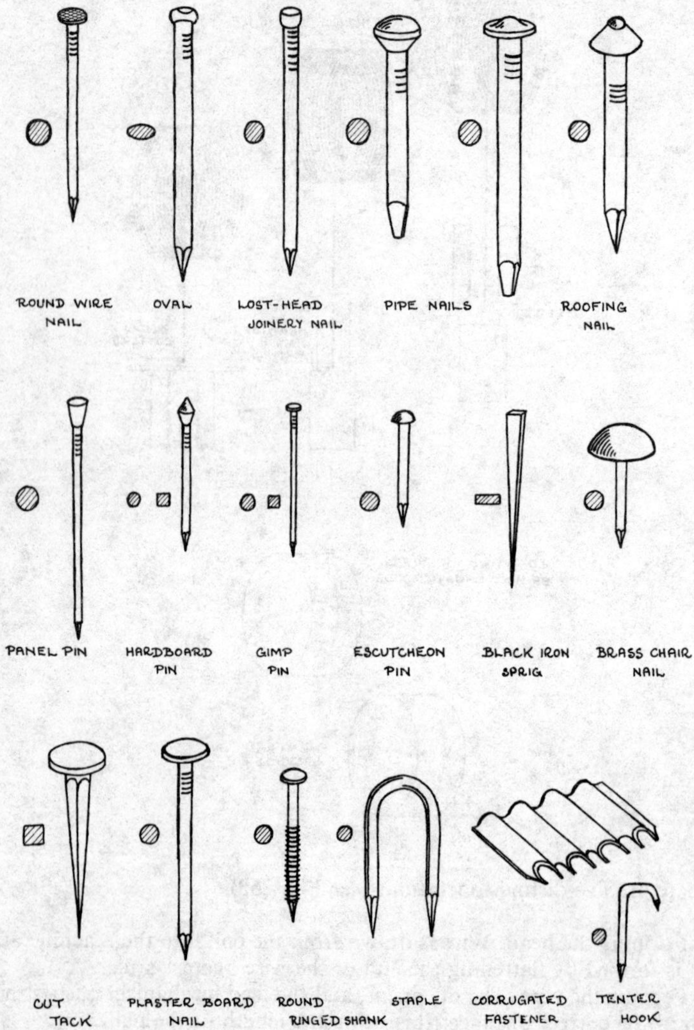

Fig. 264. Varieties of Nail.

punch, various shaped heads—diamond, brad, rose, lost, etc.—can be made while various points—pencil, chisel, diamond etc.—can be produced with suitable cutters.

Most nails are made from steel wire with a carbon content of 0·19 to 0·25 per cent, but clout nails are made from a wire with a carbon content of 0·06 to 0·13 per cent, which is softer. GKN, for example, manufacture a wide variety of nails of different lengths and gauges ranging from approximately 5 mm long × 1 mm diameter to 304·8 mm × 9·53 mm in diameter.

After forming, the nails are cleaned by being churned in a large metal barrel containing hot caustic soda. They are then polished by being churned in a second barrel which is heated by gas jets and contains sawdust. This dries the nails and gives them a bright finish. Depending upon their use they may be supplied bright, or may be galvanised in molten zinc, or be 'sherardised'. The latter process applies a corrosion-resisting coat of zinc by heating the nails to a temperature of about 300 °C in a closed container with a powder of zinc dust and zinc oxide.

Britain's largest nail factory is at Cardiff, where more than 200 fully automatic machines produce about 1,400 nails per second, or about 300 million each week. This amounts to 800 tons by weight; about half the total production of the country. Some of the very many different varieties are illustrated in Fig. 264.

Nailing is not at all difficult but a few simple techniques should be observed. Naturally, the **correct nail** for the work should be selected and a suitable weight of hammer used. The hammer head should be kept clean to avoid slipping off the nail, which in turn should be hit squarely, avoiding glancing blows which may result in a bent nail, damage to the work and injured fingers. A nail of the **correct length** should be used to give maximum strength and this is usually considered to be three to four times the thickness of the top piece of wood (see Fig. 265).

Care should be taken to **avoid splitting** the wood. Again, chosing the correct nail partially avoids this: for example, oval nails are less likely to cause splitting than are round ones because they do not force the fibres of the wood as far apart. To reduce the danger of splitting, the point of the nail may be blunted by filing or being hammered on a hard surface so that it tends to drill its own hole by tearing through the fibres of the wood rather than by pushing them apart.

Splitting may also occur if a row of nails is put in line along a piece of wood as this increases the wedging effect, and in practice they should be **staggered** (see Fig. 266), which also pulls the two pieces of wood more firmly together.

To avoid splitting where nailing is being done near the end of the wood, it is advisable to drill holes for the nails with either the bradawl or a hand drill. This may be at the corner of a box, where the nailing can be made more effective by sloping them in a **dovetail** fashion (Fig. 267).

As a general rule all nails, except those with special heads, are knocked in **level** with the surface of the wood, care being taken not to bruise the surface with the hammerhead. Where it is desirable for the nail head not to show—for example, where a painted finish is to be applied—nails with small heads should be used so that they can be **punched in** and a filler applied (see Fig. 268).

Tongued and grooved boards may be **secret nailed** so that the nail heads do

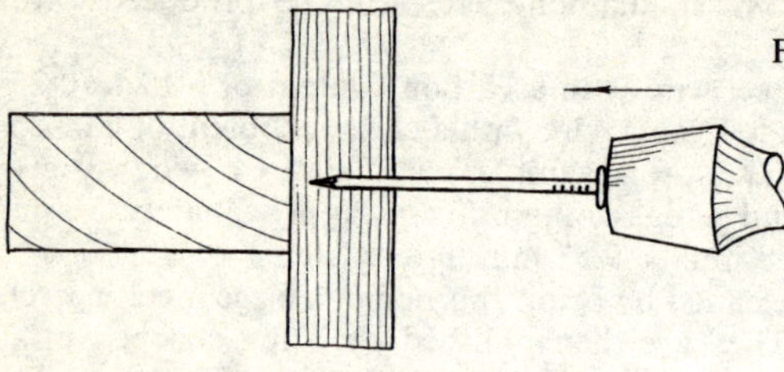

Fig. 265. Correct length of nail.

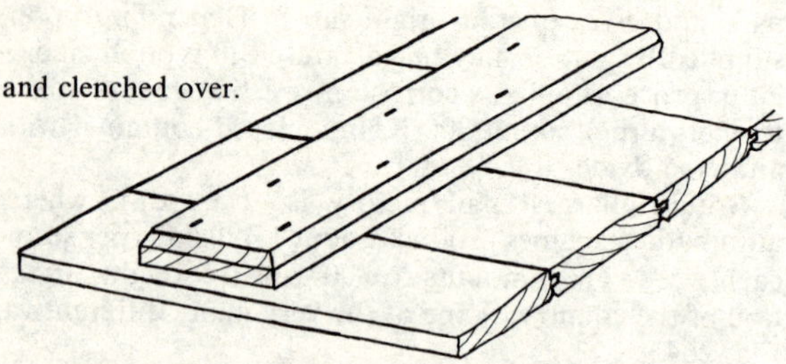

Fig. 266. Nails staggered and clenched over.

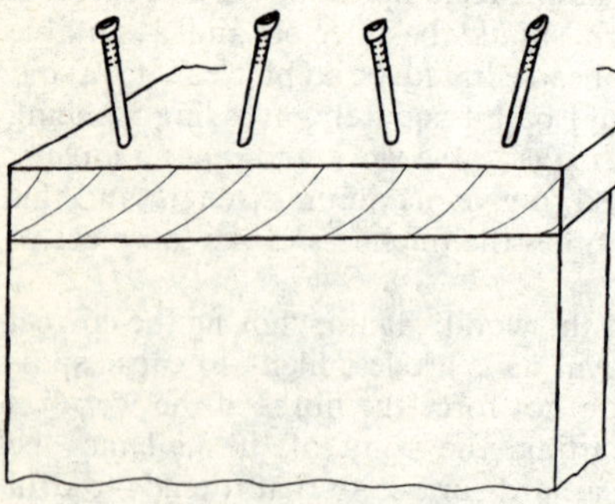

Fig. 267. Dovetail nailing.

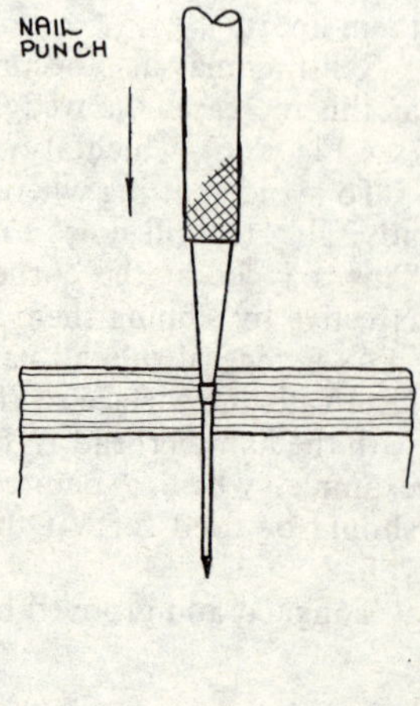

Fig. 268. Punching below the surface.

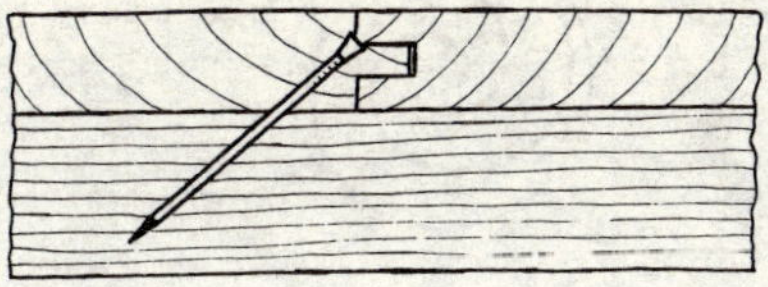

Fig. 269. Secret nailing.

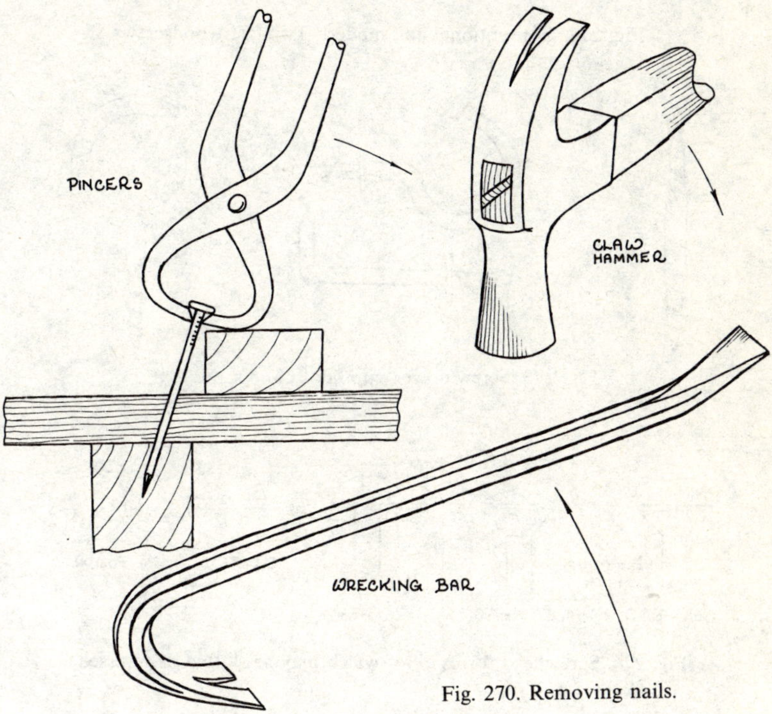

Fig. 270. Removing nails.

Fig. 271. Hardened fixing pins and washer (note point shape).

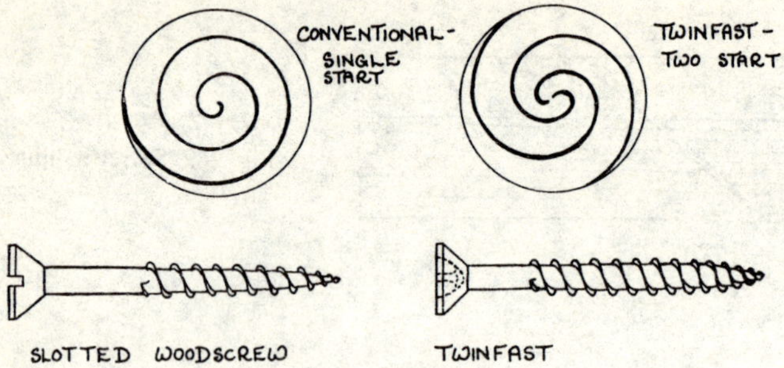

Fig. 272. Conventional and modern Twinfast woodscrews.

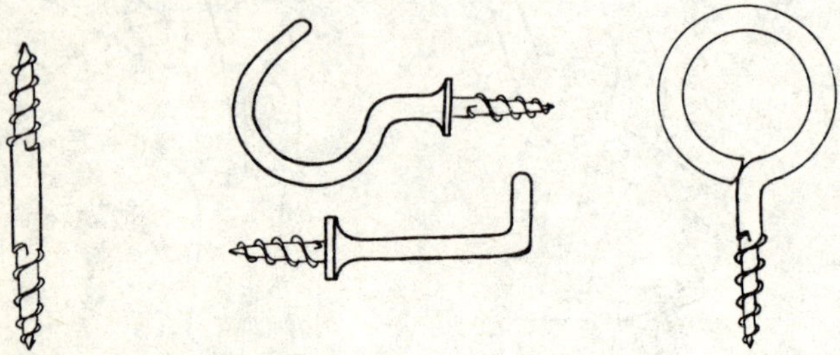

Fig. 273. Screw dowel, cup hooks and screw eye.

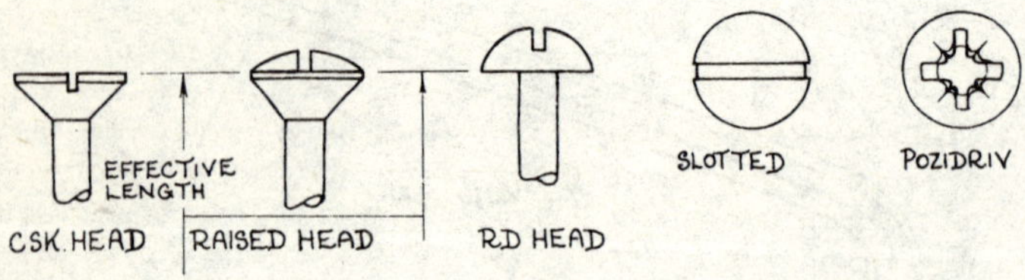

Fig. 274. Screwhead forms all of which may be slotted or recessed.

Fig. 275. Screw cups.

not show (Fig. 269). This is done through the tongue so that the groove of each succeeding board covers the nail head.

Pincers, the claw hammer, or for really heavy work the 'wrecking bar', are the tools with which to **extract** nails. To give a fulcrum on which to lever, and at the same time protect the surface, a pad of scrap wood is placed between the tool and the work (see Fig. 270).

Wooden battens, skirting boards and other wooden fixtures can be nailed directly to brickwork with the GKN **hardened fixing pin**. These are manufactured from specially selected steel which is hardened and tempered, and can be hammered direct into brickwork, breeze blocks, and average mix concrete for secure and permanent fastenings. The pins are zinc-coated to give protection against corrosion. When selecting lengths, a penetration of 16–19 mm into the solid brickwork beyond any top plaster is recommended for maximum efficiency. Initially, light hammer blows should be used to start the penetration, completing with a few straight heavy blows. To minimise possible danger from splintering it is advisable to wear safety goggles. Butt and mushroom heads are available, as are zinc-plated washers for under the head. Butt-headed pins can be obtained from $\frac{3}{4} \times \frac{1}{4}$ inch to $2\frac{1}{2}$ inch length $\times$ 2·5 mm diameter and $1\frac{1}{2} \times \frac{1}{2}$ inch to 4 inch length $\times$ 3·5 mm diameter, and mushroom heads $\frac{3}{4}$ and 1 inch length only $\times$ 2·5 mm diameter.

Woodscrews

Firm, strong joints can be made with woodscrews between wood and wood. Unlike nails (particularly if they have been clenched over), woodscrews can be removed readily without damage to the surrounding material. This allows for easy adjustment to an assembly, which is particularly useful if the screws are being used for attaching metal components such as hinges, stays, locks, etc. As a general rule woodscrews are used in high-class joinery and cabinet work, and are also preferable to nails for vehicle body or caravan construction. Because of their greater grip, woodscrews will pull glued surfaces closely together and a strong joint will be obtained.

The principle of the screw thread is one of man's major mechanical discoveries, equal in importance to the principle of the lever and wheel. The woodscrew thread is designed to form its own mating thread in the timber to which it is applied. It is a so-called spaced thread and may be grouped into two basic types: conventional (single-start) and Twinfast (two-start), as in Fig. 272.

The **conventional thread** form runs out to a gimlet point and takes up two thirds the length of the screw. The remaining one third is plain and has a shank diameter equal to the major diameter of the thread.

The **Twinfast thread** is two-start and is taken up to the head of the screw. Lengths over $1\frac{1}{4}$ inches do, however, have a plain portion under the head with a shank diameter approximately equal to the average of the minor and major diameter of the thread. The smaller shank diameter reduces the danger of splitting. This thread was designed for application to man-made boards, such as chipboard, improving the holding power and increasing the speed of assembly. The conventional woodscrew thread is also applied to screw dowels, hooks and eyes and similar products (Fig. 273).

Head shapes in common use for woodscrews are countersunk (CSK), **round (RND), and raised countersunk (RSD CSK). These may have slotted** or recessed heads. The advantages of the recessed head are:

1. The driver engages positively in the screw recess without slipping, so that the screw is easier to drive with less effort.
2. There is less risk of damaging the surface of the work, the recess or the screw driver.
3. Even in difficult places the screws can be driven safely by only using one hand.
4. It gives easier alignment.
5. It is more decorative.

The three basic head styles each have their own particular use. The **countersunk head** woodscrew is primarily used for fixing wood to wood or metal to wood. As the screw is turned the countersunk head is drawn down into a predrilled countersunk clearance hole, leaving the surface of the work completely level. **Round-headed** woodscrews are used mainly for attaching metal fittings to wood, particularly if they are thin, as the flat underside of the screw head gives extra support to the metal. The head style of the **raised countersunk** woodscrew is more aesthetically pleasing and enhances the appearance of the work; hence its frequent use in high-quality products. Both countersunk head and raised head woodscrews can be used in conjunction with brass screw cups (turned pattern) or brass or stainless steel surface screw cups (Fig. 275). Very often these improve the appearance of the work to make the screw head a decorative feature.

In choosing the **correct screw** for the work it is expected to do, the following points must be remembered.

1. Length. This depends upon the width and thickness of the timber into which it will be inserted. If the screw is fixing wood to wood its overall length should not be less than three times the thickness of the outer piece. For maximum holding, there should be seven diameters of thread engagement and certainly not less than four.
2. Diameter by screw gauge (S.G.). This should not exceed one tenth of the width of the wood into which it is inserted.
3. The screw must be of the type of metal most suited to the work it has to do, particularly with regard to the strength required to withstand any stresses and strains which may occur within the construction.
4. Head style, paying attention to what is being fixed and the appearance of the finished work.
5. Type of finish or protective plating, if any, covering the basic metal from which the screw is made. (The nature of the work and the atmospheric conditions to which the screw will be subjected must be taken into consideration.)

For example, a screw might be specified in the following way:

1¼ inch × No. 8 gauge steel: Supadriv: round-head woodscrew: black-japanned

To avoid the risk of **splitting** the timber or having to use undue force to insert the screw (which may result in damage to the screw head, consequent damage to the work, or the shearing off of the screw within the wood) pilot

Table 1. Pilot Holes for Conventional Woodscrews

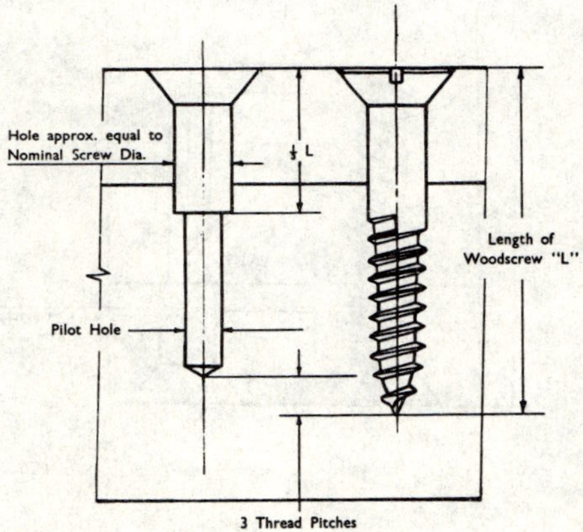

WOOD SCREW				PILOT HOLE							
Diameter		Core Dia.	3 × Pitch	Hard Woods				Soft Woods			
				Pilot Hole Dia.	Drill Sizes			Pilot Hole Dia.	Drill Sizes		
Screw Gauge	Nom.	Approx.	Approx.		Fraction	M/M	Letter or No.		Fraction	M/M	Letter or No.
0	·060	·040	$\frac{3}{32}$	·038		·975	62				
1	·070	·044	$\frac{3}{32}$	·042		1·05	58	It is not considered			
2	·082	·051	$\frac{1}{8}$	·049		1·25		necessary to have pilot			
3	·094	·059	$\frac{1}{8}$	·057		1·45		holes for these sizes.			
4	·108	·068	$\frac{1}{8}$	·066		1·70	51				
5	·122	·076	$\frac{5}{32}$	·073		1·85	49				
6	·136	·085	$\frac{5}{32}$	·082		2·10	45	·059		1·50	53
7	·150	·094	$\frac{3}{16}$	·091	$\frac{3}{32}$	2·30		·066		1·70	51
8	·164	·102	$\frac{7}{32}$	·097		2·50	40	·071		1·80	49
9	·178	·111	$\frac{1}{4}$	·103		2·65	37	·078	$\frac{5}{64}$	2·00	47
10	·192	·120	$\frac{1}{4}$	·108	$\frac{7}{64}$	2·75	35	·084		2·15	44
12	·220	·138	$\frac{5}{16}$	·124	$\frac{1}{8}$	3·15		·097		2·50	40
14	·248	·155	$\frac{11}{32}$	·140	$\frac{9}{64}$	3·60	28	·108	$\frac{7}{64}$	2·75	35
16	·276	·173	$\frac{3}{8}$	·156	$\frac{5}{32}$	4·00	22	·121		3·10	
18	·304	·190	$\frac{13}{32}$	·171	$\frac{11}{64}$	4·35	17	·131		3·35	
20	·332	·208	$\frac{7}{16}$	·187	$\frac{3}{16}$	4·75	12	·145		3·70	26
24	·388	·243	$\frac{1}{2}$	·219	$\frac{7}{32}$	5·60	2	·170	$\frac{11}{64}$	4·35	18
28	·444	·278	$\frac{9}{16}$	·250	$\frac{1}{4}$	6·40	E	·195		5·00	9
32	·500	·313	$\frac{5}{8}$	·282	$\frac{9}{32}$	7·20	K	·219	$\frac{7}{32}$	5·60	2

All dimensions are in inches unless stated otherwise.

Table 2. Pilot Holes for Twinfast Woodscrews

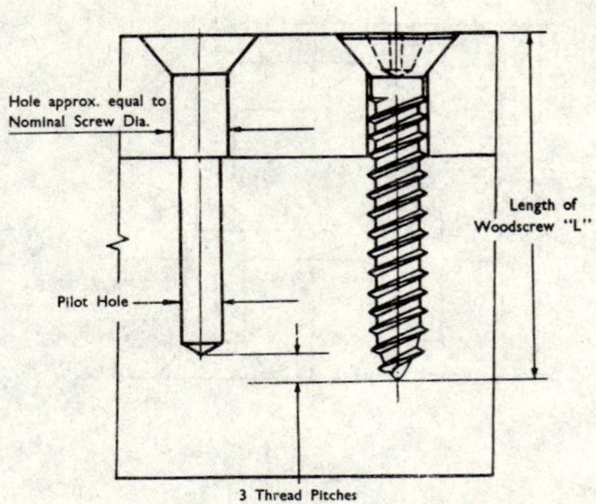

WOOD SCREW				PILOT HOLE							
Diameter		Core Dia.	3 × Pitch	Hard Woods				Soft Woods			
				Pilot Hole Dia.	Drill Sizes			Pilot Hole Dia.	Drill Sizes		
Screw Gauge	Nom.	Approx.	Approx.		Fraction	M/M	Letter or No.		Fraction	M/M	Letter or No.
4	·112	·086	·125	·070		1·80	50	·049		1·25	
5	·128	·096	·136	·082		2·10	45	·057		1·45	
6	·137	·099	·150	·093	$\frac{3}{32}$		42	·062	$\frac{1}{16}$		
7	·152	·112	·166	·106		2·70	36	·065		1·65	
8	·164	·122	·166	·116		2·95	32	·076		1·95	48
9	·176	·124	·187	·118		3·00		·082		2·10	45
10	·186	·134	·200	·125	$\frac{1}{8}$			·089		2·25	43
12	·212	·152	·231	·142		3·60		·102		2·60	38
14	·243	·177	·250	·166		4·20	19	·116		2·95	32

All dimensions are in inches unless stated otherwise.

holes should be drilled where necessary. GKN recommendations are given below and in Tables 1 and 2.

The best pilot hole for any particular application can only be determined by trial and error since it is dependent upon such variable factors as hardness and moisture content.

The following recommendations are given, however, in the belief that they will be found satisfactory for the majority of applications and will normally allow the maximum axial holding power of the woodscrews to be obtained.

Recommendations are given for both hard and soft woods; hardwoods normally include ash, beech, birch, elm, mahogany, oak and teak, while softwoods normally include cedar, fir, pine and spruce. In distinguishing between hard and soft woods, however, the relative hardness of the wood should be considered and not the botanical classification.

When the length of the woodscrew is greater than ten times the nominal diameter, a lubricant such as tallow or beeswax should be used.

If extra precautions against splitting the wood and/or lower driving torques are required the pilot hole diameter may be increased but this will result in some loss of holding power.

It is bad practice to screw into the end grain of timber. The holding power of the screws so used is very inferior since in tightening the screw the threads sever the fibres of the wood. A sudden knock will then pull the screw out. The problem can be overcome if really necessary by gluing a dowel from edge to edge of the member into which the screws are to be driven. The screw threads then engage with the side grain of the dowel and obtain a secure hold. Alternatively, fibre or plastic plugs can be inserted into holes drilled into the end of the wood. These in turn offer the screw a firm grip. Fig. 276 illustrates the two methods.

Appendix 2 contains lists of slotted and Supadriv conventional type and Twinfast screws and the finishes in which they may be obtained. Pozidriv drivers or bits will fit the new style Supadriv recess. (Size No. 1 fits 3–4 S.G.; No. 2 fits 5–10 S.G.; and No. 3 fits 12–14 S.G.)

Unframed mirrors are often screwed directly to the wall through pre-drilled holes. In such cases a **mirror screw** (Fig. 277) should be used. This has a head which is tapped and into which a chromium-plated cap is screwed to cover the head completely.

GKN supply the **Plastidome** (Fig. 277), a snap-on cover for screws. This is available chromium-plated or in black, white, red, light blue, light green, pink and yellow and may be used with any type of screw. Plastic caps (see Fig. 227) are available in a limited range of colours. These have been designed to provide a neat flush-fitting cover to conceal recessed countersunk head screws. The spigot located on the underside of the cap is lightly hammered into the recess of the head of the screw. (No. 2 is suitable for S.G. 5–10 and No. 3 for S.G. 12 and 14.)

Coach Screws, Cup Square Carriage Bolts and Nuts

For heavy constructional work where conventional woodscrews would not be sufficiently strong, **coach screws** are available (see Fig. 278). These are particularly useful for fastening heavy metal fittings to wood. A pilot hole

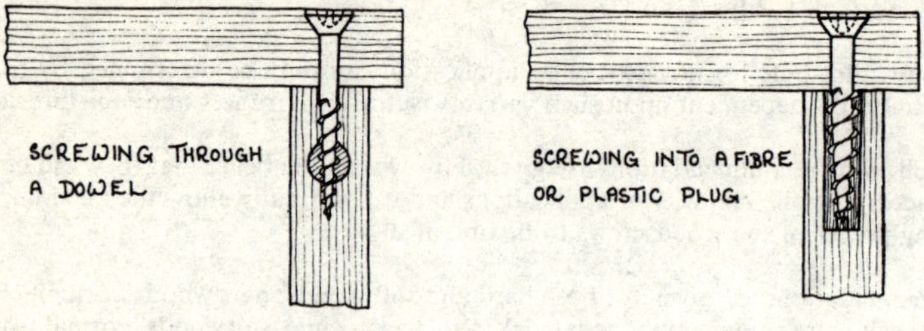

Fig. 276. Screwing into end grain.

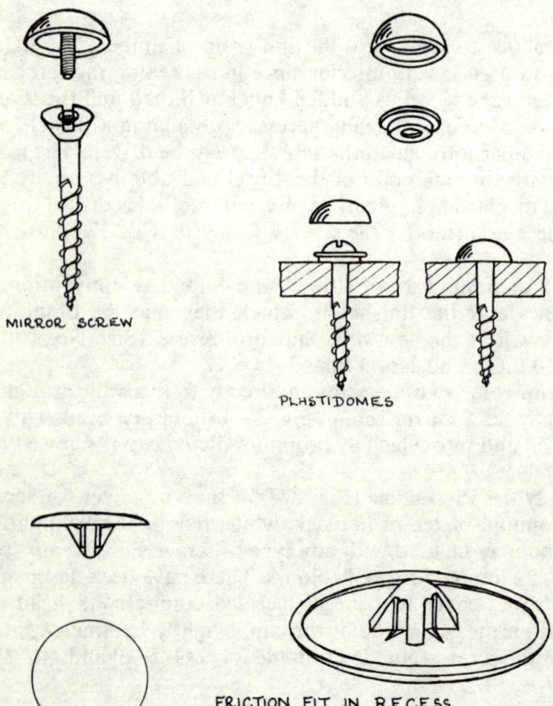

Fig. 277. Screw caps.

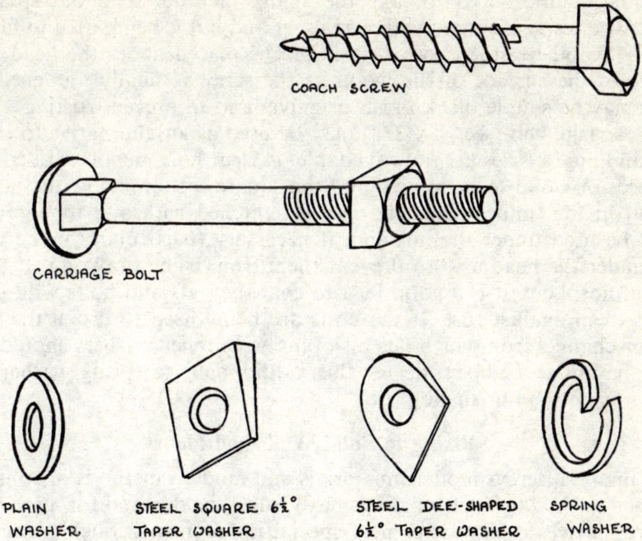

Fig. 278. The coach screw and carriage bolt.

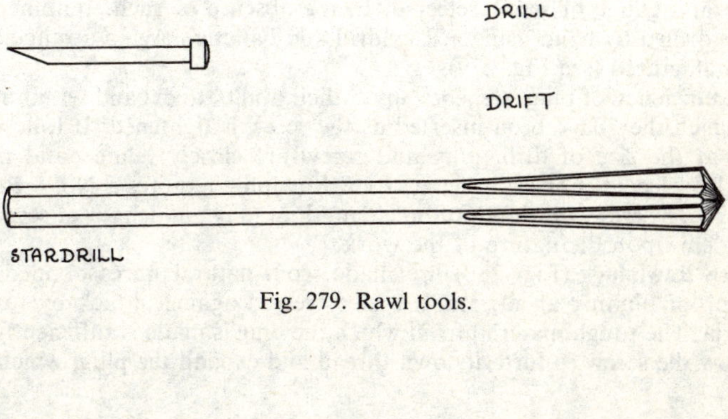

Fig. 279. Rawl tools.

should be drilled a little less than the core of the screw, and if necessary this should be counterbored to take the shank in order to avoid splitting the timber. The screw is turned with a spanner and if it is being used to fasten two pieces of wood together a washer should be placed under the head to avoid damage to the surface of the wood as the screw is finally tightened. Coach screws may be simple black finish or galvanised to prevent rusting.

The **carriage bolt** (see Fig. 278) may be used as an alternative to the coach screw and metric sizes are now available. A clear hole must be drilled through the pieces of wood to be joined, and the square section below the head locks the bolt in the timber while the nut is tightened with a spanner. A washer should be used under the nut and, if necessary (particularly if the timber is soft), under the head also to prevent them from being drawn in. If used in a damp atmosphere, it is a good idea to coat the nuts and bolts with grease to protect them against rust. If the bolts are being used to fasten the wood to angle or channel iron which has a sloping web, taper washers should be used under the nut to compensate for this; additionally, a spring washer may be used to make the nut shake-proof.

Fixing to Solid Walls and Floors

The many different modern materials and modern methods of construction now used in the fabric of buildings have led to the demand for a great variety of fixing devices designed to meet special requirements. Such fixings can be roughly divided into two categories: those for fixing to solid walls or floors and those for fixing to cavities or hollow walls where there is no access to the reverse side. The competent woodworker should then be sufficiently skilful and knowledgeable to design his work in such a way that it can be secured firmly and easily by the most appropriate method.

Modern furnishing schemes in comparatively small rooms often require that items such as cabinets, mirrors, racks and open shelves for which battens are required should be fastened to the wall, leaving the maximum amount of floor space free. Solid walls in older properties may be of masonry or brick, but in more modern homes they are likely to be of breeze or thermolite blocks. Lightweight battens can be readily fixed to these and to brick using hardened fixing pins (see p. 219), but for heavier work suitable **plugs** which will carry screws should be used. In general, holes for these are drilled with a power tool fitted with a tungsten carbide tipped masonry drill. A range of such drills is available, as is a range of plugs so that suitable sizes can be chosen for the length and gauge of screw selected. In the absence of such equipment holes can be drilled by hand using a Rawldrill and hammer. Again a range of drills is manufactured (see Fig. 279).

The efficiency of plugs depends upon their ability to expand within the hole into which they have been inserted as the screw is tightened. It follows from this that the size of drill, plug and screw are closely related and must be carefully selected. For example, a No. 8 Rawlplug requires a No. 8 Rawldrill and a No. 8 screw, the depth of hole, length of plug and length of screw being dependent upon the nature of the work.

Fibre Rawlplugs (Fig. 280) are made from natural fibres bonded with a waterproof binding agent, and are also treated against attack by fungi and bacteria. The tough material from which the plug is made is sufficiently elastic to allow the screw to form its own thread and expand the plug, which results in a strong permanent fixing. These plugs are not designed to accommodate the unthreaded shank of the screw and they should therefore be inserted well below the outer surface of the wall. This prevents damage to the area immediately around the plug and to the plug itself as the screw enters and makes it expand. This precaution is particularly necessary when the wall is plastered or of very soft blocks. Fibre plugs are made in a range of sizes for screw gauges 6 to 26 and coach screws $\frac{1}{4}$–$\frac{1}{2}$ inch diameter.

Recommended Methods of Using Plugs

1. Drill hole of correct diameter into the masonry.
2. Turn the screw a little way into the plug.
3. Holding the screw, push the plug into the hole so that it is below the surface of the masonry.
4. Turn the screw into the plug up to the shank.
5. Withdraw the screw. The plug is now expanded and forms a secure fixing within the material.
6. Place the fitment in position, enter the screw through it and tighten.

Plastic plugs of high-strength polypropylene (Fig. 281) are unaffected by corrosive atmospheres and normal temperature changes. The internal taper automatically centres the screw and the plug will accept the plain shank. Protrusions on the side prevent the plug from turning when the screw is being entered. Inserting the screw and securing the fitment should be done in one operation.

Nylon Rawlplugs (Fig. 282) have been designed to give secure fixing in soft materials and lightweight building blocks. Possible rotation of the plug in the hole as the screw is inserted is prevented by angled pins, and the plug will accept the shank of the screw if necessary. These plugs are unaffected by cold weather and will withstand temperatures up to 80 °C.

In conditions where constant high temperatures are experienced—for example, around domestic fires or in boiler houses—**metal plugs** (Fig. 283) are available. In such conditions ordinary masonry plugs may fail. Metal plugs are also recommended for extremely wet conditions such as may be found around fountains or in fixing swimming pool equipment. Although they are non-corrosive it is advisable to use stainless steel or cadmium-plated woodscrews with this type of plug. The makers advise against using brass screws.

It does happen at times, particularly in older walls, that satisfactory drill holes to accept plugs cannot be made. Irregular holes such as these may be filled with **Rawlplastic**. This is a fibrous compound which is moistened, rammed into the hole and then pierced to receive the screw. As the compound dries out the screw is firmly anchored.

Where a stronger fixing is required than can be obtained with masonry plugs, **Rawloks** (Fig. 284) are recommended. These are for use in masonry and are all-steel zinc-plated through bolt fixings, i.e. the fitment is held in position and the hole drilled through it and into the masonry behind. The Rawlok is then inserted and tightened. Windows, doorframes, handrails, etc., can be fixed in this way. A range of lengths with diameters from $\frac{1}{4}$ to $\frac{3}{4}$ inch is available. Bolts may be hexagon nut, dome head, countersunk, round head, eye bolt or hanger bolt. Hexagon heads are of stainless steel.

For very heavy fixing to walls and floors **Rawlbolts** should be used, of which

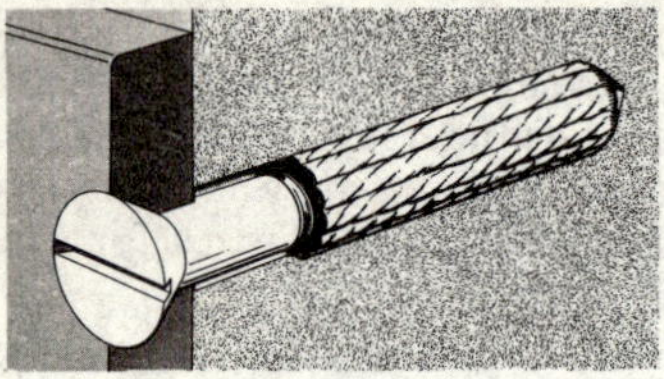

Fig. 280. Fibre Rawlplug.

Fig. 281. Plastic Rawlplug.

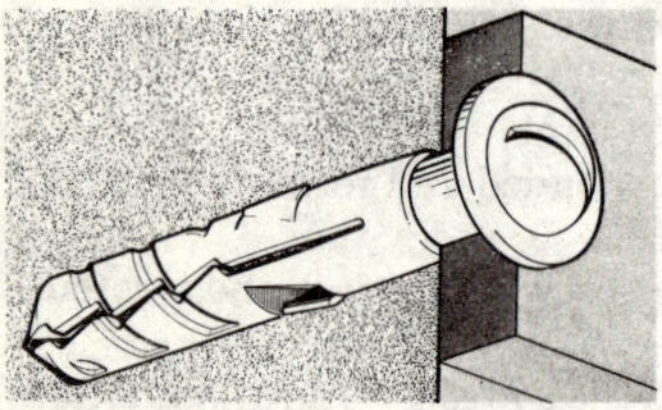

Fig. 282. Nylon Rawlplug.

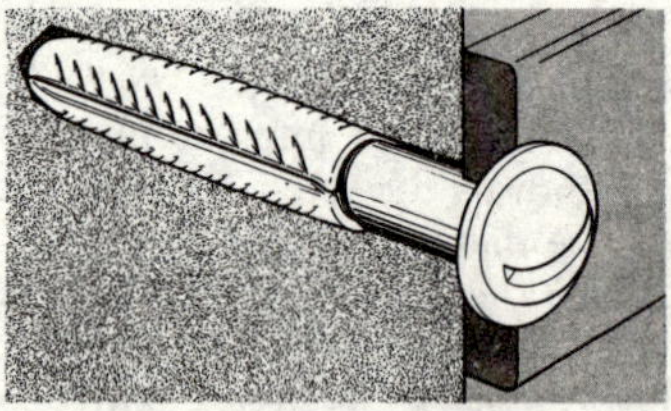

Fig. 283. Metal Rawlplug.

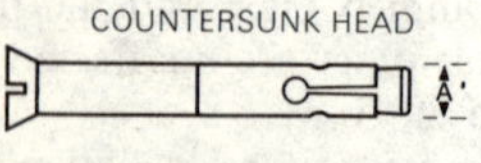

Fig. 284. Rawlok.

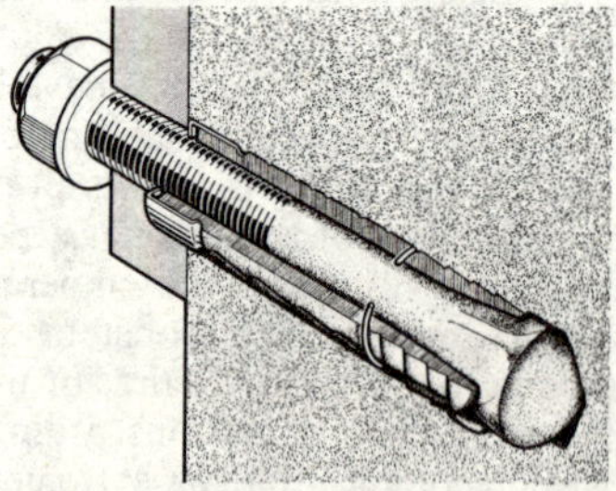

Fig. 285. Bolt projecting type Rawlbolt.

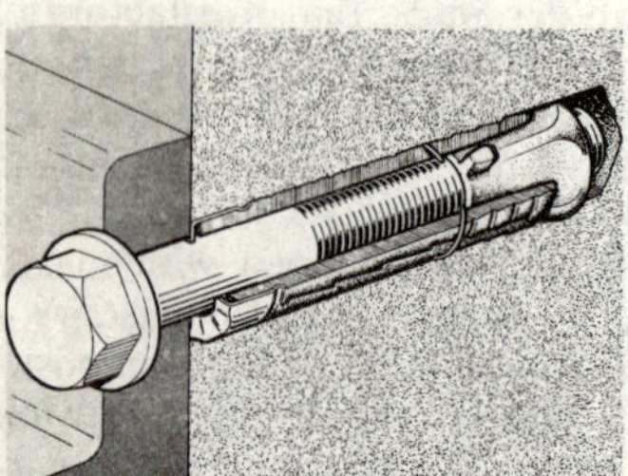

Fig. 286. Loose bolt type Rawlbolt.

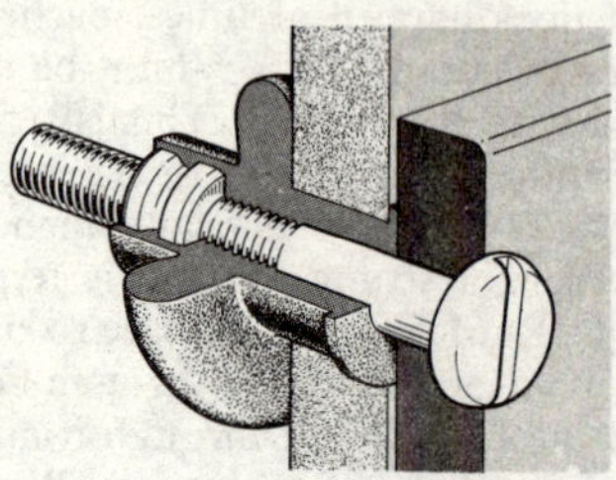

Fig. 287. Rawlnut.

there are two types. The bolt projecting variety (Fig. 285) expands the shell in the hole as the nut is tightened and cannot then be removed. It is ideal for wall fixings where the fitment can be suspended from the protruding bolt before being finally fixed in place. The fixing bolt of the loose bolt type (Fig. 286) can be removed at any time if required. This fixing is ideal for use in floors as the shell can be inserted in the hole, the item to be fixed placed over it and the bolt passed through. Tightening then draws the expander nut up into the shell forcing the segments apart. Either type is suitable for overhead or ceiling work. Bolt diameters range from 5 to 24 mm and lengths from 50 to 350 mm.

Fixing to Hollow Walls

Hollow walls may be constructed of timber frames clad with lath and plaster in older buildings, or more recently with plaster board or hollow building blocks. Where fitments have to be secured to such walls various fixings have been designed which provide automatic anchorage within the cavity.

Rawlnuts (Fig. 287) are standard-thread nuts bonded into tubes of natural rubber or Neoprene. Once inserted in the hole, as the screw is tightened the rubber tube collapses and spreads on the rear side of the wall panel. These fixings are non-corrodible, electrically insulated and water and vibration proof. As well as being suitable for use in plaster board, plywood, plastic, asbestos, glass and sheet metal, they can also be used in solid masonry if necessary.

The **spring toggle** (see Fig. 288) is an alternative to the Rawlnut. It is more suitable for use on lath and plaster that would not be strong enough to withstand the bursting strain of the Rawlnut. The toggle is passed through a hole of suitable diameter and is then forced apart by the spring. As the screw is tightened, drawing the toggle up against the side of the cavity, the load is spread over quite a large area. **Gravity toggles** (see Fig. 288) are another variation of this type of fixing. Due to gravity the anchor drops into position as it is passed through into the cavity and is then drawn back into position by the screw. Both types of toggle are zinc-plated to resist corrosion—an important consideration since they cannot easily be replaced.

Adhesives

Seen through a microscope, planed surfaces of wood which we would consider to be both flat and smooth are, in fact, quite rough and irregular. Placed together two such surfaces would not make very close contact except at a few of the high spots. To produce a permanent bond an adhesive is therefore required to fill the gaps between the two. The flatter and smoother the two surfaces are, the better will be the adhesion.

It is a common misconception that there must be penetration of the wood by the glue to obtain good adhesion. This is true to a certain extent, since the glue does penetrate the cells of the wood, but the main strength must be due to the affinity of the glue to the timber as a whole. In practice, if the joint is starved of glue by excessive penetration and insufficient glue remains to fill the gap, there will be poor adhesion.

For many years the adhesive in common use was **animal glue**, derived from the bones and hides of animals. Known as Scotch glue, its basis is the gelatine obtained from these materials which are first cleaned, treated with lime, and then boiled. The resultant liquid is filtered, evaporated and allowed to solidify, and is supplied in cake, granulated pearl or powder form. To prepare the glue, cakes should be broken up, preferably in a rag to prevent splinters flying. Whichever form is used, the glue should be soaked in water overnight before heating in a glue pot. It is essential that a double vessel of this nature is used to prevent the glue from being overheated. It should never be boiled or both strength and colour will be adversely affected. The glue is ready to use when it flows freely and in a continuous stream from a brush held a little way above the pot.

Animal glue is suitable for most indoor woodwork and for furniture-making. Rubbed joints can be readily made and surplus glue easily removed when it has jelled, or after hardening, without serious detriment to chisels and planes. Assembling has to be done quickly due to rapid jelling and the glue must not be used where there may be a humid atmosphere as it has little resistance to water or fungus attack.

Fish glue, which is usually sold ready for use as a liquid in tubes, is obtained from fish offal. Because of its relatively high cost and somewhat objectionable smell it is not used for large woodwork jobs.

Casein is a protein derived from milk. With hydrated lime and caustic soda added, the glue is available as a powder ready to mix with water, usually in the proportion of one to one. It has a better resistance to water once it has thoroughly set. Storage and mixing are simple but it is liable to stain woods containing tannic acid (e.g. some mahoganies and oak). A further disadvantage is that since the glue is not sticky it cannot be used for rubbed joints.

A modern development of the present century has been the invention and production of glues made from **synthetic resins**. In 1937, due to the need for strong, moisture-proof adhesives for bonding wooden aircraft, glues were developed from urea-formaldehyde formulations. Aero Research were pioneers in this field and now, as Ciba–Geigy (UK), market a whole range of synthetic resin glues designed to meet a variety of requirements. Widely used in woodworking, they are made from the same groups of chemicals used for making plastics. They require to be under light pressure while setting.

Ordinary glues set by chilling or by the evaporation of the solvents they contain, but synthetic resin glues set by the chemical reaction which takes place when the resin comes in contact with a recommended hardener. For this reason resin and hardener are supplied in separate containers. Ciba–Geigy synthetic resin adhesives are used extensively in the production of furniture, building materials and components, boat building and in the manufacture of sports equipment. Some grades of these adhesives are also suited to work in school and in the home. Their products meet the requirements of British Standard 1204 (Parts 1 and 2) and BS 1203, which classifies the durability of adhesives as follows:

WBP—weather and boil proof.
BR—boil resistant.
MR—moisture resistant.
INT—interior use only.

Aerodux adhesives are of the WBP type and are resorcinol-phenol-formaldehyde resins of a reddish-brown colour. Two grades are available: 500 with liquid hardener and 185 with powdered hardener. The 500 is available in three grades—fast, medium and slow setting—and is mixed 1:1 by volume with the hardener. The hardeners for 185 are in powder form and are mixed depending upon the required viscosity of the adhesive. Both Aerodux 500 and 185 are gap-filling adhesives up to 1·27 mm, as well as for close contact work, giving extremely durable weatherproof joints, which resist the attack of insects, fungi, and micro-organisms. The major use of these adhesives is in the manufacture of structural timbers using laminating techniques or the combination of plywood and solid timber for vehicle bodies and boat building.

Aerolite 300 and 306 are ureaformaldehyde resins which are gap-filling and of the MR classification. They also conform to BS 1204: Part 2 (Close Contact Adhesives). Aerolite 300 is a syrup-like liquid which is spread on one part of the joint and the hardener, which is very thin, is applied to the other. This is known as the 'separate application method' and the glue begins to set when the two parts are brought together. For school and home use the limited shelf life of the glue—three months from the date of manufacture—is a disadvantage. Aerolite 306 has the advantage of a shelf life of two years at 20 °C. It is in powder form and has only to be mixed with water. The proportions by volume are two of resin powder to one of water when the resulting liquid is identical in every way to Aerolite 300. Great care must be taken to avoid accidental contact between glue and hardener. Each should be kept in its separate bottle, which must be clearly identifiable. Neither should it be possible for the spreaders to be confused. The glue is non-staining unless contaminated by ferrous metals—e.g. nails and screws—it is colourless and clean in use and does not require a heated glue pot. It is suitable for furniture manufacture, joinery, shop fitting, boat building and car and caravan body work, aircraft construction and the making of sports goods and toys. Each may be obtained in small quantities, which is of advantage to schools and the home woodworker. Other grades of Aerolite are available for industrial use in plywood making, veneering and the manufacture of chipboard and are of the type BR.

The Borden Chemical Company manufacture a waterproof wood glue of the MR category in powder form with the resin and hardener combined under the trade name of **Cascamite**. It is best mixed by weight, using two parts of Cascamite to one part of cold water, or $3\frac{1}{2}:1$ by volume. The glue should be mixed in a glass or plastic container—copper, brass and ferrous metals are to be avoided. The powder should be stirred rapidly into half the quantity of water until it has all dissolved. The remainder of the water should then be added, again stirring until the mixture is smooth and free from lumps. The wood to be glued should be smooth and joints well fitting, the glue spread thinly and the work put under pressure while the glue is still moist—that is, within 20 minutes of spreading at higher temperatures and 30 minutes at lower temperatures. Pressure time varies from 18 hours at 10 °C to three hours at 20 °C, and the usable life of the mix from 9 hours at 10 °C to $1\frac{1}{2}$ hours at 20 °C. The Cascamite powder has a considerable shelf life if stored in a tightly closed container in a cool, dry place.

Polyvinyl acetate (PVA) adhesives such as Aerocol 4501, which meets the requirements of BS 4071 (PVA Emulsion Adhesives for Wood), is a cold-setting resin glue in the form of a fairly thick, white liquid. They are general-purpose thermoplastic adhesives suitable for furniture assembly and interior joinery. Such glues must be used for interior work and not be exposed to damp conditions. The surfaces of the wood to be bonded must be smooth, clean and free from dust and grease. Oily timbers such as teak should be wiped with a solvent such as 1.1.1-trichloroethane before bonding. The moisture content of the wood should be within the range 7–13 per cent and it is therefore good practice to store the wood in warm, dry conditions for a few days before gluing. To apply the glue, it should first be stirred thoroughly and then spread by brush or roller to one surface, or both if the wood is of a high density such as oak. The container should be firmly sealed when not in use. Pressure should be applied to the joint with cramps while the glue is still wet. As polyvinyl acetate glues set by loss of water, the clamping time depends on the temperature and absorbency of the wood, its moisture content and the pressure applied, and all these factors thus determine the thickness of the glue line. PVA glues are liable to creep and in consequence should not be used for joints subjected to continuous stress.

Epoxy Resins

A range of epoxy resins is manufactured by Ciba–Geigy under the trade name of Araldite. The adhesive and hardener, both of which are of a thick syrupy consistency, are mixed in equal quantities. The mixture has a usable life of about three hours and sets entirely by chemical reaction. Araldite is capable of bonding completely non-porous materials such as glass and metals, and has excellent adhesion to most other materials, including, wood, china, stone, rubber, leather, paper and some plastics such as bakelite. Maximum strength is reached in about three days but more rapid curing can be obtained by applying moderate heat—for example, by placing the work in a hot-water cylinder cupboard or near a radiator. Resin and hardener have a tube life of several years. Borden Power Pack is a quick-setting epoxy adhesive—five minutes at 25 °C.

In making it possible to make positive bonds between dissimilar materials and wood these epoxy resins are of utmost service to the craftsman. Synthetic glues can cause dermatitis and should not be allowed to set on the hands. A wet cloth should be readily available at all times, and the use of rubber gloves or a suitable barrier cream may be desirable.

Rubber-Based Adhesives

These impact adhesives are of no real use for constructional woodwork but are invaluable for bonding laminated plastic sheeting such as Arborite to blockboard, chipboard, etc. In practice, the adhesive is applied to both surfaces and allowed to dry for 10–15 minutes. Bonding can take place when the adhesive does not transfer if touched lightly with the knuckle, but the joint must be completed within 25 minutes of the adhesive being spread. Dunlop Thixofix, which is non-drip and very pleasant to use, and Borden Superstik allow for limited repositioning of the materials so long as pressure is avoided. The bowing of a large sheet may place excessive weight on a particular area and cause adhesion. Once the correct position has been obtained and pressure is applied, the bond is immediate. Care must be taken to avoid trapping air between the surfaces and pressure should first be applied to the centre, gradually working outwards. Appendix 2 gives detailed data charts relating to synthetic resin glues.

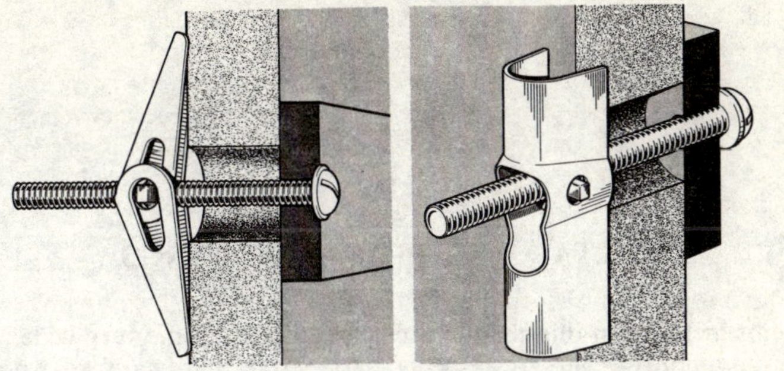

Fig. 288. Spring and gravity toggles.

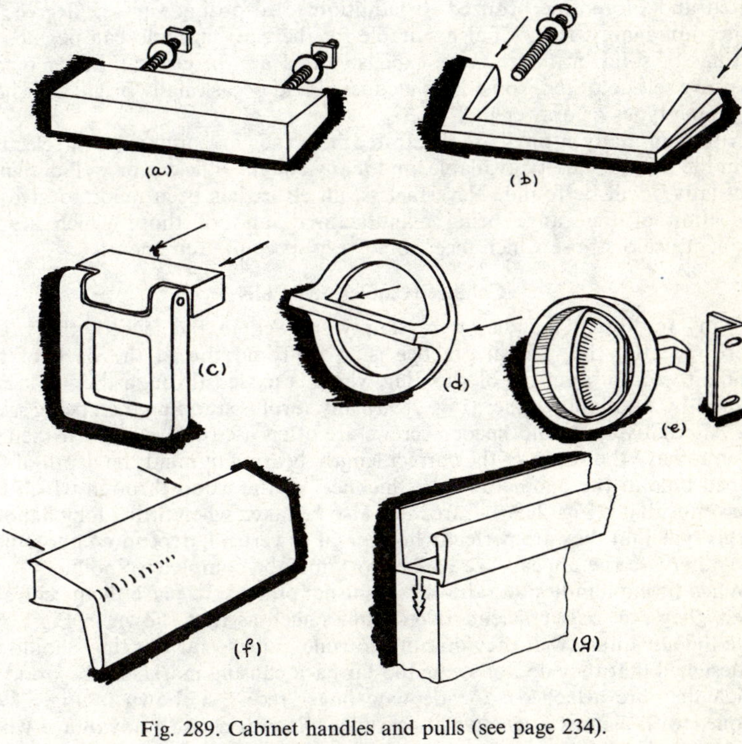

Fig. 289. Cabinet handles and pulls (see page 234).

10

METAL AND PLASTIC FITTINGS

The items included in this chapter are a selection from the very wide range of fittings commonly regarded as being part of the 'hardware' of woodwork. Traditionally they were made of steel or brass, but increasing use is being made of plastic and nylon.

Steel hardware, which is very strong, may be bright finished but is inclined to rust unless very well protected with paint; alternatively, fittings may be of brass, copper, nickel, cadmium, zinc or chromium-plated. There are also variations of these finishes, such as satin-brassed and lacquered, antique brass-plated and Florentine bronzed. In addition to affording varying degrees of protection against rust, a finish suitable for the work in hand can be chosen. Fittings of solid brass are more expensive and are, in general, better made. They are self-coloured, sometimes lacquered and occasionally bright polished, e.g. some types of drawer pull.

Although many fittings are illustrated here they are only a small selection from the infinite variety available, and many equally efficient or well designed alternatives will be found. Nevertheless, an effort has been made to give an indication of the range being manufactured, and of those which are in frequent use or those which meet some very special requirement.

Cabinet Handles and Pulls

Many traditional handles were simply screwed to the face of the work. More recently, the general practice is to drill and thread the back of the handle to accept a length of studding which is passed through the work and secured by a nut and washer (Fig. 289*a*), any surplus studding then being sawn off. Alternatively, round-headed screws are often used but care must then be taken to have the screw of the correct length, bearing in mind the depth of the tapped hole in the handle and the thickness of the wood through which the screw must pass (Fig. 289*b*). Care must also be taken when fitting long handles of this type that they are perfectly horizontal or vertical, depending upon their use, otherwise the appearance of the work may be completely spoilt.

When fitting handles to a drawer it is usual practice to place them centrally where they are most efficient. **Drop-handles** such as that shown in Fig. 289*c* have the advantage that they do not protrude quite so far but they should be so designed that they do not swing too far back causing marks on the wood to which they are attached. An adequate finger recess is shown in Fig. 289*d*, coupled with a most attractive appearance which is seen to advantage when the handle is mounted on a painted surface. The **flush handle** with integral catch (Fig. 289*e*) is fitted in a circular recess and will hold doors and drawers securely in vehicles, such as caravans, in boats and in aircraft. Pulling the

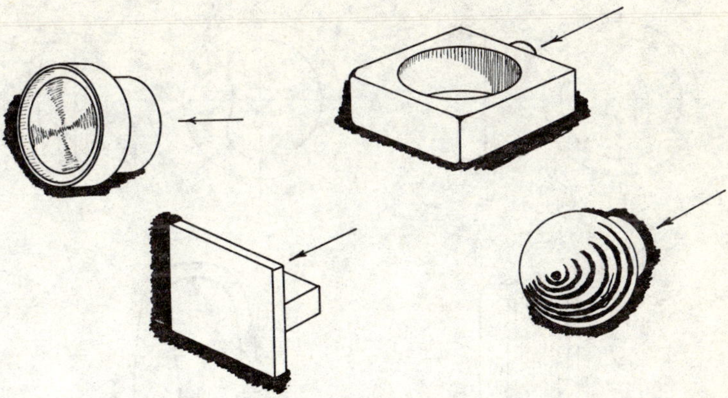

Fig. 290. Cabinet knobs.

handle releases the catch from the striker, and pushing locks it again. Figs. 289*f* and *g* show sections of **extruded aluminium alloy**, the former being available in 100 mm lengths and secured by means of two screws. Note also the protruding edges along the back which bite into the wood as the screws are tightened, thereby keeping the handle in place. The long extrusion illustrated in Fig. 289*g* is for use on the top edge of doors mounted on the fronts of cabinets. This is commonly used with manufactured boards for items such as built-in kitchen fitments. It is available in lengths up to 1·752 m to be cut to the required size and is secured by pressing the 'fir tree' section flange into a groove of a suitable width.

Furniture knobs, as their name implies, are smaller than handles and are secured by only one screw but do have small protruding spikes at the back which bite into the wood to prevent them from turning out of position. Like the handles, they may be of metal or plastic, or a combination of the two, making possible a wide range of colours (see Fig. 290).

It is also quite feasible to make your own wooden handles or knobs from a wood suited to the work. If round ones are required it will be necessary to turn them on the lathe, leaving on a peg to be glued into a pre-drilled hole. Other shapes can be fitted by mortising, by slot screwing, or by screwing from the back. In each case they should also be glued.

Flush pulls may be of plastic, wood or metal, and are usually fitted to doors of slab construction. The plastic ones shown in Fig. 291*a* and *d* are simply pressed into place and are held by serrations on the side; wooden ones (Fig. 291*b*) are glued into the door; while those of metal (Fig. 291*c*) are secured by small pins or screws. This type of handle is necessary for sliding doors to avoid fouling the movement. Note that larger handles and pulls are made for room and exterior doors.

Hinges

The most common of all hinges and the one most frequently used is the **butt hinge**, which is available in steel or brass in lengths from 25 mm to 150 mm (see Fig. 292*a*). Designed to meet many different requirements, each length of

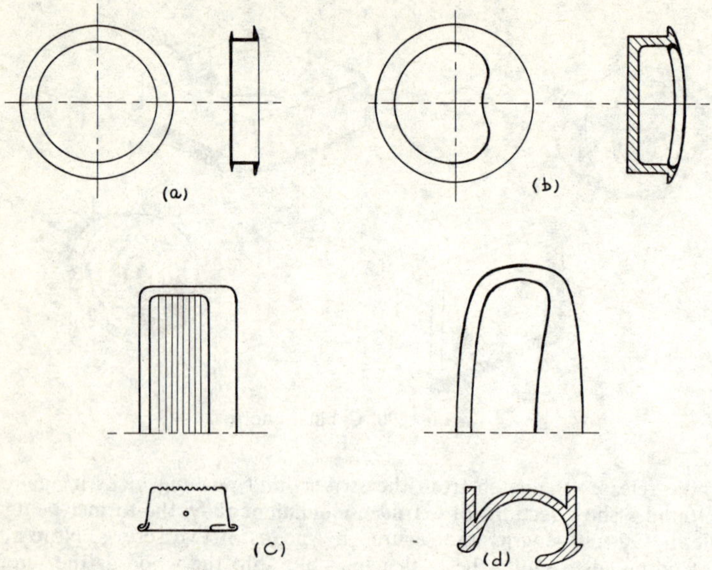

Fig. 291. Flush pulls.

butt hinge is made in different widths and strengths, the full range of each grade being referred to as a suite: for example, a 50·8 mm solid drawn brass butt, narrow suite is 22·3 mm wide when fully open; broad suite 28·6 mm; strong suite 31·8 mm; and extra broad 47·6 mm. The different widths of butt hinge are necessary due to the different thicknesses and weights of the work to be hung on them; usually cabinet, cupboard, heavy room and exterior doors, or box lids. Doors are usually designed to fit inside the carcase or frame and are made a little oversize. They must therefore be 'fitted' before they can be hung and the usual practice is to plane the hanging stile, then the top and bottom edges, leaving a little clearance at the bottom, and finally the lock stile, again allowing a little clearance. Once the door has been hung, small adjustments may still be necessary to perfect the fit. It is also common practice deliberately to inset cabinet doors slightly, because of the extreme difficulty in hanging a door so that it is perfectly flush all round the edge of the carcase. Breaking the line in this way is quite acceptable and is a principle often applied in other situations.

Steel butt hinges may have cranked or uncranked knuckles and attention must be given to this point when they are being fitted, because for satisfactory operation the knuckle must protrude either wholly or only half outside the work respectively (see Fig. 292*b*).

Hinges must be so positioned on doors that the screws do not run into the end grain of any cross members or they will soon pull out. Depending upon the design of the work and the weight of the door, butt hinges can be set wholly into the door or equally into both carcase and door, or into box and lid. The setting out must be done with great accuracy, the length of the hinges

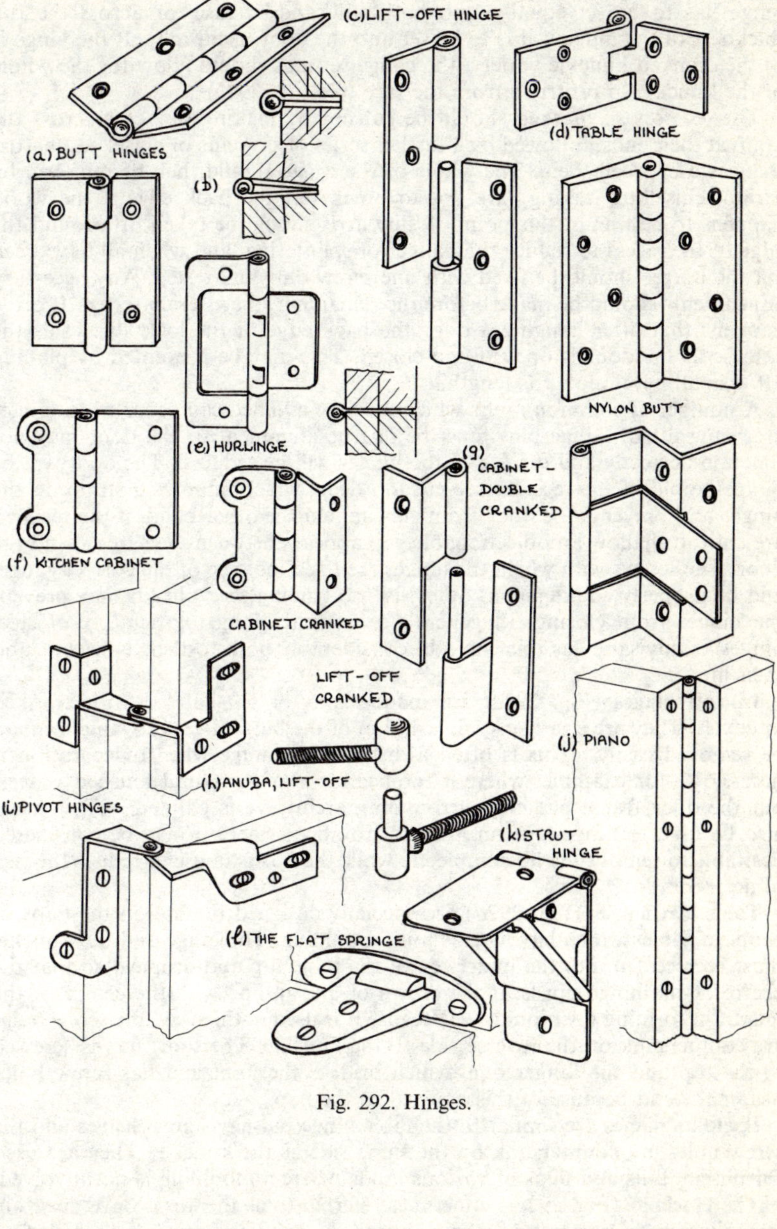

Fig. 292. Hinges.

being marked first, preferably by a cut line, and then the width and depth of the 'boxing-in' gauged with the single marking gauge. These gauge settings are taken directly from the hinge and are to the centre of the knuckle where the hinge has to be set equally into both stile and carcase, or across the full thickness of the hinge if it is to be set into the door or lid only. If the hinge is of the cranked knuckle variety, the gauge settings should allow for the whole of the knuckle to protrude from the face (see Fig. 292*b*).

The recesses so marked should be cut out by making saw cuts across the grain at their ends, followed by a further series of saw cuts or chisel cuts across the waste between them. The whole of the waste should then be removed by careful chiselling, taking care not to break out the back edge if the wood happens to be thin at this point. A tiny arris should be taken off around the edge of the recess to reduce the danger of splintering, and when all have been cut the hinges should be fixed with one screw only and tested. Any necessary adjustments should be made before the remaining screws are inserted. It often happens that after hanging a door the back edge of the lock stile fouls the carcase as the door is opened and closed. This may be prevented by planing off a small bevel along its length.

A number of common faults which must be avoided can occur when hinges are being fitted. Hinge pins must be in true alignment or the door may not function correctly and the life of the hinges will be reduced. The door will be 'hinge-bound' if the recesses are cut too deep, which imposes a strain on the hinges and prevents the door from closing. On the other hand, if the recesses are cut too shallow an objectionable gap appears between the carcase and the door. The screws with which the hinges are fixed must be of the correct gauge, and be properly countersunk, otherwise protruding screw heads may prevent the hinges from closing. In general, occasional oiling, particularly of steel hinges, is advisable, as this can add considerably both to their efficiency and their life.

Lift-off hinges (Fig. 292*c*) are made right- or left-handed with cranked knuckles. They are a very useful variation of the butt hinge, allowing doors to be removed easily. (This is often a distinct advantage when redecoration is necessary—for example, where a room door is of a natural finished veneer, but the door frame and the surrounding architrave is painted.) They could also be used to advantage on a child's toy box, where it may be considered desirable to remove the lid completely while the box is in use to reduce the risk of accidents.

Table leaf hinges (Fig. 292*d*) are specially designed for use on the flaps of dropleaf tables which have a rule-joint moulding. The hinge and the knuckle must be recessed into the underside of the table top and dropleaf so that the centre of the hinge pin is at the centre of and in line with the centre of the quadrant forming the moulding. Because it is used in this way, the screw holes are countersunk on the reverse side to the knuckle. The short flap is screwed to the top and the longer one, which bridges the joint and has screw holes nearer the end because of this, is fixed to the flap.

Backflap hinges are similar to the table hinge but have equal leaves and the screw holes are countersunk on the same side as the knuckle. They are used for bureau falls and flaps of various kinds where a moulding is not involved.

The **Hurlinge** (Fig. 292*e*), sometimes referred to as the flush hinge, has thin leaves which do not require recessing into the door or frame, and which fold one inside the other. The small projecting lugs on the small leaf automatically position the hinge on the door and it should be noted that the whole of the knuckle protrudes. It is often used on cheap whitewood furniture such as kitchen cabinets.

Cabinet hinges (Fig. 292*f*). The flat hinge is fixed easily and screws directly behind a face-mounted door and on to the carcase. The cranked version, of which there are other varieties, is for slab doors with rebated edges, and in this case the crank fits into the rebate. Both are also intended for kitchen furniture.

Cabinet double-cranked and lift-off cranked hinges (Fig. 292*g*) are intended for somewhat heavier doors, and can be used to hang doors on the face of cabinets where sides fit tight up against the wall of a room. The alternative would be to use butt hinges, in which case the door would have to be fitted within the carcase.

Screw-in lift-off hinge (Fig. 292*h*). Recommended for comparatively small rebated doors, the Anuba hinge screws firmly into manufactured boards and presents a neat appearance when assembled.

Pivot hinges (Fig. 292*i*). These are semi-concealed hinges intended for use on larger doors of slab construction, usually of the veneered chipboard which is now so popular for built-in cupboards and wardrobes. The throw-off action of the hinge allows the door to open 180 degrees across the front of the unit. As these pivot hinges are fitted near to or at the top and bottom of the door, extra long doors are liable to warp. To prevent this, pivot hinges are available which may be fitted in an intermediate position. Invariably zinc-plated on steel, these hinges are best fixed with Twinfast woodscrews, especially if used in conjunction with manufactured boards. Slotted screw holes in one leaf allow for adjustment before inserting the third screw.

The **continuous or piano hinge** (Fig. 292*j*) is manufactured in widths of 19 mm, 25 mm, 32 mm and 38 mm in brass, both polished and chromium-plated, and steel-finished Florentine bronzed, Sussex gold, nickel-plated and electro-brassed. Some widths are also available in black or white plastic. All varieties are initially 1·828 m long, and the hinge is then sawn to whatever length is required. Its main use is on wide falls, such as piano lids (hence its name), and slab-type doors of manufactured board. Running along the full length of the edge, the knuckle presents a neat appearance on the face while the evenly spaced screws provide strong fixing and ensure efficient operation.

The **strut hinge** (Fig. 292*k*) is ideal for use on work such as tool boxes, fishing tackle boxes, etc., where items may be stored in the lid, which is held open at 90 degrees by the strut.

The **flat springe** (Fig. 292*l*) is intended for use on flaps and box lids. It has three positive positions: 0, 90 and 180 degrees. This means that on, say, horizontally hung kitchen cabinet doors, they can be opened 90 degrees or vertically through 180 degrees and will remain in place, leaving both hands free until the door is closed again. The springe is recommended for use on moving vehicles and boats, and is rust-proof being made of a tough plastic.

Card table hinge (Fig. 293*a*). This is a double-jointed, solid, drawn-brass hinge obtainable with square or rounded ends. The leaves are let into the table top and flap so as to present a flush surface when opened. A side-fitting hinge is also made to be let into the edges.

Lift-off centre hinge (Fig. 293*b*). The leaves are set into the cabinet and into the top and bottom of the door and the hinge is then concealed. As the top

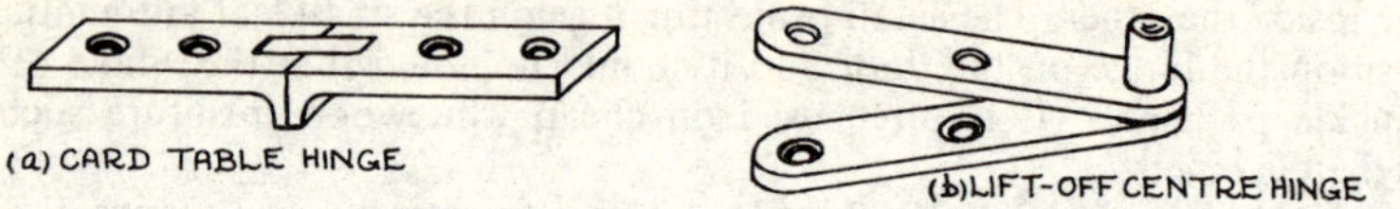

Fig. 293. Hinges.

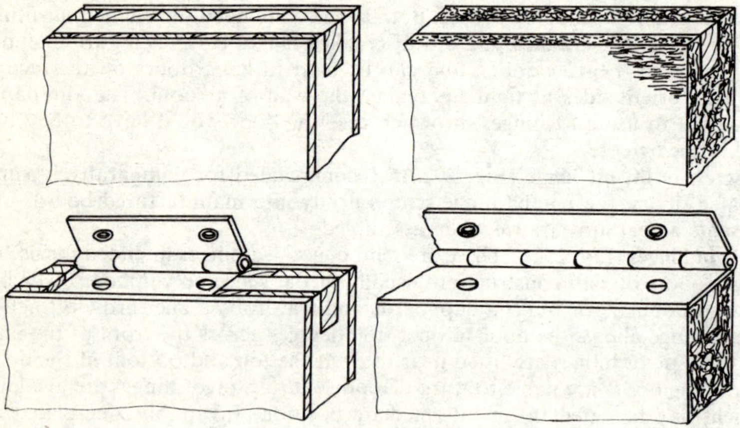

Fig. 294. Hinges.

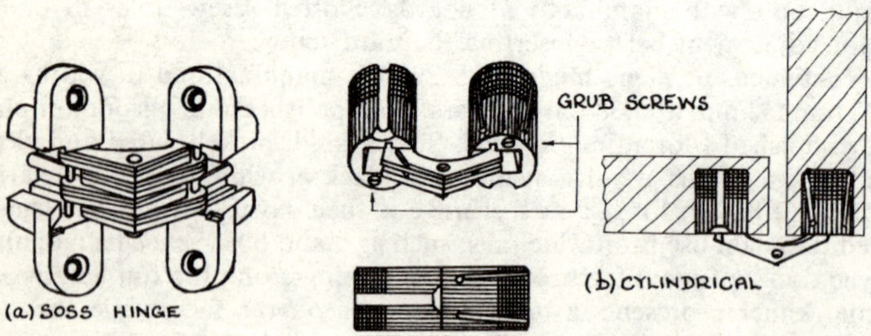

Fig. 295. Invisible hinges.

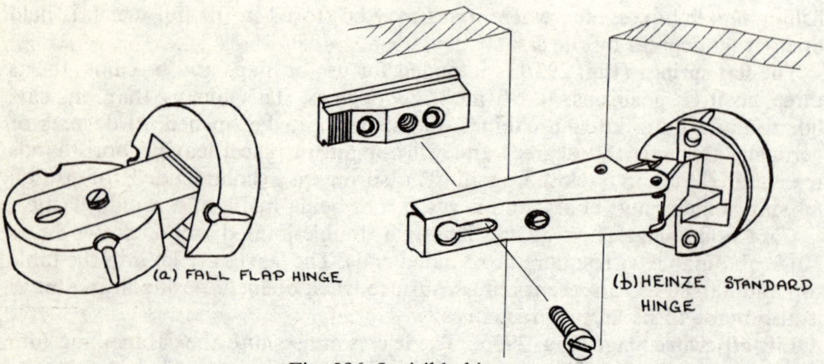

Fig. 296. Invisible hinges.

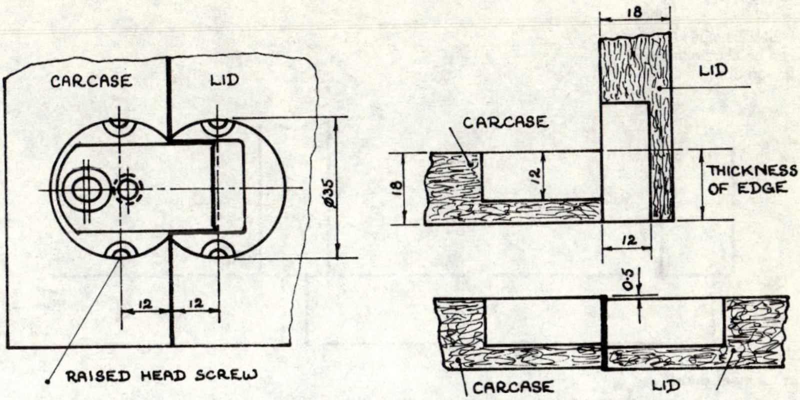

Fig. 297. Recessed hinge.

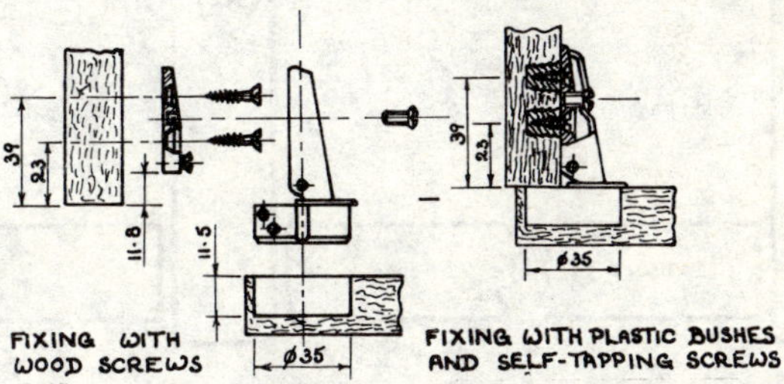

Fig. 298. The Heinze furniture hinge.

hinge is inverted the door cannot be lifted off. To prevent binding, the bottom hinge should have a thin washer placed over the pin to hold the leaves apart. Various types of centre hinge are made to meet different needs, including cranked and single-leaved versions whose pin rotates in a simple bush sunk into the door.

With manufactured boards there is often a problem in screwing hinges to their edge securely. A strip of wood glued into the edge as indicated in Fig. 294 will often prove a satisfactory method of presenting side grain into which the screws will bite. Alternatively, the door can be framed all round with plain or T-sectioned edging.

It has always been the author's practice, and the reader is advised, when fixing a hinge, to line up the screw slots along the length of the hinge whenever possible. This gives a much neater and more professional appearance. The use of Pozidriv screws, which have a recessed centre in place of the traditional slot, is also recommended.

Invisible Hinges

Invisible hinges are so called because they are completely concealed when the door on which they are used is closed. Both the **Soss hinge** (Fig. 295*a*) and the **cylindrical hinge** (Fig. 295*b*) allow for a movement of 180 degrees. Each portion of the Soss hinge is recessed into the work and is then screwed in.

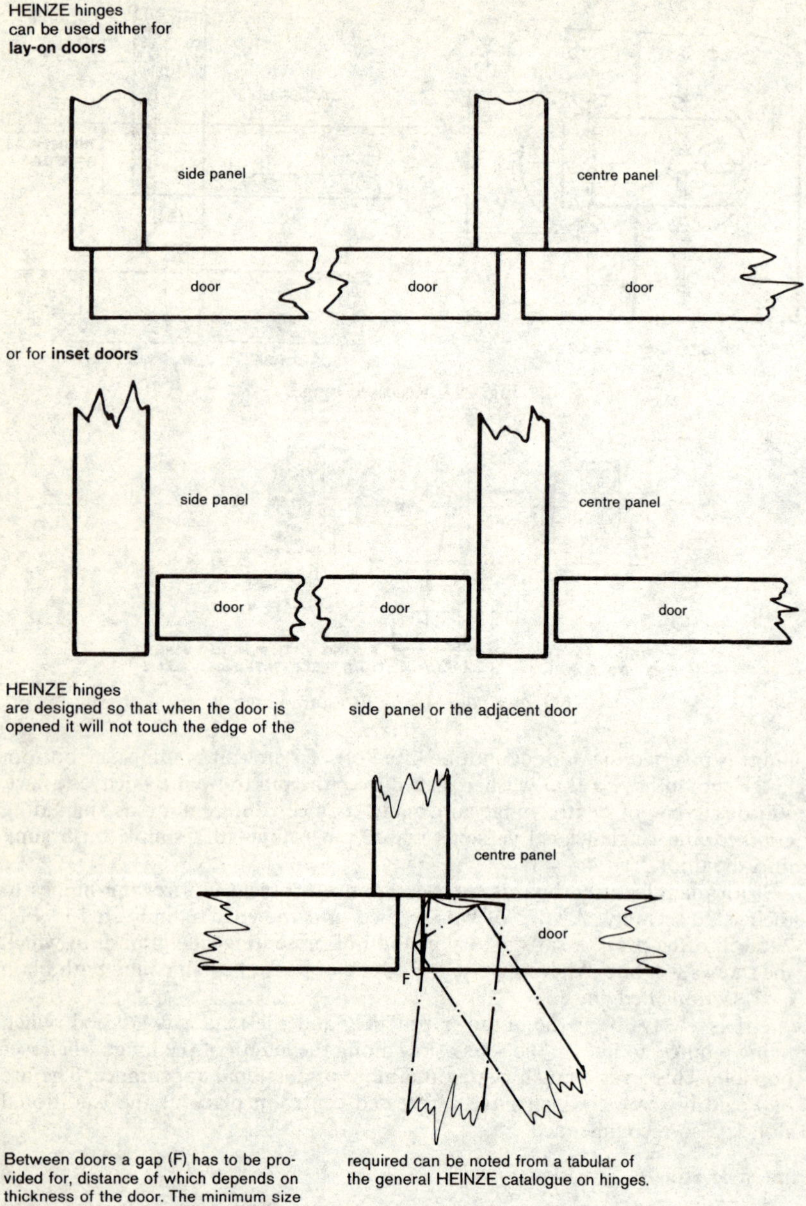

Fig. 299. Door applications of Heinze hinges.

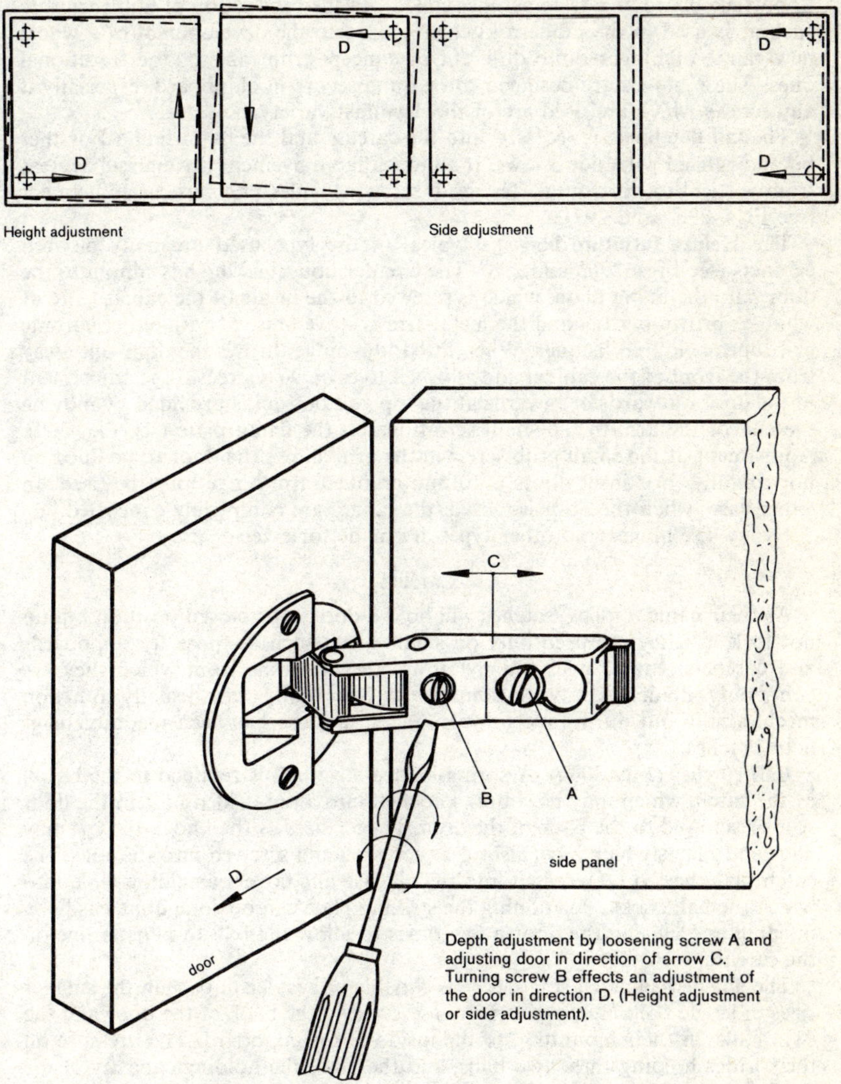

Fig. 300. Adjustment of Heinzc hinges.

The brass cylindrical hinge fits into pre-drilled holes and is prevented from turning by the screw inserted between it and the timber. The small grub screw in each part is then tightened, forcing open the wedge-shaped section, which in turn causes the serrations to bite firmly into the wood.

The ever-increasing use of manufactured boards—particularly chipboard, or particle board as it is sometimes called—in the production of unit furniture such as is used in the modern kitchen has led to the development of a whole new range of hinges quite different in concept from any of the traditional ones. These hinges are designed to be quite secure in chipboard, especially if any screws which are used are of the Twinfast variety.

The **fall flap hinge** is recessed into the carcase and the flap using a Forstner bit and is fixed with side screws. It allows a flap movement through 90 degrees from vertical to horizontal. The grub screw provides fine vertical adjustment (see Figs. 296*a* and 297).

The **Heinze furniture hinge** is typical of the type used on many modern cabinets (see Figs. 296*b* and 298). The circular housing, which is sunk into the door, and the fixing plate, which is screwed to the inside of the carcase, are of white or brown plastic, and the metal arm is stove finished with either chrome or bronze-coloured lacquer. When fitted, the hinge throws the door out away from the front of the cabinet and allows it to open 90 degrees. Fine adjustment of the door outwards or inwards at the top and bottom is provided by moving the end of the arm in the small serrations on the fixing plate (see Fig. 300). Adjustment of the small grub screw in the arm allows the door to be lined up horizontally. For inset doors a 10 mm cranked arm hinge must be used. In either case, when the door is closed, the hinges are completely concealed.

Heavy Tee hinges and other types are made for exterior use.

Catches

As their name implies, catches will hold a door in its closed position but do not lock it. They are used only on small doors such as those for cupboards and cabinets. Brass, steel and nylon are the materials from which they are commonly made. Always automatic in operation, they usually function mechanically but during recent years increasing use has been made of magnetic catches.

Ball catches (Fig. 303*a*). A spring-loaded steel ball is retained in the barrel of the catch, which may be simply knocked into a pre-drilled hole in the door stile or screwed to the back of the door. Larger sizes of the knock-in type may have end-plates which have also to be recessed and screwed into the stile. The catch plate has to be recessed into the carcase and covers a shallow hole into which the ball clicks. Positioning the striking plate can be done quite easily by opening and closing the door a few times to allow the ball to mark a line on the carcase.

The **double ball catch** (Fig. 301*b*) is capable of heavier duty than the smaller sizes of single ball. Here the striker is screwed to the back of the door and the twin balls, in their mounting, to the inside of the cupboard. The pressure on the springs holding these two balls, and therefore the holding capacity of the catch, can be adjusted by means of the grub screws in the barrels.

The **mini catch** (Fig. 301*c*) and the **rocker catch** (Fig. 301*d*) are both made of nylon and are only suitable for very light work. The mini catch and the 'rocker' simply click over the striker plate, which is screwed to the cabinet

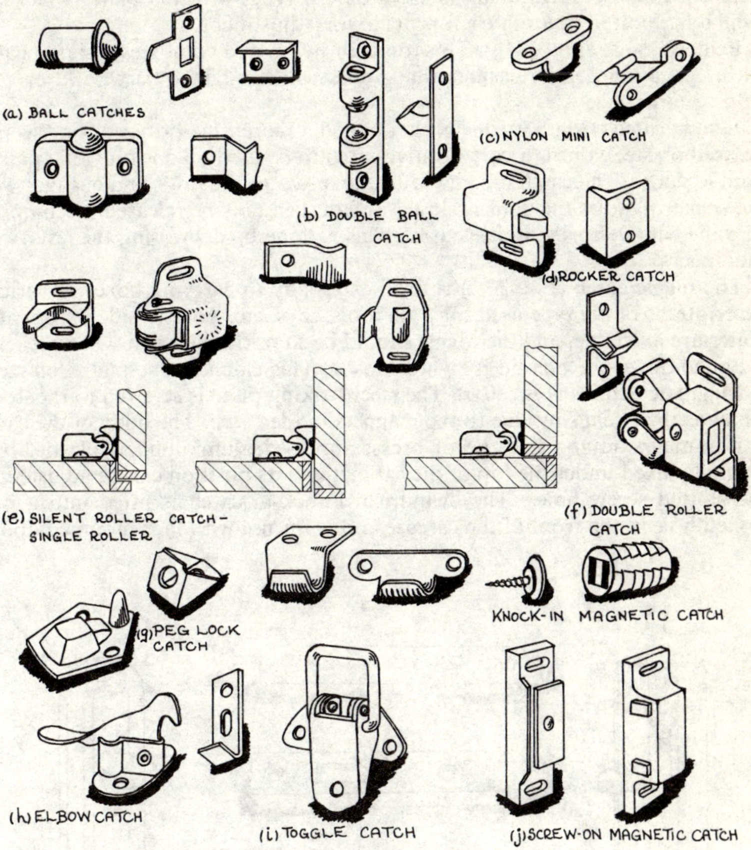

Fig. 301. Catches.

side. The 'rocker' is spring-loaded and the position of this part of the catch can be adjusted on the door by means of the slotted screw holes. Because of this it should be fixed with round-headed screws.

The **single roller catch** (Fig. 301*e*) and **double roller catch** (Fig. 301*f*) are of metal construction with nylon rollers. The use of the single roller catch on different doors is illustrated, as are different types of catch plates which are available. Slotted holes in each provide for adjustment.

Peglock catch (Fig. 301*g*). This too is of nylon and combines a spring catch with a locating peg. It ensures that doors which might otherwise 'drop' are held square.

Elbow catch (Fig. 301*h*). Nickel-plated, Florentine-bronzed or electro-brassed on steel, this is a very positive catch to be used on one only of a pair of double doors. The catch is screwed to the inside of the door and engages with the striker plate as the door is closed. It can then only be released by compressing the captive spring in the barrel. This is done by depressing the lever with the fingers.

The **toggle catch** (Fig. 301*i*) is fixed externally to carrying boxes of various descriptions of the type used for pets, tools, toys, etc. Top- or side-fixing catch plates are available, and the toggle should be so positioned that when the lever is pulled down the box lid is tightly closed. This catch is zinc-plated on steel.

Magnetic catches (Fig. 301*j*). The steel striking plate is screwed to the door, which is then held shut due to the magnets in the catch. The body of the catch is non-magnetic and may be of brass, anodised aluminium or plastic. It is normally fixed under the top of the cabinet and its position can be adjusted by the slotted screw holes. The cylindrical knock-in catch is fitted into a pre-drilled hole in the front of the carcase and is for use with face-mounted doors.

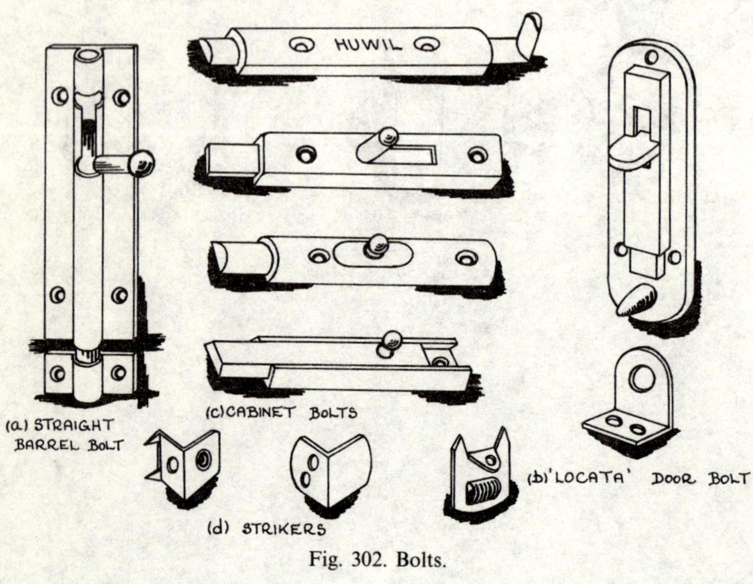

Fig. 302. Bolts.

Bolts

Large bolts are often used in addition to locks to give greater security to large doors. For cabinet work, however, much smaller ones are used and are mainly for double doors. The bolt secures one door and a lock or catch the other.

The quality of the work and its design will help to determine the choice of bolt. The **straight barrel bolt** (Fig. 302*a*), for example, might be used externally on a rabbit hutch, whereas the **Locata** (Fig. 302*b*) would be more suitable for a cupboard door. The latter automatically corrects distortion and provides alignment of doors and rigidity of the complete unit. A selection of smaller, neater cabinet bolts is illustrated in Fig. 302*c* and *d*, as well as some of the many types of striker made to meet different requirements.

Locks

As with all hardware, there is an ever-widening range of locks being made to meet varying requirements. The **cylindrical desk or drawer lock** (Fig. 303*a*) is quite a recent addition to this range, and is easily fitted through a pre-

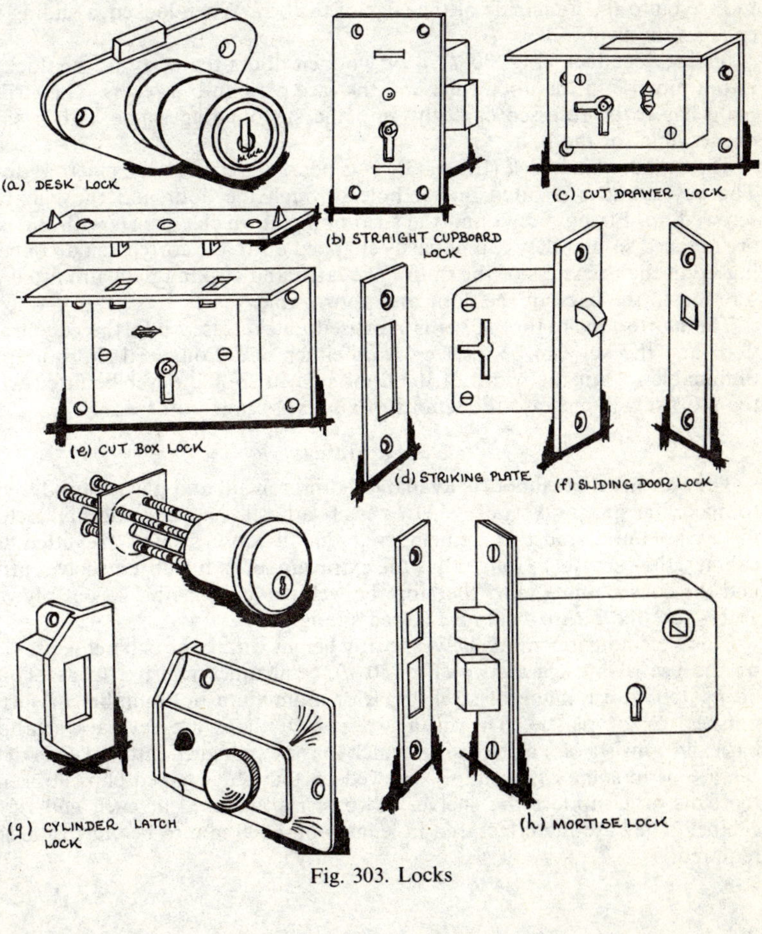

Fig. 303. Locks

drilled hole in the drawer front, the housing then being screwed to the back of the drawer. Made of plastic with a metal cylinder, 200 'differs' are available.

The **straight cupboard lock** (Fig. 303*b*) may be of mild steel or brass and is simply screwed to the back of the door after the keyhole has been cut. As the bolt is thrown both ways it can be used on right- or left-hand inset drawers.

Cut till or drawer lock (Fig. 303*c*). Care is needed in positioning this type of lock, which has to be fitted into recesses cut into the back of the drawer front. A double recess is required for the mechanism and the backplate, which must also be sunk into the top edge of the drawer front. It is sometimes advisable to do this before the drawer is finally assembled. The **cut cupboard lock** is very similar in appearance to the drawer lock but is used vertically and is 'handed: left or right'.

The above three locks all require an appropriate **striking plate** (Fig. 303*d*) fitting to the carcase into which the bolt shoots.

The **cut box lock** (Fig. 303*e*) is usually of brass and is fitted in a similar way to the drawer lock. The lock plate, which carries two hooks, needs to be recessed into the underside of the edge of the box. When locked, a sliding bolt engages the two hooks.

Sliding door lock (Fig. 303*f*). For wooden doors the body of this lock fits into a mortise in the door edge and the face plate into a recess. The striking plate has to be recessed carefully into the surrounding frame with a small, deeper hole for the bolt.

The **cylinder latch lock** (Fig. 303*g*) is generally used on large external doors. The key cylinder is fitted into a hole through the door and the backplate screwed up. Fixing screws and the strip of metal which engages with the latch are notched so that they can be easily snapped off to the correct length depending upon the thickness of the door. The latch and striking plate are fitted and screwed to the back of the door and door frame.

The **mortise lock** (Fig. 303*h*) is mortised and recessed into the edge of the door and the key can be inserted from either side. Long and short sizes are obtainable to suit the width of the door stile. It should never be fitted where the mortise will cut into the tenons of any cross rails in the door.

Shelf Fittings

The various shelf supports available both in metal and plastic are designed to make the spacing between shelves easily adjustable. They also make cleaning easier but it must be remembered that if loose shelves are fitted to a cabinet, the carcase no longer has the extra support which fixed shelves afford and the corner joints must therefore be well made. If the back is of plywood and is screwed on this will give added strength.

Complete adjustment of shelves to any height within the cabinet is provided by the use of **bookcase strip** (Fig. 304*a*). Sometimes referred to as 'Tonk's fitting', strips are made of steel, brass or aluminium in a number of surface finishes, or of plastic. The fitting, of which there are several variations, basically consists of a slotted strip which may be ploughed into the ends of the carcase or in some cases simply screwed on. Suitably shaped clips hook into the slots and support the shelves. Two strips are used at each end of the cabinet. They are manufactured in lengths of 4,000 mm to be cut to the sizes required.

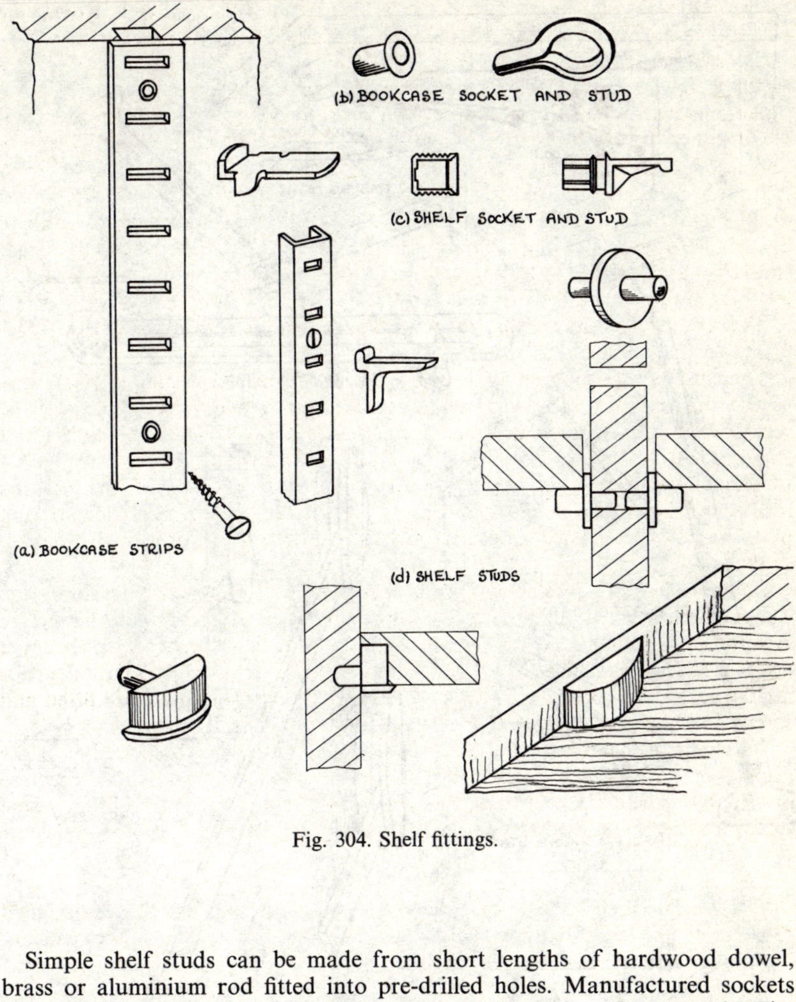

Fig. 304. Shelf fittings.

Simple shelf studs can be made from short lengths of hardwood dowel, brass or aluminium rod fitted into pre-drilled holes. Manufactured sockets and studs are obtainable made from metal or plastic (see, for example, Fig. 304*b–d*).

Stays

Stays are used to support flaps or to limit the opening of lids and doors. The strong, well designed **flap stay** shown in Fig. 305*a* is suitable for tables, wall tables, folding shelves and seats. The automatic self-locking device ensures complete safety, and prevents the flap from being released accidentally. It is made in sizes of 180 mm, 280 mm and 350 mm for flaps from 220 mm to 500 mm in width. If used with a pair of table hinges a 'rule' joint can be used, but where this is not essential the 280 and 350 mm sizes can be used without hinges.

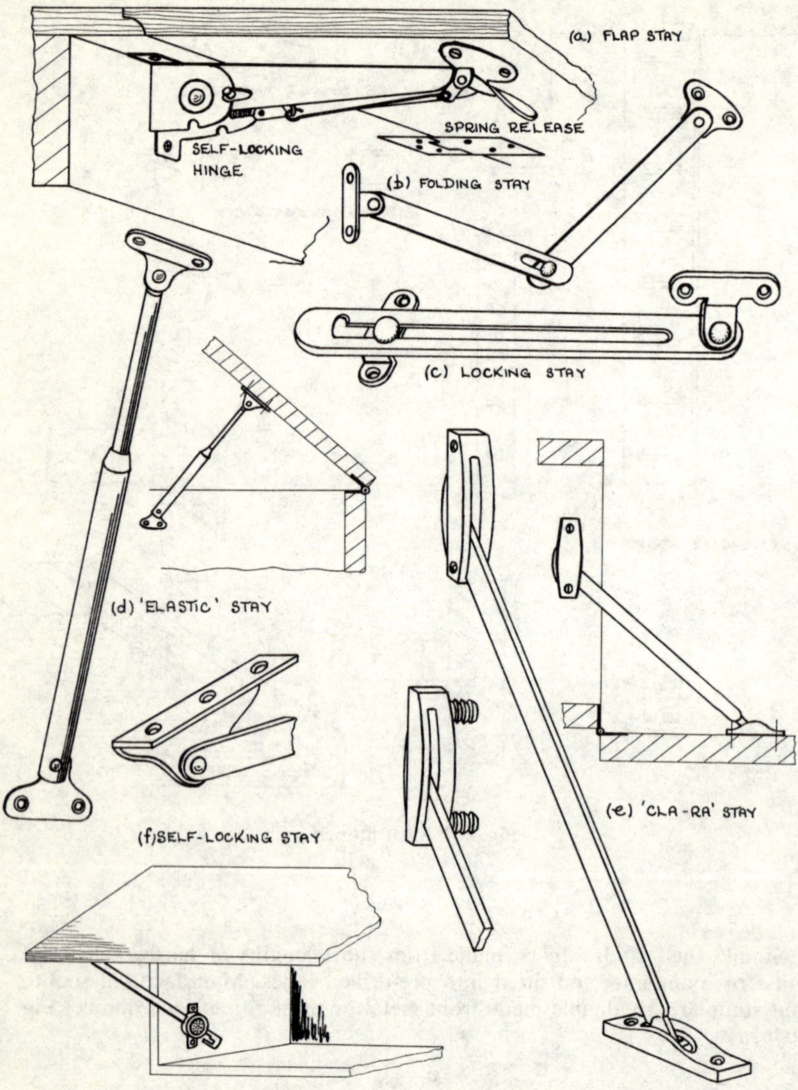

Fig. 305. Stays.

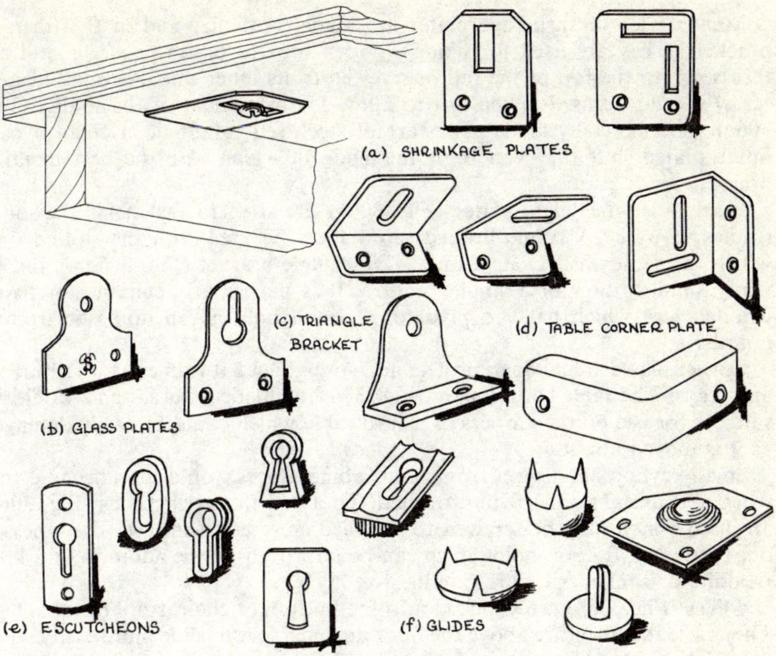

Fig. 306. Thin plates and stampings.

Lightweight **folding stays** (Fig. 305*b*) and the very similar rule-joint stay are generally used for small box lids, whereas the heavier **locking stay** (Fig. 305*c*) is suitable for such as tool chests. The arm of the stay is clicked on to the stud and released again manually, but a cam action stay is made whereby opening the stay to its full extent engages the locking mechanism, which can then be released by first lifting the lid slightly in the opening direction before closing.

'Elastic' flap stays by Huwil (Fig. 305*d*) are spring-loaded, made of brass, and have two functions: first, to hold the door or flap open in any required position; and second, when closed the spring pulls the door or flap well home. An all plastic stay with catch, the **Cla-ra** is 220 mm long and finished white (Fig. 305*e*). It can be obtained for screw fitting or with brackets having dowel fittings at 32 mm centres. Being of plastic, the arm can be twisted and inserted after the brackets have been fixed.

Specially designed for top-hung cupboard flaps, the **self-locking stay** is 200 mm long, finished in bright chrome on steel with a large three-hole fixing bracket (Fig. 305*f*).

The reader should bear in mind that some stays are suitable for both right- and left-hand fixing, but others, due to the way in which they are constructed, are restricted to either right- or left-hand patterns. Depending upon the design of the work, the correct 'hand' must be chosen.

Thin Plates and Stampings

Many styles of shrinkage plates are made, both flat and in the form of brackets. They are used for fixing wooden tops to tables or stools and are recessed into the top of the rail or screwed to its inner side. A round-headed screw should be used in the slot to allow for movement of the timber (Fig. 306*a*). Commercially made plates are of steel, self-coloured, or zinc- or cadmium-plated, but they can be home-made in which case the best metal is brass.

Plain or slotted **glass plates** (Fig. 306*b*) are used to fasten light wooden frames to walls. A round-headed screw must be used with the slotted type which drops down over its shank. The **triangle bracket** (Fig. 306*c*) is one of many small fittings of a similar nature. It is particularly suitable for fixing wooden legs which have to pivot on a small bolt, as on domestic ironing boards.

Corner plates are made to protect and strengthen flat frames as with mirrors and trays. The **table corner plate** (Fig. 306*d*) is made of brass and would be suitable for use on the corners of a card table which could be easily damaged as it is moved about.

Small keyholes in drawer fronts and cabinet doors would soon become very worn and unsightly if left unprotected. To avoid this **escutcheons** (Fig. 306*e*) are used which may be screwed to the face or recessed into it. The recessed ones rely on a friction hold which can be improved by the addition of a little Araldite or similar epoxy resin adhesive.

Glides (Fig. 306*f*) are knocked into the bottom of chair, stool or table legs. They raise the furniture above the floor and enable it to slide more easily when required, at the same time reducing the risk of small pieces being splintered off. The glides may be deep-drawn or shallow; some are made to screw across the corners of cabinets, others are of plastic to be pressed into a pre-drilled hole.

Mirror Fittings

The frequent use of vanity mirrors, adjustable and fixed mirrors on furniture and wall-mounted mirrors has led to the design of very many different mirror fittings.

The **swivelling mirror stand** (Fig. 307*a*) comprises a brass-plated solid steel pillar (10 mm diameter), a polished brass-lacquered lower sleeve which fits over the pillar, a base plate, washers and wing nut. The brackets are screwed to the wooden back of the mirror and because of their unequal lengths the mirror is given a permanent and appropriate tilt.

The **tubular mirror stand** (Fig. 307*b*) is of similar construction to the above, the brass outer tube being the full length of the pillar (300 mm) on which it fits closely to allow controlled rotation. Similarly, the mirror tilts against the friction of two fibre washers riveted between the two fixing brackets and the top of the pillar to hold it at any required angle. Universal movement is thus obtained.

Mirror clips of metal in various finishes or in clear plastic are used to fasten mirrors on to wooden backs (Fig. 307*c*).

Mirror corner plates (Fig. 307*d*) give support and protection to the corners of the mirrors. An example of their use would be in fixing a long mirror behind a wardrobe door.

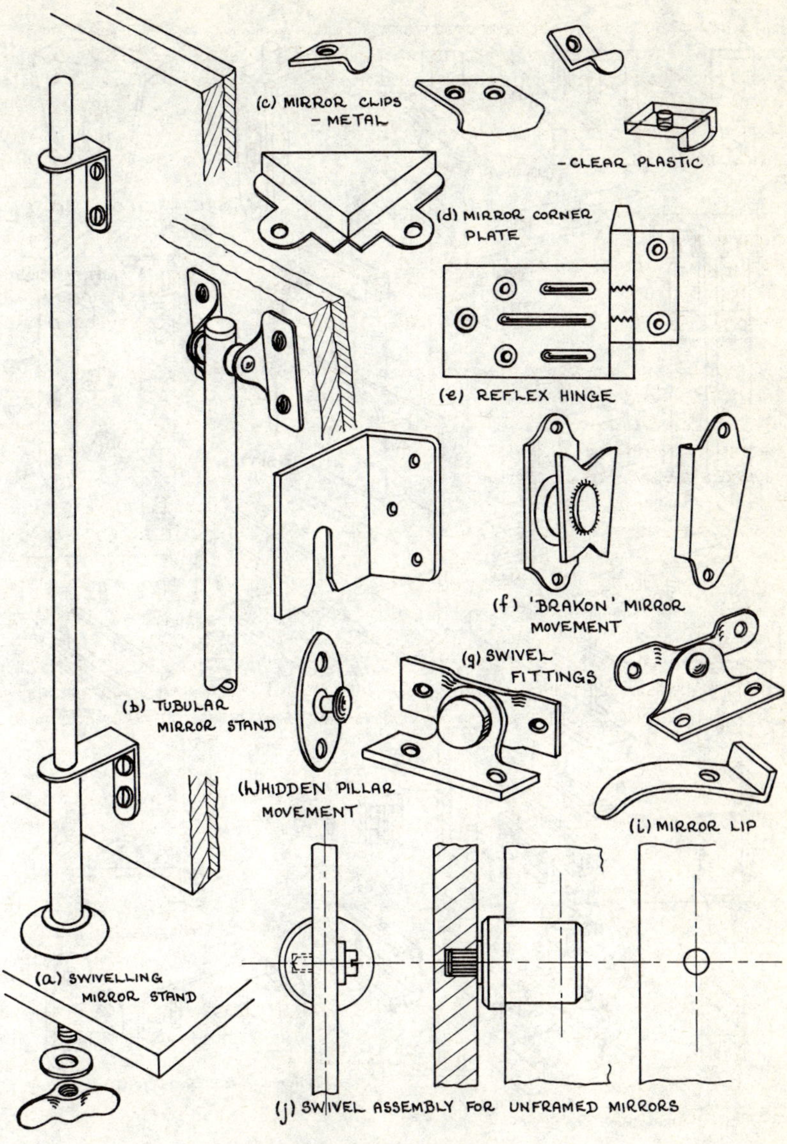

Fig. 307. Mirror fittings.

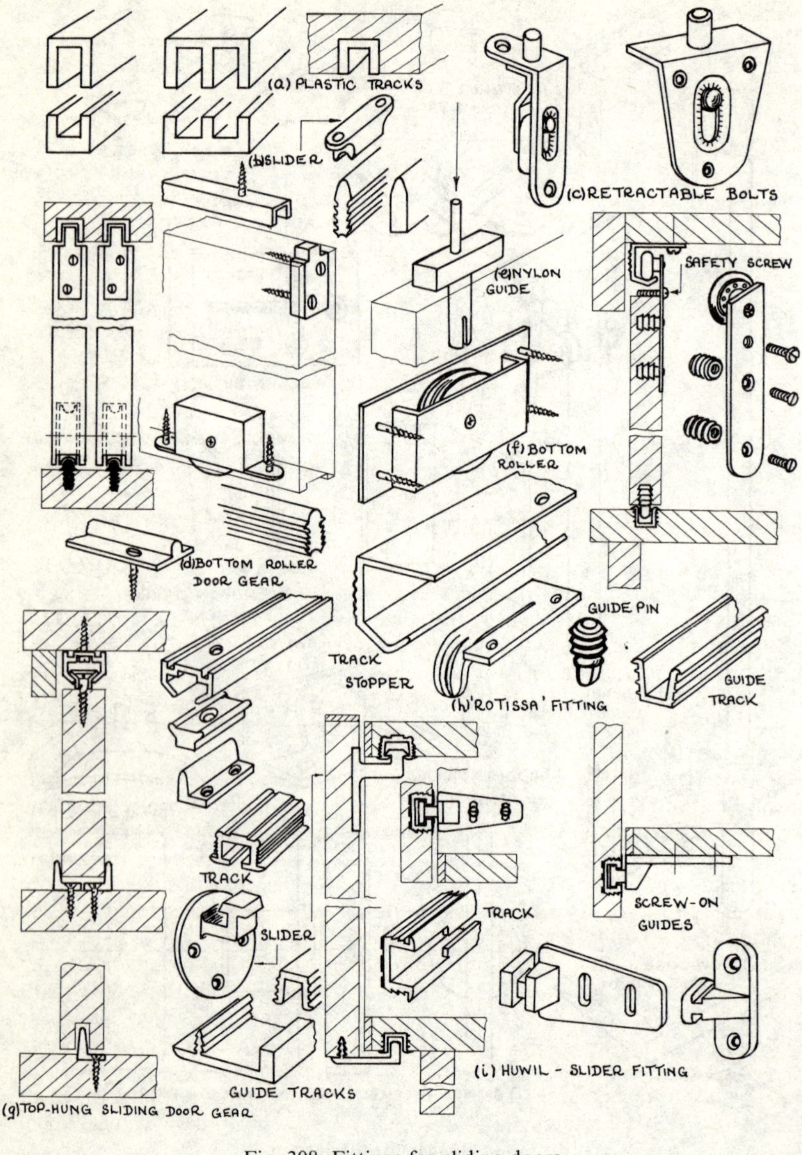

Fig. 308. Fittings for sliding doors.

Reflex hinges. A large hinge is illustrated in Fig. 307*e* and a narrow suite is also made. They are used to enable vertically hung mirrors to be rotated and, as the notches round the knuckle engage with each other, the mirror can be held at any required angle. The hinges are in left- or right-handed pairs, the long leaf of the large one being made more rigid by the protruding ridges pressed in it.

Swivel movements (Fig. 307*f–h*) are used on mirrors hung between pillars or within a frame and allow the mirror to be tilted. They are mounted centrally on the edge of the mirror so that it is balanced, and rely largely on friction to hold the mirror at the required angle. The 'Brakon' has a patented movement giving more positive adjustment.

The **mirror lip** is a small finger grip which screws under the edge of wooden framed tilting mirrors (Fig. 307*i*).

Swivel assembly (Fig. 307*j*). The mirror should be drilled with a glass drill and the fitting is then screwed directly to the mirror with the projecting stud rotating in the vertical member. This is a modern and very neat method of producing a tilting movement. Again the fitting is mounted centrally along the edge.

The reader is reminded that plastic mirrors are now manufactured which can be used to advantage in certain circumstances.

Fittings for Sliding Doors

One big advantage of sliding doors is the small amount of space they require in which to operate as opposed to hinged doors which have to swing outwards. It is an advantage to have the door as light as possible in relation to the strength required, and whereas framed and panelled doors were often used in the past it is now common practice to use flat doors of glass, plywood, blockboard, chipboard, or plastic-faced hardboard. Flush-fitting pulls of wood or plastic are recessed into them to facilitate easy handling. Glass doors usually have ground-in finger grips.

Single and double plastic tracks for thin materials (see Fig. 308*a*). These may be surface-mounted, in which case they have to be drilled, countersunk and screwed to the carcase. A neater appearance can be obtained by dropping the tracks into rebates or plough grooves. This prevents the bottom track from being an awkward protuberance on which the contents of the cabinet might catch. The top track is twice as deep as the bottom one so that the doors can be lifted up into this and dropped into place.

Small wooden doors may have nylon or plastic **sliders** (Fig. 308*b*) screwed to the underside which run on a single raised track. The **retractable bolts** shown in Fig. 308*c* would be used on doors using the slider. They are mounted at the end of, or behind, the door which is placed on the bottom track and the bolt then engaged with the top track.

The **bottom roller** (Fig. 308*d*) for this door gear is mortised into the door bottom and runs on a single track which may be ploughed in or screwed down through a flange. The edge-fitted nylon guide supports the top of the doors, or alternatively retractable bolts may be used. The bottom roller is suitable for 16 mm doors up to 23 kg.

The **nylon guide** (Fig. 308*e*) is fixed to the top of the door by inserting the peg into a pre-drilled hole and spreading it by punching in the wedge pin.

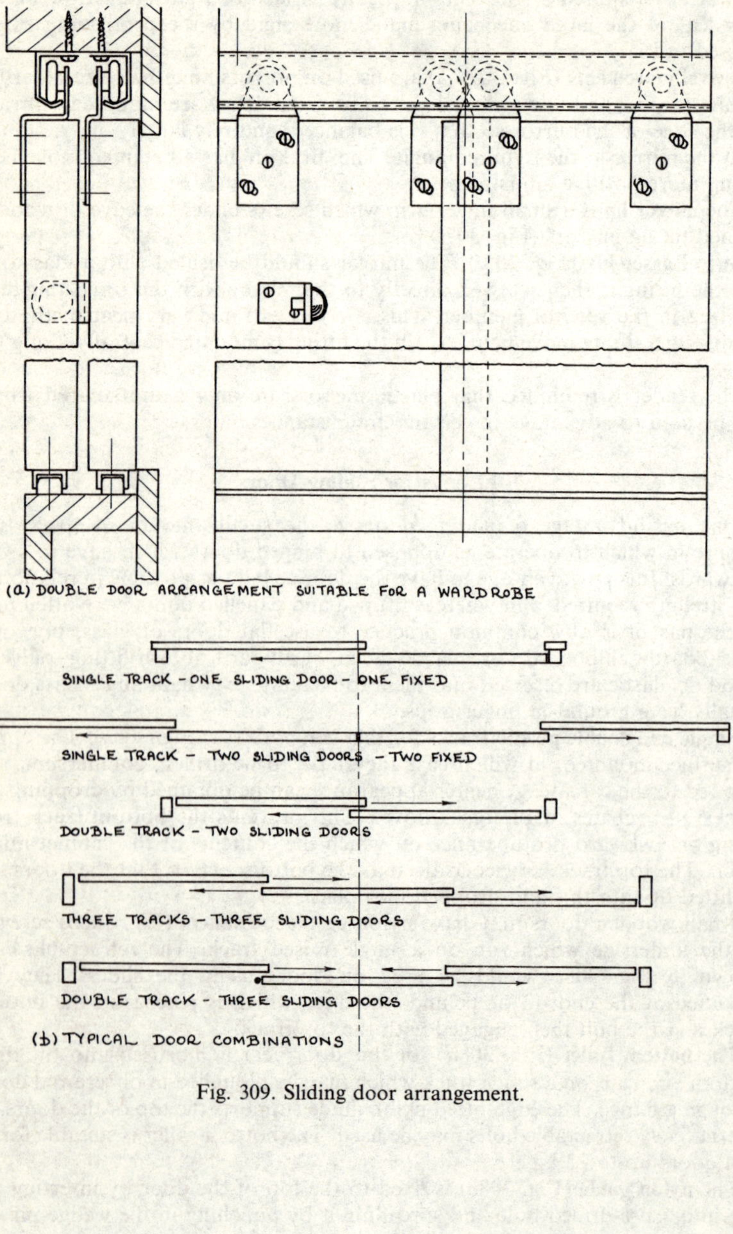

Fig. 309. Sliding door arrangement.

The **side-fixing roller** (Fig. 308*f*) can be used as an alternative to the mortise bottom roller and is suitable for 13 mm doors.

The **top-hung arrangement** (Fig. 308*g*) is suitable for doors of medium weight. They are fitted by tilting until the top hangers engage with the track. The door then hangs vertically and the bottom guides can then be screwed into place. A small piece of thin card wrapped round the bottom edge of the door will provide sufficient clearance and can be removed later. If the bottom of the door is grooved a single guide can be used instead. In either case the guides can be surface-fitting or let in flush.

The **'Rotissa' fitting** (Fig. 308*h*) is typical of many top-hung systems and uses a roller to overcome friction in the form of nylon ball bearings 22 mm in diameter which run in aluminium tracks supplied in lengths of 5,000 mm to be cut to the required measure. The roller plate is fixed to the back of the door by means of screws fitting into nylon bushes. There is also a safety screw which prevents the roller from jumping out of the track, and right- or left-handed 'stoppers' are available to be fitted to the top track if any door has to be stopped at a particular point.

The **Huwil slider fitting** (Fig. 308*i*) is available as an all-plastic system or with aluminium tracks. Various combinations of components enable it to be used for lay-on doors as illustrated, or doors running inside the carcase.

Fig. 309*a* shows a typical sliding arrangement such as might be used in any built-in cupboard or wardrobe in the home. The use of a door stop prevents the doors from overlapping, which might in some cases conceal the door pull.

Fig. 309*b* shows combinations of doors using one, two and three tracks and running between fixed doors or within a framework. Other arrangements can be worked out to meet special requirements.

Height Adjusters

Height adjusters are fitted inside the bottom corners of modern cabinets and are adjusted either by means of a screwdriver through a hole in the bottom shelf or a spanner if there is a square on the bolt, or by a combination of the two. If a spanner is used the plinth has to be removable or the fitting accessible from the back. The fittings are ideal levellers to compensate for the movement or unevenness of a wooden floor.

Fig. 310*a* shows adjustment by spanner or screwdriver, the bolt operating through a tee nut in a wooden block. This stud is screwed to the side of the cabinet, or is available in plastic with two knock-in dowels moulded on. A plastic cap is supplied to cover the hole in the bottom shelf.

The fitting in Fig. 310*b* is screwed below the bottom shelf of the unit and adjusted with a screwdriver from above. A tee nut may be used instead of the screw-on fixing plate if desired, and again a plastic cover cap is supplied. The bolt length is 50 mm.

The fitting in Fig. 310*c* is designed to screw on to a corner block behind the plinth; the bolt is available in three lengths of 80, 100 and 120 mm.

Fig. 311 illustrates a concealed hanger which can be adjusted for height or depth from within the cabinet, allowing it to be levelled on the wall and drawn tightly to it. The hanger is suitable for either right- or left-hand use. The bearing strength per hanger is 50 kg.

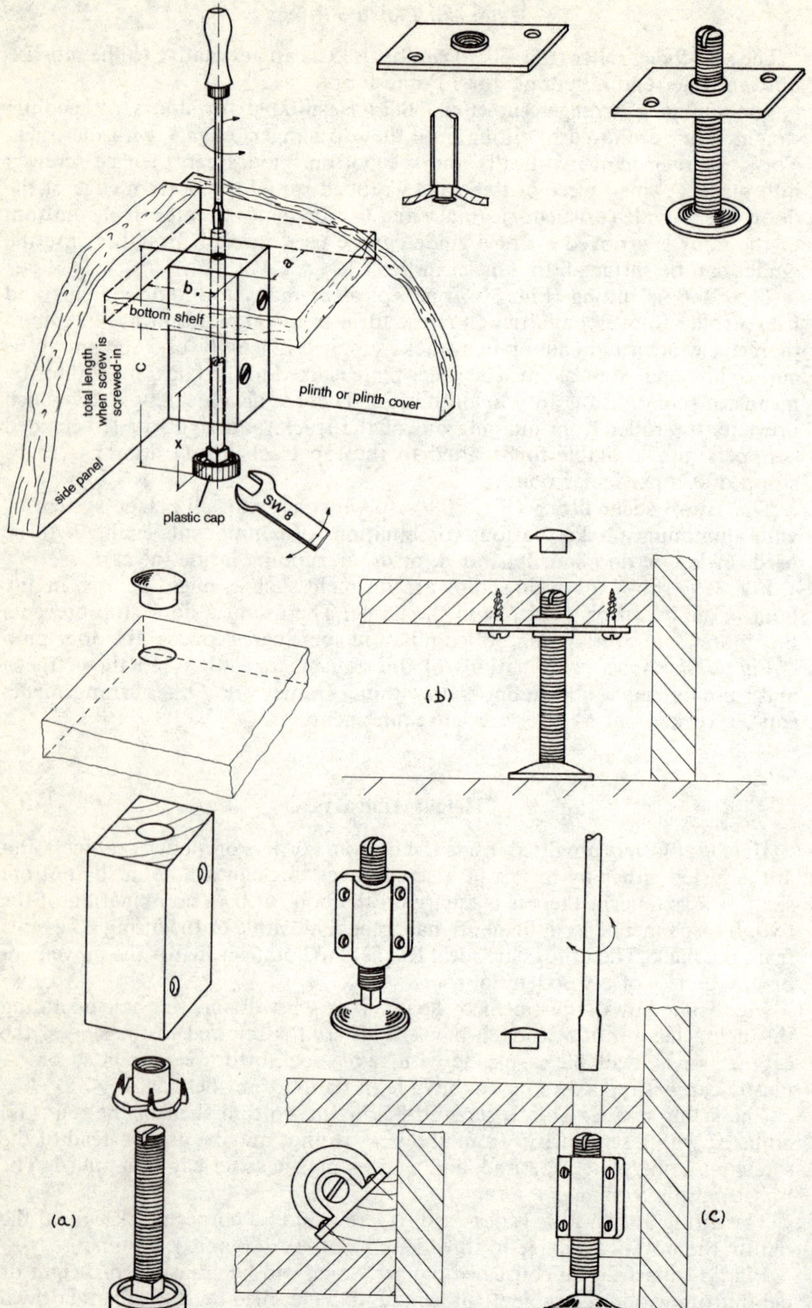

Fig. 310. Height adjusters.

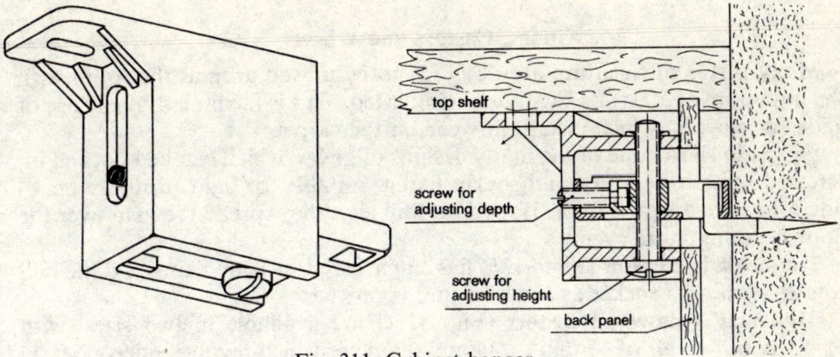

Fig. 311. Cabinet hanger.

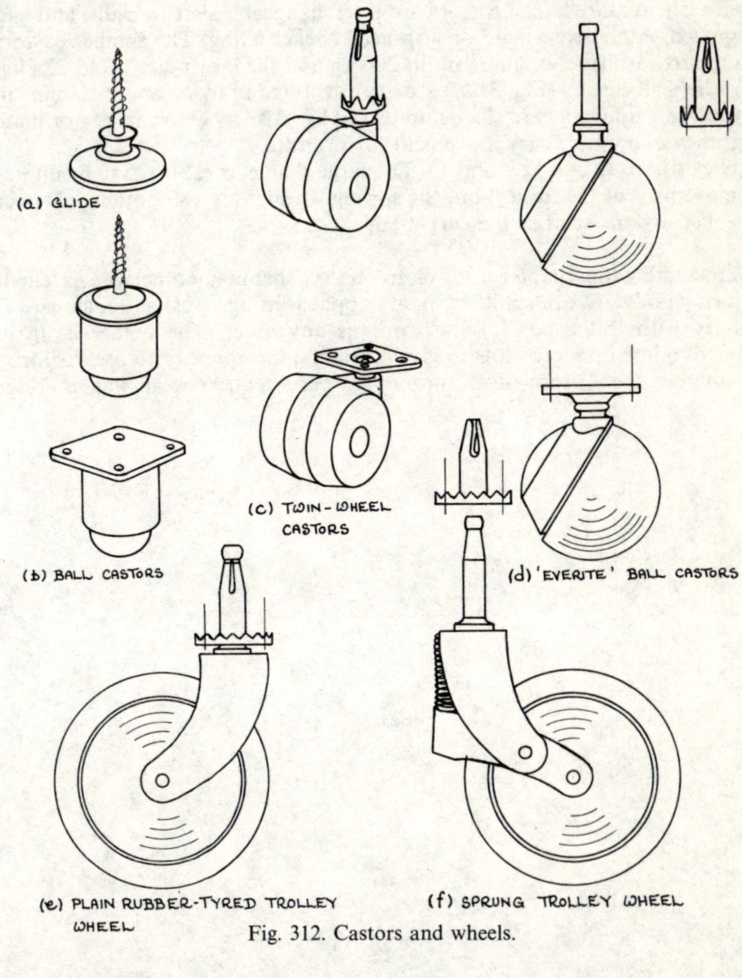

Fig. 312. Castors and wheels.

Glides, Castors and Wheels

Many pieces of furniture are designed to be moved around the room with the minimum of effort and without being lifted. This is facilitated by the use of glides or castors, which also limit wear on the carpet.

Fig. 312*a* shows one of the many designs of **glides**, which can be knocked in, screwed in or have a peg-and-socket fixing, suitable for light furniture enabling it to slide over the floor. If used on thin legs, they spread the load over the floor covering more evenly.

The **single ball castor** (Fig. 312*b*) has single-screw or plate fixing and the ball rotates within its socket as the furniture is moved.

'Diplomat' twin-wheel castors (Fig. 312*c*) are available in two sizes, with black nylon wheels of 35 mm or 44 mm diameter which revolve independently to give greater mobility and less wear on the floor coverings. No lubrication of the wheels is required. The castors are interchangeable, left to right, and can be supplied with square-plate or grip-neck socket fixing. The smaller castors will support furniture weighing up to 200 kg and the larger size up to 225 kg.

'Everite' ball castors (Fig. 312*d*) are manufactured of nylon and melamine in two-tone grey and can carry loads up to 150 kg. Also available in peg or plate fixing, they allow very easy movement of furniture.

Trolley wheels (Fig. 312 *e* and *f*). The large-diameter rubber tyre facilitates easy movement of the trolley, but the sprung wheel gives a smoother ride over small obstructions such as the carpet edge.

In concluding this chapter it is well to observe that many otherwise excellent pieces of woodwork are spoilt by badly applied fittings. Just as much care is necessary with this aspect of the work as any other. The reader is again reminded to line up screw slots to give a neater appearance or to use Pozidriv. Also, the occasional spot of oil on moving parts reduces wear and prolongs life.

11

KNOCK-DOWN (K/D) FITTINGS

For many years it has been common practice to design large pieces of furniture such as wardrobes, beds, roll-top desks and bureaux, etc., so that they can be broken down into smaller sections which may be handled more easily. This makes transportation, delivery and assembly within the home easier, and also facilitates the movement of furniture from one room to another which is necessary from time to time and might otherwise be quite impossible. Until comparatively recently this 'sectioning' of furniture was achieved mainly and quite effectively by means of woodscrews, so placed that they could be easily removed but not obtrusive when the furniture was reassembled. Few special fittings were used, but of late quite a tremendous range of metal and plastic fittings has been developed by manufacturers, mainly because of the increasing use of man-made boards. Many of these are pre-veneered or plastic faced, and because of their very nature cannot often be jointed together satisfactorily using traditional woodworking joints. The components produced for this purpose have become known collectively as 'Knock-Down' or K/D fittings. Much modern furniture is designed so that it may be delivered completely 'knocked down' in packs consisting of pre-machined slabs and other members plus a packet of fittings with which it may be assembled.

Although many K/D fittings were originally intended for use by the manufacturers of mass-produced furniture, several are quite suitable for use in the school or home workshop where perhaps only the simplest of tools are available. Even the more complicated fittings which require precise machining of the timber for them to be fully effective are now within the scope of a workshop equipped with modern portable electric tools. From experience, the author strongly advises that Twinfast screws only should be used where any such fittings are screwed to chipboard.

Corner fitting (Fig. 313). Made in two sizes of 19 mm and 25 mm, corner fittings are supplied in sets of four, two 'lefts' and two 'rights'. They have numerous uses in joinery and cabinet making and are suitable for all prefabricated and collapsible constructions, such as portable sheds, partitions, shelves, counters, packing cases, etc. The parts, which are of steel, simply slide together and a number of finishes are available.

Keyhole plates (Fig. 314). These act in a similar way to secret or slot screwing, and have to be recessed into one of the pieces. Protruding screw heads in the other piece then slide into the keyhole slot.

Taper connector (Fig. 315). This is only suitable for use where the screws enter side grain—for example, horizontal rails may be joined to legs if they are suitably recessed.

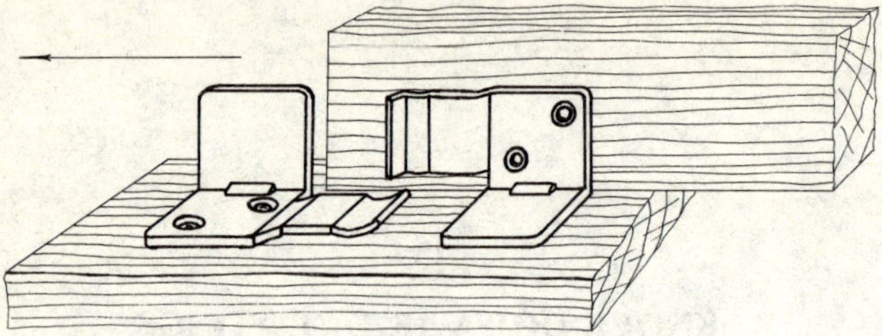

Fig. 313. K/D corner fitting.

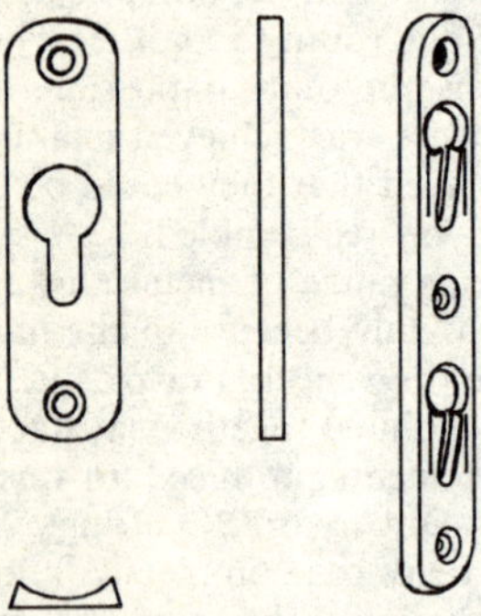

Fig. 314. Keyhole plates.

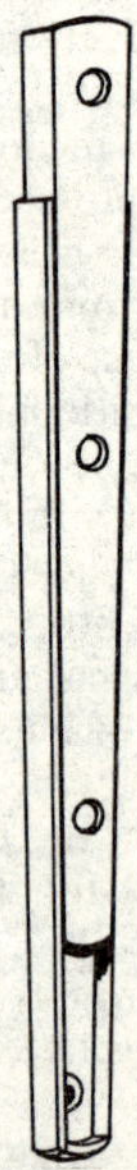

Fig. 315. Taper connector.

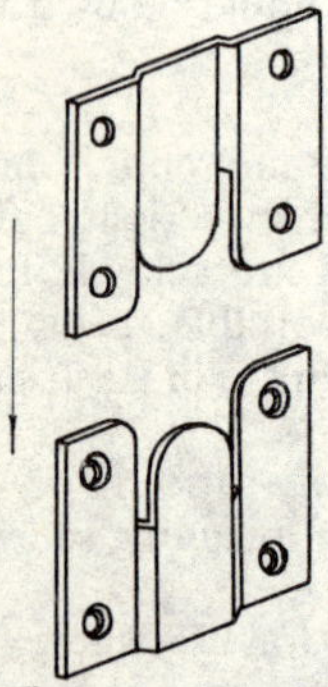

Fig. 316. Flush mount.

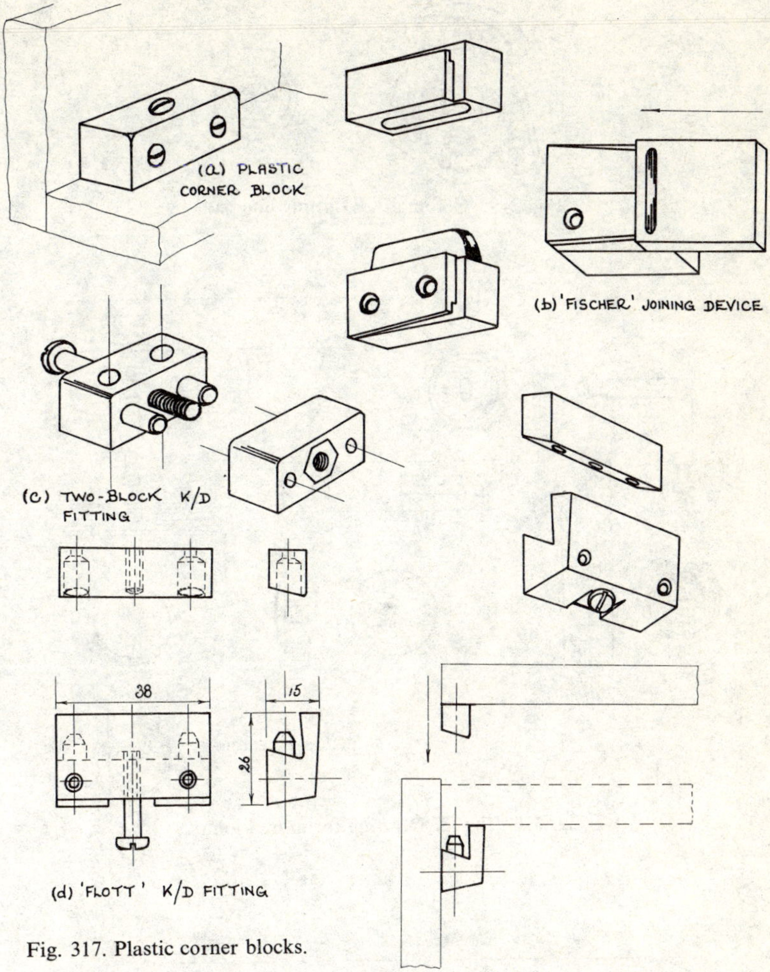

Fig. 317. Plastic corner blocks.

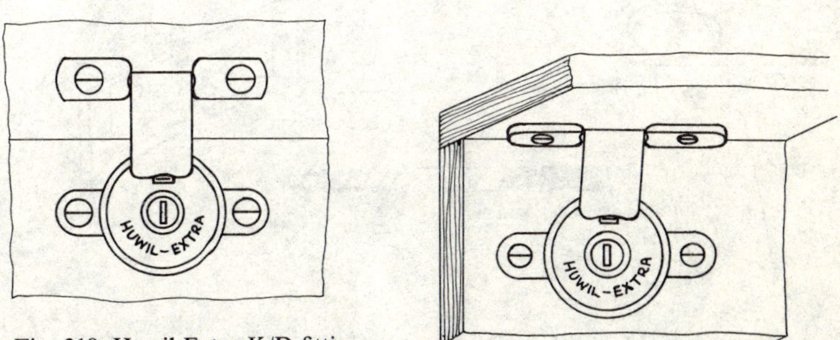

Fig. 318. Huwil Extra K/D fitting.

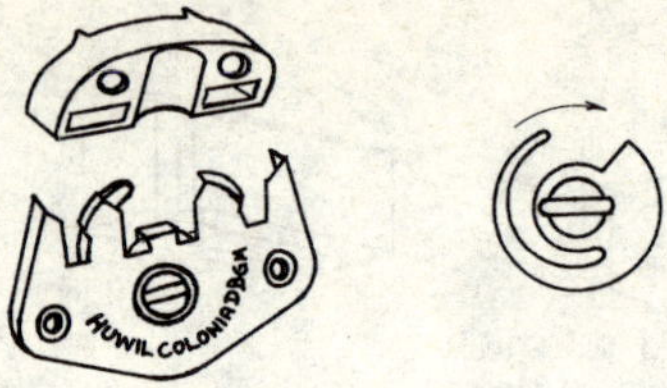

Fig. 319. 'Colonia' K/D fitting and cam.

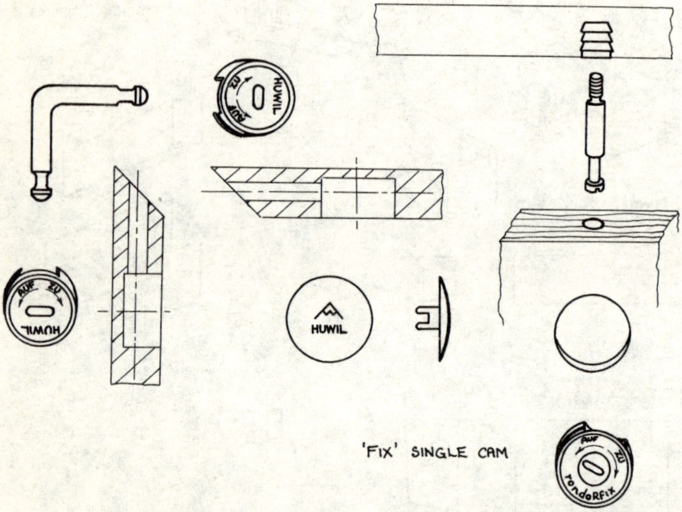

Fig. 320. 'Fix' K/D fitting for mitred joints.

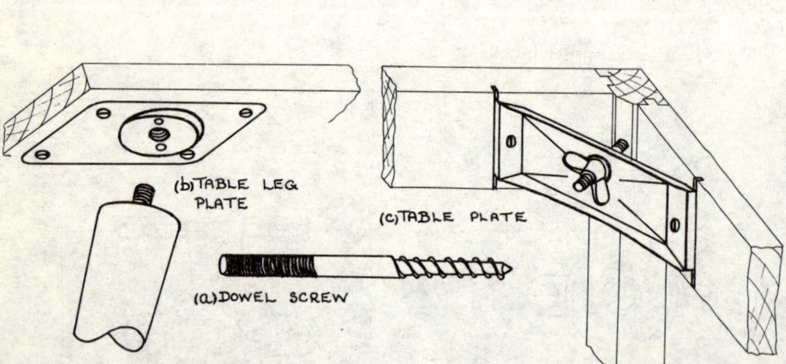

Fig. 321. Table leg fittings.

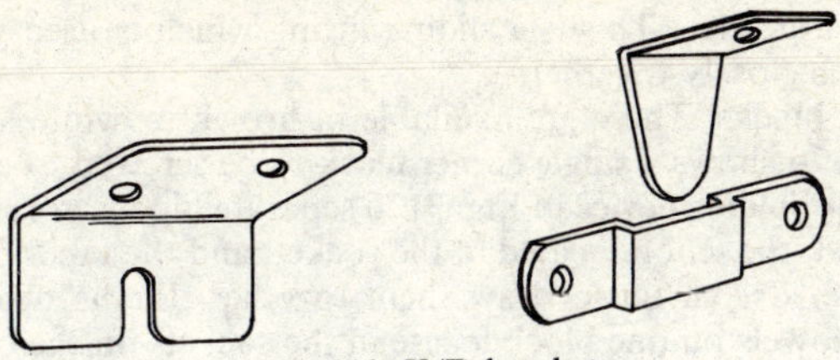

Fig. 322. K/D bracket.

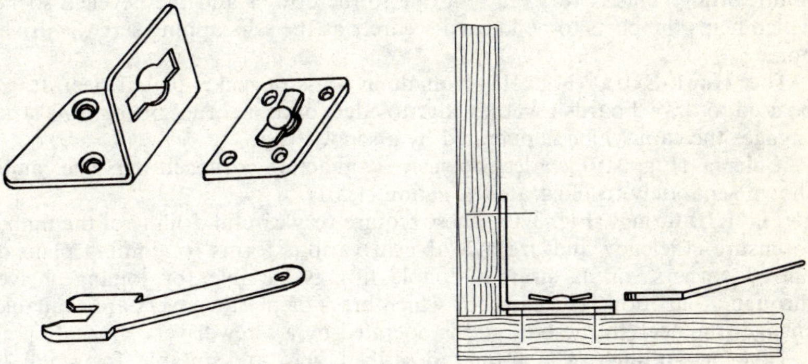

Fig. 323. K/D corner fitting (Spegelstein Ltd.)

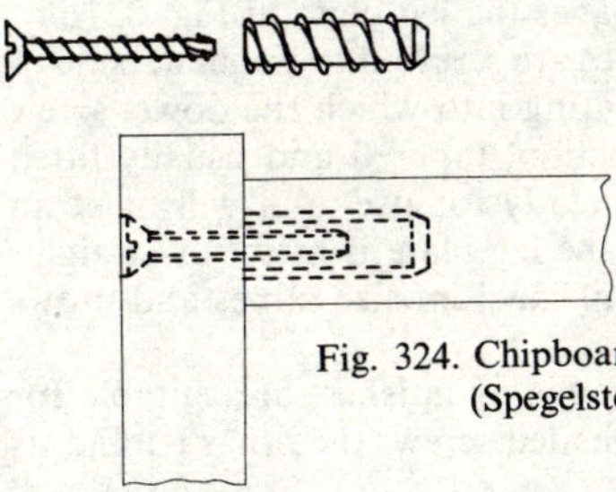

Fig. 324. Chipboard fastener (Spegelstein Ltd.)

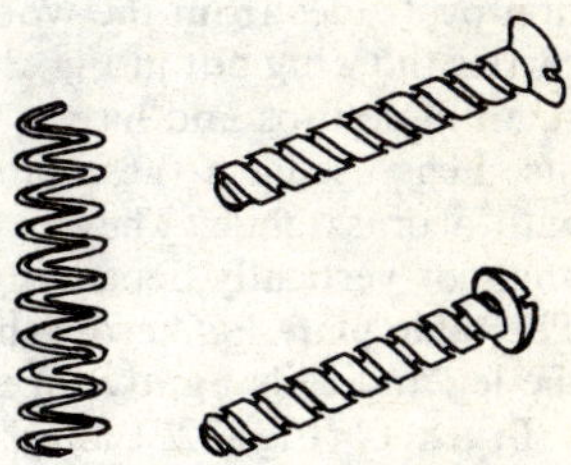

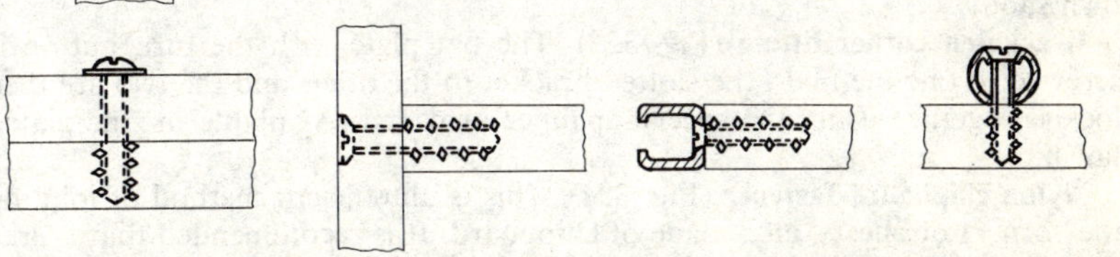

Fig. 325. Helicoil inserts and screws.

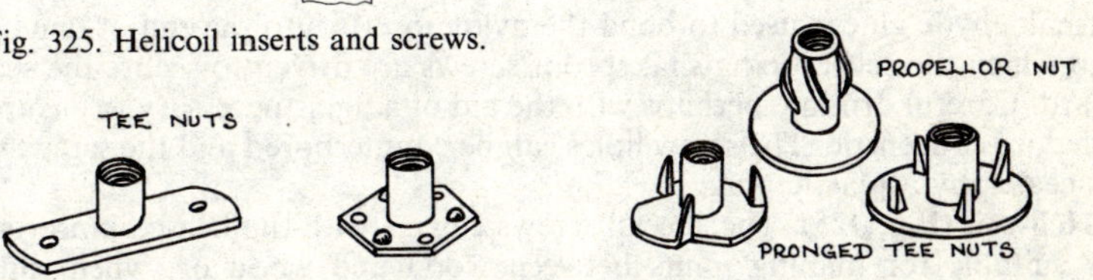

Fig. 326. Tee nuts.

Flush mount (Fig. 316). This is a sliding fitting which is used vertically and will hold sections closely together.

Plastic corner blocks. These are available in brown or white and in several varieties. Fig. 317*a* shows a **single corner block** to be screwed to each member. With the **'Fischer' joining device** in Fig. 317*b* separate blocks are screwed to the parts to be joined, the tenon located in the socket, and the taper fitting, nickel-plated steel cover driven on to draw them together. In the **two-block fitting** (Fig. 317*c*) the dowels on one block locate in the sockets on the other, and the two are drawn together by the machine screw and nut. Fig. 317*d* illustrates the **'Flott' fitting**. This is very efficient due to the dowels and the bevelled socket which helps the parts to be located securely as the self-tapping screw is driven home.

The **'Huwil-Extra'** (Fig. 318) is made in brass or nickel-plated steel. It can be used to draw boards together edge to edge, or as a corner fitting. The strap engages the cam which is operated by a screwdriver.

'Colonia' (Fig. 319) is a less obtrusive cam action corner fitting. The cam is shown separately to illustrate the action clearly.

'Fix' K/D fittings (Fig. 320). These require very careful drilling of the timber to ensure efficiency and are available in various forms for joining plain or mitred corners, or as straight double fittings suitable for joining shelves through a partition. The cam, for which brass or plastic covers are available, engages the neck in the bolt and is operated by a screwdriver.

Table leg fittings. The fittings described here are suitable for small to medium-size tables. The **dowel screw** (Fig. 321*a*) is made with wood and metal thread, steel, self-coloured zinc plated or sherardized. The metal thread portion protrudes from the wooden leg and engages the leg plate in Fig. 321*b* or carries the wing nut in Fig. 321*c*. The **leg plates** are screwed to the underside of small table tops and have a tapped raised seating into which the dowel screw fits. Legs used for these tables are round section, tapered and usually fitted with a brass glide. They may be purchased ready for use, and will fit at an angle or vertically depending upon whether the leg plate is offset or straight. The **table plate** fits across the inner corners of medium-size tables and draws the leg and rails tightly together.

Brackets (Fig. 322). Steel brackets, in a range of finishes, are suitable for shelves, pelmets, etc. One fits over a round-headed screw, the other behind its own saddle.

Bracketed corner fitting (Fig. 323). The flat plate with the turn button is screwed to one member, the slotted bracket to the other and the two are then locked together using the special spanner provided. Available in zinc-plated finish.

Nylon chipboard fastener (Fig. 324). This is an efficient method of jointing the corners of chests, etc., made of chipboard. It is recommended that a urea formaldehyde glue is used to bond the nylon inserts into the end of one board into which the self-tapping shakeproof screws are driven to secure the second board. Careful drilling, perhaps with the aid of a jig, is necessary to ensure the holes are concentric. The screw holes can be counterbored and the screw heads concealed by a plastic plug.

Heli-coil (Fig. 325). The special screws engage with the heli-coil inserts and are suitable for making joints between wood and wood or, when suitably drilled, between metal tube and wood.

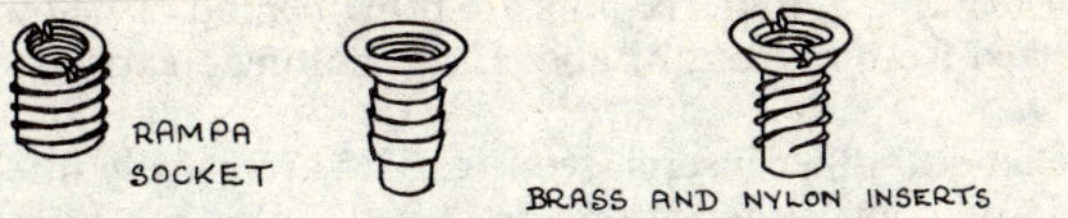

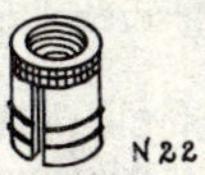

INTERNAL THREAD

N 22	METRIC	3·5	4	5	6
	HOLE SIZE	N°5	15/64"	LETTER G	21/64"

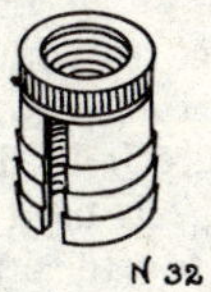

N 32	METRIC		4	5	6	8
	HOLE SIZE		9/32"	11/32"	13/32"	15/32"

Fig. 327. 'Banc-Lok' inserts.

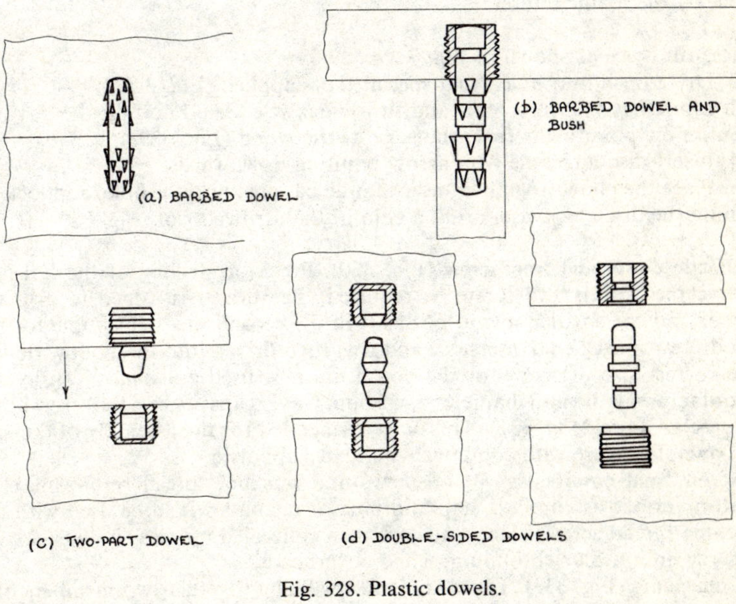

Fig. 328. Plastic dowels.

Tee nuts and threaded inserts (Fig. 326). These may be used for bolting wood to wood or metal to wood. Tee nuts are fitted behind or below the work and the bolt inserted from in front or above, e.g. bolting a carrying handle to a wooden case.

The **rampa socket** and other inserts (see Fig. 326) are usually fitted into the face of the wood and connections are made directly into them. Care must be taken to ensure that the holes into which they fit are of the correct diameter. In different sizes they are tapped to accept metal thread screws of various diameters.

Banc-lok (Fig. 327). These inserts are of brass and are suitable for wood and composition materials. Sharp fins are expanded into the material surrounding the insert, which is then anchored as the screw is driven home. The tables indicate screw capacity and hole size required for each.

Plastic dowels. Fig. 328*a* illustrates the **barbed dowel**. In white plastic this provides a permanent fixing. A variation is the **barbed dowel and bush** (Fig. 328*b*). The barbs of the dowel provide it with a secure hold in the timber, especially if a little glue of the urea formaldehyde type is used as well. The bush should also be glued in and the two then snapped together. With the **two-part dowel** (Fig. 328*c*) the components should be glued into the wood and they can then be assembled in the same way as a press-stud is clipped together, giving a firm, strong joint on light work. **Double-sided dowels** (Fig. 328*d*) work in a similar way, but have two separate bushes and a connecting piece. They are suitable for fixing the corners and shelves of carcase work. Again great accuracy is necessary in drilling the holes for these dowels.

Off-centre fitting. Suitable for large carcase work; the fitting instructions are given by the manufacturer:

1. Drill holes as shown in Fig. 329*a*.
2. Drive bush into hole using special tool supplied (Fig. 329*b*).
3. Insert bayonet into bush and turn clockwise. The hook on the bayonet should now point away from the edge of the wood (Fig. 329*c*).
4. Insert disc into hole with arrow pointing downwards.
5. Place the panels together, inserting the bayonet into the hole, and lock by turning the disc clockwise, using a coin in the arrowed slot (Fig. 329*d*).

Plastic dowel and woodscrew (Fig. 330). Precision drilling of the holes to receive the dowels and screws is required. The dowel is ridged to grip the timber and the smaller spigot locates it in the second piece. The hole for the woodscrew must be countersunk and it is then driven into the hollow dowel. The correct size of screw for the dowel must be used and that given by the manufacturer is 3·5 mm diameter × 25 mm. Cover caps conceal the screw head.

'Special' dowel (Fig. 331). This is recommended for the assembly of 'knock-ed-down' furniture with components already upholstered.

Screws and coverheads. Woodscrews and machine-thread screws may be used in various assemblies. Standard nuts or tee nuts would be used with the machine-thread screws. The heads are then concealed by press-in plaster caps or screw-in brass or chromium-plated coverheads.

Connectors (Fig. 333). These are used for fixing together two members of a frame or fitments such as wall shelf units which have to fit side by side. Those for frames consist of a length of threaded studding of a suitable length which

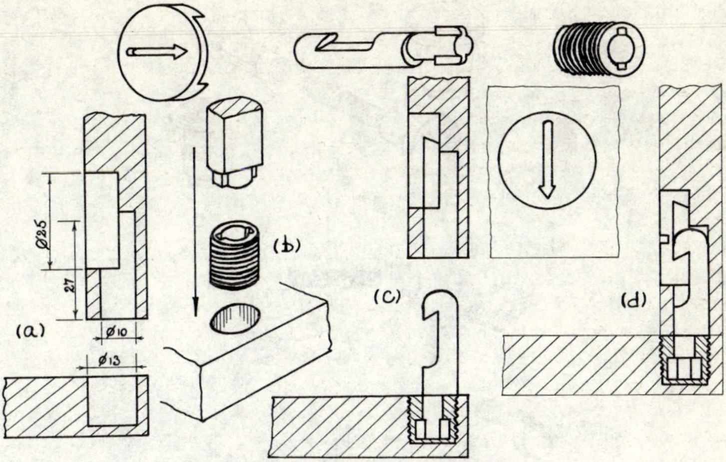

Fig. 329. Off-centre K/D fitting in nylon.

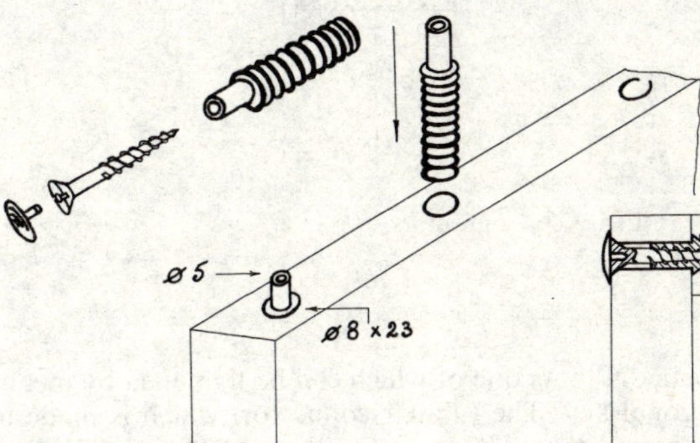

Fig. 330. Plastic dowels with woodscrew.

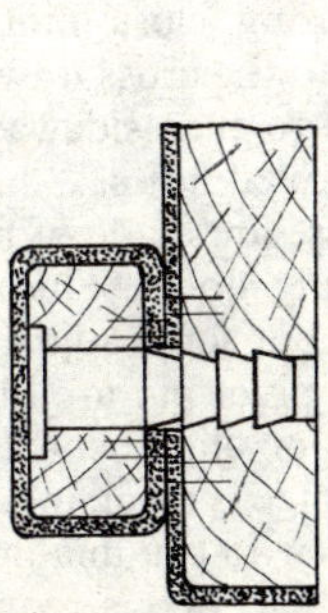

Fig. 331. Special dowel.

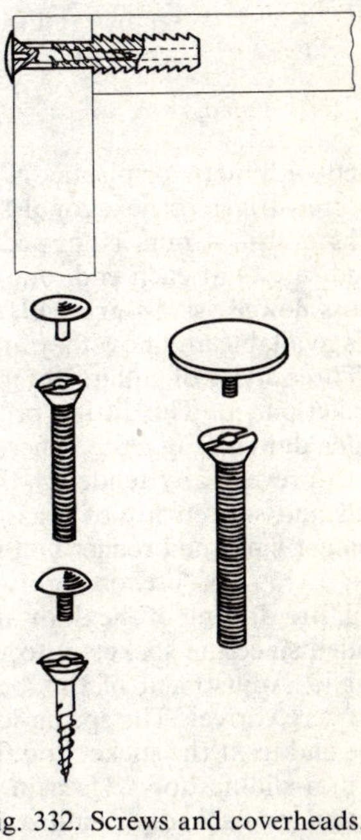

Fig. 332. Screws and coverheads.

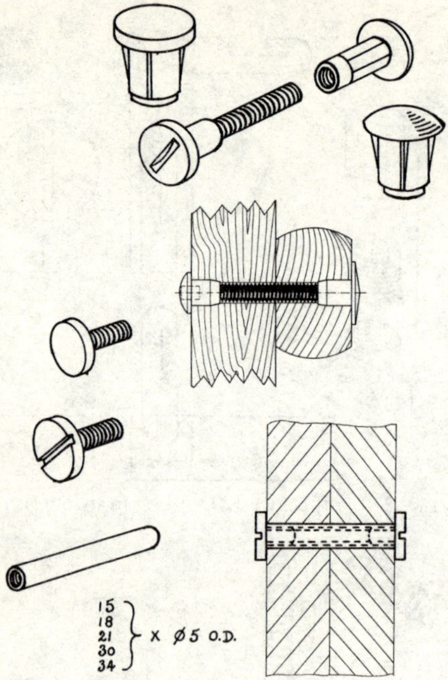

Fig. 333. Connectors.

is fitted with metal or plastic 'N' nuts one of which can be tightened by means of a screwdriver or hexagonal key. The tubular connector, which is made in lengths of 15–34 mm, is tapped throughout its length and is fitted with flat-headed screws at each end, one or both being slotted.

Cross dowels, screw and collars. Fig. 334 indicates a range of cross dowels that is available and how they are used in conjunction with an Allen screw and key. Three styles of collars are made, and finishes are black oxidised and brass or nickel-plated. This fitting provides a remarkably strong, close joint.

Guide dowels (Fig. 335). These are used in addition to the cross dowel (Fig. 334) to prevent any tendency there may be for a rail to turn sideways. The dowels and sockets are of brass and knock into pre-drilled holes.

Plunger hinge and runner bolt fittings (Fig. 336). These are made of natural-colour nylon for use on lightweight pivoted or sliding doors. Once more, careful pre-drilling of the door and carcase is essential, but some adjustment is provided since the sockets into which the plunger and pivot pin are fitted are eccentric. Adjustment of this bush, which provides door alignment, is made with a screwdriver. The spring-loaded plunger in the hinge is reversible, round at one end to fit the socket and flat-sectioned at the other to run in a groove if used in a sliding door. Used in this way as a runner bolt, one is required at each end of each door and a suitable simple track is necessary along the

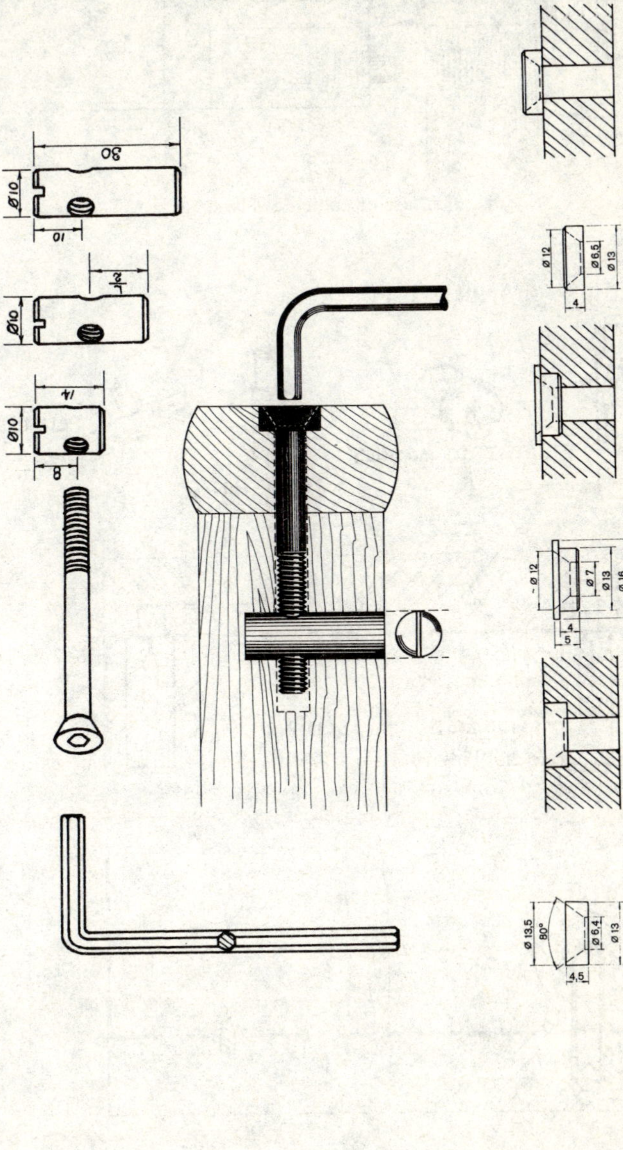

Fig. 334. Cross dowels, screw and collars.

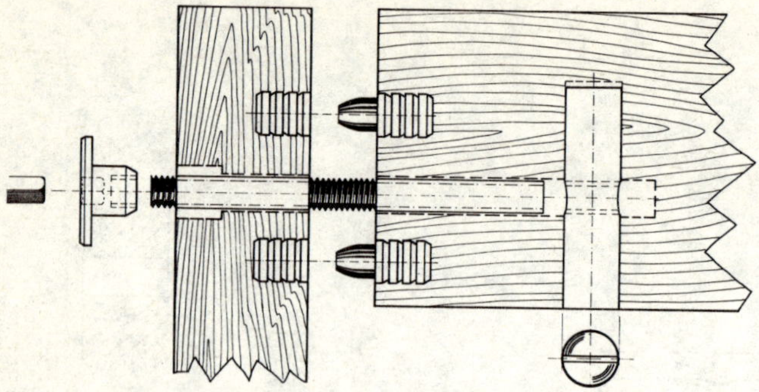

Fig. 335. Use of guide dowels.

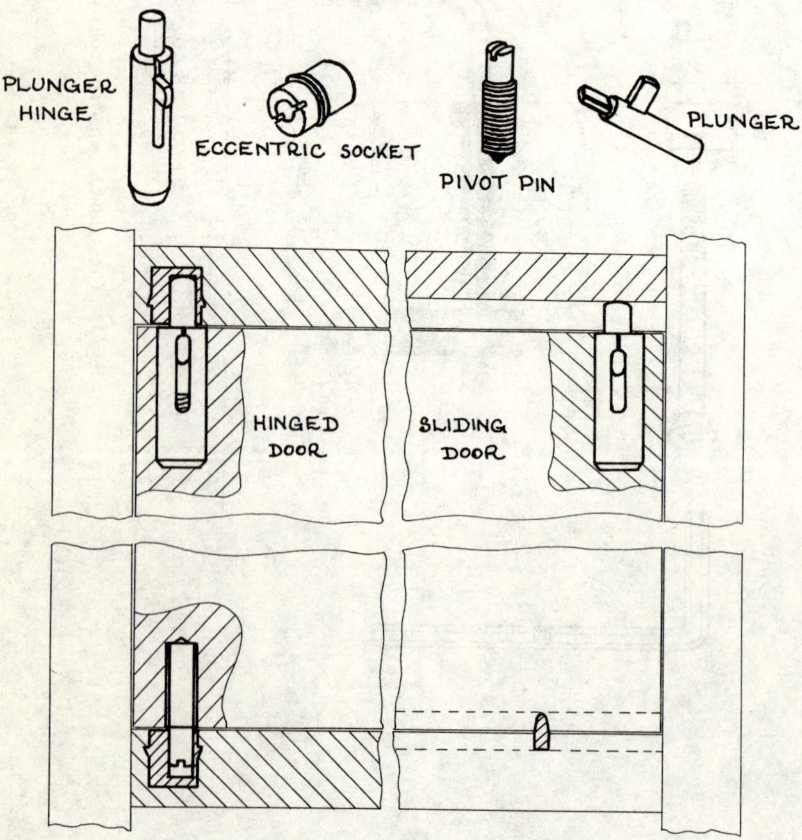

Fig. 336. Plunger hinge and runner bolt fittings.

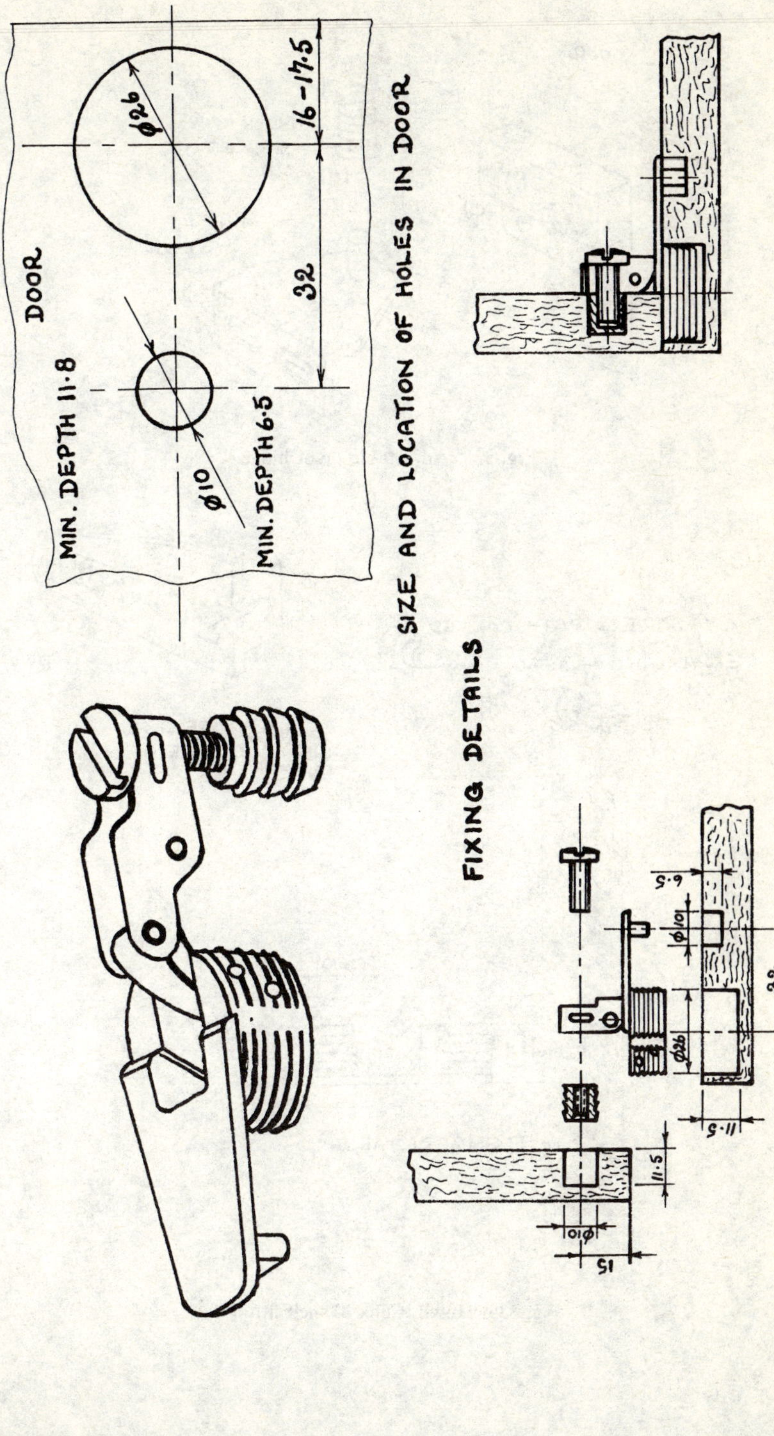

Fig. 337. Heinze K/D hinge.

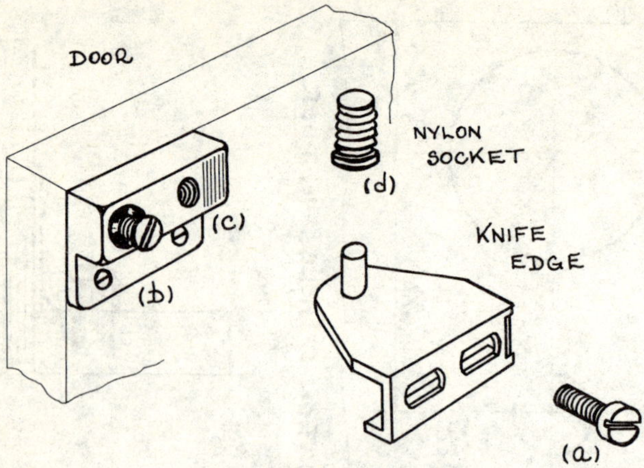

Fig. 338. Adjustable pivot hinge.

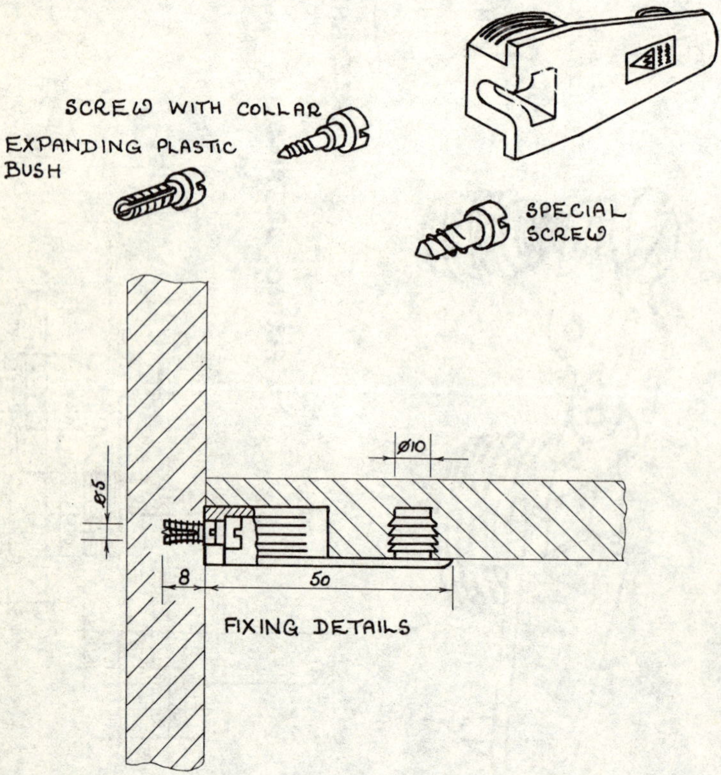

Fig. 339. Huwil 'Cefix 3' shelf fitting.

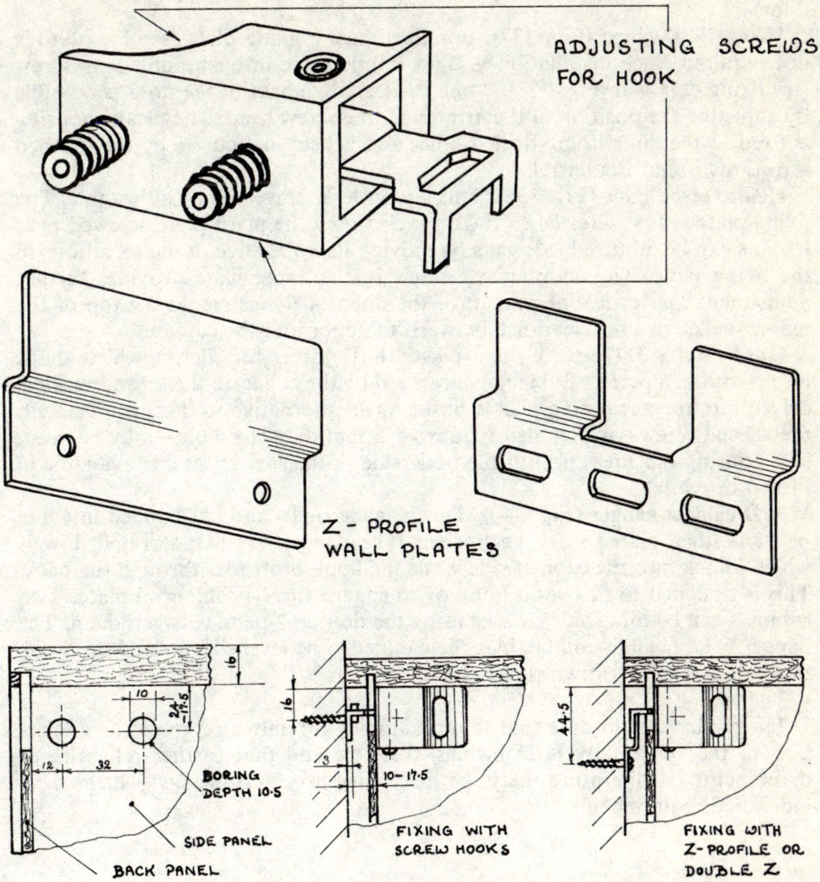

Fig. 340. Cabinet hanger with dowel fixing.

bottom. Fig. 336 illustrates the arrangement for either use, and is taken from the back, showing the plunger arm for which a slot must be cut down the door.

Heinze K/D hinge (Fig. 337). For this hinge a fixing plate (see Fig. 296) is not required since installation is by a simple drive-in bush and fixing screw (see fixing details in Fig. 337). Some vertical alignment of the door is possible by adjusting the position of the arm under the screw head. The plastic housing is fixed to the door in pre-drilled holes and is held in securely by the toothed serrations round the barrel.

Heinze pivot hinge (Fig. 338). This lay-on K/D hinge is fully adjustable. The fixing plate is first screwed to the door and then the pivot plate screwed over it. This can be adjusted sideways by moving its knife edge in the serrations in the fixing plate. The countersunk screw in the fixing plate provides further adjustment for vertical alignment of the door. A flange round the top of the nylon socket ensures clearance between the door and the carcase.

Huwil 'Cefix 3' (Fig. 339) is a plastic K/D fitting for shelves which snaps into position, a perfect fit being guaranteed by the collar on the screw, which is driven into the expanding plastic bush. As an alternative to this arrangement, the special screw—which also requires a 5 mm diameter hole—may be used. The housing is a press fit into the underside of the shelves, and is available in brown or white.

K/D cabinet hanger (Fig. 340). This is made right- and left-handed in white plastic with a plated steel mechanism. The hanger has two serrated dowels which knock into the cabinet side while the hook protrudes through the back. This is designed to fit over a hook or to engage the Z-profile wall plate. Two cabinets can be hung side by side using the double Z-plate between them. The hanger is adjustable and enables the cabinet to be levelled once it is hung on the wall and to be drawn tightly to it.

The reader should note that these examples are only a representative selection of the very many K/D fittings available and that further reference to manufacturers' literature may be necessary to find fittings which meet individual requirements.

12

WOODCARVING

Woodcarving is an aspect of woodwork that can become totally absorbing. Combining creativity and skill, it is a craft to which some devote the whole of their lives. In woodcarving the amateur or professional craftsman will find a form of expression which is both exciting and satisfying, whether the carving is used purely to embellish a piece of his work or whether is is a complete work in itself. There is a very considerable range of woodcarving tools but a limited selection will suffice for the majority of work and special shapes may be added as required.

Carving Tools

Carving tools may be divided into chisels, gouges and V tools, of which gouges are made in the largest variety of sizes as they are most frequently needed.

Chisels for woodcarving are ground and sharpened on both sides in a similar way to woodturning tools, a low angle being the average. This enables a keen strong edge to be produced by honing. This may be **square** or **skew**, of 6, 10 and 13 mm widths, while the **spoon bit** chisel has widths of 3 and 6 mm (see Fig. 341). Handles are of the carving pattern of hardwood.

There is a range of curves for each width of **gouge** (Fig. 342) from almost flat to a deep U-section. **Straight** gouges are the most common, along with the **curved** gouge which has a gentle bend throughout its length. Gouges are ground and honed so that they are square across the end, with possibly a small radius on the corners to prevent digging in. The inside curve is usually maintained but some craftsmen do prefer to produce a smaller inner bevel by honing. The **veiner** is a narrow, deep gouge with straight sides suitable for making very narrow cuts. Widths range from 3 to 16 mm in the Marples range, with a restricted choice of the larger widths, and the curved gouge is restricted to the sizes marked with an asterisk—see Fig. 343.

Both **straight and curved** V **parting tools** are made in the sizes shown in Fig. 344, the curved being in the two larger sizes only. These are really a double-sided chisel used to produce V-shaped grooves. (Reference is made in Chapter 6 to the special difficulty in sharpening these tools.)

When carving, the tools are held so that the hand steadies both blade and handle so that the cut is made with the tool under complete control. Pressure is applied with the other hand for light cuts, heavier ones being made with the assistance from the mallet (see below). When not in use, woodcarving tools should be stored carefully to protect their fine edges, either in their own racked box or in a canvas tool roll.

Tools used to remove tool marks include **scrapers**, **'rifflers'** (rasps with short curved faces at each end) and the **'half-round' cabinet file**. **Surform rasps** by

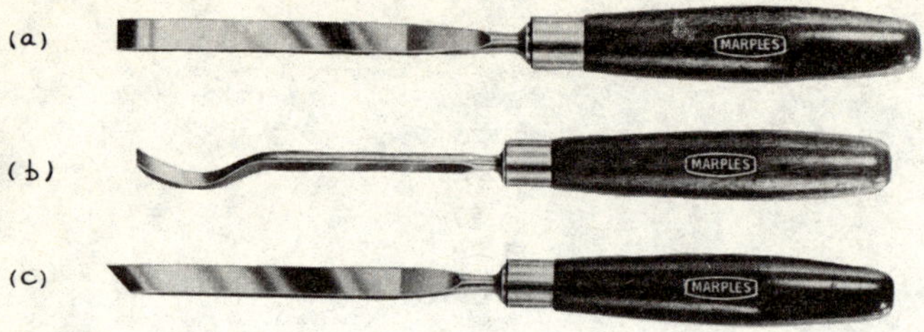

Fig. 341. (*a*) Square chisel. (*b*) Spoon-bit chisel, square. (*c*) Skew chisel.

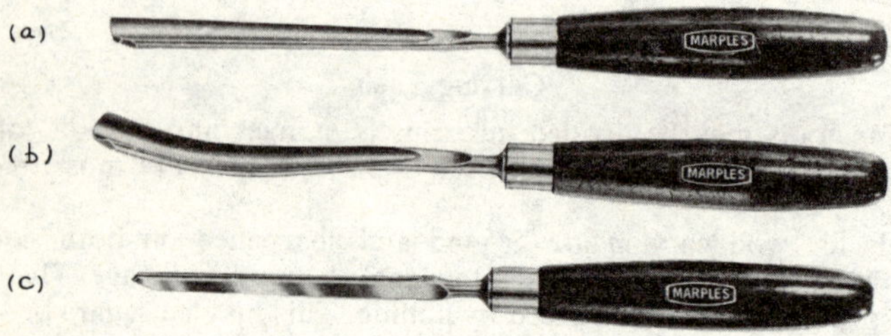

Fig. 342. (*a*) Straight gouge. (*b*) Curved gouge—sizes marked * in Fig. 343. (*c*) Veiner.

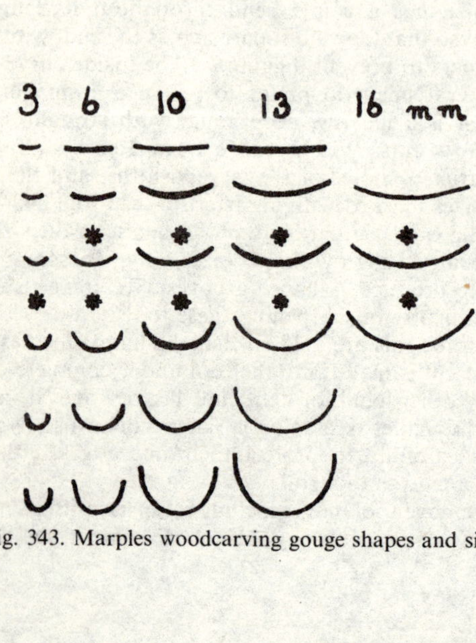

Fig. 343. Marples woodcarving gouge shapes and sizes.

Stanley Tools are abrasive tools which have made sculpture accessible to many more people than was ever previously considered feasible. The blades are perforated and each tooth ground to create a series of cutting teeth (see Chapter 4). Surform tools are safe and quick cutting so that once the bulk of the surplus wood has been removed by a suitable saw, the required shape may be achieved quite readily. After roughing out, a fine-cut Surform blade should be applied, strokes being light and with thc grain. Cabinet files, suitable engineers' files and various grades of glasspaper should then be used for final finishing.

If large three-dimensional sculpture is being undertaken, bulk waste may be removed with the **axe** (see Chapter 4) or the **woodcarving adze**. The latter is similar to the traditional adze but has a shorter handle and narrower blade. The **carver's mallet** (Fig. 345) is used in preference to the joiner's mallet for making heavy cuts with carving tools; lighter cuts are made by hand pressure alone. The mallet is usually of beech and about 100 mm in diameter.

Holding Tools

Wood being carved must be held firmly to avoid errors in cutting. If the work is rectangular or square in shape this may be done in the bench vice, but if it is irregular, or if the hardwood jaws of the bench vice are likely to cause damage to the work, then **carvers' chops** (Fig. 346) should be used. The jaws are lined with cork and buff, and the position of the chops may be adjusted on the bench screw to obtain the most suitable angle at which to work. The chops are of ash with a metal square-thread screw. Linings for the jaws are available so that badly worn ones may be replaced.

Several ways have been devised for holding wood to the bench top so that it can be worked all round. It may be glued or screwed to a baseboard which in turn is screwed or cramped to the bench. Heavy work may be held with the **carver's bench screw** (Fig. 347) which allows wood to be turned round as required, the tapered screw being driven into a suitable hole in the work. The square thread then fits through a hole in the bench top to which it is fixed with a wingnut and washer. G cramps and the bench holdfast (see Chapter 4) may also be used to hold down flat work.

Carving Techniques

The various aspects of woodcarving can be only briefly outlined here. They include **low relief carving**, basically a form of surface decoration, as are **chip carving** and **incised carving**. All three are really two-dimensional as opposed to three-dimensional sculpture, which may be in the form of treen work dishes, etc., sculptures or abstract shapes.

Virtually any wood can be carved but obviously some are more suitable than others. Lime is considered to be the best timber of all for carving. It is available in large sizes, it is close grained and cuts cleanly in almost any direction. Sycamore is excellent for domestic ware to be used in the kitchen, as is beech. The more exotic hardwoods such as rosewood, boxwood, ebony and lignum vitae, which are often only available in small quantities, are suitable for small feature items. The attractive grain of yew makes it ideally suitable for abstract shapes, as are the various species of pine, with which, as it is soft, particular care is needed to obtain a good finish but the beauty of the grain is amply rewarding.

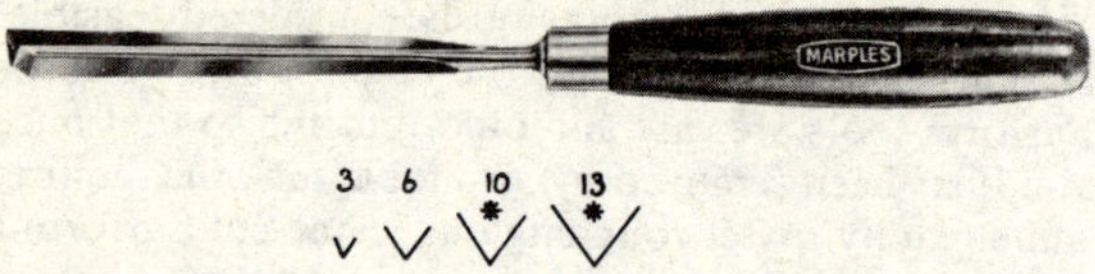

Fig. 344. Straight V parting tool; curved V parting tool marked *.

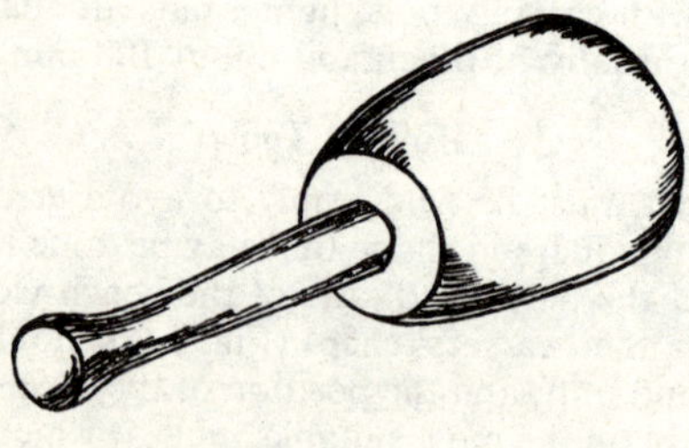
Fig. 345. Woodcarving mallet.

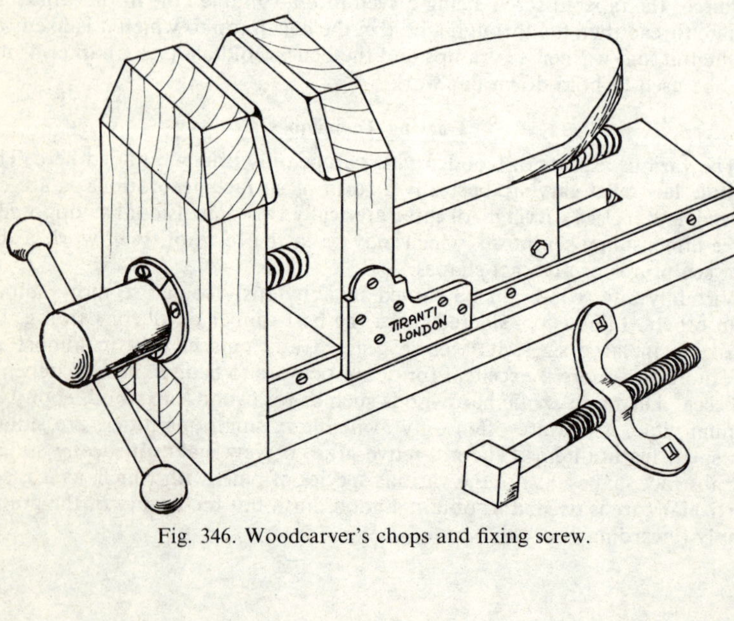

Fig. 346. Woodcarver's chops and fixing screw.

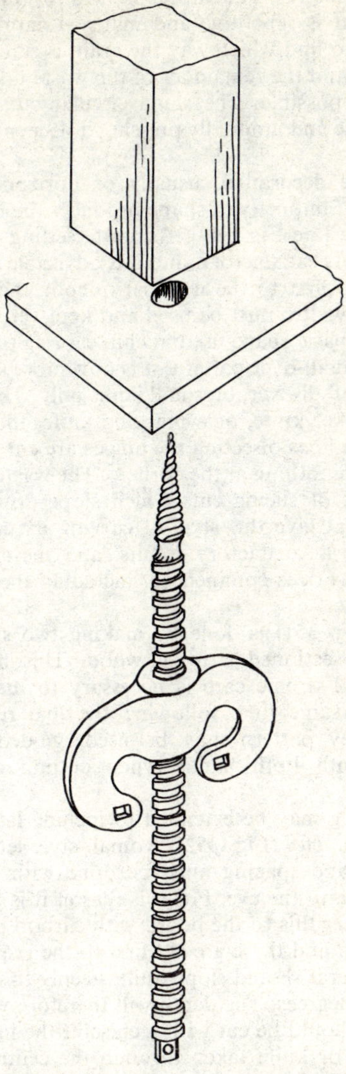

Fig. 347. Woodcarver's bench screw.

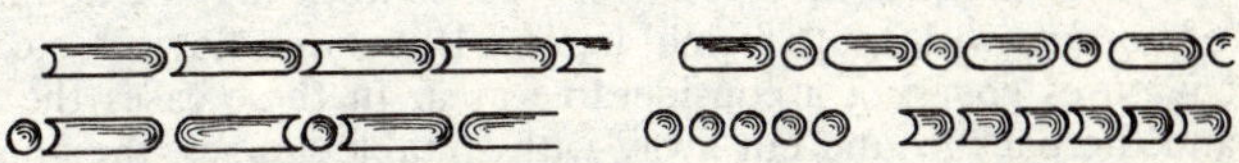

Fig. 348. Simple gouge decoration.

Simple **gouge decoration** (Fig. 348) is usually restricted to narrow surfaces such as the edges of shelves, but can be used to form a border on small table tops. The pattern cut is repetitive and many variations may be developed. Care must be taken to find which way the grain is running, the far end of the cut then being made and the remainder of the waste taken out 'with the grain' with as few cuts as possible. The small circular cuts or dots are made by rotating a small gouge and gradually pressing it deeper until the waste wood is removed.

Alternatively, **edge decoration**, usually of horizontal members, may be applied by the chisel. Simplicity of shape produces the best results, the pattern again being repetitive (see Fig. 349). Accurate setting out is essential for the results to be completely satisfactory, and it is advisable to make all the vertical cuts across the grain, first to the necessary depth and then pare into them. Chisels of a suitable width must be used and kept very sharp at all times.

The triangle is the basic shape used in chip carving (see Fig. 350). Although at one time used as an all-over pattern, it is now more acceptable as a form of edge decoration; but if all-over, on small items only. The work may be carried out using only a pocket knife, or a marking knife, the edge being kept very keen at all times. The lines bisecting the angles are cut in vertically to the full depth at the centre, to nothing at the corners. The waste is then removed from each side by a series of slicing cuts which slope down to the centre. This removes the chips that give this style of carving its name. Simple repeating patterns give the most satisfactory results, and these must be marked out carefully before the work is commenced, including the centre lines on which the first cuts are made.

Incised carving (Fig. 351) is done by making two slightly sloping cuts to remove a narrow V-sectioned strip of wood. This may be done with an acute-angled V-tool. Extreme care is necessary to maintain an even depth of cut while at the same time following the line required. Alternatively, knives of the Stanley pattern may be used, guided by a steel rule for straight cuts and with both hands when cutting curves so that freely flowing lines result.

This type of carving may be extended to include **lettering and numbers** to produce name boards, etc. (Fig. 352). Roman-style letters are most suitable and the setting out and spacing must be done with great care to give an appearance acceptable to the eye. For this reason it is best first to set out on paper and then transfer this to the board with carbon paper. The centre lines must also be drawn in and these are cut first to the required depth. The sides of each letter or numeral should slope quite steeply to give an included angle of approximately 60 degrees. The depth will therefore vary according to their size. The centre line should be cut with a chisel if the line is straight, or when curved with a gouge or knife taken through the centre of each serif to the surface of the board. The waste wood should be pared away at the required angle with the minimum of cuts to produce a clean finish, using chisels and gouges as appropriate.

The various techniques involved in low relief work may be adapted to the carving of borders with quite formal figures, leaves and flowers, etc., or more complex pictures covering a considerable area. In these cases the outline is incised and the background cut away with suitable gouges, the gouge marks left showing. Alternatively, the background may be matted with a matting

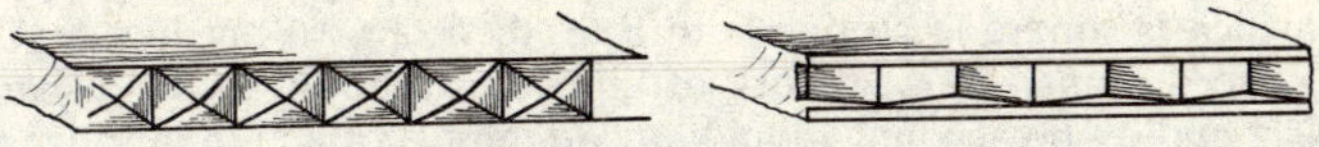

Fig. 349. Edge decoration with the chisel.

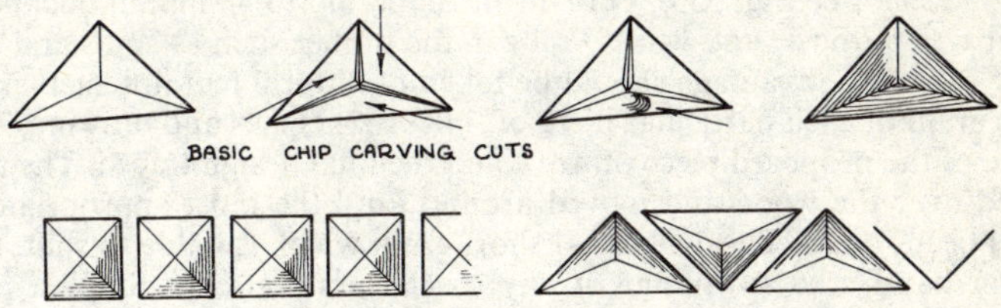

Fig. 350. Examples of chip carving.

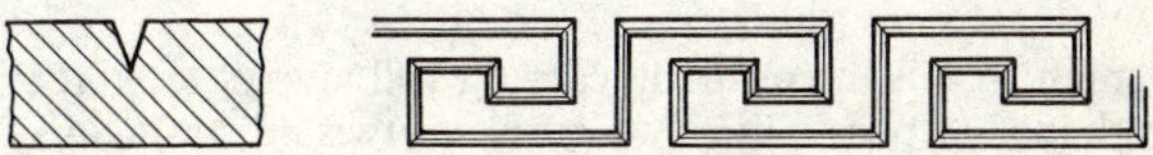

Fig. 351. Incised carving.

Fig. 352. Incised carving of letters and numbers.

Fig. 353. Simple animal, bird and fish shapes carved in wood.

punch, which is square in section with a toothed face to produce a series of regular spaced points. Carved work of this nature should have a clean, crisp tool finish, and on no account should any attempt be made to improve it with glass paper or its character will be lost.

Simple relief carving may be extended to include representative shapes from life; humans, animals, birds, fish and plant forms are readily adapted as a basis for small free-standing work or for wall mounting, the latter being left flat on one side (see Fig. 353). Off-cuts of timber up to 38 mm in thickness are ideal for this purpose, and whilst faults in the timber such as splits and shakes must be avoided, advantage should be taken of natural features such as knots and the grain of each particular piece of timber. Sketches and drawings should be made of the proposed piece of work and the final design traced. The tracing is placed over the wood and moved around until the most appropriate position has been found. This will avoid short grain which is liable to split, but on the other hand take advantage of any special grain effects. Staples, pins or Sellotape should then be used to fasten the tracing to the wood, carbon paper slipped underneath and the shape transferred to the timber. The bulk of the waste wood can then be removed by a coping saw or bow saw, followed by the rasp, until the outline is produced. Rounding-off of the surface is completed by the appropriate Surform tool, followed by fine finishing with abrasive papers.

The craftsman who is interested in carving will always look at timber carefully to weigh up its possibilities. A curly or twisted grain in off-cuts can produce intriguing effects, while oddities such as a knot on the waney edge lend themselves to imaginative treatment (see Fig. 354). The latter, for example, could readily be carved into a snail, or a bird's head. There is a wealth of natural objects which provide an unlimited source of ideas for simple carvings. For example, the pebbles illustrated in Fig. 354 are ideal shapes for touch-toys or tactiles, the grain of the wood enhancing the simple but satisfying shape. Bones too provide ideas for abstract shapes, and weathered knuckle-bones and vertebrae from sheep have intrigued the author on country walks. Weathered stones, shells, leaves, flowers, roots and branches may also be added to the list, the latter often lending themselves to carving by adaptation of shape.

Wooden assemblages (Fig. 355) are included in this chapter, although in the strict sense of the word they are not carvings. Their construction, however, does depend upon imaginative use of creative skills to produce shapes which are interesting and pleasing to the eye. Proportions are important, as is the relationship between the solid shape used and spaces created by them in order to achieve an acceptable whole which combines balance with aesthetic appeal. One big advantage in making constructions of this type is that pieces may be added or discarded depending upon their overall effect, or the position of pieces changed until an acceptable shape is produced.

Carved work and assemblages may be free-standing or mounted on a base. The way the two are joined will depend very much on the shape of the work and the type of material used for the base, since in addition to wood, metal and some thick plastics or remnants of stone and slate, etc., may also make the work more attractive. Simple shapes in the main are best, since the base should never detract from the appearance of the completed work. The appearance of wall-mounted assemblages may be enhanced by mounting them on a

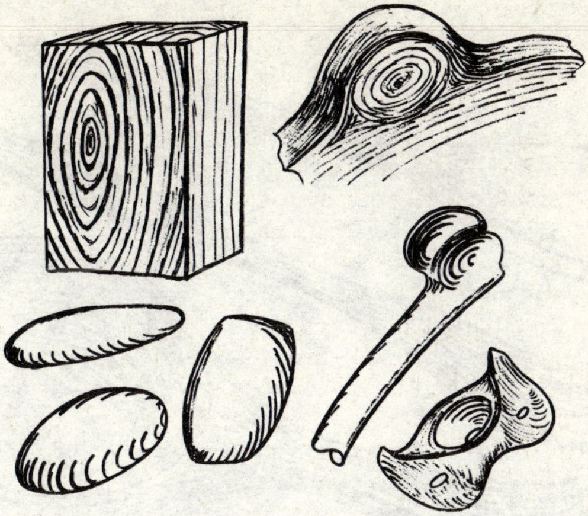

Fig. 354. Offcuts of wood or natural objects which may inspire simple carving.

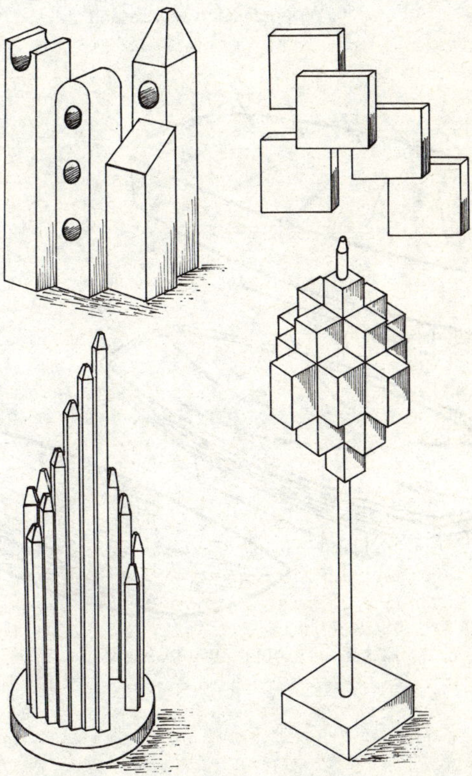

Fig. 355. Wooden assemblages.

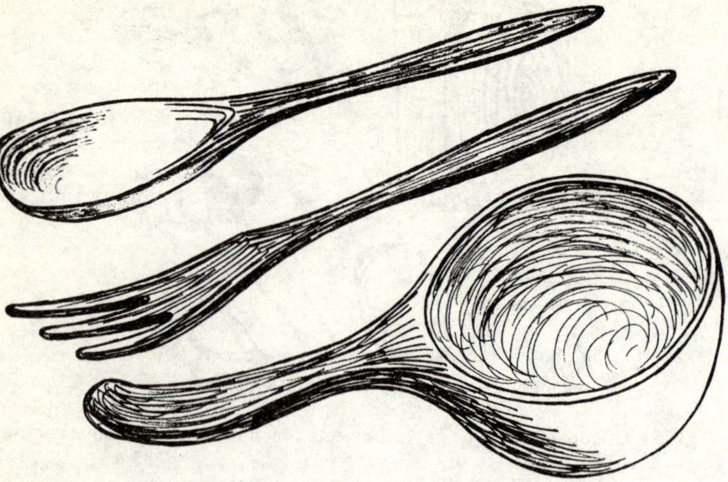

Fig. 356. Wooden salad servers and ladle.

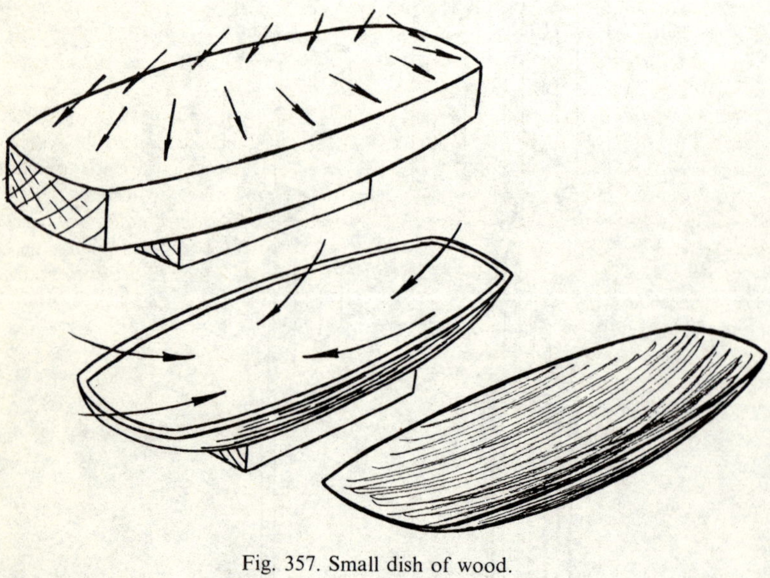

Fig. 357. Small dish of wood.

background of hessian, natural or of a suitable colour, possibly with a frame as a surround.

Treen is the term applied to small domestic items made of wood usually carved to shape by hand methods (see Fig. 356). Small off-cuts of hardwoods, pine and home-seasoned timber from the prunings of ornamental and garden fruit trees are eminently suitable. It is particularly satisfying to work in wood of known origin. An almost infinite range of work falls into this category of treen, including spoons, ladles, bowls, dishes, platters, cutting boards, condiment sets, etc. The design of this type of work is interesting, in that shape may sometimes be governed by the shape and size of the wood available and by its grain and texture. Freehand sketches, card templates and sometimes models in clay or Plasticine may all be employed in determining the final shape. Holding work of this nature while it is being fashioned is often a problem but one very sensible way is to work from wood which is a little longer than the finished item. The surplus wood can be held in the vice until almost the whole of the work has been fashioned before it is finally cut off.

Dishes and platters present a somewhat different holding problem and the usual practice is to glue a block, often with a paper separator between, first to the top of the dish and then the bottom (see Fig. 357). This can be held in the vice while the underside is shaped with chisel, gouge, Surform, file and glass-paper, then reversed to enable the inside to be gouged out, and finally finished with scrapers of suitable shapes and abrasive paper.

Because of the use to which treen work is put a suitable protective finish should be applied; this will also enhance the grain of the wood. Linseed oil diluted 1:1 with turpentine gives a satisfactory finish. The wood should first be damped to raise the grain, which is papered off when dry. The oil is then applied freely to the wood with a cloth and rubbed in with very fine glass paper, the surplus being wiped off with a cloth. A second coat is then applied, allowed to dry overnight, and polished with a smooth cloth the following day. After a period of use the finish may be renewed if necessary, first cleaning the work with turpentine. To finish treen work which may come into contact with food, medicinal paraffin oil or olive oil may be used. Eggshell or matt polyurethane varnish is a suitable finish for some items and is best applied with a soft brush. The varnish should be diluted with turpentine and only thin coats applied. (See also Chapter 15, Finishes and Finishing.)

13

VENEERING, LAMINATING AND BENDING

Veneering is another aspect of woodworking which has been practised for many thousands of years. Although it is possible to obtain almost any figured hardwood in veneer form, it is more usual for it to be cut from the more exotic woods, which are both rare and expensive. Because of this, the use of veneer is an important form of conservation. Nor should veneered work be regarded as a cheap substitute for solid wood since veneers must be laid on skilfully constructed grounds of good-quality timber. Defects in timber used for grounds—such as splits, knots, etc.—will subsequently be 'telegraphed' through the veneer. The careful selection and seasoning of timber used for grounds and the use of manufactured boards, such as chipboards and plywood, combined with modern glues, now avoid many of the difficulties previously experienced, such as warped grounds or veneers which peeled off.

Cutting and Peeling Veneers

Veneers are obtained from timber which has a particularly beautiful grain or colour, and may be from sections of the trunk itself or from crotches, burrs or stumps. They are cut by sawing, slicing or rotary peeling. Very few veneers are now sawn because of their expense (being quite thick) and an almost 50 per cent wastage in sawdust. Slicing is much more economical; the flitch is sliced either by being moved across the knife, or the knife moved across it (see Fig. 358). Prior steaming of the wood assists cutting.

Long continuous sheets of veneer are produced by rotary cutting, which is the method also used to produce the veneers for plywood manufacture. The log is rotated against a knife (Fig. 358), the veneer then having an 'open' and a 'closed' side due to the peeling effect. Whenever possible the open side should be the glue side when applied to the ground.

Applying Veneers

The grounds on to which veneers are laid must be carefully prepared, and toothed with the toothing plane (Fig. 359). This has a serrated blade which provides a key for the glue. Alternatively, a hacksaw blade may be used. End grain should be avoided below veneers as it will eventually show through. Common dovetails, for example, would not therefore be a suitable joint at the corner of a cabinet which was to be veneered. Similarly, the edges of chipboard and plywood should be lipped before being veneered. It is also advisable to veneer both sides of flat work to prevent distortion as the glue dries out and the veneer begins to pull. The balancing veneer, which may be of a cheaper quality, opposes the pull of the face veneer.

The traditional way of applying a veneer is with thin Scotch glue at about

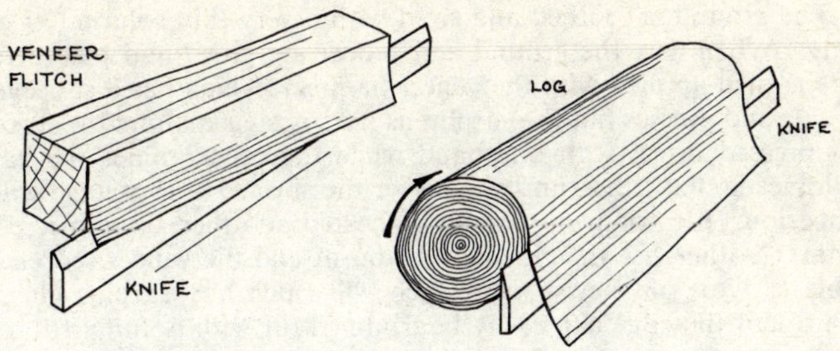

Fig. 358. Cutting and peeling veneers.

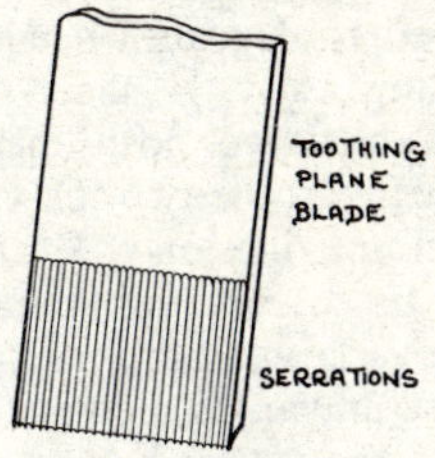

Fig. 359. The toothing plane.

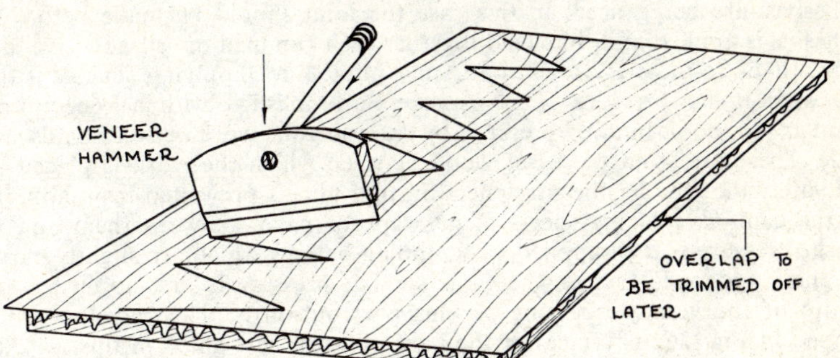

Fig. 360. Veneering.

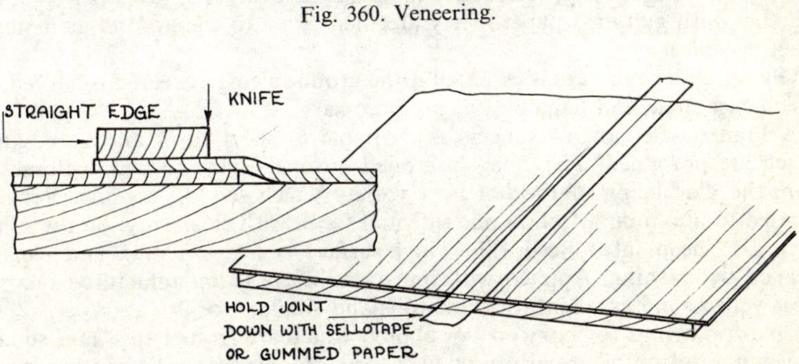

Fig. 361. Jointing veneers.

65 °C. The ground is toothed and sized with a very thin solution of glue and hot water. When dry, the ground and veneer are glued and placed together. Pressure is then applied with the veneer hammer, which has a squeegee effect on the glue and presses out the surplus as it is zigzagged along the surface. The head is pressed down with one hand while the other guides the handle. A warm domestic 'flat iron' run lightly over the surface at this stage will ensure firm adhesion. (Electric irons should be heated and then disconnected before work starts—otherwise the glue may be burnt and the veneer scorched.) It is advisable to work on newspaper which will catch any surplus glue. Excess veneer around the edge can easily be trimmed off with a knife if the work is turned over on to a cutting surface.

Impact glues such as Dunlop Thixofix may be used quite successfully to fix veneers using the same methods as for plastic laminates. Each surface must be coated and the glue allowed to dry until it can be lightly touched with the knuckle without any coming away. A sheet of newspaper should then be placed over the ground and the veneer positioned over the paper. As the paper is gently pulled out from between the two the veneer hammer should be used to press the surfaces into close adhesion.

When large areas are to be covered joints may be necessary. The two veneers should be allowed to overlap and are then cut through with a knife held against a straight edge. Both unwanted pieces of veneer are then lifted out and the joint pressed down with the veneer hammer and taped until the adhesive has finally set (see Fig. 361). This method is not suitable when impact adhesives are being used: in this case the joint should be made before the adhesive is applied and then held together with gummed or self-adhesive tape.

Synthetic resin or PVA glues are only suitable for applying veneers if they are used under pressure. This may be accomplished with a veneer press (similar to a book-binding press) or by cramping the work between cauls (Fig. 362). These are stout pieces of wood between which the work is placed immediately the glue has been applied. Surplus glue is prevented from adhering to the cauls by placing sheets of greaseproof paper between them and the work. Pressure is then applied by cramping battens which are slightly curved on their undersides across the cauls so that pressure is first applied to the centre of the work, squeezing surplus glue outwards. The chessboard illustrated in Fig. 362 is typical of the kind of work best glued in this way, the various pieces first being assembled and stuck face down on to paper or taped together with gummed paper. They are then glued to the ground as a single sheet of veneer.

Gluing under pressure is essential if the ground being veneered is curved, in which case male and female cauls are necessary.

A limited selection of veneers is available in sheet form and as edgings which are pre-glued. They may be ironed on to the ground with a domestic iron, the glue being of the hot melt variety which sets on cooling. Veneers bonded to aluminium foil on one side and faced with clear vinyl on the other have also been introduced. The vinyl surface is heat-resisting and can be cleaned by washing. Applied with impact adhesive to manufactured boards, these veneers are excellent for table tops and similar work.

Lines or strings (of boxwood or ebony) which are from 1 to 3 mm square and in metre lengths are also used as a form of decoration. So too are bandings, which are built-up patterns of contrasting woods. They may be used in

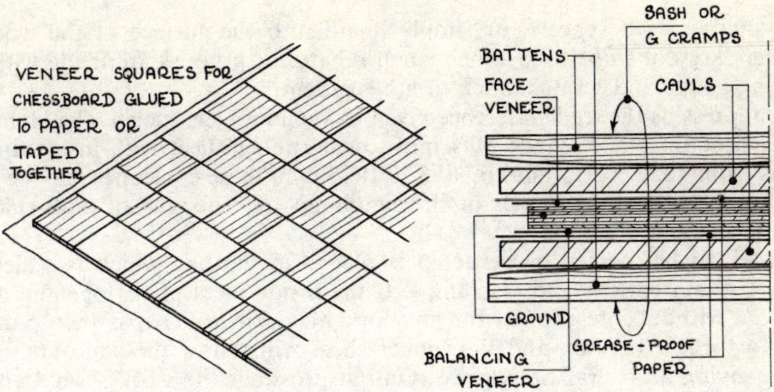

Fig. 362. Veneering between cauls.

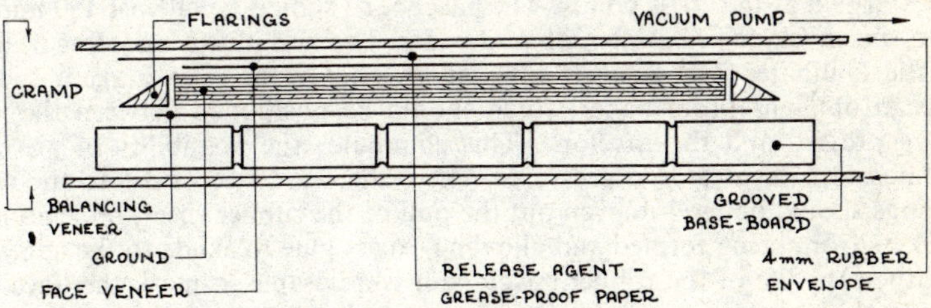

Fig. 363. Use of the bagpress.

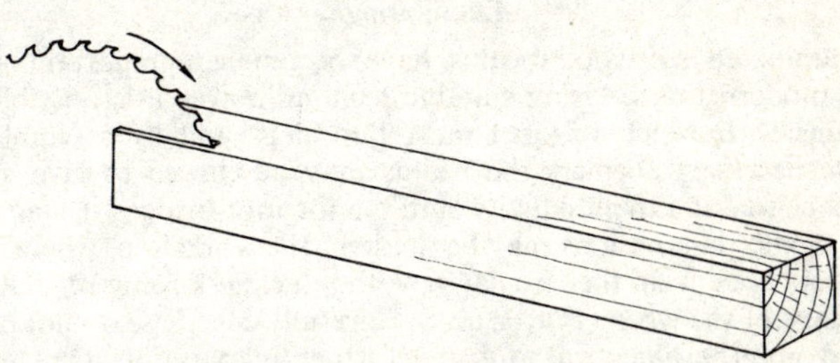

Fig. 364. Cutting constructional veneers.

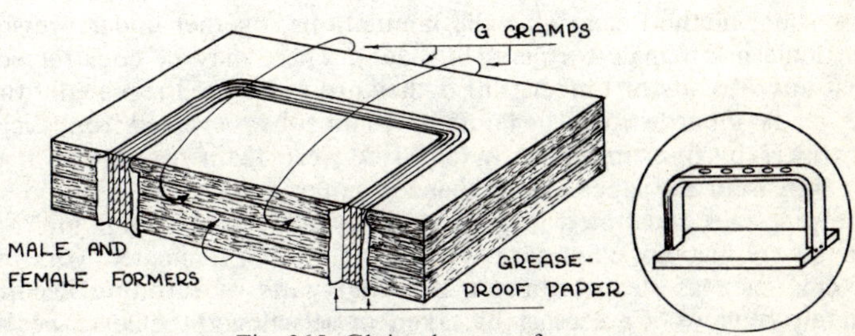

Fig. 365. Gluing between formers.

conjunction with veneers, or simply inlaid into the surface of the wood if veneers are not to be used, when small rebates or grooves are made with the cutting gauge and scratch stock to accept them.

'Bagpress' is the trade reference given to vacuum bags such as the Harefield Supasheet Envelope. Made of 4 mm tough rubber sheet with inside dimensions from 1220 × 915 mm to 3655 × 1675 mm, these envelopes may be used for veneering formed shapes or the simultaneous veneering of both sides of flat panels.

Work to be formed or veneered is placed in the bag which is sealed by 50 × 75 mm battens and G cramps. If the inside faces of the opening make contact without interruption the envelope may self-seal. Air is then pumped out to form a vacuum and the rubber sheet will follow the contours of the work giving an overall snug press. On flat pressings the work should always be placed on a base board at least 25 mm thick to prevent distortion under pressure, air channels being cut all round at intervals of 150 mm with 6 mm holes drilled at the cross points. The baseboard should be at least 150 mm less than the envelope in both length and width. Because of the smooth surface of plastic laminates it is advisable to use an open-work release agent such as hessian or greaseproof paper which should be positioned between the work being pressed and the envelope. This eliminates the possibility of air being trapped and ensures even pressure. Where there are steep sides to the work, flarings should be used to even out the pull of the rubber sheet, preventing air pockets from being formed and allowing excess glue to exude to the edges. To lengthen the life of the rubber envelope it is advisable to mark the 'face' and the 'back' and turn it over on alternate periods, cleaning the inside regularly and removing all dried glue and foreign matter.

Laminating

Large laminated softwood beams have become an important structural feature of modern times. Using suitable resin adhesives it is possible to construct beams with which to span most buildings, and by assembling them around the necessary formers the beams may be curved to give additional strength, thus making them equally suitable for foot bridges. Using the same principle, smaller laminations may be made in the workshop, where constructional veneers are cut on the circular saw, the thickness being regulated to the size and shape of the work ($1\frac{1}{2}$ to 2 mm). Carefully cut, these do not need to be planed and may be glued without any further preparation. One of the big advantages of using this technique is that strong, curved work may be built up, woods which have natural bending properties being selected.

The usual method is to glue the laminations together under pressure between male and female formers (Fig. 365). These may be constructed from almost any off-cuts of timber, but if they are to be used repeatedly they are better made of hardwood. The laminations must be prevented from sticking to the formers by inserting some material between them to serve as a release agent—greaseproof paper or polythene is suitable.

The pipe-rack illustrated in Fig. 365 is typical of a 'one-off job' and the formers were made of chipboard. The possibilities of laminated work in making items such as sledge runners, skis and parts of furniture become immediately obvious. Care must be taken in selecting the glue to be used in relation to the use to which the item is to be put and the situation in which it is to be used. Hard-setting glues such as Cascamite 'One-Shot' are satisfactory, ensuring that the work is rigid when released from the formers and does not de-laminate. It is always a good idea to assemble the work dry to ensure fitting, then apply the glue, cramping up as before.

Chair and stool seats may be built up from 1·5 mm plywood on large open formers, the plywood being cramped down beneath full-width battens (Fig. 366). This is an example of where the bagpress could possibly be used to advantage. It is also possible to make quite complex laminations around flexible steel bands which are prepared commercially. Small metal brackets are screwed to a base board in such a way that when the flexible band is screwed to them the curvature required is produced and the laminations can be G-cramped to the band. A sheet of polythene spread over the base board before the brackets are attached collects the surplus glue and prevents the work from adhering to the board.

Bending Timber

Bends made by laminating will maintain their accuracy but it is quite a lengthy process, and for some work bends made in solid timber are acceptable. It must be borne in mind that changes in atmospheric conditions may result in changes in the bends. Solid wood becomes bendable after being steamed for about one hour for every 25 mm of thickness. Large-diameter aluminium rainwater pipe is ideal from which to make a steam chest (see Fig. 367). The pipe should be lagged and plugs fitted to each end, steam from a boiler being piped through one, the other being removable to allow for the extraction of the wood. The chest should be inclined slightly downwards with a small drainpipe at the lower end.

When the timber has been steamed sufficiently, it should be bent around a suitable former without delay. As with laminations, this may be between male and female formers, but this has the disadvantage of taking a long time to dry out. Bending around a block, as in the case of the chair end illustrated in Fig. 368, is better, the wood being supported on its outer surface by means of a mild steel strip bolted to the wooden pulls. The steel strip prevents the timber from pulling apart at the corners as the bend is made, and G cramps and sash cramps are used to hold the bent wood in place. After about one hour the wood should be removed from the former, but the sash cramp and steel strip should be left on overnight until the bend has dried out thoroughly. It is always advisable to make bends to a slightly smaller radius than that required in order to allow for the natural tendency the wood has to spring back a little as the cramp is removed.

The Forest Products Research Laboratory lists the bending properties of common timbers as follows:

Very good Ash, beech, birch (Canadian yellow), cherry, elm, hickory, hornbeam, oak, sycamore, walnut.

Good European birch, chestnut, mansonia, yew, Tasmanian myrtle.

Moderate African walnut, afrormosia, iroko, makore, Queensland walnut, Tasmanian oak, Utile (Uganda).

Poor Sapele, spruce, willow.

Very poor Abura, blackbean, cedar, idigbo, African mahogany, ramin, Sitka spruce.

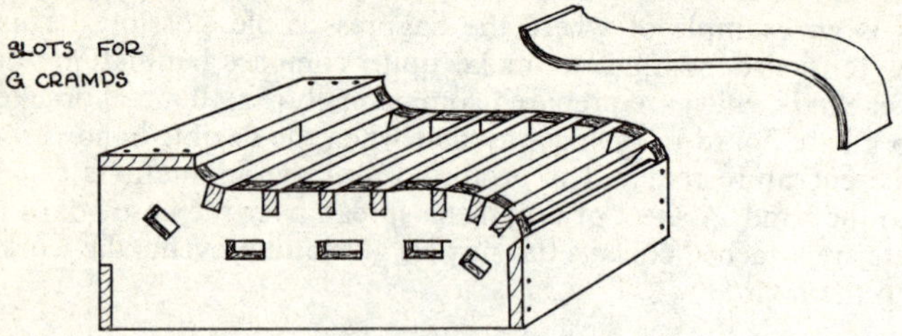

Fig. 366. Former for wide laminations (seats).

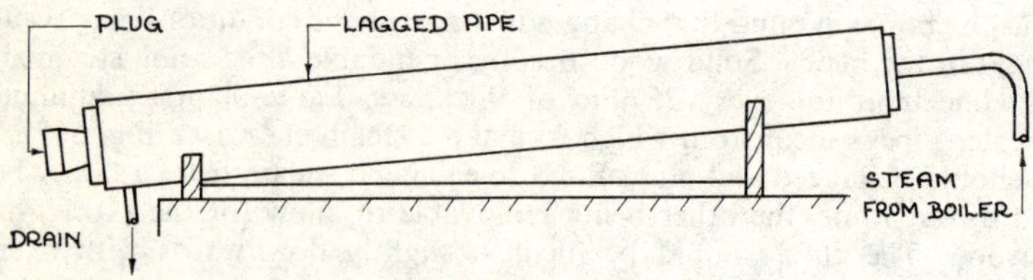

Fig. 367. Steam chest.

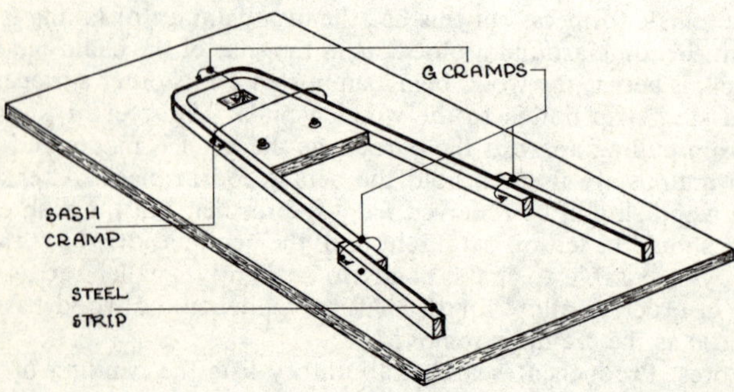

Fig. 368. Solid bending.

14

WOODTURNING

Like all aspects of woodwork, turning is very fascinating, and the ability to produce work which is truly round in section gives great satisfaction. The ancient Egyptians were skilled woodturners, rotating the timber between centres by means of a wooden bow which was moved backwards and forwards. The cord was wound round the wood causing it to rotate first one way and then the other, while the operator sat on the ground using his free hand to hold the tool and giving it added support with one foot. As with all things, the design of lathes has steadily improved throughout the ages, from pole lathes, which gave a similar action to the bow-string lathe but used an overhead pole, cord and foot pedal, to treadle lathes and wheel lathes. Wheel lathes were hand-driven by an assistant turning a large fly-wheel. It was the added pleasure to be derived from woodturning which led the author to design and make his own lathe very many years ago. Although made with the aid of only the very minimum of engineering equipment, it has given and is still giving yeoman service.

The Woodturning Lathe

All lathes consist of a **bed**, on which are mounted the **headstock**, which drives the work, the **tailstock**, which supports the end of long work, and the **tool rest**. The modern woodturning lathe, such as the 'Viceroy' (Fig. 369), also has a short bed to the left of the headstock, known as an **outrigger** which carries a further tool rest. Larger diameters can be turned by this means, and the work is mounted on an extension to the main spindle, which at this end has a left-hand thread. The bed of the lathe is a heavy-duty, rigid box section of close-grain cast iron with machined ways. Its capacity is 914 mm between centres which are 130 mm above the bed, enabling a diameter of a little over 260 mm to be turned. Cone pulleys give a range of four speeds, from 425 to 2,275 r.p.m., and both headstock and tailstock spindles are bored 20 mm and accept No. 3 Morse taper centres. The main spindle, which runs in heavy-duty ball-races, is threaded at each end so that faceplates carrying large-diameter work can be screwed on to it. The headstock, tailstock, outrigger and tool posts are of cast iron, and the rool rests of malleable iron. The lathe itself is mounted on pedestals of welded heavy-gauge steel with a height to spindle centre line of 1,016 mm.

Almost any type of timber can be turned in the lathe, but a better finish can generally be produced on hardwoods than on softwoods. Although turnery discs are available it is cheaper to buy wood in the plank and leading timber merchants list the following suitable timbers for turnery:

Home-grown: ash, lime, cherry, sweet chestnut, elm and sycamore.

Imported: African afrormosia, afzelia, agba, walnut, iroko, mahogany, sapele, utile, European beech, Japanese elm, Burma teak, East Indian rosewood and Brazilian rosewood.

Tools for Woodturning

It is important that good-quality tools are used and that they are of a suitable size for the lathe. Small tools are available for use with lightweight machines powered by the electric drill. Such machines are adequate for small work, but the tools are quite inappropriate for use on larger machines such as that described above. For heavy duty, tools which are described as long and strong should be used: long so that they may be held securely and strong so that there is no danger of the metal snapping while in use. Lathe tools must always be held so that one hand holds the front end of the blade down firmly to the tool rest and at the same time controls its forward or sideways movement. The handle is then held firmly in the other hand, which steadies the tool and assists in its correct manipulation.

Gouges are usually available in 6, 13, 16, 19 and 25 mm sizes; **chisels**, 13, 19, 25 and 35 mm; **parting tools** 4 to 6 mm wide. In addition, **round-nosed** and **diamond-point chisels** are manufactured in 13, 19 and 25 mm widths. Not all these tools are immediately necessary for the amateur, who can gradually build up his individual set. Handles should be selected ash or beech.

Use of Tools

In use, the cutting edge of the tool should always be presented to the work in such a way that it cuts to produce shavings and does not scrape, which would produce a rough surface and quickly dull the edge. This means that the tool should always be honed at the same angle as that at which it is ground (see Fig. 371), avoiding the double bevel which is quite normal with many other woodworking tools. This also means that the bevel must always bear on the surface of the wood; otherwise the tool will scrape rather than cut.

When grinding is necessary this must always be done on the face of the stone, never on its side (see Fig. 372 and Grindstones, page 149). In this way a slightly concave bevel will be formed enabling a really keen cutting edge to be produced by honing. Convex grinding must be avoided at all costs or a thick cutting edge will be formed.

For quick roughing down of wood in the lathe from square or octagonal section, gouges should be ground straight across at the end, whereas gouges intended for taking out hollows must be ground to a nose to enable them to reach into the wood without the danger of corners digging in.

The **skew chisel** and **parting tool** should also be hollow ground so that sharp cutting edges can be obtained, and it should be noted how the parting tool is tapered back from its cutting edge to prevent it from binding in the cut as it is fed into the wood.

Scrapers, as their name indicates, do not cut in the accepted way and are used to smooth difficult surfaces such as those which might be experienced due to interlocking grain or end grain (Fig. 374). This is usually confined to faceplate work only, and in use the bevel does not rub the surface, the handle being held high so that the tool is inclined downwards. They are ground at a steep angle, as much as 75–80 degrees across their edge, and because of the nature of their work, sometimes across the top also. A burnisher may be used after

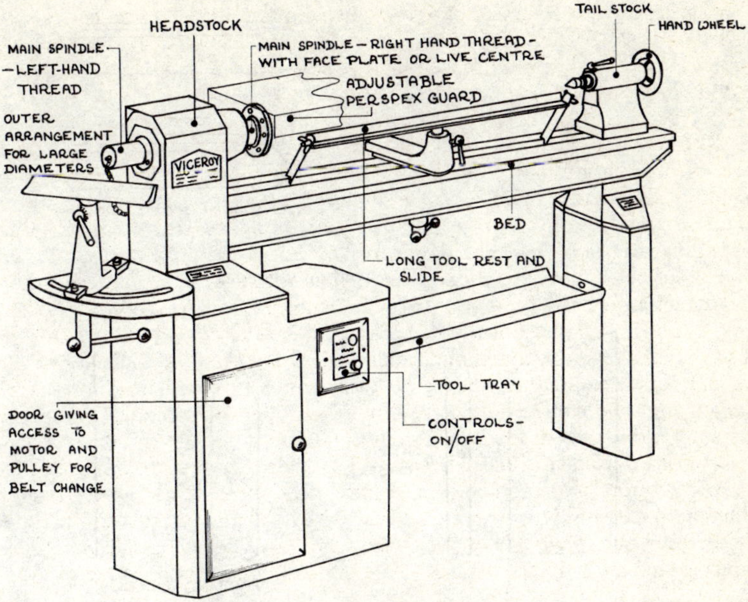

Fig. 369. Viceroy woodturning lathe.

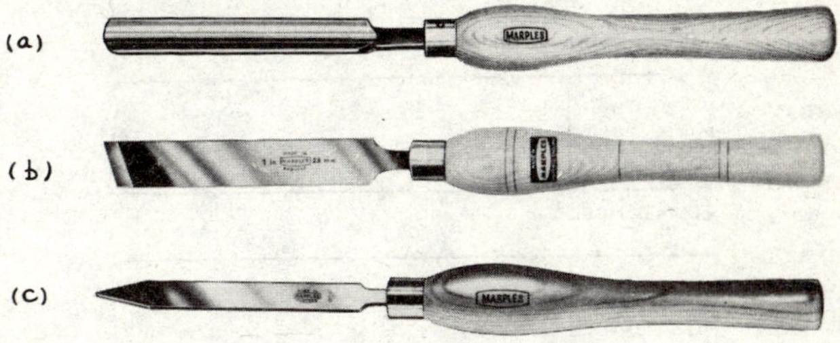

Fig. 370. Woodturning tools: (*a*) gouge; (*b*) skew chisel; (*c*) parting tool.

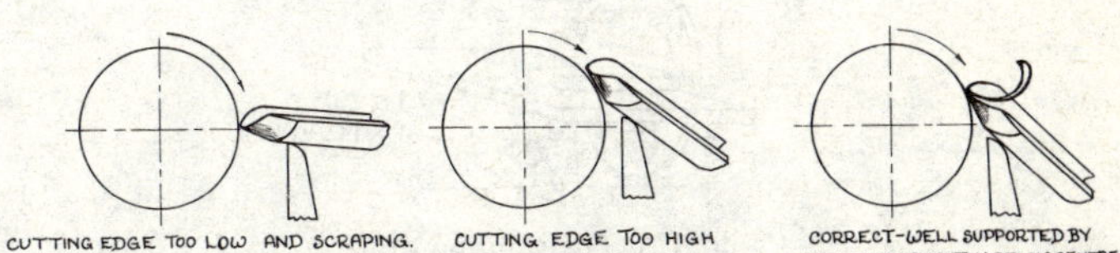

Fig. 371. Angle of cutting edge in relation to the work.

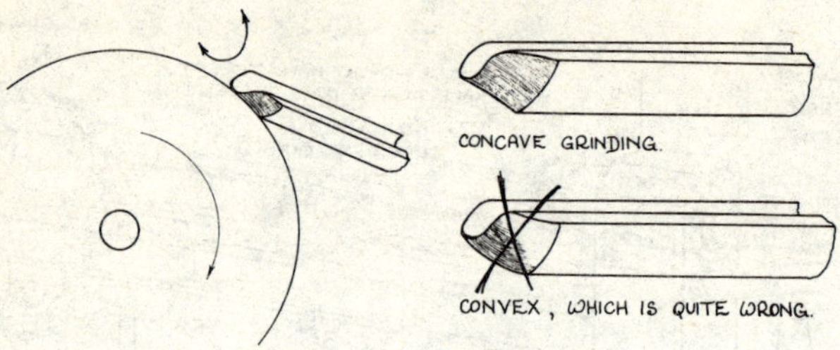

Fig. 372. Grinding a gouge.

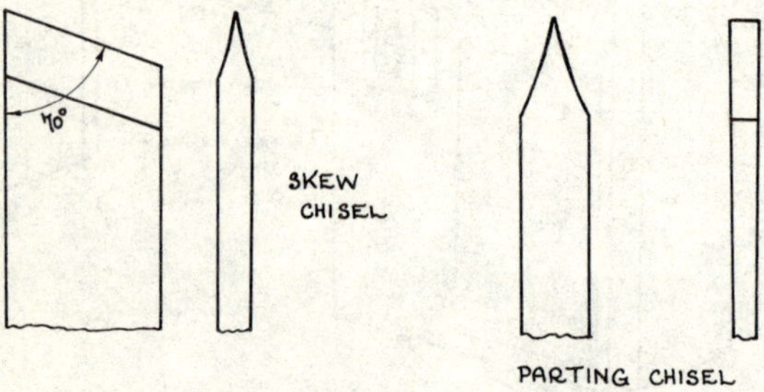

Fig. 373. Grinding the skew chisel and parting tool.

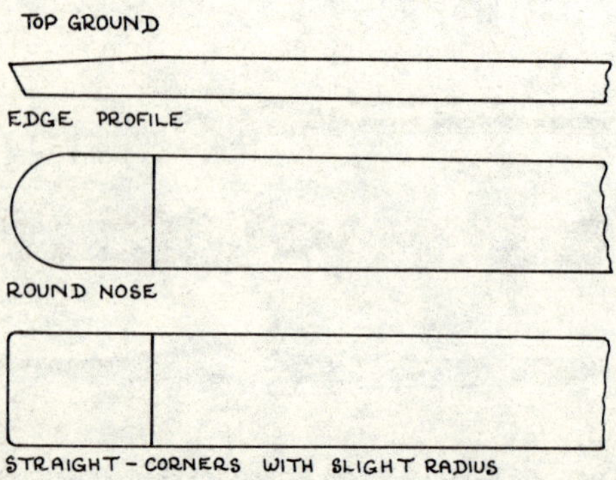

Fig. 374. Grinding of scrapers.

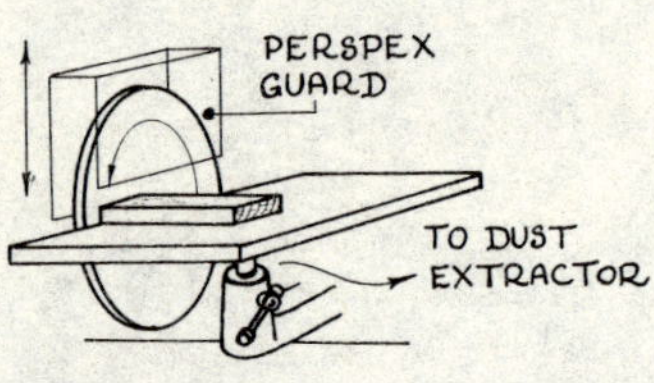

Fig. 375. The sanding disc.

grinding to form a scraper edge as for scraper plane (page 165). The round-nosed and straight scraper (which should have its corners slightly radiused) will be found to be most useful, but other shapes may be necessary also. These should always be ground to shape from blanks obtained from a reputable manufacturer and never from old files because of their brittle nature.

Garnet paper or aluminium oxide paper glued to a plywood disc which in turn is screwed to a faceplate forms a serviceable **sanding disc** (Fig. 375). A horizontal table which fits into the tool post in place of the tool rest may usually be obtained from the manufacturers or be homemade. A sliding fence mounted on the table holds work at right angles to the disc or may be adjusted to any angle. It can be used for sanding the ends of legs and K/D jointed rails, mitre joints, etc.

Should a lathe tool snap when in use because of the pressure imposed the operative could well be thrown off balance and fall on to the machine with quite serious consequences. The broken tool would almost certainly damage the work and it therefore follows that only the best of tools should be used. Good overhead lighting should be provided in the absence of natural light. Loose clothing must be avoided at all costs, and protective clothing and eye shields worn at all times. If dust is a problem a disposable filter mask should be worn to prevent irritation of the nose and throat. There should never be more than one operator near the machine, which must always be properly serviced and maintained.

All levers must be tightened securely before the machine is used and the work held firmly either between centres or on a faceplate. Tool rests must be set while the work is stationary and then tested by rotating it slowly by hand to make sure there is no obstruction. Tool rests should never be adjusted while the work is moving, or attempts made to remove the waste. Braking by hand is very dangerous and must be avoided. To avoid any danger of the hands being trapped, tool posts must be drawn well clear of the work before 'papering off' is commenced.

Sound timber, free from knots and splits, must always be used so that there is no danger of wood being flung from the machine. The most suitable speed for the work being turned should be chosen: work up to 30 mm in diameter is turned at the fastest speed (2,750 r.p.m.) and 200 mm plus at the slowest (425 r.p.m.). Electrical safety must be observed at all times, and modern lathes such as the Viceroy are so designed that when belt changes are being made the machine is electrically isolated.

Turning Between Centres

Long work is turned between centres, the ends of the timber having been dimpled with a bradawl at the point where the diagonals cross. Small square-sectioned material may be roughed down on the lathe with a suitable straight-ended gouge. With larger sections it may be advisable to plane off the corners first. At the headstock the wood is supported and driven by the morse-tapered forked centre which fits into the main spindle, while at the tailstock it rotates on the 'dead' centre. This is so called because it does not revolve and therefore the centre of the wood should have a little grease applied to it. After a time pressure on the wood from this centre and the cutting action may cause the wood to become loose on the centre, causing chatter and inaccuracy; frequent checking and retightening may therefore be necessary.

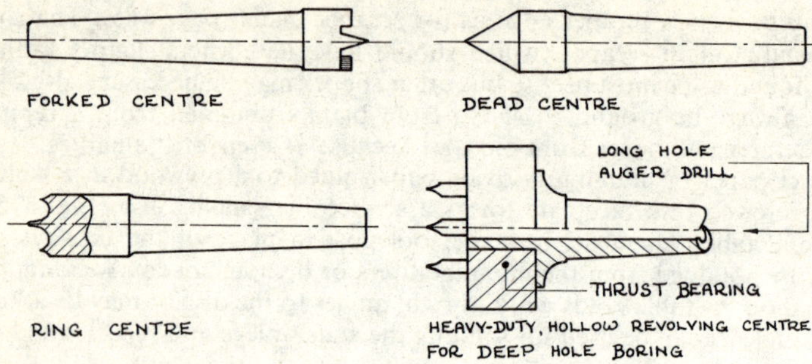

Fig. 376. Centres with which to support long work.

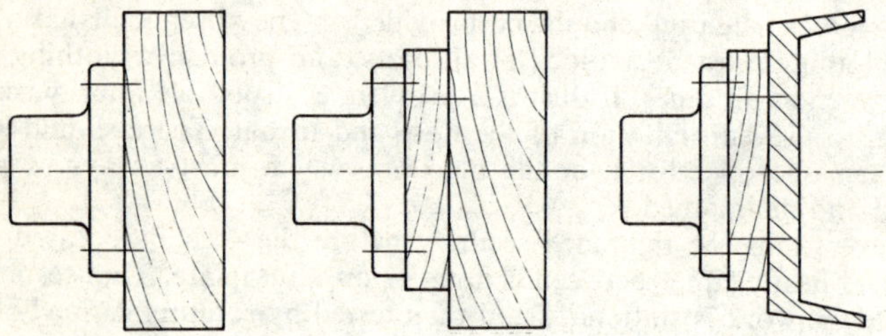

Fig. 377. Single chucking.

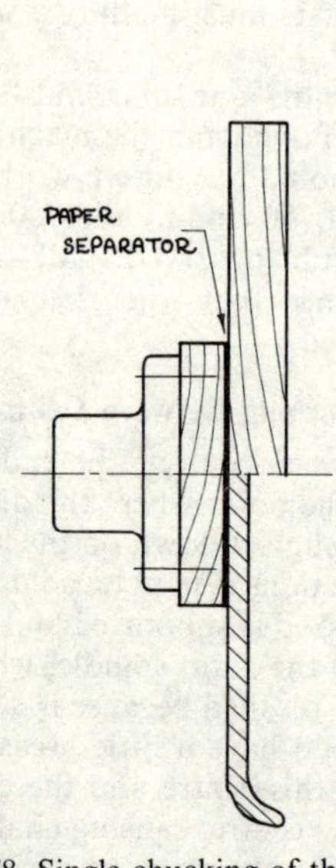

Fig. 378. Single chucking of thin work.

The tool rest should be set a little below centre so that the gouge will cut smoothly when the tool is held at the correct angle (Fig. 371). Roughing down is then done with a suitably sized gouge, starting the cut near to, but not at, the right-hand end, and working to the left. After two or three cuts the remaining wood is turned off, this time working from left to right. The process is repeated until almost the correct diameter is obtained as measured with outside calipers.

Final smoothing to give a perfect cylinder is done with the skew chisel, using the centre of the blade to avoid corners digging in. For this operation the tool rest should be lifted so that it is almost level with the top of the work, and cutting can be in either direction, both hands moving steadily with the chisel so that the angle of cut, once begun, is not changed. Turned on edge and held at the appropriate angle, the skew chisel can be used for making Vee grooves or convex curves—for example, that on the end of a handle, in which case the chisel handle must be swung in a sweeping curve in order to guide the cutting edge in the required arc. It can also be used to square off end grain, again being held on its edge with the point advancing into the work and the appropriate bevel at right angles to the axis. The tool rest should once more be slightly below centre.

Beads are produced with the skew chisel, cutting 'with the grain' from the high point to right and left. Hollows are also cut 'with the grain', this time with the gouge, working inwards from left and right until the required width and depth are obtained.

Ring centres are sometimes preferred to the plain dead centre since they offer more support, and various rotating centres are available which help to cut down friction. One such centre (Fig. 376) is also hollow so that a long auger of similar diameter can be inserted. By this means table lamps and sections for standard lamps can be bored, the auger being withdrawn regularly to clear the chips. In most cases, so long as suitable waste is left at the ends, the wood should be reversed so that boring is carried out from each end.

Faceplate Work

Items turned at the headstock of the lathe and supported by that part of the machine only are usually referred to as faceplate work, although there are other means of securing the wood to the machine than by simply screwing it to a faceplate. Platters, dishes and deeper bowls are the type of article associated with this aspect of turning, and because of the inherent beauty of wood the finished article is almost always pleasing.

Single chucking (Fig. 377) by screwing the block to the faceplate, is the most direct way of mounting. The design of the bowl must be such that the whole of its shape may be turned before it is taken off the faceplate. This may limit the possible shape because of the danger of turning into the edge of the faceplate, or because the base has to be left thick to avoid turning into the fixing screws. What will be the base of the bowl must be planed flat before the faceplate is attached with heavy-gauge screws, which if allowed a minimum penetration of 13 mm will hold quite well as they are going into side grain. The bulk of the waste wood should be removed from the circumference of the bowl either by sawing off the corners, or, if a band saw is available, by cutting out the disc. Small diameters may be turned at faster speeds, but as the diameter increases so too does the peripheral speed. Should this be too high

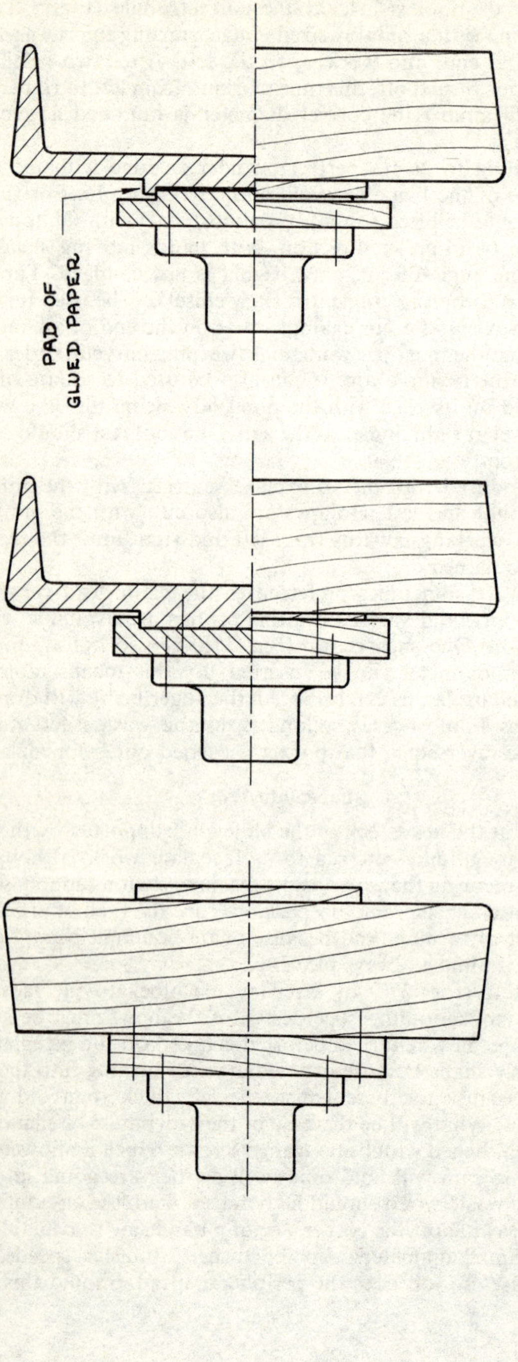

Fig. 379. Double chucking a bowl—alternative methods.

excessive vibrations will be set up, and in addition the turning tool will have difficulty in cutting the wood efficiently. It is with this sort of work that the advantage of the heaviness and strength of woodturning tools will be really appreciated as they bite into the wood.

The outer profile of the bowl is turned first, using a deep fluted gouge of about 13 mm. For the tool to be at the correct angle to cut the wood, the handle must be held low and given extra support by placing it against the hips. This also means that the tool rest must be set quite low and at a suitable angle. The direction of cutting should whenever possible be with the grain, but in bowl turning it is inevitable that in some places it will be against the grain, and if at that time a smooth finish becomes really difficult to obtain, then the scraper should be used.

To take out the inside of the bowl, the tool rest must be moved across the face, again at a suitable height to allow the gouge to cut. A few light cuts should be used to true the face, and then a deep groove turned out, working alternately from its opposite edges until the required shape for the wall of the bowl has been produced. The lower corner (see Fig. 377) is squared out with skew chisel and straight scraper. Taking out this wide groove leaves a large centre boss which assists the smooth rotation of the work, but once the shape of the wall is completed, it must be gradually turned away until the full inner shape has been produced.

The danger of turning into the faceplate when single chucking is used can be avoided by screwing a softwood pad to the blank, and then in turn screwing the faceplate to it. This provides waste material which can be cut into if necessary in order to achieve the correct shape for the bowl, and at the same time provides a little more working space by moving the blank forward.

Small or thin work, where the use of screws would be quite impossible, may be glued to a similar softwood pad, with paper between the two (Fig. 378)—polyvinyl acetate is a suitable adhesive. When complete the work can be removed quite easily. A wide firmer chisel tapped smartly with a mallet will split the paper, the remains of which can then be glasspapered away.

Double Chucking

In many ways double chucking is a superior way of turning a bowl. The faceplate may be screwed directly to the upper face of the wood, or with a wooden pad between them to enable the outer profile to be turned more easily. However, since the work must now be reversed care is necessary in recentring and two methods are shown in Fig. 379. In the first, a recess turned into the pad accepts the plinth of the bowl, which can then be screwed into place, taking care in choosing the length of screws and in positioning them. Alternatively, the plinth may be recessed and the wooden pad turned to fit into this. The two can then be glued together using a paper separator; this avoids the use of screws and enables the bowl to be turned out to a greater depth. A blunt hardwood wedge driven between the wooden pad and bowl easily separates them on completion. If the bowl is flat-bottomed a shallow recess may still be made into which the wooden pad can be fitted. The recess is then fitted with a felt pad on completion of the work.

When the outer profile of large bowls is being turned the tailstock and dead centre can be used to give added support to the timber.

Screw Chucks

Screw chucks of different types are available on which to mount small items (Fig. 380). Generally the wood into which the screw is entered is wasted and allowance must be made for this. Also, since the screw often goes into end grain, which is not good basic woodworking practice, excessive force applied to the timber can loosen it from the screw. Jacobs' pattern drill chucks with morse taper arbors to fit the lathe spindles (basically a metalworker's tool) are also extremely useful for holding small items, a spigot of wood being turned on the work which will then fit into the chuck. Metal cup chucks into which a spigot can be driven to hold the work in place are obtainable, but it is also quite easy to turn these from short ends of wood mounted on the screw chuck when special sizes are required. Serviette rings turned to their outer diameter on a tapered mandrel held between centres, can be tapped into a homemade wooden cup chuck of this nature so that their inner surface can be trued, glass-papered and polished.

Measuring Tools

Measuring tools such as the steel rule, dividers, wing compasses, inside and outside calipers, depth gauge and Vernier caliper, as used by engineers, are a necessary part of the wood turner's equipment.

Card or thin metal templates are also advisable with which to test shapes being produced, particularly if there are several of the same item. The Copydex Mimic (see Chapter 4) is also a useful tool for this purpose.

Tool Rests

In addition to tee rests for general use, there are tool rests specifically designed for use when turning out the inside of bowls. They are made both left-hand and right-hand for use to the left or right of the headstock, and can be positioned to reach deep into the bowl to give better support to the turning tool.

Finishing

In finishing turned work some papering off is almost always necessary, although ideally the work should come straight from the gouge or chisel. Open-coat aluminium oxide paper is recommended as it does not clog readily and retains its keenness. Coarse grades must be avoided or deep scratches will be made in the work. The tool rest must be removed, and for straight work between centres the paper should be wrapped round a length of scrap wood or a cork block. This also applies to convex surfaces such as the outside of bowls, whereas for concave surfaces it is usually sufficient to hold the paper in the hand.

Small cracks such as those around knots may be filled with a proprietary filler which will accept the final polish. It may sometimes be considered advisable to raise the grain by damping with a wet cloth followed by subsequent papering off. The ends of long work may be finished on the disc sander.

Finally, various finishes such as those indicated in Chapter 15 may be used to seal the surface, some of which should be applied while the work is still rotating at slow or medium speeds in the lathe—for example, those normally applied with a rubber, and oils and waxes. Carnauba wax applied directly to the work, or mixed with beeswax and turpentine, is particularly recommended for turned work, producing a good polish when buffed with a clean soft cloth. The author has found that olive oil is a practical finish for work which will be in contact with food and may at times require to be washed. Cheese boards, bread and meat boards, fruit and salad bowls are in this category, and readily respond to a further application of oil after washing, particularly if made of teak.

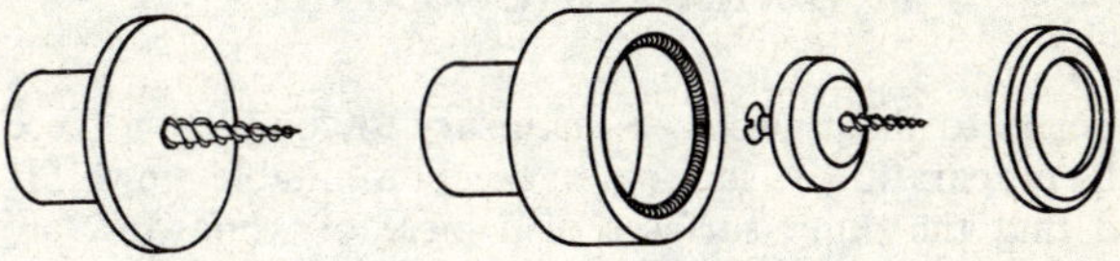

Fig. 380. The screw chuck (*left*) and combination coil grip chuck (*right*).

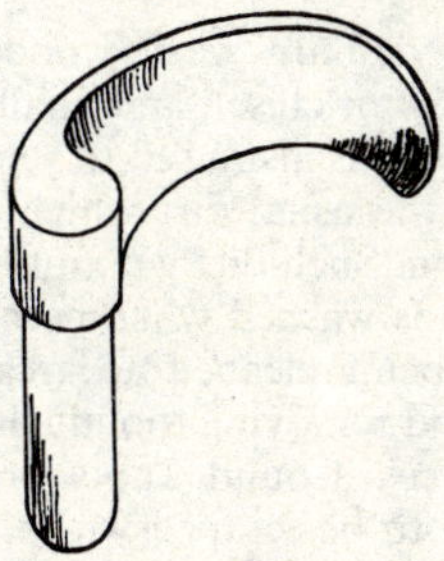

Fig. 381. The inside tool rest (left-hand or right-hand).

15

FINISHING AND FINISHES

'Finishing' refers to those processes necessary to complete a piece of woodwork and the preparation of surfaces to accept a suitable 'finish'. It should be remembered that the outer surfaces of a piece of woodwork are generally 'cleaned up' after the work is finally assembled. Inside surfaces, however, must almost invariably be cleaned up before being assembled and glued.

Cleaning Up

'Cleaning up' entails removing any waste wood left protruding from joints, which may be done with a saw or chisel, and finally levelling with the smoothing plane. The smoothing plane is also used to remove surplus pencil lines left from setting out as well as the usual dirt which accumulates from dust and hands during the construction. Such dirt will not be excessive if the bench and vice are kept clean, and hands washed when necessary.

When inner surfaces are being cleaned up great care must be exercised at and around the joints to avoid removing too much material and affecting their close fitting. Difficult surfaces around knots or where there is crossed or interlocking grain may need to be scraped with the cabinet scraper.

Final finishing is done with an abrasive paper, always working with the grain. Rubbing across the grain will produce deep scratches which are difficult to remove. It is sometimes desirable to cover the wood near to a joint with a strip of Sellotape once the cleaning up has been completed. This protects the surface from any surplus glue which may squeeze out of the joint during assembly; this can then be wiped away quite easily with a damp cloth, and the Sellotape removed once the glue in the joint has set.

Abrasives

Abrasive papers for the final smoothing of surfaces on wood are made from five types of grit, four of which are stuck to backing sheets of paper or cloth with animal and/or resin glues. They are termed 'close coat' or 'open coat' depending upon whether the grains completely cover the sheet or are spaced out. **Glasspaper** is the most common of these, the usual sheets measuring 280 × 230 mm and of close grain. Although it will produce a very smooth surface, since glass is comparatively soft it does wear rapidly and soon becomes choked.

Garnet paper is red in colour and although harder than glass and therefore longer lasting, it still tends to choke quite rapidly even though it is often manufactured as an open-grain paper. Garnet is a natural mineral which is crushed to give the grit sizes required.

Aluminium oxide is a tough, hardwearing artificial abrasive usually used for machine sanding rather than hand use, and is particularly good on hardwoods. Generally open-grain, sheets are made for use in sanding machines and discs for use with electric drills.

'Wet and dry' papers are made from **silicon carbide**, which is also an artificial abrasive. It is produced by subjecting quartz sand to heat and is the same material used in making some oilstones. The backing paper is waterproof, as is the resin glue used to secure the grits, and it can therefore be used with water or white spirit. If lubricated in this way the paper does not choke readily and the dust is checked. Being used wet, it cannot be employed on unfinished wood but is suitable for rubbing down resin varnishes or cellulose paints.

Tungsten carbide grits have a life more than 100 times that of glass and give good results on fibreglass, plastic laminates, etc., as well as wood. The grits are near the hardness of diamond and do not crush or fracture easily; they are fixed permanently to a steel backing by means of copper brazing. Being open-grain, they do not clog easily and can be cleaned with a stiff bristle or wire brush, or a solvent such as paint stripper. Three grades—coarse, medium and fine—are available. (See Appendix 2 for grit grades for abrasive papers.)

Abrasive papers should be used wrapped around a cork block which is sufficiently resilient to maintain the uniformity of a surface. The tungsten carbide metal sheets should be tacked or stapled to a wooden block for easy handling.

Steel wool of various grades and 3M Scotchbrite pads are also useful finishing abrasives.

Surface Preparation

It should be remembered that any surface defect tends to be exaggerated and become more unsightly after the finish is applied and therefore the preparation of the surface must be done thoroughly.

Surfaces must be smooth and clear of pencil marks, oil and grease stains, dents due to accidental damage, tool marks and scratches, etc. Occasionally, faint oil or grease stains may be removed by rubbing with turpentine substitute or more difficult ones with trichloroethane.

The first application of any liquid finish may cause the grain of the wood to swell and produce a rough surface which must be completely papered off. Some craftsmen, however, prefer to 'raise the grain' before applying the finish by lightly damping the surface with a wet cloth, allowing it to dry and then rubbing down.

Where it has been necessary to use nails or panel pins in the construction these should be punched below the surface and the hole filled with a suitable wood filler. This must match the colour of the timber if a 'natural finish' is required. Open-grain timbers such as oak may need to be filled in order to obtain an even overall finish. This is best done with a proprietary brand filler, rubbing it in across the grain with a cloth and removing any surplus filler in the same way before it dries. Final rubbing down is then necessary with fine glasspaper along the grain. If the wood is to be stained later it may be necessary to tint the filler with a little of the stain before application.

Choice of Finish

Once the work has been prepared satisfactorily it is ready to receive its 'finish', which may vary tremendously depending upon the nature of the work, what it has to do, the kind of wood, existing decor, etc. The choice of finish is part of the design and as such demands careful consideration on the part of the designer.

The primary purpose of a finish is to afford protection to the surface of the work and in varying degrees to the timber itself. All finishes do protect against dirt and make cleaning easier. All to some extent protect against moisture, some are heat-resisting, others protect against insect or fungus attack and are termed preservatives. The modern trend with furniture is to enhance the inherent beauty of the wood by giving it a 'natural finish', but occasionally stains are used to change the colour or to give emphasis to the grain. High-gloss surfaces, eggshell or matt may be obtained with clear finishes, or paints if these are used where solid colour is required.

Finishing Tools

The tools with which finishes are applied are few and simple. **Clean rags** of linen and soft cloth are used to make up polishing 'rubbers' or pads with cotton wool or polisher's wadding. The rags should be free from fluff and loose threads. Foam pads are suitable for the application of cream spirit stains.

Good-quality flat **varnish brushes** are available in a range of widths from 12 mm upwards. Cheap brushes with coarse bristles should be avoided as they tend to leave brush marks on the work and bristles break off and stick to the surface. **Thinners** suited to the finish being applied can also be used to clean brushes. These will include white spirit, methylated spirits, cellulose thinners and any special ones necessary for lacquers of proprietary brands. A plentiful supply of labelled jars and containers should be available in which to clean brushes and keep partially used thinners. Any brushes used for oil-based finishes may be kept soft in water as a temporary measure between coats, but should then be thoroughly cleaned when the work is completed. Fine **abrasive papers** or **steel wool** should be available for rubbing down between coats where necessary, the dust being removed carefully before a further coat is applied.

Newspapers should be at hand on which to place the work and to catch any accidental drips or spills as well as small blocks of wood to place under the work to prevent it from sticking to the paper. Brushing should always be towards the edge of the work, and brushes should never be dragged over an edge or their contents will be squeezed out causing a considerable build-up of liquid and consequent unsightly trickling.

French Polish

The choice of finish will be made from a very large number of liquids and pastes which are on the market. French polish, which is very traditional, is included here for the benefit of any reader who may be involved in the renovation of furniture. (Modern finishes have almost entirely replaced it since it is neither heat- nor spirit-resistant.)

French polish is made by dissolving shellac in methylated spirits with hardening additives (the resins benzoin from the East Indies, and sandarac, from a tree native to Morocco). There are numerous types of french polish, common ones being button, yellow, slightly opaque, garnet, brown, white, milky for light woods, and transparent. It is also available tinted with dyes of black and red. The aim is to produce a mirror finish by the application of numerous coats of polish, which requires patience and considerable skill acquired from experience.

1. Using full strength polish, apply a brush coat along the grain and leave to dry (about 30 minutes at room temperature).
2. Rub down with flour-grade glasspaper or 000 steel wool, and dust off.
3. Make up a rubber from dry cotton wool or wadding, about the size of a cricket ball, folded into a piece of linen such as that used for handkerchiefs. The wadding should be charged with polish from the bottle. The amount can be controlled easily if a glass tube is fitted through the cork. The linen is then drawn up round the wadding and the ends twisted together to form a rubber, free from creases, which fits the hand. Polish strength at this stage should be 3 to 1 of methylated spirits.
4. First using long sweeps along the length of the work, and then shorter looping sweeps gradually moving along the wood, successive coats of polish should be applied over a period of one to two hours. It will be necessary to recharge the rubber regularly during this stage and to lubricate it occasionally with a spot of linseed oil applied with the finger tip.
5. After drying and hardening for one whole day, the work should be papered down and dusted once more.
6. Repeat 4 and 5 above using a polish strength of 2 to 1.
7. Using a dry, clean rubber free from polish, 'spirit off' with a solution of 1 to 2 of methylated spirits. In this case the mixture is sprinkled over the sole of the rubber, which is then moved quickly and carefully in loops along the work finishing off with long straight strokes. The object of spiriting off is to remove traces of linseed oil and any previous rubber marks. This is a difficult operation and if not carried out successfully first time, further coats of polish may have to be added and the process repeated.

Ebonising, which is usually done on sycamore, mahogany or birch, is carried out in the same way as above, using black french polish over a coat of black stain.

After use, rubbers should be stored suspended in an airtight jar with a little methylated spirits in the bottom.

There are many other types of finish available, some quite traditional and others very modern. It is quite impossible to list each brand name but the following is a useful general selection:

1. Paints
2. Oil polishing
3. Wax polishing
4. Semi-wax polishing
5. Clear varnishes
6. Cellulose lacquer
7. Polyurethane varnish and paints
8. Plastic coating
9. Stains
10. Preservatives

Paints

Paints are generally used on softwoods only, and provide a durable and colourful protective coating for their somewhat vulnerable surface. Conditions for painting are often far from ideal, particularly out of doors, but it is essential that the surface to be painted is dry, clean, and free from grease. There should be good natural light, good ventilation, a dust-free atmosphere and a temperature of about 15 °C. A huge variety of colours and shades is obtainable but it is essential to ensure that the paint selected is suitable for the work it has to do, whether internal or external. When painting new wood the usual sequence is as follows:

1. The surface prepared as above.
2. Knotting is applied to knots and end grain. This coat of shellac seals the surface and prevents resin bleeding through at some later date. Rub down when dry.
3. Brush on a priming coat, either of the traditional oil-based type or the more modern alkyd or acrylic water-borne types which are fast drying. Dulux aluminium sealer and wood primer is recommended for use on end grain and resinous timbers to minimise discoloration due to resin bleed. Children's toys and furniture may be primed with Dulux wood primer (white or pink), aluminium sealer or acrylic primer. The first two are 'low lead paints' (as defined by BS 4310: 1968) and the last two are lead-free. When dry the primer should be rubbed down.
4. Make good all cracks, nail holes, open joints, etc., with a suitable stopping.
5. Apply a thin undercoat of the type specified for the final coat. Leave to dry thoroughly.
6. Paper off and dust. Take care not to rub the paint off at corners.
7. Apply the final coat, which may have a gloss, eggshell or matt surface as required.

Paint is best applied in thin, even coats. Extra coats may be added if required or as the paint ages and becomes worn. Cleaning and rubbing down is necessary on each occasion. The new synthetic resin paints with a polyurethane base give good results, and the non-drip types are simple and pleasant to apply. Special lead-free paints must always be used for children's toys and furniture.

After use the paint tin must be *firmly sealed* to prevent evaporation and skinning. Evaporation can be further retarded if the tin is stored upside down. Brushes should be washed out in white spirit and then washed in hot soapy water and laid out to dry. They must not be stood on the bristles, which would cause them to become distorted. Some modern paints are such that the brush can be washed out in water immediately without the use of turps substitute.

Oil Polishing

The traditional oil for this kind of finish is linseed. By applying numerous coats, matt, satin or gloss surfaces may be obtained, the resulting finish being very beautiful and durable. It is particularly suitable for such woods as oak, enhancing both the grain and the colour.

Either boiled or raw linseed oil may be used and it should be simmered for 15 minutes in a double pan, after which turpentine in the ratio of 1:8 should be added to speed up drying. The oil should be applied with a clean cloth and rubbed in with a felt pad. It must then be allowed to dry for at least one day, rubbed down with fine glasspaper, dusted and a further coat applied. Several coats should be applied in this way with perhaps as much as a week's drying time between each. This is a suitable finish for exterior use on garden furniture, for example, but further applications are necessary annually.

Modern teak or Danish oils supplied by Rustin's produce pleasant matt finishes, sealing the wood and 'bringing out the grain'. Danish oil is more viscous and does not dry to a gloss even on wood which has already been heavily oiled. They are based on vegetable oils and synthetic resins to give a quick-drying, penetrating seal to teak, oak, mahogany, walnut, cedar, other hard and softwoods and veneered surfaces. Danish oil may be used over Rustin's matt wood stains if required. It also primes and fills wood, and will at a later date accept either varnish or paint. The rags with which these oils are applied soon harden and are best destroyed immediately after use.

Wax Polishing

A waxed finish may be built up by applying successive coats of polish directly to the bare wood, as with oils. This is obviously more successful on hardwoods than softwoods, which would absorb the wax more readily.

The wax polish is applied evenly with a cloth and then rubbed to a pleasant sheen with a soft duster. Proprietary brands are available which are ready for use, many of which have additives to speed up drying so that the final finish is obtained more quickly.

For the craftsman who wishes to prepare his own polish, shredded unbleached beeswax should be mixed with an equal volume of pure turpentine, a double container being used for this purpose, the outer one of which contains hot water. The mixture is very inflammable and should be kept away from naked flames. The thickness of the resulting paste may be controlled by varying the volume of turpentine. A lighter-coloured polish may be produced by using bleached beeswax, or a brown polish by stirring in small quantities of burnt umber powder. The addition of lamp black produces an 'antique' black polish.

Semi-Wax Polishing

This is a convenient way of producing a satisfactory finish in much less time. The wood is sealed by rubbing on two coats of cellulose sanding sealer with a cloth, papering down between coats. Drying time is quite rapid, and the second coat should be rubbed down with fine-grade steel wool to which the wax polish has been applied. The final burnishing to produce the finish required is done with a soft cloth.

If an oil-based stain has been used on the work wax polish should not be applied directly to it or the stain may be lifted by the turpentine in the polish. The stain should first be sealed with french polish.

Although waxed finishes are acceptable for many items of furniture they should not be subjected to rough use, and not being resistant to heat or water they are not really suitable for table tops.

Clear Varnishes and Lacquers

Many traditional finishes of this kind have been replaced by modern products, but care must be exercised when using these to follow the manufacturers' instructions, particularly if stains and fillers have been used.

For a 'natural' finish on external woodwork there is still much to be said for the traditional **copal oak varnish**. Applied when the wood is warm and dry, it produces a tough resilient finish which is weatherproof. Providing it is properly rubbed down and cleaned with white spirit, several coats can be applied over the years as they become necessary before it must finally be stripped off and renewed completely.

Great care must be taken if modern **polyurethane varnish** is used externally. Various brands are available which may be 'one-pot', which is used straight from the can, or 'two-pot', in which one is the base and the other the hardener, to be mixed before use. The wood to be sealed must be dry and the varnish applied to cover the whole surface thoroughly, taking particular care in the region of joints, edges and end grain. Although polyurethanes are quite waterproof, if moisture does penetrate the film it will 'creep' and destroy the bond between the wood and the varnish, which will then peel off. Gloss finish should be used externally and Rustin's recommend that for maximum protection and durability as many as five coats should be applied. Rustin's polyurethanes are pale in colour and darken very little with age, so preserving the natural appearance of the wood. They are resistant to heat and liquids, and are available in gloss or matt finishes. A satin or eggshell finish may be obtained by mixing two parts matt with one of gloss. They may be thinned with white spirits, in which brushes also should be cleaned.

Cellulose lacquers may, according to their composition, be applied by brush or rubber. Industrial application is most often by spraying. To produce a gloss finish on wood at least four brush coats should be applied. Each coat must be applied quickly as the cellulose is quick-drying, and over-brushing must therefore be avoided. A drying time of about one hour should be allowed between first and second coats, and a day between second, third and fourth. Rubbing down between coats should be with progressively smoother grades of glasspaper and lastly with fine-grade flatting paste on a pad. The final high gloss is produced by rubbing vigorously with a smooth cloth to which a little burnishing cream has been applied. Brushes should be cleaned immediately after use in cellulose thinners. Readers are reminded that both lacquer and thinners are extremely inflammable. Cellulose lacquers are suitable for internal use only.

Acid-catalysed and **precatalysed lacquers** are also for internal use. In the former, the acid hardener is added to the resin lacquer in the proportion recommended by the manufacturer, and mixed. This should then be applied to the work quickly and without over-brushing. Two or three coats if necessary should be applied, allowing a drying time of at least one hour between coats and overnight for the final one. Fine-grade wet and dry silicon carbide paper may be used for rubbing down between coats; the final gloss finish is produced with a suitable burnishing paste. A matt finish can be obtained by rubbing down with fine wire wool and wax polish, and catalysed lacquers are also available in black, white and pale tints, and as enamels with gloss, satin or matt finishes. The plastic coatings obtained with these lacquers are ideal for table tops as they are impervious to heat and liquids, and are extremely hard and scratch-resistant. They are also suitable for use on hardboard, cane and cork, and may be applied by brush, roller or spray. Catalysed lacquers are also grain-filling, so that the use of a normal filler is not necessary, and clear grades therefore produce an even more 'natural finish'. Special thinners are available which can also be used for cleaning brushes.

Stains

Modern clear finishes enhance the natural beauty of wood, its colour and its grain. It is generally recommended, therefore, that the use of stains is to be avoided. This is not always possible, however, if restoration work is being carried out, or work is being done to match existing pieces. The range of Rustin's matt wood stains in eight colours from golden oak to ebony, all of which are inter-mixable to give an infinite variety of shades, is sufficient to meet most requirements. Light and dark teak stains are also made, and all are penetrating, quick-drying and do not raise the grain. They can all be used on bare wood and may be finished with wax, oil, varnish, polyurethane or catalysed lacquer. Filling and staining can be done in one operation, the stain being used to thin the grain filler instead of white spirit. Grain fillers and wood stoppings are produced in the same range of colours as the stains.

Within the furniture trade some stains are still made up in the workshop from traditional recipes, usually producing shades of brown with chemicals such as Vandyke crystals and bichromate of potash, which are mixed with water, while sulphate of iron produces a grey tone on oak. A brown oil stain can be made by dissolving asphaltum in turpentine, while various rather cold shades of brown can be produced on oak by **fuming**. Here the article is placed in an airtight wooden box in which there are dishes of 'point eight-eighty' ammonia. Various types of oak respond at different rates and regular observations must be made to check the colour produced.

Aniline dyes suitable for mixing with water, methylated spirit or turpentine may be obtained to produce shades of brown, yellow, blue, green, red, etc., and are suitable for use on items such as wooden toys.

Oxalic acid crystals dissolved in hot water in the proportion of approximately 25 grams to one quarter litre of water, make a useful bleach for lightening odd areas of wood or removing stains. It is a poison and should not be allowed to get on to the hands; all traces must be removed from the work by washing with a weak solution of borax and water to avoid any detrimental effect on the final finish.

Western red cedar used externally for cladding may be left untreated and will 'weather' to a rather beautiful silver-grey colour. If desired, however, its colour may be renewed by the use of a suitable restorative such as Sanderson's 'Colorbac'.

Preservatives

Preservatives is the term given to those solutions designed to protect timber from insect or fungal attack. The most common of the **insects** is the furniture beetle, which may attack structural timbers as well as domestic furniture and fittings. Eggs are laid by the adult females in cracks and splits in bare wood, and the grubs which hatch out after about three weeks bore into the wood. This is continued for about two years or more before the grub pupates and becomes a mature beetle, leaving the timber through a small round flight hole. Unfortunately, the attack may not be discovered until this stage is reached and the holes become visible, when considerable damage will have been done. Small attacks can, however, be contained and eradicated using proprietary brands of insecticide which can be brushed over the infected timber and injected into boreholes to ensure deep penetration which kills any remaining larvae. Repeated applications may be necessary before there is complete success, but once treated the timber is protected against further attack. Badly affected timbers may have to be replaced in which case those removed should be burnt.

There are a number of wood destroying **fungi** which attack standing timber, felled timber and converted timber. Conditions for their growth vary depending upon the species, but in buildings the lack of good ventilation and the presence of dampness bringing the moisture content of the timber to more than 20 per cent provide a situation where such fungi could develop. If this does occur then treatment by experts is almost invariably necessary, and should be sought immediately. The source of dampness will be located and made good, ventilation improved, decayed timber destroyed, sound timber cut back to at least 1 m from the attack and surrounding walls, etc., sterilised. New and remaining timbers will then be treated with a suitable fungicidal preservative.

Timber preservation within the timber trade and allied industries is now accepted as an integral part of wood processing and utilisation, and for many years it has been possible to have structural timbers treated with preservatives under pressure to ensure deep penetration. Any untreated surfaces which are exposed during working are then brush-coated. Proprietary brands of preservatives are available, some of which are coloured so as to be decorative on external woodwork.

Creosote, which is a tar-oil, is a useful preservative for exterior work such as fences. It usually produces a pleasant brown colour on new timber, annual applications being advisable. Once applied, it becomes virtually impossible to paint the timber and this should be remembered before creosote is used.

Stripping

Redecoration of domestic fitments, painted or polished furniture, or renovation often involves the complete removal of the previous finish. On large items and on exterior woodwork which has been painted this may entail using a blowlamp and appropriate scraper to burn it away. Smaller items such as furniture may be cleared using proprietary brands of **stripper** such as 'Nitromors' or Rustin's 'Stripit'. These solutions are brushed on and almost immediately 'lift' the finish, enabling it to be scraped and washed away. In obstinate cases more than one application may be necessary.

A strong solution of common soda in hot water will remove french polish, which can also be softened with methylated spirits so that it can be scraped off. Point eight-eighty ammonia will soften old polish and varnish enabling it to be scraped off, as will a solution of caustic potash on paint.

Caution is necessary when using strippers to avoid splashes and the use of protective rubber gloves is advisable. The work should always be washed thoroughly to remove completely all traces of the stripper to prevent adverse effects on any subsequent finish.

Finishes suited to work produced on the lathe are dealt with in Chapter 14.

16

UPHOLSTERY

Upholstery is practised as a craft in its own right as are many other aspects of woodworking. The amount of information that can be given here is therefore restricted to what is necessary to enable the amateur craftsman, whether at school or at home, to upholster his work in an efficient and professional manner. Unless the amateur is prepared to do some upholstery it is quite obvious that his choice of work is going to be restricted, but with the modern materials which are now available many earlier difficulties have been minimised and simple work can be undertaken with confidence.

Upholstery Tools

The tools required are few and of a simple nature, and include the upholstery hammer with suitable nails, mainly **cut tacks** and **gimp pins** (see Fig. 382). Tacks are from 10 to 16 mm in length, heavy-gauge tacks of the larger sizes being used to fasten upholstery webbings and the smaller for hessian and calico covers. Gimp pins are of similar lengths and are used for fixing braids and outer covers such as those on chair backs. The modern **upholsterer's hammer**, such as the one illustrated, is magnetic so that the material may be held in place by one hand while the nail is lightly positioned with the hammer and then finally driven in. The head is light, weighing only 170–200 grams, and the face is small in diameter to facilitate the accurate positioning of nails and to avoid damage to the surrounding material. Nails wrongly positioned or bent may be extracted with the claw, and the shaft is of steel fitted with a rubber grip.

Much of the work previously done by hammer is now done with the **staple gun**, the advantage being that it can be operated by one hand, leaving the other free to adjust and position the material.

Tailor's chalk, with which a clear line may be made when marking and setting out; a steel tape; Stanley knives; straight edge; scissors; strong needles and threads of suitable colours; adhesives and a long, really sharp knife will also be necessary at different times.

Adhesives must be selected carefully and manufacturer's instructions followed to ensure efficient results in view of the varied composition of modern upholstery materials.

Foams

The knife will be found effective in cutting the foam filler materials which have now largely replaced the traditional stuffings of horse hair and vegetable fibres, which were overlaid by a wadding made of cotton waste. Foams are of two types: latex or plastic. **Latex foam** (Fig. 383) is a mixture of natural and

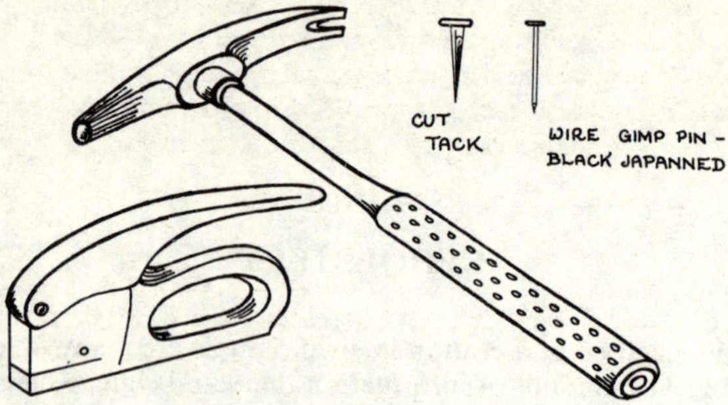

Fig. 382. The upholstery hammer and staple gun.

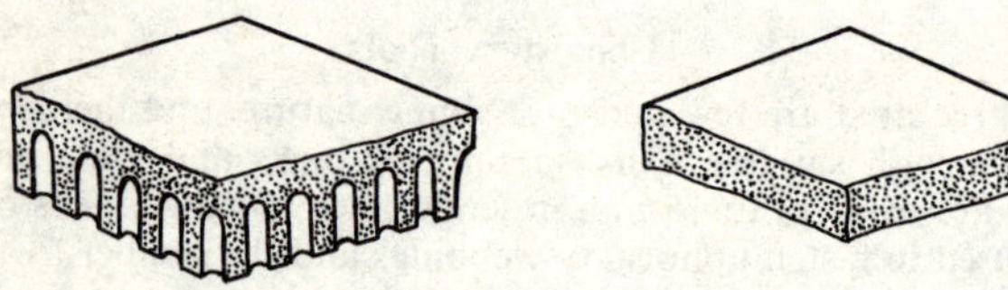

Fig. 383. Latex foam: cavity and plain sheet.

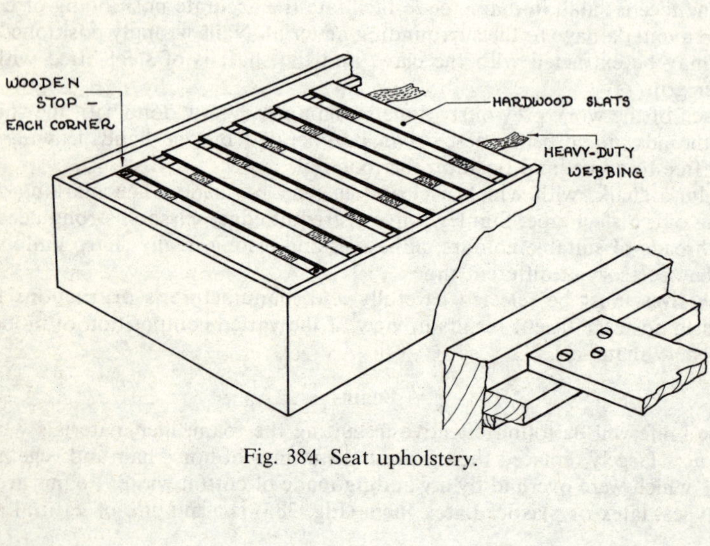

Fig. 384. Seat upholstery.

synthetic rubbers made in a variety of sizes, specially moulded shapes or larger slabs which can be cut to size, and is available in cavity or plain sheets from 25 to 100 mm thick. Latex is rather more expensive but has better powers of recovery to its original shape after being sat upon than has **polyether plastic foam**. This too, is available already moulded into cushion shapes and sizes, or as sheets of different thicknesses and grades of hardness.

Covering Materials

It is usual practice to cover the foam with an inner lining of calico, which is made of cotton, or with hessian. Such a lining is particularly necessary if the outer cover is of a woven material. The outer cover may be of natural fibres such as wool or mohair, from which moquettes are made, or artificial fibres of rayon or nylon, which have the additional advantage of being colour-fast and easily washable. There is also a wide range of PVC sheets from which to choose outer covers, and many colours, surface textures and finishes are manufactured. The most suitable for use by the amateur are those with knitted base fabrics of cotton such as Ambla and Cirrus. These have high stretch properties which enable them to be formed more readily to the shape of the cushion. Good recovery after being sat upon is also one of their characteristics, and they are easy to stitch and staple.

Natural leather is the most expensive outer cover of all, and is reserved for the very best of work. Leather is able to 'breathe', it is resistant to 'stitch tear', has a high tensile strength and elasticity, is resistant to abrasion of the surface and is very hygienic since it is easily cleaned in the same way as PVC sheets—that is, with a cloth damped with a soft soap or mild detergent solution and finished when dry with a proprietary brand finish.

Supports

Upholstered seats are supported on a flexible or rigid base, depending upon their use. One particularly convenient form used by the author on both large and small work is **hardwood slats** (see Fig. 384). These need to be of good-quality timber with straight grain and free from knots; ash, oak and beech have been found to be suitable. Their sectional size is determined by the work expected of them. The slats may be spaced equally along two lengths of webbing; the webbing being tacked to them, in which case a small stop is required in each corner to keep the webbing in tension and the slats equally spaced. The slats are loose and may be lifted out to provide useful storage space below if the work is so designed. Alternatively, each slat may be screwed down at its ends, the number of screws depending upon the size of slat, to provide a more rigid base.

More flexible support is provided by the use of resilient **webbing**, such as that manufactured by Pirelli (Fig. 385), which consists of rayon cords bonded together with rubber. Several grades and widths are available suitable for stools, chairs, settees and beds, each being identified by its colour. The ends of each piece of webbing are terminated by a self-grip clip which may be pressed on to it in the vice. The clip has a protruding lip on one edge by which it may be inserted into the stopped mortise. Teeth on the lower edge then prevent it from withdrawing.

Rather similar clips may be used to secure this type of webbing into through mortises (Fig. 386). Once inserted and doubled back on the webbing, the clip

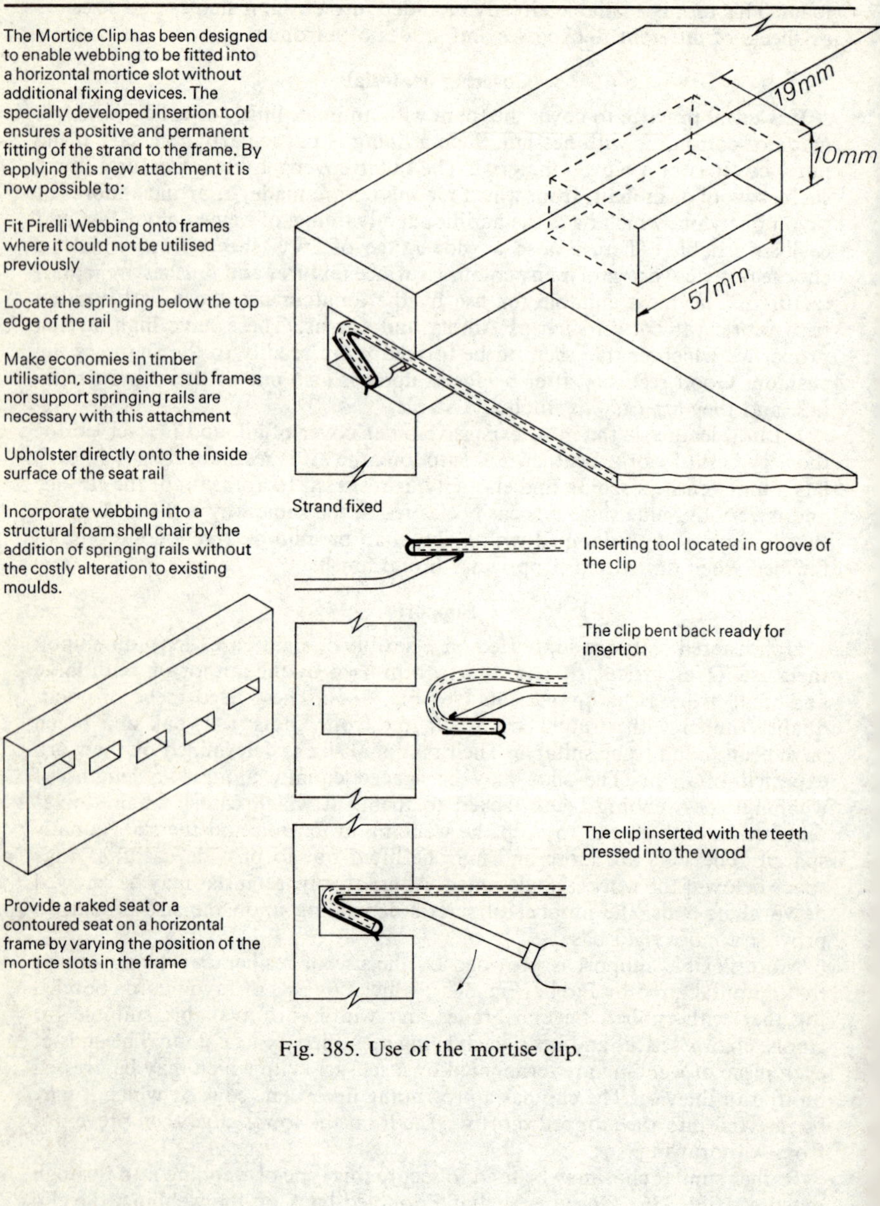

Fig. 385. Use of the mortise clip.

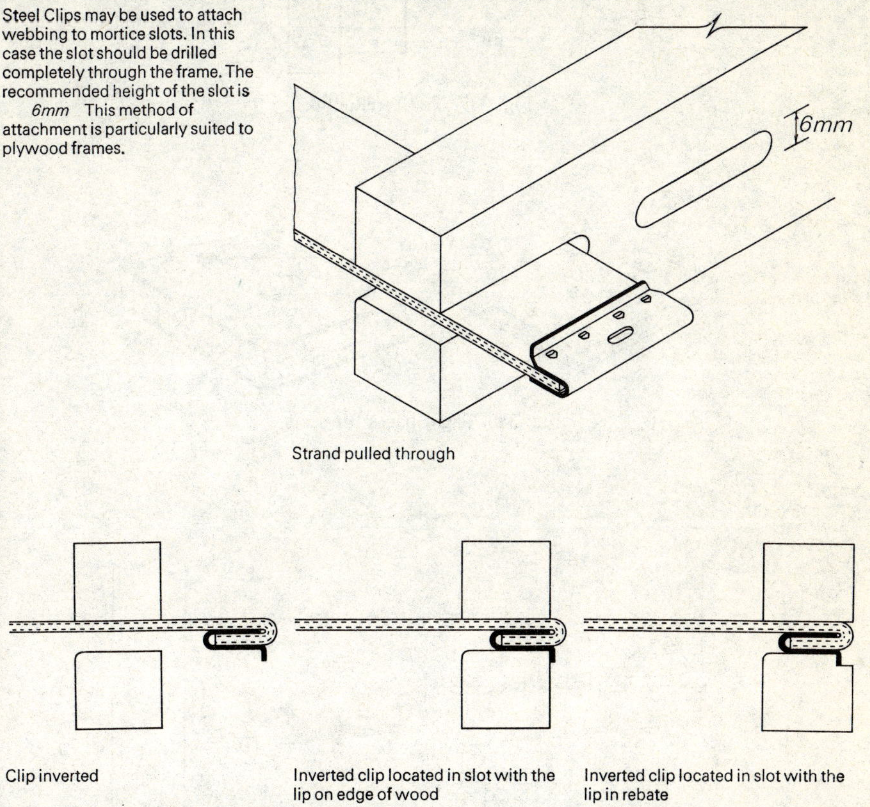

Fig. 386. Use of the steel clip in upholstery.

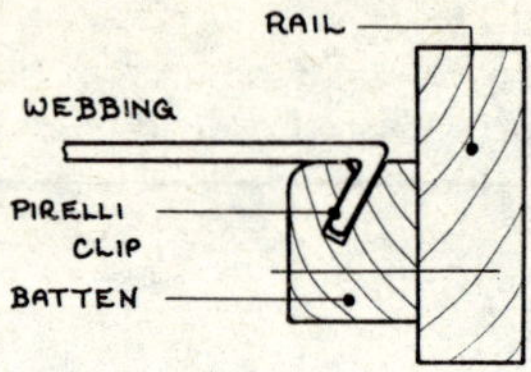

Fig. 387. The Pirelli clip.

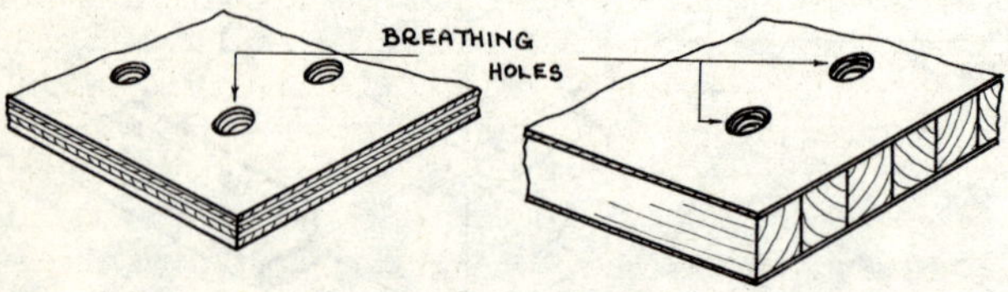

Fig. 388. Rigid bases for seats.

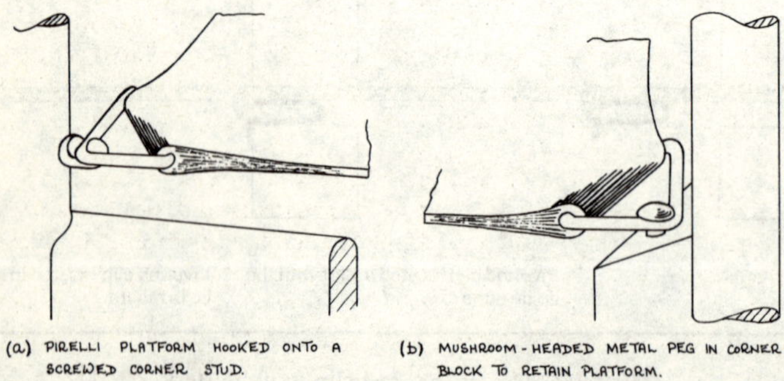

Fig. 389. The Pirelli four-point platform.

anchors the end firmly. If a flush surface is required the bottom edge of the mortise should be rebated.

The same pattern of clip may also be used in the above way by pressing it down into an inclined groove where it is held by tension (Fig. 387). The batten must be of hardwood so that there is no danger of it splitting, and the top edge must be rounded off to avoid the webbing being worn due to its movements when the seat is in use.

All three methods of fixing the webbing allow the upholstery covers to be attached to the seat rail as is traditional, or the webbing may be taken over the seat rail and tacked to the inside (see Fig. 392). In a similar way it may be tacked to the top of hardwood frames for loose seats.

Rigid bases of **plywood** or **blockboard**, from 12 to 19 mm thick depending on the seat area to be supported, are often used for 'loose' or 'drop-in' seats (see Fig. 388). These rest on battens fixed to the inside of the seat rails, or more often in rebates around the inside of their top edges. Because the support is solid, a number of breathing holes must be drilled—particularly if the outer cover is of PVC—to provide ventilation and to allow air to escape when the seat is sat on and be drawn back afterwards so that the seat recovers its shape quickly.

Pirelli **four-point platforms** (Fig. 389) are a comparatively recent introduction made of tough, load-bearing rubber into which is moulded a triangular steel ring at each corner. These rings are hooked on to slotted steel studs which are screwed into each leg or are hooked over the dome heads of metal pegs fitted into bevelled corner blocks or rails. The bevel is to allow for the downward movement of the platform when in use. Seven sizes are available ranging from 360 mm to 490 mm square, which at their maximum extension are 410 mm and 530 mm square respectively. In addition, there are two rectangular sizes, 380 × 430 mm and 420 × 485 mm. The company also manufacture special tools with which to insert the slotted studs and to stretch the platform to make fitting simpler.

Cushions and Seats

The slatted platform and the Pirelli rubber platform are designed to support loose cushions, the general form of which is indicated in Fig. 390. The slab of seating foam has a calico cover fitted to it, and the outer cover is made to contain the two. Cushions which have PVC covers may be cleaned simply by sponging. Fabric covers, however, are usually fitted with a zip fastener so that they may be removed for washing, which may be positioned along one edge as shown in Fig. 390 so that the cushion is reversible.

The making of covers for loose cushions requires a certain amount of sewing, which may be done by hand or machine after suitable advice has been obtained. Upholstered studs and 'piped' edges are often used by professional upholsterers to add to the decorative construction of cushions and seats.

Loose seats on rigid platforms of plywood or blockboard are usually flat with vertical sides or crowned (see Fig. 391). The arrangement of the foam is important. To ensure that the flat seat retains its vertical sides, the softer seating foam should be reinforced along each edge with a hard-grade foam, all the pieces then being held in position with an inner lining of calico tacked or stapled to the under side of the platform. Crowned seats are produced by placing a piece of plain sheet under the centre of the seating foam. This should

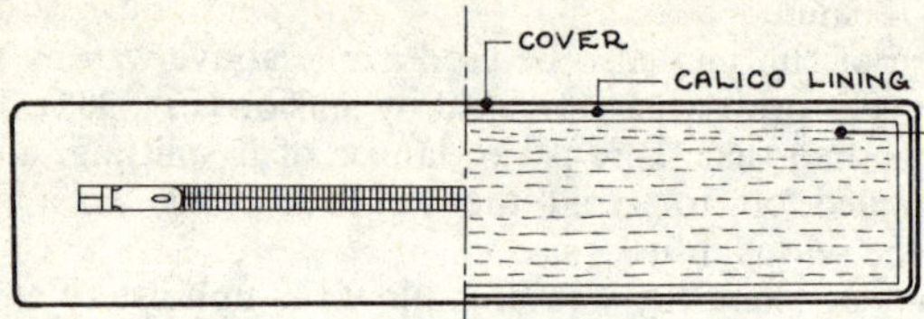

Fig. 390. Loose cushion.

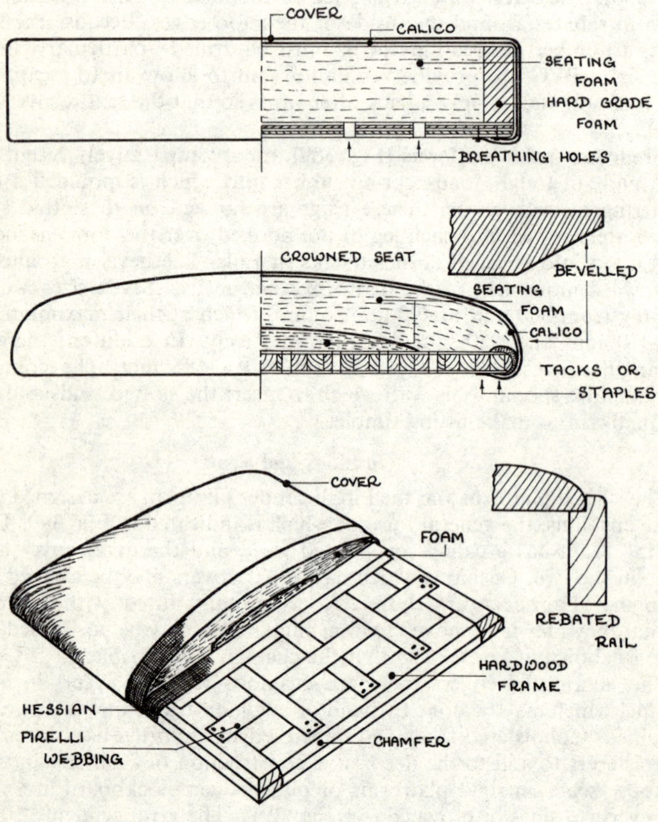

Fig. 391. Loose seats.

be glued to the base or the seating foam to prevent possible movement in use. To further assist the doming effect, the seating foam should be undercut along each edge which is then pulled down into place by the inner cover. In this case it is also advisable to 'soften' the edge of the platform with a thin sheet of foam, which may be either glued or stapled into place. A similar seat is often constructed for use on chairs, the platform being built up of webbing tacked to a hardwood frame. In this case hessian or calico is used both above and below the seating foam to give it the necessary support.

The neat fitting of the outer covers of seats is of the utmost importance as their appearance will 'make or mar' the finished work. Fabrics are more readily manipulated than PVC covers, although those with the double-stretch qualities of knitted cotton backs can be drawn into shape relatively easily. Corners are the biggest problem and it is advisable to fasten these down last, having first secured opposite sides. Some stitching may be necessary, particularly at the corners of the flat seat where the cutting of a paper pattern is often advisable, and in every case an effort should be made to ensure the neatness of the underside. Since loose seats always fit into a frame—usually in a rebate but may be carried on an inner batten or corner blocks as an alternative—when making the platform allowance must always be made for the thickness of the covers around the edge. This method of upholstery can often be adapted for use on certain styles of chair arms and backs where the constructional woods serve as a base.

An alternative style of platform may be formed by taking the webbing round the seat rails, and tacking it to their inner sides. Thin foam sheets are then used to pad out any small irregularities so formed, and depending upon the construction of the work and the preference of the craftsman the foam and outer cover are either trimmed around the leg or taken over it. The seat is then completed by fitting a base cloth across the underside of the rails.

One final aspect to remember in all cases is that foams are compressed during fitting and allowance should be made for this in length, width and thickness when cutting to size.

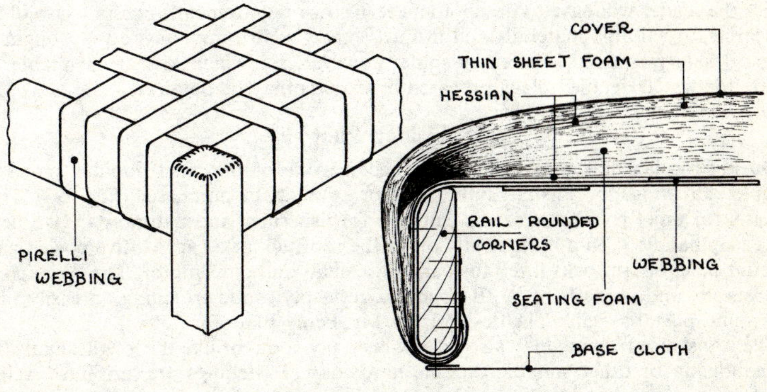

Fig. 392. Webbing attached to seat rails.

APPENDIX 1

SUGGESTIONS FOR MAKING LEISURE-TIME EQUIPMENT

The amateur craftsman and senior pupils at school should not necessarily restrict their work to furniture making, turning and carving, etc. Wood is an excellent medium from which to make items to further leisure time pursuits. Not only does this create greater enthusiasm for one's work but there is also added pleasure in having produced the article oneself. For the amateur, modern materials, glues and fittings now make possible what could only be done commercially a few years ago. The design of the work and all the research which it entails give even more interest to each project. The following list gives some indication of the wide variety of work of this nature.

Garden: certain tools such as grass and leaf rakes, seats, summer house, sheds, cold frames, greenhouse, wheelbarrow.

Pets: huts, kennels, hutches, carrying boxes, nesting boxes, breeding boxes, feeding boxes.

Hobbies: work tables, collecting boxes, light fitments, display units, record racks, cassette holders, jewellery, brush making, beehives.

Model Making: layouts, scale models of cars, ships, aircraft, etc., architectural models.

Musical Instruments: castanets, slit drum, psaltery, glockenspiel, xylophone, recorder, guitar, violin.

Fishing: rods, floats, creels.

Outdoor Pursuits: skis, toboggans, trolleys, bows and arrows, cricket bat, stumps, croquet set, car trailer to carry camping equipment, etc., caravans.

Within the compass of this book it is not possible to discuss these suggestions in detail, but much of the satisfaction of the work is in 'finding out'. For many of the topics the reader will have to design to meet his own requirements; possibly he will have to search for suitable materials and fittings, expert advice may have to be sought and physical safety ensured. There are some, however, for which kits are available, and others for which detailed plans prepared by experts may be obtained.

Fishing Punt

During the last few years sailing has become one of the most popular sports and complete drawings for a fishing punt may, for example, be purchased (Fig. 393). This is a vessel for quiet rivers and canals, suitable for fishermen and naturalists. Two people can easily handle it, and it fits neatly on to the roofrack of a car. Motive power can be by punt pole, or rowlocks fitted for oars, or a small outboard motor. The Woodcrest is very stable, and is made of WPB-bonded Cresta plywood, providing an easily made, cheap and portable punt. The design is by Mr. Percy Blandford.

The transverse framing may also be of Cresta plywood, or like the longitudinal strips, of mahogany or other suitable durable hardwood. Fastenings are 'grip-fast' nails or brass screws, and Aerolite 306 or Cascamite waterproof glues are suitable for bonding the components.

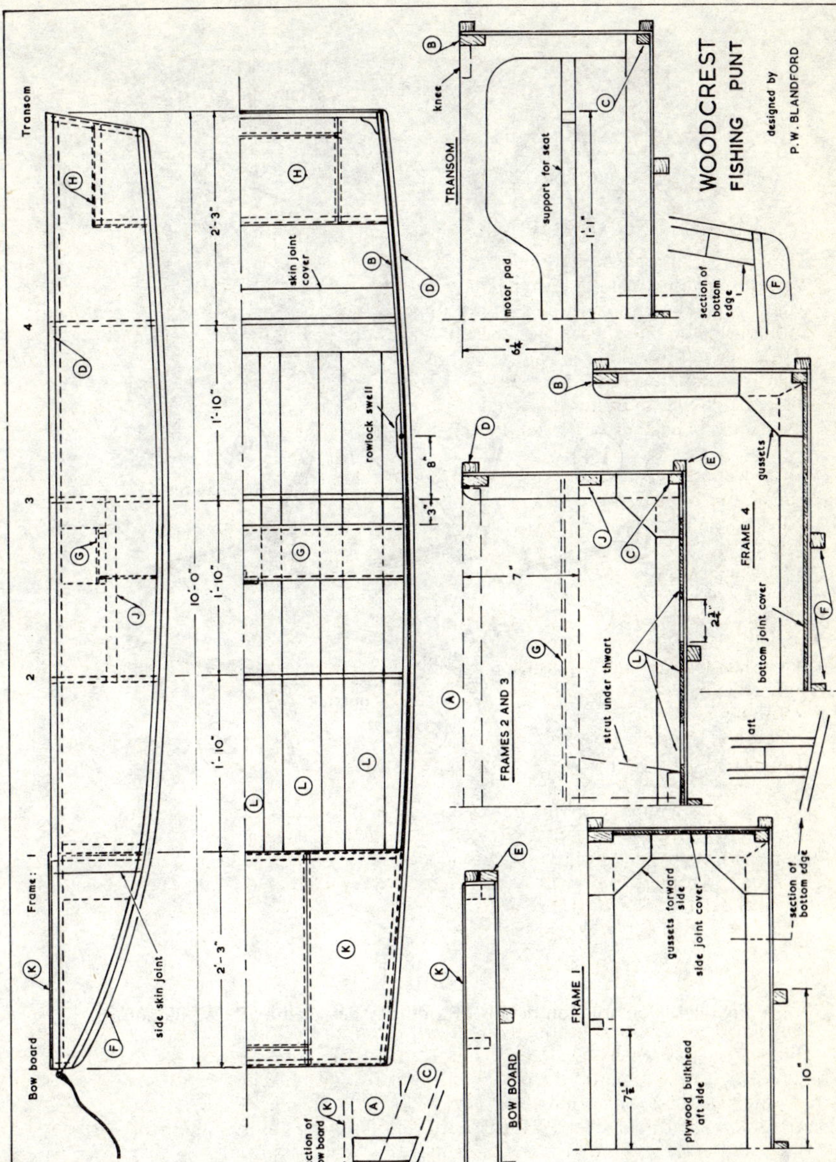

Fig. 393. The Woodcrest fishing punt designed by P. W. Blandford.

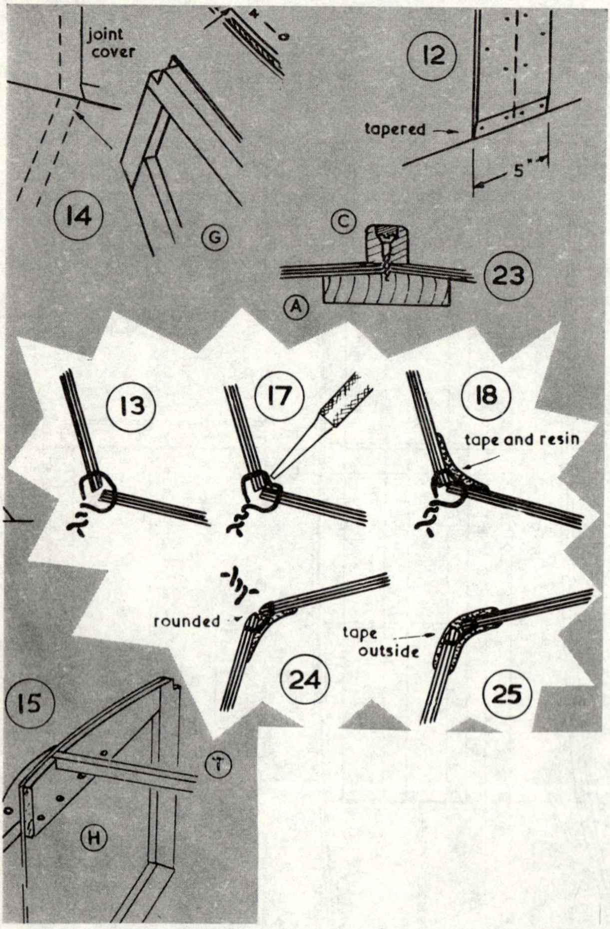

Fig. 394. Construction details of a dinghy designed by P. W. Blandford.

Dinghy

Also designed by Mr. Blandford, the Cresta dinghy is a useful introductory craft in which to learn the rudiments of sailing on inland waterways. Fig. 394 indicates how details of construction are clearly drawn on the plans so that they may be followed in complete confidence by the amateur boat builder. Illustrated are the joints between the plywood sheets, which are wire stitched and covered with resin-bonded glass fibre. The manufacturers of Cresta plywood do point out that finishes applied to wood destined for exposed use should effectively and completely seal the boards, particularly on end grain and the edges.

The above are but two of many boats designed by Mr. Blandford, and if particularly interested in this aspect of woodwork the reader will be well advised to contact him (see Acknowledgements).

APPENDIX 2

REFERENCE TABLES

General Sizes and Thicknesses of Manufactured Boards

Board		*Width* (mm)	*Length* (mm)	*Thickness* (mm)
Plywood		Combinations of the following dimensions 3660, 3050, 2745, 2440, 2135, 1830, 1525, 1220, 915 × 1830, 1525, 1270, 1220, 915 Length, i.e. dimension along the grain of the face veneer, must be given first		3–25 Special 1·5
Blockboard/ Laminboard		1220, 1525, 1830, 2050, 2500	1830, 2135, 2440, 3660, 5220	12, 16, 18, 22, 25
Chipboard		1220, 1525, 1830	1830, 2440, 2595, 2745, 3660	9, 12, 15, 18, 22, 25, 30
Hard-board	Standard	1220, 1525, 1600	Up to 3660	2–12·7
	Tempered	1220, 1525, 1600	Up to 3660	2·5–12·7
	Medium	610, 915, 1220, 1830	Up to 3660	6·4–19
Insulating board		1220	2440, 3050, 3660	11–25
Plastic laminates		1220 ×	3050	
		1220 ×	2745	0·8 Light duty—especially vertical faces
		1220 ×	2440	
		1070 ×	3050	
		915 ×	3050	
		915 ×	2440	1·2 Moderate duty
		760 ×	3050	
		760 ×	2440	1·5 Heavy duty
		1525 × Limited range of patterns only	3660	

Further slight variation of sizes may be found depending upon country of origin.

Woodscrews

	Steel						Brass						Stainless steel					
	Pizidriv			*Slotted*			*Supadriv*			*Slotted*			*Supadriv*			*Slotted*		
	Csk.	*Rd.*	*Rai. Csk.*	*Csk.*	*Rd.*	*Rai. Csk.*	*Csk.*	*Rd.*	*Rai. Csk.*	*Csk.*	*Rd.*	*Rai. Csk.*	*Csk.*	*Rd.*	*Rai. Csk.*	*Csk.*	*Rd.*	*Rai. Csk.*
¼″ × 1										●								
2					●					●								
4		●			●													
⅜″ × 1										●								
2				●	●					●	●							
3	●	●		●	●		●	●		●	●							
4	●	●		●	●		●	●		●	●							
5		●			●													
6		●			●													
½″ × 2				●						●	●					●		
3	●	●		●	●					●	●	●				●		●
4	●	●	●	●	●	●	●	●	●	●	●	●	●	●	●	●	●	●
5	●	●		●	●		●	●	●	●	●	●				●		●
6	●	●		●	●		●	●	●	●	●	●	●		●	●	●	●
7	●			●	●													
8	●	●		●	●												●	
12											●							
⅝″ × 3				●						●								
4	●	●	●	●	●	●	●	●	●	●	●	●	●			●	●	●
5	●	●	●	●	●	●	●	●	●	●	●	●				●		●
6	●	●	●	●	●	●	●	●	●	●	●	●	●	●	●	●	●	●
7	●			●	●													
8	●	●		●	●											●	●	●
10		●			●													
¾″ × 4	●	●	●	●	●	●	●	●	●	●	●	●	●		●	●	●	●
5	●	●	●	●	●	●	●	●	●	●	●	●				●		●
6	●	●	●	●	●	●	●	●	●	●	●	●	●	●	●	●	●	●
7	●	●		●	●		●			●	●	●				●		
8	●	●	●	●	●	●	●	●	●	●	●	●	●		●	●	●	●
9	●			●														
10	●	●		●	●		●			●						●	●	
⅞″ × 6	●			●														
7	●			●														
8	●	●		●	●													
1″ × 4	●	●		●	●				●	●		●				●	●	●
5	●			●						●								
6	●	●	●	●	●	●	●	●	●	●	●	●	●	●	●	●	●	●
7	●			●	●					●	●	●				●		
8	●	●	●	●	●	●	●	●	●	●	●	●	●	●	●	●	●	●
9	●			●						●								
10	●	●	●	●	●	●	●			●	●	●	●			●	●	●
12	●	●		●	●					●	●					●	●	●
1¼″ × 6	●	●	●	●	●	●	●		●	●	●	●			●	●	●	●
7	●			●	●					●								
8	●	●	●	●	●	●	●	●	●	●	●	●	●	●	●	●	●	●
9	●			●						●								
10	●	●	●	●	●	●	●			●	●	●	●		●	●	●	●
12	●			●			●			●	●	●				●	●	
14				●							●							

Stock Sizes (BS 1210 preferred sizes)

	Steel						Brass						Stainless steel					
	Supadriv			*Slotted*			*Supadriv*			*Slotted*			*Supadriv*			*Slotted*		
	Csk.	*Rd.*	*Rai. Csk.*	*Csk.*	*Rd.*	*Rai. Csk.*	*Csk.*	*Rd.*	*Rai. Csk.*	*Csk.*	*Rd.*	*Rai. Csk.*	*Csk.*	*Rd.*	*Rai. Csk.*	*Csk.*	*Rd.*	*Rai. Csk.*
1½″ × 6	●	●		●	●					●						●	●	●
7	●			●														
8	●	●		●	●		●	●	●	●	●	●	●	●	●	●	●	●
9	●			●						●								
10	●	●	●	●	●	●	●			●	●	●	●	●	●	●	●	●
12	●	●		●	●					●	●		●	●		●	●	●
14	●			●	●					●						●	●	
16				●														
18				●														
1¾″ × 8	●	●		●	●											●		●
9	●			●														
10	●	●		●	●		●		●	●						●		
12	●			●						●						●		●
14				●														
16				●														
18				●														
2″ × 6	●			●														
8	●			●	●		●			●						●	●	●
9	●			●														
10	●	●		●	●		●			●			●	●		●	●	●
12	●	●		●	●					●	●					●	●	●
14	●			●	●					●	●					●		
16				●														
18				●														
20				●														
2¼″ × 10	●			●														
12	●			●														
14	●			●														
2½″ × 8	●			●														
10	●			●	●					●						●		●
12	●			●						●						●	●	●
14	●			●						●						●		
16				●														
20				●														
3″ × 8	●			●														
10	●			●												●		
12	●			●						●						●	●	
14	●			●						●						●		
16				●														
18				●														
20				●														
3½″ × 12				●														
14	●			●												●		
16				●														
4″ × 12				●														
14				●												●		
16				●														
18				●														
20				●														

Only self-colour (unplated) stock sizes are shown. A large number of sizes are also available from stock in plated or coloured finishes. There is also a range of aluminium alloy woodscrews and silicon-bronze woodscrews.

Stock range of finishes for Supadriv Twinfast woodscrews

Length and diameter	*Electro-brassed C'sk. 113-8*	*Electro-brassed Rnd. 114-8*	*Sherardized C'sk. 113-29*	*Dark Florentine bronzed C'sk. 113-42*	*Bright zinc plated C'sk. 113-81*	*Bright zinc plated Rnd. 114-81*
¾" × 4					●	●
½"	●	●		●	●	●
⅝"	●				●	●
¾"					●	
1"					●	
½" × 5	●			●	●	●
⅝"	●	●			●	●
¾"					●	
1"					●	
⅜" × 6						●
½"		●			●	●
⅝"					●	●
¾"	●				●	●
1"	●		●		●	●
1¼"					●	●
1½"					●	●
⅝" × 7					●	
¾"					●	
1"			●		●	
1¼"					●	
½" × 8					●	
⅝"					●	●
¾"					●	●
⅞"					●	
1"					●	●
1¼"					●	●
1½"					●	●
1¾"					●	
2"					●	
1" × 10					●	●
1¼"					●	
1½"					●	●
1¾"					●	
1½" × 12					●	
2"					●	

Supadriv Twinfast Steel: Self-Colour

	3 Csk.	*3 Rd.*	*3 Rai. Csk.*	*4 Csk.*	*4 Rd.*	*4 Rai. Csk.*	*5 Csk.*	*5 Rd.*	*5 Rai. Csk.*	*6 Csk.*	*6 Rd.*	*6 Rai. Csk.*	*7 Csk.*	*7 Rd.*	*7 Rai. Csk.*	*8 Csk.*	*8 Rd.*	*8 Rai. Csk.*	*10 Csk.*	*10 Rd.*	*10 Rai. Csk.*	*12 Csk.*
5/16"					●																	
⅜"				●	●	⊙	●	●		●	●						⊙					
½"	●			●	●	●	●	●	⊙	●	●	⊙	●			●	●			⊙		
⅝"	●			●	●	●	●	●		●	●	●	●			●	●	⊙	⊙	●		
¾"				●	●	●	●	●		●	●	●	●			●	●	●	●	●		
⅞"							⊙			●	⊙					●			⊙	⊙		
1"				●		⊙	●			●	●	⊙	●			●	●	●	●	●		●
1⅛"													⊙			⊙		⊙				
1¼"							⊙			●	●	●	●			●	●	●	●	●	●	●
1½"										●	●					●	●	⊙	●	●	●	●
1¾"										⊙						●		⊙	●	●	⊙	●
2"										●						●		⊙	●	●		●
2¼"																⊙			●			●
2½"																●			●			●

⊙ Indicates not-preferred size.

Finishes for Screws

Screw material and finish	*Appearance*	*Suitable applications*
Steel + Bright zinc plate	Bright attractive protective coating	All dry interior applications and where a paint finish is applied, indoor or outdoor
Sherardized (zinc)	Dull grey protective coating. May turn brown unless painted	Most exterior fasteners for buildings. A good surface for painting
Nickel plate	Bright reflective finish —may tarnish	Dry interior fasteners, e.g. shelves, heaters
Chromium plate	Attractive bright reflective finish	Fairly dry interior work. Kitchens, most domestic appliances
Brass plate (electro-brass)	Reflective bright yellow finish	Cupboards and furniture for matching against brass. Dry interior work only
Bronze metal antique	Dark brown finish	For interior use with oxidised copper fittings
Dark Florentine bronze	Near black finish	For interior use with oxidised copper fittings
Antique copper bronze	Uniform bronze colour	For interior use with copper, bronze and matching timber finishes
Black japanned	Overall black enamel finish	General interior use; re-painting necessary outdoors for protection
Berlin blacked	Overall black enamel finish duller than japanned	General interior use; re-painting necessary outdoors for protection
Steel + Blue and oiled	Dark blue/black oxide coating, protective lubricating oil finish	Temporary protection only and requires painting in most applications
Brass	Uniform bright yellow Does not rust	All timber fastenings, brass hinges and door furniture
Chromium plate	Brilliant reflective finish	With all chromium plated domestic goods, e.g. dome-head mirror screws
Silicon bronze	Uniform dark brown colour	All exterior timber fastenings including boat building screws. Screws for copper and bronze components
Aluminium alloy (anodised and lubricated) with lanolin)	Matt silver-grey finish	All fasteners for aluminium articles, e.g. door furniture, bathroom fittings
Stainless Steel, 18/8 type	Bright attractive finish	All construction applications, where long term durability and freedom from rust staining is essential. May be used with aluminium components

Spacing of Woodscrews

	Driven without pre-drilled holes	*Driven into pre-drilled holes*
Distance from end	20 D	10 D
Distance from edge	5 D	5 D
Distance between lines of screws	10 D	3 D
Distance along the grain, between adjacent screws	20 D	10 D

D = Diameter of woodscrew.

Abrasives: Comparison of Grit Numbers

Approximate Grade	*Aluminium oxide/ Silicon carbide*	*Garnet*	*Glass*	*Tungsten carbide*
Very fine	P600/360 P400/320 P320–nearest 280 P280/240 P220/220	10/0 9/0 8/0 7/0 6/0		Three grades only 'Open coat'
Fine	P180/180 P150/150 P120/120	5/0 4/0 3/0	00 0 1	Fine
Medium	P100/100 P80/80 P60/60	2/0 0 ½	1½ F2 M2	Medium
Coarse	P50/50 P40/40 P36/36	1 1½ 2	S2 2½ 3	Coarse
Very coarse	P30/30 P24/24 P20/20 P16/16 P12/12	2½ 3 3½ 4 4½		

Summary of Gap-Filling Adhesives (Aerodux and Aerolite)

Resin and hardener	*Form*	*Principal characteristics and applications*	*British Standard Specification*
Aerodux 185 resorcinol-phenol-formaldehyde resin + HRP hardeners	Liquid resin Powder hardeners	Cold-setting weatherproof adhesive system. Aerodux 185 used with (*a*) Hardener HRP.155 for bonding wood, asbestos-based boards and decorative laminates, (*b*) Hardener HRP 150 where a more viscous glue mix is required to limit flow, (*c*) Hardener HRP.151 for scarf and finger joints. Shelf life is 18 months for Aerodux 185 and considerably longer for the hardener.	BS 1204: Parts 1 and 2 (Type WBP) BS 1203 (Type WBP)
Aerodux 500 resorcinol-phenol-formaldehyde resin + Hardener 501	Liquid resin Liquid hardener	Cold-setting weatherproof adhesive system. The resin, which is used with Hardener 501, is supplied in three grades fast, medium and slow. It is a two-liquid system with a simple 1 : 1 mixing ratio. It allows longer assembly times than Aerodux 185. Shelf life is at least one year for Aerodux 500 and Hardener 501.	BS 1204: Parts 1 and 2 (Type WBP) BS 1203 (Type WBP)
Aerolite 300 urea-formaldehyde resin + Hardener GBP.X or GBQ.X	Liquid resin Liquid hardener	Fast-setting separate-application adhesive system suitable for joinery and small-scale assembly applications and for boat-building. Shelf life is at least three months for Aerolite 300 and considerably longer for the hardeners. This adhesive is not suitable for export.	BS 1204: Part 1 (Type MR)
Aerolite 303.SM urea-formaldehyde resin + GS Hardeners	Liquid resin Liquid hardener	Mixed-application system, suitable for joinery and small-scale assembly applications, especially where better wetting-out characteristics are advantageous. Shelf life is at least six months for Aerolite 303.SM and longer for the hardener. This adhesive is not suitable for export.	BS 1204: Parts 2 and 2 (Type MR)
Aerolite 306 urea-formaldehyde resin + Hardener GBP.X or GBQ.X	Powder resin Liquid hardener	Alternatives to Aerolite 300 with GB hardeners. Powder resin requires mixing with water before use but has the advantage of considerably longer life—the powder can be stored for at least two years.	BS 1204: Parts 1 and 2 (Type MR)
Aerolite 311 urea-formaldehyde resin + LB Hardeners	Liquid resin Liquid hardeners	Adhesive system for laminated beams. Tolerates considerable assembly time. Hardener LB.4 usually used. LB.2 recommended for low workshop temperatures. LB 15 exceptionally fast hardener and used to give quick curing of finger and scarf joints. Shelf life: at least 6 months for Aerolite 311, considerably longer for the hardener. This adhesive is not suitable for export.	BS 1204: Parts 1 and 2 (Type MR)

Resin and hardener	*Form*	*Principal characteristics and applications*	*British Standard Specification*
Aerolite 308 urea-formaldehyde resin + Hardener GBP.X or GBQ.X	Powder resin Liquid hardener	May be used by mixed-application or separate-application method. Gives light-coloured glue-line with considerable resistance to heat and tolerates some exposure to weathering. Shelf life is at least one year for Aerolite 308 and considerably longer for the hardeners.	BS 1204: Part 1 (Type BR)

Handling precautions. Precautions to be taken when handling and processing Ciba–Geigy formaldehyde-based products are given in the individual instructions sheets and in Sheet No. AD. 2 *Handling Precautions for Formaldehyde-based Products.*

Storage. Resins and hardeners should be stored in a cool dry place sealed in their original containers. The storage figures quoted relate to these conditions.

Structural adhesives must comply with the gap-filling requirements of British Standard Specification BS 1204: Part 1.

BS 1204 has been drawn up to determine the suitability of phenolic and aminoplastic adhesives for particular uses. Part 1: 1964 relates to the gap-filling types used in construction work and Part 2: 1965 is concerned with close contact adhesives. British Standard Specification 1203 relates to the use of adhesives for plywood manufacture.

Type WBP: weatherproof and boil proof. This indicates that joints are highly resistant to weather, micro-organisms, cold and boiling water and dry heat.

Type BR: boil resistant. This specification implies a good resistance to weather and to boiling water but failure under the very prolonged exposure to weather that Type WBP adhesives will survive. Joints will withstand cold water for many years and are highly resistant to micro-organisms.

Type MR: moisture-resistant and moderately weather-resistant. Joints made with these adhesives will survive full exposure to weather for only a few years. They will withstand cold water for a long period and hot water for a limited time, but fail under the boiling water test. They are resistant to attack by micro-organisms.

Aerodux

Resorcinol-phenol-formaldehyde resins. Aerodux resins are used with great success for bonding wood to most building materials, including brick, concrete, cement and asbestos-cement. (In contrast to urea-formaldehyde adhesives, Aerodux sets in neutral or slightly alkaline conditions.) When bonding to such uneven substrates the addition of mineral filler is advantageous in reducing shrinkage stresses which may occur in thick glue lines—the filler addition also reduces glue-line costs.

Aerodux is excellent for bonding building boards—including asbestos-based building boards and ships' boards. Many plastics—laminated, moulded or expanded—are successfully bonded with Aerodux to porous substrates.

Aerolite

Urea-formaldehyde resins. Aerolite resins are dependable and durable glues for joinery and timber construction, for boat-building, for laminated work and for the making of plywood and wood chipboard. They are highly resistant to moisture and are not attacked by insects, moulds or other micro-organisms. They are colourless and non-staining.

Further Information

Technical service. Information or advice on the use of adhesives for specific applications and projects is readily available from Ciba–Geigy. Enquiries are welcomed and are given prompt attention by staff specialising in technical advisory service.

INDEX

Abrasives
- aluminium oxide paper, 299, 304, 306, 333
- garnet paper, 306
- glasspaper, 306
- 'papering off', 299, 304
- ScotchBrite pads, 307
- silicon carbide, 307
- steel wool, 307, 308, 311
- tungsten carbide, 307

Adhesives, 14, 16, 199, 208, 229, 232, 303, 315, 334, 335
Adze, 166, 279
Aerosol sprays, 167
Ammonia, 313
Angle divider, 42
Angles, grinding and sharpening, 152
Arrises, 83
Asbestos, 168
Assemblages, wooden, 284
Axe, 166, 279

Back, framed and panelled, 207
Bandings, 290
Bare-faced tenon, 183
Barrel bolts, 247
Battens, 202, 207, 226
Beading, edge and centre, 77
Bench
- hook, 50, 112, 169
- holdfast, 279
- stop, 104, 110
- woodwork, 102

Blind holes, 87
Blockboard, 16, 203, 321
Blocks
- breeze, 226
- cork, 304
- corner, 203, 266

Board, insulating and hard, 17, 82
Bolts, carriage, 102, 226
Bookcase strip, Tonk's fittings, 248
Borax, 313
Bowls, 301
Brace bits
- centre, 87, 157
- countersink, 89
- expansive, 88
- Forstner pattern, 88
- Jennings pattern, 88
- plain, 83
- ratchet, 85
- Stanley screw mate range, 89
- turnscrew, 89
- twist or auger, 87, 88, 157

Bradawl, 38, 99, 166, 173, 299
Bronze, 211
Buffing, 305
Bull nose work, 73
Burnishing tool (ticketer), 161
Burr, 69, 161, 169
Brushes
- paint, 310
- varnish, 308

Cabinet files, 279
- hanger, 276

Calico, 317, 323
Calipers, Vernier, 301, 304
Carcase, 207, 208, 236
Carving
- bench screw, 279
- chip, 279, 282
- incised, 279
- low relief, 279, 284

Carving tools
- chisels, 277
- chops, 279
- gouge, 277
- veiner, 277
- V parting tool, 277

Castors, 260
Catches
- ball, 244
- double ball, 244
- elbow, 246
- magnetic, 246
- mini, 244
- peglock, 246
- roller, 246
- toggle, 246

Cauls, 290

Chalkline reel, 41
Chamfering, 79
Chatter, 299
Chipboard, 16
  fastener, 266
  pre-veneered, 203
Chip effect, 69
Chisels
  bevel edged, 61
  firmer, 59, 60, 61, 153
  hollow square, 139
  mortise, 61
  paring, 61
  register, 63
  sash mortise, 63
Chuck, 83, 146
Clamp
  frame, 110
  the jet, 107
  hand, 110
  mitre Copydex, 110
Cocked bead, 207
Cog, 192, 207
Compasses, wing, 36, 304
Contraction, 207
Copper, 211
Copydex Jointmaster, 119
  Mimic, 115, 304
Cornering tool, 83
Corrugated fastener, 173
Counterboring, 207
Countersinking, 202
Cradle, 119
Cramps
  corner, 110
  edging, 105
  G, 105, 279, 292, 293
  heads, 107
  mitre, 177
  sash, 105, 199, 293
  T bar, 107
Creosote, 314
Cross members, 208
Cushions, 321

Dadoing, 77
Depth gauge, 304
  stop, 71, 85
Dividers, wing, 38, 304
Domestic iron, 207, 290
Doors, 207
  flush, 208
  framed and panelled, 208
  glass, 208
  slab, 208
  sliding, 208
Dovetail pins, 187
  half pins, 187
Dowelling jig, 115, 119, 202
Dowell plate, 202
Dowells, 173, 202, 203, 223
  cross, 270
  guide, 270
  plastic, 268
Drawer fronts, 207
  slips, 195
Drilling machine bits, 122, 124
Drilling machine pedestal, 122, 169
Drill
  masonry, 159, 226
  mortise, 139
  portable electric, 136
    woodboring bits, 137, 138
  stand, 139
  twist, 83, 157
Drum sander, 143
'Dry' assembled, 202
Dry rot, 143
Dust respirator, 168, 299
Dyes, aniline, 313

Ebonising, 309
Electric tools, double-insulated, 146
End clamps, 203, 207
End trimmer, 177
Escutcheons, 252
Expansion, 207
Extension cables, 144, 170
Eye shield, 152

Face edge, 41
  side, 41
Fence, 71, 77, 119
File, cabinet, 58
File cuts, 58
Files, 56
File, saw, 159
Filler, 307
Finishes, 307, 308, 309
Finishing, 306
  surface preparation, 307
Fillet, cross-grained hardwood, 202
Fillister, 71, 77
Finger recesses, 208
Flexidisc, 143
Floorboards, 211
Flush mount, 266
Foams
  latex, 315
  polyether, 317
Formers, male and female, 293
Foxtail wedging, 180

French polish, 308, 309
  rubbers, 309
Friction, 211
Fulcrum, 219
Fuming, 313
Furniture beetle, 313

Galvanised, 215, 226
Gauges
  butt, 41
  cutting, 39, 292
  mortise, 39
  single marking, 38, 202
Gimlet point, 219
Girdled, 11
Glassfibre, 167
Glass plates, 252
Glides, 252
Glue
  Cascamite, 293
  casein, 230
  fish, 230
  hot press, 207, 290
  impact, 290
  PVA, 290
  scotch, 229, 288
  synthetic resins, 230, 231, 232, 290
Goggles, protective, 152, 168
Gougers
  firmer, 63, 153, 157
  paring or scribing, 63, 153
Grain
  across the, 282
  against the, 303
  bringing out the, 311
  curly, 69
  end, 68, 79, 223
  filling, 312
  raise, 304, 307
  run with the, 85
  with the, 77, 282, 301, 303
Grease, 299
Grindstone, 149
Grooves, 208
Grounds, 288
Gunstock joint, 183

Hammer
  claw, 93, 219
  club, 93
  engineer's, 93
  peins, 94
  shaft, 91
  Stanley soft-faced, 94
  upholsterer's, 315
  Warrington pattern, 93
Hand drill, 83
Handles
  drop, 234
  flush, 234
Hardened fixing pin, 219
Hardening and tempering, 219
Hardwood buttons, 207
Hatchet, Canada, 94
Haunch, 180, 183
Height adjuster, 257
Hessian, 317, 323
Hinges
  back flap, 238
  butt, 207, 235
  cabinet, 239
  cylindrical, 241
  Heinze, 241, 242, 243, 244, 273, 276
  hurling, 238
  lift off, 238
  piano, 239
  pivot, 239, 276
  plunger, 270, 272
  reflex, 255
  soss, 241
  strut, 239
  table leaf, 238
  tee, 207
Honing, 69, 149, 152, 153
Horn, 180, 185, 199
Housing, 77, 82

Iron, 211

Jig Saw
  blades, 125
  portable, 124, 143
Joints
  bridle, 177
  butt, 173, 183, 203
  corner, 185
  corner tongued and grooved, 185
  dovetail, 187, 192, 195, 288
  dowelled, 173, 199
  finger or comb, 187
  housing, 185, 187
  halvings, 173
  lap, 203
  mitre, 177, 203
  mortise and tenon, 171, 180, 183, 203
  pinned, 187
  rebated, 185
  secret screwed, 202
  tongued and grooved, 202

Kerf, saw, 36, 44, 177
Kicker, 197

Knife
  marking, 36, 153, 190, 282
  pocket, 282
  trimming, 99, 100
Knitted base fabrics, 317, 323
Knives, Stanley, 315
Knock-down fittings, 261
  corner, 261, 262, 263, 264, 265
Knots
  short grain, 284
  splits, 288, 299
Knotting, 310

Lacquers
  acid-catalysed, 312
  cellulose, 312
  pre-catalysed, 312
Lambswool polishing bonnet, 143
Laminating, 292
Laminboard, 16
Lathe
  bed, 295
  centres, hollow, 301
  'dead' centres, 299, 304
  headstock, 295
  morse taper, 304
  outrigger, 295
  ring, 301
  rotating, 301
  tailstock, 295
  tool rest, 295, 304
Lathe, woodturning, 169, 295
  between centres, 299
  chucks, 304
  double chucking, 303
  face plate, 301, 303
  'Roughing down', 301
  single chucking, 301, 303
  speeds, 299
Leather, 317
Ledged and battened doors, 183
Lids, 207
Lipped edges, 199, 203, 207, 208, 288
Locks, 219
  box, 248
  cupboard, 248
  cylinder latch, 248
  drawer, 247, 248
  mortise, 248
  sliding door, 248

Machine planes, portable, 129
Machine router, 130
Machine router blades, 133
Mallet
  joiner's, 94
  woodcarving, 277, 279
Masonry, 211, 226
Matting punch, 282
Mirror
  clips, 252
  corner plates, 252
  lip, 255
  movements swivel, 255
  stand, 252
Mitre block, 112
  box, 50, 112
  square, 42
Mitres, 50
Mohair, 317
Moquettes, 317
Moulding, 77, 79

Nailing, 215
  secret, 215
Nails, 211
  clout, 215
  cut, 211
  cut tacks, 315
  gimp pins, 315
  oval, 215

Oil
  Danish, 311
  linseed, 287, 311
  paraffin, medicinal, 287
  machine, thin, 69, 149
  olive, 287, 305
  teak, 311
  thin machine, 69, 149
Oilstone, 69, 147
  boxes, 147, 161
Oxalic acid, 313

Paint, 310
  stirring, 143
  stripping, 314
Panel dust, 197
  fielded or raised, 197, 208
Paraffin, 149
Pilot hole, 221, 222, 223
Pincers, 100, 219
Piped edges, 321
Pirelli platforms, 321
  webbing, 317
Planes
  block, 68, 79, 153
  bullnose, 76, 153
  circular or compass, 79
  fibreboard, 82
  fore, 68, 70

Planes—*contd.*
- jack, 41, 68, 69, 71, 153
- multiplane, 77, 153
- plough, 76, 202
- rebate, 70, 71, 76, 153
- shoulder, 73, 153
- smoothing, 68, 69, 147, 153, 192, 306
- technical, 70, 115
- toothing, 288
- try or jointer, 41, 68, 70

Planes, adjustment, 66, 67
- blade, 65, 68, 153
- cap iron, 66, 68, 69
- frog, 67, 68, 73
- honing, 68
- mouth, 67
- sole, 67, 68

Plasticene, 287
Plastic caps for screws, 223, 224
Plastic laminates, 17, 290, 292
Plastidome, 223
Platters, 301
Pliers, combination, 33, 102
Ploughing, 77
Plugs
- fibre and plastic, 223, 226, 227
- metal, 227

Plywood, 13, 173, 183, 197, 199, 202, 203, 207, 293, 321, 325
- stoutheart, 15, 203

Pocket screwing, 207
Polishing wax, 311
Protective clothing, 299
Punches
- centre, 166
- nail, 102, 106
- pin, 102

Pushpin, 100

Rasp
- cabinet, 58, 284
- wood, 58

Rawlbolts, 227
Rawldrill, 226
Rebates, 73, 77, 79, 207, 292
Release agents, 292
Resin glues, 167
Rubbed joints, 195, 197, 199
Rule
- bench, 33
- folding, 35
- steel, 33, 79, 304

Sander, belt, 132
- orbital, 142, 143

Sanding disc, 131, 299, 304

Saws
- band, 301
- bead, 51
- bow, 53, 284
- circular, 8, 126, 203
- compass, 55
- coping, 51, 53, 284
- cross-cut, 45, 47
- dovetail, 51
- fleamtooth, 56
- general purpose, 55
- hacksaw, 56
  - junior, 56
- jeweller's, 51
- log, 51
- pad (keyhole), 55
- panel, 45
- ripsaw, 8, 45, 47
- tenon, 49
- veneer, 51

Saws, circular
- bench, 141
- blades, 127

Saws, gullet (teeth), 161
- set, 44, 47
- toe and heel, 49
- toothguard, 45

Scrapers
- cabinet, 161, 277, 306
- Skarsten, 161
- woodturning, 296

Scratch stock, 83, 183, 292
Screwdrivers, 33
- cabinet, 95
- London pattern, 95
- offset, 99
- Pozidriv, 99
- ratchet, 95

Screws
- coach, 102, 223, 225
- wood, 219, 220, 223, 329, 330, 331, 332, 333
  - single start, 219
  - 'Twinfast', 16, 219, 223

Screws, machine thread and cover head, 268
- mirror, 223, 224

Shank, 202, 213, 219, 227
Shelves, 207
Sherardised, 215
Shooting board, 79, 112
- mitre, 115, 177

Shrinking plates, 207, 252
Silver sand, 149
Sizing, 290
Slabs, 8, 171, 203
Slats, 317

Sliding bevel, 42
Slitting, 77
Slot-screwed, 197, 202, 235
Spanner adjustable, 102
Spigot, 223
Spirit level, 102
Spoke shaves, metal, 100, 153
  wooden, 100, 153
Spur, 71, 77, 87
Stains, 313
Staple gun, 315
Stays, 219, 249, 251
Steam bending, 293
Steel bands flexible for laminating, 293
Straight edge, 35, 315
Stretcher rails, 173
'Strings', 290
Studs, upholstered, 321
Square (out of), 42
Supadriv screws, 97, 99, 182, 220, 223, 329, 330, 331
Surform, 59, 277, 284

Table leg fittings, 266
  tops, 207
Tactiles, touchtoys, 284
Tailor's chalk, 315
Tang, 87
Tape, steel, 35, 315
Teflon*S, 50
Tempering, 44
Templates
  card, 287, 304
  dovetail, 115, 190
  mitre, 115
  square, 115
Tenon, 73
Thinners, 308
Timber
  annual rings, 1
  bark, 3
  bast, 3
  burrs, 288
  cambium layer, 3
  crotches, 288
  dry rot, 12
  end grain, 68
  hardwoods, 3
  heartwood, 3
  kiln dried, 11
  medullary rays, 1
  moisture content, 8
  pith, 1
  sapwood, 3
  shakes, 12
  softwoods, 3
  stumps, 288
  timber pests, 12
  warping, 11
  wany edge, 12, 284
Toggle,
  gravity, 229
  spring, 229
Tool roll, 166, 277
Tools, woodturning
  auger, 301
  chisels, 296, 301, 304
  gouges, 296, 299, 301, 303, 304
  parting, 296
  scraper, 296, 298, 299
Tongue, cross grained, 203
  loose, 202
Topping saw teeth, 159
Tracking, nylon or plastic, 208, 255, 257
Trammel heads, 38
Treen work, 279, 287
Trenching, 77
Trestle-sawing, 47, 112
Trichloroethane, 167
Try square, 41, 49, 202
Turpentine, 287

Vacuum bag, 292
Varnish
  copal oak, 312
  polyurethane, 287
Veneers
  balancing, 203, 288
  'closed', 288
  constructional, 291, 292
  flitch, 288
  hammer, 290
  press, 290
  rotary peeling, 288
  sawing, 288
  slicing, 288
  telegraphing, 288
  veneers, 13, 14
Vice, woodwork, 55, 104

Walls, cavity, 226
Washers, 226
  spring, 226
  taper, 226
Wax
  beeswax, 311
  Carnauba, 304, 305
Webbing, 317, 321, 323
Wedges, 180
Wheels, trolley, 260
Winding strips, 36

Wire brush, 143
Woodcarving tools, 157
Woods
  abura, 294
  African mahogany, 293, 296, 309, 311
  African walnut, 293
  afzelia, 296
  agba, 296
  Afrormosia, 296
  ash, 293, 296, 317
  beech, 293, 296, 317
  birch, 293, 309
  blackbean, 294
  boxwood, 279, 290
  cedar, 296, 311, 313
  cherry, 293, 296
  chestnut, 293, 296
  ebony, 279, 290
  elm, 293, 296
  hickory, 293
  hornbeam, 293
  idigbo, 293
  iroko, 293, 296
  lignum vitae, 279
  lime, 279, 296
  makore, 293
  mansonia, 293
  oak, 293, 311, 317
  pine, 279
  Queensland walnut, 293, 296, 311
  ramin, 293
  rosewood, 279, 296
  sapele, 293, 296
  sitka spruce, 293
  spruce, 293
  sycamore, 293, 296, 309
  Tasmanian myrtle, 293
  Tasmanian oak, 293
  teak, 296, 311
  utile, 293, 296
  walnut, 293, 311
  willow, 293
  yew, 279, 293
Workshop dress, 168

Zip fastener, 321